Two week

THE FINANCIAL SERVICES
AND MARKETS ACT:
A PRACTICAL LEGAL GUIDE

AUSTRALIA
Law Book Co.
Sydney

CANADA and USA
Carswell
Toronto

HONG KONG
Sweet & Maxwell Asia

NEW ZEALAND
Brookers
Auckland

SINGAPORE and MALAYSIA
Sweet & Maxwell Asia
Singapore and Kuala Lumpur

THE FINANCIAL SERVICES
AND MARKETS ACT:
A PRACTICAL LEGAL GUIDE

ASHURST MORRIS CRISP, LONDON

Edited by
James Perry

LONDON
SWEET & MAXWELL
2001

Published in 2001 by
Sweet & Maxwell Limited of
100 Avenue Road,
London NW3 3PF
(http://www.sweetandmaxwell.co.uk)

Typeset by J&L Composition Ltd, Filey, North Yorkshire
Printed in Great Britain by
Athenæum Press Ltd, Gateshead, Tyne & Wear

No natural forests were destroyed to make this product; only farmed
timber was used and replanted

ISBN 0 421 679 905

A CIP catalogue record for this book is available from the British Library

ISBN 0-421-67990-5

9 780421 679900

Foreword

The relatively short history of financial services regulation in the U.K. has produced its own side industry of books, articles and comment. This book strides boldly into that already bustling marketplace.

In covering the FSA and the Financial Services and Markets Act, it enters the expanded areas for debate and discussion that have been created by such a step-change in financial services regulation. The importance of this change has not gone unnoticed—Parliament, the industry, consumer groups and other interested parties, not least the legal community, have all discussed it at great length with varying degrees of pleasure and enthusiasm. Nor has this debate been confined to the U.K.—the model of a single regulator for financial services is becoming a fast-growing export industry as other countries seek to adapt our structure for their own use.

It is sometimes easy to forget that, although the FSA has been up and running for four years, we have had to continue to work under the various regulatory regimes of the past with their different legal foundations, rulebooks and panoplies of powers. Now that the midnight hour has struck and the new Act has come into force, we can operate a single regime in the full hope that it will mean a better system of regulation—one that is not only responsive, risk-based and cost-effective but also considerably less confusing.

The four years in waiting have not seen us standing idly by for the Act to come into force. We have, as you will know to your personal cost of bleary eyes and late nights, been busy publishing consultation papers containing proposals on the detailed regime we will put into operation, including our single Handbook of rules and guidance. I apologise for the amount of paper that we have produced—frankly I wish it could have been less—but we are grateful for the responses we have received and have taken full account of them. As a regulator, we recognise the importance of well-informed debate and constructive dialogue with all interested groups and I know that the legal community will continue to play its full part in this.

I therefore welcome the appearance of this book, under its distinguished editorship as a contribution to that debate. No reader would expect me to say that I agree with all that it contains, but I hope it will play a part in developing an understanding of our powers and the checks and balances that apply, as well as bringing together in one place the main features of the legislation. I look forward to the ongoing debate.

Sir Howard Davies, Chairman of the Financial Services Authority

Preface

There have been moments during the past four and a half years when many a student of the Financial Services and Markets Act 2000 must have felt like the hero in a poem by Robert Browning, valiantly striving to reach a destination and nearly, but never quite, reaching it. Whatever one's view of the new Act and the statutory regulator, the journey from the Chancellor's announcement on May 20, 1997 to 'N2' has certainly been a long and arduous one for all concerned; along the way, as Lord Saatchi, a senior member of the Conservative team on the Bill observed, grown men have been seen weeping (though it is not clear whether this was in Parliament, Whitehall, Canary Wharf or the City). The regulated community has now, thankfully, reached some kind of resting place with the coming into force of most of the Act, and the advent of the new statutory regulator, on December 1, 2001.

The long period of gestation which the FSMA has undergone only partly hints at the difficulties which an author of this kind of work has faced. A brief perusal of the Act will confirm that the FSMA itself is, in essence, a framework; most of the detail sits in orders made by H.M. Treasury and principles, rules and guidance made by the FSA. These have been heavily consulted upon—with finality being achieved, in many cases, only in spring or summer this year (or, in some cases, even later). Some orders—for example, that relating to Control of Business Transfers—had yet to be published or made by the time that this work went to press. As a result, we have endeavoured to capture late development in the legislative and rule-making processes after May 2001 but have not succeeded in every case. We hope, nonetheless, that the reader will find that our efforts to reflect late changes (and new material) have borne some fruit.

For whom is this work intended? We hope, of course, that this work will have as wide-ranging an appeal as possible; however, if pressed, we would admit that the people most in our minds' eye while writing were those hard-pressed regulated and 'perimeter' firms which, for whatever reason, did not play an active part in the consultation process. These are the firms which seem most in need of a little guidance (written or otherwise) in the months following N2.

It would be wrong not to include here a customary word of thanks to certain people who have helped, in different ways, to realise this book. I am immensely grateful to my colleagues at Ashursts who have contributed individual chapters; they receive just recognition at the beginning of their work. I am also grateful to other colleagues who have read different sections of the manuscript and have made helpful comments. My personal debt is to David Toube and Jai Chavda, who have been as vigilant, supportive and knowledgeable as I could have wished (and then more). We are all, of course, in debt to our publishers, Sweet & Maxwell, whose enthusiasm and encouragement have been a source of inspiration (and occasional fear in the latter stages!). On a personal note, I would like to thank my wife, Andrea, and daughters, Melissa and Abigail, for their constant understanding and support and for remaining calm when I had seemingly disappeared under hundreds of draft orders and consultation papers.

We must add two final caveats that the process of change will continue after N2, though this edition is constant; and that the general comments in this work are not intended as a substitute for specific advice.

James Perry
September 2001

Contents

Table of Cases

Table of Statutes

Table of Statutory Instruments

Table of SIB Rules

Table of Rules

Table of European Legislation

Note to Treaty of Rome: new (*i.e.* post-Treaty of Amsterdam) numbering is given, with old (*i.e.* pre-Treaty of Amsterdam) numbering in brackets.

CHAPTER 1

Background to U.K. Regulation

DAVID TOUBE

THE PROPER ENDS OF REGULATION

1.01 In 1999, the financial services sector contributed 5.8 per cent of the Gross Domestic Product of the United Kingdom, and employed over one million people.[1] However, somewhat surprisingly, given the pre-eminence of the United Kingdom as a world financial centre, and the importance of this sector to the economy, workers in the financial services industry are not always as well loved as they might be. Samuel Johnson defined a stock jobber in his 1755 Dictionary as:

"a low wretch who makes money by buying and selling shares in a fund."

In some ways, attitudes have not significantly changed in the 250 years since Johnson penned that epigram. In bull markets, City professionals are painted as the fat cats, supping on the surplus value of the honest worker's labour. In bear markets, they are cast as irresponsible gamblers, playing the ponies with the public's hard earned savings. All in all, those active in financial services sometime seem to occupy a position in the public imagination only slightly below journalists, although admittedly somewhat above that of the lawyers. Yet, despite the opprobrium heaped upon the poor financial services worker, the take-up of financial services of all varieties by the public has never been more widespread.

FINANCIAL SERVICES REGULATION: 1697 TO NOVEMBER 30, 2001

1.02 In order to understand both the form and the impact of the FSMA upon the financial services marketplace, it is helpful to know something of what has come before. Viewed from the wrong end of the telescope, the road to the constitution of the FSA as "the broadest financial regulator in the world"[2] appears to stretch back almost infinitely. Although this book is not a history of regulation or the United Kingdom financial markets, context is useful if the form and impact of the present regime is to be understood properly.[3] As we have seen, the urge to police

---

[1] International Financial Services, London, *www.britishinvisibles.co.uk.*
[2] p.5, FSA Occasional Paper Series No.2, "The Rationale for a Single National Financial Services Regulator", Clive Briault, May 1999.
[3] For an extensive history of the City of London, see David Kynaston's four-volume work: *The City of London Vol 1: A World of Its Own 1815–1890*; *The City of London Vol. II: Golden Years 1890–1914*; *The City of London Vol. III: Illusions of Gold: 1914–1945*; *The City of London Vol. IV: A Club No More: 1945–2000*, Chatto and Windus.

the financial markets is not new. Instructively, regulatory initiatives have typically coincided with periods of feverish speculation and headline-grabbing scandal. The late seventeenth and eighteenth centuries, for example, saw both a fascination both with investment, regulation and scandal which in many ways is reminiscent of the furore over the Maxwell pensions affair, the collapse of Barings Bank, and the pensions misselling fiasco which formed the backdrop against which the present reforms were debated and drafted.

No introduction to the regulation of the securities markets is complete without a mention of the 1697 "Act to restrain the number and ill practices of brokers and stock-jobbers" which required brokers to be licensed and to enter into a bond of £500, forfeitable in the event of misconduct. The same year saw the expulsion of stock jobbers from the Royal Exchange, from where they moved to the coffee houses which surrounded St Paul's Cathedral. However, licensing and eviction did not dampen the appetite for speculation. The public were content to pour their wealth into ventures aimed variously at inventing a "wheel for perpetual motion", for "the transmutation of quicksilver into a malleable fine metal" and, most famously of all, for "carrying on an undertaking of great advantage, but nobody to know what it is".[4] The British enthusiasm for speculation survived even the collapse of South Sea Bubble—an ultimately unsustainable boom in the stock of a company originally formed to trade slaves with Spanish America, which had outbid the Bank of England to take over the national debt. The fallout from the South Sea Bubble adventure paved the road for Sir John Barnard's "Act to prevent the infamous practice of stock-jobbing", which effectively outlawed options trading for a century, and rendered certain transactions illegal and therefore void and unenforceable.

However, the modern starting-point for the statutory regulation of the securities market at least is conventionally held to be the Prevention of Fraud (Investments) Act 1958. That Act empowered the Department of Trade and Industry (DTI) to license all securities dealers with the exception of members of recognised stock exchanges and various other persons who were exempted from the licensing requirement by the DTI. The DTI were also invested with the authority to make rules which bound those persons which they licensed. However, the role of the DTI as a regulator of the securities markets was not dominant: the system was essentially still self-policed. Accordingly, the Council of the Stock Exchange largely eclipsed the DTI as a nexus of power. Additionally, the Stock Exchange made provision for investor compensation (through the mutual and unlimited liability of all firms for each other's debts), public dissemination of market-sensitive information (provided for by a Listing Agreement with firms whose securities were traded on the Exchange), the avoidance of conflicts of interests (institutionalised by the division between jobbers and brokers) and the preservation of fixed commissions.

1.03 Control of the banking industry, by contrast, was even less formal. The Bank of England—which had been nationalised in 1946—played a central supervisory role. However, although the Bank of England Act 1946 gave the Bank of England limited statutory authority to control other banks, the power of the Bank of England was essentially a matter of convention, in which real authority was

---

[4] Charles Mackay, *Extraordinary Popular Delusions & the Madness of Crowds* (Three Rivers Press, 1980, first published in 1841).

exercised by the Bank of England's Discount Office. Even in recent years, the Bank of England's style of regulation did not, in general, rely on a detailed prescriptive rule book (though detailed regulations were issued governing capital adequacy). Instead, the Bank operated chiefly through the provision of regular information to banks operating in the United Kingdom, and through the judgment and discretion of the Bank of England's Supervision and Surveillance Department. This approach came in for considerable criticism after the fall of Barings.

The authority of the Bank of England to regulate the "deposit-taking" activities of retail, commercial and investment banks were strengthened by the direct statutory powers derived from the Banking Act 1987. In addition, the Bank of England supervised the dealing activities of banks and other firms using the wholesale money markets through its quasi-legal "London Code of Conduct". By contrast, building societies were regulated comparatively early on under a succession of Building Societies Acts from 1836 onwards.

Although Lloyd's of London had been established under successive Acts of Parliament from 1971 onwards, which proclaimed that the object of the Society of Lloyd's included "the advancement and protection of the interests of the Members of the Society", Lloyd's was also largely self-regulated, with authority flowing from the Committee of Lloyd's. Individual "Names"—that is, members or investors—were sponsored by another existing Name, and were required to demonstrate net worth of a certain level. Somewhat ironically, the cornerstone of protection for the insured—the unlimited personal liability of Names—ultimately turned out to be a fatal source of weakness; by the late 1980s, Names were increasingly unsophisticated retail investors.

The regulation of other aspects of the financial services industry was equally piecemeal but, by contrast, was premised upon statutory powers invested in governmental regulators. Friendly Societies originally fell under the auspices of a Registrar of Friendly Societies. The Board of Trade was made responsible for the regulation of life assurance companies under the Life Assurance Companies Act 1870; ultimately, the DTI was constituted as the prudential regulator of life and general insurance companies in the United Kingdom. The DTI's powers were derived from the Insurance Companies Act 1982. However, it was not responsible for their selling and marketing activities, which partially fell under the auspices of the Insurance Brokers Registration Council (a body created by the Insurance Brokers Registration Act 1977 which operated a code of conduct and registration system which applied only to those insurance intermediaries which chose to call themselves insurance brokers).

1.04 The catalyst for reform of at least part of this patchwork quilt was the publication of Part 1 of the Gower Report[5] in 1984, which had been commissioned by the Tory Government three years previously to canvass options for reform of the regulation of investment business. In a nutshell, Gower's view was that the Prevention of Fraud (Investments) Act 1958 no longer provided a proper foundation for regulation. Accordingly, he saw a need for self-regulatory organisations with a semi-public status, by which all significant actors in investment business would be licensed. The self-regulatory bodies would in turn have been regulated by a single statutory regulatory body, or by the DTI.

---

[5] L.C.B Gower, "Review of Investor Protection: Report Part I", January 1984, Cmnd. 9125.

The Gower Report was, however, somewhat overtaken by the publication one year later by the Government of its own proposals for reform, contained in the White Paper, "Financial Services in the United Kingdom: A New Framework for Investor Protection".[6] The White Paper followed the broad thrust of the Gower Report, but proposed dividing the powers at the top level of regulation between two organisations: a Securities and Investment Board (the "SIB") and a Marketing of Investments Board. The bifurcation of regulatory responsibilities was dropped by the Government by the time that the Financial Services Bill was published, and only the SIB was ultimately created. Although the most important statutory powers were vested in the Secretary of State (that is, originally the DTI, but ultimately H.M. Treasury), powers were delegated to the SIB which became—if not quite the replica of the SEC that the City feared—at least a considerably more powerful regulator than the DTI had ever been. The Financial Services Act 1986 received Royal Assent in November 1986 and came into force a year and a half later, in April 1988.

The Financial Services Act 1986 required persons who engaged in investment business in the United Kingdom—that is, the business of engaging in certain specified activities in relation to listed classes of investments—to be authorised. Authorisation was chiefly to be achieved by membership of one of four self-regulatory organisations ("SRO")[7]: the Securities and Futures Authority[8] (which regulated securities firms, merchant banks, corporate finance houses and others), the Investment Management Regulatory Organisation (which primarily regulated fund managers and other portfolio managers and advisers), the Financial Intermediaries, Managers and Brokers Regulatory Association, and the Life Assurance and Unit Trust Regulatory Organisation. The latter two SROs were ultimately replaced in 1994 at the recommendation of Sir Kenneth Clucas by a single SRO, the Personal Investment Authority (which regulated the marketing of life assurance, unit trusts and other retail products). However, accountants, actuaries and lawyers which engaged in investment business were to be regulated through membership of their trade associations which under the 1986 Act became Recognised Professional Bodies.[9] Additionally, the SIB was given certain indirect powers to regulate Recognised Investment Exchanges and Recognised Clearing Houses which were rendered "exempted" persons in relation to any of its activities as exchanges or clearing houses which constituted investment business.[10]

Nevertheless, though the paradigm shift which the Financial Services Act 1986 represented was palpable, the Act reformed only the aspect of the financial services industry which became known as "investment business". The "patchwork quilt" approach has subsisted in law at least until December 1, 2001, the date upon which the FSMA comes into force, although the relevant regulators from the bodies which have now been abolished were relatively quickly transferred to the SIB—which was renamed the Financial Services Authority, which took over their

---

[6] "Financial Services in the United Kingdom: A New Framework for Investor Protection", Department of Trade and Industry, January 1985, Cmnd. 9432.
[7] Financial Services Act 1986, s.7.
[8] It was originally The Securities Association (TSA) and the Association of Futures, Brokers and Dealers (AFBD) which merged to become SFA.
[9] Financial Services Act 1986, s.15.
[10] Financial Services Act 1986, Pt IV.

functions either as a result of orders made under the Deregulation and Contracting Out Act 1994, or under contract.

1.05 The cultural earthquake inherent in the new Labour Government's proposals for reform of the regulatory system was substantially more far-reaching. The Government fought the 1997 general election, at least in part, on a promise to make the SIB the direct regulator of the investment business sector of the financial services industry. Accordingly, it promised in its Business Manifesto, "Equipping Britain for the future" that it would bring self-regulation to an end, and replace the existing structure with a single regulatory tier. That said, little in the manifesto prefigured the wholesale reform which was announced by Gordon Brown, the Chancellor of the Exchequer, on May 20, 1997. The most unexpected aspect of the proposed blueprint for reform was that it went well beyond the limited aim of ending self-regulation as the objective of the legislation and replaced that goal with that of creating what the Government termed "one stop regulation".[11] Indeed, one of the most revolutionary—and somewhat unexpected—aspects of the new regime was that the Bank of England was to lose its historic responsibility for banking regulation. Alan Milburn, then the Chief Secretary to the Treasury, later explained the rationale behind the reform thus:

"Nowadays, banks, securities firms and insurance companies all play in the same pond. But while the traditional sectoral boundaries are disappearing, the old regulatory structures have failed to keep pace. The result is the worst of all worlds—heavy-handed and confused regulation, with more than one supervisor, all with different rules and procedures, seeking to regulate the self-same firm. That is not just a recipe for confusion; it is costly and inefficient and, ironically, it can dilute the impact of effective regulation."[12]

A notable feature of the legislative process which gave rise to the passage of the FSMA was the degree of scrutiny and debate which the procedures adopted were designed to engender. Indeed, the breadth, quality and thoroughness of the debate which reform engendered was unprecedented in recent political history, even when measured against the theoretically rich approach to regulation of investment business of Part 1 of Professor Gower's Review of Investor Protection. The Bill itself was published in a preliminary draft form for consultation in July 1998. That Bill was then subjected to extensive scrutiny, first by the Treasury Committee[13] and then by the Joint Committee on Financial Services and Markets—a joint committee of the House of Commons and the House of Lords—under the Chairmanship of Lord Burns, which took live and written submissions from industry participants, interest groups and constitutional lawyers, and ultimately published two detailed reports on the Bill. The First Report,[14] published on April 27, 1999, focused upon:

---

[11] See, Alan Milburn HC Deb, Jun 28, 1999, c.35.

[12] Alan Milburn HC Deb, Jun 28, 1999, c.37.

[13] Financial Services Regulation, Treasury Committee, HC, 73-I 1998–99.

[14] HC, 328 1998–99.

- the scope of the FSMA regime;

- proposed arrangements for the accountability of the FSA;

- the statutory objectives and principles of the Financial Services Authority;

- discipline, enforcement and the role of the proposed Tribunal;

- market abuse;

- the role of the Ombudsman and Compensation Scheme.

During the course of the Joint Committee's deliberations on the market abuse and enforcement aspects of the Bill, significant constitutional questions were raised in relation to the compatibility of the legislation with the European Convention on Human Rights. Accordingly, the Joint Committee took further evidence and published a second report on May 27, 1999.[15]

1.06   Extensive consultation was also carried out by H.M. Treasury, notably in March[16] and October 1999,[17] on the content of the draft Financial Promotion order and, in February 1999,[18] on the draft Regulated Activities Order. The FSA in turn published over one hundred Consultation Papers, revisiting the more important aspects of the proposed regime on three or more occasions. At the same time, the FSA organised a series of official "roadshows": conferences which were, at least in part, consultation exercises in their own right. Paradoxically, it has been alleged in some quarters that the consultation exercise was itself "a bit of a fraud"[19]: that so much material was published that it became impossible for all but the most committed to identify those issues which really mattered. Furthermore, the process of consultation itself has been the subject of separate consideration, under the auspices of the Hansard Society, by means of a separate committee chaired, again, by Lord Burns.[20]

At the same time, the progress of the Bill was subject to intense, critical and often constructive scrutiny in the press and by industry figures. Andrew Tyrie MP and Martin McElwee published a polemical pamphlet, "Leviathan at Large", for the right-wing think tank, the Centre for Policy Studies.[21] David Lascelles published a report for the Centre for the Study of Financial Innovation, which surveyed the attitudes and concerns of the City arising from the new regime.[22] With the exception, perhaps, of the two great constitutional Acts of the late 1990s—the Scotland Act 1998 and the Human Rights Act—it is hard to think of any Act in recent times which has been subject to so much well-informed public consideration.

---

[15] HC, 465 1998–99.

[16] H.M. Treasury, *Financial Services And Markets Bill Financial Promotion—A Consultation Document*, March 1999.

[17] H.M. Treasury, *Financial Services And Markets Bill Financial Promotion—Second Consultation Document, A New Approach For The Information Age*, February 1999.

[18] *Financial Services And Markets Bill, Regulated Activities—A Consultation Document.*

[19] p.1, "Waking up to the FSA, How the City views its new regulator", David Lascelles, Centre for the Study of Financial Innovation, May 2001.

[20] *www.hansard-society.org.uk/parlReform_dlb2.htm.*

[21] "Leviathan at Large", Andrew Tyrie MP and Martin McElwee, Centre for Policy Studies.

[22] "Waking up to the FSA, How the City views its new regulator", David Lascelles, Centre for the Study of Financial Innovation, May 2001.

1.3 KEY THEMES

1.07 The tricky theoretical issues were by no means ignored during the passage of the Act. Indeed, the three-year process of reform gave rise to a particularly rich and sophisticated debate on the future of the United Kingdom's financial services industry, and raised foundational questions related to the purposes of regulation. Precisely because the debate was so wide-ranging, it is difficult to list the key issues around which debate centred in a manner sensitive to the subtleties of the different positions. Nevertheless, a brief guide to the debate can provide a helpful benchmark against which the regime may be judged.

First, although there was general agreement by all involved that there were many advantages in creating a single regulator, it was feared that the FSA would need to ensure that the centralisation of the regulatory function did not lead to an artificial "one size fits all" approach to the regulation of institutions which performed very different functions. In the event, a differentiated approach to regulation was retained by the FSA; nevertheless, the concern is as much directed to the culture of supervision as to the content of the rules themselves. An associated argument focused upon the importance of ensuring that the FSA did not find itself in the grip of institutional inertia when called upon to deal in an innovative manner with novel developments in the financial services marketplace. In fact, one of the more palpable manifestations of the concern to maintain the flexibility of the new regime can be seen in H.M. Treasury's lengthy consideration of the impact of the internet upon the promotion of financial services, and its emphasis upon the drafting of a "technology-neutral" approach.

Secondly, commentators on the new regime focused upon the importance of maintaining accountability of the regulator. At its most extreme, some critics of the FSA feared that it would become a "behemoth" by virtue of its sheer size and by the breadth of its powers. However, the concern was more generally to ensure that its actions could be adequately scrutinised and, if necessary, that the FSA could be called to account.

Thirdly, critics of the FSMA were concerned that the Act would give rise to a significant increase in the compliance burden of regulated firms: that the costs would both be passed on to customers, and moreover might damage the competitive position of the United Kingdom in the international financial marketplace. The flip side of the argument—which indeed was hard-wired into the FSMA itself in the form of one of the regulatory objectives—was that under-regulation itself would lead to a loss of confidence in the markets. A variation on this argument suggested that the FSA, in attempting to set out clearly the nature of its processes and limits of its powers, had replaced a principle-based system of regulation with one which depended excessively upon rules. The concern is that firms will be increasingly wary of acting without receiving expert advice upon its duties under the FSA Handbook, and that anxiousness about breaching the rules will lead both to reluctance to innovate by regulated firms and to spiralling indirect compliance costs.

1.08 The fourth major theme which ran through the public debate was the interplay between the principle of *caveat emptor* and the role of the state as the protector of the consumer. A related concern is that intensive regulation may promote "moral hazard", the concern that institutions and consumers alike will be lulled into a false sense of security, leading to a failure properly to assess the risks to which they are exposed.[23]

The fifth theme centred around the constitutional propriety of the FSA's enforcement and market abuse powers. Specifically, debate focused upon two major issues. The first aspect was the separation of function between the investigation and "prosecution" processes carried out by the FSA. The second focused upon the issue of process rights and the status, under the European Convention of Human Rights, of certain aspects of the regime which were avowedly civil in form but which might plausibly be seen as criminal in substance.

It will of course take time before it is possible to say how well the FSA has lived up to the hopes and met the concerns of those with an interest in the regulation of financial services. One of the perils of creating a super-regulator is, as the Equitable affair has already taught us, that the more powerful a regulator is perceived to be, the more vulnerable it is to criticism when it fails. Furthermore, the broader a regulator's authority, the greater danger there is that failure in one sphere of regulation will undermine confidence in another. The position of the FSA is in some respects akin to a high-wire artist performing without a safety net. It will fail if it does not gauge correctly the proper balance to strike between competing principles, and it will be severely damaged if it misjudges its step, yet it is compelled constantly to move forward.

---

[23] FSA Occasional Paper Series No.1, "The Economic Rationale for Financial Regulation", David Llewellyn, April 1999.

CHAPTER 2

Introduction to the FSMA
and the
Financial Services Authority

DAVID TOUBE

THE REGULATORY OBJECTIVES

2.01   The FSMA is an Act which wears its heart on its sleeve: it contains within its body—and not merely its short title—a comprehensive statement of the regulatory objectives which underpin the Financial Services Authority ("FSA"). The regulatory objectives are:

- market confidence;
- public awareness;
- the protection of consumers; and
- the reduction of financial crime.[1]

These regulatory objectives are not empty aspirations. They are not just a statutory "mission statement" for the FSA, imposing a framework within which it is empowered to exercise its public law powers, although this is of course an important function of the objectives. Rather, Sir Howard Davies characterised the objectives as a "very effective discipline on our internal processes",[2] and contrasted the FSMA favorably with the status quo under the existing financial regulatory legislation which, he observed, had upon occasion left the previous regulators in some difficulty in identifying the ends to which they ought to apply their powers. However, the legal effect of the regulatory objectives is also to describe the boundaries within which the FSA is authorised to act, and are the benchmark against which the Financial Services and Markets Tribunal ("Tribunal") and (if there is an appeal from the Tribunal on a point of law) the courts will judge the lawfulness of the FSA's conduct.[3] Of course, the manner in which the regulatory objectives are

---

[1] FSMA, s. 2(2).
[2] Joint Committee on Financial Services and Markets, *First Report, Minutes of Evidence* (March 16, 1999), para. 22.
[3] Delegated Powers and Deregulation Committee, Draft Financial Services and Markets Bill, para. 11; Joint Committee on Financial Services and Markets, *First Report, op. int.*, Annex B.

drafted may well provide little meat for the High Court on appeal from the Tribunal or in an application for judicial review. Nevertheless, the objectives are a tool for achieving both internal and, at least formally, external accountability of the FSA.

Specifically, the FSMA provides that in discharging its general functions, the FSA must act in a manner which is compatible with the regulatory objectives.[4] However, the FSA is given a relatively high degree of discretion in meeting those regulatory objectives. First, the FSA is constrained to act in a compatible manner only "so far as is reasonably possible". Secondly, the FSA is itself invested with the primary responsibility for determining which measures are "most appropriate for the purpose of meeting those objectives". Thirdly, the FSA's general functions—which are specified as its power to make rules, to prepare and issue codes, to give general guidance, and to determine the general policy and principles which govern the performance of particular functions[5]—are "to be considered as a whole", with the exception of the final general function which is qualified by the term "general". Accordingly, if a person seeks to review judicially or otherwise to challenge a specific exercise of power by the FSA by reference to its compatibility with the regulatory objectives, the Tribunal or court will need to consider that exercise of power in the context of all other exercises of power falling under the same head of "general function". It may well be possible to persuade the Tribunal or court to embark upon such an exercise. However, the effect of this qualification will be to render the exercise somewhat open-textured and to afford the FSA a relatively broad freedom of manoeuvre.

Finally, the absolute character of the regulatory objectives are tempered of further by the requirement that the FSA have regard to a further set of "principles of good regulation"[6]:

- the need for the FSA to use its resources in the most efficient and economic way;

- the responsibilities of those who manage the affairs of authorised persons;

- the principle that a burden or restriction which is imposed on a person, or on the carrying on of an activity, should be proportionate to the benefits, considered in general terms, which are expected to result from the imposition of that burden or restriction;

- the desirability of facilitating innovation in connection with regulated activities;

- the international character of financial services and markets and the desirability of maintaining the competitive position of the United Kingdom;

- the need to minimise the adverse effects on competition that may arise from anything done in the discharge of those functions; and

- the desirability of facilitating competition between those who are subject to any form of regulation by the FSA.

---

[4] FSMA, s. 2(1).
[5] FSMA, s. 2(4).
[6] FSMA, s. 2(3).

Certain of these principles are close to semi-independent statutory objectives: for example, the Joint Committee considered whether competition and competitiveness ought to be given the status of regulatory objectives, and concluded that they should not[7] although it would not have been unreasonable to include these policy goals within the regulatory objectives.[8] Other principles impose high level considerations which are of general application in the exercise of all aspects of the FSA's general function: for example, the European law concept of proportionality is included within the principles. The FSA has developed a "risk model", the central feature of which is that it enables the FSA to assess, in a consistent and integrated manner, potential risks to its objectives occurring measured against the probability of their happening in the first place and against the backdrop of their impact upon the financial system.[9]

Finally, the regulatory objectives themselves operate at a relatively high level of generality. They are further defined within the FSMA as follows:

(a) Market confidence

2.02   The market confidence objective is identified as that of "maintaining confidence in the financial system".[10] The financial system is defined as the United Kingdom financial system, including:

- financial markets and exchanges;
- regulated activities; and
- other activities connected with financial markets and exchanges.

Although the banking sector is not specifically mentioned as an aspect of the financial system, during the passage through Parliament of the FSMA, banking was said to be "swept up" within the final head of the definition of the financial system.[11] The FSA has indicated that it regards its role as limited, in part, to ensuring a "low incidence of failures" of regulated firms and markets: it sensibly regards achieving zero failure as incompatible with the principles of good regulation.[12]

During the pre-legislative scrutiny of the FSMA by the Joint Committee on Financial Services and Markets, extensive consideration was given to the question of whether systemic risk should be included as a fifth regulatory objective. Systemic risk—i.e. the risk presented to financial stability by the failures of financial institutions—is clearly related to market confidence, to the extent that such a failure would certainly contribute to a loss of market confidence. However, systemic risk is a distinct and separate hazard from loss of market confidence, and—as Sir Howard Davies pointed out to the Joint Committee—is the subject of a separate Memorandum of Understanding between the Treasury, the

---

[7] Joint Committee on Financial Services and Markets, *First Report*, para. 51.
[8] Competition is also dealt with separately under Part X, Chapter III of the FSMA.
[9] Annual Report 1999/2000, p. 11.
[10] FSMA, s. 3.
[11] House of Commons, Standing Committee A (c. 164) July 13, 1999. Accepting deposits is itself a regulated activity.
[12] Annual Report 1999/2000.

Bank of England and the FSA[13] which sets out the division of responsibility between the FSA and these two authorities in meeting "the common objective of financial stability".

The course of action favoured by the Joint Committee—which was charged with conducting a pre-legislative review of the draft Bill—was the incorporation of systemic risk within an expanded definition of the market confidence objective. Specifically, the Joint Committee recommended that:

> "the market confidence objective should refer to maintaining confidence in the *soundness* of the financial system, and should be expanded to include a reference to the management of systemic risk, in collaboration with the Treasury and the Bank of England."[14]

Ultimately, however, the Government rejected the Joint Committee's recommendation, in part at least on the grounds that to include systemic risk within the objectives would be to create the misleading impression that systemic risk was the sole responsibility of the FSA, rather than an objective that is shared between three agencies.

(b) Public awareness

2.03   Public awareness is further defined as the promotion of public understanding of the financial system,[15] including:

- promoting awareness of the benefits and risks associated with different kinds of investment or other financial dealing; and

- the provision of appropriate information and advice.

The absence of widespread public awareness of the manner in which the financial sector operates is not simply a matter of abstract pedagogical concern: it was properly perceived by the Government as a potential source of risk to consumers and as a significant obstacle to sound regulation of the financial sector. The improvement of public awareness was therefore a particularly important policy goal, especially when viewed against the backdrop of the move from state to private pension provision. Improving consumer awareness of financial services is a daunting task. For example, in preparing for the reform of the polarisation rules, the FSA discovered that 30 per cent of consumers were of the view that the best source of "independent" financial advice was banks, despite the fact that most banks are tied to a single product provider.[16] The task which faces the FSA should not be underestimated.

Accordingly, the FSA has now taken the first steps towards fulfilling this regulatory objective. The FSA's strategy is set out in the Policy Statement, "Consumer Education: A strategy for promoting public understanding of the financial system",[17]

---

[13] *Financial Services Authority: An Outline,* (1997), App. 2.
[14] Joint Committee on Financial Services and Markets, *First Report,* para. 45.
[15] FSMA, s. 4.
[16] Consultation Paper 80, *Reforming Polarisation: First steps,* para. 4.3.
[17] May 1999.

and certain of the proposals set out in that document are already in place. In summary, the FSA has identified its consumer education role as comprising:

- the promotion both of specific messages and generally of the importance of consumer education as a subject;

- the provision of information tailored to specific audiences; and

- facilitating educational work, in collaboration with other bodies where possible.[18]

Specifically, the FSA proposes to establish educational programmes and publish educational materials for all consumers of financial services in a fashion which—given the inclusion of prepaid funeral plans within the scope of the FSMA—can properly be characterised as "cradle to grave" in nature. Additionally, the FSA has begun to provide generic information and advice—in the form of paper publications[19] and an interactive consumer website—to assist consumers in making intelligent choices in relation to their finances. Most importantly, the FSA has embarked upon a work programme of consumer research intended to identify the core problems which face consumers, their needs of and the role which the FSA can play in addressing those problems and needs. The programme of research is already well underway.[20]

(c) Consumer protection

2.04 In determining the "appropriate degree of protection for consumers, the FSA is obliged to consider the spectrum of risk presented by different transactions, consumers' needs for advice and the range of experience and expertise that different consumers are likely to have in relation to various regulated activities".[21] Given that "consumers" in this context means not only private users of financial services, but broadly speaking "all those with an interest in regulated services", and includes both ordinary members of the public and professional investors, the final consideration is apt and permeates the FSA's approach to the regulation of authorised persons.[22] Furthermore, the definition of consumers includes all persons who are using, have used, or are even contemplating the use of services provided by authorised persons, appointed

---

[18] *Financial Services Authority: an outline* (1997), para. 28.

[19] See, *e.g.*, FSA, *Guide to financial advice*, (May 2000); FSA, *Guide to ISAs*. (May 2000); FSA, *Guide to the risks of pension transfers* (August 2000); FSA, *Factsheet: Endowment Mortgage Complaints* (October 2000); FSA, *Is an endowment mortgage right for you?* (January 2001); FSA, *Guide to making a complaint* (January 2001); FSA, *Factsheet: Stakeholder pensions and decision trees* (March 2001); FSA, *You and Your Money* (March 2001).

[20] See, *e.g.*, Consumer research 1: *Better informed consumers* (April 2000); Consumer research 2: *Stakeholder pensions decision trees* (June 2000); Consumer research 3: *In or out?* (July 2000); Consumer Research 4: *A cycle of disadvantage? Financial exclusion in childhood* (November 2000); Consumer research 5: *Informed decisions?* (November 2000); Consumer research 6: *Persisting—why consumers stop paying into policies* (December 2000); Consumer research 7: *Women and personal finance: the reality of the gender gap* (April 2001).

[21] FSMA, s. 5.

[22] *e.g.*, the FSA has published a separate Inter-Professional Conduct chapter of the *Market Conduct Sourcebook* which proceeds on the basis that a lower degree of protection should be provided in relation to transactions in inter-professional investments undertaken with or for a market counter-party.

representatives,[23] or persons who are unregulated but are nevertheless carrying out regulated activities,[24] and all those whose rights or interests are indirectly derived from or are attributed to such services.

The final consideration in this context is the general principle that consumers should take responsibility for their decisions. During the course of public consultation, the *caveat emptor* provisions resulted in a not wholly unexpected but sharp divergence between the responses from advocates with the interests of consumers on the one hand, and those of the regulated community on the other. The latter argued that the absence of such a provision would result in moral hazard for consumers who would be mistakenly led to believe that the FSA would be able entirely to remove the element of risk from financial services. During the final stages of the bill, an attempt was made by Lord Borrie to qualify the consumer protection objective, by recasting the principle as requiring consumers to take "reasonable responsibility for their decisions".[25] That amendment was not accepted. Nevertheless, the dual requirement that the FSA meet the second regulatory objective of promoting public understanding and the introduction into the FSMA of the obligation that the FSA have regard, in meeting the third regulatory objective, to consumers' needs for advice go some way to providing consumers with some of the necessary tools if they are to take responsibility for their financial decisions.

(d) The reduction of financial crime

2.05   The FSA is required to have regard to the extent to which it is possible for businesses carried on by authorised persons, recognised investment exchanges, recognised clearing houses[26] or unauthorised persons unlawfully carrying on regulated activities[27] to be used for a purpose connected with financial crime. "Financial crime" is defined as including any offence—including acts and omissions carried out outside the United Kingdom which would fall within the definition of financial crime if it took place in the United Kingdom[28]—involving fraud or dishonesty, handling the proceeds of crime or misconduct in, or misuse of information relating to, a financial market.[29] The FSA is also obliged to have regard to the desirability of regulated persons being aware of the risks of involvement in financial crime, and taking "appropriate" measures to prevent, detect and monitor financial crime.[30]

The FSA has sought to meet this regulatory objective, principally in two ways. First, the FSA has a firefighting role; it is empowered to bring proceedings in relation to a broad range of criminal offences which fall within the definition of financial crime.[31] Secondly, the FSA has a firewatching role and has integrated measures into the various rules, guidance and codes which it has produced and designed to ensure that regulated persons have adequate systems in place for the prevention and detection of financial crime.

---

[23] FSMA, s. 138(7).
[24] FSMA, s. 5(3).
[25] House of Commons. (c. 31), March 20, 2000.
[26] FSMA, s. 6(5).
[27] FSMA, s. 6(1).
[28] FSMA, s. 6(4).
[29] FSMA, s. 6(3).
[30] FSMA, s. 6(2).
[31] See, *e.g.*, FSMA, ss. 401 and 402.

THE FSA'S RISK-BASED APPROACH TO REGULATION

2.06   At the heart of the FSA's approach to regulation is the concept of "risk".[32] By risk, the FSA specifically means risks to their statutory objectives. In short, the FSA sees its approach to regulation as moving away from an individualised and isolated focus on regulatory problems presented by specific institutions to a holistic methodology premised upon identifying and pre-empting risks to the regulatory objectives as a whole. The FSA has identified 15 risks to their statutory objectives which are as follows:

- market confidence:
    - o lack of understanding of what the regulator can and cannot achieve;
    - o financial collapse of significant participants in the financial system;
    - o widespread misconduct by, or mismanagement of, institutions;
    - o significant market malfunction; and
    - o financial crime or market abuse on a major scale;

- public awareness:
    - o inadequate general financial literacy of the public; and
    - o inadequate understanding by consumers of specific products and services;

- the protection of consumers:
    - o misconduct by, or mismanagement of, institutions;
    - o market malfunction;
    - o financial crime or market abuse; and
    - o inadequate understanding by consumers of specific products and services;

- the reduction of financial crime:
    - o misconduct in, or misuse of information relating to, a financial market;
    - o fraud or dishonesty; and
    - o handling the proceeds of crime.

   The FSA has stated that its general approach to prioritising these various risks will be premised upon a consideration both of the *impact* of the risk upon the FSA's objectives if it manifests itself, and of the *probability* of the feared event occurring. Accordingly, the FSA has carried out an "impact analysis", which has taken the form of allocating institutions to four "impact bands", in part upon the judgment of regulators and in part by reference to set criteria, which differ for each industry sector. These indicators include, for example, the number of registered individuals and annual turnover of investment advisory firms, and the funds under

---

[32] FSA, *Building the new regulator—Progress Report 1* (December 2000).

management of fund management firms. In a pilot exercise, the FSA has also calculated the probability element of the equation by reference to the likelihood of problems occurring in relation to various specified business and control risks and the likely effect of such problems upon the FSA's consumer protection, public awareness and financial crime objectives.

The ultimate purpose of the risk assessment exercise, is that firms will be allocated to four categories: A, B, C, and D[33] which will determine the nature and intensity of supervision to they will be subject. A Category A regulatory relationship represents the highest level of supervision; a Category D relationship, the lowest. The FSA has suggested that the practical impact upon individual firms of its risk-based approach to regulation is as follows:

- institutions with low risk assessment profiles will no longer enjoy the same level of "close continuous interaction with FSA staff";

- routine monitoring visits will cease, but will be replaced by "sample" visits carried out for the purpose of keeping tabs on sectoral or cross-sectoral compliance standards, and specific visits to deal with issues which have been revealed by a firms returns to the FSA; and

- it will in principle be possible for a firm to reduce its regulatory burden by following the recommendations of the FSA for lowering its risk assessment.[34]

THE DUTIES AND RESPONSIBILITIES OF THE FSA

2.07   The remainder of this work will consider, in greater detail, the particular elements and key aspects of the FSA's duties and responsibilities under the FSMA. However, it is useful at this point to take a broad overview of the regulatory regime created under the FSMA and the functions of the FSA, some of which in essence predate the FSMA, but some of which are recast and expanded, and others of which are wholly novel.

(a) Regulated activities and the general prohibition

2.08   The starting point for any consideration of the nature of the FSA's role is the regulated activities and the general prohibition. Put simply, the general prohibition provides that no person may carry on a regulated activity in the United Kingdom, or purport to do so, unless he is an authorised person or an exempt person.[35] A person is authorised if:

- it has been granted a "permission" under Part IV of the FSMA to carry on regulated activities;

- it is a qualifying "EEA firm"[36];

---

[33] FSA, *Building the new regulator—Progress Report 1* (December 2000), para. 56.
[34] *ibid.*, para. 62.
[35] FSMA, s. 19.
[36] FSMA, Sched. 3.

- it is a qualifying "Treaty firm"[37]; or
- is otherwise authorised under the FSMA.

A person is an "exempt person" if it has not been granted a permission and it is:

- an appointed representative[38];
- a "recognised investment exchange" or "recognised clearing house"; or
- the subject of an exemption order.[39]

Breach of the general prohibition is both a criminal offence[40] and also may result in the person acting unlawfully being subject to civil action taken against them by the public[41] or by the FSA.[42]

(b) Financial Promotion

2.09 Secondly, the FSMA introduces a new regime which performs a similar role to the the "cold calling" and "investment advertisement" regimes under the 1986 Act. The FSMA prohibits the communication in the course of business of invitations or inducements to engage in investment activity otherwise than by authorised persons, unless the contents of the communication are approved by an authorised person.[43] The process of approval may require the authorised person to verify its contents, and to comply with various content and form requirements. The financial promotion regime applies not only to communications issued from the United Kingdom but also to communications which are "capable of having an effect in the United Kingdom". The FSA polices the financial promotion regime as it applies to both authorised and unauthorised persons.

(c) Single authorisation procedure

2.10 Thirdly, the FSA operates a single authorisation procedure for all persons who need to become authorised persons because they are carrying on a regulated activity. A person is an authorised person if it has been granted specific permission or permission to carry on regulated activities by the FSA under Part IV of the FSMA. The FSA is empowered to describe or limit the scope of any permission.[44] In granting or varying a permission, the FSA must ensure that the authorised person meets five "Threshold Conditions" in relation to the activities which it will carry out, which include fitness and propriety and adequacy of resources.

Separately, the FSMA establishes a new "approved persons" regime.[45] Put very briefly, authorised persons are obliged to secure the approval of the FSA before any

---

[37] FSMA, Sched. 4.
[38] FSMA, s. 39.
[39] FSMA, s. 38.
[40] FSMA, s. 23.
[41] FSMA, ss. 26–29.
[42] FSMA, ss. 380 and 382.
[43] FSMA, s. 19.
[44] FSMA, s. 46.
[45] FSMA, s. 59.

person employed by or who provides services for the authorised person performs a controlled function under an arrangement entered into by the authorised person in relation to the carrying on by that authorised person of a regulated activity. Controlled functions fall into the following three categories:

- the exercise of a significant influence on the conduct of the authorised person's affairs;
- dealing with customers of the authorised person; and
- dealing with property of customers of the authorised person;

in a manner substantially connected with the carrying on of the regulated activity. The FSA has expanded extensively upon the nature of the roles that are caught in the Supervision Manual.

(d) Single regulator

2.11   Fourthly, the FSMA constitutes the FSA as the single regulator for all authorised persons and approved persons. As such, it is empowered to make rules, issue guidance and codes in relation to a wide variety of matters,[46] including those which govern the conduct of business by authorised persons and the prudential supervision of authorised persons. The FSA is also invested with formidable investigatory[47] and disciplinary[48] powers which may be exercised against authorised persons.

Separately, the FSA is responsible for the recognition and supervision of investment exchanges and clearing houses.[49]

In addition, the FSA has a role to play in relation to the authorisation and recognition of certain collective investment schemes.[50] The FSMA itself governs the operation and promotion of collective investment schemes more generally.

(e) Criminal offences and market abuse

2.12   Fifthly, the FSA is invested with the power to prosecute a broad range of offences concerning the financial markets.[51]

The FSMA also creates a regulatory "offence" of "market abuse": behaviour which occurs in relation to "qualifying" investments "traded on" a prescribed market, which a regular user of that market[52] would regard as amounting to a failure to observe "the standard of behaviour reasonably expected of a person in his or their position in relation to the market". Although in many ways the market abuse procedure resembles a domestic disciplinary regime, it applies not only to authorised persons who can be said to have voluntarily submitted to the jurisdiction

---

[46] FSMA, Pt X.
[47] FSMA, Pt XI
[48] FSMA, Pt XIV.
[49] FSMA, Pt XVIII.
[50] FSMA, Pt XVII.
[51] FSMA, Pt XXVII.
[52] A "regular user" is defined as a reasonable person who regularly deals on that market in investments of the kind in question: FSMA, s. 118(10).

of the FSA, but also unauthorised members of the public. Once the FSA has decided to impose a sanction upon a market abuser, and if the matter is referred by the "defendant", the case is tried not by a criminal court but by the Tribunal.

(f) UK Listing Authority

2.13 Finally, under the FSMA the FSA is the "competent authority",[53] responsible for the maintenance of the official list.

ACCOUNTABILITY

2.14 For those familiar with the patchwork quilt of regulation which preceded the FSMA, when considering the breadth of the FSA's responsibilities set out, it is easy to see why the FSA has been characterised neutrally as a "super-regulator" and less charitably as both a "behemoth"[54] and a "leviathan".[55] The thinking behind such uncomplimentary bestial comparisons was that the FSA would, if not subject to proper safeguards upon its powers, grow into an all-powerful supervisor, answerable in practice to nobody, which would risk declining into the sort of bureaucratic monster to which Lord Acton's familiar caveat in relation to persons who exercise absolute power might appear apposite. Broadly speaking, the concerns of those who opposed the FSMA were directed, at the micro level, to the disciplinary sanctions which the FSA was empowered to exercise in relation to regulated persons, and at a macro level, to the effect which the FSA would have upon the financial system as a whole. In short, it was feared that, were the FSA invested with broad unchecked rule-making powers, it would succumb to the natural bureaucratic tendency to over-regulation of its subjects. Over-regulation in turn, it was feared, might ultimately lead to a decline in the United Kingdom's position as a player in global financial markets as players in those markets engaged in regulatory arbitrage and exercised their right to establish themselves in jurisdictions which imposed a more tolerable regulatory burden.

The answer to these concerns is in part that under-regulation itself presents a threat to the stability and reputation of financial markets. Equally, it has been argued that the consolidation of regulators into a single "super-regulator" is itself a solution to over-regulation. A single regulator deriving its powers from a single piece of legislation covering the majority of financial services business is in a better position to deliver focused, integrated and coherent regulation across the range of various disparate financial service activities in a cost effective manner than a patchwork quilt of regulators, each imposing different regulatory requirements upon firms with a set of multiple authorisations.

However, a partial and practical solution to the problem of misapplication of power and over-regulation is accountability. The FSMA provides for a broad range of checks and balances upon the powers of the FSMA at every level of operation.

---

[53] FSMA, Pt VI.
[54] House of Commons c. 365, vol. 344 HC, February 9, 2000.
[55] ibid., c. 369 McElwee, Martin and Tyrie, Andrew, *Leviathan at large: the new regulator for the financial markets* (Centre for Policy Studies, 2000).

(a) Judicial oversight

2.15   Although judicial oversight undoubtedly has a role to play in restraining the use of power by the FSA, it is clearly not the option most favoured by the FSMA for reasons which are transparently related to the resource implications of litigation, the delay and uncertainty associated with a legal challenge, and the danger that a vulnerable FSA would practise "defensive" regulation, taking unnecessary precautions in order to minimise the threat of litigation.[56] Accordingly, as we have seen, the limits upon the power of the FSA contained within the regulatory objectives are drafted so as to provide relatively lean pickings in an application for judicial review of the FSA.

Moreover, the FSA and its staff, members and officers are granted statutory immunity[57] from liability in damages in respect of act or omissions in relation to the discharge of the FSA's functions. Statutory immunity does not extend to instances of bad faith.[58] Neither does it prevent an award of damages which is unlawful under the Human Rights Act 1998.[59]

Although the provisions giving statutory immunity to the FSA largely reproduced a similar stipulation in the 1986 Act, statutory immunity emerged as a source of contention during the passage of the FSMA. Opponents of the provision sought to limit the statutory immunity of the FSA so that it would render the FSA liable if it acted unreasonably, recklessly or negligently.[60] Indeed, the Joint Committee had concluded that statutory immunity should remain as drafted, only subject to their recommendations relating to the strengthening of the powers of the complaints committee, which included a suggestion that the Investigator be empowered to award compensation to businesses or their employees damaged by the maladministration of the FSA. However, that particular recommendation was not implemented.

The difficulty presented by the statutory immunity provision and the likely difficulty in making a successful application for judicial review is in part compensated for by the presence in the FSMA of a significant number of rights of reference to the Tribunal. In summary, a person may refer a matter to the Tribunal in a wide variety of circumstances, including:

- following the refusal an application for permission to carry on regulated activities[61];

---

[56] See, e.g., the argument presented by the Economic Secretary, Patricia Hewitt, in the House of Commons, Standing Committee A, on Tuesday July 13, 1999 at 5. 45 p.m.

[57] FSMA, Sched. 1, para. 19.

[58] See, e.g., *Three Rivers District Council v. Governor and Co. of the Bank of England* (2000) UKHL/16: in that case, a strikeout of the claimant's action failed. The claimant alleged misfeasance in a public office by the Bank of England which is in some respects analogous, but not identical, to bad faith.

[59] See *Osman v. United Kingdom* (1998), Application No. 00023452/94 which held that the blanket immunity from suit in respect civil proceedings against the police was in breach of Article 6(1). Although the application of Osman to actions in the tort of negligence against public bodies has recently been significantly cut down by *Z and others v. the United Kingdom* (Application No. 000/29392/95), it is not at all clear whether a statutory blanket immunity will meet the "fair, just and reasonable" test required by Article 6.

[60] c. 147, House of Commons, Standing Committee A, July 13, 1999.

[61] FSMA, s. 55.

- following the making of a prohibition order[62];

- following an unsuccessful application for the variation or revocation of a prohibition notice[63];

- following the refusal of an application for approval to perform a controlled function[64];

- following the withdrawal of the FSA's approval[65];

- following the decision to take disciplinary action against a person[66];

- in market abuse cases, following the service of a decision notice stating that the FSA will impose a penalty upon or issue a statement in respect of a person[67];

- various powers to refer matters to the Tribunal relating to the promotion and recognition of collective investment schemes constituted in other EEA states.[68]

The nature and operation of the Tribunal is set out in greater detail at Chapter 10, below. However, it should be noted that during the progress of the FSMA through Parliament, the Tribunal developed from a purely appellate and essentially domestic creature to an independent body, forming part of the Courts Service, whose rules are made by the Lord Chancellor[69] and whose Chairmen are drawn from a panel appointed by the Lord Chancellor[70] and whose President and Deputy President are also appointed by the Lord Chancellor.[71] Persons accused of market abuse who exercise their right to refer a decision notice issued by the FSA to the Tribunal may also qualify for legal assistance[72] to meet the costs of legal advice before the Tribunal.

(b) Public Consultation

2.16 At a second level, accountability is achieved by public consultation. The FSA is subject to a general duty to put in place "effective arrangements" for consulting with both practitioners and consumers on the consistency of its general policies with its general statutory duties.[73]

These arrangements must include, but are not limited to, the establishment of both a Practitioner Panel and a Consumer Panel,[74] which are given teeth by an obligation on the FSA not only to consider any representations in relation to the FSA's

---

[62] FSMA, s. 57(5).
[63] FSMA, s. 58(5).
[64] FSMA, s. 62(4).
[65] FSMA, s. 63(4).
[66] FSMA, s. 67(7).
[67] FSMA, s. 129(4).
[68] FSMA, ss. 265(5), 269(3), 271(3), 276(2), 280(2).
[69] FSMA, s. 132.
[70] FSMA, Sched. 13, para. 3
[71] FSMA, Sched. 13, para. 2
[72] FSMA, s. 134.
[73] FSMA, s. 8.
[74] FSMA, ss. 9–10.

general policies which the Panels may make, but also to set out in writing the FSA's reasons for disagreeing with any representation made by the Panels.[75] The Practitioner Panel must include representatives of authorised individuals, authorised firms, recognised investment exchanges and recognised clearing houses. Although authorised persons are within the scope of the statutory definition of "consumer", they are excluded from membership of the Consumer Panel. In the first instance, the FSA is responsible for appointing the members of these two Panels; however, their independence is partially safeguarded by the requirement for the approval of the Treasury for the appointment or dismissal of their Chairmen.

Additionally, before the FSA is permitted to make rules under Part X of the FSMA, to publish a statement or code setting out the conduct to be expected by approved persons,[76] or to make an insurance market direction in respect of the Lloyds market,[77] a direction to the Council, to Society of Lloyds,[78] or a to make direction in relation to an exemption varying the scope of application of the limited exemption from general prohibition in relation to financial services provided by lawyers, accountants and actuaries,[79] it is obliged to publish those provisions in draft. An analogous procedure applies to the publication of draft statements of procedure which govern the process for issuing supervisory or warning notices in disciplinary cases,[80] and the issuing of draft statements of policy which set out the FSA's policy in relation to the imposition and calculation of penalties for breach of the Listing Rules,[81] under the market abuse[82] regime and in respect of other disciplinary penalties.[83] A similar consultation exercise must be carried out in relation to the FSA's own internal complaints scheme.[84]

When certain draft documents are published, the FSA is obliged both to explain the purpose of those provisions and set out why it is of the view that the rules are compatible with its general duties under the FSMA.[85] The FSA is also generally obliged to have regard to representations which are made to it during the course of consultation exercises, to publish the representations which it receives, to set out its response, and—if the FSA amends its draft rules in the light of the consultation process—to set out the details of the amendments.[86] The FSA has in fact consulted extensively upon all aspects of the exercise of its rule making powers, well before the FSMA came into force (although in fairness, the FSA was motivated not only by a desire to enhance the general transparency of the process but also by the need

---

[75] FSMA, s. 11.
[76] FSMA, s. 64.
[77] FSMA, s. 316.
[78] FSMA, s. 318.
[79] FSMA, s. 328.
[80] FSMA, s. 396.
[81] FSMA, s. 93.
[82] FSMA, s. 125.
[83] FSMA, s. 210.
[84] FSMA, Sched. 1, para. 7(5).
[85] The obligation to explain the compatibility of draft material with the FSA's general duties only applies to the publication of rules under Part X of the FSMA.
[86] FSMA, s. 155. The analogous procedure governing codes and statements of principle applying to Approved persons is contained in s. 65. In respect of directions made in relation to Lloyd's, the procedure is set out at s. 319 of the FSMA. In relation to directions made in respect of members of the professions, the consultation procedure is set out in s. 330 of the FSMA. The procedure in relation to penalties for breach of the Listing Rules is at s. 94 of the FSMA, in respect of market abuse, at section 125, FSMA and in respect of disciplinary penalties, at s. 211.

to conduct and conclude the consultation process in a timely manner). By virtue of a transitional order made under the FSMA,[87] all consultations properly carried out before the Act came into force are deemed to be valid. The consultation processes resulted in changes which were sometimes significantly being made to their subject matter, and afforded the FSA with the considerable benefit of the respondents' experiences of the financial system in practice. The process also enabled the FSA to identify and remedy a series of relatively small but important accidental omissions and drafting errors in early versions of the rules, codes and guidance.

The FSA is also obliged to include with certain draft consultation documents, a "cost benefit analysis",[88] *i.e.* an estimate of both the costs and the benefits arising from the making of the rules.[89] A cost benefit analysis must also accompany any revised rules published following the consultation exercise.[90] However, the FSA is excused from this obligation if it concludes that there will be no, or only a minimal, increase in costs.[91]

The cost benefit analysis is an important method of ensuring that the FSA does not subject the financial system to over-regulation.[92] Compliance is not a cost-free matter. Each new rule potentially places direct or indirect compliance costs upon regulated persons which either arise from compliance with the rules themselves, or are passed on to regulated bodies in the form of fees levied by the FSA, both of which in turn are potentially passed on to consumers. Equally, such costs may in turn impact upon the competitiveness of the United Kingdom financial system, and therefore may conflict with the principle which requires the FSA to have regard to the need to minimise the adverse effects on competition presented by anything done in the discharge of its general functions.[93]

Finally, the FSA is obliged to hold an Annual Meeting within three months of the publication of its Annual Report,[94] and to publish a report of that meeting.[95] At the Annual Meeting, the FSA must allow for a general discussion of the contents of the Annual Report, and provide for questions to be put to the FSA relating to its exercise of powers during the period under scrutiny.

(c) The Treasury

2.17   At a third level, the FSA is accountable to the Treasury. At the most basic level, the FSA is obliged to provide copies of any rules,[96] general guidance[97] and codes and statements of principle[98] which it makes to the Treasury. The Treasury is also empowered to direct the FSA to take certain steps to remedy an adverse

---

[87] Part III of the Financial Services and Markets Act 2000 (Transitional Provisions and Savings (Rules) Order 2001).
[88] FSMA, s. 155(2)(a).
[89] FSMA, s. 155(10).
[90] FSMA, s. 155(6)(b).
[91] FSMA, s. 155(8).
[92] For a discussion of the FSA's methods, see Occasional Paper Series 3, "Cost-Benefit Analysis in Financial Regulation: How to do it and how it adds value" by Isaac Alfon and Peter Andrews, FSA (September 1999).
[93] FSMA, s. 2(3)(f).
[94] FSMA, Sched. 1, para. 11.
[95] FSMA, Sched. 1, para. 12.
[96] FSMA, s. 152.
[97] FSMA, s. 158.
[98] FSMA, s. 64.

effect on competition[99] identified by the Competition Commission. Indeed, the Treasury has an undoubted but probably theoretical power to make subordinate legislation in place of the FSA.[1] Neither should it be forgotten that the Treasury is responsible for the appointment (and the dismissing) of the Chairman and the governing body of the FSA.[2]

However, the keystone in the process of accountability is the Annual Report.[3] The Annual Report must contain an account of:

- the discharge by the FSA of its functions;

- the extent to which, the FSA's regulatory objectives have been met; and

- its consideration of the manner in which it has observed the principles.

Additionally, the Annual Report must contain the report of the Chairman of the Non-Executive Committee of the Governing Body of the FSA. The Treasury is also empowered to direct that an Annual Report address any additional matters, reports or information that it is minded to require be included. Indeed, the FSA agreed with HM Treasury in 1999 the contents of the Annual Report which will be published in 2002[4]: that Report will consider a broad range of matters, including such general issues as the "major policy decisions taken during the year and the reasons for them", but also specific information including, for example, data relating to the authorisation of firms and enforcement matters, and a comparative assessment of the compliance costs imposed by the regime, measured against the costs in other jurisdictions.[5] Once the Annual Report has been published, it must be laid before Parliament.

The Treasury is also equipped with what might be termed emergency powers to hold the FSA—and indeed the financial system—to account. The Treasury is empowered to appoint an independent person to conduct a Review solely of the economy, efficiency and effectiveness with which the Authority has used its resources in discharging its functions,[6] although that person is not empowered to consider the merits of the Authority's general policy or principles, or the FSA's role as the Listing Authority. Within those boundaries, however, the Treasury may set the terms of the Review: the report may consider either the functions of the FSA as a whole, or it may be limited to specific functions only of the FSA. The investigator has the power to call for persons and papers to be made available to it.[7] At the conclusion of these inquiries, the investigator is required to make a written report to the Treasury, which must then be published.

The Treasury is also able to set up two species of Inquiry. In the first type of Inquiry, the Treasury may order an investigation into a collective investment

---

[99] FSMA, ss. 163 and 307.

[1] See s. 426 of the FSMA, which is an archetypal "Henry the VIII" clause.

[2] FSMA, Sched. 1, para. 2.

[3] FSMA, Sched. 1, para. 10.

[4] FSA Press release, FSA/PN/064/1999.

[5] Indeed, somewhat out of date comparative information was published in FSA, *A new regulator for the new millennium* (January 2000).

[6] FSMA, s. 12.

[7] FSMA, s. 13.

scheme[8] or a person who is carrying out a regulated activity which either presented or could have presented a "grave risk" to the financial system or caused or could have caused significant damage to the interests of consumers, which was at least partly attributable to either operation of the regulatory regime established under the FSMA, or the regime itself. Secondly, the Treasury is empowered to set up an Inquiry into a serious failure in the regulation of listed securities as a result of events relating to listed securities or their issuers which presented at least the risk of serious damage to their holders.[9] If such an inquiry is to be held, the Treasury will appoint an investigator invested with the powers of the High Court to order the production of documents and the giving of evidence,[10] and with the power to refer any refusal to assist to the High Court for punishment as a contempt of court.[11] The Treasury may at its discretion withhold publication of all or part of such a report of the Inquiry.[12]

As a footnote, there is no explicit provision for accountability of the FSA to Parliament, although certain orders made under the FSMA are subject to parliamentary approval.[13] A constitutionally innovative attempt to introduce a higher degree of Parliamentary accountability was made by Lord Kingsland during the committee stage of the FSMA in the House of Lords.[14] It was proposed that the appointments of the chairman, the chief executive and the non-executive deputy chairman of the FSA should be subject to confirmation by the House of Commons Treasury Select Committee following a public hearing. That amendment was withdrawn. It should be mentioned that according to the ordinary constitutional principles of ministerial responsibility, the Minister is accountable to Parliament: the FSA is therefore accountable, at one stage removed, to Parliament.

(d) The Complaints Scheme

2.18   At the fourth level, the FSA is obliged to operate and publish details of a complaints scheme to investigate complaints against itself[15] and to appoint an independent complaints investigator,[16] whose independence from the FSA is assured by the requirement for Treasury approval before that person is appointed or dismissed. When presented with a complaint, the FSA may either investigate the matter itself, refer the matter to the investigator, or determine that the complaint should be dealt with in a manner which it considers more appropriate (in which case it must at least inform the investigator, who may nevertheless take the case up).[17] The investigator is empowered to recommend remedial action, and/or make an ex gratia payment to the complainant. It should be noted that the Joint Committee took the view that, the wide ranging statutory immunity enjoyed by the FSA gave rise to a good argument that the investigator be empowered to award compensation in cases involving

---

[8] *cf.* the LTCM crisis, which threatened global markets.
[9] FSMA, s. 14.
[10] FSMA, s. 15.
[11] FSMA, s. 18.
[12] FSMA, s. 17.
[13] FSMA, s. 429.
[14] c. 1721, House of Lords, March 16, 2000.
[15] FSMA, Sched. 1, para. 7(1)(a).
[16] FSMA, Sched. 1, para. 7(1)(b).
[17] FSMA, Sched. 1, para. 8.

maladministration, and that the appointment of the investigator be approved by the Lord Chancellor.[18] Neither suggestion was accepted by the Government.

(e) The FSA Board

2.19   The fifth and final level at which the FSA is rendered accountable is by means of its own governing body. At the highest level of generality, the FSA is obliged to have regard to the principles of good corporate governance "as it is reasonable to regard as applicable to it".[19] Because this requirement is a statutory obligation, the chief forum for holding the FSA to account in this respect may well be the Annual Meeting. However, a more structured and permanent level of scrutiny is provided by the governing body of the FSA, a majority of whose members must be non-executive. These non executive members are appointed by the FSA, although the Chairman is selected from those members by the Treasury.[20] The function of non-executive members is to:

- scrutinise on a permanent basis whether the FSA is deploying its resources efficiently and economically in carrying out its functions in accordance with decisions of its governing body;

- overseeing the proper conduct of the FSA's financial affairs; and

- setting the salaries of the Chairman and the executive members of the FSA.

OTHER INSTITUTIONS

2.20   We have considered the important role played by some of the most important bodies, mechanisms and other institutions established under the FSMA in ensuring the accountability of the FSMA. There are, however, two bodies whose function is directed not at checking excesses of power or misadministration by the FSA, but rather in providing cheap and quick redress for customers against the firms. Those two bodies are the Financial Services Ombudsman Scheme ("Ombudsman") and the Financial Services Compensation Scheme ("Compensation Scheme").

(a) The Ombudsman

2.21   The Ombudsman established under the FSMA[21] replaced eight separate ombudsman schemes in operation under the pre-FSMA regime: the Banking Ombudsman, the Building Societies Ombudsman, the Insurance Ombudsman, the Office of the Investment Ombudsman, the Personal Insurance Arbitration Service, the PIA Ombudsman Bureau, the SFA Complaints Bureau and Arbitration Services, and the FSA Independent Investigator. The new Ombudsman is administered by an independent body corporate, the board of which is appointed by the

---

[18] Joint Committee on Financial Services and Markets, *First Report*, para. 146.
[19] FSMA, s. 7.
[20] FSMA, Sched. 1, para. 3.
[21] FSMA, Pt XVI.

FSA but whose Chairman is subject to Treasury approval.[22] The FSA has a certain role to play in relation to determining the scope of the Ombudsman scheme, setting fees, and approving rules which govern the scope of and access to the Ombudsman. However, the Ombudsman is operationally independent from the FSA.

The Ombudsman has oversight over complaints falling within two categories: the "compulsory jurisdiction"[23] which in principle covers both the regulated and potentially regulated activities of authorised firms, and the "voluntary jurisdiction", which is in principle also open to unauthorised firms (for example, members of the self-regulatory General Insurance Standards Council) and to those potentially regulated activities of authorised firms not brought within the Compulsory Jurisdiction. The Ombudsman scheme is open only to private individuals and to certain small businesses (although Lloyd's Members are excluded from access to the Ombudsman scheme).

The function of the Ombudsman is to provide a quick, informal, flexible, cost effective, accessible and efficient dispute resolution service with the power to order firms to pay "fair" compensation for loss and damage[24] which in the case of the Compulsory Jurisdiction may be enforced by a County Court[25] and additionally may order the firm to take steps, enforceable by an injunction[26] which the Ombudsman considers to be "just and appropriate" to remedy the complaint. It should be noted, however, that under the *Conduct of Business Sourcebook*, a firm is required to inform its customer of its internal complaints procedure, and of the right of access to the Ombudsman[27] which is envisaged as the first port of call for a customer with a complaint.

A person may use the Ombudsman scheme if:

- the complainant is eligible and it wishes to have the complaint dealt with under the Ombudsman scheme; and

- at the time that the act or omission to which the complaint relates,

  — the Compulsory Jurisdiction rules were in force in relation to the activity in question and the respondent was an authorised person at the time of the act or omission to which the complaint relates; or
  — the respondent was participating in the Voluntary Jurisdiction of the scheme and the Voluntary Jurisdiction rules were in force at the time of the act or omission to which the complaint relates occurred and the respondent was participating in the scheme, and the complaint cannot be dealt with under the compulsory jurisdiction.[28]

The Ombudsman is empowered to call for documents and information to be provided to it.[29] Failure to comply with a request for documents or information may

---

[22] FSMA, Sched. 17, para. 3(2).
[23] FSMA, s. 226.
[24] FSMA, s. 229.
[25] FSMA, Sched. 17, para. 16.
[26] FSMA, s. 229(9).
[27] See, *e.g.*, Table COB 4.2(9)R of the COBS.
[28] FSMA, ss. 226–227.
[29] FSMA, s. 231.

be referred to the High Court which can treat the failure to comply as a contempt of court. The Ombudsman is also obliged to provide an Annual Report to the FSA.[30] The Ombudsman's powers and procedures are further circumscribed by the Ombudsman scheme rules[31] which are subject to a public consultation requirement.[32]

(b) The Compensation Scheme

2.22   The "alphabet soup" of regulators which existed prior to the FSMA was mirrored by a parallel jumble of compensation schemes.

- deposit taking was covered by two schemes: the Deposit Protection Scheme for banks and the Building Societies Investor Protection Scheme covering building societies;

- investment business was covered by the Investors Compensation Scheme;

- most insurance business was covered by the Policyholders Protection Scheme with the exception of that carried on by Friendly Societies, which was originally covered by the Friendly Societies Protection Scheme.

Further, the United Kingdom is subject to two European Directives which set the standards for Deposit Guarantee Schemes[33] and Investor Compensation Schemes.[34]

Under the FSMA,[35] a new statutory scheme has been established by the FSA, which is operated by a scheme manager, the Financial Services Compensation Scheme Limited. The scheme covers all firms authorised by the FSA (including, ultimately the deposit taking activities of Credit Unions), with the exception of:

- service companies;

- some EEA firms (United Kingdom branches of passporting EEA firms may in certain circumstances apply to participate in the Compensation Scheme);

- the Society of Lloyd's and firms carrying on Lloyd's business only; and

- FSA regulated professional firms.

The last two species of firms are covered by a separate compensation scheme.

The Compensation Scheme is divided into three sub-schemes: Accepting Deposits, Insurance Business and Investment Business. Within each sub-scheme, the following conditions must be met if compensation is to be paid:

- there must be an application for compensation which relates to business covered by the Scheme conducted by an authorised or passported firm in default; and

---

[30] FSMA, Sched. 17, para. 7.
[31] FSMA, Sched. 17, para 14.
[32] FSMA, Sched. 17, para. 22.
[33] Directive 94/19.
[34] Directive 97/9.
[35] FSMA, Pt XV.

- the claimant must, if required to do so, assign its rights in respect of the claim to the scheme manager.

Broadly speaking, only small businesses and private individuals qualify for compensation.[36] The Compensation Scheme also provides, in particular circumstances for caps on compensation to be paid, and also sets certain limits on the proportion of the claim which can be awarded.

The funding of the Compensation Scheme is divided between three subschemes. Each subscheme is further subdivided into "contribution groups" of firms offering similar products and services, designed to minimise cross subsidy between firms whose business was not similar; the contribution groups largely mirror the FSA fee categories into which the firms fall. Within each contribution group, liabilities are "weighted" to firms which do business with consumers who are eligible to receive compensation. Compensation costs largely fall, as far as possible, on the individual contribution groups within which the default occurs. All firms will additionally contribute to the base costs of running the Compensation Scheme.

SELF-REGULATION OF GENERAL INSURANCE INTERMEDIARIES

2.23 The FSMA has also resulted in the deregulation of general insurance broking—*i.e.* the broking of contracts of insurance which are not regulated investments— with the repeal of the Insurance Brokers (Registration) Act 1977 and the abolition of the Insurance Brokers Registration Council ("IBRC"), which follows the creation by the industry of the non-statutory and truly self regulatory organisation, the General Insurance Standards Council ("GISC"). There was prior to the repeal of the 1977 Act no requirement that a person who acted as an intermediary in the arrangement of general insurance cover or the provision of advice in relation to such non-regulated products be licensed. There was, however, a prohibition upon any person describing himself as an insurance broker, unless he was registered with the IBRC.

GISC was launched on July 3, 2000. Membership of GISC is entirely voluntary, although the ABI and GISC have been working towards creating a consensus under which insurers will not deal with brokers unless they are members of GISC. GISC itself provides to customers the following protections:

- a Private Customer Code which sets out minimum standards of good practice by which all Members of GISC are required to abide when dealing with consumers. The Private Customer Code is decidedly "light touch". Nevertheless, it does provide useful protections to consumers including a 14-day cooling-off period. In addition, GISC has published guidance for use in Terms of Business which, though optional, is intended to provide assistance to GISC members which wish to meet their obligations under the Code;

- a Commercial Code governing the conduct of GISC members in their dealings with commercial customers;

---

[36] The Compensation Scheme rules set out the categories of circumstances in which a claim is excluded.

- independent monitoring by GISC;

- an independent complaints procedure and dispute resolution scheme; and

- GISC Rules, containing in addition to the matters listed above, provisions governing training and competence, intervention and enforcement, client money handing, solvency and the maintenance of professional indemnity insurance.

GISC's scope does not cover all unregulated products, but covers only the general insurance contracts originally listed in Schedule 2 to the Insurance Companies Act 1982.

CHAPTER 3

Regulated Activities and the "General Prohibition"

JAMES PERRY

INTRODUCTION

3.01 The "regulated activities" are the core of the FSMA. The definition and scope of the regulated activities which will determine, in most cases, whether different kinds of businesses will require authorisation under the Act. Broadly speaking, the answer to the question of whether a person will need authorisation under the FSMA will be answered by the following analysis:

(a) Will activities be carried on which are regulated activities under the Act?

(b) Is any such activity carried on by way of business?

(c) Is any such activity carried on within the United Kingdom territorial scope of the Act?

(d) Is the relevant person exempt or does an exemption apply?

If the answer to the first three questions is "yes" and to the fourth question is "no", then (subject to the position in relation to firms which are covered by the European single market directives or which are "Treaty firms", which will be discussed later) FSMA authorisation is very likely to be required. This chapter discusses these issues, as they apply to banking, insurance and investment businesses, in more detail.

THE GENERAL PROHIBITION

3.02 The requirement for FSMA authorisation stems from the so-called "general prohibition" in section 19 of the Act. This states that no person may carry on a regulated activity in the United Kingdom, or purport to do so, unless he is an authorised person or an exempt person. An "authorised person" is defined by section 31(1) as a person who has a "permission" under Part IV of the FSMA to carry on one or more regulated activities; an "EEA firm" or a "Treaty firm" qualifying for authorisation under, respectively, Schedules 3 or 4 of the Act; or a person who is otherwise authorised by a provision in or under the Act. Conversely, an "exempt person" may either be exempt because of who he is (for example, the European Community and the International Monetary Fund are exempt except in relation to insurance business) or, in relation to relevant activities, because he falls within a category of persons specified under the FSMA as being exempt (section 38).

A person who breaches the general prohibition is guilty of a criminal offence and may be tried summarily or on indictment. On conviction on indictment, a person is liable to imprisonment for two years or a fine, or both (section 23(1)). As was the case under the 1986 Act, it is a defence for the accused to show that he took all reasonable precautions and exercised all due diligence to avoid committing the offence (section 23(3)). In practice, this has normally been taken to mean that a person should seek legal advice where appropriate; that he should check the status of a person with whom he is dealing where that is relevant (such as, for example, in a case where a person wishes to deal in derivative contracts and relies on the authorisation of his broker to avoid contravening the general prohibition); and that he should take reasonable care not to exceed the terms of any exemption or "safe harbour" on which he is relying. In addition, the FSA can often provide helpful guidance on the requirement for authorisation to those on the "perimeter" of regulation, though such guidance will always be given subject to the (understandable) caveats that the FSA's view is not a substitute for taking independent legal advice and that the interpretation of legislation (both primary and secondary) is ultimately a matter for the courts. The FSA has already issued "perimeter guidance" in Chapter 2 and Appendix 1 of the Authorisation manual (part of the FSA Handbook).

Significantly, a breach of the general prohibition may also result in agreements being unenforceable against the other party (this is discussed below).

"HOLDING OUT"

3.03   As was the case under section 4 of the 1986 Act, the general prohibition catches persons who "purport" to carry on a regulated activity in the United Kingdom when they are neither authorised nor exempt. As a policy matter for the protection of depositors, investors and others, it must be correct to penalise those who give the outward impression of carrying on a regulated activity, even if they do not commit the substantive offence.

This provision is augmented by a new offence which catches a person who is neither authorised nor (in relation to the particular activity) exempt and who describes himself (in whatever terms) as an authorised person or an exempt person, or who behaves, or otherwise holds himself out, in a manner which indicates (or which is reasonably likely to be understood as indicating) that he is authorised or exempt (section 24(1)). This offence has its root in the Banking Acts—mostly recently, sections 67 and 69 of the Banking Act 1987—which prohibited any person apart from an authorised institution from holding itself out as a "bank". In the overall context of the rationalisation of financial services regulation in the United Kingdom, the sensible decision has been taken to extend this "holding out" offence to any regulated activity under the FSMA, including insurance and investment business. As with the general prohibition, a statutory defence is provided for an accused person who can prove that he took all reasonable precautions and exercised all due diligence to avoid committing the offence (section 24(2)). It is suggested that the onus of this defence may be difficult to shift in some cases; for example, an overseas firm marketing to United Kingdom persons may apparently commit the offence without any fault on its part and will then only be relieved from liability if it does everything necessary to avoid creating the impression that it is United Kingdom authorised. This might well include, for example, stating that the firm is not United Kingdom authorised on all relevant pages of a web-based advertisement. In due course, some guidance from the FSA on the steps required in particular situations would be useful.

REGULATED ACTIVITIES UNDER THE FSMA

3.04   An interested reader studying the FSMA for the first time would, perhaps, expect to see the new "regulated activities" laid before him, in full detail, in the primary legislation. If that expectation did exist, the reader would be sorely disappointed. Section 22(1) provides that a "regulated activity" is an activity of a "specified kind" which is carried on by way of business and—

(a) relates to an investment of a specified kind; or

(b) in the case of some specified activities, is carried on in relation to property of any kind.

This vague description is then supplemented by a lengthy Schedule which recites various "regulated activities" and "investments", but only in terms which make it clear that they merely reflect matters which may be included in orders made by H.M. Treasury (Schedule 2 of the FSMA). Therefore, though many of the potential "regulated activities" specified in Schedule 2 hark back to the 1986 Act, they do not even appear to be a starting point, since section 22(3) provides that nothing in Schedule 2 limits the broad power conferred on H.M. Treasury by section 22(1) (which is amplified in Part III of Schedule 2) to "specify" regulated activities and investments. Section 22(4) completes this lack of definition by asserting that an "investment" includes any asset, right or interest.

Some commentators have argued that, in theory, H.M. Treasury could in future take advantage of the highly permissive nature of section 22 to bring within the ambit of regulation some kinds of property which would not currently be thought of as being proper subjects for financial regulation—such as land, paintings, antique furniture or wine. On its face, the FSMA does not seem to prevent this. Against this, however, it has been argued that Schedule 2 effectively sets the "four corners" of statutory regulation beyond which the Treasury, by order, may not stray. As a matter of strict statutory interpretation, this seems doubtful, though it would be helpful if the Treasury adopts this approach when considering possible amendments in the future.

As it is, the "investments" and "regulated activities" at the heart of the FSMA have been prescribed by the Regulated Activities Order ("RAO") of which much more is said later in this chapter.

BUSINESS

3.05 Early drafts of section 22 caused considerable disquiet by omitting any requirement for regulated activities to be carried on by way of business. A similar omission was made in relation to "financial promotion" (see Chapter 6, below). H.M. Treasury justified this by saying that, though the "business test" would be included in the Regulated Activities Order, its omission from the Bill was appropriate since the test did not apply uniformly to all regulated activities (for example, section 191 of the 1986 Act made the management of occupational pension schemes a regulated activity, whether or not it was carried on by way of business). The Treasury's logic also seemed to suggest that other kinds of private dealings might become regulated, for policy reasons, in the future. Ultimately, however, the Government relented and the requirement for activities to be carried on "by way of business" was included on the face of the Act in section 22.

Though, in most cases, it will not be difficult to conclude that the "business test" is satisfied, this issue will be important, and difficult, in some marginal cases. It is interesting in this regard to note that, in a recent case, the Court of Appeal noted "the varied approach of the courts in differing areas of the law to the question of which is or is not done in the course of a trade or business".[1] This seems to suggest the potential for some uncertainty, though it is true to say that most legal authorities recognise the existence of "business" where an activity is undertaken regularly or continuously, with a view to profit and not wholly or substantially for the purpose of pleasure or social enjoyment.[2]

The potential for uncertainty is augmented by the fact that banking, insurance and investment businesses were respectively subject to different "business tests" under prior legislation. In relation to investment business, the 1986 Act caught activities carried on in a way constituting the carrying on of *a business* in the United Kingdom. This formulation might well lead to a different conclusion in particular cases than if the "by way of business" test is applied (for example where a person carries out an investment-related activity as a "one-off" and incidentally to his existing business; in such a case, it does not seem certain that the activity itself would constitute the carrying on of a business).

Conversely, banking legislation adopted neither of the above formulations, but regulated persons "holding themselves out as accepting deposits on a day-to-day basis", and solely where deposits were not accepted "only on particular occasions". Insurance legislation required a person carrying "insurance business" to be authorised, but did not define exclusively what was meant by this. In view of these historic differences, the Treasury wisely exercised its statutory power under section 419 of the FSMA to change the "business test" for different kinds of regulated activities with the intention that they should, in essence, correspond to the business tests existing under previous legislation.[3] The previous business tests for deposit taking and investment business are largely replicated in the "Business Order".[4] The business test for the activities of effecting or carrying out contracts

---

[1] *Stevenson v. Rogers* [1999] 2 W.L.R. 1064, *per* Potter L.J.
[2] *H.M. Customs and Excise v. Lord Fisher* [1981] 2 All E.R. 147.
[3] The Financial Services and Markets Act 2000 (Carrying on Regulated Activities by Way of Business) Order 2001 (S.I. 2001 No. 1177).
[4] Arts 2 and 3.

of insurance and for some of the "new" regulated activities (including Lloyd's and regulated mortgate-related activities) is that the activities are carried on by way of business. Also, the Business Order contains provisions relating to the management of occupational pension schemes ("OPS"), which are mainly intended to mirror section 191 of the 1986 Act—which required trustees of OPS to become authorised unless they delegated day-to-day investment decisions, irrespective of the business test.[5] In one important respect, however, the new order gives more freedom to OPS trustees: under the 1986 Act, trustees had faced a problem with investing in venture capital funds, since (if authorisation was to be avoided) a trustee was required to engage a professional to manage its shares or interests in the fund itself (as opposed to the investments within the fund, which are managed by the venture capital firm sponsoring the fund). The Myners Report on United Kingdom investment management recommended that a change be made in this respect.[6] The Business Order now allows OPS trustees to make investment decisions in relation to holdings in venture capital funds, provided (inter alia) the decision is made in accordance with advice received from a FSMA authorised or exempt person or an overseas investment professional. The "advisory" condition has already been criticised for reducing the usefulness of the liberalisation.[7] Also, the relaxation will not apply at all if the fund itself is not managed by an authorised, exempt or "overseas" person (which could be the case for some funds run on an "advisory" basis).

TERRITORIAL SCOPE OF THE FSMA

3.06 The general prohibition refers to the carrying on of regulated activities in the United Kingdom. At a time when the internet and other means of electronic communication are bringing a global marketplace closer to practical reality, clear geographical limitations on the scope of the Act are obviously of critical importance. Regrettably, the FSMA does not deliver a clear statement of its territorial ambit. Though not perfect, most commentators have regarded the 1986 Act as providing a relatively clear starting-point for consideration of its territorial scope. It provided, broadly, that a person would not be regarded as engaging in a regulated activity unless he engaged in such an activity:

(a) from a permanent place of business maintained by him in the United Kingdom; or

(b) [otherwise] in a way which constitutes the carrying on by him of a business in the United Kingdom.

Paragraph (a) above generally caught United Kingdom-based offices, subject to the "permanent" and "maintained" qualifications. Paragraph (b) caught overseas businesses without a permanent United Kingdom presence, but subject to the important exemptions in favour of "overseas persons" (paragraphs 26 and 27 of Schedule 1 to the 1986 Act).

---

[5] Art. 4.
[6] "Institutional Investment in the United Kingdom: A Review", March 6, 2001. See in particular Chapter 12 of the report, on "Private Equity".
[7] House of Commons, Tenth Standing Committee on Delegated Legislation (March 15, 2001).

The FSMA contains no such clear statement. Instead, the Act merely contains a rather difficult section (section 418) describing four "cases" where a person is to be "deemed" to be carrying on an activity in the United Kingdom even if, in fact, he is not. A review of the four "cases" might suggest that the Treasury's intention is to broaden significantly the potential territorial scope of United Kingdom regulation; the Treasury has refuted this, stating that "it is not the Government's intention to extend the regulatory jurisdiction but . . . to clarify it . . . " and that (in relation to the vexed question of the outward application of the Act) "the Government proposes to make explicit that, subject to full compliance with the relevant European Directives, the authorisation requirement contained in the Bill [now the FSMA] extends to activities actually carried on or directed from a United Kingdom place of business, rather than to all regulated activities carried on by firms with their head offices in the United Kingdom".[8]

It is most helpful to consider the territorial scope of the Act further by reference to, separately, business carried on *from* the United Kingdom and business carried on *in* (or into) the United Kingdom.

(a) Business Carried on from the United Kingdom

3.07 The four cases described in section 418 establish the so-called "outward" application of the FSMA, whereby persons based in the United Kingdom who carry on regulated activities overseas need to be regulated in the United Kingdom.

Case 1

3.08 applies where a person has his registered office (or, if he does not have a registered office, his head office) in the United Kingdom, is entitled to exercise rights under an EEA "single market directive" as a United Kingdom firm, and carries on in another EEA state a regulated activity to which that directive applies. This case will therefore apply, for example, to a United Kingdom-incorporated company whose only business is to pass orders in relation to securities on behalf of, and to give investment advice to, French or Italian clients. Such a company would be entitled to "passport" its services to France or Italy under the terms of the ISD[9] (by reason of its providing the "core investment service" of passing orders) once it has obtained United Kingdom authorisation. It is clear that this case is intended to ensure that the FSMA is consistent with the single market directives (namely ISD, BCD[10] and the third life and non-life directives), under which a firm incorporated in one Member State is prohibited from having its head office in a different Member State, and where the state of incorporation is required as the "home Member State" of the entity concerned to make access to regulated business subject to home authorisation requirements.[11]

---

[8] *Financial Services and Markets Bill: Consultation Document on the Regulated Activities Order* (Explanatory Notes) February 1999.
[9] 93/22/EC.
[10] The Banking Consolidation Directive (2000/12) has consolidated and replaced the various banking co-ordination directives. See further Chapter 4, below, in relation to EEA rights and "Treaty firms".
[11] *e.g.*, see Art. 3 of the ISD.

Case 2

3.09 is the corollary of Case 1 in relation to the managers of collective investment schemes. This provides that a United Kingdom incorporated manager of a collective investment scheme which is entitled to enjoy the rights conferred by a relevant "Community instrument" will be regarded as carrying on a regulated activity in the United Kingdom where persons in another EEA State are invited to become participants in the scheme. "Community instruments" may be prescribed under the Act, but will for the time being be confined to the UCITS Directive,[12] under which collective investment undertakings constituted in EEA Member States and complying with minimum criteria may be marketed to the public in other EEA Member States, subject to formal recognition of the undertaking in the host State. Though Case 2 may appear at first glance to be a superfluous addition to Case 1, that is not true because collective investment undertakings and their managers are exempted from the ISD[13] and thus are not entitled to exercise rights under a "single market directive" as prescribed by Case 1. However, the UCITS Directive imposes in practice similar "single market" requirements in relation to collective investment undertakings and their managers which are intended to ensure that a "host" Member State should not impede the legitimate marketing of a qualifying scheme in its territory by means of special licensing requirements either for the undertaking concerned or for its manager.[14] Consequently, section 24 of the 1986 Act prescribed the operator or trustee of a recognised EEA scheme as a United Kingdom authorised person as regards any investment business carried on by him in connection with or for the purposes of that scheme, and that special authorisation is repeated in the FSMA.[15] However, conversely, United Kingdom incorporated managers intending to benefit from UCITS recognition for their schemes in other EEA Member States will now be deemed to carry on a United Kingdom regulated activity by reason of that overseas marketing, though it is very likely that they would require authorisation in any event for their United Kingdom scheme management activities.

Case 3

3.10 provides that all persons who have their registered or head office in the United Kingdom will need to be authorised if responsibility for the day-to-day management of the carrying on of a regulated activity is the responsibility of that office or another establishment maintained by the relevant person in the United Kingdom. This case seems mainly intended to cover businesses whose only regulated activities are carried out in overseas, non-EEA states (since Case 1 covers United Kingdom incorporated companies which carry on regulated activities within the EEA, irrespective of any "day-to-day management" in the United Kingdom), though it could also apply to firms doing business in the EEA outside the single market directives (*e.g.* a commodities broker). It is not entirely clear why the Treasury has felt it necessary to draft a "case" applying to non-EEA/non-directive

---

[12] European Communities Directive for the co-ordination of undertakings for collective investment in transferable securities (UCITS) (85/611).
[13] ISD, Art. 2(2)(h).
[14] Art. 1(6) of the UCITS Directive (see n. 12, above).
[15] FSMA, Sched. 5.

activities in this way. Further, the interpretation and practical consequences of this case seem much more uncertain and potentially difficult than Cases 1 or 2. First, and importantly, what is meant by "day-to-day management"?

Though the position will be uncertain until there is some direct authority on the meaning of this section, it seems likely this phrase can be interpreted to include the practical implementation and administration of strategic, corporate decisions (distinguishing, for this purpose, the place where a company has its "central management and control" from the place (or places) where "day-to-day management" is carried out).[16] If this is correct then, for example, the European head office of a U.S. or Japanese bank could be caught under Case 3. Secondly, it is noticeable that the Case refers to day-to-day management being the responsibility of the United Kingdom registered office (or head office) or another "establishment" maintained in the United Kingdom, without any requirement for that establishment to be "permanent", as was the case under the 1986 Act.[17] This seems to imply that temporary (or permanent) establishments may now be subject to "outward regulation" in the United Kingdom, which is certainly a change from the *status quo ante* under the 1986 Act. While there seems to be some legal authority that an "establishment" implies some degree of permanence in any event,[18] it is not difficult to think of examples, such as the plethora of temporary serviced office accommodation in London, which may lead to the conclusion that a company temporarily located in the United Kingdom (*e.g.* for a specific project) has become sufficiently associated with an office location to be deemed "established" there. Thirdly, it should be noted that a person will fall within this Case where he has *responsibility* for the day-to-day management of a particular regulated activity; it does not refer to the actual (day-to-day) direction of such an activity, as H.M. Treasury's comments on this section imply. United Kingdom Businesses which are responsible for day-to-day management, but which delegate it, are apparently at risk. Last (but not least) there is, of course, no requirement for the activity itself to be carried on from a United Kingdom office, since Case 3 is essentially a provision which deems an activity to be carried on in the United Kingdom when, in fact, it is not.

As a practical matter, it appears that Case 3 could lead some United Kingdom incorporated businesses to abandon or modify an overseas branch structure (since the day-to-day activities of an overseas branch could apparently land the United Kingdom company with a United Kingdom authorisation requirement) in favour of the incorporation of overseas subsidiaries. However, this will probably not prevent odd, and presumably unintended, consequences from time to time. The policy justification of this new deemed United Kingdom business is, however, not entirely clear. Is it right that a United Kingdom company should need United Kingdom authorisation to accept deposits in Australia?

Case 4

3.11 covers the more straightforward case where a person does not have its registered or head office in United Kingdom, but carries on an activity from an establishment maintained by it in the United Kingdom. This is not very different

---

[16] *Untelrab Ltd v. McGregor* [1996] S.T.C. (S.C.D.) 1.
[17] The relevant requirement under s.1(3)(a) of the FSA 1986 was a "permanent place of business".
[18] *c.f., e.g. The Oriel Ltd* (1986) 1 W.L.R. 180.

from the "outward" regulation applied under section 1(3) of the 1986 Act, with the notable exception again that there is no requirement for the establishment to be "permanent". This Case could potentially be more difficult for mainstream financial businesses than the others, in that it could result in (for example) an overseas banking or insurance company requiring authorisation purely by reason of visits to leased United Kingdom premises to direct or transact particular types of business.

In all of these Cases a firm will therefore need to apply to the FSA for permission under Part IV of the FSMA, even though the relevant regulated activity is actually carried on by a non-United Kingdom branch or on a cross-border basis.

(b) Business carried on in (or into) the United Kingdom

3.12 As referred to above, the starting point for overseas investment businesses considering their position under the 1986 Act was section 1(3)(b), under which a person without a permanent place of business in the United Kingdom would only require authorisation to carry on an activity if he engaged in the activity in a way which constituted the carrying on by him of a business in the United Kingdom. This was complemented by the "overseas person exemptions" in paragraphs 26 and 27 of Schedule 1 to the 1986 Act, whose basic effect was to exclude "overseas persons" (*i.e.* persons without a permanent place of business maintained in the United Kingdom) who:

(i)   deal or arrange deals in investments only with or through authorised persons or exempt persons; and/or

(ii) carry on the regulated activities of dealing in investments, offering or agreeing to arrange deals, managing investments or giving investment advice without contravening the provisions of the 1986 Act regarding cold calling (section 56) and investment advertising (section 57).

"Overseas person" status, however, was lost once a firm carried on any regulated activity from a permanent office maintained by it in the United Kingdom, even if other regulated activities were carried on from overseas. As far as regulated investment firms have been concerned, however, the practical consequences of this have been reduced by the relevant rules of the self-regulating organisations ("SROs") which have largely been drafted to prevent conduct of business regulation from applying to overseas branches and offices.[19]

The overseas person exemptions for firms carrying on "investment business" under the 1986 Act have been retained, substantially unaltered, in the Regulated Activities Order. As noted below, an overseas person continues to be a person without a permanent place of business maintained by him the United Kingdom. Interestingly, business falling within one of these exemptions is now treated as *not* being a regulated activity; under the 1986 Act, it *was* "investment business", but was exempted because it was treated as carried on outside the United Kingdom.[20]

---

[19] *e.g.*, see Rule 5.1(2) of the Rules of the Securities and Futures Authority. This position has been maintained in FSA's *Conduct of Business Sourcebook* (see COB 1.4.3R, 5.5.7R (U.K. customers) and 5.5.8 (overseas customers)).

[20] RAO, para. 4(3).

It should be noted in this regard that section 418 (discussed above) only bites where a regulated activity is carried on (albeit outside the United Kingdom); consequently, there may be cases where the overseas person exemptions will narrow the application of section 418.

Very significantly, the final version of the RAO "ironed out" a major limitation in the application of the overseas person exemptions, which threatened to cause great difficulties for inter-professional business carried on between overseas firms and United Kingdom firms. The penultimate draft of the RAO (and, indeed, a prior draft) excluded the exemptions in the case of "investment firms" (EEA and non-EEA) providing "core investment services" as defined in the ISD. This was certainly not the case under the 1986 Act, which preserved the exemptions for EEA and non-EEA firms.[21] If this provision had remained, overseas firms providing core investment services[22] in the United Kingdom institutional markets—including discretionary investment managers and broker/dealers—would have required United Kingdom authorisation for the first time. The Treasury corrected this, however, in the final RAO, and the *status quo ante* has been retained (Art.4(4)). Consequently, among other benefits flowing from the exemptions, EEA investment firms eligible for "passporting" under the ISD or BCD will still be able to take account of these exemptions when deciding whether a notification to the FSA is required.

The overseas person exemptions do not apply to deposit-taking. The Treasury has stated that this is because section 5(3) of the Banking Act 1987, which exempted deposits taken from persons who themselves have "permission" to take deposits in the United Kingdom, has been preserved in the Regulated Activities Order[23] (thus enabling overseas deposit-takers to have access to the United Kingdom wholesale money markets without obtaining authorisation). Further, the activity of "accepting deposits" is only caught where the acceptance takes place in the United Kingdom. Consequently, in normal circumstances, deposit-taking will only be regulated if the account in which the deposit is accepted is maintained in the United Kingdom.[24] Notwithstanding this, it would have been desirable for the playing field between deposit-taking and investment business to have been levelled.

H.M. Treasury flagged early in the consultation process on the draft Order that it intended to extend the overseas person exemptions so that they covered some reinsurance activities. Subsequently, this did not happen, and the exemptions thus do not apply to effecting or carrying on contracts of insurance or reinsurance.

(c) In the United Kingdom or outside?

3.13 While the overseas person exemptions in the Regulated Activities Order will certainly be helpful in maintaining the United Kingdom's competitive position as a territory in which (for example) inter-professional financial dealings attract light regulation, they do not answer the more fundamental question of where any particular regulated activity will be deemed to be carried on. If, for example, a

---

[21] Art. 6 of the Financial Services Act 1986 (Investment Services) (Extension of Scope Act) Order 1995 (S.I. 1995 No. 3271) disapplied exclusions in Part III of Schedule 1 to the 1986 Act—but not the overseas person exemptions, which were in Part IV of that Schedule.
[22] But not including firms exempted under Art. 2.2 of the ISD.
[23] RAO, Art. 6(1).
[24] This was the historic analysis under the Banking Acts; see below.

regulated activity such as accepting a deposit, establishing a collective investment scheme or arranging a securities deal can properly be said to be carried on overseas (*i.e.* not "in the United Kingdom"), the overseas person exemptions will not matter anyway and United Kingdom regulation will only apply to the extent of the "financial promotion" regime, unless, of course, an overseas business with a registered or head office or an "establishment" in the United Kingdom is caught by the "deemed United Kingdom business" tests in section 418.

The question of where particular activities are actually carried on can be extremely difficult to determine, but a brief guide to the likely position in relation to various regulated activities is as follows:

(i)   A deposit is normally taken to have been accepted at the place where the liability to repay it has been assumed, which would be expected to be the bank branch or office where the deposit account is held.[25] An early draft of the Regulated Activities Order actually defined "accepting" a deposit as "assuming the liability to repay" it; though this definition was subsequently deleted, this was the accepted definition under the Banking Act in any event. There seems to be no good reason why the position should differ in the case of "on-line" banks which market their deposit-taking services through the internet rather than through traditional methods.

(ii) In relation to contracts of insurance, a person requires FSMA authorisation if he effects *or* carries out a contract of insurance in the United Kingdom. In this regard, as far as English law is concerned, the location of the risk (even in relation to general business) is irrelevant to the question of where either activity is carried on.[26] It is necessary in each case to determine where the relevant activity is carried on as a matter of fact. The question of where a contract of insurance is effected can be complex, and will depend on factors including the requirements of the governing law of the contract and (if English law governs) where communication of acceptance of an offer takes place and whether communication of acceptance has been dispensed with under the terms of the contract.[27] In most cases, however, it seems likely that an overseas insurer will be able to arrange for contracts to be concluded outside the United Kingdom. A contract of insurance will be carried out at the place where its rights are normally exercised and its obligations are performed[28]; consequently, factors such as the location of an insurer's claims administration centre are likely to the relevant in determining where the activity is carried on.

(iii) Transactions in securities and other investment products have traditionally been taken to be concluded at the place where acceptance of an offer is received by the offering party if communication of the acceptance is instantaneous,[29] and at the place of "posting" where communication of

[25] *Joachimson v. Swiss Bank Corp.* (1921) 3 K.B. 110.
[26] *Re United General Commercial Insurance Corp.* (1927) 2 Ch. 51
[27] *Carlill v. Carbolic Smoke Ball Company* (1893) 1 Q.B. 256.
[28] *Scher v. Policyholders Protection Board* (1993) 3 All E.R. 384.
[29] *Entores Ltd. v. Miles Far East Corp.* [1955] 2 Q.B. 327.

acceptance is delayed.[30] However, within these broad propositions the analysis (and the court's view) can differ depending on the precise facts. It will be interesting to see if case law develops to deal with internet-related issues such as delayed e-mails.

(iv) The managing of investments is normally taken to be carried on at the place where the investment manager is physically present when he reviews portfolios and takes investment decisions. This view was supported by the Securities and Investments Board (now the FSA) in a guidance paper issued shortly after the 1986 Act came in force.[31] Similar reasoning should, it is suggested, apply to the activity of establishing, operating and winding-up a collective investment scheme.

(v) The FSA is understood to consider that the activity of "arranging deals in investments" is normally carried on at the place where the arranger is present when the arrangements in question are made. This seems logical when applied, for example, to the ISD activity of "receiving and transmitting orders" (which is similar to the United Kingdom regulated activity of "arranging a deal"[32]), which should be performed at the place of "reception and transmission", rather than either at the place where a person places the order or at the place to where the order is transmitted. This view also seems to be consistent in the European context with the published opinion of the European Commission in relation to the performance of "cross-border" services under the BCD; in the Commission's view, a service is provided at its place of "characteristic performance", which will differ depending on the circumstances but which suggests that, in many cases, a service will actually be provided in a firm's "home state" and not cross-border (so that, to that extent, an ISD or BCD notification to a host state would not be required).[33] It is suggested that similar reasoning can be applied to the safeguarding and administration of investments (custody services).

(vi) It is submitted that investment advice should be treated as being "given" at the place where it is received. It is understood that the FSA has taken this view in the past, particularly in the context of the territorial scope of the 1986 Act and the ISD requirement to notify the Authority of the provision of services on a cross-border basis. However, it is equally possible to take the view that advice is also given at the place of origination, though this is likely to be less material because investment advisers with a United Kingdom permanent place of business will generally need to be authorised anyway, and overseas firms will normally only need authorisation if their advice to United Kingdom customers is treated as given where it is received (assuming that this is in the United Kingdom).

---

[30] *Adams v. Lindsell* (1818) 1 B.&Ald. 681.

[31] Securities and Investments Board, Consultative Paper No. 19 *Carrying on Investment Business in the United Kingdom* (March 1989).

[32] RAO, Art. 25(1).

[33] Commission of the European Communities, Interpretative Communication, *Freedom to provide services and the interest of the general good in the Second Banking Directive* (SEC (97) 1193), June 1997.

THE REGULATED ACTIVITIES ORDER

3.14   The Regulated Activities Order ("RAO") itself has been made by H.M. Treasury pursuant to its power under section 22(5) of the FSMA.[34]   The broad purpose of the Order, as with the Act itself, is to amalgamate and rationalise the previously separate statutory regimes for banking, insurance and investment business, and to carry through the specific policy changes which the Government has deemed necessary (*e.g.* in relation to mortgages, funeral plans and the Society of Lloyd's).

The FSMA contains wide powers conferred on the Treasury to make orders to specify regulated activities and to amend or supplement any such order (paragraph 25 of Schedule 2 of the FSMA).   The breadth of these powers of prescription and amendment were criticised by many commentators during early consultation on the Bill, since it was felt that more detail should be included in the Bill itself and thereby be subjected to Parliamentary scrutiny.

Against this, it was argued—with some merit—that including all of the new regulated activities within the new Act would be inflexible and would be likely to result in piece-meal changes of the kind which blighted the 1986 Act.   There was the further risk that the time taken to introduce and pass amendments to the primary legislation could simply result in the Act failing to keep pace with market-related and technological changes.

The compromise reached was that procedures were introduced into the Act (paragraph 26 of Schedule 2) which made certain changes to the RAO subject to the so-called "affirmative resolution procedure" in Parliament.   This procedure involves any relevant new order being laid before Parliament when it is made, after which it will cease to have any effect at the end of a period of 28 days unless, before the end of that period, the order is approved by resolution of each House of Parliament.   However, this procedure will only apply to orders which contain a statement by the Treasury that, in their opinion, the effect of the order is that a new regulated activity is thereby created.

SCHEME OF THE REGULATED ACTIVITIES ORDER

3.15   The Treasury repeatedly stated during the passage of the Bill, and the consultation process on the RAO, that it was not their intention to make major changes at this stage to the scope of financial regulation, except for those well-publicised examples such as the Lloyd's insurance market and the conduct of mortgage lending where radical change has been deemed in the public interest.   Consequently, there is much in the RAO which will be very familiar to financial services businesses and their advisers, even if the lay-out and some of the definitions used are new.

The RAO is divided into four Parts and three Schedules.   The main body of the Order contains definitions (Part I); the regulated activities themselves, and the related exclusions (Part II); the "investments" in relation to which regulated activities may be carried on (though a few of these, such as general insurance contracts,

---

[34] The Financial Services and Markets Act 2000 (Regulated Activities) Order 2001 (S.I. 2001 No. 544). The RAO was made by the Treasury on February 26, 2001 and was laid before Parliament the following day.

are not really "investments") (Part III) and some consequential changes to the Consumer Credit Act 1974 in relation to regulated mortgage contracts (Part IV). The Schedules contain the classes of general and long-term insurance business formerly found in the Insurance Companies Act 1982 (Schedule 1); the Annex to the ISD (Schedule 2); and Article 2.2 of the ISD (Schedule 3).

The insertion of the Annex to the ISD as a mere Schedule to the RAO is significant. The Annex contains the lists of core and non-core services, and investments, which are relevant to the definition of an "investment firm", and the availability of the EEA passport, under the ISD. Since the ISD was enacted into United Kingdom law in 1995,[35] practitioners have advocated that United Kingdom definitions of "investment business" should become more closely aligned with the ISD "investment services", to afford greater certainty to United Kingdom businesses and to avoid undue difficulties for overseas businesses wishing to provide services in the United Kingdom. The example most frequently quoted where the United Kingdom definition is broader and far less clear than the ISD equivalent is the activity of "arranging deals in investments" (formerly in paragraph 13 of Schedule 1 of the 1986 Act), which has led in practice to many applications for "precautionary authorisation". The argument against the ISD approach has often been that the ISD does not treat United Kingdom regulated activities such as investment advice and safe custody of investments as "core investment services" (the carrying on of at least one of which is the trigger to the availability of the ISD passport), so that the adoption of ISD definitions would in any event require some modifications to be made. However, there seems to be no reason why these activities could not have been added to the "core investment services" by appropriate provisions purely for the purpose of United Kingdom regulation (as the United Kingdom is at liberty to do).

Notwithstanding all this, the Government has resisted aligning United Kingdom regulated investment business with the ISD, which will mean in practice that firms will continue to have to study two parallel regimes to work out their position in relation to, respectively, United Kingdom regulation and EEA passporting. In addition, it means that certain exclusions from the definitions of regulated activities will continue to have to be read subject to the overriding qualification that they will not exclude ISD "investment firms" whose regular occupation or business is the provision of investment services to third parties on a professional basis (Art. 4(4) of the RAO). These exclusions, some of which exactly or closely follow former exclusions in Part III of Schedule 1 to the 1986 Act, have not been re-drafted so that they are internally consistent with the ISD requirement that the provision of "core investment services" in an EEA State must be subject to regulation.[36] For example, the regulated activity of dealings in investments as principal will continue to be qualified by the implied rule that United Kingdom incorporated investment firms which provide the "core investment service" of "dealing as principal" will require United Kingdom authorisation in any event, even though there must be doubt as to whether persons dealing as principal in many cases provide a "service" to third parties at all. By the same token, the relevant exclusion from the "dealing as principal" activity in favour of persons who do not act as market

---

[35] Under the Investment Services Regulations 1995 (S.I. 1995 No. 3275).
[36] ISD, Art. 3.

makers or buy with a view to sale or regularly solicit members of the public[37] is expressly disapplied in the case of "investment firms" (United Kingdom, EEA and non-EEA), even though it seems that a person in the "regular occupation or business of the provision of core investment services to third parties on a professional basis" would surely not fall within the exclusion anyway. As a result, the law lacks the clarity which would have been afforded by more explicit consistency with the ISD.

Most issues arising from the RAO's definitions can conveniently be discussed in relation to particular regulated activities or investments. However, it is worth mentioning separately the odd-looking definition of "contractually-based investments", which comprises the heterogeneous components of some long-term insurance contracts, derivatives, funeral plan contracts and rights in respect of each of them. The "long-term insurance contracts" in question are those which used to be "investments" under the 1986 Act (paragraph 10 of Schedule 1), which excludes long-term policies without an investment element (including, for example, PHI policies and term assurance). In addition to such long-term policies and derivatives (futures, options and contracts for differences), funeral plan contracts have been added, presumably because such contracts involve the pre-payment of money in return for the contractual promise of services. These "investments" are the subject of a specific exclusion[38] which reflects the former exemption for dealings in these investments (apart from funeral plan contracts) as principal under the 1986 Act.[39] Similarly, there is a new definition of "securities" which incorporates shares, "instruments creating or acknowledging indebtedness" (e.g. debentures and loan stock), government and public securities, "instruments giving entitlements to investments" (e.g. warrants), certificates representing securities and units in collective investment schemes, as well as the new "rights under a stakeholder pension scheme". Dealings in these "securities" continue to be subject to separate exclusions (in Article 15 of the RAO) from those relating to "contractually based investments" (Article 16).

REGULATED ACTIVITIES

3.16 As stated above, the new "regulated activities" are in fact mostly an aggregation of the existing regulated activities under United Kingdom banking, insurance and financial services legislation, with a few well-publicised additions. Briefly, the activities are:

- Accepting deposits.
- Effecting contracts of insurance.
- Carrying out contracts of insurance.
- Dealing in investments as principal.

---

[37] RAO, Art. 15.
[38] RAO, Art. 16.
[39] Para. 17(4) of Sched. 1 of the 1986 Act.

- Dealing in investments as agent.

- Arranging deals in investments.

- Managing investments.

- Safeguarding and administering investments (safe custody).

- Sending dematerialised instructions by means of a "relevant system".

- Establishing, operating or winding-up a collective investment scheme.

- Establishing, operating or winding-up a stakeholder pension scheme.

- Advising on investments.

- Advice on syndicate participation at Lloyd's.

- Managing the underwriting capacity of a Lloyd's syndicate.

- Arranging deals in contracts of insurance written at Lloyd's.

- Entering as provider into a funeral plan contract.

- Entering into or administering a regulated mortgage contract.

- Agreeing to engage in any of the above activities, save for accepting deposits or effecting or carrying out contracts of insurance and the activities relating to collective investment schemes and stakeholder pension schemes.

The bulk of this list comprises the investment activities which were regulated under the 1986 Act, but there are important new regulated activities in relation to Lloyd's "investments", funeral plan contracts, regulated mortgages and stakeholder pension schemes. The investment activities under the 1986 Act—such as dealing in, arranging, managing or advising on, and acting as custodian of, investments—have not been extended to deposits, general insurance or "pure protection policies". However, in addition to the specific new activities indicated above, various 1986 Act activities have also been extended to cover the new "investments". For example, the "arranging" activity has been extended to include Lloyd's underwriting capacity and syndicate membership; and most of the activities now cover stakeholder pension schemes and funeral plan contracts (with the notable exception of the "dealing" activities in relation to funeral plan contracts). It is not clear in every case that these extensions are necessary.

The final activity referred to above—*agreeing* to engage in a regulated activity—has been carried over from the 1986 Act. It does not apply, though, to the deposit-taking and insurance activities, or to the activities of establishing, etc., a collective investment scheme or a stakeholder pension scheme (though an earlier draft of the RAO did extend the activity to agreeing to establish, operate or wind-up a collective investment scheme—which would have been a very unwelcome change). However, "*offering*" to engage in a regulated activity, which was a regulated activity in its own right under the 1986 Act, has not been carried forward to the new legislation. This is certainly to be welcomed, since the "offering" activity frequently gave rise to problems in practice—particularly in relation to offers of units or shares in collective investment schemes and other securities by overseas firms. The regulation of "offering activities" will be dealt with in future under the financial promotion regime.

In addition to the above list, it seems likely that effecting "long-term care insurance" will become specifically regulated at some point after N2. Though, to some extent, long term care products will be regulated at N2 (for example, in the guise of equity release mortgages, pure insurance contracts or investment bonds), the Government is in favour of specific regulation so as to extend "CAT standards" to these products and to enable the FSA to prescribe conduct of business rules in relation to marketing and advice.[40]

Since many of the activities referred to above closely follow the definitions previously included in (respectively) the Banking Act 1987, the Insurance Companies Act 1982 and the Financial Services Act 1986, attention is particularly drawn below to those activities, and features of activities, where material changes have been made.

Regulated Mortgages

3.17 For most consumers, the inclusion of mortgage contracts as regulated investments will be the most significant change to the scope of financial regulation under the FSMA. The debate which accompanied its introduction was, however, somewhat protracted and at times fierce.

The RAO[41] specifies *entering into* a regulated mortgage contract, and *administering* a regulated mortgage contract, as separate regulated activities. The definition of a "regulated mortgage contract" is crucial and has been the source of much debate. It is, broadly, a contract under which:

(i)   the lender provides credit to a borrower who is/are an *individual* or *trustees*;

(ii) the obligation to repay is secured by a *first legal mortgage* on land (other than timeshare accommodation) *in the United Kingdom*, at least 40 per cent of which is used, or is intended to be used, as or in connection with a *dwelling* by the *borrower* (or, in the case of trustees, their beneficiary) or by a *related person* (emphasis supplied).

The words highlighted suggest a number of important concepts. Most commercial mortgages are excluded, as are "buy-to-let" arrangements. Loans secured on overseas properties, second mortgages and equitable mortgages are all excluded. However, "equity release" mortgages are covered; this was the subject of discussion during the Treasury's consultation on the new regulated activity, since the first draft definition only caught loans for a term of five years or more—which would not have caught some equity release products (because the loans are not necessarily for a fixed period). The five-year condition was therefore dropped.[42]

The definition of a "related person" has been cast (following lobbying) so that it includes relationships (whether or not between persons of the opposite sex) which "have the characteristics of the relationship between husband and wife".

---

[40] HM Treasury, *Long Term Care Insurance* (December 2000).
[41] RAO, Art. 61.
[42] H.M. Treasury, *Policy changes following responses to the Treasury consultation document "Regulating Mortgages"* (February 2001).

Though entering into a regulated mortgage contract—agreeing to lend—is the primary regulated activity, the activity of "administration" is also to be regulated. This was introduced into the final draft of the RAO, in place of the previous concept of acting as "rights holder" in connection with a mortgage. The "rights holder" concept was dispensed with because it seemed likely seriously to compromise the securitisation market, where "special purpose vehicles" ("SPVs") and trustees normally hold rights to enforce and operate the subject mortgages.[43] The new definition of administration covers either or both of:

(i)   notifying the borrower of changes in interest rates or payments due under the contract, or of other matters of which the contract requires him to be notified; and

(ii)   taking any necessary steps for the purposes of recovering payments due under the contract from the borrower.

Importantly, though, a person will not need to be authorised to administer regulated mortgage contracts pursuant to an agreement with an authorised person who has permission to carry on that activity.[44] This means that unauthorised administrators will continue to be able to exercise functions on behalf of regulated banks and building societies under "outsourcing" and similar arrangements, without needing to apply to the FSA for permission. The Treasury has also provided a further exclusion[45] which is intended to allow an SPV or a securitisation trustee to arrange for administration by an authorised person, or to administer regulated contracts for not more than one month after such an arrangement comes to an end. The first limb of the exclusion seems odd, since "arranging" administration is not part of the regulated activity anyway; and in the second limb, the provision of one month to appoint an alternative authorised administrator does not appear generous.

A key "transitional" point is that the "administration" activity only applies to regulated contracts entered into *after* N2; and thus loans entered into *before* N2 which are subsequently varied after N2 will not be regulated under the FSMA regime. The industry argued successfully during consultation with the Treasury[46] that applying two different regimes (*e.g.* Consumer Credit Act and FSMA) at different times to the same loan contract would be potentially confusing for consumers and costly for lenders.

The relationship of the new FSMA regime to the Consumer Credit Act 1974 ("CCA"), which was unclear in earlier definitions of the new regulated activity, has been clarified in the RAO.[47] This has been achieved by a number of amendments to the CCA and subordinate legislation which, in essence, carve FSMA regulated mortgage contracts out of the CCA provisions regarding duties to display information, advertisements, quotations, extortionate credit bargains and others (by treating FSMA regulated contracts as CCA "exempt agreements"). However, pre-N2 loans will continue to be regulated by the Office of Fair Trading ("OFT"); and

---

[43] *ibid*. para. 15.
[44] RAO, Art. 63.
[45] RAO, Art. 62.
[46] H.M. Treasury, *op. cit.* paras 5–11.
[47] RAO, Arts 90–91.

it is certainly possible that different elements of a "loan package" will still be regulated by the FSA *and* the OFT (for example, loans with secured and unsecured elements).

The treatment of mortgage advice was one of the most heated areas of discussion in relation to the Act. Ultimately, arranging mortgage loans and giving mortgage advice will not be separate regulated activities (though, of course, services in relation to the life policy component of an endowment mortgage have been regulated since 1988). In practice, the regulation of such arranging and advisory services by means of full authorisation for service providers would have been an enormous undertaking,[48] and the Government does not seem to have been persuaded that the cost (direct and indirect) would have been proportionate to the benefits obtained.

Whatever the merits of the respective arguments, the net result of the new regime is that banks, building societies and other mortgage lenders will now need to obtain permission from the FSA to enter into regulated contracts, and will be subject to the new FSA rules on promotion, information, product features and contract terms which are to be incorporated in FSA's *Handbook of Rules and Guidance*.[49] The key new FSMA requirement is that mortgage promotions must be issued or approved by an authorised person; consequently, though some mortgage intermediaries will remain unregulated, they will face the additional burden and cost of arranging for their marketing (except for generic promotions) to be approved by an authorised lender. Conversely, authorised intermediaries will be permitted by the FSA to approve promotions in relation to mortgages provided they have the necessary expertise, even though, as such, they will not generally provide FSMA regulated services in relation to regulated mortgage contracts.[50]

Since obtaining FSA permission and devising new compliance procedures will be time-consuming for mortgage lenders, the Treasury has extended the transitional arrangements for the new regulated activity so that FSMA permission will not be required until the date which is nine months after N2 (generally known as "N3"). It may still be necessary for additional transitional arrangements to be made, either generally or for some lenders, in due course.[51]

Stakeholder Pension Schemes

3.18 The concept of the stakeholder pension scheme ("SHP") was introduced by the Government under the Welfare Reform and Pensions Act 1999 in order to widen public access to pension savings and to oblige United Kingdom employers, subject to certain exceptions, to provide employees with access to a contributory pension scheme complying with statutory requirements. The broad provisions of the 1999 Act have been supplemented by regulations[52] which provide for important

---

[48] Though, interestingly, a cost benefit analysis of regulating this area did not conclude that the regulatory cost would be disproportionate (FSA, October 1999).

[49] Discussed in FSA *Consultation Paper 70 on Mortgage Regulation* (November 2000); see also Chapter 6 below.

[50] *ibid.*, para. 5.65.

[51] H.M. Treasury, *op. cit.* paras 24–25.

[52] The Stakeholder Pension Schemes Regulations 2000 (S.I. 2000 No. 1403); the Stakeholder Pension Schemes (Amendment) Regulations 2001 (S.I. 2001 No. 104); and the Stakeholder Pension Schemes (Amendment) (No. 2) Regulations 2001 (S.I. 2001 No. 934).

matters such as limiting the charges which may be deducted from scheme property (broadly, the limit is set at 1 per cent per annum) and regulating the making of contributions and the provision of information to scheme members. The manager of a SHP is required to be a United Kingdom authorised person.[53] Though one might have expected that the management of this kind of scheme would, in any event, have involved carrying on regulated business (most obviously, managing investments and giving investment advice), the Treasury decided to make the establishment, operation and winding-up of a SHP a regulated activity in its own right.[54] Also, as noted above, rights under a SHP are treated as a regulated investment for the purpose of various of the other regulated investment activities—including the dealing, arranging, managing, advising and custody activities. It seems that the separate prescription of a SHP as an investment, with a related investment activity, has been designed so that it will filter down to the FSA conduct of business and prudential rules for the managers of stakeholder schemes.

In practice, most operators of SHPs are substantial United Kingdom regulated life companies and asset managers, many of whom have spent considerable time and resource designing their stakeholder pensions initiatives in time for the implementation of the new product on April 6, 2001. Since these schemes may be constituted by trust or contract, it is of course possible that other persons, including scheme trustees, might choose to seek permission in order to carry on the new regulated activity after N2 (and indeed existing regulated activities under the 1986 Act prior to N2), though such cases will probably be infrequent. The FSA has helpfully recorded its understanding that employers should not require authorisation in order to "designate" a scheme pursuant to the Stakeholder Pension Scheme Regulations.[55] However, an employer may require authorisation if it becomes involved in the arranging or operation of a scheme, or arranging investments in a scheme, depending (*inter alia*) on whether it derives any commercial benefit from the activities in question.[56]

The process of authorising firms as managers of SHPs has actually begun well before N2. However, given that the FSA has not had its FSMA statutory powers during this period, "temporary" authorisation has been provided by the SROs (SFA, IMRO and PIA), mainly through an appropriate amendment to the permitted business profiles of existing member firms which have applied for this new status. Firms which have thus been authorised as SHP managers prior to N2 will have this authorisation "grandfathered" across into the new regime (see Chapter 4, below, in relation to transitional provisions generally).

As an incidental point, it should be noted that SHPs will not be collective investment schemes, since they are pension schemes for the purposes of the Pensions Act 1993[57]; consequently, as one would expect, the restrictions on promotion applying to unregulated CISs do not apply to SHPs.

---

[53] See reg. 2 of S.I. 2001 No. 104.
[54] RAO, Art. 52.
[55] Financial Services Authority Policy Statement, *Regulation of Stakeholder Pensions* (February 2001), para. 4.5.
[56] *ibid.*
[57] Art. 20 of the Financial Services and Markets Act 2000 (Collective Investment Schemes) Order 2001 (S.I. 2001 No. 1062).

Funeral Plan Contracts

3.19 Pre-paid funeral plan contracts, which were not regulated under the 1986 Act, have been specified in the RAO as an "investment", and the activity of entering as provider into such a contract has become a regulated activity. The Government signalled its intention in early 1999 to regulate the pre-paid funeral industry.[58] Pre-paid funeral plans are typically offered by funeral directors or specialist plan providers, who offer to provide or procure the provision of a funeral in exchange for advance payment, either by way of a lump sum or by instalments for a period of up to 10 years. The Government was clearly persuaded that such contracts, which are typically bought by persons of relatively modest means, needed to be regulated so that some control might be exercised over the terms of such plans and the holding and investment of fees paid to providers.

A contract is a regulated funeral plan contract under the RAO[59] if, under that contract:

(i) a customer makes one or more payments to the provider; and

(ii) the provider undertakes to provide, or secure that another person provides, a funeral in the United Kingdom for the customer (or another living person) on his death,

unless at the time of the contract both parties intend or expect the funeral to occur within one month. This limitation was included so that funeral directors who accept short-term advance payments from terminally ill patients should not thereby require authorisation.

Since the purpose of regulation is mainly to ensure that a customer's advance payments are used for the purpose intended, the RAO provides exclusions for contracts providing for the taking out of whole life insurance from an authorised person or for sums paid to be held in trust by persons most of whom are unconnected with the provider and to be managed by an independent authorised person.[60]

The new regime for funeral plan contracts will come into effect on January 1, 2002 (which is expected to be one month after N2). Interestingly, the FSA has said that its assumption is that most plan providers will organise their product in such a way that authorisation will not be required.

Deposit-taking

3.20 Accepting deposits is a regulated activity if (as was the case under section 5 of the Banking Act 1987) (a) money received by way of deposit is lent to others; or (b) any other activity of the person accepting the deposit is financed, wholly or to any material extent, out of the capital of or interest on money received by way of deposit (Article 5 of the RAO). "Accepting" is not explicitly defined, though the first draft of the RAO did define it explicitly as "assuming the liability to repay". However, since this is the generally understood meaning of the word under existing law and banking practice, the absence of a definition does not seem

---

[58] H.M. Treasury Consultation document, *Regulation of the Pre-Paid Funeral Industry* (January 1999).
[59] RAO, Art. 59.
[60] RAO, Art. 60.

problematic. The real problem with this definition, which is not new, is its second limb, which brings within the potential scope of banking regulation the host of commercial companies which issue debt securities in the capital markets to fund their businesses, and have no intention of lending as credit institutions do. This point was previously addressed by an array of exemptions under the Banking Act 1987 (Exempt Transactions) Regulations 1997[61] in favour of some companies whose equity or debt securities were, or were to be, listed on an EEA investment exchange. In its *Consultation Paper on the RAO* published in February 1999, however, the Treasury impliedly acknowledged that this approach had its limitations, and floated the possibility of a simpler, broader exemption for the acceptance of money in return for the issue of debt securities.

After a somewhat complex first attempt at liberalising the regime,[62] the final version of the RAO contains a remarkably straightforward exclusion of any sum which is received by a person as consideration for the issue of an Article 77 (instruments creating or acknowledging indebtedness) or Article 78 (government securities) investment.[63] This new exclusion removes the various complications which existed under the Banking Act regulations in relation to, inter alia, non-corporate issuers; net assets requirements for issuers; minimum denominations for longer-term securities; and requirements relating to listing on an investment exchange. The only qualification of the straightforward new exclusion is that commercial paper—defined as an Article 77 or 78 investment which must be redeemed before the first anniversary of its issue—will only be excluded if it is issued exclusively to professionals and in denominations of not less than £100,000 (or equivalent). The Treasury has evidently taken the view that this is satisfactory because the commercial paper market is essentially a "professionals-only" one, but this special treatment seems at odds with the general philosophy of the new exclusion. All in all, though, Article 9 represents a considerable improvement on the *status quo ante*.

Dealing as Principal

3.21   One of the striking features of the 1986 Act when compared to overseas equivalents was that, subject to various exemptions, any investor needed authorisation to buy and sell investments if he did so from a United Kingdom place of business.[64] However, the 1986 Act also provided a general exemption for all persons dealing in shares, debentures and other "securities" as principal except where a person either (a) held himself out as willing to enter into transactions at prices determined by him generally and continuously rather than in respect of each particular transaction; or (b) held himself out as engaging in the business of buying investments of the relevant kind with a view to selling them; or (c) regularly solicited members of the public for the purpose of inducing them to enter into transactions in securities and relevant transactions resulted from such solicitations.[65] In relation to regulated long-term insurance contracts (*i.e.* those with an

---

[61] S.I. 1997 No. 817.
[62] See H.M. Treasury's *Second Consultation Document on the RAO* (October 2000); the exclusions depended on the characterisation of debt securities as "longer-term" or commercial paper, and included numerous conditions relating to (*inter alia*) EEA listing and "offers to the public".
[63] RAO, Art. 9.
[64] 1986 Act, Sched. 1, para. 12.
[65] *ibid.*, Sched. 1, para. 17(1).

"investment element") and the three kinds of regulated derivative contracts—futures, options and contracts for differences—the 1986 Act provided a separate exemption for unauthorised persons dealing as principal with or through an authorised, exempted or permitted person or (in some circumstances) an overseas investment professional.[66]

The RAO has maintained the substance of this position, by providing for a broad, regulated "dealing" activity[67] and separate exclusions for dealings in securities[68] and dealings in "contractually based investments" (i.e. long-term insurance contracts and derivatives).[69] There are, however, some new significant features. First, the exclusion for dealings in securities also applies to assignments of "qualifying contracts of insurance" (i.e. long-term insurance except for reinsurance and direct insurance without the required investment element); therefore, an additional exclusion is now available for some unauthorised persons who sell second-hand life policies, where they act as principal, irrespective of whether they sell to or through an authorised person. Second, because a "stakeholder pension scheme" is defined as a "security", the dealing activity and the related exclusion for dealings in securities will apply to dealings in interests in such schemes (though it is not entirely clear how relevant this will be in practice). Finally, and perhaps most importantly, the exclusion for dealings in securities will no longer apply to any person who holds himself out as engaging in the business of underwriting investments. The exclusion has presumably been limited in this way to ensure the RAO's compatibility with the ISD, which prescribes the underwriting of issues of transferable securities and units in CISs as a "core investment service".[70] It is a pity, however, that the Treasury did not take the opportunity to re-draft the entire regulated activity of "dealing" to make it fully consistent with the ISD and to remove old concepts from the 1986 Act. Further, if compatibility with the ISD was the object of this change, the reference in the RAO to underwriting should have been accompanied by a further reference to "placing" (which is also an ISD core investment service).

Certain other exclusions to the activity of dealing as principal—including the important new "risk management" exclusion—are discussed below.

Dealing as Agent

3.22 The new regulated activity of "dealing as agent" has been specified in the RAO separately from the "dealing as principal" activity. It covers all regulated securities (including stakeholder pension schemes) and contractually-based investments (other than funeral plan contracts). It does not, however, extend to deposits, non-qualifying insurance contracts, Lloyd's underwriting capacity and syndicate membership and regulated mortgage contracts. The "dealing as agent" activity will unfortunately continue to catch a person who merely signs an investment agreement on behalf of a party to the agreement, but who is not himself a party and who has no discretion regarding the terms or execution of the agreement.

---

[66] ibid., Sched. 1, para. 17(4).
[67] RAO, Art. 14.
[68] RAO, Art. 15 (Absence of holding out, etc.).
[69] RAO, Art. 16 (Dealing in contractually based investments).
[70] See Sched. 2 to the RAO, which sets out in full the Annex to the ISD.

There seems to be no investor protection ground for the regulation of such an activity, but the FSA evidently regards such an activity as "dealing as agent".[71]

Arranging deals in investments

3.23   The 1986 Act contained a definition of "arranging deals in investments" with two limbs.[72] The first limb referred to the making of arrangements with a view to another person buying, selling, subscribing for or underwriting an investment. The scope of this limb was reduced substantially by a note in the 1986 Act to the effect that the arrangements had to be such that they brought about or would have brought about the transaction in question; consequently, arrangements were not caught under this head unless a direct causal link existed between the arrangement and the transaction in question. Therefore, this excluded many kinds of arrangements which were remote from any transaction (for example arranging for the distribution of "mail-shot" advertising) and normally excluded mere introductions. The second limb caught (more remote) arrangements made with a view to a participant buying, selling, subscribing for or underwriting investments (as opposed to a particular investment).

The substance of the existing position has, again, been retained in the RAO,[73] and an earlier attempt to turn the first and second limbs of "arranging" into separate regulated activities (with different exclusions) was dropped by the Treasury. In relation to the activity of arranging a particular investment deal, a helpful drafting change has been made. The words "with a view to" (which appeared in the 1986 Act) have been replaced by the word "for", which emphasises the requirement for a causal link between the arrangement and a transaction, and excludes any consideration of the intention of the arranger. In addition, arrangements under this head will continue not to be caught unless they bring about or would bring about the transaction to which the arrangements relate. It is generally considered (including by the FSA, which has given guidance to such effect in Chapter 2 and Appendix 1 of its Authorisation manual) that a person will be caught under Article 25(1) only if his involvement in the chain of events leading to the transaction is of sufficient importance that without that involvement the transaction would not take place.

It is also worth noting that the FSA has stated in a recent guidance paper that, in its view, the regulated activity of arranging a particular investment deal corresponds to the ISD activity of "receiving and transmitting orders" in relation to investments (which also requires a causal link between the activity and the transaction).[74] In this paper, which related to corporate finance services, the FSA also gave some helpful guidance (in the context of such services) on those activities which, either alone or when taken in conjunction, would be sufficient to amount to regulated "arrangements". It seems that the FSA takes the view that a simple introduction of one person to another does not, without more, amount to a regulated arrangement. This is helpful, but this view probably explains why the exclusion

---

[71] See *Hansard*, March 16, 2001 (vol. 623, col. 1107).
[72] 1986 Act, Sched. 1, para. 13.
[73] RAO, Art. 25. The two limbs appear in, respectively, Arts 25(1) and 25(2).
[74] FSA, *The Raising of Corporate Finance under the Financial Services Act 1986* (Guidance Release 3/98).

under the 1986 Act for introductions to authorised persons and others with a view to the provision of investment advice or discretionary investment management services now only applies to the (more remote) Article 25(2) regulated activity— whereas it used to apply to both kinds of "arrangements".[75] In the absence of a clear statement in the FSMA or the RAO regarding the status of introductions, this seems to create an unfortunate element of uncertainty, though it is true that most definitions of "arrangements" would exclude introductions made without additional activity or assistance (such as assistance with negotiations).

The former second limb of the definition of "arranging deals" under the 1986 Act[76] now appears in Article 25(2) of the RAO. It is fair to say that it has attracted more criticism during previous years than any other investment activity due to its relatively broad and uncertain scope. Under the 1986 Act, paragraph 13(b) caught "arrangements with a view to a person who participates in the arrangements buying, selling, subscribing for or underwriting investments". Since the definition referred to investments generally and not to a particular investment, it was generally considered that paragraph 13(b) would catch many kinds of preparatory arrangements, such as the engagement of an investment bank by a company to seek out investment opportunities, or an agreement between a fund manager and a distributor to refer clients for potential investment in unit trusts or ISAs. Since, in these and other examples, regulated arrangements relating to specific investment transactions would follow in due course, it seems doubtful that there is any real justification on policy grounds for a separate, broad regulated activity of this kind. Nonetheless, this activity has been retained in the RAO with a similar scope. Helpfully, an attempt in the first draft of the RAO to move the words "with a view" so that the relevant "view" would be that of the participant rather than the arranger was not proceeded with. Consequently, for the purposes of Article 25(2), it is the intention of the arranger which is of prime importance, though in most cases the arranger will of course be aware of the participant's intentions also (but not always!).

If Article 25(2) had been consigned to history, few tears would have been shed. It is submitted that the regulation of deal arrangers in relation to specific deals, and of investment exchanges in relation to trading platforms and similar facilities (through Part XVIII of the FSMA), should be sufficient. However, this regulated activity is likely to increase in importance with the growing use of the internet as a selling medium, since numerous financial services and product providers will continue to enter into arrangements with the operators of on-line "financial supermarkets" and portals and with internet service providers ("ISPs") for the placing of advertising, offering material and hyperlinks on websites. For the on-line service provider, this head of regulated activity is a real trap for the unwary, though some relief was provided when the Treasury introduced into the final version of the RAO a special new exclusion for persons who merely provide a "means of communication"[77]; this is discussed in more detail below, together with the new exclusion for "arranging deals with or through authorised persons".

---

[75] 1986 Act, Sched. 1, para. 13, note 6; see also the section entitled "Introducing", below.
[76] *ibid.*, Sched. 1, para. 13(b).
[77] RAO, Art. 27.

As a final point, the two heads of "arranging" now include arrangements relating to deals in Lloyd's underwriting capacity and membership of syndicates. These new activities are in addition to the special new Lloyd's activities of advising on syndicate participation[78] and managing the underwriting capacity of a Lloyd's syndicate.[79] Consequently, both Lloyd's managing agents and members' agents are likely to require permission to carry on general "arranging" activities as well.

Managing Investments

3.24 The important change to the 1986 Act definition of "managing investments"[80] is that the RAO now states expressly that the management must involve the exercise of discretion (Article 37 of the RAO). Therefore, the intention of the RAO is clearly that advisory management of investments will be regulated under the head of "investment advice" and not as investment management. Because the 1986 Act definition did not refer to "discretionary" management of investments, advisory management appeared to be caught, though it is understood that the FSA took the view that, under the 1986 Act, only arrangements conferring discretionary authority were caught under this head. The change is also welcome because it means that the United Kingdom definition of "managing investments" will be more obviously consistent with the corresponding ISD definition (which refers to discretionary management).

However, some element of doubt remains because the relevant paragraph does not expressly tie the exercise of discretion to the taking of decisions to buy or sell investments; consequently, if an investment firm gives advice on the composition of a portfolio but exercises discretion in relation to voting rights, it is not entirely clear whether it would be managing investments or giving investment advice. This is not an academic point since some of the exclusions in the RAO—for example, the "group exemptions"—may not apply to the same extent if the adviser is in fact a manager.

Further, it remains unclear what the precise components of "managing investments" are. Based on experience under the 1986 Act and on the new RAO definition, it is suggested that this activity will include:

(a) keeping a portfolio of assets consisting of or including investments under continuous or regular review (since "management" implies some continuity) and taking investment decisions on a discretionary basis; and

(b) having the right to implement, or to instruct the customer or a third party to implement, any such investment decision (*e.g.* by placing an order with a broker or custodian).

However, does "management" also include activities involved in the implementation of an investment deal, including "dealing" or "arranging a deal"? The intention appears to be that it does not since, again, the exclusions relating to,

---

[78] RAO, Art. 56
[79] RAO, Art. 57
[80] 1986 Act, Sched. 1, para. 14.

respectively, dealing in or arranging deals in investments and managing investments are not identical and there is no obvious reason for that disparity if the "managing" function also includes dealing or arranging. In addition, it is not entirely clear whether incidental activities, such as reporting to customers on the performance of a portfolio, are included in the overall definition. This point could be of significance to overseas investment managers who periodically meet clients in the United Kingdom to discuss investment performance, but who take all decisions offshore; the common view taken in the past, which still seems preferable, is that the location of the investment manager when he takes investment decisions is the relevant place when considering whether the "overseas exemption" will apply (Article 72 of the RAO, discussed further below).

Safeguarding and administering investments (Safe Custody)

3.25   This activity still incorporates the separate regulated activity of "arranging for the safeguarding and administration of assets belonging to another" (Article 40 of the RAO).   In this regard, it is still worth revisiting the helpful guidance which the FSA gave on this activity in 1997[81]; this confirmed, for example, that a person would be regarded as "arranging custody" where he safeguards investments (*e.g.* by holding certificates in a safe deposit box) and arranges for a third party to carry on administration functions such as receiving and disbursing income and dealing with corporate actions, such as rights issues or takeover offers (though, in that case, the third party would not be carrying on regulated custody business because he would not be safeguarding investments).

The exclusions relating to this activity are broadly those which appeared in the 1986 Act, including an exclusion for persons who introduce investors to independent United Kingdom authorised custodians.   Unfortunately, a new exclusion for the custody of unquoted investments, which appeared in the first two drafts of the RAO, was omitted from the final version.   Since the exclusion was apparently aimed mainly at professional firms providing occasional safe custody services for clients in relation to unquoted shares, the view seems to have been taken that the special regime for the professions under Part XX of the FSMA, together with other RAO exclusions, is sufficient to avoid any need for "precautionary authorisation" in this connection. While it might be argued that separate treatment for the custody of unquoted investments is unnecessary, it is equally arguable that this exclusion might have benefited other types of persons as well, such as some venture capital firms which arrange custody of unquoted shares for clients and third parties.

Acting in relation to Collective Investment Schemes

3.26   Under the 1986 Act, authorisation was required by a person establishing, operating or winding-up a collective investment scheme ("CIS"), including acting as trustee of an authorised unit trust scheme or as depositary or sole director of an investment company with variable capital.   Ultimately, the RAO has not extended the scope of this regulated activity, though two previous drafts threatened to extend it fundamentally.   For example, the Treasury originally suggested a new

---

[81] The Securities and Investments Board (now the FSA), *Custody of Investments under the Financial Services Act 1986* (Guidance Release, June 1997).

definition of "establishing" a CIS, which would "include" engaging the operator of the relevant CIS and/or determining the constitution of the CIS. This seemed to suggest a broader definition of "establishing" a CIS than was hitherto suspected, and it is to be hoped that a court would not view this as an appropriate starting-point. Also, it is to be noted that "agreeing" to act in any of the defined ways in relation to a CIS has not become a regulated activity, despite its appearing in drafts of the RAO. This would have been a potential trap for the unwary in relation to offshore CISs, since it has generally been assumed that offshore status in relation to the establishing and operation of the CIS will be maintained as long as relevant individuals are outside the United Kingdom when they undertake the activities in question, even if they agree to do so while in the United Kingdom.

Investment Advice

3.27   The broad definition of "giving investment advice", and the definition of the "investments" concerned, remain similar (though the latter now includes stakeholder pension schemes and funeral plan contracts in addition to 1986 Act investments), but a couple of interesting, clarificatory amendments have been made to the definition in the 1986 Act (Article 53 of the RAO). First, advice will be regulated if it is given to a person in his capacity as an investor or a potential investor, *or in his capacity as agent for an investor or potential investor* (emphasis supplied). This change has been made since it has sometimes been argued that advice given to, for example, a discretionary investment manager is not investment advice because the manager is a professional intermediary and not an investor. Given the agency relationship which commonly exists between investment managers and their clients, however, this was a doubtful argument and the common view under the 1986 Act has been that (for example) advice given by a United Kingdom investment adviser to an offshore investment manager was regulated investment advice. This point has now been settled.

Secondly, the new definition refers to advice being given on the merits of buying, etc., "a *particular* investment", rather than simply "an investment". In its *Consultation Paper on the RAO* in February 1999, the Treasury pointed to this change as being one of substance, adding that it ought to assist in reducing the number of "precautionary authorisations" required by members of the professions, including solicitors and accountants. In fact, the former definition in the 1986 Act[82] had been widely assumed not to catch generic advice (*e.g.* the merits of shares versus bonds, or a recommendation to "get a pension policy") as opposed to a recommendation regarding a particular investment. Nonetheless, the clarification in the RAO is welcome, though the status of the professions has had to be dealt with in different ways from those originally envisaged (see below).

Lloyd's Activities

3.28   The new regulation of the Lloyd's insurance market is one of the main features of the new Act. The general exemption for Lloyd's related activities[83] has been swept away, and the traditional activities of Lloyd's managing agents and

---

[82] 1986 Act, Sched. 1, para. 15.
[83] 1986 Act, s. 43.

members' agents—namely managing underwriting capacity of a Lloyd's syndicate and advising persons on syndicate participation—have become regulated activities. In addition, other investment activities of Lloyd's professionals—such as investment management or advice—will of course be regulated in the normal way. In addition, as noted above, Lloyd's professionals will need a separate permission in order to arrange deals in syndicate participation and (apparently) underwriting capacity. The Society of Lloyd's also requires authorisation in order to arrange deals in contracts of insurance written at Lloyd's.[84]

The new regime for Lloyd's is discussed in more detail in Chapter 15.

REGULATED INVESTMENTS

3.29 The "investments" are now grouped together in Part III of the RAO (Articles 74–89, inclusive), beginning with deposits and rights under contracts of insurance (general and long-term). These are followed by the list of "investments" mainly as drafted in the 1986 Act, and the new prescribed investments, being stakeholder pension schemes, Lloyd's syndicate capacity and syndicate membership, funeral plan contracts and regulated mortgage contracts. As was the case under the 1986 Act,[85] there is a general "sweeper" investment comprising any rights to or interests in investments though, interestingly, this residual investment now includes rights to and interests in deposits, insurance contracts (general and long-term) and the new prescribed investments other than regulated mortgage contracts. It is not entirely clear what the policy reason for this extension is. The difficulties encountered in interpreting this provision under the 1986 Act may well now be extended.

Since most of the definitions of investments are unchanged from the previous banking, insurance and financial services legislation, they will not be rehearsed in full below. Some material changes and points of interest are, however, highlighted.

Deposits

3.30 The basic definition of a "deposit" which was contained in the Banking Act 1987[86] is retained. Since a sum paid to a third party will only be a deposit if it is so paid on terms that *it* will be repaid, "certainty of capital" is required in order for a payment to be deposit. Consequently, sub-participations of loans (where the "seller" of the sub-participation agrees to pay to the participant sums linked to actual payments of principal and interest by the borrower under the loan in question), and some kinds of guaranteed investment entitling the holder to the return of part only of the principal advanced (together with potential stock market returns), will not be deposits. Articles 6 to 9 (inclusive) of the RAO then list a number of exclusions from the basic definition, most of which have been drawn from the 1987 Act and the orders made under it, including one in respect of sums received from other authorised deposit-takers or from insurance companies.

---

[84] RAO, Art. 58.
[85] 1986 Act, Sched. 1, para. 11.
[86] 1987 Act, s. 5.

However, there are also two significant changes. First, as noted above, the exclusion for sums received pursuant to issues of debt securities has been considerably liberalised, except in relation to issues of commercial paper. Secondly, there is a new exclusion, which was included for the first time in the final version of the RAO, in relation to sums received by authorised or exempt persons with permission to carry on regulated dealing, arranging, managing, CIS or stakeholder pension activities, where such receipt is in the course of, or for the purpose of, carrying on that activity with or on behalf of the person by, or on behalf of whom, the sum is paid.[87] While, on its face, this exclusion appears helpful, it had seemed that, for example, a cash sum received from a customer by a stockbroker or an asset manager would not be a deposit because that sum would be "referable to the provision of property (*e.g.* the purchase of investments) or services (*e.g.* investment management services) or the giving of security (*e.g.* margin or collateral)".[88] However, the exclusion is presumably intended to remove any doubt which may exist as a result of the limitation on the "property or services" exclusion in Article 5(3) of the RAO (which also appeared in the 1987 Act), which seems to require a contract to be in place in order for a sum not to constitute a deposit.

Shares

3.31   The definition of "shares" includes shares in any unincorporated body constituted under the law of a country or territory outside the United Kingdom.[89] This would presumably include interests in an overseas collective investment scheme which is not a body corporate, such as a Bermudan or Channel Islands limited partnership. Therefore, rather strangely, promotions of shares in such vehicles might appear to be subject both to the regime for securities under the Public Offers of Securities Regulations 1995 (which cross-refers to this definition) and to the regime for the promotion of collective investment schemes under section 238 of the FSMA. An amendment is to be made before N2, however, which will exclude units in collective investment schemes from the regime relating to offers of securities.

Futures

3.32   The definition of a "future" continues to contain a list of conclusive and indicative features to determine, or a to help to determine, whether a particular contract is made for investment purposes or for commercial purposes.[90] Therefore, for example, contracts traded on a recognised investment exchange continue to be regarded conclusively as made for investment purposes. However, an interesting change has been made to the provision that a contract which is not traded on an investment exchange shall be regarded as made for commercial purposes (and will therefore not be an investment) if under the terms of the contract delivery is to be made within seven days. A new provision has been inserted that this conclusive

---

[87] RAO, Art. 8.
[88] RAO, Art. 5(2)(b).
[89] RAO, Arti. 76(1)(b).
[90] RAO, Art. 84.

presumption will not apply if it can be shown that there existed an understanding that, notwithstanding the express terms of the contract, delivery would not be made within seven days. This change had its genesis a few years ago when a number of unregulated foreign exchange firms began to offer to their customers short-term (*i.e.* less than seven day) currency contracts which were, in practice, usually or invariably "rolled-over" before the end of each successive seven-day period with profits or losses being allocated to the customer. Since the written terms of the contracts in question were usually (and unsurprisingly!) explicit that delivery would always be required within seven days, SIB (now FSA) elected to issue guidance[91] which stated, *inter alia*, that SIB regarded such contracts which were issued on the "understanding" that they would be automatically extended after seven days as being regulated futures, with the result that the unregulated brokers who traded these contracts were required to become authorised. Though it may be open to debate whether such guidance could alter the legal position under the 1986 Act, the position has now been made clear by this change.

Contracts for Differences

3.33   There is a new exclusion to the definition of a contract for differences which applies to rights under a contract under which money is received by way of deposit on terms that any interest or other return to be paid on the sum deposited will be calculated by reference to fluctuations in an index or other factor. This is a helpful exclusion in relation to some index-linked deposit products offered by banks which will, of course, constitute deposit-taking under the FSMA. The exclusion is drafted widely enough to accommodate deposits offering index-linked capital return as well as (or instead of) interest. Nonetheless, apparently any such product must constitute a "deposit" in order to qualify; consequently, products which do not offer "certainty of capital" will not be excluded; nor will sums paid which are not deposits because of any of the exclusions in Articles 6 to 9 (inclusive) of the RAO.

Certificates representing securities

3.34   The former definition under the 1986 Act has been re-drafted, though the changes are evidently intended to be largely clarificatory. Certificates or other instruments are now covered if they confer contractual or property rights (a) in respect of shares, bonds, government securities or warrants where the investment is held by a person other than the person on whom the rights are conferred by the certificate or instrument and (b) the transfer of those rights may be effected without requiring the consent of that person (*i.e.* the holder of the underlying investment). This fits more closely the typical "certificate", such as an American Depository Receipt ("ADR"), which is freely tradable independently from the underlying securities which are held by the custodian bank.

---

[91] The Securities and Investments Board, *Foreign Exchange and the Financial Services Act 1986* (Guidance Release 1/96).

EXCLUSIONS FROM THE REGULATED ACTIVITIES

3.35   The exclusions from each regulated activity are to be found in two places in the RAO. First, the definition of each regulated activity in Part II of the RAO is accompanied by those exclusions which apply solely to that activity. Secondly, those exclusions which apply to several different kinds of activity—including the "groups and joint enterprises", "sale of body corporate" and "overseas persons" exclusions—are grouped together at the end of Part II. This is a considerable improvement on the first draft of the RAO, in which the exclusions applying to any particular regulated activity were placed together in separate, exhaustive categories; though intended to be helpful, this approach made the draft RAO unnecessarily lengthy and repetitive.

The exclusions in Part II of the RAO contain some important changes, including new exemptions as well as specific exclusions from the deposit-taking and insurance activities (some of which have been referred to above). The exclusions are, of course, of critical importance to the many businesses which reside at or around the "perimeter" of financial services regulation and which are currently unregulated; such businesses should study Part II mindful of the fact that the FSA has already consulted on its future approach to policing this perimeter pursuant to its statutory objectives and powers.[92] The exclusions are also of relevance to many regulated businesses, since their obligations under FSA conduct of business rules are likely to be reduced in respect of activities which are excluded under the RAO. In its *Conduct of Business Sourcebook*, the FSA prescribes that the Conduct of Business ("COB") Rules will not apply to any aspect of a firm's business which falls within an exclusion in Part II of the RAO, subject to the application of the COB Rules to "non-regulated activities".[93]

"Occasional" deposit-taking

3.36   The important new exclusions from the deposit-taking activity in the cases of issues of securities and sums received by investment businesses have been discussed above. Apart from these changes, the most striking aspect of the exclusions relating to deposit-taking is that the former exemption under the Banking Act for a person who accepted deposits only on "particular occasions" (without holding himself out as accepting deposits on a day-to-day basis) is missing. Thankfully, this is only because the Treasury has decided to put the exclusion into a different statutory instrument—namely the so-called "Business Order".[94] It seems that deposits which are excluded pursuant to Articles 6 to 9 (inclusive) of the RAO may be disregarded when determining the "particular occasions" on which deposits are accepted for this purpose.

Community Co-Insurers

3.37   There is a special exclusion for EEA insurers who effect or carry on a contract of insurance in the United Kingdom other than through a United Kingdom

---

[92] FSA, *Enforcing the perimeter* Consultation Paper 35 (December 1999).
[93] FSA, *The Conduct of Business Sourcebook* (COB 1.3.1R and 1.3.2G(3)). See also Chapter 10 below.
[94] The Financial Services and Markets Act 2000 (Carrying on Regulated Activities by Way of Business) Order 2001 (S.I. 2001 No. 1177).

branch, pursuant to a European Community co-insurance operation in which the firm is participating otherwise than as the leading insurer.[95] This gives effect to the E.C. Directive on co-insurance.[96] Given the general policy elsewhere in the FSMA and the RAO not to discriminate between EEA and non-EEA businesses, it might also have been useful to broaden this exclusion so that it applied equally to non-EEA insurers authorised in "approved" jurisdictions.

Exclusions from Dealing as Principal

(i) General

3.38 As noted above, the former exemptions under paragraphs 17(1) and 17(4) of Schedule 1 of the 1986 Act in relation to dealings as principal have been retained in broadly the same form.[97] The exemption in the 1986 Act for accepting "instruments creating or acknowledging indebtedness" (*e.g.* debentures or loan agreements) has also been carried forward.[98]

(ii) Companies issuing securities

3.39 As was the case under the 1986 Act,[99] the RAO contains an exclusion[1] which means that companies do not need to be authorised in order to issue their own shares or debentures (or warrants in relation to either). However, this is now framed as an exclusion to the dealing activity, and not (as was the case under the 1986 Act) a provision that issuing securities is not to be regarded as "selling" or "disposing". Without more, this would have meant that issuing equity and debt securities would in effect be part of the regulated activity, and that—unlike the position under the 1986 Act—arranging for a company to issue securities would be a regulated activity, even where the "arranger's" services do not extend to making arrangements with investors. This point was addressed by the Treasury in the final version of the RAO by expanding one of the exclusions relating to the "arranging" activities to provide that (inter alia) a company would not be treated as selling shares or debentures, or warrants, by reason of its issuing them.[2] The only change is now that, because of the broad definition of "shares", arranging for the issue of shares by a non-United Kingdom unincorporated body will be a regulated activity.

(iii) Risk Management (and former Permitted Persons)

3.40 The "permitted person" regime under the 1986 Act[3] has been discontinued. This exclusion was intended to benefit persons who dealt in investments either as principal or as agent for other group companies and whose main business was not investment business. Most permitted persons were either public companies acting through their corporate treasury departments, or energy companies dealing in

---

[95] RAO, Art. 11.
[96] Directive No. 78/473.
[97] RAO, Arts 15 and 16.
[98] RAO, Art. 17; *cf.* note 1 to para. 12 of Schedule 1 to the 1986 Act. This exclusion is intended to take ordinary lending activities outside "dealing".
[99] 1986 Act, Sched. 1, para. 28(3).
[1] RAO, Art. 18.
[2] RAO, Art. 34.
[3] 1986 Act, Sched. 1, para. 23.

energy-related derivatives (*e.g.* electricity, gas or oil futures or contracts for differ-ences). Apparently, the number of permitted persons who had applied to the FSA for certification as such dwindled and the Treasury decided not to continue the spe-cial regime.

However, having made this decision (apparently on the ground that companies such as power generators would probably not need authorisation anyway), the Treasury received some concerted lobbying by some "permitted persons", and others, with a view to a satisfactory new exclusion being drafted to replace the permitted persons regime. Ultimately, the Treasury came up with the "Risk Man-agement" exclusion,[4] the final version of which is a considerable improvement on the first draft, entitled "Hedging", which appeared in October 2000.[5] The exclu-sion applies to a transaction in futures, options or contracts for differences entered into by a person as principal provided neither party is an individual and that the "sole or main purpose" of the relevant party in relation to the transac-tion (either by itself or in combination with other such transactions) is that of limiting the extent to which a "relevant business" will be affected by an "identi-fiable risk" arising otherwise than as a result of carrying on a regulated activity. The "relevant business" must consist of activities other than regulated activities (or activities which would be regulated but for an exclusion) and must be a busi-ness of the relevant party or a member of its group or a participant with it in a joint enterprise.

Though the exclusion is now more helpful than it was originally, it still contains some difficulties. In particular, the exclusion applies to transactions taken indi-vidually or in combination with other transactions, rather than to companies or businesses; it is suggested that it may sometimes be difficult for companies to "group" particular transactions so that, for example, a profitable transaction entered into partly (but perhaps not mainly) to limit a risk can fall within the exclusion as part of a group of deals forming part of a risk management strategy. However, one positive aspect of the exclusion is that it covers both transactional risks—such as changes in interest rates, exchange rates or prices—and non-transactional ones, such as climate change or natural disasters.

The exclusion applies both to the activity of *dealing as principal* and *dealing as agent*. In relation to the latter, it is particularly important that the "relevant busi-ness" which must mainly consist of non-regulated activities can be that of a fellow group company on whose behalf the transacting party is dealing. This may well allow some services companies providing treasury and dealing functions within energy or industrial groups to avoid authorisation. Though, it should be noted, there is no "Risk Management" exclusion for "arranging" activities, this may not be a problem in practice since—in addition to the Risk Management exclusion for dealings as agent—a services company might be able to rely on the "groups and joint enterprises" exclusion, or the exclusion for deals arranged with or through authorised persons, in relation to any arrangements for other group companies where it is not a party to relevant transactions.[6]

---

[4] RAO, Art. 19.

[5] See the Treasury's *Second Consultation Document on the RAO* (October 2000).

[6] RAO, Arts 29 and 69. In relation to the "groups" exclusion, the impact of Art. 4(4) of the RAO (dis-cussed above) always needs to be considered.

If an energy company (or a member of its group) requires authorisation notwithstanding this exclusion, the practical consequences have been reduced to some extent by a new "energy market participant" regime introduced by the FSA, which is similar to the "oil market participant" regime operated for some years by the SFA.[7] Energy market participants will be subject to a modified regulatory regime.

Exclusions from Arranging Deals

(i) General

3.41 A number of the exclusions contained in the 1986 Act in relation to the "arranging" activities have been carried forward in the RAO—including those relating to arrangements in connection with loans (including those made on the security of insurance policies) and the provision of finance for investments.[8] The exclusion for introductions to independent advisers and discretionary investment managers is also retained[9] though, as noted below, it only applies to the activity of making "general" arrangements under Article 25(2), and not to "deal-specific" arrangements under Article 25(1). As was the case under the 1986 Act, a person does not need authorisation to arrange a transaction to which he is a party (as principal or as agent).[10]

(ii) "Enabling Parties to Communicate"

3.42 One of the key issues during consultation on the RAO was the position of internet portals and internet service providers ("ISPs"), and other on-line intermediaries, whose main businesses are not financial services but who provide a "hub" or "link" between customers and product providers. Much attention centred on the relevant provisions of the Financial Promotion Order,[11] but (as professional advisers know well) the definitions of the activities of investment advice and arranging deals have frequently resulted in precautionary authorisations under the 1986 Act for on-line businesses, and are of at least equal concern. In relation to arranging deals, the exemption for transactions with or through authorised persons (discussed immediately below) contains a major limitation and thus, without more, the RAO would certainly not have achieved the Government's stated aim of "media neutrality".[12] Presumably with this in mind, the Treasury introduced an exclusion in the final version of the RAO which exempts a person from the Article 25(2) "general arrangements" activity if he merely provides means by which one party to a transaction (or potential transaction) is able to communicate with other such parties. Though this exemption clearly applies to traditional as well as new media, it should enable many ISPs and internet portals to avoid authorisation. More generally, the exclusion is presumably intended to enable a person whose web-site contains a "hyperlink" to an investment product provider's web-site to

---

[7] Securities and Futures Authority, Board Notice 585 (May 18, 2001).
[8] RAO, Arts 30–32.
[9] RAO, Art. 33.
[10] RAO, Art. 28.
[11] See Chapter 6, below.
[12] See H.M. Treasury, *Consultation Paper on the RAO* (February 1999).

avoid authorisation unless that person's site also contains investment advice or a financial promotion.

This exclusion is certainly to be welcomed, but with two caveats. First, it does not provide an exclusion from "arranging a particular transaction" under Article 25(1). Consequently, providing a hyperlink from an unregulated site to (say) a securities firm's site for the purpose of executing specific deals may amount to a regulated activity under Article 25(1) (even if a financial promotion for that purpose on the unregulated site has been approved by the authorised securities firm). Secondly, the FSA has already given guidance (in Chapter 2 and Appendix 1 of its Authorisation manual) that it regards the use of the word "merely" in Article 27 as crucial. Consequently, an ISP which "co-brands" an investment service or product jointly with its provider or endorses it may well find that the exclusion will not apply, though the payment of volume-based commissions to the ISP should not of itself have this effect.

(iii) Arranging deals with or through authorised persons

3.43 This new exclusion[13] was evidently designed to help both professional firms and internet businesses to avoid the need for authorisation by reason of "arranging deals", provided that the arrangements (under Article 25(1) or (2)) are made with a view to a transaction by a person (in the RAO, called "the client") with or through an authorised person if:

(a) the transaction is or is to be entered into on advice given to the client by an authorised person; or

(b) it is clear in all the circumstances that the client, in his capacity as an investor, is not seeking and has not sought advice from the relevant person as to the merits of the client's entering into the transaction (or, if such advice was sought, the request was declined and the client was recommended to seek advice from an authorised person).

While the exclusion will be useful in some cases and is certainly to be welcomed, it seems likely to be of limited benefit to professionals and the world of e-commerce alike. As far as lawyers and accountants are concerned, Article 29 does not really address the need for a fuller exemption for transaction-related negotiation and administration undertaken in the course of providing professional services[14]; and, most obviously, the exclusion simply will not work in the many cases where a transaction will be concluded without the intervention of an authorised person. As far as on-line firms are concerned, the exclusion carries the major problem that it does not apply if the person in question receives from any person other than the client any pecuniary reward or other advantage, for which he does not account to the client, arising out of his making the arrangements. Although this limitation was drafted with professional firms in mind, it has had the effect that the exclusion will not be available, for example, to a portal which receives fees or commissions from a product provider (perhaps on the basis of volume of business referred).

---

[13] RAO, Art. 29.
[14] See also the section on "Professional firms", below.

Though the exclusion for "providing means of communication" should nonetheless help in many cases, there will probably be others where precautionary authorisation will now be required and which might have been avoided, if, for example, the exclusion had permitted receipt of fees or commissions subject to disclosure being made to the client. As a final point, unlike the "Introducing" exclusion referred to below, this exclusion does not extend to arrangements with a view to transactions with exempt persons or overseas professionals. The reason for this omission is not clear.

(iv) Introducing

3.44 As mentioned above, the ambit of the "introducer" exemption in the 1986 Act[15] has been narrowed. This applies to arrangements for the introduction of persons to another person, where that person is an authorised or exempted person or an overseas investment professional lawfully carrying on regulated activities in the United Kingdom (*i.e.* under the overseas person exemptions), and the introduction is made with a view to the provision by that other person of independent advice or discretionary investment management services.[16] However, this exemption has been retained for Article 25(2) "general" arrangements but not for the activity of arranging particular transactions under Article 25(1). The Treasury's explanation of this is that such introductions would not be capable of constituting the regulated activity of arranging a particular transaction because they would be very unlikely to cause the transaction itself to happen[17]; arrangements not causing a deal to happen are excluded under this head anyway.[18] The Treasury's explanation is persuasive, but it seems that there would have been no harm in extending the exclusion in view of the doubt which must remain. As a result of this, some persons who from time to time provide "company marriage broking" introductions, but who do not provide advice or any other regulated services, may require "precautionary" authorisation (particularly if Article 29 does not help because no authorised person is involved), though the extended "sales of bodies corporate" exclusion may also be useful.

Professional Firms

3.45 The 1986 Act contained exemptions in favour of professional firms, such as solicitors and accountants, in respect of the regulated activities of "arranging deals in investments" and "giving investment advice", which only applied to services:

(a) given or made in the course of the carrying on of any profession not otherwise constituting investment business; and

(b) the giving of which is a necessary part of other advice or services given in the course of carrying on that profession.

---

[15] 1986 Act, Sched. 1, para. 13, note 6.
[16] Art. 33.
[17] H.M. Treasury, *Consultation Document on the RAO* (February 1999).
[18] RAO, Art. 26.

The use of the words "necessary part", and other doubts about the scope of the exemption, led most professional firms to obtain authorisation under 1986 Act, though very many carried on little or no mainstream investment business,[19] and even less were separately remunerated for such business. The professional firms were regulated in the conduct of their investment business by the "recognised professional bodies" ("RPBs"), which were the same bodies which regulated the professions themselves (such as the Institute of Chartered Accountants of England and Wales and the Law Society of England and Wales).

The Treasury stated in its *Consultation Paper on the RAO* in February 1999 that the Government believed that the FSA's remit should extend to the regulation of all firms offering investment advice and services to their clients, including professionals, so that consumers might benefit from a consistent regulatory approach irrespective of who provides them with financial services. However, in addition to this basic policy objective, the Government recognised that there was little merit in forcing the great majority of the professional firms to maintain what was, in reality, no more than "precautionary authorisation". Unfortunately, the Treasury's first attempt to deal with this problem in the draft RAO which appeared in February 1999 was not entirely successful, because the relevant "professionals" exclusion retained the use of the word "necessary" (which caused precautionary authorisation in the first place), and merely qualified it by the use of the word "reasonable", so that arrangements or advice were to be exempted if (*inter alia*) they "[might]" reasonably be regarded as a necessary part of other services provided in the course of carrying on that other profession or business". This solution was not received favourably by the professions, though the exclusion (referred to again below) was retained and now appears as Article 67 of the RAO. Ultimately, the Government announced on October, 13 1999 a special regime for "exempt regulated activities" carried on by members of a profession supervised and regulated by a "designated professional body". Again, however, this proposed exclusion contained a significant qualification in that it required (*inter alia*) that any regulated activity should be "ancillary and subordinate" to professional services provided for a client, as well as that any such activity should be provided in an "incidental manner" in the course of a professional activity.

After further discussion with interested parties, a modified version of this special regime was inserted in the Financial Services and Markets Bill, which now appears as Part XX of the FSMA (sections 325 to 333 inclusive). This contains the important change that the "ancillary and subordinate" condition no longer appears. Instead, the exclusion to the general prohibition provides that "the manner of the provision by [a person] of any service in the course of carrying on the [regulated] activities must be incidental to the provision by him of professional services".[20] "Professional services" are defined as services which do not constitute carrying on a regulated activity, and the provision of which is supervised and regulated by a "designated professional body". The new formulation has sensibly been based on Article 2.2(c) of the ISD, which excludes investment services provided

---

[19] In its Consultation Paper 30, *The FSA's Regulation of Professional Firms* (October 1999), the FSA estimates that only 2,000 out of the 15,000 professional firms in the U.K. carry on what it terms "mainstream investment business".
[20] FSMA, s. 327(4).

"in an incidental manner in the course of a professional activity". However, the FSMA contains the additional conditions that:

(a) the professional firm must not receive from a person other than his client any pecuniary reward or other advantage for which he does not account to his client arising from the carrying on of any of the regulated activities; and

(b) the professional firm must not carry on, or hold itself out as carrying on, a regulated activity other than one which rules made by the relevant designated professional body allow the firm to carry on.

In addition, the Act allows the Treasury to designate "prohibited" investments or activities for non-FSA regulated professional firms (section 327(6)). The Treasury has specified numerous non-exempt activities,[21] including accepting deposits, insurance activities, dealing as principal and establishing, etc., a collective investment scheme. Major limitations are also placed on discretionary management and the giving of investment advice.

The Act also places the FSA under a statutory duty to "keep itself informed" about the way in which designated professional bodies supervise and regulate the carrying on of exempt regulated activities by their members (section 326(1)). The Treasury is empowered by order to designate professional bodies for the purposes of the new professionals regime and has duly designated authorities including the various United Kingdom legal and accounting bodies.[22]

The consequence of the complicated structure summarised above is as follows. The starting-point for any professional firm is Article 67 of the RAO, which provides an exclusion from the dealing as agent, arranging, custody and investment advice activities (but *not* including activities such as dealing as principal or managing investments) if any such activity "may reasonably be regarded as a necessary part" of other professional services. Unfortunately, this formulation remains somewhat uncertain, and the RAO contains no provision (as the Treasury suggested it might[23]) specifically excluding administrative, transaction-related services provided by solicitors and accountants. Consequently, many legal and accounting firms seem likely to opt for the Part XX "designated professional body" regime, which is in some respects not unlike the *status quo ante*, but which involves firms in effect declaring that they are carrying a regulated activities (though, in fact, they may not be). This route also carries the contingent risk that the Treasury (under section 327(6)) or the FSA (by direction under section 328) might decide to subject a particular activity or activities to direct FSA regulation. However, perhaps the most difficult choice is that faced by those United Kingdom firms which are not members of a United Kingdom "designated professional body", such as many of the U.S. law firms now resident in London; they must choose between the Article 67 exclusion and direct FSA regulation.

---

[21] The Financial Services and Markets Act 2000 (Professions) (Non-Exempt Activities) Order 2001 (S.I. 2001 No. 1227).

[22] The Financial Services and Markets Act 2000 (Designated Professional Bodies) Order 2001 (S.I. 2001 No. 1226).

[23] See H.M. Treasury, *Consultation Paper on the RAO* (February 1999); and the *Minutes of the Tenth Standing Committee on Delegated Legislation* (March 15, 2001).

Professional firms should also refer to the Financial Promotion Order when considering their need for authorisation (see Chapter 6 below). At the time of writing, many City of London solicitors' firms in particular were concerned that the financial promotion regime would lead them to "precautionary authorisation". Any firm which concludes that direct FSA regulation is or may be required can "opt-in" to automatic authorisation under the FSMA pursuant to transitional arrangements, provided it is a member of a "recognised professional body" (RPB) (see further Chapter 4 below).

Managing Investments: Attorneys

3.46   There is a special exemption in respect of the regulated activity of "managing investments" when it is conducted by a person appointed to carry on that activity under an enduring or limited power of attorney.[24] This was a provision designed to assist professionals, such as solicitors or accountants, who are given authority to manage their clients' assets and affairs, and it only applies if all routine or day-to-day decisions relating to investments are taken by an authorised or exempt person.   However, this exclusion is likely to be of limited use in practice since there is no corresponding exclusion for attorneys who also act in conjunction with an investment professional to arrange or implement a dealing consequent upon an investment decision being made.

Advice Given in Publications

3.47   The former exclusion (in paragraph 25 of Schedule 1 of the 1986 Act) in relation to investment advice given in newspapers, journals, magazines and other "periodical publications", whose "principal purpose" is not to lead or enable persons to deal in investments, has been retained in Article 54 of the RAO (but with the added proviso that the principal purpose must also not be the giving of investment advice).   The exclusion has, however, been extended to cover any other "service comprising regularly updated news or information", which most obviously refers to teletext and other news services, but which will also catch many websites carrying financial news (Article 54(1)).   Unfortunately though, the exclusion as a whole retains the concepts of "periodicals" and "regularly updated" information, which has caused a problem in practice for some websites which are not necessarily issued or updated regularly or periodically.   Also, the new extended definition for news services may not help the kind of financial website which offers opinion, research and comment, as well as news and information.   A separate exclusion in relation to websites, which appeared in the Treasury's *Second Consultation Paper on the RAO* (October 2000), did not appear in the final version.

The exclusion in favour of television and radio programmes which appeared in the 1986 Act has also been retained in Article 54, but it will now apply only if the principal purpose of the service, taken as a whole and including any advertisements or other promotional material, is not to give investment advice or to lead to investment transactions (Article 54(2)).

---

[24] RAO, Art. 38.

The FSA may certify on application being made that Article 54 applies to a particular publication or service, though a certificate is not necessary for the exclusions to apply. As under the 1986 Act, however, a certificate is conclusive evidence of the matters certified (Article 54(4)). In practice, the FSA is understood to have been reluctant, in the past, to grant certification to on-line services; it remains to be seen how and whether this practice develops. Helpfully, the FSA has already given detailed guidance in Chapter 7 of its Authorisation manual regarding the scope of the Article 54 exclusion and the availability and process of certification.

Groups and Joint Enterprises

3.48 These important exclusions under the 1986 Act[25] have benefited many intra-group and commercial joint venture activities, including (for example) investment management or investment advisory services provided by a company solely to members of its group, and arranging services provided by a participant in a joint venture to other participants. The exclusions are substantially repeated in the RAO,[26] and apply to all of the regulated activities carried forward from the 1986 Act, though no exclusions appear to have been provided for "agreements" between group companies and joint enterprise participants (as used to be the case in relation to "arranging" and "management" activities under the 1986 Act).

The exclusions are very similar to those contained in paragraph 18 of Schedule 1 of the 1986 Act, but there are minor differences. Perhaps most significantly, the group exemption for "arranging deals" has apparently been narrowed so that it will clearly only apply where the arrangements are for another group company to invest *as principal*, and not as agent (though it is possible to interpret the existing exemption[27] as having the same meaning). This change could have practical consequences, for example, for some United Kingdom-based investment advisers to offshore private equity fund managers within the same group. Such advisers have sometimes remained unregulated on the basis that the 1986 Act exempted arrangements carried out for group companies entering into investment transactions as agent for limited partnerships or other customers.

Sales of bodies corporate

3.49 The exemptions for investment services provided in relation to sales of companies (including overseas incorporated companies) have had something of a chequered past. When they came into force in 1988,[28] many corporate finance advisers in the mergers and acquisitions market (particularly "boutiques" and niche firms such as subsidiaries of management consultants and surveyors) could have been forgiven for reading the exemptions quickly (as some perhaps did) and reaching the conclusion that this exemption represented their ticket out of financial services regulation. Unfortunately, a closer inspection revealed that the exemption had significant limitations. First, it only applied to acquisitions or disposals of at least 75 per cent of the voting share capital of companies. Secondly, and most

---

[25] 1986 Act, Sched. 1, para. 18.
[26] RAO, Art. 69 .
[27] 1986 Act, Sched. 1, para. 18(3)(a).
[28] *ibid.*, Sched. 1, para. 21.

significantly, it only applied where the acquisition or disposal was, or was to be, between parties each of whom was a body corporate, a partnership, a single individual or a group of "connected individuals" (being, broadly, directors, managers and their close relatives). Unfortunately, the drafting of this latter limitation was not transparently clear and different interpretations were possible; the most favoured interpretation was probably that, to come within the exemption, each of the vendor and the purchaser had to fall within one (and not more than one) of the permitted categories, so that the exemption would not apply (for example) if a group of connected individuals sold a company to two partnerships. However, some practitioners regarded such a transaction as falling within the exemption, as long as each party to it fell within one of the stated categories. Whichever interpretation was preferred, however, the exemption would not apply if (for example) the vendors were a group of "connected individuals" together with some unconnected individuals. It clearly did not apply to public takeovers.

Subsequently, the exemption was further narrowed following the enactment of the ISD in the United Kingdom, which provided that none of the specified exemptions in Part III of Schedule 1 of the 1986 Act had the effect that a person whose regular occupation or business was the provision of investment services to third parties on a professional basis was not to be regarded as carrying on a regulated activity, if that person was an ISD investment firm.[29] The Securities and Futures Authority is believed to have suggested that the ISD had in effect removed the "sale of body corporate" exemption, though it subsequently altered this position in a letter to its member firms. Interestingly, the view of SFA was subsequently that services relating to transactions falling within the exemption would be entirely *outside* the ISD (and that, therefore, the exemption would apply in full) if the relevant firm's regulated activities all fell within the "sale of body corporate" exemption. This appears to be on the basis that such services relate in substance to the sale of a "business" rather than the sale of transferable securities, so that the ISD does not apply.

The RAO continues to apply the exemption to the same list of regulated activities as previously,[30] but with the important change that the 75 per cent threshold is lowered to 50 per cent. Even more significantly, the exclusion may now apply if the stated conditions relating to the 50 per cent threshold and the limited range of parties are satisfied, or even where they are not, provided "the object of the transaction may nevertheless reasonably be regarded as being the acquisition or disposal of day-to-day control of the affairs of the body corporate". The main significance of this is that many corporate acquisitions from multiple vendors will now fall within the exclusion, irrespective of the number and identity of the vendors, as long as the "day-to-day control" test is met.

Trustees and Personal Representatives

3.50 The 1986 Act contained an important exclusion for trustees and personal representatives who provide arranging, custodial, investment management or investment advisory services, or send dematerialised instructions in their capacity

---

[29] Art. 6 of the Financial Services Act 1986 (Investment Services) (Extension of Scope of Act) Order 1995 (S.I. 1995 No. 3271).
[30] RAO, Art. 70.

as trustees or PRs.[31] This exclusion was subject to the important qualification that the trustee or PR should not be remunerated for such an investment service in addition to any remuneration received for carrying out his duties as trustee or personal representative. This qualification was problematic to professional trustees and PRs (such as solicitors executing wills), since such persons would normally receive independent remuneration for professional services, and it was not clear that such remuneration was permissible under the terms of the exclusion. The Securities and Investments Board (now the FSA) gave helpful guidance to the effect that the exclusion would indeed, in SIB's opinion, apply unless the additional remuneration was received in respect of investment services (as opposed to professional services such as those of a solicitor), but the law required some clarification.

The RAO has now clarified the position[32] by providing that, for these purposes, a person is not to be regarded as in receipt of additional remuneration merely because his remuneration is calculated by reference to time spent (which may include, for example, time spent arranging for the sale of investments to pay taxes and expenses). This is likely to be helpful for solicitors, accountants and other professionals acting as executors or PRs.

It should be noted that the "bare trustee" exclusion in respect of dealing in investments as principal (formerly in paragraph 22(1) in Schedule 1 of the 1986 Act) has been carried forward.[33] This exclusion continues to apply where bare trustees or, in Scotland, nominees for other persons act on such other persons' instructions and do not hold themselves out as providing a service of buying and selling investments.

Overseas Persons

3.51 The "overseas persons" exemptions have already been discussed in connection with the territorial scope of the FSMA (see above). Though the general intention of the Treasury has clearly been to reproduce insofar as possible the exemptions formerly provided under the 1986 Act and to extend the exemptions to other regulated activities where appropriate (for example, the extension in respect of arrangements concerning regulated Lloyd's investments, because such arrangements are now regulated under Article 25(1) and (2)), some concerns remain.

Most important is the fact that no overseas persons exemption has been provided for the deposit-taking and insurance activities (Articles 5 and 10). Particularly in relation to deposit-taking, the argument against extending the exemptions seems to have been partly that it was unnecessary, since the normal definition of "accepting a deposit" places the relevant activity in the United Kingdom only if the customer's account is opened in United Kingdom (see above). Also, the Treasury argued that taking deposits in the wholesale markets would be excluded anyway (under Article 6 of the RAO). While these arguments are relevant, they are not entirely conclusive; and it seems strange that an Act which was intended to abolish many of the artificial distinctions between the regulation of different financial services should continue to treat (for example) deposit and bond products offered by an offshore bank differently.

---

[31] 1986 Act, Sched. 1, para. 22.
[32] RAO, Art. 66(7).
[33] RAO, Art. 66(1).

There are also more minor points on the drafting of the exclusions in Article 72, including that agreeing to provide investment advice (which is a regulated activity) has no overseas person exemption. However, more positively, the definition itself of an "overseas person" was changed in the final version of the RAO so that it continues to refer to the absence of a "permanent place of business maintained by [the person] in the United Kingdom", which was the formulation under the 1986 Act. A more uncertain reference to an "establishment"(permanent or otherwise) in the United Kingdom was deleted for this purpose.

Also as noted above, the overseas person exemptions continue to be available to EEA and non-EEA "investment firms", which—in the case of EEA firms—may result in passporting notifications to the FSA being avoided in some cases.

Other Exclusions

3.52 In addition to the above, various other exclusions appearing in the 1986 Act are retained in the RAO either intact or subject to limited drafting changes. These include the exclusions for sales of goods and supplies of services[34]; employees' share schemes[35]; special exclusions in relation to custody activities, including for introductions to authorised United Kingdom custodians and for arrangements where a "primary custodian" undertakes responsibility to a customer[36]; and special exclusions relating to sending dematerialised instructions or causing them to be sent.[37] There are also exclusions for arrangements made for the purpose of carrying out the functions of an international securities self-regulating organisation.[38]

In addition to the exclusions located in the RAO, various persons are specifically exempted in respect of all or certain regulated activities.[39] These exemptions are intended largely to mirror the exemptions previously conferred on various public bodies and commercial companies under the Banking Act 1987 and the 1986 Act.[40] Various banking authorities and regulators (including the European Central Bank) are exempted in relation to all regulated activities other than insurance business, and numerous bodies are exempted for deposit-taking business. There are also exemptions for (among others) enterprise schemes, gas companies, trade unions, charities, local authorities, housing associations and former members of Lloyd's in relation to particular regulated activities. Some exemptions, however, have apparently not been carried forward (including those in favour of universities). The Exemption Order contains a transitional exemption for credit unions insofar as they accept deposits. This exemption will cease to have effect on July 1, 2002.

Recognised investment exchanges and recognised clearing houses continue to be exempt from authorisation in relation to their core activities (see further Chapter 14, below).

---

[34] RAO, Art. 68.
[35] RAO, Art. 71.
[36] RAO, Arts 41 and 42.
[37] RAO, Arts 46–49.
[38] RAO, Art. 35.
[39] The Financial Services and Markets Act 2000 (Exemption) Order 2001 (S.I. 2001 No. 1201).
[40] Including those exemptions formerly located in Schedule 2 of the 1987 Act and the Banking Act 1987 (Exempt Transactions) Regulations 1997 (S.I. 1997 No. 817) and the Financial Services Act 1986 (Miscellaneous Exemptions) Order 1988 (S.I. 1988 No. 350).

Wholesale money markets

3.53 The former regime for listed "money market" institutions under section 43 of the 1986 Act has been discontinued. This section exempted from the authorisation requirement dealings in specified currency, debt and derivative instruments by participants in the wholesale money markets. Exempted participants were known generally as "listed institutions" because they appeared on a list maintained originally by the Bank of England and latterly by the FSA, either as principals or as brokers. In fact, most of the listed institutions were firms authorised under the 1986 Act, banks authorised under the Banking Act 1987 and EEA investment firms and credit institutions passported under, respectively, the ISD and BCD. However, listed institution status was useful because it exempted these banks and investment firms from compliance with the conduct of business rules of the SFA in respect of dealings with counterparties. Instead, institutions admitted to the list were regulated under the *London Code of Conduct*, which was a far shorter (but evidently effective) set of rules for dealings with professional and other institutional customers and by the so-called "Grey Paper" which set out the requirements for admission to the list. The wholesale money market exemption survived the implementation in the United Kingdom of the ISD since, although the regime covered "core investment services" subject to the ISD (*e.g.* dealings in money market instruments and financial futures and options), the Bank of England and then the FSA was designated as the "ISD regulator" of the section 43 list.[41]

Following enactment of the FSMA, dealings between wholesale counterparties formerly regulated under the section 43 list will now be regulated by the new Inter-Professionals regime forming part of the FSA's *Market Conduct Sourcebook*.[42] The Inter-Professionals regime, which is reviewed in more detail in Chapter 10 below, sets out (mostly in the form of FSA guidance) similar principles of good practice and conduct to those found in the *London Code of Conduct*, without applying many of the requirements aimed at consumer protection which are set out in FSA's *Conduct of Business Sourcebook*. In addition, the Bank of England has co-ordinated a new "Non-Investment Products Code" ("NIPs"), which is intended to regulate (on a non-statutory basis) dealings in those money market products which used to be covered by the Grey Paper regime but which fall outside the ambit of the FSMA.

Appointed representatives

3.54 The FSMA continues the exemption for "appointed representatives" of authorised persons (section 39(1)). The logic of the exemption remains that an unauthorised person may carry on a limited range of regulated activities provided he is a party to a contract with an authorised person (his "principal") under which he is permitted or required to carry on certain regulated activities and his principal has accepted responsibility for those activities. The unauthorised person is accordingly exempted in respect of regulated activities for which the authorised

---

[41] Investment Services Regulations 1995, para. 26.
[42] Announced in FSA's Consultation Paper 45, *The Conduct of Business Sourcebook* (February 2000).

person has accepted responsibility. For this purpose (as with other purposes under the FSMA), an "authorised person" includes an EEA investment firm qualifying for United Kingdom authorisation under its European passport and a "Treaty firm".

The Treasury is empowered to prescribe types of business for which authorised persons may accept responsibility, and to prescribe requirements for appointed representative contracts. As was the case under the 1986 Act,[43] the exemption will be limited to arranging and advisory activities (including arranging custody of investments), and thus will not permit appointed representatives to deal in investments as principal or as agent or to manage investments on a discretionary basis.[44] Apart from limiting the scope of the exemption as a matter of policy, this restriction is consistent with the genesis of the appointed representative regime, which was to provide regulatory "cover" to the armies of self-employed salesmen who traditionally sold life policies, pensions and unit trusts for insurance companies and other product providers. Subsequently, the exemption came to be used by large "marketing groups" including life companies, banks, fund managers and financial advisers, which caused the potentially significant regulatory problem that large numbers of individuals could be selling a product provider's investments within different exempted companies.

The FSMA has tightened the regulation of such arrangements. Under the new regime for "approved persons", an authorised person has to take reasonable care to ensure that "controlled functions" are not performed by a person under an arrangement entered into by a contractor of the authorised person (*i.e.* an appointed representative firm) unless the FSA has "approved" the performance of that controlled function by that person (section 59(2) of the FSMA). The FSA has specified various "customer functions" (to the extent that they are performed in a manner substantially connected with a firm's regulated activities) as controlled functions for this purpose[45]; consequently, individuals who are employees of appointed representative firms, and individuals who are self-employed appointed representatives, will have to become "approved persons" of an authorised firm if they perform any such controlled function under an arrangement entered into by the firm or the appointed representative in relation to a regulated activity of the authorised firm.

The appointed representative exemption was narrowed by the ISD in respect of exempted firms which are also EEA investment firms (for example, because such a firm receives and transmits orders in relation to transferable securities). Such an ISD appointed representative has not been exempted unless it provides services solely for the account of an ISD investment firm (or for a firm which would be an ISD investment firm if it was a United Kingdom incorporated firm).[46] This means, therefore, that a firm which passes orders to a second firm whose sole business is the management of unregulated collective investment schemes will not be able to

---

[43] s. 44.
[44] The Financial Services and Markets Act 2000 (Appointed Representatives) Regulations 2001 (S.I. 2001 No.1217).
[45] SUP 10.3.1R and 10.10 (Supervision Manual in the FSA, *Handbook of Rules and Guidance*). The customer functions include the "investment adviser function" and the "customer trading" function (which includes the activity of arranging investment transactions).
[46] See the Investment Services Regulations 1995, para. 27.

claim the appointed representative exemption (because managers of collective investment undertakings are excluded from the ISD[47]). This limitation has been carried forward by order of the Treasury under the new regime.[48] In most cases, however, it is likely that the "principal" will be an ISD investment firm and that the exemption will be available.

BREACH OF THE GENERAL PROHIBITION: UNENFORCEABLE CONTRACTS

3.55 The FSMA contains important provisions similar to those in the 1986 Act[49] in relation to the enforceability of contracts. Under section 26(1), an agreement made by a person in the course of carrying on a regulated activity in contravention of the general prohibition is unenforceable against the other party. The other party is entitled to recover any money paid or transferred by him under the agreement, together with compensation for any loss sustained by him as a result of having parted with it (section 26(2)). The section does not apply to the regulated activity of accepting deposits (section 26(4)), since, in that case, the best interests of the depositor will most likely be served simply by the prompt recovery of his deposit rather than the statutory device of making his contract unenforceable. Consequently, section 29 provides for a depositor to apply to the court for the recovery of a deposit which has been accepted in breach of the general prohibition, if he is not already entitled to recover the deposit without delay.

Like the 1986 Act, the FSMA also invalidates contracts entered into by authorised persons in consequence of something said or done by another person in the course of a regulated activity carried on by the third party in contravention of the general prohibition (section 27(1)). This provision is a particular cause of concern for product providers, securities dealers and others since, without more, it will result in the invalidity of contracts entered into by a customer in consequence of, for example, unlawful investment advice or arrangements by a third party. Consequently, there was considerable debate during the early stages of the Bill on the circumstances when authorised providers should be entitled to enforce contracts notwithstanding unlawful conduct by a third party. At one stage, the Bill required that the authorised person "did not believe, and had no grounds for suspecting, that the third party was contravening the general prohibition"; this was self-evidently a very difficult test to meet, since the authorised person may well be actually unaware of the involvement (or even existence) of the third party in question. Subsequently, the Bill was amended to permit (and the Act now permits) enforceability where the court is satisfied that the authorised person did not know that the third party was (in carrying on the regulated activity) contravening the general prohibition. However, the position is still not entirely satisfactory for the authorised person, since (under section 28(6)) enforcement of any contract in these circumstances is not an entitlement, and will depend on a court being satisfied that it is just and equitable in the circumstances of the case to allow the agreement to

---

[47] ISD, Art. 2.2.(h).
[48] The Financial Services and Markets Act 2000 (Appointed Representatives) (Amendment) Regulations 2001 (S.I. 2001 No. 2508).
[49] 1986 Act, s. 5.

be enforced or money or property paid or transferred under the agreement to be retained (section 28(3)), though the court is required to "have regard to" the relevant knowledge of the authorised person. The court's flexibility to order what is "just and equitable" in the circumstances does mean, however, that a court might elect to permit the enforcement of a contract even where the authorised person knew of the involvement of a third party, if (for example) it is satisfied that the authorised person took all reasonable steps open to it to prevent the third party's breach of the general prohibition.

The court is also given discretion to permit the enforcement of an agreement entered into by an authorised person himself in breach of the general prohibition. In this case, the court is required to have regard to the issue of whether the person carrying on the regulated activity reasonably believed that he was not contravening the general prohibition by making the agreement (section 28(5)). Since a similar provision was contained in the 1986 Act, it is safe to assume that the question of what is likely to be "reasonable" in this context has been frequently considered; in the author's view, it will be prudent in most circumstances for persons in doubt to seek legal advice, and perhaps also to consult the FSA if the facts give rise to particular uncertainty or a difficult question of statutory interpretation or policy.

Agreements may also be rendered unenforceable in consequence of unlawful financial promotions; this is considered further in Chapter 6 below.

CHAPTER 4

Authorisation and "Permission"

JAMES PERRY

INTRODUCTION

4.01 The single system of authorisation, covering banking, insurance and investment services, is a cornerstone of the new regime. Until the introduction of the Act, regulation of financial services in the United Kingdom had been the preserve of a veritable "alphabet soup" of regulators as follows:

- the Bank of England, through its Supervision and Surveillance Branch, which regulated the deposit-taking activities of wholesale and retail banks and formerly the "wholesale money market regime" under section 43 of the 1986 Act;

- the Building Societies Commission ("BSC");

- the Friendly Societies Commission and the Registry of Friendly Societies;

- the Treasury's Insurance Directorate, which regulated the prudential and solvency requirements applying to long-term and general insurance companies (having assumed these responsibilities in 1997 from the DTI);

- the Financial Services Authority ("FSA"), formerly the Securities and Investments Board ("SIB"), which had various statutory responsibilities under the 1986 Act including the recognition of the SROs;

- the various self-regulating organisations ("SROs") recognised under the 1986 Act, being the Investment Management Regulatory Organisation ("IMRO"); the Personal Investment Authority ("PIA"); and the Securities and Futures Authority ("SFA"); and

- the "recognised professional bodies" ("RPBs"), including the Law Society of England and Wales and the Institute of Chartered Accountants of England and Wales.

These regulators policed a range of different authorisation regimes under the Banking Act 1987; the Insurance Companies Act 1982; the Financial Services Act 1986; the Building Societies Act 1986; the Friendly Societies Act 1992; and the Credit Unions Act 1979. In addition, professional members of the Lloyd's insurance market were regulated by the Council of Lloyd's under the Lloyd's Acts;

general insurance brokers could obtain registration under the Insurance Brokers (Registration) Act 1977; consumer credit providers and brokers were (and still are) registered under the Consumer Credit Act 1974; and mortgage providers were not, as such, subject to statutory regulation but were subject to the voluntary Mortgage Code.

This added up to formidable complexity for regulated firms—and indeed for their customers, who had a difficult task to know what protections they were offered for which kinds of business.

Since May 1997, various steps have been taken to transfer responsibility for overall regulation of United Kingdom financial services to the FSA. Responsibility for the authorisation and supervision of banks was transferred to the FSA in June 1998,[1] though the primary legislation conferring powers on the regulator remained the Banking Act 1987. The FSA also entered into arrangements with the Treasury and the SROs to perform regulatory functions—including authorisation—on behalf of the regulators concerned.[2] The FSMA has now completed this process by providing the full statutory framework for authorisation and regulation.

SINGLE AUTHORISATION

4.02 Parts III and IV of the Act set out who is to be authorised, and how authorisation is to be obtained. Part III also provides the statutory mechanism for the Treasury to make orders providing specified persons, or kinds of persons, with exemption under the Act (section 38). It also provides for the "appointed representative" regime carried over from the 1986 Act (section 39, discussed in Chapter 3, above).

The concept of single authorisation has been central to the Treasury's and the FSA's vision of the new regime. Single authorisation flows from the general prohibition in section 19 of the Act, which applies to the carrying on of any regulated activity by way of business in the United Kingdom. However, perhaps confusingly on a first reading, the new legislation does not proceed expressly on the basis of "single authorisation" as such, but on the basis of "permissions" to carry on regulated activities. Part III begins by stating that the persons "authorised" for the purposes of the Act are:

- a person who has a Part IV permission to carry on one or more regulated activities;

- an EEA firm or a Treaty firm qualifying for authorisation under, respectively, Schedule 3 or Schedule 4; and

- a person who is otherwise authorised under or pursuant to the Act (section 31).

---

[1] Under the Bank of England Act 1998.
[2] Responsibility for the authorisation and supervision of insurance companies was assumed by the FSA by a delegation from the Treasury under the Deregulation (Contracting Out) Regulations 1994. FSA agreed by contract to provide services to the SROs in relation to the SROs' functions under the 1986 Act.

EEA firms and Treaty firms are discussed below. The final category referred to above might cover any number of persons, or persons of a specified kind, who are prescribed as authorised in the Act or by Treasury order. Initially, the category includes the operators, trustees and depositories of recognised EEA collective investment schemes, for limited purposes connected with such schemes (section 264 and Schedule 5).

Under the new Act, there is no such thing as an application for *authorisation*; rather, an application may be made to the FSA (under Part IV) for *permission* to carry on one or more regulated activities. Once a person receives a permission to carry on at least one regulated activity, he is automatically deemed to be an "authorised person" (section 31(2)). Conversely, when an authorised person's last Part IV permission is cancelled and, as a result, there is no regulated activity for which he has permission, his status as an authorised person will be withdrawn (section 33). To some extent, therefore, the difference between "authorisation" and "permission" is actually more about word-play than real substance, though it is important in that it is the basis on which the Act legislates for different regulated activities to be carried on within the overall concept of single authorisation. Under the 1986 Act, authorisation was required to carry on "investment business", while it was only in the rules of the SROs (established under contract with their members) that one found the "permitted business" activities that the SROs actually authorised firms to carry on. These permitted business activities certainly did not correspond in all cases to the different kinds of "investment business" specified in Schedule 1 to the 1986 Act. The FSMA, therefore, provides a far more explicit link, on a full statutory basis, between authorisation (on the one hand) and obtaining permission to carry on different activities (on the other).[3]

However, if a firm has an existing Part IV permission (and is therefore an authorised person), it cannot apply as such under section 40 for "permission" to carry on one or more new activities (section 40(2)). Rather, the firm is required to apply to "vary" its permission by adding a regulated activity to those for which the FSA has already given permission (section 44(1)(a)). Strictly, therefore, "permission", like authorisation, may only be obtained once; in reality, however, FSA regards itself as being empowered to grant "permissions" across the range of regulated activities, and it is rather more helpful to think of the relationship between "permission" and "regulated activities" in this way.

CARRYING ON REGULATED ACTIVITIES WITHOUT PERMISSION

4.03 What are the consequences of carrying on business without a required permission? The potential consequences of breaching the general prohibition are very clear; a person is liable to commit a criminal offence and agreements entered into in the course of or in consequence of the illegal activity will be unenforceable (sections 26, 27 and 28), subject to the residual discretion of the court to permit enforcement. However, what if an authorised person with a Part IV permission carries on another regulated activity without "varying" his permission as required

---

[3] It should be noted in this regard that the FSA has broadly followed the list of regulated activities in its regime for granting permissions, but with some differences. See below.

by section 44 of the Act? Under the 1986 Act, an authorised person would not have faced the criminal and civil consequences referred to above, but would have been liable to disciplinary action under the rules of the SRO of which he was a member. He would also have been liable to potential actions by private investors in respect of losses flowing from the breach of SRO rules.[4] This position is broadly replicated in the FSMA but with important differences. Section 20 provides that, in these circumstances, an authorised person is to be taken to have contravened a requirement imposed on him by the FSA under the Act, but the contravention does not make a person guilty of an offence or make any transaction void or voidable (section 20(2)). Transactions will therefore not be affected whether they constitute the regulated activity (*e.g.* dealing in shares) or *result* from the regulated activity (*e.g.* investment advice). This position is reinforced in relation to FSA rules (as opposed to permission requirements) by section 151, which states that a person is not guilty of an offence by reason of a contravention of an FSA rule, and that no such contravention makes any transaction void or voidable.

Further, section 20(2)(c) states that any contravention by an authorised person will not give rise to a right of action for breach of statutory duty *except* in cases which may be prescribed by the Treasury. Section 20(3) goes on to say that an action for breach of statutory duty will lie "in prescribed cases" at the suit of "a person who suffers loss as a result of the contravention". One might have expected that the "prescribed cases" would have mirrored the statutory rights given to private investors under the 1986 Act. However, initially, the Treasury evidently interpreted the absence in section 20(3) of any reference to "private" persons as necessarily broadening the class of persons entitled to include "non-private" persons (*e.g.* corporations) as well.[5] Following consultation, however, the Treasury used its regulations effectively to replicate the position under the 1986 Act, so that a right of action is conferred only on private persons and fiduciaries or representatives for private persons. A breach of a requirement in relation to permission will be actionable at the suit of such persons *except* for contraventions of a Part IV financial resources requirement.[6] In addition, these rights of action will now be available against banking and insurance businesses, as well as firms formerly regulated under the 1986 Act—which is a logical consequence of the new unitary regime.

FSA's Powers in Relation to Permission

4.04   The single application procedure for "permission" is set out in Part IV of the Act (sections 51 to 53 (inclusive)). As one might expect in an Act which essentially provides the broad framework for regulation (the detail of which is then prescribed by numerous orders and rules outside the statute), the FSMA confers extremely broad powers on the FSA to determine the procedure for applications and much of the substantive detail attaching to the granting of permissions. When

---

[4] See ss. 62 and 62A of the 1986 Act, and the Financial Services Act 1986 (Restriction of Rights of Action) Regulations 1991.
[5] See the Treasury's *Consultation Document on "Rights of Action"* (December 2000), para. 1. 13. Conversely, s. 150 expressly refers to "private persons" in the cases of rights to sue for breaches of FSA rules.
[6] The Financial Services and Markets Act 2000 (Rights of Action) Regulations 2001 S.I. 2001 No. 2256. See reg. 4(2).

it grants permissions, the FSA is required to specify the permitted regulated activity or activities, but may describe them in such manner as it thinks appropriate (section 42(6)). The FSA also has power to incorporate in the description of a regulated activity such *limitations* as it considers appropriate, and to specify a narrower or wider description of regulated activity than that to which the application relates (section 42(7)). For example, therefore, the FSA may *limit* the kinds of customers with whom a regulated activity may be carried on (*e.g.* "intermediate" customers and market counterparties only[7]), or even limit the number of customers a firm may deal with.[8] The FSA has also said that it will limit the activities of some firms so that they fall within specific light regulatory regimes carried over from the 1986 Act, such as those applying to oil market and energy participants, corporate finance advisers, service companies and journalists/publishers; however, these restrictions will take the form of "requirements" imposed by the FSA (as to which see below).

The FSA may include such *"requirements"* in connection with a Part IV permission as it considers appropriate (section 43(1)). The distinction between *limitations* on the one hand and *requirements* on the other is evidently that a limitation will normally be designed to be specific to a particular regulated activity, while requirements may relate to a range of regulated, or unregulated, activities.[9] In its Authorisation Manual ("AUTH"), the FSA has noted[10] that "requirements" in this context might include:

- a requirement regarding the payment of dividends;

- a requirement to submit to periodic independent compliance reviews during the first months or years of business. Such a requirement would be consistent with the practice of IMRO, which generally required newly authorised firms without significant regulatory compliance experience to arrange for (normally) quarterly compliance reviews to confirm that relevant rules were being adhered to; and

- a requirement to submit financial returns more frequently than normal (*e.g.* during the period immediately following a firm's authorisation), or to submit audited accounts of a parent company.

Though this is clearly an illustrative and not an exhaustive list, it shows the potential diversity of requirements which the FSA might impose under section 43. As noted above, a requirement may extend to activities which are not regulated activities (section 43(3)). Therefore, for example, a requirement may be imposed not to hold client money or property (which would not, of itself, constitute a regulated activity unless it involves the safeguarding and administration of assets including investments); or possibly a requirement relating to the organisation or staffing of "back office" administrative activities. A requirement may also be imposed by

---

[7] For a definition of "intermediate" customers, see Chapter 10, below.
[8] The FSA has stated in 3.6.3G of its Authorisation Manual ("AUTH") that it may in some cases wish to limit the number of a firm's customers in its early period of trading post-authorisation, for example because its systems are not yet adequate to handle a high volume of transactions.
[9] See AUTH 3.6.2G (limitations) and 3.7.2(G) (requirements).
[10] AUTH, 3.7.6G.

reference to a person's relationship with his group or members of his group (section 43(4)). This provision may be used (for example) to prohibit or limit intra-group transactions or exposures; or to require the provision of specified information by members of a group of which an applicant forms part. In reality, however, though the Act itself is drafted to empower the FSA to "impose" limitations and requirements, it will in many cases be the applicant itself which suggests such restrictions in its application—for example, by stating that it has no intention to deal with private customers or to hold client money or assets. The applicant would usually do this, where its business plan so dictates, in order to avoid the additional systems and procedures which would be required if its Part IV permission was broader.[11]

In addition, section 48 provides that requirements imposed by the FSA may include a so-called "assets requirement", which means a section 43 requirement (*inter alia*) prohibiting or restricting dealings in assets (whether in the United Kingdom or elsewhere) or requiring the transfer of a firm's or its customer's assets to a trustee approved by the FSA. The section goes on to make supplemental provisions regarding such requirements, including that any charge purported to be created by the relevant regulated firm in respect of assets held under trust will be void (section 48(7)).

The FSA may also vary or cancel a Part IV permission on its own initiative if an authorised person fails (or is likely to fail) to satisfy the threshold conditions in relation to one or more regulated activities; if an authorised person has failed to carry on a particular regulated activity during a period of at least 12 months; or if the FSA believes that it is desirable to vary or cancel the permission in the interests of consumers (section 45(1)). For this purpose, a "variation" may include, *inter alia*, varying the description of the regulated activity for which the FSA gives permission (*e.g.* narrowing a permission so that it only relates to specified kinds of customers or investments) or varying a requirement imposed under section 43 (section 44(1)). These "own-initiative powers" may also be exercised at the request of, or for the purpose of assisting, an overseas regulator of a kind prescribed by the Treasury (section 47(1)), which may be a regulator within the European Community (section 47(3)) or outside it (section 47(4)).[12]

Interestingly, the FSA's powers to impose requirements under this Part are extended in certain circumstances to EEA firms and Treaty firms passported into the United Kingdom (section 196).

Taken as a whole, the FSA's arsenal of powers in relation to granting, varying and cancelling of permissions is formidable indeed. It is to be hoped that the Authority will interpret and exercise these powers over time with consistency, and in accordance with practices of previous regulators (including the SROs) with which regulated firms are reasonably familiar.

APPLICATIONS FOR PERMISSION

4.05 The procedure for application for a Part IV permission is stated in the Act at the highest level of generality, and on the basis that the FSA is given very considerable

---

[11] See the FSA's comments in paras 3.47–3.50 of its *Response to Consultation Paper* 29 (August 2000).
[12] The Treasury has prescribed overseas regulators by statutory instrument (made under the Negative Resolution Procedure). See The Financial Services and Markets Act (Own-initiative Power) (Overseas Regulators) Regulations 2001 (S.I. 2001 No. 2639).

discretion. Applications must be made in such manner as the Authority directs and, in addition to a statement of the regulated activities for which permission is sought, must contain (or be accompanied by) such information as the Authority may require (section 51(3)). Applicants may of course be required to provide further information once an application has been received (section 51(4)), and to verify it in such a way as the FSA directs (section 51(6)).

The FSA has put flesh on these statutory bones in its Authorisation Manual (which is part of Block 3 (Regulatory Processes) in the FSA's *Handbook of Rules and Guidance*, and is known by the abbreviation "AUTH"). The Authorisation Manual, in fact, consists almost entirely of guidance made under section 157 of the Act, though there are also a few high level "directions" included at appropriate points (such as the direction that applicants for authorisation must complete the FSA's standard application pack).[13] This guidance fleshes out the FSA's policy on substantive issues such as the descriptions of "regulated activities" and "specified investments" for the purpose of applications for Part IV permission (as to which, see below), as well as providing important procedural guidance. This Chapter refers to the Authorisation Manual at appropriate points.

How long will an application take? Perhaps worryingly, the Act prescribes relatively lengthy periods for the determination of applications. The FSA is given a maximum of *six months*, beginning with the date on which it receives a *completed* application, to determine it (section 52(1)); and the FSA must in any event determine an *incomplete* application within *twelve months* beginning with the date on which it received the application (section 52(2)). These periods are consistent with those previously prescribed under the Banking Act 1987,[14] but are lengthy when compared to the periods within which the SROs could normally be expected to process applications (being, typically, some three to four months from the date of application). The FSA has responded to these concerns, during consultation and in its Authorisation Manual, by stating its expectation that most applications will be processed well within the time limits set out in the Act, though the length of the process will relate directly to the complexity of the application. The Authority will also publish standard response times on its website, along with details of its performance against these standards.[15] Helpfully, the FSA has indicated that its "median" time to process applications will be in the region of *three months*, though this will vary from case to case according to risk and complexity.

Unfortunately, the Act does not expressly cater for the helpful practice operated by some former regulators—including the Bank of England—of receiving applications "in draft", so as to enable applicants to discuss and resolve issues with the regulator on an informal basis before a formal application was submitted, and any statutory period for the determination of the application began to run (though it is equally true to say that the Banking Act 1987 did not expressly refer to the Bank of England's practice in this regard either). This means that any informal consultation prior to an application being made will continue to have no effect on the statutory period for determination, which may in turn prompt some applicants to submit applications before the Authority's views have been canvassed, simply in

---

[13] AUTH 3.9.3D. AUTH was made by the FSA on June 21, 2001 by the Authorisation Manual Instrument 2001.
[14] 1987 Act, s. 10(6).
[15] AUTH 3.9.30G.

order to ensure that "the clock is ticking". This seems likely to be unwise, since the FSA has encouraged all applicants to make early contact with the Corporate Authorisation department to discuss their application before any forms are submitted.[16] The FSA has also stressed that the application process will be an interactive one.[17]

The FSA has, helpfully, given detailed guidance in the Authorisation Manual regarding the procedure for applications for permission to undertake regulated activities for the first time (excluding EEA firms and Treaty firms).[18] Applications will be submitted to the Corporate Authorisation Department of the FSA on standard application forms, together with the prescribed fee. Though these forms are not all available at the time of writing, they will be based on elements of the application forms previously used by the SROs, and will therefore require (*inter alia*) general corporate and other information about the applicant and its directors, controllers and group companies; a "business plan" describing the applicant's proposed regulated and non-regulated activities; projected financial information, demonstrating that the applicant will comply with the FSA's financial resources requirements; information on the applicant's proposals for compliance with FSA rules; and questionnaires completed by proposed "approved persons" of the applicant. The application must also contain detail regarding systems to be used, which will include completion of a special questionnaire in the case of e-commerce-based businesses. However, systems do not have to be in place at the time of application.[19] Information will also be required regarding "controllers" of the applicant, including individuals or firms which, directly or indirectly, hold 10 per cent or more of the applicant's share capital, as well as other "connected persons" of the applicant.[20] Once it has received an application, the FSA will determine whether the applicant meets the "threshold conditions" for authorisation in Schedule 6 (see below) and will probably request further information and at least one meeting with the applicant. The FSA may visit the premises which the applicant intends to use as its place of business.[21] Where the applicant or members of its group hold existing authorisations or licences in overseas countries, the FSA is likely in most cases to seek relevant information from the overseas regulator on a confidential basis.[22] When an application for permission is granted, the FSA will notify the applicant concerned, specifying the date when permission will take effect. The newly authorised firm will then appear on the FSA's register of authorised persons.[23] Where an application for Part IV permission is granted on the terms applied for (including any limitations or requirements applied for or which are agreed between the FSA and the applicant), the decision to grant permission will be made by FSA staff, usually with the endorsement of a senior individual or more than one individual.[24] This procedure may well be more flexible in practice than the

---

[16] AUTH 3.9.1G.
[17] AUTH 3.9.14G.
[18] AUTH 3.9.
[19] AUTH 3.9.9G(3).
[20] AUTH 3.9.22G. Examples of "connected persons" might include group companies, and firms with whom the Applicant has or will have an outsourcing agreement.
[21] AUTH 3.9.15G(5). It is likely that this power will almost invariably be used.
[22] AUTH 3.9.15G
[23] Maintained under s. 347 of the FSMA.
[24] AUTH 8.2.6G.

authorisation committee procedures operated by the SROs. However, if it is proposed to refuse the application, or to grant it with a narrower description of regulated activities than those applied for or (perhaps more likely) subject to limitations or requirements which were not applied for, the application will be referred to the FSA's Regulatory Decisions Committee ("RDC") (see below).

VARIATIONS TO PART IV PERMISSION

4.06 As noted above, section 44 provides the mechanism for the FSA to "vary" a firm's Part IV permission in specified ways. A firm can apply to:

- undertake one or more further regulated activities;
- reduce the number of regulated activities it is permitted to undertake;
- vary the description of a regulated activity for which the FSA has given permission;
- cancel a requirement imposed under section 43; and
- vary any such requirement.

Section 44, therefore, provides the means for a firm to make relatively minor adjustments to its regulated business profile (*e.g.* a manager of regulated collective investment schemes applying to extend its permission to cover establishing, operating and winding-up unregulated schemes), or major changes (*e.g.* a securities firm applying for permission to accept deposits). This facility for adding "permissions" through the making of applications to a single regulator was one of the chief attractions of the new regime when it was announced in 1997 by the Chancellor, Gordon Brown. Some may therefore be disappointed that the maximum periods for determining applications to vary an existing permission are precisely the same as those prescribed for first-time applications (namely *six months* for complete applications and *12 months* in any event for incomplete ones) (section 52(1) and (2)). However, given that the procedure for variations has to cater for the possibility of an authorised person making fundamental changes which, in reality, constitute the commencement of a new business, it is hard to see that the statutory waiting periods could be different from those relating to first-time applications unless, perhaps, the legislation aimed to define "material" and "non-material" variations (which would certainly be difficult). This in itself suggests a reality underlying the new regulatory system, namely that the existence of a single regulator is unlikely, in many cases, to enable companies to extend their businesses to encompass new regulated activities more quickly than would have been the case under the previous, fragmented system. It is clear that a firm wishing to undertake deposit-taking or insurance business for the first time can expect to receive very similar requests to complete application forms, containing business plans and financial information, as those which a new applicant will receive; this must be correct, since the firm's compliance with the Schedule 6 threshold conditions in respect of its existing business may be largely irrelevant to the question of whether those conditions will continue to be satisfied if a new deposit-taking or insurance activity is carried on. It is hoped, however, that the new concept of single authorisation will help firms which wish to expand their businesses in more marginal ways. For example, an asset manager formerly regulated by IMRO might well have required a separate authorisation from PIA to undertake retail marketing of funds; this made little sense at the time, and it is likely that firms will be able to add investment advisory activities to investment management in a relatively short timescale and without undue difficulty (except, perhaps, when the firm wishes to advise private customers for the first time).

The FSA has helpfully indicated that an authorised firm will not be required to submit a full set of new application forms in order to vary its permission, though it may be required to complete appropriate parts of the application pack if the variation requested would "cause a significant change in the firm's business or risk profile".[25]

An application for a variation must be sent to a firm's FSA supervision team, which will decide the information required to be submitted on a case-by-case basis. For example, if carrying on a new regulatory activity would require the applicant firm to increase its regulatory capital, it is very likely that FSA will require the firm to submit a financial projection showing the effect of the changes over a 12-month period. If the applicant wishes to extend its business into a significantly different area (a move into deposit-taking is the most obvious example), the firm's supervision team is likely to call on the resources of one of FSA's other supervision teams. The FSA has indicated that, not surprisingly, the length of time taken to process an application will relate directly to the complexity of the variation requested.[26] The Authority has undertaken, however, to publish standard response times on its website.[27]

REFUSAL OF APPLICATION FOR PERMISSION

4.07   It is to be expected that most firms which apply for a Part IV permission will be granted it (this has certainly been the position in relation to authorisations under the 1986 Act and other previous legislation). The FSA has, however, the power to refuse applications (section 52(7)), which is likely to be exercised where, *inter alia*, the FSA considers that to do so is necessary in view of the statutory "market confidence" or "protection of consumers" objectives (sections 3 and 5). Section 52(7) provides that a person whose application is to be refused must be given a warning notice complying with section 387 of the Act. This procedure does not apply, however, in the case of EEA firms exercising their right to passport into the United Kingdom to provide services cross-border or through the establishment of a branch (section 52(8)). Apparently, though, a warning notice would be required in the case of European firms asserting rights to exercise "Treaty rights" under Schedule 4 to the Act (see below). Any warning notice will have to state the FSA's reasons for deciding to reject the application. If the Authority is not subsequently persuaded by the applicant that the grounds for the

---

[25] SUP 6.3.20G in the FSA's *Supervision Manual*.
[26] SUP 6.3.25G sets out a non-exclusive list of the information which may be required.
[27] SUP 6.3.37G.

warning notice will be addressed in such a way that permission may safely be granted, it will confirm its warning notice by the issue of a formal decision notice (section 52(9)). The warning notice procedure also applies where FSA's staff decide to impose limitations or requirements other than those applied for, or to specify a different (probably narrower) description of permitted regulated activities (section 52(9)).

The question of what should happen if the FSA's executive staff decide in principle to exercise these powers was the subject of some debate in the lead-up to the enactment of FSMA. Initially, the FSA argued that disappointed applicants should not have the same right as authorised firms which are threatened by disciplinary action or the withdrawal of authorisation, namely the right to have their case considered by an independent committee before the FSA completes its determination of the case (*i.e.* before a section 52(9) decision notice is finally sent to applicant)[28]. In this case, the independent committee is the FSA's Regulatory Decisions Committee ("RDC"), which is a body outside the Authority's management structure and of which none of the members—other than the Chairman—is an employee of the FSA.[29] Subsequently, however, the FSA was evidently persuaded that the refusal or limitation of authorisation was a serious enough matter (which it certainly is) to warrant the use of a formal procedure before any final decision is taken. Consequently, the Authority has proposed to use a procedure which involves the approval of any warning notice by the RDC prior to its issue, and a right for the applicant to make written and/or oral representations to the RDC (based on a review, if the applicant wishes, of the evidence on which the FSA has relied in reaching its conclusions) within a specified period, which may not be less than 28 business days from the date of receipt of the notice.[30] The RDC will then consider any representation and may either grant the application or direct FSA staff to issue a decision notice.[31] If a decision notice is issued, the applicant has the right to refer the matter to the Financial Services and Markets Tribunal. Any decision made by the Tribunal may be the subject of an appeal on a point of law, though it is to be expected that such appeals will be very rare and that the Tribunal will represent an applicant's last realistic chance of reversing a decision notice. In the case of an application for a variation of a Part IV permission, however, the warning and decision notice procedure may be operated by *either* FSA executives *or* by the RDC; the RDC is only likely in practice to become involved in cases where a proposed variation, if granted, would make a fundamental change to the nature of the Part IV permission.[32] Even in cases where executives operate the procedure, however, the Authority is obliged to ensure that the decision-taker(s) are not the same individuals as those who are directly involved in establishing the evidence on which the decision is based (section 395(2) of the FSMA).

---

[28] FSA Consultation Paper 17, *Financial Services Regulation: Enforcing the new regime* (December 1998).
[29] AUTH 8.2.9G and 8.2.10G.
[30] AUTH 8.3.2–8.3.6G.
[31] AUTH 8.3.9G.
[32] SUP 6.3.39G. See also DEC, Chapter 2, Annex 1.

THE THRESHOLD CONDITIONS

4.08 The FSMA imposes an obligation on the Authority in giving or varying a permission, or imposing or varying any requirement, to ensure that the person concerned will satisfy, and continue to satisfy, the "Threshold Conditions" in relation to all of the regulated activities for which he has or will have permission (section 41(2)). These conditions are located in Schedule 6 to the Act. They were originally termed by the FSA as the "Qualifying Conditions for Authorisation", or "QCAs", but this was subsequently dropped in favour of the statutory terminology.

The Threshold Conditions represent the minimum criteria which a person must satisfy to obtain and keep authorisation. It is not correct to say that they are only of relevance to new applicants for authorisation; on the contrary, compliance, or failure to comply, with any of the Threshold Conditions will determine whether the FSA is entitled to exercise its own-initiative power to vary or cancel a permission under section 45(1)(a) of the FSMA. Further, failure to comply with the Threshold Conditions may give rise to other types of statutory or disciplinary intervention against an authorised firm. Interestingly, the FSA has already addressed the question, which is relevant for authorised firms, of the relationship between the Threshold Conditions and the FSA Principles for Businesses. Though there are differences in detail between the Threshold Conditions and the Principles, and the Threshold Conditions are statutory while the Principles are FSA "requirements" made under the Act, the FSA has confirmed the sensible practical conclusion that the general kind of behaviour needed to meet the Threshold Conditions will also be required by the Principles (and vice-versa).[33] Therefore, in determining whether a firm satisfies the Threshold Conditions, the FSA will also take into account whether the firm is ready, willing and organised to comply, on a continuing basis, with the Principles and the FSA's rules (the Principles are considered in more detail in Chapter 9, below).

The Threshold Conditions are, in essence, a statutory distillation of the high-level requirements for authorisation which have previously been applied under different financial services legislation. Those familiar with the 1986 Act, however, will recall that it did not contain an exhaustive (or even brief) list of threshold conditions, since the determination of "fitness and properness" was largely left to the rules of the SROs. Conversely, the Insurance Companies Act 1982 contained "Criteria for Sound and Prudent Management" which were required to be considered by the Treasury when determining applications by prospective insurance companies (Schedule 2A), and the Banking Act 1987 contained its familiar "Minimum Criteria for Authorisation" (Schedule 3 to the 1987 Act). Not surprisingly, the Threshold Conditions do not represent any sort of attempt to "cut and paste" these statutory requirements, which were developed to address particular prudential issues (including, in the case of banks, requirements reflecting their traditionally important role in the United Kingdom's financial system). Consequently, the Threshold Conditions do not contain the former statutory requirements for a bank to have at least two individuals effectively directing the bank's business (known as the "four eyes" rule) and sufficient appropriately qualified non-executive directors,

---

[33] FSA, *"Feedback Statement"* on its Consultation Paper for the QCAs (October 1999).

or a minimum capital requirement of £5 million. Similarly, the requirements for insurance companies to supervise the activities of their subsidiary undertakings with due care and diligence so as to main proper "systems of control" does not, as such, survive (though the requirements of Schedule 2A of the 1982 Act were couched in very general terms in any event).

Notwithstanding these differences, it is inconceivable that the FSA will in practice interpret the Threshold Conditions as lowering or raising the hurdle of "fitness and properness" in any material way. Instead, it is likely that the FSA will use the specific prudential requirements and supervisory policies applying to banks and insurance companies (under the FSA's Rules and Guidance) to continue many of the requirements and practices which have up to now been applied. The flexibility afforded by dealing with such matters through rules, guidance and the exercise of discretion, rather than by primary legislation, should be to the benefit of the regulated community in most cases. In particular, the former statutory requirements for banks and insurance companies to maintain proper systems and controls will, without doubt, continue to be applied by the FSA in its day-to-day supervision of these kinds of institutions.[34]

There are five Threshold Conditions in Schedule 6. The first two Threshold Conditions (Legal Status and Location of Offices) set out absolute, legal tests, while the final three confer discretion on the FSA. The FSA has decided to issue guidance pursuant to section 157 of the Act in relation to all of these Threshold Conditions.[35] In brief, the Threshold Conditions are as follows:

Threshold Condition 1: Legal Status

4.09 Insurance contracts may only be effected or carried out by a body corporate, a registered friendly society or a member of Lloyd's. Only bodies corporate or partnerships may take deposits (paragraph 1(1) and (2) of Schedule 6). This implements the requirements of the European banking and insurance directives in relation to EEA persons, though it extends these requirements to non-EEA firms, and other firms outside the scope of the directives, as well.

Threshold Condition 2: Location of Offices

4.10 This Threshold Condition implements the requirement of the "Post-BCCI Directive"[36] that EEA authorised firms should have their head office in the country in which they have their registered office. This requirement is now applied to firms outside the scope of the EEA single market directives. If a person does not have a registered office (for example, in the case of those partnerships constituted in or outside the United Kingdom which are not required to have a registered office), it must have its head office in the United Kingdom *and* carry on business in the United Kingdom. Unfortunately, neither the Post-BCCI Directive nor the

---

[34] In the case of banks, these requirements have already been set out in considerable detail in FSA's Banking Supervisory Policies.

[35] This guidance can be found in the part of the "High Level Standards" part (Block 1) of the FSA's *Handbook of Rules and Guidance,* known as "COND". COND was made by the FSA on June 21, 2001 by the Threshold Conditions Instrument 2001.

[36] Directive 95/26 of June 29, 1995. The Directive was enacted in the U.K. by the Financial Institutions (Prudential Supervision) Regulations 1996 (S.I. 1996 No. 1669).

FSMA define what is meant by a "head office"; however, the FSA has given guidance[37] that (while each instance will be judged on a case-by-case basis) the key issue will be to determine where "central management and control" is exercised, which is (the FSA says) where the main management decisions on a day-to-day business are taken and the central administrative controls of the firm are located. This definition seems to have been deliberately crafted to avoid catching offices from which "strategic" direction (as opposed to day-to-day management and control) is exercised.

Threshold Condition 3: Close Links

4.11 As in the case of the previous Threshold Condition, this condition is derived from the Post-BCCI Directive, and requires the FSA to be satisfied that it can effectively supervise a firm taking into account the structure of a group to which it belongs, or other firms to which it has "close links", and the laws, regulations or administrative provisions of any non-EEA country to which such "close links persons" may be subject. In this regard, "close links" mean (i) the links between parent and subsidiary undertakings (as defined in the Seventh Company Law Directive and, in the United Kingdom, in section 258 of the Companies Act 1985[38]), or (ii) an equivalent degree of control in relation to unincorporated persons, or (iii) the holding or control of 20 per cent or more of the voting rights or capital of a firm. The Act requires the FSA to be satisfied that such close links are not likely to prevent the Authority's effective supervision of a firm, and that the laws, regulations or administrative provisions relating to a "close links person" in a non-EEA state will not prevent effective supervision either. The FSA has decided to give guidance on this Threshold Condition, but has not ventured to provide an explanation of the kinds of group structures or ownership arrangements which may not, in the FSA's view, satisfy the condition. However, the FSA has given guidance that it will consider (*inter alia*) whether the structure and geographical spread of a group might hinder adequate and reliable flows of information to the FSA; and whether group companies have different accounting dates and do not share common auditors.[39]

During consultation with the FSA, some respondents were concerned that the FSA might take into account for these purposes, and in relation to Threshold Conditions 4 and 5, matters of relatively minor significance. The FSA has tried to address these concerns by giving guidance[40] that it will take into account for the purposes of Threshold Conditions 3, 4 and 5 relevant matters only insofar as they are significant, and that "significance" will be weighed in the context of the FSA's ability adequately to supervise the firm, having regard to the regulatory objectives in section 2 of the FSMA.

Threshold Condition 4: Adequate Resources

4.12 This Threshold Condition, and the final Threshold Condition relating to suitability, represent the bedrock on which most of the detailed rules in the FSA's

---

[37] COND 2.2.3G.
[38] FSMA, Sched. 6, para. 3(3). See Seventh Council Directive 1983/349.
[39] COND 2.3.3G.
[40] COND 2.3.5G, 2.4.4G(3) and 2.5.4G(3).

Handbook are built. The Act says, in brief, that the resources of a firm must be adequate in relation to regulated activities it seeks to carry on or carries on; and that the FSA may take into account or have regard to the provision a person makes in respect of liabilities (actual, future and contingent), the means by which it manages the incidence of risk in its business and any effects of a person's membership of a group.

This latter definition is, of course, inclusive rather than exclusive, and both the Treasury and the FSA have made it clear that the concept of "adequacy of resources" is very broad indeed, covering financial resources (including any event of insolvency affecting a firm or any of its controllers, directors or "close links persons"[41]), and non-financial matters such as management and other human resources and the installation of appropriate control systems for the purpose of prudent management. Consequently, this Threshold Condition is developed in the FSA's rules covering capital adequacy, training and competence, management and internal organisation, systems and provision of information. FSA's guidance on Threshold Condition 4 states that the Authority may have regard, when assessing a firm's resources, to whether it has "conducted sufficient enquiries" into the financial services sector in which it intends to conduct business to establish that the firm has access to adequate capital to cover any early losses and that client money and assets, deposits or policy holders' right will not be placed at risk if the business fails. The FSA may also need to be convinced that an applicant has a "well-constructed business plan or strategy plan for its product and service" which "has been sufficiently tested".[42] All in all, this may look like an attempt by the FSA to "second-guess" the commercial judgment of others but (after some criticism of an earlier draft of this guidance) the FSA has clarified that its interest is confined to the need to satisfy relevant regulatory requirements; and it has also, rightly, said that it expects the level of detail in a business plan to be proportional to the complexity of proposed regulated activities (and unregulated activities) and the risks they pose.[43] This suggests that, for example, applicants for deposit-taking permissions may expect the kind of close scrutiny of the adequacy of a business plan which was a feature of the Bank of England's supervision.

Threshold Condition 5: Suitability

4.13 The final Threshold Condition recites the requirement that authorised persons must be "fit and proper". For this purpose, the Act provides that the Authority must be satisfied, *inter alia*, by a person's "connection" with any other person, which suggests some overlap with both Threshold Conditions 3 and 4. However, FSA's guidance on the Threshold Condition focuses more broadly on a number of detailed considerations under the two headings of:

- Conduct of business with integrity and in compliance with proper standards; and

- Competent and prudent management and exercise of due skill, care and diligence.

---

[41] COND 2.4.3G.
[42] COND 2.4.4G and 2.4.6G.
[43] COND 2.4.6G(3).

Under these headings, the FSA has stated in its guidance that it will focus upon numerous key issues (whether arising in the United Kingdom or elsewhere) such as the installation of compliance procedures and employees' awareness of those procedures; procedures for a firm's "approved persons" to be made aware of the regulatory requirements applying to them; whether a firm demonstrates readiness to comply with FSA's regulatory requirements; whether there are arrangements for proper systems of internal control to comply with regulatory standards and requirements to be put in place; whether reasonable care has been taken to ensure that robust information and reporting systems have been developed, tested and properly installed; and whether a firm has made sufficient enquiries to give reasonable assurance that it will not pose unacceptable risks to consumers or the United Kingdom financial system.[44] Broadly, however, these issues will be very familiar to most regulated firms which have been subject to one or more of the regulatory regimes which FSMA has replaced. It is also helpful that the FSA's guidance on the suitability condition has largely been drafted so as to omit some of the absolute requirements which appeared in the first version sent out for consultation (for example, reference is now made in certain places to firms putting in place procedures which are "designed reasonably to ensure" a particular outcome; absolute obligations to procure employees' compliance have been deleted).

An interesting point in the FSA's guidance is that the Authority may take particular account of whether the firm has appointed auditors (or, in the case of insurance companies, actuaries) who have sufficient experience in the areas of business to be conducted. The role of accountants is likely to be particularly relevant to deposit-taking activities; the commissioning of accountants' reports under section 39 of the Banking Act 1987 has been an important feature of the Bank of England's, and then the FSA's, supervision of banks. The Authority's statutory power to commission such reports has been extended in the Act to cover firms carrying on any regulated activity and to include reports by any "skilled person" (section 166).[45]

Additional Conditions

4.14   The Treasury is also given power in Schedule 6 to the Act to prescribe additional conditions for non-EEA insurance companies.[46] Accordingly, the Treasury has prescribed[47] certain conditions applying specifically to insurance companies with their head office outside the EEA (other than Swiss general insurers), including requirements to maintain in the United Kingdom assets of a specified value and (other than in the case of reinsurance) to make a deposit of such amount and with such a person as may be specified. The FSA will prescribe relevant requirements in its interim prudential sourcebook for insurance companies (IPRU (INS)).

---

[44] COND 2.5.6G and 2.5.7G.
[45] See also Chapters 3 (Auditors) and 4 (Actuaries) of the Supervision Manual.
[46] See para. 8.
[47] In the Financial Services and Markets Act 2000 (Variation of Threshold Conditions) Order 2001 (S.I. 2001 No. 2507).

ELEMENTS OF THE PERMISSION REGIME

4.15   Under section 42(6) of the Act, the FSA is given discretion to specify the regulated activity or activities which a person is permitted to carry on, "described in such manner as the Authority considers appropriate". The FSA has confirmed how it intends to exercise this discretion.[48] The permission granted to a firm will consist of three elements:

- a *description of the activities* the firm can carry on, including any section 42(7)(a) *"limitations"*;

- the *specified investments* involved; and, where appropriate;

- any section 43(1) *"requirements"*.

As such, a firm's notice of scope of permission will be devised as a matrix. This matrix structure will be familiar in principle to many firms which were regulated by one or more of the SROs, though it is true to say that there were differences between the SROs in the ways in which, respectively, they regulated firms' "permitted business". The SFA was perhaps closest to the "matrix" model which the FSA has in mind, but its categories of investment activity were broad and largely followed the "investment business" activities specified in Schedule 1 to the 1986 Act. On the other hand, IMRO's method was more obviously tailored to the types of asset management and advisory firms which it regulated, and included separate permitted business categories for activities such as "marketing unregulated collective investment schemes" and "venture capital activities". The concept of "permitted business" was clearly not relevant for banks in relation to their deposit-taking activities or for insurance companies in relation to general or non-investment-linked long-term insurance (though banks and insurers were, more often than not, also members of at least one SRO in connection with their investment business).

The FSA's *Authorisation Manual* says that the *regulated activities* for which permission must be sought will, with three exceptions, mirror exactly the categories set out in the Regulated Activities Order ("RAO").[49] The differences will be a separate category for giving investment advice on pension transfers and opt-outs (because the pensions mis-selling debacle has persuaded the FSA that separate treatment is required); different categories of establishing and operating, respectively, regulated and unregulated collective investment schemes (because of the different rules, characteristics and risks applying to the different types of scheme); and separate categories for safeguarding and administration of assets (without arranging) and arranging safeguarding and administration of assets (because some firms, and in particular investment managers, will arrange custody without intending to provide the service itself).

Similarly, the description of *specified investments* in the Authorisation Manual closely follows the RAO,[50] though the FSA has decided sub-divide certain categories of derivatives so that commodity futures and options, spread bets and

---

[48] AUTH 3.3–3.5 (inclusive).
[49] AUTH 3.4.1G.
[50] AUTH 3.5.1G.

rolling spot forex contracts are distinguished. In the case of commodity derivatives, this is largely because these investments are not covered by the ISD and it is
helpful to clarify that this activity may not be included in a firm's EEA "passport".
Spread bets and rolling spot forex contracts have probably been included separately
because they are marketed to a retail audience, as opposed to the largely
professional and institutional investor base which deals in the exchange and OTC
derivative markets. Rolling spot forex contracts have been the subject of regulatory
intervention in the past (see Chapter 3, above).

The nature and scope of the *"limitations"* and *"requirements"* which may be
imposed in relation to a firm's Part IV permission have been discussed above. The
FSA's original scheme was to include the types of customers with whom a firm would
be permitted to deal as the third element of the regime; in the event, it was decided
that customer types would be included among the limitations which may be
imposed on a firm's permitted activities (the first element referred to above).
Requirements (and indeed limitations) are likely to be sought in some instances by
applicants as well as imposed by the FSA; for example, a firm might apply for a
requirement not to hold or control client money in order to benefit from lower financial and other prudential requirements. Requirements will also be used by the FSA
to control a few specified activities which are deemed to entail special risks for firms
and their customers: these activities are ISA or PEP management, operating an
investment trust savings scheme and broker fund management.[51] This means that an
investment manager who is allowed to deal with private customers will be subject to
"requirements" not to carry on these activities unless he wishes to do so and can satisfy the FSA that he has adequate systems and controls for the purpose. Of course,
each of the activities will necessarily involve a firm in carrying on one or more RAO
regulated activities in any event (*e.g.* managing investments and dealing as agent).

EEA PASSPORT RIGHTS

4.16 The FSMA's harmonisation of financial services regulation extends to the
integration of the various "passporting" regimes which existed under previous
legislation. These regimes were the product of the basic principles of "freedom of
establishment" and "freedom to provide services" enshrined in the Treaty of
Rome.[52] As a result of political and other factors, the European directives giving
effect to these basic freedoms in the field of financial services came into force at
various times between 1973 and 1993; the directives in question being the Second
Banking Co-ordination Directive ("2BCD") for banks and other credit institutions,[53] the Third Life and Non-Life Directives for insurance companies (including
friendly societies and other mutual insurers),[54] and the Investment Services Directive
("ISD") for investment firms.[55] (The Banking Co-ordination Directives have now

---

[51] AUTH 3.7.3.G(2).

[52] Arts 52 and 59 (now Arts 43 and 49 respectively) of the Treaty establishing the European Community.

[53] Directive 89/646, amending Directive 77/780. The various Banking Directives have now been consolidated into and repealed by the Banking Consolidation Directive 2000/12.

[54] Directive 92/96, amending Directive 79/267 and Directive 90/619 (the Life Directives); and Directive
92/49, amending Directive 73/239 and Directive 88/357 (the Non-Life Directives).

[55] Directive 93/22.

been consolidated into and repealed by the Banking Consolidation Directive 2000 ("BCD")). These directives, referred to in the FSMA as "the single market directives",[56] introduced the concept of the single market "passport", which would enable financial services firms to establish branches or provide cross-border services in different EEA states without the need to obtain a licence or authorisation in each relevant EEA state (Member States being forbidden by the directives from implementing laws which would impede these freedoms). The regulatory premise of all of the single market directives was that the EEA state in which a firm had its registered office and head office (the "home state") would be responsible for the authorisation of the firm in accordance with common EEA standards and for the prudential regulation of the firm (including financial supervision and the determination of "fitness and properness" of directors and controllers). Any other EEA state in which that firm established a branch or provided services (a "host state") would be permitted to impose rules or restrictions on activities carried on in the host state only to the extent that they were "justified by the general good".[57] In practice, this meant that the host state could impose local conduct of business regulation on the passported EEA firm, but little else.

The single market directives were enacted in the United Kingdom at different times, culminating in the enactment of the ISD through the Investment Services Regulations 1995.[58] The practical implementation of the ISD in the United Kingdom was not helped by the fact that the lead United Kingdom regulator of financial services (the SIB, now the FSA) adopted the practice of requiring firms wishing to establish a branch to apply for membership of one of the three SROs recognised at that time under the 1986 Act (namely SFA, IMRO and PIA), evidently because its policy was to avoid direct SIB/FSA regulation wherever possible. Although the SRO rules in a number of areas were disapplied in the case of incoming EEA firms, such firms might nonetheless have been forgiven if they felt that the United Kingdom could have made the practical implementation of the ISD a little easier for them.

Such concerns have now, happily, been consigned to history with the advent of the new statutory regulator. The procedure for the exercise of passport rights for "EEA firms"—that is, investment firms, credit institutions (and certain "financial institution" subsidiaries specified in the BCD) and direct insurers which are covered by the single market directives and which do not have their head office in the United Kingdom[59]—is set out in Schedule 3 to the Act. A firm eligible to be passported pursuant to this Schedule is referred to in the Act as "qualifying for authorisation" and is treated as an authorised person (section 31(1)(b) of the Act). The automatic nature of the application for United Kingdom authorisation by an EEA firm, once it has obtained the consent of its home state regulator, is emphasised by the fact that, so long as an EEA firm retains its home state authorisation, the FSA may not remove its Schedule 3 authorisation. Section 34 of the Act confirms that only the withdrawal of home state authorisation, or ceasing to have an

---

[56] FSMA, Sched. 3, para.1.
[57] See *European Commission v. France* [1986] E.C.R. 3663.
[58] S.I. 1995 No. 3272
[59] 1986 Act, Sched. 3, para. 5.

"EEA right"[60] in circumstances where EEA authorisation is not required, will result in an EEA firm ceasing to qualify for United Kingdom authorisation. If, however, an EEA firm has a Part IV permission, it will not cease to be an authorised person because it no longer has an EEA right (section 34(3)). For example, therefore, a United Kingdom branch of a German firm dealing in commodity derivatives as well as financial futures and other ISD investments, which has a Part IV permission for its activities relating to commodity futures (not ISD investments), would not lose that permission just because its home state authorisation is terminated.

Passporting into the United Kingdom

4.17   The procedures set out in Schedule 3 for passporting by EEA firms are derived from the single market directives and therefore do not differ materially from those previously set out in the different sets of regulations covering banking, insurance and investment services. An EEA firm wishing to establish a branch must satisfy "the establishment conditions", which are that the FSA must receive a "consent notice" from the EEA firm's home state regulator (given in accordance with the relevant single market directive) stating that consent has been given to establish a branch in the United Kingdom, identifying the activities to which the consent relates and including such other information as the FSA may prescribe (paragraph 13). This wide power to prescribe further information must be exercised by the Authority "in the general good" in accordance with the principles derived from the Treaty.[61] The FSA then has two months in which to inform the EEA firm of the (United Kingdom) host state rules (if any) with which the firm is required to comply when carrying on a regulated activity through its United Kingdom branch; if no such notice is received, the United Kingdom branch may be established notwithstanding. Not surprisingly, the "service conditions" to be satisfied by an EEA firm wishing to provide services cross-border are more straightforward still, and require in all cases that the firm should give notice of its intention to provide services in the United Kingdom to its home state regulator (paragraph 14). In the case of investment firms and direct insurance companies, the FSA must also receive a notice from the home state regulator containing prescribed information.[62] Again, the FSA has two months in which to inform an EEA firm of "applicable provisions", calculated from the date on which the Authority receives the EEA regulator's notice or (where no such notice is required, in the case of credit institutions or subsidiary "financial institutions"), from the date on which the Authority is informed of the firm's intention to provide services in the United Kingdom. However, in the case of cross-border services, the incoming firm is at liberty to carry on business in the United Kingdom (within the two month period) before it receives any such information from the FSA as long as the "service conditions" have been satisfied.

---

[60] An "EEA right" in this context is the entitlement of an EEA firm to establish a branch or provide services in the United Kingdom pursuant to the Treaty of Rome and subject to the single market directives (para. 7 of Sched. 3).

[61] *European Commission v. France* [1986] E.C.R.

[62] This reflects the differing requirements of the respective single market directives: under Art. 21 of the BCD an institution merely has to notify its home state authority in order to use the BCD passport for cross-border services.

It is important to note that an EEA firm qualifying for authorisation under Schedule 3 may also decide to apply for a Part IV permission to carry on a regulated activity outside its EEA passport (for example, a permission to carry on the activity of making "general arrangements" for a person to deal in investments under Article 25(2) of the RAO, which is not a core or ancillary ISD investment service). As noted above, if an EEA firm obtains a separate Part IV permission, it will not lose it merely because it ceases to qualify as an authorised person under Schedule 3, though, as a practical matter, it may well be the case that any factors which caused the firm to lose home state authorisation will be equally relevant to its Part IV permission. In addition, and significantly, an EEA firm without a United Kingdom branch whose activities fall within the "overseas persons exemptions" in the RAO[63] will not need to use the Schedule 3 passport (or indeed Schedule 4 "Treaty rights", as to which see below), because the exempted activities are not treated as being "regulated activities" at all.[64] Therefore, for example, an EEA firm whose only United Kingdom activities are providing dealing and advisory services on a cross-border basis solely to institutional investors will be able to carry on those activities without satisfying the "service conditions" and without being subject to United Kingdom conduct of business rules.

One technical issue which was raised in the Houses of Parliament during debates on the Bill was the way in which the legislation should deal with the imperfect dove-tailing between the respective services specified in the Annexes to the BCD and the ISD. The specific problem is that credit institutions passporting into the United Kingdom under the BCD will not, by virtue of the BCD passport, be entitled to provide certain services which are covered by the ISD but not by the BCD. The services in question include "receiving and transmitting orders" in relation to ISD investments. This problem had in the past been resolved by the Treasury voluntarily granting the equivalent of an ISD passport to qualifying EEA credit institutions using a BCD passport (often known as the "top up" passport). At the Committee stages of the Bill, the Conservative Opposition argued for an amendment to Schedule 4, the effect of which would have been that an EEA credit institution whose home state authorisation covered one or more ISD investment services would have been treated as entitled to provide those services in the United Kingdom as a "Treaty firm" (see below), even though its BCD passport did not cover the relevant activities.[65] Regrettably, this amendment was not accepted by the Government and, on the face of it, Part IV permissions may now be required by EEA credit institutions providing the relevant services in the United Kingdom (though the Treasury may well carry forward its previous, voluntary practice; and see below in relation to Treaty rights).

Passporting out of the United Kingdom

4.18   Part III of Schedule 3 covers the "outward" passporting of United Kingdom firms which are authorised to provide services under the single market directives. The procedure specified will be familiar to many United Kingdom regulated firms;

---

[63] RAO, Art. 72.
[64] RAO, Art. 4(3).
[65] *Hansard, House of Lords Official Report*, March 21, 2000 (Vol. 611, No. 61, cols 150–151)

in essence, in the case of establishment of non-United Kingdom branches, the FSA has three months following receipt of a notice of intention from a United Kingdom firm to establish an EEA branch in which to determine whether to issue a consent notice to the host state regulator (paragraph 19(2), (4) and (12)). The host state regulator has the statutory two-month period after receiving the FSA's consent notice in which to inform the United Kingdom firm (or, in the case of insurance companies, the FSA) of its "applicable provisions"[66] (this accordingly implies a maximum five month regulatory timetable in order to establish an EEA branch). In the case of the provision of cross-border services, a United Kingdom firm may exercise its EEA right as soon as it has given the FSA notice of its intention to provide services; a provision in Schedule 3 which suggested that an investment firm would have to wait up to one month for the FSA to inform it that a copy of the notice had been sent to the relevant EEA regulator was subsequently omitted.[67]

General

4.19　It will be evident that Schedule 3 retains some technical differences between the passporting regimes under each of the single market directives. EEA credit institutions passporting under BCD[68] into the United Kingdom to provide services, do not have to wait for their home state regulator to notify the FSA before exercising their rights, while investment firms and direct insurance companies must wait. In relation to the establishment of an EEA branch of a United Kingdom insurance company, the FSA may refuse consent if it has reason to question the reputation, qualifications or experience of the directors or managers of the firm or the person proposed as the branch's authorised agent, which is not a relevant consideration in the cases of investment firms or credit institutions.[69] In the main, however, the procedures and rights are very similar and follow the single market directives themselves.

The FSA's *Authorisation Manual* will give some guidance to EEA firms wishing to provide services in or into the United Kingdom. Interestingly, in an early draft of this guidance, there was no reference to the completion of forms of application by firms wishing to establish a branch, as used to be required by the SROs. This is, clearly, more consistent with the "automatic" nature of authorisation under the single market directives and—if reproduced in the FSA's final guidance—would be welcomed.

As a final point on Schedule 3, it should be noted that not all United Kingdom firms using the outward EEA passport will be FSA regulated. For example, a firm holding a full licence under the Consumer Credit Act 1974 may have an EEA right to carry on lending business covered by its CCA licence in another EEA state, and will to that extent be able to use the BCD passport for that purpose.

---

[66] See para. 19(5) of Sched. 3.
[67] See para. 20(5). This provision was deleted by Regulation 2(5) of the Financial Services (EEA Passport Rights) Regulations 2001 (S.I. 2001 No. 1376).
[68] Schedule 3 has been amended to refer to the BCD, in place of the 2BCD; see the Banking Consolidation Directive (Consequential Amendments) Regulations 2000 (S.I. 2000 No. 2952).
[69] See para. 19(7)(b) of Sched. 3.

TREATY RIGHTS

4.20   Schedule 4 to the Act explicitly introduces into United Kingdom law the concept of a "Treaty firm". In essence, a Treaty firm is a firm authorised to carry on a regulated activity in an EEA state in which it also has its head office, but which has no "EEA right" under any of the single market directives to carry on that activity by "passport" in the manner in which it seeks to carry it on. Schedule 4 provides a specific procedure for such firms to qualify for United Kingdom authorisation.

It may seem curious that this new concept has been added to the Act now, when the single market directives have been enacted in United Kingdom law for some years. There are three possible answers to this. First, it is arguable that the power conferred on the Treasury to specify regulated activities by order (section 22) is broad enough to take the potential scope of the Act well beyond the services covered by the single market directives, with the result that EEA firms' basic freedoms under the Treaty of Rome (namely freedoms of establishment and to provide services) might be prejudiced. It may be objected against this that the scope of the 1986 Act was also wider than the ISD,[70] but an effective prohibition on the carrying on of a particular activity, through a United Kingdom authorisation requirement, would be at odds with the Treaty. Secondly, an EEA right under the single market directives will only be exercisable in the United Kingdom in relation to a particular activity if, within the meaning of the directives, a branch is established or services are provided in the United Kingdom. In the case of services provided cross-border, the directives do not precisely define, in any case, where services are to be taken to be provided (and, of course, the answer to this may well be different depending, *inter alia*, on whether services are provided in person or through a remote medium, including telephone, fax or the internet). In this regard, the European Commission provided some helpful guidance in an interpretative communication relating to the 2BCD,[71] which concluded that distance banking services (*e.g.* through the internet) should not require prior notification to a host state under the 2BCD since services are not in such circumstances provided in the customer's territory (*i.e.* it is not the place of "characteristic performance" of the activity). The Commission's view was also that mere advertising or promotion in a host state (whether by remote means or in person) did not generally amount to the "characteristic performance" of a service in that state. Though this guidance is limited to banking services,[72] and has evidently not been adopted in practice by some EEA states, the result of the Commission's guidance is that an EEA right may well not exist in cases where FSMA authorisation may otherwise be required because of the Act's own territorial scope and broader regulated activities (*e.g.* in relation to agreements to provide services). Schedule 4 is intended to fill this gap.[73]

---

[70] *e.g.* regulated arrangements under para. 13(b) of Sched. 1 to the 1986 Act were not a core or non-core service under the ISD, and it is arguable that many U.K. authorised "own-account dealers" in investments are not providing a "service" within the meaning of the ISD.

[71] Commission of the European Communities, Interpretative Communication, *Freedom to provide services and the interest of the general good in the Second Banking Directive* (SEC (97) 1193), June 1997.

[72] It is understood that officers of Internal Markets DG have expressed the view that the Commission's guidance should apply equally to investment services under the ISD.

[73] This point was debated in the House of Lords at the Committee Stage: see *Hansard, House of Lords Official Report* March 21, 2000 (Vol. 611, No. 61, col. 151ff).

Thirdly, and lastly, the concept of Treaty rights is *not* entirely new to United Kingdom financial services legislation; section 31 of the 1986 Act conferred automatic authorisation on an E.U. authorised firm provided that the law of its home state recognised it as a national of that or another Member State, and it was authorised to carry on investment business either generally or of any particular kind. Section 31 did not, however, apply to investment firms and banks coming within the ISD or 2BCD. Some of the provisions of section 31 were strikingly similar to Schedule 4, though there are significant differences, perhaps the most important being that section 31 did not apply to any European firm if it transacted investment business from a permanent place of business maintained by it in the United Kingdom (section 31(2) of the 1986 Act). Schedule 4 contains no such limitation, and may therefore apply to the establishment of a branch or the provision of cross-border services. In one respect, though, Schedule 4 is narrower than its predecessor; section 31 appeared automatically to authorise a European firm in relation to *all* investment business, even if it carried on a much narrower range of qualifying business in its home state. Schedule 4, conversely, expressly limits the application of Treaty rights to the carrying on in the United Kingdom of particular permitted activities which are authorised in the firm's home state (paragraphs 3(1) and 4(1) of Schedule 4).

Not all EEA firms with a home state authorisation and no available EEA right will qualify as Treaty firms. The Act prescribes as a further condition (as section 31 of the 1986 Act did) that the relevant provisions of the law of the home state must "afford equivalent protection or satisfy the conditions laid down by a Community instrument for the coordination or approximation of laws, regulations or administrative provisions of Member States relating to the carrying on of that activity or those activities" (paragraph 3(1)(b) of Schedule 4). Thus the FSA has discretion, in theory at least, to refuse a Treaty-based application from a firm resident in a jurisdiction where regulation of the activity in question is less developed than in the United Kingdom and the conditions of a single market directive are not satisfied.

The passporting regime under the single market directives govern the position in relation to the services which the directives purport to cover. Consequently, an EEA firm cannot avoid the notification procedure prescribed by Schedule 3 where any of the directives apply. However, an interesting amendment was made to the Bill in the House of Lords as a result of which a Treaty right may now be invoked where an EEA firm has "no EEA right to carry on that activity *in the manner in which it is seeking to carry it on*" (paragraph 3(1)(c) of Schedule 4, emphasis added). This underlined phrase, which may seem somewhat obscure, evidently represents recognition on the part of the Government that an EEA firm may not be able to use the passporting procedure under Schedule 3 because of the manner in which it proposes to carry on an activity covered by a single market directive. This is because the European Commission's guidance in relation to the 2BCD referred to above is that an EEA right cannot be used where a person provides services by means of a remote communication from outside the Member State where the customer or counter-party resides, even if that right would exist if the service were to be provided through a branch or by a personal visit. It appears that the new Treaty rights procedure is intended to be used in circumstances such as these.

The procedure prescribed by Schedule 4 is straightforward when compared to the passporting procedure under Schedule 3. A Treaty firm qualifying for authorisation must not carry on a regulated activity in the United Kingdom until after the expiry of seven days beginning with the day on which it notifies the FSA of its intention to do so. It appears that the Treasury has endeavoured to provide a simple procedure which will not represent a potential infringement of rights under the Treaty. However, if the European Commission's view on the position of remote communications under all or some of the single market directives is accepted, Schedule 3 and 4 would seem to create very different procedures for the authorisation of potentially similar activities.

At the time of writing, the FSA's *Authorisation Manual* (most of which was made on June 21, 2001 and took effect on September 3, 2001) had yet to include provisions for the exercise of Treaty rights. An early draft suggested that, if a Treaty firm wished to carry on regulated activities in or into the United Kingdom as such, it would have to give the FSA notice in writing, by completing and submitting an application pack to be provided by the Authority. Though it remains to be seen whether this special application pack will ultimately be prescribed, such requirements would sit a little uneasily alongside the confident proclamation in Schedule 4 that a Treaty firm may commence a regulated activity in the United Kingdom seven days after it gives notice to the FSA.

Who will use Schedule 4 in practice? It is clearly a little early to tell with certainty (and, indeed, Schedule 4 may be a part of the Act which is discussed more in text books than in real life!), but the principal candidates would seem to be insurance companies in respect of their reinsurance business; some kinds of automated trading systems ("ATSs") or online broker/dealers whose services are only provided on a "remote" basis and not through a physical presence in a host state; commodity futures and options brokers, who do not (as yet) fall within the ISD at all; and possibly some firms which pass orders in relation to transferable securities and shares or units in collective funds. The common factor in all these cases, of course, is that the relevant firms will not, or may not, have an EEA right in relation to these activities (or, at least, an EEA right in relation to the activities in the manner that they are carried on).

TRANSITIONAL PROVISIONS AND "GRANDFATHERING"

4.21 Nobody—least of all, one suspects, the FSA—would have wanted all existing authorised firms to have had to re-apply for Part IV permission. Therefore, the FSMA makes provision for the Treasury to make transitional provisions regarding, among other things, the authorisation and permission of persons who before the commencement of the Act were entitled to carry on activities (sections 426 and 427). This is colloquially known as the "grandfathering" process; and it is, by any standards, a complex and intricate procedure, since it needs to be broad and flexible enough to carry over the existing authorisations or exemptions of:

- *regulated firms*;
- *individuals* who will be *"approved persons"*;
- *recognised investment exchanges* and *clearing houses*;

- *exempt persons*, including section 43 firms and some "appointed representatives"; and

- *collective investment schemes.*

In relation to authorisation and permission under Part IV, the basic position is simple enough. Any person who before "commencement" of the Act (the date normally known as "N2") was authorised under previous legislation to carry on a regulated activity is automatically given at N2 a Part IV permission to carry on that activity in the United Kingdom.[74] This automatic authorisation extends to, among others, banks, insurance companies and friendly societies, as well as to firms formerly authorised under the 1986 Act. In the case of the latter, the effect of the Transitionals Order is not to allow any firm to broaden the scope of its permission by avoiding any limitations or restrictions which previously applied to its regulated activities; the automatic authorisation only applies to activities which the firm was able to carry on in the United Kingdom "without contravening any rules of a recognised self-regulating organisation of the kind described in section 10(3) of [the 1986] Act".[75] For example, therefore, a firm which was permitted to give investment advice only to "non-private customers" will not become automatically authorised to give such advice to private customers as well.

This last point, however, suggests a potential problem in the grandfathering process. The FSMA is not the same as the different pieces of legislation which preceded it. It is in some respects broader and in others narrower; and it uses different language, concepts and definitions. At a basic level, the Treasury has rightly decided that grandfathering must take place by reference to the definitions used in the RAO[76] though the FSA may describe the regulated activities for which a person has permission "in such a manner as [it] considers appropriate".[77] This means, for example, that a firm's automatic Part IV permission may contain section 42 "limitations" or section 43 "requirements" which have effectively been drawn from the firm's existing scope or terms of authorisation (*e.g.* a requirement not to hold client money; or directions or requirements previously imposed by the Treasury or the FSA on insurance companies pursuant to the Insurance Companies Act 1982). A section 42 limitation may also be used effectively to circumscribe a regulated activity in the same way as under the previous regime (*e.g.*, a requirement to provide discretionary management services in relation to venture capital investments only).[78] However, the basic position runs into difficulty where there are subtle differences between the definitions or concepts used in the FSMA or the RAO and those formerly used in (for example) SRO rules. Using the "non-private customer" example once more, the new corresponding definition of an "intermediate customer" is somewhat broader, but it is not immediately apparent that the FSA is given discretion effectively to "relax" a limitation or requirement imposed on a firm where this is a direct consequence of definitional changes, though the FSA's "final view

---

[74] Financial Services and Markets Act 2000 (Transitional Provisions) (Authorised Persons etc.) Order 2001 (S.I. 2001 No. 2636) (the "Transitionals Order").
[75] *ibid.*, Art. 4(1).
[76] *ibid.*, Art. 55.
[77] *ibid.*, Art.55(2).
[78] *ibid.*, Art.55(5).

notice" is definitive of a firm's position (see below). To some extent, therefore, firms will need to be on their guard during the grandfathering procedure (described below) to ensure that restrictions imposed are appropriate.

Apart from existing authorised firms, automatic authorisation is also conferred on "listed institutions" formerly exempted under section 43 of the 1986 Act, since this exemption no longer appears in the FSMA.[79] Also, because a person can no longer be authorised to carry on an activity and also be exempted as an "appointed representative" (under section 39 of the FSMA, formerly section 44 of the 1986 Act), appointed representatives who have been granted a Part IV permission at N2 are also given permission to carry on regulated activities which were previously exempt under section 44 of the 1986 Act.[80] In addition, professional firms which are unable to (or which doubt whether they can) benefit from the exemption in section 327 of the FSMA—probably because they carry on "mainstream invest-ment business"[81] or may communicate financial promotions—are granted auto-matic authorisation provided that (in the case of members of "designated professional bodies" such as the Law Society) a firm holds a certificate issued by the DPB entitling it to authorisation immediately before N2 and that it serves a notice on the FSA at least one month before N2 stating that it wishes to have a Part IV permission.

Detailed transitional provisions are also included for EEA firms having EEA passporting rights under the single market directives and for "Treaty firms" which were previously authorised under section 31 of the 1986 Act or which are insurance or reinsurance companies. Lloyd's underwriting agents are also provided with automatic permission to carry on any regulated activities which they were autho-rised to carry prior to N2 under the Lloyd's Act 1982.[82]

The new extra-territorial reach of the FSMA under section 418 (which deems activities to be carried on in the United Kingdom even when they are not) has necessitated a series of automatic permissions for investment, banking and insur-ance firms authorised prior to N2 (but which did not previously need authorisation for non-United Kingdom business).

The actual procedure by which "grandfathering" is achieved involves the FSA serving a "scope of permission notice" on each regulated firm. This notice is required to state which regulated activities the Authority considers that the firm has permission to carry on at N2 (described in such manner as the FSA considers appro-priate), and the "requirements" (if any) to which it is subject to at that time. It must also specify a period of not less than three months for the firm to signify its agree-ment, or otherwise, to the contents of the notice.[83] Though the Transitionals Order only requires the FSA to use "best endeavors" (sic) to send out scope of permission notices before N2,[84] the Authority planned from an early stage to issue notices around three months prior to N2 (from September 3, 2001 onwards).[85] In most cases, it is likely that the scope of a firm's permission will be agreed amicably between the

---

[79] Transitionals Order, Art. 6.
[80] Transitionals Order, Art. 9.
[81] See Chapter 3 above in relation to the regime for professionals.
[82] ibid., Art.7.
[83] ibid., Art.56.
[84] ibid., Art.55(3).
[85] See the FSA's paper, "Countdown to N2: Grandfathering" (July 2001).

firm and the FSA before N2, which is clearly desirable in view of the benefits brought by certainty. If no agreement is reached (bearing in mind that the FSA may serve more than one "scope of permission" notice on a firm in order to reach agreement), the FSA is required to serve a "final view notice" stating its conclusions and indicating that the firm has the right to refer the matter to the Financial Services and Markets Tribunal.[86] This process may be concluded after N2, but is likely in most cases to happen more quickly; the FSA set a target of October 2001 for responses to scope of permission notices (though firms could take longer to respond if they wished), and expected most final view notices to be issued prior to N2.

It might be supposed that a firm's entitlement to "grandfathering" will not be derived from the FSA's opinion of the facts, but from the Transitionals Order and the factual details of the firm's pre-N2 authorisation. This does not, however, appear to be the case; once the FSA issues a final view notice, the regulated activities which a person has permission to carry on a N2 are to be taken to be as stated in the final view notice, notwithstanding any other provision of the Transitionals Order.[87] Therefore, firms will have to take particular care to check the details contained in scope of permission notices, since an error on the part of the FSA which goes unchallenged and is repeated in a final view notice could have serious consequences. More helpfully, for the purposes of grandfathering, it is not relevant that a firm has not actually been carrying on a particular activity, as long as it is authorised to do so; therefore, some firms are likely to find that they will be grandfathered to carry on activities which were part of an original business plan but which have not been implemented in practice.

The Transitionals Order focuses upon regulated firms, individuals and products and makes provision for them. The same is not true for unregulated persons who will now require authorisation because of the wider scope of the FSMA. However, as when the 1986 Act was introduced, interim authorisation will be available for existing businesses which require authorisation for the first time, but only where an application for authorisation is received by the FSA between September 3 and October 31, 2001.[88] This nonetheless puts a burden on affected firms to take advice as quickly as possible and to apply for a Part IV permission where necessary.

APPLICATION FEES

4.22 The FSA has proposed a new system for charging fees to new applicants for permission and to existing authorised firms which wish to vary their permission (e.g. by adding a new regulated activity). The basic two principles of the new system are that the regulatory costs of processing applications should be split between, respectively, applicants on the one hand and the existing regulated community on the other; and that the amount charged should depend upon the complexity of the application.[89] For this purpose, the FSA has divided the

---

[86] Transitionals Order, Art. 58.
[87] ibid., Arts 57, 59 and 60.
[88] See The Financial Services and Markets Act 2000 (Interim Permissions) Order 2001 (S.I. 2001 No. 3374).
[89] See in this regard FSA, *Consultation Papers 79* (December 2000) and 95 (May 2001) in relation to fee-raising arrangements.

regulated community into three so-called "fee-blocks", according to the perceived complexity of different types of businesses (which, it is thought, will also largely determine the complexity of applications for permission). The three blocks are "straight-forward", "moderately complex" and "complex". By way of example, independent advisers, corporate finance firms and some "arrangers" will fall into the first category; fund managers and execution-only brokers into the second; and deposit-takers (excluding credit unions) and insurance companies into the third.[90] The FSA's costs incurred in applications will effectively be divided between applicants and existing regulated firms within each fee-block, with the relative percentage to be borne by applicants being higher in the case of "moderately complex" and "complex" applications (being 70 per cent and 90 per cent of the total cost respectively, as opposed to 50 per cent in the case of straight-forward applications). Though the amount actually charged by the FSA in any individual case will only be known once the Authority's annual budgets are set, the fees for each fee-band have been set at "indicative" levels of £2,000, £5,000 and £25,000.[91] EEA passported firms will not be charged application fees; Treaty firms will receive a substantial discount to the fees otherwise payable.[92] Fees for applications for variation of permission will only be charged in the case of "significant" changes, which will occur where the applicant will fall into a new fee-block (or blocks) as a result of the application (e.g. if a fund manager or securities firm applies for deposit-taking permission, or even vice-versa). The FSA plans to charge permission variation fees at half the rate of equivalent authorisation fees.[93]

---

[90] See Chapter 4 of the Authorisation manual.
[91] AUTH 4 Ann IR, Part 1.
[92] AUTH 4 Ann IR, Part 4.
[93] FSA, *Consultation Paper 95*, para. 8.25.

CHAPTER 5

Approved Persons

JAMES PERRY

THE HISTORIC POSITION

5.01 It is not surprising that the regulation of individuals working in the financial sector has suffered in the past from similar weaknesses to those which have affected the regulation of the firms for which they have worked. Before the enactment of the FSMA, these weaknesses had two principal causes.

First, the separate legislation covering each of the banking, insurance and investment industries created different systems for the registration, control and discipline of regulated individuals. To a considerable extent, these reflected the historic roots and quirks of the respective sectors. Broadly, the statutory regulators of banking and insurance (including, for this purpose, building societies with banks, and friendly societies with insurance companies) applied their own notification and "vetting" requirements to directors, senior managers and certain persons having management or other specified responsibilities. For example, banks authorised under the Banking Act 1987 were required to notify their chief executive, managing director, directors (including non-executive directors), and managers reporting directly to the board of directors or the chief executive. Similar requirements applied to insurance companies, though in their case notification was also required for the "main agents" through whom insurance business was conducted (which was a historic feature of the development of parts of the insurance industry[1]). However, the statutory regimes contained the common features that:

- in most cases, individuals did not require prior approval from the regulator before taking up a particular position or function;

- notification was not required for non-managerial staff involved in a firm's deposit-taking, insurance or other business activities; and

- there was no provision for disciplinary action to be taken against individuals (as opposed to the firms for whom they worked), although the legislation allowed the regulators effectively to bar an individual from working in a regulated industry in the United Kingdom if the individual ceased to be "fit and proper".

By contrast, the self-regulating organisations ("SROs") recognised under the 1986 Act operated systems of individual registration pursuant to their own respective sets of rules, each of which provided that an individual was not permitted to

---

[1] Previously codified in s. 64 of the Insurance Companies Act 1982.

assume registrable functions until registration had occurred. Since registration would not occur unless the regulator was satisfied that the individual was "fit and proper", the regulator's approval was in effect required. However, the respective scopes of the SROs' registration requirements differed; this was partly a function of the different kinds of investment business regulated by the respective SROs, but was also a consequence of policy initiatives undertaken separately. For example, IMRO had its own registration requirements for individuals who "supervised a firm's administration functions" for customers. SFA had particular rules and policies relating to the "senior executive officer" function.[2] Each SRO had its own procedures for taking disciplinary action against its member firms.

The second key problem lay in the regulatory structure created by the 1986 Act, which conferred limited, high-level powers on the Securities and Investments Board ("SIB", now the FSA), along with the duty to recognise SROs if they met the minimum statutory criteria.[3] However, the 1986 Act did not confer on either the SIB, or the SROs, statutory powers to take disciplinary action against individuals who were registered persons working for regulated firms (though section 59 of the 1986 Act did allow the SIB to make "prohibition orders" barring a person from working in an investment business in the United Kingdom). As a result, disciplinary action fell to be taken by SROs under their rules, which were binding on member firms by contract with the regulator. The rules were also, in general, made binding upon registered individuals by means of the written undertakings which were required to be signed by such individuals when they applied to be registered by an SRO (as a director or other representative of the sponsoring firm[4]). However, this contractual basis for disciplinary action was undeniably less satisfactory than a proper statutory framework. Against this background, the FSMA has introduced the concept of "approved persons".

THE BASIS OF THE APPROVED PERSONS REGIME

5.02   The source of the new regime for the registration of individuals is section 59 of the FSMA, which requires an authorised person ("A") to take reasonable care to ensure that no person performs a "controlled function" under an arrangement:

- entered into by A in relation to the carrying on by A of a regulated activity (subsection 1); or

- entered into by a contractor of A in relation to the carrying on by A of a regulated activity (subsection 2),

unless the FSA approves the performance by that person of the controlled function to which the arrangement relates. For this purpose, the "regulated activities" are those which are defined in the Regulated Activities Order made under section 22.[5] "Controlled functions", the performance of which will trigger the

---

[2] See in particular rr. 2–24 and 2–28 of the Rules of the SFA.
[3] 1986 Act, Sched. 2.
[4] e.g., the SFA required individuals to undertake, inter alia, to be "fully bound by and subject to the rules of SFA for the time being in force and as amended from time to time".
[5] See Chapter 3, above.

requirement for approval, are to be specified in rules made by the Authority (section 59(3); see further 5.03 below).

As indicated above, section 59 catches the performance of controlled functions by direct employees of an authorised person and by other persons under an arrangement between a firm and a "contractor". The most obvious example of an arrangement between an authorised person and a contractor, with which students of the 1986 Act will be familiar, is a contract with an "appointed representative" of an authorised person pursuant to section 39 of the Act.[6] Appointed representatives may be individuals, partnerships or companies and will generally be engaged by an authorised firm to market and/or advise on regulated investments under a contract for services (rather than a contract of service). In relation to such appointed representatives, section 59(2) will essentially carry forward the existing practices of the SROs, which required an appointed representative firm or individual to obtain registration as the representative of the authorised firm which engaged him or it, and extended individual registration and "training and competence" requirements to individuals who were, or who were employees of, appointed representatives. However, the new regime will extend the existing registration requirements to include directors and senior managers of appointed representative firms, irrespective of whether they perform regulated activities in connection with an authorised firm's business.[7] The more interesting question was whether the FSA would use section 59(2) to extend the requirement for approval to:

- relevant individuals employed by authorised firm B which performs services for authorised firm A under a sub-contract arrangement (e.g. a delegated investment management arrangement, or an outsourcing of custodial functions); and/or

- persons who are not authorised or exempted under the FSMA and who perform services for an authorised firm.

In the first case, the FSA originally interpreted section 59(2) as requiring an individual employed by B which is providing services under sub-contract to A to be approved in respect of *both* A and B. This seemed a little surprising as a general proposition since, in many such cases, B will be acting as a third party contractor of A—and not as an agent—and the individual will surely regard himself or herself as being "B's representative". The FSA subsequently altered this proposal to a requirement for the outsourced firm (B) to ensure that functions it carries out for another authorised firm (A) are undertaken by approved persons. A will be required to comply with the FSA's outsourcing policies in relation to the sub-contract arrangement[8] which includes an obligation for firms outsourcing the performance of controlled functions to take reasonable care to ensure that FSA approval is obtained. In the second case, the answer is that an unauthorised subcontractor of any authorised person is likely in most cases to breach the general prohibition in section 19 if it carries on a regulated activity, even where this is

---

[6] Formerly s. 44 of the 1986 Act.
[7] See para. 84 of the FSA, *Consultation Paper 26: The Regulation of Approved Persons* (July 1999); and paras 10.1.16R and 10.1.17G of FSA, *Supervision Manual* ("SUP").
[8] Chapter 10 in the SUP contains these policies: see SUP 10.12.3G and 10.12.4G.

done in connection with the regulated business of an authorised person (since the unauthorised person would normally be acting as principal in this regard, and not, like an employee, as the agent of the authorised person in question). Consequently, an authorised firm would not expect to have a section 59(2) arrangement with an unauthorised contractor for the performance of regulated business. However, it is possible in theory for management functions for which FSA approval is required (section 59(5), and see 5.04 below) to be performed by employees of unauthorised sub-contractors. This is indeed sometimes the case in complex groups where senior managers are employed by one or more companies other than the authorised firm(s) in the group. In the case of any such group arrangement, the FSA will expect to approve any individual employed by (say) a holding company or a group service company who exercises senior managerial functions in relation to the authorised person. However, in the case of other outsourcings to a third party non-authorised company, the FSA will require A to comply with its outsourcing policies but will *not* normally require an employee of B to become an approved person of A.[9]

Before leaving section 59(1) and (2), it is worth noting that both subsections require an authorised person to "take reasonable care" to secure the prior approval of the FSA where it is required. Initial drafts of the Bill imposed an absolute obligation to procure approval in the case of employees (under what is now section 59(1) of the Act). Interestingly, this clause was amended in Standing Committee in the House of Lords so as to impose the same requirement to take reasonable care as that which appears in section 59(2). This is a helpful amendment in view of the potential disciplinary and other consequences which may be visited on a firm which (innocently) fails to obtain prior approval for a particular employee; these consequences may also include an action for breach of statutory duty at the suit of an aggrieved "private person" who has suffered loss as a result of the contravention (section 71(1)).[10] This represents a significant change for banks and insurance companies, which were not subject to such rights of action under previous legislation.

THE "CONTROLLED FUNCTIONS"

5.03   FSA approval is required where a person is to perform a "controlled function" in relation to the carrying on of a regulated activity by an authorised person. The FSA's power to designate controlled functions by rules (section 59(3)) is circumscribed by section 59(4), which provides that the Authority may only specify a description of a function if (in relation to the carrying on of a regulated activity) it satisfies one of three conditions prescribed in section 59(5), (6) and (7) of the Act. These three conditions, taken together, effectively define the scope of the Approved Persons regime. In any case, a function must:

---

[9] See para. 3.14 of the FSA, *Policy Statement on the Regulation of Approved Persons: Controlled functions* (February 2001).

[10] The Treasury has also prescribed pursuant to s. 71(2) of the Act that a "non-private person" acting in a fiduciary or representative capacity on behalf of a private person may also sue under s. 71(1). This would include investment managers or brokers acting for private customers. See reg. 4 of the Financial Services and Markets Act 2000 (Rights of Action) Regulations 2001 (S.I. 2001 No. 2256).

- be likely to enable the person responsible for its performance to *exercise a significant influence* on the conduct of the authorised person's affairs, so far as relating to the regulated activity; or

- involve the person performing it in *dealing with customers* of the authorised person in a manner substantially connected with the carrying on of the regulated activity; or

- involve the person performing it in *dealing with property of customers* of the authorised person in a manner substantially connected with the carrying on of the regulated activity.

These three key conditions, and the FSA's interpretation of their scope, need to be examined in turn.

Significant Influence

5.04 The top level at which the approved person regime operates is that of the governing bodies (*e.g.* boards of directors), and the senior managers, of financial services businesses. Under both the old and the new regulatory regimes, the Government and the FSA have been at pains to stress the critical importance of organised and effective management of regulated businesses. Indeed, section 2(3)(b) of the Act requires the Authority to "have regard to" the responsibilities of those who manage the affairs of authorised persons, when discharging its own functions. Though the objective of sound and prudent management of regulated businesses is also pursued elsewhere in the new regime—notably in the FSA's requirements for senior management arrangements, systems and controls[11]—the requirement for those responsible for directing or influencing a business to be "approved persons" is also central to the FSA's plans for prudential supervision. As far as regulated persons are concerned, however, the key question is what is meant in practice by the exercise of "significant influence"? The FSA's response has been to specify no fewer than 20 controlled functions under the head of "significant influence", which are grouped under the sub-headings of:

- governing functions;

- required functions;

- systems and controls functions (finance, risk assessment and internal audit); and

- significant management functions.

The "*Governing Functions*" include, separately, the "*director function*" (which excludes non-executives), the "*non-executive director function*" and the "*chief executive function*", as well as other functions relating to particular types of business organisations such as partnerships. The FSA believes that, in most firms,

---

[11] The FSA set out its policy thinking on these subjects in its *Consultation Paper* 35 (December 1999) and its *Policy Statements* "High Level Standards for firms and individuals" (June 2000 and February 2001).

it is the governing body that wields significant influence, to the exclusion of more junior or intermediate managers. Though this approach does not represent a change from the respective practices of the former statutory regulators and SROs, it seems rather doubtful that a particular individual (who may be a non-executive) on a large board of directors can truly be said in all cases to wield a "significant influence" in relation to a firm's regulated activities. Even if the principle of the universal approval of directors is accepted, the responsibilities placed on them as approved persons may appear onerous (see below). The "chief executive function" has been included as a separate function and will apply to any individual who, under the immediate authority of the governing body, has responsibility for the whole of a firm's business (or, in the case of a United Kingdom branch of an overseas firm, for all relevant United Kingdom business).[12] A person may therefore be required to be approved as "chief executive" even though he has a different job title—such as "Managing Director" or "United Kingdom Regional Head". However, the prime significance which the SFA afforded to the function of the chief executive officer has not been carried forward in the new regime; FSA guidance makes it clear that some firms may not fill the chief executive function[13] and the overall responsibility for apportioning management responsibilities and controls has now been allocated to the new "apportionment and oversight function" (see below), one of the "required functions".

The *required functions*, as their name implies, are controlled functions in respect of each of which an authorised firm is obliged to have at least one approved person.[14] The relevant functions are the apportionment and oversight function; the EEA investment business oversight function; the compliance oversight function; the money laundering reporting function; and, in the case of long-term insurers only, the appointed actuary function. The *apportionment and oversight function* ("A&O") is the consequence of the requirement in FSA's provisions for "senior management arrangements, systems and controls" ("SYSC")[15] that a firm must appropriately allocate to one or more individuals the functions of dealing with the apportionment of responsibilities under SYSC[16] and of overseeing the establishment and maintenance of systems and controls.[17] The FSA has indicated that there is no upper limit on the number of individuals to whom this function may be allocated, provided that the allocation is "appropriate",[18] however, the consequence of allocation to a number of individuals is that they must all be approved persons. Therefore, this function might be undertaken by the board of directors of a company, though each director would need to be separately approved for this purpose, or by a number of senior executives within a "matrix management" structure operated by a larger, international firm. If a firm has a chief executive, he or she must be one of the individuals to whom the A&O function is allocated (unless the function

---

[12] SUP 10.6.13G.

[13] SUP 10.6.15G.

[14] SUP 10.7.2G.

[15] These requirements are contained in the High Level Standards block of FSA's *Handbook of Rules and Guidance*. SYSC was made by the FSA in the Senior Management Arrangements, Systems and Controls Instrument 2001.

[16] SYSC 2.1.1R and 2.1.3R.

[17] SYSC 3.1.1R.

[18] FSA, *Policy Statement: "High Level Standards for firms and individuals"* (June 2000), para. 3.16. The FSA has also warned firms that too many individuals sharing this responsibility risks the possibility of "responsibility falling between the cracks" (*Policy Statement*, February 2001).

is allocated to someone of greater seniority).[19] In most cases, it is expected that one or a small number of individuals in a firm will exercise the A&O function. The *compliance oversight function* is again the product of a requirement in SYSC, that a firm carrying on "designated investment business" (as defined in the COB Rules—see Chapter 10) must delegate to a director or a senior executive the responsibility for oversight of the firm's compliance, and for reporting to the governing body in respect of that responsibility.[20] Again, the FSA has given guidance that this function might be carried out by more than one person, particularly where a firm has a complex structure.[21] However, guidance is also given that the appointment of an external compliance consultant (a common occurrence, particularly among smaller firms) will not relieve a firm from the responsibility of allocating this function to a director or a senior manager.[22] This function was originally called "the compliance function", but the word "oversight" was added to allay concerns that firms would routinely seek approval for junior compliance officers. A further concern was that the scope of this function would include responsibility for all or most of the principles and rules in the FSA's *Handbook*; again, this point has been met by narrowing the compliance oversight function to responsibility for conduct of business ("COB") and collective investment scheme ("CIS") Rules only.[23]

The *EEA investment business oversight function* was included in the final list of functions to meet the point that, as host state regulator of "passported" EEA branches in the United Kingdom, the FSA has no responsibility for "prudential" regulation (*e.g.* "fitness and propriety" of most senior managers; capital adequacy, etc.). Therefore, this function has been specified to cover the person(s) within EEA firms responsible for overseeing systems and controls *but only* insofar as they relate to "designated investment business"[24] carried on from a United Kingdom branch. The FSA has anticipated arguments that even this limited specification may go beyond its remit as host state regulator, and has given guidance that the individual carrying out this function will normally be located in the United Kingdom.[25]

The *money laundering reporting function* is new, though firms will of course already have appointed a "Money Laundering Reporting Officer" ("MLRO") pursuant to the requirements of the Money Laundering Regulations 1993. The MLRO now becomes an "approved person" in consequence of the FSA's new powers to make rules in relation to money laundering.[26] In many organisations, the MLRO is likely also to be the Compliance Officer, though not necessarily so.

The *"systems and controls functions" of finance, risk assessment and internal audit* are not "required functions" and may, or may not, be relevant for a regulated firm. Senior managers with job titles such as "Financial Controller" or "Head of Risk" may now require FSA approval.

---

[19] SUP 10.7.2G.
[20] SYSC 3.2.8R.
[21] SUP 10.7.11G.
[22] SUP 10.7.12G.
[23] SYSC 3.2.8R. The FSA also anticipates that some firms will voluntarily elect to include oversight of the Principles ("PRIN") and the Market Conduct sourcebook ("MAR") in their compliance function (see SUP, 10.7.10G).
[24] SUP 10.7.6R
[25] SUP 10.7.7G.
[26] FSMA s. 146.

The *Significant Management Functions*, which comprise controlled functions relating to significant influence over (respectively) designated investment business, other business, insurance underwriting, financial resources and settlements, are likely to be relevant only to a few firms with large-scale operations or more complex structures. In most cases, such management functions would be undertaken by the firm's governing body, or by a small number of senior executives, such as the Chief Executive and the Finance Officer. During consultation on the approved persons regime, many larger firms were concerned that these "significant management functions" might result in the approval (for reasons of caution) of numerous middle managers, who in reality did not wield "significant influence".[27] The FSA has tried to avoid this consequence by providing that only "senior managers" of "significant business units" might be caught and giving guidance on the limited circumstances where a business unit might be "significant"[28]; and by voicing its expectation that such senior managers would, in most cases, report directly to the governing body or CEO of the firm (or equivalent within a group).[29] This should mean that layers of "middle management" and administration within larger firms will not require FSA approval, though some uncertainty will probably exist during the early stages of the new regime (particularly in relation to "matrix management" structures devised to control multiple, international business lines). In particular, some banks should be able to reduce the number of "managers" who are registered with the FSA at present. It should also be noted in this regard that the FSA is expressly permitted by the Act to take into account the likely consequences of a failure to discharge a function properly when deciding if the "significant influence" test is met (section 59(9)).

Dealing with Customers/Dealing with Property of Customers

5.05   Section 59(6) brings within the scope of the approved persons regime, in theory, any person who deals—or "interfaces"—with customers of an authorised firm. Similarly, section 59(7) covers persons dealing with *any* property of a customer. When framing its proposals for the controlled functions under these subsections, however, the FSA was clearly aware of the immense implications of casting the regulatory net too widely, so as to include, for example, a bank's branch staff involved in deposit-taking, or general insurance salesmen.[30] Following consultation on the approved persons regime, the FSA concluded that two factors were of prime importance when determining the scope of functions under sections 59(6) and 59(7):

- the reliance the customer places on an adviser or the advice given; and

- whether a United Kingdom regulatory conduct of business regime applies to the activities of the individual.[31]

---

[27] FSA, *Consultation Paper 53: The Regulation of Approved Persons, Controlled Functions* (June 2000) (CP53), para. 3.2.6.
[28] See SUP 10.9.3G and 10.9.4G; *e.g.*, FSA expects that these functions will only apply to investment business units employing in excess of 100 approved individuals or to general insurance businesses where gross written premiums exceed £100 million.
[29] FSA, CP53, para. 3.32.
[30] In this regard, the FSA acknowledged its responsibility under s. 2(3)(c) of the Act to have regard to the principle that the regulatory burden should be proportionate to the expected benefits.
[31] FSA, CP53, para. 3.46.

Consequently, the seven "customer functions" are focused upon individuals who give advice or provide other services in relation to (with one exception) "designated investments" as defined in the COB Rules. This excludes advisory or other services relating to (*inter alia*) deposits and general insurance or "pure protection policies", which are not, in general, the subject of COB Rules. The one exception is advice given to members of Lloyd's in relation to participation in syndicates.[32] The other key issue which the FSA had to address during consultation on the new regime was the number of advisory and other functions to be specified. The Authority's initial attempt[33] did not meet with widespread acclaim, because it specified different "controlled functions" for some activities which were similar or related. For example, the investment management function (specified under section 59(7)) did not include related investment advice (section 59(6)) or customer trading (section 59(7)), so that any discretionary investment manager, it appeared, might require two or three separate approvals for the same job. Also, a variety of separate "adviser" functions were specified for different products (*e.g.* life policies and pensions). The FSA responded to criticism that multiple "approvals" were now likely to be required by removing (for the purposes of FSA rules) the distinction between section 59(6) and 59(7) functions; by dispensing with some functions (*e.g.* Life and Pensions Adviser); and by broadening the description of the seven "customer functions" which remained. For example, therefore, the *"investment adviser" function* now incorporates "customer trading" in connection with the giving of investment advice; and the *"investment management" function* incorporates customer trading and investment advice (ancillary to investment management). As a result, the need for separate approvals has been reduced, though some firms may find that some customer-facing staff will fall within more than one function. The *"customer trading" function* covers dealing and arranging deals in investments for, with or in connection with, private customers and intermediate customers, but not investment advice or investment management (and thus only execution-only traders or arrangers will perform such a function). The FSA has given guidance that the customer trading function does not extend to merely introducing a customer to the firm or distributing advertisements, or simply inputting orders into an automatic execution system[34] (in the latter case, this is presumably because such an action may properly be regarded as an administrative rather than a dealing function). *Corporate finance advice* is also the subject of a controlled function, reflecting the special treatment of that activity which has historically been accorded by the SFA Rules (see also Chapter 10 in relation to the treatment of corporate finance in the FSA's Conduct of Business Rules).[35] An individual whose advisory activities are broader than purely corporate finance will need to seek approval as an investment adviser rather than a corporate finance adviser, but a separate approval for corporate finance will not be required.

During consultation on the regime, there was some debate on the special position of "Proprietary Traders", since they did not appear automatically to fall within any of the three heads of controlled functions in section 59. In the event,

---

[32] SUP 10.10.15R.
[33] See CP53.
[34] SUP 10.10.19G.
[35] SUP 10.10.13R.

such traders have not been specifically included under any head, though some senior proprietary traders may require approval under the *"significant manager (other business operations) function"*, if they have the power to manage, or materially influence the commitment of, their firms' resources.[36]

INCOMING FIRMS AND OVERSEAS BRANCHES

5.06 The Approved Persons regime does not apply to a person if his "fitness and properness" to perform the function in question is reserved under one of the single market directives[37] to an authority in another EEA territory (the "home state") (section 59(8)). In practice, this means that the governing body of an EEA firm, and any branch managers notified to the FSA, do not have to be approved persons. However, under the single market directives, the FSA is responsible as "host state" regulator of business carried on in the United Kingdom. As a result, individuals carrying on controlled functions within section 59(6) or 59(7) for a United Kingdom branch of an incoming EEA firm will clearly fall within the approved persons regime. The FSA has had to consider very carefully, though, which "significant influence" functions under section 59(5) should apply. In the event, it has decided that a United Kingdom branch of an EEA firm needs to allocate to an approved person the function of oversight of systems and controls (SYSC 2.1.3R(2)), but that function will only be "controlled" to the extent that systems and controls relate to "designated investment business" within FSA's remit as host state regulator. This "EEA investment business oversight" function consequently applies to the exclusion of the "apportionment and oversight" function which applies to other United Kingdom firms. In addition, the money laundering reporting function, the compliance oversight function and those significant management functions which relate to "designated investment business" will apply to an incoming EEA firm (as well as the customer functions). If an incoming EEA firm needs a "top-up" Part IV permission (*e.g.*, in order to carry on trading in commodity derivatives), then the "required functions" will apply in relation to those activities[38] other than the apportionment and oversight function.

Home/host state considerations do not apply to non-EEA incorporated firms which have one or more branch offices in the United Kingdom. The FSA has endeavoured, however, to limit the application of the significant influence functions to these firms in a similar way to the regime for incoming EEA firms. Consequently, the same controlled functions will apply to non-EEA firms with United Kingdom branches, except that the chief executive function and the required functions (including the full A&O function) will also apply.[39] The FSA believes that overseas-based managers with some responsibility for United Kingdom designated investment business would not normally require approval, because the exercise of the "apportionment and oversight" function will limit the influence which such overseas individuals may have.[40] While this is helpful as a general statement of

---

[36] SUP 10.9.13G.
[37] See para. 4.17 in Chapter 4, above.
[38] SUP 10.1.14R.
[39] SUP 10.1.7R.
[40] FSA, CP53, para. 4.14.

policy, it is not entirely clear why this logic could not equally be applied to some United Kingdom-based senior managers of United Kingdom incorporated firms— who are certainly intended to fall within the new regime. The FSA has also noted that overseas chief executives and "global heads" of functions will tend to fall outside the United Kingdom regime where they have delegated the implementation of global strategy in the United Kingdom to United Kingdom-based executives.[41] Though the members of the governing body of a non-EEA firm will not be required to become approved persons, it is intended that the fitness and propriety of such persons will be assessed when the firm applies for United Kingdom authorisation, to ascertain whether the firm itself meets the Threshold Conditions for authorisation. In addition, the FSA has required that changes to the worldwide chief executive officer and certain other senior managers will have to be notified to the FSA (but without any requirement to obtain FSA's consent to any such change).[42] Any such changes may, of course, affect the firm's continuing compliance with the Threshold Conditions.

In the case of section 59(6) (dealing with customers) and section 59(7) (dealing with property of customers), the FSA will require individuals carrying out controlled functions in the United Kingdom for the overseas firm (EEA or non-EEA) to become approved persons. This raises the question of when a controlled function will be deemed to be carried on in the United Kingdom, when any particular individual is normally based overseas. The SFA used to operate a useful and flexible "30-day rule" whereby individuals visiting the United Kingdom on a temporary basis (e.g. to take part in client presentations, when investment advice might be given) would not be required to become registered provided that they were not physically present in the United Kingdom for such purposes for more than one month in any calendar year, and that they were properly supervised by a registered individual when present in the United Kingdom.[43] Helpfully, the final draft of the controlled functions was amended to incorporate the 30-day rule into the investment adviser function (though, as under the SFA regime, the supervision of an approved person who is an investment adviser is required).[44] Further, in response to questions raised during consultation on the new regime, the FSA has excluded from the definition of the "significant influence" functions activities which are undertaken by a person for fewer than 12 weeks in any consecutive 12-month period.[45] This acknowledges, for example, that some international firms might have to second an overseas-based individual to the United Kingdom for a short period to cover a senior manager vacancy. The 12-week period was increased from eight weeks following consultation. However, the FSA has said that it will review the relaxation of the rules after two years to satisfy itself that the new rule is not being abused.[46]

In the case of the overseas branch offices of United Kingdom incorporated firms, the FSA has decided to apply the "customer functions" under section 59(6) and (7) (and the Statements of Principle and Code of Practice discussed below, to the

---

[41] FSA, *Policy Statement* (February 2001), paras 3.32 and 3.33.
[42] SUP 15.4.1R. Apart from the worldwide CEO, any change in the person within the firm responsible for U.K. operations and (in the case of a bank branch) the persons filling the "four eyes" requirement have to be notified.
[43] SFA r. 5.51(6)(c).
[44] SUP 10.10.7R(3).
[45] SUP 10.5.5R.
[46] FSA, *Policy Statement* (February 2001), para. 3.99.

extent that they concern dealings with customers) only in those cases where United Kingdom conduct of business rules apply.[47] Since the FSA's Conduct of Business Rules are largely disapplied in the case of business carried on by overseas branch offices,[48] this is likely to mean that overseas branch staff will in most cases not be subject to the approved persons regime. Senior management of an overseas branch office may, however, perform a significant influence function within section 59(5) (though the FSA seems to regard this as unlikely, as stated above).

APPLICATIONS FOR APPROVAL

5.07 The application for approval of any employee of an authorised person or a contractor should be made by the authorised person itself (section 60(1)). An applicant for a Part IV permission is treated as an authorised person for this purpose (section 60(6)). An application will be made on the FSA's standard form (normally "Form A", a specimen copy of which is included at the end of Chapter 10 of SUP) designed for the purpose. The FSA has a period of three months beginning with the date on which it receives the application to determine whether to grant the application or to give a warning notice under section 62(2) (section 61(3)). The warning notice may state either that the FSA is minded to refuse the application or that it intends to impose particular requirements on the person who is the subject of the application,[49] though in practice it is likely that the FSA will discuss the application with the authorised person, and possibly the person who is the subject of the application, before any such notice is given. The three-month period in which to determine applications is very lengthy; the practice of the SROs was normally to process applications for individual registration within two to three weeks, and often more quickly. Further, the Act does not prescribe any faster procedure for an existing approved person whose employer applies for him to undertake a new controlled function (e.g. an investment adviser who intends to move into investment management with the same firm). With these and other factors in mind, the FSA has proposed some "standard response times" for the processing of applications for approval. It is proposed, *inter alia*, that a "new, routine fully completed application form" for section 59(5) functions will be processed within seven days, and section 59(6) and 59(7) functions within four days; but, in any case, applications requiring checks to be made overseas might take two to four weeks or longer.[50]

The FSA permits a shortened version of the application form for use in relation to, in general:

- an individual performing different or additional controlled functions within the same firm (in this case, it is not mandatory to complete all parts of Form A, unless the individual is applying to perform a "significant influence" function for the first time); and

---

[47] SUP 10.10.1R.

[48] FSA, *Conduct of Business ("COB") Sourcebook,* COB 1.4 and Table 1.4.3R.

[49] As noted in Chapter 4, above a warning notice must (*inter alia*) state the FSA's reasons for its decision, allow the person access to relevant evidence on which the FSA has relied and must give any recipient a reasonable period of not less than 28 days in which to make representations before the decision notice is issued (section 387).

[50] FSA, CP53, Chapter 7. See also SUP 10.12.5G

- a person moving from one firm to another but performing the same controlled function(s), as long as the application is made within six months after the FSA receives notice of his/her leaving the former employer.

It is also proposed that such shortened applications will be processed more quickly than standard ones. Though these measures are of course helpful, they do not entirely address the problem that the new array of "controlled functions" will, without doubt, lead in many cases to one individual requiring numerous "separate approvals" to carry on different functions (though the application will be made on a single "Form A" where the approvals are being sought simultaneously). It also seems likely that senior individuals within smaller firms will in some cases suffer disproportionately, since they will frequently take on a variety of roles in the absence of greater resources; for example, a director and chief executive of a small corporate finance or IFA firm with two or three full time staff could find himself performing five or more controlled functions—and requiring approval for each! It also seems likely that senior managers within larger organisations may require new or different approvals as their focus of responsibility changes (*e.g.* from responsibility for particular areas of investment business to responsibility for general operations).

If the Authority ultimately decides to refuse an application it must give a decision notice to each interested party (who will normally be the relevant individual and the authorised person who made the application) (section 62(3)). A refusal may be referred to the Financial Services and Markets Tribunal (section 62(4)).

FITNESS AND PROPRIETY OF APPROVED PERSONS

5.08   As was the case under the individual registration regimes operated by the SROs, the FSA may only grant an application for approval if it is satisfied that the candidate is fit and proper to perform the controlled function to which the application relates (section 61(1)). The Act does not define which matters the FSA should take into account when determining fitness and propriety, although section 61(2) does state that the Authority may have regard (among other things) to the qualification, training or competence of the candidate when measured against the FSA's requirements for the controlled function in question. As a matter of law, therefore, the FSA may take into account all matters which a reasonable body in its position would consider relevant,[51] and may weigh the relative importance of different matters according to similar considerations.[52] It is worth bearing in mind in this regard that the burden of proving fitness and propriety rests with the firm making the application (though that burden is shifted to the Authority if it proposes to withdraw an approval under section 63 of the Act).

The Authority has published its criteria for assessing the fitness and propriety of approved persons.[53] It is not surprising either that these criteria are not exclusive, or that they do not differ markedly from the criteria used by the SROs pursuant to

---

[51] *Associated Provincial Picture Houses Ltd v. Wednesbury Corp.* [1947] 1 K.B.D. 498.
[52] *R. v. Barnet & Camden Rent Tribunal, ex.p Frey Investments Ltd* [1972] 2 Q.B. 342.
[53] The Fit and Proper test for Approved Persons (FIT) Within "High Level Standards for firms and individuals" in the *Handbook of Rules and Guidance*.

the 1986 Act. Briefly, the FSA will take three key factors into account when assessing fitness and propriety, being:

- honesty, integrity and reputation;
- competence and capability; and
- financial soundness.

The last of these factors is perhaps the only one which has given rise to some controversy; the FSA has observed that, if an individual is in financial difficulty, he may be tempted to put his interests above those of his customers to "boost his own earnings".[54] While this statement might be fair in some cases, it tended to suggest that the FSA might become involved in investigations of the financial soundness of individuals, and making judgements on available evidence, which would probably be impractical for a regulator in its position. The FSA has taken account of these concerns by acknowledging in FIT that the fact that a person may be of limited financial means will not, in itself, affect his suitability to perform a controlled function[55]; and by providing that a candidate will not normally be required to supply a statement of assets or liabilities. However, the FSA has explicitly stated that it will "look beyond bankruptcy and court orders in making a full assessment of financial soundness"[56]; this rather begs the question, however, of the evidence on which the FSA will base any such judgment. It seems preferable for the regulator to work solely on the basis of clear evidence such as bankruptcy orders or unsatisfied county court judgments, and only to decide against an individual on this ground in the clearest circumstances.

In relation to the "honesty" requirement, some exceptions are to be made to the Rehabilitation of Offenders Act to enable the FSA and employers in the financial services industry to take certain spent convictions into account in the context of the approved persons regime.[57]

STATEMENTS OF PRINCIPLE FOR APPROVED PERSONS AND THE CODE OF PRACTICE

5.09   Section 64 of the FSMA empowers the FSA to issue "statements of principle" with respect to the conduct expected of approved persons. The statements of principle are not to be confused with the FSA's Principles for Businesses (discussed further in Chapter 9, below), though the two sets of principles are complementary; the Principles for Businesses are addressed to authorised firms themselves, while the section 64 Principles are intended to set out, in general terms, the personal responsibilities expected of approved persons when performing controlled functions. There is also some similarity between the sanctions for breaches of the respective sets of principles, in that both may give rise to disciplinary action by the

---

[54] FSA, *Consultation Paper 26* (July 1999), para. 91.
[55] FIT 2.3.2G.
[56] FSA, *Policy Statement, "High Level Standards for firms and individuals"* (June 2000), para. 4.66.
[57] The relevant statutory instrument is due to be made in late 2001. This issue was discussed in FSA, CP26 (Annex A).

FSA, but neither will give rise to any right of civil action by a person affected or will affect the validity of any transaction (section 64(8)). If the Authority chooses to issue a statement of principle under section 64 it must also issue a "code of practice for the purpose of helping to determine whether or not a person's conduct complies with the statement of principle" (section 64(2)). A code issued under this section may specify descriptions of conduct which, in the FSA's opinion, comply or do not comply with a statement of principle, or factors which are to be taken into account in determining whether or not a person's conduct complies with a statement of principle (section 64(3)). Though compliance with an express provision of the code, or at least avoidance of a prohibited kind of conduct referred to in the code, will have evidential value in any disciplinary proceedings brought by the Authority against an approved person (section 64(7)), the Act does not provide that compliance with a provision of the code will be deemed to constitute compliance with the principle to which it relates. In the absence of a "safe harbour" provision,[58] therefore, such a code has practical value but no conclusive legal weight. Further, when determining if an approved person's conduct complies with the statements of principles, the fact that the conduct is consistent with requirements imposed on his firm is a consideration to be taken into account[59]; but, again, it is not a safe harbour, though the FSA has said that this is "likely to show compliance with the statements of principle".[60]

Following a lengthy series of consultations,[61] *Statements of Principle* and a *Code of Practice* have been issued by FSA under section 64. The *Statements of Principle* are written as high-level, general statements of the FSA's expectation of the conduct of individuals. There are four principles which are to apply to every approved person, requiring any such person to act with integrity in carrying out his controlled function (Principle 1); to act with due skill care and diligence in carrying out his controlled function (Principle 2); to observe proper standards of market conduct (Principle 3); and to deal with the FSA and other relevant regulators in an open and co-operative way and to disclose appropriately any information of which the FSA would reasonably expect notice. (Principle 4). There are also three additional principles applicable only to persons approved to perform a "significant influence" function under section 59(5), which require any such person to take reasonable steps to ensure that the regulated business for which he is responsible is organised so that it can be controlled effectively and that it complies with relevant regulatory requirements, and to exercise due skill, care and diligence in managing the business for which he is responsible in his controlled function (Principles 5, 6 and 7).[62] It is noticeable that the concepts used in these principles clearly follow similar concepts used in the FSA Principles for Businesses referred to above. Further, importantly, the principles focus on behaviour carried on in connection with *controlled functions*; as a result, they have no direct application to individuals

---

[58] *cf.* s. 122(1), which provides a safe harbour for persons who behave in a way which is stated in the Code of Market Conduct (within MAR) as not amounting to market abuse.

[59] APER 3.2.1 E(2). APER is the section in the "High Level Standards" block of the *Handbook* which contains the statements of principle and code of practice for approved persons, and was made in the Statements of Principle and Code of Practice for Approved Persons Instrument 2001.

[60] FSA, Policy Statement (June 2000), para. 4.24.

[61] FSA, *Consultation Papers 26, 35* and *53*, and a *Policy Statement*, contained discussion regarding the principles and the code for approved persons.

[62] See APER 2.1.2G.

carrying on activities falling outside the boundaries of the controlled functions, such as bank administrators who accept deposits or general insurance salespersons in the case of Principles 1 to 4 (though the principles apply in full to the management of banking and insurance businesses).

Given the regulatory emphasis on senior management responsibility, and the potential disciplinary consequences for breach of these principles, it is helpful that Principles 5, 6 and 7 impose a duty of care on senior managers rather than absolute standards. However, these principles for senior managers do not sit easily with the practical reality for many financial services businesses that important decisions are taken on a collective basis by a board of directors or an executive committee; in such cases, how is one to determine (in accordance with these principles) "the business of the firm for which [a particular individual] is responsible in his controlled function"? This problem seems particularly acute in the case of non-executive directors (whose presence on a board was a legal requirement under the Banking Act 1987), who will not as such be "responsible" for any particular business area. The FSA has attempted to deal with this concern for non-executive directors by including guidance in the section of SYSC relating to apportionment of responsibilities that the responsibility of a non-executive will be limited to the role which he actually undertakes; provided that he has personally taken due care in his role, a non-executive would not be held disciplinarily liable either for the failings of his firm or for those of other individuals (*e.g.* senior managers) within the firm.[63] Consequently, a non-executive director who sits on (for example) an audit or asset/liability management committee might apparently incur more significant potential liabilities than a non-executive whose role is limited to attendance at board meetings.

The *Code of Practice* published by the FSA contains a considerable amount of detail. Its general style is to specify a kind of behaviour or conduct in relation to a principle, and then to give examples or illustrations of that conduct to amplify the point made. For example, the FSA states that it considers that a person will not have behaved with integrity (Principle 1) where (*inter alia*) he deliberately misleads a customer, his firm (or its auditors or appointed actuary) or the FSA. Various examples of such misleading conduct are then given, ranging from falsifying documents to mismarking the value of investments or trading positions.[64] However, despite this large amount of detail, the Authority has decided not to specify any descriptions of conduct which, in its opinion, actually comply with a statement of principle (section 64(3)(a)) except in relation to Principle 3. Instead, in relation to most of the principles, it has published descriptions of conduct which are, in the opinion of the FSA, non-compliant. When added to the absence of any "safe harbour", this omission seems likely to trigger numerous requests for guidance from authorised persons (and their approved persons) pursuant to section 157 of the Act. Though descriptions of "compliant conduct" are not generally given in the code, the code does contain "factors" which in the opinion of the FSA are to be taken into account when assessing compliance (pursuant to section 64(3)(c)). In relation to Principle 3, compliance with the Inter-Professional Conduct section of the *Market Conduct Sourcebook* ("IPC"), the *Code of Market Conduct*

---

[63] SYSC 2.1.2G.
[64] APER 4.1.4E.

("COMC") and relevant market codes and exchange rules have been specified as a "factor" in determining whether or not particular conduct complies with this principle.[65] Again, however, this falls short of the safe harbour which many interested parties requested during consultation on the Code.

A recurrent criticism of the new regime made by some commentators has been the perceived tendency of the FSA towards "micromanaging" regulated firms or "second guessing" their managers. This criticism was particularly levelled—with some justification—at the first draft of the code of practice, which contained a very long list of evidential "factors" to be taken into account in relation to Principles 5, 6, 7 and many detailed examples of non-compliant behaviour (e.g. a dozen cases of delegation without due care). The FSA rightly concluded after consultation that this level of detail was not required in order to maintain the Code's effectiveness, and the subsequent and final versions were far shorter and less prescriptive. The Code nonetheless contains a significant amount of useful detail which will be mandatory reading for approved persons; in particular, the Code contains important guidance which senior managers will need to bear in mind at all times, including the need to clarify reporting lines, areas of responsibility and authorisation limits and issues in relation to delegations of responsibility.[66]

DISCIPLINARY POWERS

5.10 Under the 1986 Act, such powers as the SROs had to take disciplinary action against individuals employed by regulated firms were founded in contract.[67] As a separate matter, the SIB (now the FSA) had the power to make "disqualification directions" against individuals who were deemed not to be fit and proper persons, pursuant to section 59 of the 1986 Act.[68] This power to disqualify individuals from working in the investment industry looked fearsome when it was introduced, but in practice was used sparingly by the SIB.[69] Under the regulatory system created by the 1986 Act, the powers exercisable by the SIB against individuals in respect of regulated investment business were undeniably somewhat limited, though certain of the SROs used the contractual powers available to them to take severe disciplinary action against individuals when they considered that the circumstances warranted it. In general, however, the powers available to the SROs were used to take such disciplinary action only where the individual(s) concerned had caused their employer to be in breach of one or more FSA Principles or SRO Rules.

The FSMA changes the position radically by supplying significant new powers for the Authority to take action against individuals. Section 66(1) provides that action may be taken by the Authority against an individual if, being an approved person, he is "guilty of misconduct", which is defined as *either* failing to comply with a statement of principle issued under section 64 *or* being "knowingly concerned" in a contravention by the relevant authorised person of a requirement

---

[65] APER 4.3.3E; and see APER 1.2.3G.

[66] *e.g.*, see APER 4.5.11–14G, 4.6.12G and 4.6.13G.

[67] See para. 5.01, above.

[68] The Secretary of State's power under s. 59 was transferred to the SIB by the Financial Services Act 1986 (Delegation) Order 1987 (S.I. 1987 No. 942).

[69] It is believed that the power under s. 59 had been used in thirty cases by the SIB/FSA as at March 12, 2001.

imposed on that authorised person under the FSMA (section 66(2)). A person found guilty of misconduct is liable to pay a penalty of such amount as the Authority considers appropriate; and the Authority may publish a statement of his misconduct (section 66(3)). In view of the unlimited power to impose penalties conferred by the Act, it is not surprising that the Authority is required to issue a statement of its policy with respect to the imposition and amount of penalties under section 66, which must have regard to factors including whether the person on whom the penalty is to be imposed is an individual[70] (section 69(2)(c)). The FSA has indicated, however, that it will not be adopting a "tariff" of penalties for different kinds of breach, except possibly for minor breaches.[71]

The FSA has stated that, in assessing the appropriate level of a fine in any case, it will take account of factors including the amount of profits accrued or loss avoided; the conduct of the firm or approved person following the contravention; what action the FSA has taken in relation to previous similar behaviour; and what action has been taken by other regulatory authorities.[72] The costs incurred by the FSA are not a relevant factor. The FSA believes that this approach will provide appropriate flexibility in operating the new regime[73] (the new Enforcement Regime is considered more broadly in Chapter 13, below).

As noted above, the definition of "misconduct" given by section 66(2) has two limbs; though the second of these limbs requires a contravention by an authorised firm in order for an approved person to be potentially liable, the first contains no such limitation. Thus, an approved person apparently might be liable to disciplinary action under section 66 when no such action is taken against the firm of which he is a director or employee. This represents a departure from the previous practices of the SROs, and gave rise to some criticism from commentators during the Bill's passage through Parliament. There is also some disparity between the requirements of the two limbs of this section, since the second requires a person to be "knowingly concerned" before he may be guilty of misconduct, while the first simply requires a breach of a section 64 principle; as discussed above, these principles in general impose a standard of reasonable care on senior managers and financial professionals so that, it seems, such a person might be guilty under section 64(2)(a) where he fails to exercise such care but is unaware of relevant conduct by his firm or other approved persons (a form of "statutory negligence"). The FSA has attempted to address these concerns by giving guidance in the code of practice that an approved person will only be in breach of a statement of principle where he is "personally culpable", which will arise where the approved person's conduct was:

- deliberate; or
- below the standard which would be reasonable in all the circumstances.[74] (A reference in an early draft of the code to the FSA's view of reasonableness was subsequently omitted.)

[70] An approved person may also be a body corporate; see below.
[71] FSA, *Response to Consultation Paper 17 on Financial Services Regulation: Enforcing the new regime* (July 1999), para. 37.
[72] FSA, *Enforcement Manual* ("ENF") 13.3.3G.
[73] FSA, *Consultation Paper 65*, Annex A.
[74] APER 3.1.4 G(1). See also ENF 11.5.3G (Action against Approved Persons).

In addition, the FSA's *Enforcement Manual* confirms that, since the primary responsibility for ensuring compliance with a firm's regulatory obligations rests with the firm itself, the main disciplinary focus will be on the firm rather than on approved persons.[75] Though this is clearly of some comfort, it does not entirely address the additional risk to which approved persons will evidently be subject under section 64(2)(a), or the question of how the Authority will determine in any particular case which individuals are indeed personally culpable. Senior directors and managers have particular cause to be wary, though the FSA's answer to such persons is that it is the responsibility of each regulated firm, from the governing body downwards, to organise a system of accountabilities which makes it clear what is expected of each person within the organisation (including directors). This is of course sound guidance, though it remains to be seen what effect—if any—the new regime will have on individuals' willingness to serve on the boards of directors of United Kingdom regulated firms.

If the FSA proposes to take action against a person under section 66, it must give him a warning notice, complying with the requirements of section 387 (section 67(1)). Any subsequent decision by the Authority to take disciplinary action will be the subject of a separate decision notice (section 67(4)), which will entitle the individual in question to refer the matter to the Financial Services and Markets Tribunal (section 67(7)). If, at the end of the disciplinary process, a penalty is imposed on an approved person, the FSA will normally as a matter of policy make the penalty public in a statement.[76] The Authority will only refrain from publishing its disciplinary action in exceptional circumstances and for "compelling regulatory reasons"[77] (which may, for example, be where it would be unfair to the person on whom the financial penalty is imposed, or prejudicial to the interests of consumers[78]).

COMPANIES

5.11 This Chapter has almost exclusively referred to approved persons as "individuals", which in the overwhelming majority of cases will be true. However, it is possible that a person with "significant influence" over an authorised person's affairs, which requires FSA approval under section 59(5), may be a company rather than an individual. For example, some firms may choose to have corporate directors as part of a strategy to limit the perceived risk of individuals incurring personal liability. The FSA has acknowledged that bodies corporate may be regulated under section 59(5).[79] Of course, it is not possible for a company to be an approved person under section 59(6) or 59(7); companies which deal with customers or with property of customers will normally require authorisation themselves, rather than approval under either of these subsections.

---

[75] ENF 11.5.1G.
[76] FSA, *Response to CP17*, para. 61. See also ENF 13.4.2G.
[77] FSA *Consultation Paper 17* (December 1998).
[78] ENF, 13.4.2G.
[79] See in particular SUP 10.6.7G in relation to the Director function.

GRANDFATHERING

5.12   As might be expected, the new regime for approved persons has not automatically obliged all individuals registered with the statutory banking and insurance regulators or with the SROs to seek fresh approval from the FSA. In general,
senior managers and employees who were vetted and registered with the former
regulators of financial services in the United Kingdom have not been required to
re-apply for approval.

The principles for the grandfathering of approved persons are, in general, the
same as those for authorised firms (see Chapter 4, above). An individual carrying
on "controlled functions" prior to "N2" is able to carry on the same controlled
functions, subject to any conditions or stipulations applying to the individual's
existing registration (*e.g.* a restriction on the types of customer with whom the
individual may deal).[80] The position has not been entirely straightforward for firms
and individuals, though, because the new controlled functions do not correlate
exactly to the system of registrations and approvals under the previous legislation;
for example, the apportionment and oversight, compliance oversight and money
laundering functions are new, but conversely the "significant management" functions seem potentially narrower than their counterparts under previous banking
and insurance legislation. The FSA's practical answer has been to send to each
authorised firm around three months prior to N2 (or N2–3, expected at the time
of writing to be September 2001) a list of expected approved persons together with
their controlled functions, and a list of "unallocated" individuals for whom
controlled functions could not be derived directly from existing registrations/
approvals. Each firm has then been required to respond advising the FSA whether
the controlled functions assigned to individuals are correct, and whether particular
individuals will carry on new controlled functions or should, alternatively, be
removed from the list. The confirmed lists of approved persons are then to be consolidated into a register which the FSA proposes to publish on the internet. It is
expected that this process will result in some debate between the Authority and
authorised firms, particularly (in the case of the larger firms) in relation to the significant management functions and the position of overseas executives, where the
position may not always be clear.

Though the transitional system of grandfathering approved persons is similar to
that used for Part IV permissions, the Treasury has not granted the FSA a specific
power—as it has in the case of permission—to require specific classes of persons
to reapply for approval if the Authority so directs,[81] since the Treasury evidently
regarded such a power as disproportionate.[82] However, it is clearly, open to the
FSA, notwithstanding this, to withdraw a person's approval after N2 if it considers that the person is not "fit and proper" to perform the controlled function(s) in
question.[83]

---

[80] See Arts 72 and 73 of the Financial Services and Markets Act 2000 (Transitional Provisions)(Authorised Persons etc.) Order 2001 (S.I. 2001 No. 2636).
[81] *ibid.*, Art. 63.
[82] H.M. Treasury *Consultation Paper on Repeals, Transitional Provisions and Savings* (December 2000),
Pt. X, para. 10.3.
[83] Under s. 56(1) of the Act.

NUMBERS OF APPROVED PERSONS

5.13 During its consultation on the new approved persons regime, the FSA estimated that the changes would result in cost savings for all kinds of firms (banking, insurance and investment) as a result of fewer individuals needing to be approved/registered and the duplicate registrations required by statutory regulators and SROs being removed.[84] In particular, the FSA calculated that the aggregate number of approved persons would be some 15,000 less than under an extension of the current, differing regimes; this reduction, representing some 13 to 14 per cent of the individuals working in the financial services industry, was apparent across all constituencies within the sector.[85] It appears that most benefits are assumed by the FSA to result from the "de-registration" of some intermediate managers in banks, insurance companies and larger securities firms, as well as some "execution-only" arrangers and traders. While this prognosis is certainly welcome for the industry, its full realisation is likely to be dependent to a major extent on firms feeling sufficiently confident in the ambit of the new system and its definitions to avoid "protective" or "cautious" applications for approval. It is suggested that the "significant management" functions, and the translation into practice of territorial principles, will be key in this respect. For example, the practical application of the "apportionment and oversight function" seems likely to be very important (as the FSA has said) in diminishing the number of cases where intermediate and overseas managers can be said to wield "significant influence". In addition, some firms will remain to be convinced that the boundaries of some of the controlled functions (in particular those relating to significant influence) have been set wide enough to minimise the occasions where multiple or new approvals will be required.

---

[84] FSA, see CP53, Chapter 8.
[85] *ibid.*, para. 8.24

CHAPTER 6

Financial Promotion

VIVIENNE DE CHERMONT

INTRODUCTION

6.01   It has often been said of financial products that they are sold, not bought. It is undoubtedly the case that many people need to be persuaded of their need for certain investment products, not least because of their complexity and the long term commitment to them, which is frequently required.

The ability to market financial products is crucial to the financial services industry and, given that dependence, it was always to be expected that the new regime introduced by the FSMA would follow in the footsteps of the 1986 Act by paying particular attention to the promotion of financial services.

There are many parallels between the FSMA's approach to the type of activities, which it seeks to regulate and the type of promotions, which it seeks to restrict. The inclusion within the FSMA framework of the requirement for those conducting business at Lloyd's and lenders under the majority of mortgage contracts to obtain an authorisation is one key example of where the financial promotion regime mirrors and even extends that applicable to regulated activities. As a result, regulation of the marketing of these products and services has for the first time been put on a par with the regime already applied to other investments.

In the Treasury's *Second Consultation Document on Financial Promotion* issued in October 1999,[1] the Government confirmed that its approach to the financial marketing regime to be embodied in the FSMA was driven by two key aims:

- the need to ensure a "technology neutral" approach to the regulation of advertising and other promotional activities in the context of regulated activities; and

- the desire to harmonise the legislative framework for the marketing of deposits, insurance and investments in the United Kingdom.

It is difficult to fault the first of these objectives. Given the growing use of technology such as the internet and interactive television as sales media, artificial distinctions in regulation based on the method of delivery of the relevant promotional activity have become unhelpful to both consumers and the financial services community.

The second was destined to present something of a challenge to those tasked with producing the substantive rules on financial promotion. Previous legislative

---

[1] H.M. Treasury, Financial Services and Markets Bill, *Financial Promotion: Second Consultation Document: "A New Approach for the Information Age"* (October 1999).

controls on the marketing of insurance and deposit accounts have by no means been aligned and have been scattered amongst various statues.[2] These controls have largely been quite limited and justifiably so; while some financial products clearly warrant a substantial degree of control over their promotion, others are much simpler in nature. Bank accounts and general insurance products have become very much a part of everyday life and, in this area, the Government's stated commitment to "light touch regulation where possible" must be particularly appropriate.

These objectives have led to the introduction of two further significant legislative changes in the context of financial services marketing. The first is the abandonment of the distinction which existed under the 1986 Act between "advertisements" and "unsolicited calls" and its replacement by a new, broader restriction on the "communication" of "an invitation or inducement to engage in investment activity"—the so-called financial promotion restriction, embodied in section 21 of the FSMA.

The second is the application of the new regime for "financial promotion" to promotional activities conducted in relation to deposit taking and general insurance. In its *Third Consultation Document on Financial Promotion*,[3] the Treasury confirmed its intention " . . . broadly to maintain the current position in respect of promotion of deposits and insurance". However, the Treasury acknowledged in that same document that it was not possible ". . . to map precisely from the previous frameworks to the new regime" and there have therefore been some changes to regulation in this area.

Other noteworthy aspects of the new legislation are its approach to "inwards" and "outwards" cross-border promotions and the introduction of some new exemptions to the controls on financial marketing to encourage investment participation by so-called "business angels" (all of which are considered below).

Collective investment schemes continue to be the subject of a separate but similar marketing regime, which is considered in Chapter 12.

THE LEGISLATIVE STRUCTURE

6.02   The Treasury made no secret of its wish to avoid having to return to Parliament to enact frequent amendments to the new legislation, in the light of future European initiatives likely to adopt a "home state" approach to regulation (similar to that embraced by the E-commerce Directive[4]). The Treasury was also keen to avoid the new legislation being quickly overtaken by rapid changes in the forms and use of technology. As a result, the FSMA itself establishes only a framework for the regulation of financial promotion, much as in the case of regulated activities and relies on secondary legislation for the detail of the new regulation. The Treasury's view, as expressed in its Third Consultation Document, was that this would allow ". . . updating of the regime via secondary legislation while subject to the safeguard that the boundaries of regulation are the direct responsibility

---

[2] See, *e.g.*, s. 130 of the 1986 Act in relation to advertisements for long-term insurance contracts; s. 72 of the Insurance Companies Act 1982 in relation to advertisements for general insurance contracts; and s. 32 of the Banking Act 1987 in relation to deposit advertisements.
[3] Published October 2000.
[4] Directive 2000/3/EC of June, 8 2000.

of Treasury Ministers rather than the FSA". Despite some criticism of its approach,[5] the Treasury persisted in structuring the FSMA's financial promotion provisions in the widest possible terms, leaving it to secondary legislation to restrict the scope of these.

Section 21(1) of the FSMA thus embodies only the starting point for the restrictions on financial promotion. It prohibits a person, in the course of business, from communicating "an invitation or inducement to engage in investment activity" (and section 25 makes contravention of this provision a criminal offence). This is referred to in the FSMA as the financial promotion restriction. Section 21(2) then immediately disapplies the restriction where the person communicating the invitation or inducement is an authorised person or the content of the communication is approved by an authorised person. Section 21(3) further limits the application of the restriction, in the case of communications originating outside the United Kingdom, to circumstances in which the communication is "capable of having an effect" in the United Kingdom (although by virtue of section 21(7), the Treasury may by order repeal this subsection).

Having barely established some ground rules, the FSMA hands over to secondary legislation. Section 21(4) empowers the Treasury to specify when a person is and is not acting in the course of a business. Section 21(5) gives the Treasury a general power to specify circumstances in which the section 21(1) restriction does not apply. Section 21(6) gives the Treasury similar power to exempt certain types of communication or to exempt communications originating outside the United Kingdom (including on a "specified country or territory" basis) from the financial promotion restriction.

Finally, subsections (8), (9) and (10) in combination effectively give the Treasury power to specify by order those activities which fall within the definition of "engaging in investment activities" and which are thus caught by section 21(1) restriction in the first place. Section 21(8) defines engaging in investment activities as *either* entering (or offering to enter into) an agreement the making or performance of which constitutes a "controlled activity" *or* exercising any rights conferred by a "controlled investment" to acquire, dispose of, underwrite or convert a controlled investment. Section 21(9) and (10) give the Treasury power to specify what constitutes a "controlled activity" and a "controlled investment".

In short, the Treasury has the power, using secondary legislation, to determine:

- those activities which are within the ambit of the financial promotion restriction;

- those activities which, although prima facie covered by the financial promotion restriction, are nevertheless to be specifically exempted; and

- those "communications" originating outside the United Kingdom, which are capable of having effect in the United Kingdom but which are nevertheless to be exempt from the financial promotion restriction.

---

[5] See, *e.g.*, the comments of the Law Society's Company Law Committee in its Memoranda entitled "Financial Services and Markets Bill: Financial Promotion" issued in January 2000 and "Financial Services and Markets Act 2001: Financial Promotion" issued in December 2000.

It is clear that, in terms of structure, the FSMA has partially built on the approach introduced by the 1986 Act in relation to the regulation of investment advertisements, through the requirement that communications inviting or inducing people to engage in investment activity must:

- be made by an authorised person; or

- have their content approved by an authorised person; or

- fall within an exemption,

failing which a criminal offence will have been committed.

However, the significance of secondary legislation in regulating financial promotion is deliberately greater than under the 1986 Act and is one of the reasons for the delay between the FSMA's receiving the Royal Assent on June 14, 2000 and its coming into force. The Treasury's powers under section 21(5), (9) and (10) (although not section 21(4) or (6)) have now been exercised in the form of the Financial Services and Markets Acts 2000 (Financial Promotion) Order 2001, which was made on April 2, 2001[6] and in the Financial Services and Markets Act 2000 (Financial Promotion) (Amendment) Order 2001, which followed swiftly in the wake of the Financial Promotion Order.[7]

RELATIONSHIP BETWEEN THE FSMA PROVISIONS AND THE FSA

6.03　It is important to stress at the outset that, just as section 57 of the 1986 Act (relating to investment advertisements) had little direct impact on persons who were authorised for the purposes of that Act, section 21(1) of the FSMA also prohibits only communications made by unauthorised persons in non-exempt circumstances; it will therefore be of little practical significance for the vast majority of firms in the financial sector who will, by and large, need to be authorised and regulated by the FSA in order to conduct their businesses. Promotional activities conducted by such firms will, instead, be subject to the FSA's own rules in the form of the *Conduct of Business Sourcebook* ("COB"), which contains detailed conduct of business requirements for authorised firms. Section 145 of the FSMA gives the FSA specific power to make rules for authorised persons concerning their own financial promotions or the approval by them of the financial promotions of others. Failure to comply with these rules will not amount to a criminal offence but will render authorised firms subject to disciplinary and enforcement action from the FSA.

The COB provisions relating to financial promotion are considered in more detail in Chapter 10, below. Many of the definitions and other terminology used in these provisions are similar, if not identical, to those used in the FSMA and the Financial Promotion Order, which should help to reduce areas of potential ambiguity or overlap between the two.

---

[6] S.I. 2001 No. 1335, referred to in this Chapter as the "Financial Promotion Order".
[7] S.I. 2001 No. 2633 made on July 20, 2001, referred to in this Chapter as the "Second Financial Promotion Order".

It is worth noting here the restriction placed by section 145 of the FSMA on the FSA's powers to make financial promotion rules. Such rules may only apply to communications which would contravene the section 21(1) restriction if made by an unauthorised person (or if not approved by an authorised person). The FSA is thus specifically disempowered from making rules which cover communications which do not invite or induce defined "investment activity" or which do but are exempt.

Note also that the Treasury has power under section 145(5) to impose further restrictions on the FSA's rule-making ability in relation to financial promotion legislation. It is clear from the Treasury's *Second Consultation Document on Financial Promotion* that this power would be most likely to be used to limit the FSA's rule-making powers in relation to deposit and general insurance advertisements, if the Treasury considered that appropriate.

THE FSMA PROVISIONS

6.04 Although the Financial Promotion Order is at the heart of the new financial promotion regime, it is difficult to make such sense of its provisions without some understanding of the primary legislation and the issues which it raises.

Promotion

6.05 Interestingly, the expression "financial promotion" appears in the heading to section 21 but is not used in section 21 itself nor is it actually defined as such in the FSMA or in the Financial Promotion Order. Concern was expressed throughout the FSMA consultation process that section 21(1) failed to embody the necessary "intention to promote" in the activity which the Treasury was seeking to regulate. The Treasury made some concession to this concern by amending the original wording of section 21(1) so as to include the requirement for an "invitation or inducement" to be contained within the communication and, in its *Second Consultation Document*, explained:

> "It is intended that the clause [21] prohibition should therefore apply only to communications containing a degree of incitement and not to communications comprising purely factual information where the facts are presented in such a way that they do not also amount to an invitation or inducement."

Various statements made on behalf of the Government during the course of parliamentary debate on this part of the FSMA confirmed the Government's view that some element of design or persuasion would have to be contained in a communication before it would be caught by the section 21(1) restriction. The definition of "investment advertisement" contained in section 57 of the 1986 Act used the terms "invite" and information "calculated to lead directly or indirectly" and it is likely that, in using the term "inducement", the Government was looking to retain the purposive element inherent in "calculation" in the type of communications to be caught by the section 21(1) restriction. However, as many respondents during the consultation process pointed out, the dictionary definition of an inducement would cover a situation in which the *effect* of a communication was to cause a person to take a particular course of action, even if that was not the *intention* of the communicator.

It is also difficult to see why, if the existence of inducement is all a matter of context (as the Treasury suggested in its *Third Consultation Document*), it was necessary for the Financial Promotion Order to contain some of its specific exemptions, for example, the exemption for communications consisting simply of a company's annual accounts and directors' report. In theory, it should have been perfectly possible to assess, from the circumstances in which these were used, whether an invitation or inducement was being made. Perhaps this was merely an excess of caution on the Treasury's part; since similar exemptions often existed in regulations made under the 1986 Act, removing them under the new regime might well have given rise to concern and confusion, which was best avoided.

In the Course of Business

6.06 If the communication is not made "in the course of business", section 21(1) does not apply. This limitation was added to the draft Bill on its way through Parliament (as happened in a similar way in relation to section 22 and regulated activities) in response to concern that informal communications between individuals in a purely personal capacity would otherwise be caught and would require a specific exemption from the regime in the Financial Promotion Order (as, indeed, was the case in relation to section 57 of the 1986 Act).

Section 21 contains no definition of this expression, although subsection (4) does allow the Treasury to specify by statutory instrument what does or does not meet this criterion. The Financial Promotion Order does not do so nor does there appear to be any current intention on the part of the Treasury to issue an order under subsection (4). In its *Second Consultation Document on Financial Promotion*, the Treasury stated that:

> "In the absence of the Treasury exercising that power, it is intended that the phrase in the course of business will be given its ordinary meaning and that it will be for the courts to determine whether or not a person has been acting in the course of a business in the light of the relevant circumstances."

In this context, neither section 22(1) of the FSMA nor the Financial Services and Markets Act 2000 (Carrying on Regulated Activities by Way of Business) Order 2001 are of much help. Section 22(1) defines regulated activities as those of the specified kind which are ". . . carried on *by way of* business". This is a very different test (and a harder one to satisfy) than that contained in section 21(1).

The wording of section 21(1) is sufficiently wide that the communication may be made in the course of *any* business and still be caught by the financial promotion restriction; the restriction is not limited in its application to communications made in the course of conducting a regulated activity or even a business which consists of promoting investments. The example often cited to justify this approach is the case of a company seeking to market its own shares—the fact that the company's business does not consist of conducting a regulated activity or of promoting its own shares or other investments does not allow marketing of its shares to escape regulation.

The wording of section 21(1) does not require the communication to be made "for the purposes" of a business either; thus, the fact that the communication was not designed to benefit the business being conducted makes no difference to whether or not section 21(1) applies.

In essence, there are two issues to be considered:

- is a business being carried on at all?
- if so, was the communication made in the course of it?

There may be instances when a communication of the type intended to be covered by the financial promotion restriction is made but it is not clear that the person making it is, in fact, conducting a business of any kind. In those circumstances, previous cases in the context of VAT and consumer protection legislation[8] suggest that an activity would have to be conducted by way of occupation (as opposed to for pleasure or social enjoyment), in circumstances where money is intended to change hands and with some degree of regularity before it would be construed as a "business".

In practice, the first limb of the phrase will be largely irrelevant to commercial enterprises, who will most certainly be conducting a business of some kind, whether they conduct financial services business or not. It is the second limb which is more likely to require some careful analysis. When will a director or employee communicating an invitation to engage in investment activity be viewed as doing so in the course of business—when the communication is made from office premises, during office hours, on company notepaper or using company telephones? Will the answer depend on the identity of the recipient or the nature of the employee's duties for the employer? For the moment, the only conclusion to be drawn is that any link, however tenuous, between the communication of a financial promotion and a business may well be sufficient to trigger the application of the section 21(1) restriction.

Communicate

Causing a communication to be made

6.07 Neither "communicate" nor "communication" are defined expressions. Section 21(13) merely says the term includes "causing a communication to be made", which encompasses an entirely incidental role in the process of conducting a promotion. It would certainly cover the activities of telecommunications companies, internet service providers, direct mail agencies, postal authorities and any other entity, which has some involvement in the process of physical or electronic transmission or publication of a promotion. It was not the Treasury's intention to catch "mere conduits" of a communication within the scope of the financial promotion restriction but, instead of making this clear in the FSMA itself, the Treasury left it to the Financial Promotion Order to include a new exemption to cover these entities (this is discussed later in this Chapter).

In a somewhat different position are advertising agencies, production companies and the like who may not be in the position of mere conduits (since they will

---

[8] See, e.g., *Stevenson and Rogers* [1999] 2 W.L.R. 1064; *Customs and Excise v. Lord Fisher* [1981] 2 All E.R. 147; and *Customs and Excise Commissioners v. Morrisons Academy* [1978] S.T.C. 1.

usually be involved in the creative process by which the communication is devised and made and will often be responsible for giving instructions to mere conduits to print or transmit a promotion) but who will not generally be authorised persons.

The Treasury confirmed, in its *Third Consultation Document on Financial Promotion*, that responsibility for communications should generally lie with the "originator" but did not clarify whom it envisaged as being within that term. The only comfort that "non-conduits" were given was in the Treasury's statement that:

". . . provided that the financial promotion which they communicate is still in the form originally approved or communicated by an authorised person, then all parties who participated in the communication will not be caught by the financial promotion restriction."

In other words, to be sure to avoid falling foul of the section 21(1) restriction, entities in the position of advertising agencies and production companies will generally want to ensure that, if not clearly exempt, the communication has already been approved by an authorised person. Indeed, a similar situation already prevails to a considerable extent in relation to investment advertisements under section 57 of the 1986 Act and has prompted the widespread requirement by for written evidence of approval of the relevant material by a compliance officer or similar representative of an authorised person before instructions are given to transmit or despatch the advertisement.

Section 25(2) of the FSMA does incorporate a defence to any charge of having committed a criminal offence through a breach of section 21(1) where a person:

(a) believed on reasonable grounds that the content of the communication was prepared, or approved for the purposes of section 21, by an authorised person; or

(b) took all reasonable precautions and exercised all due diligence to avoid committing the offence.

The reference to "prepared" as an alternative to "approved" in section 25(2)(a) suggests, on the face of it, that requiring evidence of formal approval may be excessive and that less stringent due diligence would be necessary to trigger the application of the defence. However, given that advertising agencies and production companies are themselves involved in "preparing" a communication, it would still seem prudent for them to ensure that they have written confirmation from an authorised person that the material is approved for the purposes of section 21(1).

It will also be important for an unauthorised person to ensure that, once approved, a promotion is not materially altered prior to or at the point of communication. If it is, the protective effect of the original approval will be lost.

Communication contrasted with calls

6.08 Because the use of the term "communication" in section 21(1) encompasses both an "advertisement" and a "call", it throws some up some differences of principle between the new legislation and the old:

- under section 56(1) of the 1986 Act, unsolicited calls were, to all intents and purposes, prohibited except to the extent that they were made in the circumstances permitted by secondary legislation[9] (an investment agreement entered into as a result of an unsolicited call was generally unenforceable against the customer). However, section 56(1) did not make it a criminal offence to make unsolicited calls in circumstances other than those prescribed in the CUCRs. Failure to comply with the section 21(1) the FSMA restriction, on the other hand, certainly is;

- section 56(1) of the 1986 Act did not cover solicited calls at all and there was nothing to prevent an unauthorised person from making them (so long as they did not in doing so conduct activities for which an authorisation under the 1986 Act was required or stray into "investment advertisement" territory). The use of the term "communication" in the FSMA, however, brings solicited calls into the section 21(1) regime and has drawn with it the requirement for some exemptions in the Financial Promotion Order to prevent solicited calls having to be approved by an authorised person in situations where this was not previously the case;

- section 56(1) of the 1986 Act and the CUCRs applied directly to authorised and unauthorised persons. As a result of section 21(1) of the FSMA, authorised persons are now subject only to the FSA's COB Rules in relation to unsolicited promotions (except to the extent that an exemption is available for them under the Financial Promotion Order);

- in theory, section 21(1) now allows unsolicited (and solicited) calls and indeed any other form of oral promotion where their content has been approved by an authorised person. Quite how an authorised person can be expected to approve the content of a face-to-face discussion or telephone conversation (or provide evidence that he has done so) is unclear. In fact, the FSA has taken the view that allowing an authorised firm to approve an oral promotion is unworkable. Thus, COB 3.12.2R now prohibits a firm from approving any real time financial promotion on behalf of an unauthorised (or overseas) person. In practice, only the exemptions for real time communications contained in the Financial Promotion Order will be available to unauthorised persons wishing to conduct oral promotions.

Communications by potential investors

6.09 Strangely, the wording of section 21(1) is wide enough to encompass circumstances in which a person communicates, in the course of his (non-investment) business, an invitation or inducement to engage in investment activity, where it is the *receiving* party for whom the making or performance of that agreement would constitute a regulated activity. This would catch (for example) a telephone call by a businessman outside the financial services industry with funds to invest for the benefit of his business to an investment firm, whom he wished to manage or invest those funds.

---

[9] The Common Unsolicited Calls Regulations 1991 (referred to in this Chapter as "CUCRs").

The Treasury acknowledged, after the FSMA had received the Royal Assent, that this was not its intention[10] and included a specific exemption in the Financial Promotion Order at a late stage, to deal with this.[11]

"Engage in" investment activity

6.10   The definition of this expression contained in section 21(8) of the FSMA appears to require the communication to contain an invitation or inducement for the recipient to take some positive action. In particular, section 21(8)(b) encompasses exercising any rights conferred by a controlled investment to acquire, dispose of, underwrite or convert a controlled investment, which would not cover an invitation or inducement merely to *refrain* from doing any of those acts. By way of example, a communication from a company in financial or other difficulties to its existing shareholders, urging them not to sell up would not, apparently, be covered by the restriction. This was also the position under section 57 of the 1986 Act.

Territorial Scope of section 21

6.11   The FSMA's approach to the regulation of inwards (originating outside but made to recipients within the United Kingdom) and outwards (originating inside but made to recipients outside the United Kingdom) promotions provoked more comment and debate during the Bill's passage through Parliament than almost any other single aspect of the new financial promotion regime. It is not difficult to see why. The effect of section 21(3) of the FSMA is to ensure that:

- all communications originating in the United Kingdom (regardless of their target market) are subject to the financial promotion restriction; and

- all communications originating outside the United Kingdom which are capable of having an effect within the United Kingdom are subject to the financial promotion restriction.

The only financial promotions which are wholly outside the United Kingdom's new regime are effectively those which both originate from and are receivable only outside the United Kingdom. The Government's intention was to draft the territorial scope provisions of the FSMA in a way which would catch any promotions with a United Kingdom link, regardless of the medium of delivery. It appears to have done so. Internet communications and many European television broadcasts are therefore potentially within the ambit of the primary legislation regardless of their country of origin or target market because they are "capable of having an effect" in the United Kingdom. The same is true of magazine and newspaper promotions (whether or not in the English language or circulated generally within the United Kingdom) because they may be brought into the country and would thus be capable of having an effect in the United Kingdom.

The Treasury was well aware that, in drafting the primary legislative provisions in such broad terms, it was setting little by way of real boundaries to the scope of United Kingdom regulation and that these would need to be established by

---

[10] See para. 2.44 of the Treasury's *Third Consultation Document*.
[11] This exemption appears at Art. 13 of the Financial Promotion Order and is discussed later in this Chapter.

secondary legislation to make the provisions workable in practice. Many respondents to the Treasury's Consultation Documents criticised this approach and urged the Treasury to incorporate whatever restrictions were to be applied to the territorial scope of the financial promotion regime in the FSMA itself, rather than leaving this to the Financial Promotion Order.

Nevertheless, the Treasury stood its ground. Although conscious that reserving to the United Kingdom authorities a power to regulate any inwards promotion capable of having an effect in the United Kingdom appeared to fly in the face of the "home state regulates" principle, which the Government was keen to support, the Treasury declared itself unsatisfied that the necessary degree of consistency in regulation had yet been achieved even within the European Union to allow the United Kingdom authorities to step back entirely from regulating inwards promotion. The Treasury also made the perfectly valid point that, even after that harmonisation process was complete, the United Kingdom would still expect to exercise control over inwards promotions originating from outside the European Union.

It was with similar thoughts as to the future developments in the area of "home state/host state" regulation that the Treasury opted not to provide a specific exclusion in the FSMA itself for "outward bound only" promotions by unauthorised persons. Under section 57(1) of the 1986 Act, it was generally accepted that outward bound only promotions were not caught by the investment advertisement regime because they were not generally viewed as having been "issued" in the United Kingdom. Section 21(1) does not use the expression "issue" and it was certainly the Treasury's intention that financial promotions by unauthorised persons, which originate from the United Kingdom, should be subject to the basic financial promotion restriction, even where the target market is non-United Kingdom. This view was based on the hope and expectation (the logic of which it is difficult to question) of the ultimate extension throughout the European Union of the "home states regulates" principle, which would make the United Kingdom authorities responsible for the supervision and control of such promotions.

The Treasury did, however, acknowledge the potential (at least in the short term) for double regulation of outward bound promotions (which would have to comply with host state conduct of business regulations too) in a way which would not have been the case under the 1986 Act and has addressed the issue via the exemptions contained in Article 12 of the Financial Promotion Order. The Treasury also confirmed its expectation that, where an unauthorised person was obliged to seek approval for a promotion from an authorised person because the former could not claim the benefit of the Article 12 exemption, the FSA would have an important role to play in reducing the statutory overlap, by developing a "lighter touch regime" in its rules for promotions being approved (or issued) by United Kingdom authorised persons which related to overseas recipients and by exercising its own judgment as to the degree of control which it felt necessary to exert over inward bound promotions, depending on the level of regulation already applied by the home state.

FINANCIAL PROMOTION ORDER

6.12 The Financial Promotion Order contains much of the meat of the new regulation of financial promotion. It first sets out those investments and investment activities the promotion of which triggers the application of the section 21(1) prohibition in the first place and then specifies those types of communication which would (or might) be caught by the prohibition but which are nevertheless to be exempt.

Relationship between Controlled Activities/Controlled Investments and Regulated Activities

6.13 In its *Second Consultation Document on Financial Promotion*, the Treasury confirmed its intention to ensure that the controlled activities which were to be subject to the financial promotion regime should be ". . . broadly the same as those activities contained in the scope of regulated activities under the Bill (but before any exclusions to those activities are applied)".

This approach gives rise to more than just the superficial difficulty of having two similar but distinct sets of defined activities to wrestle with under the Regulated Activities Order and the Financial Promotions Order. It means that any person who escapes the need for an authorisation for their activities under the FSMA by virtue of an exclusion in the Regulated Activities Order will still have to give separate consideration to any attempt to conduct any financial promotion of or in the course of those activities to avoid committing a criminal offence. In particular, anyone who now takes advantage of an exclusion under the Regulated Activities Order (or an exemption under the Financial Services Markets Act 2000 (Exemptions) Order 2001) which did not previously exist under the 1986 Act will find themselves in the position of being no longer able to issue or approve financial promotions caught by section 21(1) because they will no longer be authorised persons. This is particularly significant for professional firms, such as solicitors, who may either be able to claim an exclusion under the Regulated Activities Order or an exemption under the FSMA from the need for authorisation for their non-mainstream financial services activities[12] but who may previously (as authorised persons) have approved investment advertisements for clients. Their position is considered in more detail later in this Chapter.

On a similar point, businesses which may be outwith the section 19(1) general prohibition because they are not conducted in the United Kingdom but who nevertheless carry on promotional activities which are "capable of having an effect" in the United Kingdom will also need to ensure that they take advantage of an exemption in the Financial Promotion Order or find an authorised person to approve the relevant material.

As was the case under the 1986 Act, anyone seeking to carry out financial promotional activities, who is not authorised under the FSMA, will also need to consider whether, notwithstanding the existence of an exemption in the Financial Promotion Order which covers them, the extent of those activities actually brings them within the ambit of the Regulated Activities Order because (for example) they may actually be viewed as arranging or agreeing to arrange deals, rather than just promoting them.

---

[12] See Art. 67 of the Regulated Activities Order and s. 327 of the FSMA.

Controlled Activities and Controlled Investments

6.14   Article 4 of Schedule 1 to the Financial Promotion Order defines "controlled activity" (in paragraphs 1 to 11 of Schedule 1) and "controlled investment" (in paragraphs 12 to 27). By and large, these definitions are readily recognisable from those which appear in the Regulated Activities Order, which themselves largely reproduce the investment activities regulated under the 1986 Act. What is important to note, here as in the context of regulated activities, is the inclusion in the new marketing regime of:

- the activity of accepting deposits and the deposits themselves (paragraphs 1 and 12 respectively of Schedule 1);

- effecting and carrying out contracts of insurance and rights under a contract of insurance (paragraphs 2 and 13 respectively of Schedule 1);

- advising on syndicate participation at Lloyd's, underwriting capacity of a Lloyd's syndicate and membership (or prospective membership) of a Lloyd's syndicate (paragraphs 8 and 24 respectively of Schedule 1);

- providing a qualifying funeral plan contract and rights under such a contract (paragraphs 9 and 25 respectively of Schedule 1); and

- providing qualifying credit and rights under an agreement for qualifying credit (paragraphs 10 and 26 respectively of Schedule 1); and

- rights under a stakeholder pension scheme (paragraph 20 of Schedule 1).

Promotion of these activities and/or products thus now brings with it for the first time the requirement to meet the criteria for an exemption or to have the promotion issued or approved by an authorised person.[13]

The other activities and contracts listed in Schedule 1 to the Financial Promotion Order are broadly similar to those contained in the Regulated Activities Order. As such, they have already been examined in Chapter 3, above and are not considered in detail here. It is, however, worth noting two particular points:

- although "offering" to engage in a regulated activity is no longer a regulated activity in its own right prompting the need for authorisation under the FSMA, offering to enter into an agreement the making or performance of which is a controlled activity *is* caught by the financial promotion restrictions in section 21(1) of the FSMA. This makes a good deal of sense. However, the wording of section 21 in this respect is interesting. Applying the "offering" part of the section 21(8)(a) definition of engaging in investment activity to the section 21(1) restriction, it seems that a person must not in the course of business communicate an invitation or inducement to offer to enter into an agreement the making or performance of which by either party constitutes a controlled activity. The wording is rather clumsy and

---

[13] Note that paras 9 and 25 of Sched. 1 relating to funeral plan contracts do not come into force until January, 1 2002 and paras 10 and 26 of Sched. 1 do not come into force until nine months after N2, *i.e.* September 1, 2002.

appears to have been drafted on the assumption that the person communi-cating the invitation or inducement is also the person who would be enter-ing or offering to enter into the relevant agreement. Of course, many financial promotions may be conducted by intermediaries who may not themselves be authorised (mortgage brokers who do not also arrange endowment policies, for example) and who will not be one of the parties to the agreement constituting the controlled activity.

Despite the less than easy read produced by the interaction of these two subsec-tions, "offering" type promotions effected by someone other than the product or service provider referred to in the promotion were certainly intended to be caught by the financial promotion restriction and a non-authorised promoter should certainly seek an applicable exemption or authorised person approval before proceeding;

- Article 61 of the Regulated Activities Order defines a "regulated mortgage contract" as one under which the lender provides credit to an individual (or trustee) borrower and the borrower's repayment obligation is secured by a first legal mortgage on land in the United Kingdom at least 40 per cent of which is to be used as or in connection with a dwelling by the borrower (or trust beneficiary) or a related person. By contrast, paragraph 10 of Sched-ule 1 to the Financial Promotion Order uses the expression "qualifying credit" and seeks to define this more widely. The intention is to bring within the scope of the Financial Promotion Order promotion of any credit agree-ment under which the lender is a person who requires authorisation under Article 61 of the Regulated Activities Order and where the obligations of the borrower are wholly or partly secured on land. Use of at least 40 per cent of the land as a dwelling is *not* required, nor is it necessary that the credit agreement being promoted is specifically one which would require the lender to be authorised under Article 61. "Buy-to-let" mortgages are the obvious example of a mortgage which would not satisfy the definition of a regulated mortgage contract but would be qualifying credit and subject to the financial promotion restriction.

Exemptions

6.15 In broad terms, the exemptions in the Financial Promotion Order are intended to replicate within the new FSMA framework and using the new FSMA terminology the exemptions which previously existed under section 58 of the 1986 Act (and the statutory instruments made under it) in relation to investment advertisements and under the CUCRs (with some improvements and clarifications).

The approach adopted by the Financial Promotion Order in relation to exemp-tions is first to set out those exemptions of general application to all controlled activities (Part IV), then to deal with the new set of exemptions required to preserve (so far as possible) the largely unregulated status of promotions for deposits and insurance (Part V) and finally to set out a lengthy list of exemptions applicable in the context only of certain types of controlled activities (Part VI). In fact, many of the exemptions in Part VI are also of general application, in the sense that they are not restricted to a particular category of controlled activity, but are applicable only in certain factual circumstances or to certain types of target.

A considerable number of the exemptions contained in the Financial Promotions Order (particularly in Part VI) repeat in substance those previously provided under the 1986 Act. What follows focuses on material changes to or new features of the exemptions.

Real Time and Non-Real Time Communications

6.16 Although the FSMA has abandoned the concepts of "advertisement" and "unsolicited calls" at the level of primary legislation, it is not a complete surprise to find that something closely akin to this distinction has been re-introduced in the Financial Promotion Order. The Treasury's rationale for this (with which it is difficult to argue) is that ". . . the immediacy of a financial promotion and in particular extent to which a consumer has time to consider his response, should be a determining factor in the extent of regulation".[14] Article 7(1) defines a real time communication as "any communication made in the course of a personal visit, telephone conversation or other interactive dialogue". A non-real time communication is defined as any other type of communication and Article 7(3) cites communications made by letter, e-mail or in published form as examples. Article 7 goes on to list certain other indicia of non-real time communications but does not seek to pin down this category of communications conclusively.

Despite concerns that these definitions left the status of communication methods such as internet chat rooms and WAP telephone uncertain, the Government refused to limit the definition of real time communications to those involving either face to face communication or direct oral communications (and rightly so). However, the list of the factors which are likely to place a communication in the category of non-real time is not as helpful as it might be. These factors (listed in Article 7(5)) are where the communication is:

- made to or directed at more than one recipient in identical terms (though there is no requirement that this should happen simultaneously, as might have been expected—on the face of it, this description could be applied to a sequence of scripted telephone promotions, which are clearly real time communications);

- made or directed by a system which normally constitutes or creates a record of it (interactive internet transactions, which must be real time communications, generally produce some kind of record or audit trail and telephone calls may be automatically recorded);

- made or directed by a system which does not normally enable or require the recipient to respond immediately to it (e-mail, which is specifically stated to be a non-real time communication, arguably fails to meet this criterion, since it does normally allow an immediate response, if the recipient is minded to give it).

---

[14] See the Treasury's *Third Consultation Document on Financial Promotion*, para. 2.5.

Solicited and unsolicited communications

6.17 The rationale for applying a greater degree of regulation to unsolicited promotions remains as strong as ever. The distinction between solicited and unsolicited real time communications crops up frequently in the Financial Promotion Order exemptions and a number of the exemptions are specifically restricted in their application to non-real time and solicited real time communications so as to preserve the substance of existing restrictions on unsolicited calls.

Article 8 sets the parameters for "solicited" and "unsolicited" real time (although not non-real time) communications. A real-time communication is solicited if it is made in the course of a "personal visit, telephone call or other interactive dialogue" if the call, visit or dialogue:

- was initiated at the request of the recipient of the communication; or

- takes place in response to an express request from the recipient of the communication.

Unsolicited real-time communications are those made in any other circumstances.

Under section 56(8) of the 1986 Act, the concept of "unsolicited" was conveyed by the words "without express invitation". It was generally accepted that, so long as the personal visit or oral communication had been expressly invited, it was not necessary for the promotion of investments or investment business during the course of it to have been specifically requested. Thus, if a broker was asked by a customer to telephone with a view to discussing a service already being provided by the broker to the customer but then took the opportunity to discuss some other aspect of investment business with the customer, the call would not be regarded as "unsolicited".

It is not clear that this will still be the case. Article 8(3) of the Financial Promotion Order goes on to state that a communication will only be taken as solicited ". . . if it is clear from all the circumstances when the call, visit or dialogue is initiated or requested that during the course of the visit, call or dialogue communications will be made concerning the kind of controlled activities or investments to which the communications in fact made relate".

The Government certainly took the view that it was broadening slightly the definition of unsolicited call previously contained in section 56 of the 1986 Act and has sought to close some loopholes previously exploited in this area. Article 8(3) makes it clear that the communication will not be deemed to be solicited simply because the recipient has omitted to indicate (for example, by ticking the appropriate box) that he does not wish to receive any communication or because he has signed up to standard terms of business containing a consent. Real or "informed" consent to a financial promotion will therefore be required before it will be classed as solicited.

This potential increase in the scope of what will be regarded as unsolicited needs to be borne in mind by anyone looking to take advantage of parallel exemptions as between the old legislation and the new.

Territorial Scope Exemptions

6.18 Article 12 narrows considerably the scope of the section 21(1) restriction in relation to promotions intended to have effect outside the United Kingdom.

Article 12(1)(a) exempts communications made to a person who receives the communication outside the United Kingdom (note, there is no suggestion that the person must be a non-United Kingdom resident, merely that he must be outside the United Kingdom when the communication is received). Article 12(1)(b) exempts communications which are "directed" only at persons outside the United Kingdom.

In either case, it does not matter whether the communications are made from inside or outside the United Kingdom. However, the Article 12(1)(a) exemption was intended principally to deal with outwards only promotions from the United Kingdom. The Article 12(1)(b) exemption is clearly aimed at promotions originating outside the United Kingdom, which may be received in but which are not actually intended for the United Kingdom market, although it applies equally to promotions originating in the United Kingdom. Article 12(2) adds two further requirements which must be satisfied by all unsolicited real time communications before they may take advantage of the Article 12(1) exemption:

- they must be made from a place outside the United Kingdom; and

- be made for the purposes of a business carried on entirely outside the United Kingdom.

Thus, only unsolicited real time communications with no United Kingdom link are wholly outside the ambit of section 21(1). All other unsolicited real time communications will need to satisfy the requirements of some other exemption, if they can.

The Treasury ultimately acceded to requests to include "safe harbour" criteria in this exemption for the purposes of determining when a communication is "directed only at persons outside the United Kingdom". These are set out in Article 12(4). They are:

(a) the communication is accompanied by an indication that it is directed only at persons outside the United Kingdom;

(b) the communication is accompanied by an indication that it must not be acted upon by persons in the United Kingdom;

(c) the communication is not referred to in, or directly accessible from, any other communication which is made to a person or directed at persons in the United Kingdom; and

(d) there are in place proper systems and procedures to prevent recipients in the United Kingdom (other than those to whom the communication might otherwise lawfully have been made) engaging in the investment activity to which the communication relates with the person directing the communication (or certain other parties closely aligned to him).

In applying a "directed at" test of this kind with the evidential factors set out in Article 12(4), the Government has followed the non-enforcement policy adopted by the FSA in recent years in response to the increasing use of the internet as a business medium, which was itself based on what the Government termed "internationally recommended regulatory best practice", including that endorsed by the International Organisation of Securities Commissions ("IOSCO").

All four of these criteria must be satisfied where the communication is directed from within the United Kingdom before the safe harbour will apply. An understandably lesser requirement (being (c) and (d) of these criteria) is applied where the communication is directed from outside the United Kingdom. Satisfaction of any of these criteria will still be an evidential factor in determining whether the communication is "directed" outside the United Kingdom.

Article 12(4)(e) contains a fifth factor (which will be indicative only) designed to deal with the problem (highlighted earlier in this Chapter) of newspapers or other publications and television or radio broadcasts which happen to be brought or transmitted into the United Kingdom in circumstances where the United Kingdom was not the target market. These are now within the scope of the financial promotion restriction. It applies where the communication is included *either* in a web site, newspaper, journal, magazine or periodical publication principally accessed in or intended for a non-United Kingdom market *or* in a radio or television broadcast or teletext service transmitted principally for reception outside the United Kingdom. Although falling within the terms of Article 12(4)(e) does not guarantee exemption from the financial promotion restriction, it is difficult to imagine circumstances in which an essentially non-United Kingdom type of promotion falling within its terms would in practice be considered to have been caught by it unless some other factor demonstrated a real United Kingdom link or target.

Note that some of the exemptions which previously existed in respect of overseas communications (together with a new exemption in respect of solicited real time communications) have been reproduced in substance in the Financial Promotion Order. These are referred to below.

It is also worth bearing in mind that, while the FSA's COB, r. 3.3 is generally consistent with the territorial scope provisions contained in the Financial Promotion Order, some of its provisions will nevertheless apply in circumstances where an authorised person approves a financial promotion that would otherwise be exempt under Article 12. The justification for this approach is the potential reliance that consumers could place on such approval.

Mere Conduits

6.19   The expression "causing a communication to be made" used in section 21 of the FSMA does (as noted earlier in this Chapter) cover anyone with a role to play in ensuring the passage of a communication from its point of origin to the recipient. The effect of this is alleviated to some extent by the "mere conduit" exemption contained in Article 18 of the Financial Promotion Order.

A person will be acting as a mere conduit for a communication if—

- he communicates it in the course of a business which he carries on, whose principal purpose is transmitting or receiving material provided to him by others;

- the content of the communication is wholly devised by another person; and

- the nature of the service provided by him in relation to the communication is such that he does not select, modify or otherwise exercise control over its content prior to its transmission or receipt.

The exemption was aimed only at passive communication providers such as internet service providers, postal services and telecommunications companies. It will not be available to a financial services intermediary, for example, since the first limb of the exemption would not then be satisfied. The limitations on the usefulness of this exemption for persons who may play some (albeit a restricted) role in devising content have already been considered.

At one stage, the draft exemption required the communication to be devised by the customer of the conduit but, in the light of responses received to its *Second Consultation Document on Financial Promotion*, the Treasury amended this requirement, so that the exemption will apply as long as the content of the communication is devised by someone other than the person claiming the exemption.

Generic Promotions

6.20 Given the definition of "engaging in investment activity" contained in section 21(8) of the FSMA, it is arguable that financial promotions, which do not refer to specific agreements or investments (so-called "awareness" advertising), are not caught by the section 21(1) restriction in the first place.

However, by including in Article 17 of the Financial Promotion Order a generic promotion exemption, the Treasury by implication takes the view that they are and sets out the circumstances in which an exemption for them may be claimed. Essentially, the exemption will be available where no specific product provider or service provider is mentioned. The example given by the Treasury of what it was seeking to allow was the generic promotion by a trade association of unit trusts or ISAs—in other words, a specific type of investment product or service but not a named provider.

Conversely, the type of "brand awareness" promotion carried out by many product providers, in which their name is mentioned but not in the context of any particular product or service, will *not* benefit from the exemption. Indeed, such advertising was not previously exempt under section 57 of the 1986 Act. However, the FSA's COB 3.2.5R does exempt from the FSA's own financial promotion rules a promotion which contains only one or more of the following:

- the name of the firm;
- the name of an investment;
- a contact point (address/e-mail address/telephone or facsimile number);
- a logo;
- a brief, factual description of the firm's activities;
- a brief, factual description of the firm's fees;
- a brief, factual description of the firm's investment products;
- the price of yields of investments and the charges.

Thus, authorised persons will be able to issue their own short corporate image advertisements without reference to either the Financial Promotion Order or the full rigour of the COB financial promotion regime.

Journalists

6.21 The exemption contained in Article 20 of the Financial Promotion Order was not included until the third consultation draft of the Order. It replaces (and expands considerably on) Article 15 of the Financial Services Act 1986 (Investment Advertisements) (Exemptions) Order 1996. The presence of a specific exclusion in the Regulated Activities Order for advice given in newspapers[15] prompted the Treasury to seek parity for financial promotions contained in such publications and the wording of the exemption is similar to that contained in the Regulated Activities Order. There is considerable merit in this, since it would have been difficult in the context of material included in a generally available publication to draw a dividing line between advice and promotion.

Although it is possible to argue that factual reporting should not fall within the ambit of section 21(1) of the FSMA in the first place, the very fact that the exemption is included is likely to mean, in practice, that all financial journalists writing about particular products or services from named providers will seek to comply with the terms of this exemption, since to do otherwise could easily be viewed (by the Treasury, at least) as a breach of the section 21(1) restriction.

The exemption requires certain conditions to be satisfied before it will apply:

- the content of the communication must be devised by a person acting in the capacity of a journalist. It is not clear from the Financial Promotion Order (or from the Treasury Consultation Documents) exactly what the expression "acting in the capacity of a journalist" means. Could anyone writing in a newspaper be viewed in that way? If factual reporting is the essence of journalism, why would section 21(1) be applicable in the first place? Many newspaper articles are based on press releases issued by product or service providers themselves. Simple regurgitation of such releases is, arguably, not within the spirit of the exemption but, since it is what many journalists do, will the wording of the exemption allow it? Since the exemption uses the word "devised", rather than "written", the answer is presumably that it will.

- the communication must be contained in a qualifying publication. Not surprisingly, Article 20 cross-refers to Article 54 of the Regulated Activities Order for the definition of "qualifying publication". Essentially, the term encompasses newspapers, magazines or other periodical publications, and television and radio broadcasts, if their purpose, taken as a whole, is neither the giving of advice nor leading or enabling persons to buy, sell, subscribe for or underwrite securities or contractually based investments. Article 54(3) of the Regulated Activities Order allows "the proprietor" of the relevant publication to apply to the FSA for a certificate confirming that it falls within the terms of the exemption. Any such certificate will also be good for the purposes of the qualifying publication definition in Article 20 of the Financial Promotion Order.

---

[15] See Art. 54 of the Regulated Activities Order.

- any communication "requiring disclosure" will only be exempt if certain other criteria are satisfied. According to Article 20(3)(b), a communication requires disclosure if an author of the communication or a close relative of his is likely to obtain a financial benefit or avoid a financial loss if people act in accordance with the invitation or inducement contained in the communication. In those circumstances, the exemption may only be claimed where:

  — the communication is accompanied by an indication explaining the nature of the author's financial interest (or that of his close relative); or

  — the authors are subject to proper systems and procedures which prevent the publication of communications requiring disclosure without such an indication; or

  — the publication in which the communication appears falls within the Code of Practice issued by the Press Complaints Commission.

The last of these three criteria was included only shortly before the Financial Promotion Order was made. There was concern that, if it were excluded, the criteria contained in the new financial promotion regime would differ from those applied in similar circumstances by the Press Complaints Commission's ("PCC") Code of Practice, with journalists left in an uncertain position in the middle. Now, compliance with the PCC Code of Practice where there is a disclosure requirement will suffice to attract the exemption. The key difference between Article 20(2)(a) and the PCC Code of Practice appears to be that the latter would permit journalists to trade in shares or securities about which they had written provided the trading was disclosed to the editor or financial editor, whereas Article 20(2)(a) will require disclosure to the readership as a whole.

Article 20(3)(a) also includes a definition of the term "authors". These are the person who devises the content of the communication (*i.e.* the journalist) *and* the person who is responsible for deciding to include it in the qualifying publication (*i.e.* the financial editor or editor). The disclosure requirement will therefore apply if either journalist or editor stands to receive a financial benefit or avoid a financial loss through putting out the communication.

The inclusion of a requirement for the journalist to indicate his status an unauthorised person was, at one stage, proposed but subsequently abandoned in the latter stages of the consultation process for the Financial Promotion Order.

Exempt Persons

6.22 The exemption contained in Article 16 is not new in substance. It is designed to carry over to the FSMA regime, with appropriate changes in terminology, a similar exemption to that contained in section 58(1)(b) of the 1986 Act.

However, it is worth considering in the context of professional firms. Those firms are no longer automatically authorised by virtue of membership of their RPB. Article 67 of the Regulated Activities Order excludes certain activities which would otherwise be regulated where they may reasonably be regarded as a necessary part of services provided in the course of a profession, while section 327 of the FSMA exempts non-mainstream financial services activities as conducted by such firms from the need for authorisation under the FSMA, where the firm is supervised and regulated by a designated professional body. Professional firms can therefore claim exempt status if they wish but, if they do, they will no longer be able themselves to issue financial promotions unless they can find a suitable exemption for them.

On the face of it, the exempt persons exemption in Article 16 looks as if it might assist. It exempts from the financial promotion restriction any communication which:

- is a non-real time communication or is a solicited real time communication;

- is made or directed by an exempt person; and

- is for the purposes of that exempt person's business of carrying on a controlled activity which is also a regulated activity in relation to which he is an exempt person.

The logic behind this exemption is clearly to align the financial promotion regime with that applicable to regulated activities. However, for professional firms who might seek to claim the benefit of Article 16 precisely because their main business is exempt, it raises a number of difficulties:

- professional firms are unlikely to issue promotions which relate solely to their non-mainstream business and a promotion which is made for the purposes of some other business does not seem to be within the scope of the exemption;

- a professional firm which did issue a promotion relating solely to its exempt business might find it difficult to argue that this had not become mainstream business for which authorisation was, after all, required. Indeed, the Treasury said that it would be "questionable whether promotions of exempt regulated activities could be reconciled with the requirement that they be incidental or ancillary to the provisions of professional services".[16]

The Treasury subsequently confirmed that it did not intend professional firms to benefit from the exempt persons exemption and suggested that professional firms should be able to make use of other generally available exemptions, such as the new "one-off communications" exemption for promotions conducted by them in the course of their business.

The Government was initially resistant to the idea of including any specific exemptions for promotions by professional firms but did ultimately make some concessions on this point by including in the Financial Promotion Order and in the Second Financial Promotion Order exemptions for communications by members of the professions, which are specifically linked to section 327 of the FSMA and it is these, rather than the exempt persons exemption, which are more likely to be of potential use to such firms. However, the position of professional firms and their ability in practice to take advantage of exempt status under the new regime has been the subject of some controversy. This, along with the professional firm exemptions, is considered further below.

---

[16] See the Treasury's *Third Consultation Document*, para. 2.33.

Communications from customers and potential customers

6.23 Article 13 was included in the Financial Promotion Order at a late stage in response to concerns that the wording of the section 21(1) financial promotion restriction would actually prohibit unapproved requests for information *from* actual or potential business investors made *to* product or service providers.

It disapplies the financial promotion restriction where the communication is made by or on behalf of a customer "to one other person ("supplier")" to obtain information about controlled investments or controlled services (*i.e.* a service consisting of engaging in a controlled activity) available from the supplier.

It is not clear why the exemption applies only where the communication is made to one other person. On the face of it, this would seem to keep outside the ambit of the exemption a situation in which a potential investor contacts a number of different product or service suppliers to try and ascertain the best terms for an investment before proceeding. That cannot have been the intention and it is submitted that the exemption should be viewed as applying on each separate occasion to a series of communications constituting requests for such information.

Introductions

6.24 The exemption contained in Article 15 was originally intended to mirror very closely the corresponding exclusion from the scope of the Regulated Activities Order.[17] However, its scope was narrowed somewhat during the consultation process for the Financial Promotion Order. In its final form, it is restricted in its application to real time communications made with a view to or for the purposes of introducing the recipient to either an authorised or exempt person. Such communications will be exempt only if the following criteria are satisfied:

- the person making the communication is not a close relative of or in the same group as the person to whom the introduction is made;

- the introducer receives no "pecuniary reward or other advantage" from anyone other than the recipient of the communication; and

- it is clear in all the circumstances either that the recipient has not sought advice from the introducer as to the merits of engaging in investment activity or that, if he has, the introducer has declined to give it but has recommended that the recipient seek advice from an authorised person.

Article 15(2)(c) uses the expression "client", in place of "recipient" in one place; this is indicative of the Treasury's view that professional firms, such as solicitors and accountants, were likely to find this exemption particularly useful, given that they could now avoid the need to be authorised under the FSMA for their incidental financial services activities. In practice, it adds little to the professional firms' armoury of exemptions which is not already available under the "communications by members of the professions" exemptions considered below.

---

[17] See the Regulated Activities Order, Art. 29.

One Off Communications

6.25   Article 28 of the Financial Promotion Order contains a new exemption applicable to all one off non-real time communications and to solicited real time communications. Article 28(3) sets out the conditions which must be satisfied before the communication will be regarded as "one off". These are that:

- the communication is made only to one recipient (or group of recipients in the expectation that they would jointly engage in investment activity);

- the identity of the product or service to which the communication relates has been determined having regard to the particular circumstances of the recipient; and

- the communication is not part of an organised marketing campaign.

The exemption was introduced in response to concerns that, notwithstanding the introduction of the words "invitation or inducement" in section 21(1) of the FSMA, the concept of a communication would still catch tailored communications to individuals made in the course of a business, which would not previously have been classed as "advertisements" for the purposes of section 57 of the 1986 Act. The Treasury clearly accepted that the exemption might be used more than once in relation to the same recipient so long as all the conditions of the exemption were satisfied.[18] There was some criticism of the use of the expression "co-ordinated promotional strategy" in an earlier draft of the Order, which lead to its replacement by the term "organised marketing campaign" in the final version of the Order. There is no definition of this expression. However, its relevance must be questionable anyway; if the communication can only be made to one recipient or group of recipients, it is arguable that this of itself precludes anything resembling an "organised marketing campaign" from ever being effected.

The exclusion from the ambit of this exemption of all unsolicited real time communications prompted some criticism, not least from professional firms, who saw themselves being unable to take advantage of the Article 28 exemption when telephoning a potential purchase of or investor in a business, for example at their client's request. As a result, the Treasury introduced an additional exemption in the Second Financial Promotion Order (as a new Article 28A to the first) specifically covering one-off unsolicited real time communications.

The exemption will apply if the communication meets the "one-off" requirements of Article 28(3), if the person making it believes on reasonable grounds that the recipient understands the risk associated with engaging in the activity to which the communication relates *and* the communicator has reasonable grounds for believing that the point in time in which the communication is made, that the recipeient would be expected to be contacted by him. A similarly worded exemption was introduced in the Second Financial Promotion Order in relation to collective investment schemes.

This still leaves professional firms opting not to apply for a FSMA authorisation with some difficulty, in that they will have to form a value judgment (and be

---

[18] See the Treasury's *Third Consultation Document*, para. 2.21.

exposed if it is wrong) as to whether someone who is not their client is likely to have sufficient understanding of the risks associated with the particular investment activity to allow the exemption to apply.

Overseas Communicators

6.26 Since solicited calls have now been brought within the ambit of the section 21(1) financial promotion restriction, it was necessary (to preserve the regulatory status quo) to introduce a specific exemption for solicited real time communications made by an "overseas communicator" from outside the United Kingdom for the purposes of his non-U.K. investment business. This exemption appears in Article 30 of the Financial Promotion Order.

Article 32, dealing with non-real time communications to previously overseas customers, derives from Article 10 of the Financial Services Act 1986 (Investment Advertisements) (Exemptions) Order 1996. Articles 32 and 33 (which respectively cover unsolicited real time communications to previously overseas customers and unsolicited real time communications to knowledgeable customers, in each case by overseas communicators) have their origins in regulations 1 and 4 of the CUCRs.

Qualifying Credit to Bodies Corporate

6.27 In order to preserve for "qualifying credit" the current position under the Consumer Credit Act 1974 in relation to mortgage advertising, Article 46 of the Financial Promotion Order exempts from the section 21(1) financial promotion restriction those promotions relating to qualifying credit which are either:

- made to or directed at bodies corporate only; or

- accompanied by an indication that the qualifying credit to which they relate is only available to bodies corporate.

In practice, this exemption is likely to be just as insignificant for the general run of mortgage advertising (which is heavily slanted towards the retail market) as the equivalent Consumer Credit Act 1974 provisions.

This is the only exemption provided specifically in relation to the advertising of qualifying credit. This means that all detailed promotions of qualifying credit are likely, by and large, to be issued only in accordance with the FSA's COB Rules, either because they are being issued by an authorised person (the lender or an FSMA authorised intermediary) or because they must first be approved by an authorised person for a non-FSMA authorised intermediary.

There is, however, one exemption from the financial promotion restriction, which is likely to be of significance to non-authorised mortgage intermediaries and that is the generic promotions exemption contained in Article 17. This would allow a mortgage broker, who wished merely to publicise his expertise in arranging mortgages but without naming any specific mortgage provider, to do so without having to have the promotion approved by an authorised person. However, reference to specific mortgage deals available from particular lenders, will bring with it a requirement for the promotion to be approved, potentially by all the lenders referred to, if each refuses to accept responsibility for approving references to the others' products.

Although a promotion which makes no reference to a particular mortgage provider, should fall within the Article 17 generic promotion exemption, the position is less clear where no mortgage provider is mentioned but the promotion refers to a specific product only available from a particular lender. Could the promotion be said to have identified a lender indirectly, thus taking it outside the ambit of the exemption? In all likelihood, the answer will be that it has. Contrast this with a promotion in which several different mortgage rates are quoted, each of which may be available from a number of different lenders (it being impossible to tell whom from the promotion itself). It is submitted that the exemption should still apply, on the basis that no product provider can be identified from the promotion.

A mortgage promotion for which an exemption is available under the Financial Promotion Order may nevertheless fall within the ambit of the Consumer Credit Act 1974. The Government's intention was to create no overlap between the control of promotion regimes contained in the two pieces of legislation (unless a particular product has features of both qualifying and other credit) but to ensure that all currently regulated mortgage marketing continues to be covered by one or other set of provisions.

At the time of writing, the FSA's consultation process on mortgage regulation had not concluded. However, indications were that the FSA's COB Rules:

- would not seek to prevent mortgage intermediaries with an FSMA authorisation from approving their own mortgage advertisements (which had been suggested as a possible means of creating a level playing field between authorised and unauthorised intermediaries);

- would allow an authorised person not actually conducting regulated mortgage business to approve mortgage advertisements as a service to others, provided suitably qualified staff were employed; and

- would impose content requirements (and, in some instances, form and content requirements) for the promotion of qualifying credit, which would be less complex than those currently applied by the Consumer Credit Act 1974.

High Net Worth Individuals

6.28   In keeping with the Government's wish to avoid unnecessary impediments to raising finance for industry, Article 48 of the Financial Promotion Order introduces a new exemption for unapproved promotions to certain individuals not felt to require the full complement of investor protection measures (one of the categories of "business angel" specifically targeted by new exemptions).

The exemption does not apply to unsolicited real time communications but, in relation to other methods of promotion, allows them to be made to "a certified high net worth individual" where they do not invite or induce the recipient to engage in investment activity with the person who signed the certificate of net worth. The exemption is also restricted to the promotion of certain types of investments, listed in Article 48(5). These are essentially stocks or shares in an unlisted company, instruments acknowledging the indebtedness of an unlisted company and products linked to these (such as warrants, units in a collective investment scheme, options, etc. which relate to unlisted company stocks or shares and debt instruments).

The key point about such investments is that the investor must *not*, under their terms, be made to pay more than he commits by way of investment (though there is no need for this to appear as an express term of the investment contract).

The definition of "certified high net worth individual" in Article 48(2) has two limbs, both of which must be satisfied before the exemption may be claimed. Firstly, the individual has to have a current certificate of high net worth. This means there must be something in writing "... or other legible form" (which would therefore include electronic communication), signed and dated in the period of twelve months prior to the making of the communication, stating that, in the opinion of the person signing the certificate, the individual had in the financial year immediately preceding the date of signature of the certificate either an annual income of at least £100,000 or net assets (throughout that year) of at least £250,000 (excluding the individual's primary residence or any loan secured on it, rights under a qualifying contract of insurance and pension/death in service benefits to which he may be entitled). The signature must be provided either by the individual's accountant or employer.

Secondly, the individual must himself have signed a statement in the form set out in Article 48(2)(b) within the period of twelve months ending on the date the communication is made. In the statement, the individual is required to confirm that he qualifies as a high net worth individual, that he understands the promotion may not have been approved by an authorised person and that he is aware of his option to seek advice on his investment from an authorised person if he chooses.

Finally, the communication itself must fulfil the requirements of Article 48(4). These are essentially disclosure requirements, which require the communication to confirm its exempt status, state the requirements for qualification as a certified high net worth individual, confirm the absence of approval by an authorised person, and include both a risk warning and a recommendation to seek advice, if in doubt.

Sophisticated Investors

6.29 The second of the so-called "business angel" exemptions is contained in Article 50 in respect of promotions to a "certified sophisticated investor". Its terms are similar but somewhat broader than the high net worth individual exemption. In particular, there is no restriction on the type of investment covered by the communication nor are unsolicited real time communications carved out of its terms (presumably by analogy with the CUCRs, which permitted unsolicited calls on non-private investors).

The certificate (which, again, may be in writing or other legible form) must be signed by an authorised person (other than the person with whom the investor is being invited or induced to engage in investment activity) and must confirm that the investor is "sufficiently knowledgeable to understand the risks associated with" whatever type of investment the communication relates to. The Treasury's reasoning for requiring certification by an authorised person was that the FSA would be able to ensure consistency in the treatment of different categories of investor for all purposes and, in particular, to require authorised persons to ascertain the appropriate level of sophistication for a particular investment, before providing the certificate.

There is a requirement in Article 50(1)(b) for the investor to provide a similar statement to that required for the Article 48 exemption and for the communication to be accompanied by similar disclosure requirements. Note, though, that a "current" certificate for the purposes of Article 50 is one signed and dated in the three years prior to the communication (rather than twelve months, as in Article 48).

Communications by Members of the Professions

6.30 Chapter 3 above discusses the FSMA's approach to professional firms, in particular, the exemptions from the need for authorisation which are now available to them and the fact that there is a rather complicated structure for this part of the new FSMA regime. In essence, Article 67 of the Regulated Activities Order provides an exclusion from the ambit of regulated activities in respect of certain activities which ". . . may reasonably be regarded as a necessary part of other services provided in the course of . . . " a profession or non-investment business, so long as these activities are not separately remunerated. In a concession to its original view that the FSA should regulate directly *all* firms offering investment advice and services, including professionals, the Treasury ultimately allowed a special regime for such firms where regulated activities are carried out incidentally to the provision of professional services and the provision of those professional services is supervised and regulated by a designated professional body. This regime is contained in Part XX of the FSMA and, in particular, section 327.

This somewhat piecemeal approach to professional firms carried over to the Financial Promotion Order. The Treasury's original view was that no specific exemptions for such firms would be included in the Order, pointing to the availability of general exemptions such as that applicable to one-off communications. Ultimately, however, the Treasury conceded that there was a case for allowing certain specific exemptions in relation to communications made by a professional firm carrying on a regulated activity to which the general prohibition was disapplied under section 327 of the FSMA. These appear in Articles 55 and 55A[19] of the Financial Promotion Order.

The Article 55 exemption applies to real time communication so long as the person making the communication has been engaged to provide professional services before the communication is made and so long as the controlled activity which is the subject of the communication is an excluded activity, which would be undertaken by the firm "for the purposes of, and incidental to, the provision by him of professional services to or at the request of the recipient". However, it is restricted in its application to communications to persons who could be regarded as clients, since services must be provided "to or at the request of" the person receiving the communication.

The Article 55A exemption applies to non-real time communications (solicited or unsolicited) by members of professions and allows firms to include information about their Part XX activities in an exempt communication. It prescribes the form of statement which such firms may use as follows:

---

[19] Article 55A was added by the Second Financial Promotion Order.

"This [firm/company] is not authorised under the Financial Services and Markets Act 2000 but we are able in certain circumstances to offer a limited range of investment services to clients because we are members of [relevant designated professional body]. We can provide these investment services if they are an incidental part of the professional services we have been engaged to provide".

Article 55(A)(3) does allow firms, in addition, to set out the Part XX activities which they can offer their clients.

The pressure for the inclusion of a specific exemption from the financial promotion regime for professional firms arose from respondents to the Treasury's Consultation Documents, in particular the Law Society's Company Law Committee. Absent such an exemption, the Committee foresaw difficulties for solicitors who telephoned clients without express invitation to discuss a sale of shares, for example, or who sent out documentation to the other party to a transaction. The inclusion of these exemptions addresses the problem in part but not entirely. There is still the possibility that solicitors sending e-mails or draft documents to (or telephoning) the other party to a transaction will not be able to satisfy the requirements of either of these exemptions and may still feel obliged to seek a precautionary authorisation in any event.

Perhaps the most glaring omission from the exemptions in the Financial Promotion Order is that none of them allow a professional firm to approve (as opposed to issue) a financial promotion without an FSA authorisation. This point was the subject of much adverse comment during the consultation process for the Financial Promotion Order. The activities of many professional firms in the context of investment advertisements consisted not of issuing their own but of approving them on behalf of clients in their capacity as authorised persons. Although the Regulated Activities Order and the FSMA itself now offer such firms the opportunity to avoid having to apply for an FSA authorisation simply to conduct incidental financial services business, the absence of any specific provisions in the Financial Promotion Order or elsewhere in the new regime allowing them to approve communications on behalf of others means that, in practice, many such firms may end up applying for an FSA authorisation anyway, just to be able to carry on business as before.

Follow Up Communications

6.31   Article 14 allows a person making or directing a communication, which is exempt because it is accompanied by certain indications or contains certain information, to claim an exemption for any subsequent communication if the subsequent communication satisfies the following conditions:

- it is a non-real time communication or a solicited real time communication;
- it is made by the same person who made the first communication;
- it is made to the recipient of the first communication;
- it relates to the same controlled activity and the same controlled investment as the first communication; and
- it is made within 12 months of the recipient receiving the first communication.

Deposits and Insurance

6.32 Part V of the Financial Promotion Order sets out the exemptions applicable to the promotion of deposits and insurance. The first task of Article 21 is to make it clear that the exemptions do *not* apply to a "qualifying contract of insurance" as defined in the Regulated Activities Order. Such contracts are essentially long-term insurance contracts (*i.e.* those set out in Part II of Schedule 1 to the Regulated Activities Order) subject to certain exceptions.[20] The intention behind excluding qualifying contracts of insurance from the Financial Promotion Order insurance exemptions was to ensure that the exemptions apply only to contracts of insurance which did not fall within the definition of "investments" for the purposes of the 1986 Act, thus preserving the effect of section 130 of the Insurance Companies Act 1982.

The exemptions for both deposits and insurance divide into those which are relevant to real time communications and those which are relevant to non-real time communications. Real time communications (whether solicited or not) relating to both deposit-taking and to the carrying out or effecting of non-qualifying contracts of insurance are totally exempted from the section 21(1) financial promotion restriction. What the FSMA imposes with one hand, the Financial Promotion Order therefore removes with the other.

Non-real time communications relating to both deposits and insurance are also exempt, provided certain disclosure requirements are satisfied. These requirements appear in Articles 22(2) and 24(2) respectively of the Financial Promotion Order and are limited to matters such as the identity of the deposit-taker/insurer, country of incorporation and principal place of business, name of regulator, existence of a dispute resolution or deposit guarantee scheme and extent of capitalisation. Some of these requirements will already be familiar to anyone in the banking and building society industry. For the general insurance industry, they will generally represent something of a stepping up (albeit a modest one) in disclosure requirements.

In relation to reinsurance and insurance contracts covering large risks, there is a further specific exemption in Article 25. Non-real time communications are entirely exempt from the financial promotion restrictions if they relate only to reinsurance contracts or if they relate to "large risks" insurance contracts as defined in Article 25(2).

Any unauthorised person wishing to put out an advertisement for general insurance products or deposit accounts who does not wish to satisfy the disclosure requirements contained in the Financial Promotion Order can have the material approved by an authorised person instead. Since the requirements of Article 21 are hardly onerous, it is difficult to see the attraction of this. An authorised person issuing or approving a promotion for this type of product might, however, wish to structure the advertisement in such a way as to take advantage of the exemption from the financial promotion rules contained in COB 3.2.5R.

The existence of the Article 14 exemption for follow up communications is likely to be of particular assistance in relation to deposit and insurance-related promotions which were originally within the Article 21 exemption, since these will have had to contain exactly the type of "indications" or "information" required under Article 14.

---

[20] Essentially, the exceptions are reinsurance contracts, certain life and term assurance contracts and contracts providing benefits in the event of sickness or infirmity.

Overview of other changes to exemptions

6.33 Some exemptions, which existed under the 1986 Act regime, are not reproduced in the Financial Promotion Order at all, often as a result of the structural changes introduced by the FSMA. Others appear in a slightly different form for the same reason (typically, to carve what were "unsolicited calls" out of their ambit) or to accommodate deliberate refinements frequently mirrored in the Regulated Activities Order. By way of example:

- there are no exemptions in respect of non-geared packaged products and the acquisition of investment business (previously regulations 2 and 5 of the CUCRs) nor in respect of public takeovers (regulation 6 of the CUCRs) essentially because in all cases an authorised person will now be responsible for approving or supervising the relevant promotion. The substance of the CUCRs restrictions on/permissions for unsolicited calls in this (and indeed other) respects is largely maintained in the COB Rules;

- the "investment professional" exemption previously encompassed in Article 11 of the Financial Services Act 1986 (Investment Advertisements) (Exemptions) Order 1996 still appears in Article 19 of the Financial Promotions Order but now adopts a "made to/directed at" approach similar to that adopted in relation to overseas communications (with safe harbour status for a communication in which all three of the specified conditions are met);

- the sale of a body corporate exemption previously contained in Article 5 of the Financial Services Act 1986 (Investment Advertisements) (Exemptions) (No. 2) Order 1995 now appears, in a somewhat broader form, in Article 62 of the Financial Promotion Order, in order to align it with the similar exemption in the Regulated Activities Order (this is discussed in Chapter 3, above). Article 62 applies to communications issued by (but *not*, apparently, on behalf of) a body corporate, a partnership, a single individual or a group of connected individuals in respect of a transaction which meets certain specified criteria (such as the shares the subject of the transaction comprising 50 per cent or more of the voting shares in the company—see Article 62(3)) or (if those conditions are not met) where ". . . the object of the transaction may nevertheless reasonably be regarded as being the acquisition of day to day control of the affairs of the body corporate";

- there is no longer a specific exemption for communications made by companies promoting industry, commerce or enterprise akin to that contained in Article 3 of the Financial Services Act 1986 (Investment Advertisements) (Exemptions) (No. 2) Order 1995. Such companies can now claim the benefit of an exemption from the need for authorisation under paragraph 40 of the Schedule to the Financial Services and Markets Act 2000 (Exemptions) Order 2001 and will thus be able to take advantage of the exempt persons provisions in Article 16 of the Financial Promotion Order;

- the specific exemptions for management buy-outs and buy-ins previously contained in regulation 7 of the CUCRs appear to have been effectively subsumed into Article 62 of the Financial Promotion Order dealing with the sale of a body corporate. The Article 62 exemption applies to all types of communications, whether real time, non-real time, solicited or not; and

- the exemptions contained in regulation 10 of the CUCRs for unsolicited calls in respect of contracts to manage the assets of an occupational pension scheme has not been reproduced in the new regime. The Treasury's view was that promotions of this nature would only be made in practice to investment professionals and would thus be covered by the exemption in Article 19 of the Financial Promotion Order. Again, the Article 19 exemption applies to all types of communication, whether real time, non-real time solicited or not.

Other Exemptions

6.34   Virtually all the other exemptions contained in the Financial Promotion Order have their genesis in either the 1986 Act (or the investment advertisement regulations made under it) or the CUCRs. These include exemptions for promotions made by or relating to:

- sale of goods and supply of services (Article 61);
- annual accounts and directors' report (Article 59);
- participation in employee share schemes (Article 60);
- members and creditors of certain bodies corporate (Article 43);
- group companies (Article 45);
- persons in the business of disseminating information (Article 47);
- high net worth companies (Article 49);
- governments, central banks, etc. (Article 34);
- financial markets meeting certain criteria (Article 37);
- common interest group of a company (Article 52); and
- listing particulars and public offers of unlisted securities (Articles 70–73 inclusive).

It is worth mentioning one exemption which was not ultimately included in the Financial Promotion Order, in respect of hypertext links. At one stage, the Treasury took the view that a simple (not in itself promotional) hypertext link from one website to a second, where the second contained a financial promotion, might itself be viewed as causing that financial promotion to be communicated. This would have brought the hypertext link itself within the ambit of section 21(1), with criminal consequences for the owner/operator of the first website, if the second contained an unlawful financial promotion. There was a good deal of adverse comment on this point and a number of respondents to the Treasury's Consultation Documents campaigned for retention of the hypertext link exemption.

The Treasury did not concede this point. It took the view that, with the addition of the "invitation or inducement" wording in section 21 of the FSMA, this was not necessary; either the hypertext link itself contained material constituting an invitation or inducement to engage in investment activity (in which case it would, as it deserved, be caught by section 21) or it would not (and so did not need an exemption).

Although the Treasury subsequently appeared to dispel the concerns it had raised as to possible criminal liability by suggesting that responsibility for a communication should be with the originator (in this situation, presumably the person responsible for the second website), the absence of any specific exemption in respect of hypertext links has left the position in some doubt. In practice, those wishing to establish hypertext links between their own unregulated websites and those of financial product or service providers are likely (if they cannot be sure of claiming some other exemption) to require evidence that the linked website has been approved by an authorised person for the purposes of section 21.

CONSEQUENCES OF NON-COMPLIANCE WITH SECTION 21

Criminal Offence

6.35   The criminal sanction for breach of the financial promotion restriction was referred to earlier in this Chapter. Section 25(1) makes a person who contravenes section 21(1) liable to a term of imprisonment of up to two years or a fine or both. The section 25(2) defence to a criminal charge has two limbs:

- the accused believed on reasonable grounds that the content of the communication was prepared, or approved for the purposes of section 21, by an authorised person; or

- the accused took all reasonable precautions and exercised all due diligence to avoid committing the offence.

The first limb of the defence has already been considered briefly in the context of non-authorised persons involved in creating or producing promotions, who cannot claim the mere conduit exemption in Article 18 of the Financial Promotion Order. There are evidently two separate means of establishing the first limb of the defence:

- show reasonable grounds for a belief that the content of the communication was prepared by an authorised person; or

- show reasonable grounds for a belief that the content of the communication was approved for the purposes of section 21 by an authorised person.

The second of these is entirely consistent with the wording of section 21(2), which requires the content of the communication " to be approved for the purposes of this section by an authorised person". The most reasonable grounds for a belief that such approval has been given will generally be written evidence of approval (by a suitably qualified representative of the authorised person) with a specific reference to its being given for the purposes of section 21 of the FSMA.

It is less easy to see the logic behind the "prepared by" defence. It may lie in the Treasury's view that primary responsibility for a promotion remains with the originator and unwitting intermediaries in the communication chain should not be criminally penalised if they had no substantial role to play in creating it. As noted earlier in this Chapter, it would be unwise for anyone who did perform some creative or other role in producing the communication to seek to rely on the "prepared by" defence.

The second limb of the defence mirrors the defence contained in section 23(3) of the FSMA in relation to regulated activities and a breach of the general prohibition. In practice, the best form of "reasonable precautions" and "due diligence" is, again, likely to be written evidence of approval of a promotion by an authorised person but the broader wording of this limb suggests that other factors (checking that the originator was authorised, for example) may suffice.

Unenforceability of agreements

6.36 Section 30(2) of the FSMA provides that, if a communication made in breach of the financial promotion restriction gives rise to a "controlled agreement", the agreement is unenforceable against the person entering into it "as a customer". Section 30(3) tackles the alternative situation in which a person exercises any rights conferred by a "controlled investment" as a result of an unlawful communication. No obligation to which such person is subject as a result of exercising such rights is enforceable against him.

The expression "as a customer" used in section 30(2) is not defined. It is evidently aimed at a situation in which the unlawful financial promotion is carried out by or on behalf of the other party to the controlled agreement, in other words, a person whose business is the conduct of a regulated activity. It is not clear how this would apply, for example, to a person who invests in shares in a company following an unlawful promotion by the company—would the investor be acting "as a customer" of the company?

The expression is not repeated in section 30(3), the thinking (presumably) being that the only person who may exercise any rights in relation to a "controlled investment" is the customer. The definition of "controlled investment" is linked, via sections 30(1) and 21(10), to the definitions contained in Part II of Schedule 1 to the Financial Promotion Order. "Controlled agreement" is defined as "an agreement the making or performance of which by either party is a controlled activity for the purposes of" section 21 and is thus linked via section 21(9) to the definitions contained in Part I of Schedule 1 to the Financial Promotion Order.

In addition to these rights, section 30(2) and (3) also allow the person affected by the unlawful communication to recover any money or property paid or transferred by him *and* to claim compensation for any loss sustained by him through having parted with it in the first place. Loss of interest or costs associated with the realisation of funds to invest are the obvious examples of a possible compensation claim under section 30 but there is clearly scope for others. If the parties cannot agree the amount of compensation, the court may decide for them (section 30(10)).

If a person elects not to proceed with an agreement or exercise of rights, section 30(11) and (12) require him, in turn, to repay any money or property received, so as to achieve effective restitution between the parties.

Note that it is not necessary, for the purposes of section 30(2) or (3), that the person with whom the recipient of the unlawful communication contracts or deals should be the same as the person who made the communication. Thus, if an intermediary issues a mortgage advertisement which has not been approved by an authorised person (and which cannot claim the benefit of an exemption under the Financial Promotion Order), the lender is in theory vulnerable under section 30 even though he may have had no hand in devising or issuing the offending material.

However, under section 30(4), the court is given power to allow enforcement of the relevant agreement or obligation (or retention of money or property paid or transferred) where it is satisfied that it is just and equitable in all the circumstances of the case. Section 30(5) specifically requires the court to take certain factors into account when deciding whether to exercise its discretion under section 30(4). These are:

- where the person seeking to enforce the contract or obligation is also the person who made the unlawful communication, whether he "reasonably believed that he was not making such a communication" (section 30(6)); or

- where the person seeking to enforce is different from the person making the unlawful communication, ". . . whether he knew the agreement was entered into in consequence of such a communication" (section 30(7)).

Under section 30(6), the issue appears to be whether there are grounds upon which the person making the communication could argue that he believed on reasonable grounds that it was lawful. In practice, the factors relevant here must be similar to those which would be taken into account in any criminal proceedings brought against him.

Under section 30(7), there appear to be two separate issues:

- whether the person seeking enforcement knew the communication was unlawful; and

- whether he knew the agreement or dealing was being entered into as a result of it.

Knowledge of the unlawful nature of the communication is apparently a subjective test. The wording of section 30(7) does *not* say, for example, "ought on reasonable grounds to have known". Thus, even proving that a copy of the offending communication was at some stage in the possession of the person seeking enforcement would not necessarily be sufficient to establish that he "knew" of its unlawful nature.

Furthermore, it will frequently be the case that communications are issued in the press, on television or in other circumstances where it is difficult, if not impossible, to establish any real causal link between the promotion and the end contract or dealing, such as would be required by the "in consequence" aspect of section 30(7).

Neither section 30(6) or 30(7) is expressed to be decisive, such that the court must allow enforcement or retention if the applicant for enforcement can show that he had the requisite reasonable belief or lacked the relevant knowledge (or, conversely, that the court is automatically precluded from making an enforcement or retention order where these conditions are not met). However, these subsections were evidently meant as clear indications to the court and it is difficult to envisage them not being extremely persuasive in practice. It should not, in practice, be an onerous task for the lender in the earlier example to take advantage of section 30(7), particularly if he has effectively negated the effect of the unlawful communication by conducting full and accurate pre-sale disclosure in relation to the credit provided.

The wording of section 30(2) may well render section 30 generally of less use to the recipients of unlawful communications than first appears. Section 30(2) says that the relevant agreement or obligation will be "unenforceable" against the customer but leaves open what is meant by "enforcement". In other contexts (notably under the Consumer Credit Act 1974), the same issue has given rise to considerable debate. It seems likely that merely continuing to correspond with the customer and even to collect regular payments from him, if that is what the contract requires, would not *per se* amount to "enforcement" but that issuing proceedings (or a letter before action) would. Whilst the latter action may turn out to prove necessary for the recovery of monies under, say, a regulated mortgage contract, it does not feature greatly in the sphere of investments, deposits or insurance contracts.

If that is so, then in most cases the customer will in practice, have to be aware both that he has received an unlawful communication and that he can refuse to proceed with an agreement or obligation arising in consequence of it, before section 30 will be of any real relevance. Even then, it looks as if the burden of proof will be on the recipient of the communication to establish that the agreement or dealing arose "in consequence" of the unlawful communication.

It is interesting to note that the "carve out" from the unenforceability provisions in respect of deposit-taking, which appears in section 26(4) of the FSMA in relation to agreements entered into in breach of the general prohibition, does not appear in section 30. If the rationale for including special provisions in section 26 in respect of deposit-taking is that the customer has a contractual right to recover his money anyway and that a requirement to perform the agreement is actually of more benefit to the customer (since he will then often be entitled to insist on payment of interest at the contractual rate as well as the return of his deposit), it is difficult to see why similar provisions were not built into section 30.

Other enforcement issues

6.37   The FSA and the Secretary of State are each given a general power under section 380(1) of the FSMA to seek a restraining order from the court if the court is satisfied that:

- there is a reasonable likelihood that any person will contravene a "relevant requirement"; or

- there has been a contravention of a relevant requirement and there is a reasonable likelihood of its continuation or repetition.

Subsections (2) and (3) confer similar powers to apply to the court for an order requiring a person to take steps to remedy contravention of a relevant requirement or an order restraining dealings with assets following contravention of a relevant requirement.

"Relevant requirement" is defined in section 380(6) as (*inter alia*) a requirement imposed by the FSMA. The financial promotion restriction in section 21(1) probably counts as a requirement (although, strictly speaking, it is a restriction, rather than an obligation to take any positive action).

Section 382 contains similar powers for the court, on the application of the FSA or the Secretary of State, to make restitution orders where a relevant requirement has been breached.

CHAPTER 7

The Official Listing of Securities

WILLIAM CHALK

INTRODUCTION

7.01   Part VI of the Act supersedes the legal and regulatory regime relating to the official listing of securities laid down by Part IV of the Financial Services Act 1986 (the "1986 Act"). In order to understand how the Act governs the listing and trading of securities in the United Kingdom, it is necessary to understand how the legal and regulatory regime worked prior to the Act coming into force. To complete the picture, it is also necessary to understand how the changes that took place on May 1, 2000 in relation to the London Stock Exchange ("LSE"), precipitated by its demutualisation and the consequential transfer of the United Kingdom Listing Authority (the "UKLA") function to the Financial Services Authority (the "FSA"), have affected the role of the UKLA or "Competent Authority".

THE HISTORIC POSITION

7.02   The statutory basis for the regulation of the offering of securities in the United Kingdom was originally found in the Companies Act 1985,[1] the rules made by the Competent Authority from time to time (the "Listing Rules") and the 1984 Listing Regulations (the "Listing Regulations").[2] In addition, any proposed listing of securities required the issuing company to enter into an agreement with the LSE[3] and to disclose certain information to the market pursuant to that agreement, over and above the minimum requirements of the Companies Act 1985. The Listing Regulations were replaced by Part IV of the 1986 Act which itself only applied to investments set out in Schedule 1 to the 1986 Act.

The regime was modified further as a consequence of the introduction of the minimum requirements for the listing of securities contained in three European Directives: the Admissions Directive, the Listing Particulars Directive and the Interim Reports Directive (the "Directives").[4] The Directives ultimately found their

---

[1] Companies Act 1985, Pt III. This was subsequently repealed variously by the 1986 Act and the POS Regulation (as defined below).
[2] The Stock Exchange (Listing) Regulations 1984, (S.I. 1989 No. 716).
[3] The signing of this agreement also meant that the issuing company had to comply with the continuing obligations of the LSE.
[4] Admissions Directive 1979/279/EEC—this established the minimum conditions that all securities must meet before admission to the official list on any stock exchange within a Member State can take

way into United Kingdom law in Part IV of the 1986 Act, which addressed three central issues: the marketing of securities, the framework for the listing of securities and the restrictions placed on the investments for which an exchange may operate as a market. Part IV of the 1986 Act also appointed the LSE as the Competent Authority for listing in the United Kingdom.[5] The basic principle underpinning the production of offering documentation at this time was that persons responsible had to ensure that any document contained all such information as investors and their professional advisers would reasonably require[6] irrespective of whether specific disclosure was required under the Listing Rules.

The Public Offers of Securities Regulations[7] (the "POS Regulations") implemented the Public Offers Directive and in doing so amended Part IV of the 1986 Act in relation to the admission of securities to the list maintained as the official list by the UKLA (the "Official List").[8] To the extent that there was a public element to an offer, the POS Regulations clarified when an issuing company would be required to produce a prospectus.[9] If there was no public element to the offer, the 1986 Act and the Listing Rules still required listing particulars to be produced in relation to the admission of securities to the Official List.[10] When deciding whether listing particulars or a prospectus was required, the starting point was to ascertain whether or not there was an offer to the public. The POS Regulations introduced Schedule 11A of the 1986 Act which defined what constituted an "offer to the public" for the purposes of listed securities. This has not changed materially under the Act; Schedule 11A of the 1986 Act is carried forward by Schedule 11 to the Act.[11]

The POS Regulations also introduced a regime governing the issue of securities to the public in the United Kingdom which were not to be admitted to the Official List under Part IV of the 1986 Act, in other words "unlisted securities". Subject to certain restrictions and exemptions, such offers require the production of a prospectus in accordance with the POS Regulations. In addition, the LSE has stipulated that any such securities brought to trading on the Alternative Investment

---

place and includes conditions relating to the status of an issuer and its shares (including their negotiability) and the size of companies; Listing Particulars Directive 1980/390/EEC—this co-ordinates the requirements for the drafting, scrutiny and distribution of listing particulars and makes the admission of securities to the official list on a stock exchange within a Member State conditional on the publication of "listing particulars" which must "enable investors and their advisers to make an informed assessment of the assets and liabilities, financial position, profits and losses and prospects of the issuer and of rights attaching to securities" (Art. 4(1)); Interim Reports Directive 1982/121/EEC—this requires companies admitted to the official list to publish certain information on a regular basis including yearly and half yearly reports. These Directives have now been consolidated into Directive 2001/34/EC which came into force on July 26, 2001 but did not make any substantive amendment to the Directives themselves.

[5] 1986 Act, s. 142(6).

[6] 1986 Act, s. 146.

[7] Public Offers of Securities Regulations 1995 (S.I. 1995 No. 1537) as amended by the POS (Amendment) Regulations 1999 (S.I. 1999 No. 734). These regulations are in Pt V of the 1986 Act (POS Regulations, Sched. 2, Pt II, para. 4) and Pt III of the Companies Act 1985.

[8] Public Offers Directive 1989/298/EEC—this sets out the requirements for the issue of prospectuses for the initial public offerings of securities which are not already listed on a stock exchange of a Member State.

[9] See POS Regulations, Pt I, para. 3(1).

[10] See Para. 7.07, below as to the exceptions to this general principle.

[11] Sched. 11 FSMA partly implements provisions of Council Directive 89/298/EEC on the publication of a prospectus when transferable securities are offered to the public. Sched. 11 has been subsequently amended by the Public Offers of Securities (Exemptions) Regulations 2001 (S.I. 2001 No. 2955). See para. 7.14 below.

Market ("AIM") (even if securities of the same class had been issued to the public previously) would also require, subject to certain exemptions, a document containing equivalent information to a prospectus, whether or not there was a public element to the offer (an "admission document"). (For the impact of the Act on the unlisted securities regime in the United Kingdom, see paragraph 7.25, below).

As Competent Authority, the LSE was responsible not only for supervising the running of its own markets but also for supervising admission of securities to the Official List in accordance with the minimum standards laid down in the Directives and statute, chiefly the 1986 Act, and as set out in the Listing Rules themselves. In addition, the LSE (in particular, the Council of the LSE) was empowered to codify and apply its own rules for listing going beyond the minimum standards. This means that the Listing Rules have developed as a combination of established and codified market and accounting procedure and practice as well as being based on statute. They impose additional and more stringent standards and conditions on issuers of securities than the minimum requirements of the Directives and reflect a view of appropriate standards that have developed over time.[12]

As discussed, until relatively recently, the LSE was not just an RIE authorised for the purposes of Part I of the 1986 Act to run an investment exchange trading in securities in the United Kingdom; it was also the Competent Authority[13] for admitting securities to the Official List.[14] In comparison to the regimes in force in other major financial centres around the world this was somewhat anomalous; the LSE's role as a regulator, on the one hand, charged as it was by the Treasury to ensure that the securities being granted Official List status were of the requisite quality, potentially conflicting with the LSE's desire, on the other, to maximise the number of companies on the market from which it derives its revenues.

THE POSITION NOW

7.03 On May 1, 2000, the function of competent authority for admission and listing of securities to the Official List was transferred from the LSE to the FSA.[15] The change was made as a consequence of the LSE's announcement that it was to demutualise and turn itself into a public company and the fact that the LSE and the Treasury felt that, as a result, it would no longer be appropriate for the LSE to continue to exercise the Competent Authority function.[16]

In replacing Part IV of the 1986 Act, the further changes implemented by the Act would certainly not have been nearly so wide reaching were it not for this transfer of Competent Authority function; the FSA and the Treasury saw the coincidence

---

[12] The Listing Rules should not be confused with the Rules of the London Stock Exchange (the "Rules") which deal with the rules of admittance and conduct of member firms dealing in securities on the LSE's markets, nor with *AIM's: Rules for Companies* which regulate the admission of securities and continuing obligations of issuers admitted to AIM. The latter used to be incorporated as Chapter 16 of the Rules but are now found in a "stand alone" document.

[13] 1986 Act, s. 142(6).

[14] 1986 Act, s. 142(1).

[15] The Official Listing of Securities (Change of Competent Authority) Regulations 2000 (S.I. 2000 No. 968).

[16] For a full discussion of investment exchanges and demutualisation, see IOSCO Technical Committee, *Consultation Draft: Discussion Paper on Stock Exchange Demutualisation* (December 2000).

of the demutualisation and the introduction of the Act as an opportunity to review the approach to listing of securities in the United Kingdom.

The changing role of the UKLA

7.04   The role of Competent Authority transferred from the LSE to the FSA pursuant to the Official Listing of Securities (Change of Competent Authority) Regulations 2000.[17]

The Competent Authority's role has not changed to any great extent following the implementation of the Act or pursuant to the role being assumed by the FSA. It is still responsible for setting minimum standards for listing and the continuing obligations to be observed by listed companies. It also continues to be responsible for the enforcement of all continuing obligations, including monitoring the dissemination of price sensitive information, approving documentation issued by listed companies,[18] providing guidance on and investigating breaches of the Listing Rules, suspending and removing companies from the Official List, regulating sponsors and ensuring that the Listing Rules keep pace with market developments, thus ensuring that they, and it, remain competitive both in the domestic and the global market. However, the implementation of the Act has meant that its powers have expanded to include, for example, the imposition of financial penalties on individuals as well as issuers (in addition to the power of censure) and wider powers of investigation of breaches of the Listing Rules and contraventions of certain provisions of Part VI of the Act.

"Admission to Listing" and "Admission to Trading"

7.05   The transfer of the Competent Authority function to the FSA has served to highlight the once semantic difference between the "admission to listing" of securities and the "admission to trading" of those securities. Admission to listing reflects the process of being listed in accordance with the relevant minimum standards laid down by the Directives and United Kingdom legislation. This ensures that minimum standards are in place for investor protection and that the mutual recognition of listing particulars and prospectuses across the EEA can take place. Issuers that meet these minimum standards, as well as any additional standards that the designated competent authority in a Member State may impose (and as enshrined in the United Kingdom in the Listing Rules), are admitted to the "Official List". Post transfer, the FSA, acting in its capacity as the UKLA, is responsible for admitting securities to listing.

The LSE retains separate responsibility for the admission of securities to trading on its own markets with the result that being "listed on the LSE" does not mean the same thing as being "on the Official List".

The split has arguably opened the way for other primary investment exchanges to enter the United Kingdom market and to set their own standards for admission to trading, provide greater choice and, possibly, ease of listing for issuers of securities as competition between such exchanges intensifies. This manifested itself in

---

[17] S.I. 2000 No. 968.
[18] The Competent Authority does not itself investigate or verify the accuracy or completeness of the information in such documents nor does it check the sources of, or verify, the information.

the changes made to the Listing Rules immediately after the transfer of the Competent Authority function to the FSA and, in particular, in the new general reference to RIEs.[19]

In turn, the FSA has recognised that its requirements in relation to admission to listing must continue to guarantee the minimum acceptable standards for securities in the event of an RIE deciding not to require adherence to any additional admission to trading rules (for example, not implementing an equivalent of the LSE's Admission and Disclosure Standards (the "Standards")). However, the FSA has also committed itself to conducting a "root and branch" review of the Listing Rules, precipitated not only by the transfer of the Competent Authority function to it but also by the consolidation of stock exchanges in global financial centres. It has yet to indicate a timetable for this review and the ensuing consultation process.

The impact of the Act on the Competent Authority function

7.06 The Act sets out the general functions of the UKLA as Competent Authority.[20] These include making rules (being the Listing Rules), giving general guidance and determining the general policy and principles by reference to which it performs particular functions under Part VI of the Act. In addition, the Competent Authority is specifically charged with determining which securities should be admitted to listing and, where relevant, which listings should be cancelled or suspended. As regards the overall principles of regulation introduced by the Act, the FSA, as Competent Authority, is not governed by the four statutory objectives (dealt with in more detail in Chapter 2, above). It must, however, have regard to six of the seven principles repeated in relation to Part VI of the Act in section 73,[21] albeit that these have been modified to a minor extent and do not mirror exactly the main "restraining principles" which set out the parameters and goals of the FSA's regulatory existence.[22] Further, section 155 of the Act requires the FSA, in making rules as Competent Authority, to publish proposed rules together with an explanation of proposed amendments, their compatibility with the general principles in section 73(1) and a cost benefit analysis of the proposed rules.

To ensure that competition considerations are given sufficient weight in formulating rules and practices that may be applied to regulated firms (dealt with in more detail in Chapter 10, below), the Treasury may by order require a person

---

[19] Only minor changes to the Listing Rules were made immediately after the transfer of the Competent Authority function from the LSE to the FSA. The amendments made were only those deemed necessary to reflect this transfer, including splitting the concepts of "admission to trading" and "admission to listing". Further, for securities to be admitted to listing, they must have also been admitted to trading (Listing Rules, para. 3.14A). As a continuing obligation, issuers are also required to notify the Competent Authority if they request an RIE to cancel or suspend any listed securities or if they are informed by an RIE that their listed securities will be cancelled or suspended from trading.

[20] s. 72(3) gives the Treasury power to transfer these functions to another body/person in accordance with the provisions of Sched. 8 of the Act. Such a transfer may be effected if, *inter alia*, the FSA agrees in writing or if the Treasury believes that performance of the transferred functions would be significantly improved by the transfer. The application of the Act to the Competent Authority is modified by Sched. 7 to the Act itself, in relation to the general functions of the Competent Authority, its duty to consult in making statements of policy, the imposition of penalties and the levying of fees.

[21] These criteria include the principle that the benefit of regulation should not be disproportionate to the burden as well as requiring the Competent Authority to be aware of the international nature of capital markets and the desirability of maintaining the competitive position of the U.K.

[22] FSMA, s. 2(3).

to keep under review the regulating provisions[23] (*i.e.* the Listing Rules and any guidance) and practices[24] (in exercising its functions) of the Competent Authority to ensure that they do not have a significantly adverse effect on competition or require or encourage exploitation of the strength of a market position.[25] It is likely that the "person" who is charged with this responsibility will be the DGFT and the corresponding provisions under Part X, Chapter III and Part XVIII, Chapter II of the Act (though not limited to these) will equally apply to the regulating provisions and practices of the Competent Authority.

The Act also sets out in far more detail than the 1986 Act the way in which the FSA, as Competent Authority, may cover its costs by levying fees on issuers and sponsors alike both on an initial and an on-going basis.[26] In fixing the level of these fees, the Competent Authority may not, however, take into account any sums which it receives, or expects to receive, by way of any financial penalties it has imposed (see paragraph 7.20 below).[27]

The impact of the Act on the listing regime[28]

7.07   The Act provides that the Competent Authority may admit "such securities and other instruments that it considers appropriate"[29] to the Official List. This represents an important change between the Act and the former regime. Part IV of the 1986 Act only applied to certain types of security,[30] although the Competent Authority admitted to listing securities falling outside the scope of Part IV on a non-statutory basis ("non-Part IV securities"),[31] which could generally be categorised as those securities which fell outside the Listing Particular's Directive.[32] Non-Part IV securities were brought to listing by issuing an "equivalent offering document" as opposed to listing particulars or a prospectus, meaning, in turn, that such securities were not subject to the general duty of disclosure,[33] provisions relating to compensation for false or misleading particulars nor those relating to responsibility for particulars.[34]

In essence, therefore, section 74 of the Act means that non-Part IV securities will now be listed on a statutory basis and, as Part VI will apply to any such listing, will mean that certain securities (for example, those listed in accordance with Chapter 24 of the Listing Rules) will now require listing particulars or a prospectus to be

---

[23] FSMA, s. 95(1)(a).
[24] FSMA, s. 95(1)(b).
[25] As to when regulating provisions and practices have a "significantly adverse effect on competition", see FSMA, s. 95(6).
[26] FSMA, s. 99 as compared with the 1986 Act, s. 155. The Act also allows the UKLA, in determining the level of these fees, not just to cover its costs but also to provide for the maintenance of adequate reserves and repay any sums borrowed or otherwise outstanding and incurred in connection with its assumption of the Competent Authority role.
[27] FSMA, s. 99(3).
[28] See also para. 7.14 below.
[29] FSMA, s. 74(2). The Treasury may veto, by order, the admission to listing of certain securities and/or instruments; see FSMA, s. 74(3)(b).
[30] 1986 Act, Sched. 1.
[31] Non-Part IV securities included securities listed in accordance with Chapter 24 of the Listing Rules, securities issued by a state or its regional or local authorities and certain securities issued by open-ended investment trusts.
[32] The exception to this would be securities listed in accordance with Chapter 24 of the Listing Rules.
[33] 1986 Act, s. 146.
[34] 1986 Act, ss. 150–152 and see paras 7.14 and 7.20 below.

published in order to bring them to the list. Such securities will, therefore, be subject to the full provisions of Part VI, including the general duty of disclosure.

However, section 79(1)(b) of the Act grants the Competent Authority a discretion to allow issuers of certain securities to continue to list securities by way of equivalent offering document and the UKLA has proposed that this continue to be the case for specified securities which do *not* fall within the ambit of the Listing Particulars Directive.[35]

The Transitional Provisions Order[36]

7.08 The Act already contains certain transitional provisions to ensure that any securities that have been admitted to the Official List prior to the Act coming into force will continue to be Officially Listed thereafter.[37] The Transitional Provisions Order lays down further transitional provisions and ensures that applications for listing made prior to the commencement of the Act, whether under Part IV of the 1986 Act or in relation to non-Part IV securities, are treated as applications for listing under the Act.[38] In addition, listing particulars and/or prospectuses published before N2 are deemed subject to the requirements of the Act relating to the obligation to publish supplementary details of subsequent changes to information disclosed and the obligation to pay compensation for loss arising from misleading particulars.[39]

The Transitional Provisions Order also provides that where an issuer, sponsor and/or director of an issuer was the subject of disciplinary action before commencement of the Act due to a contravention of the Listing Rules, the FSA is empowered to act against such sponsor, issuer and/or director in accordance with the relevant provisions of the FSMA after its commencement. If a case has reached a subsequent appeal stage under the Listing Rules, the existing appeal body is empowered to continue to hear the appeal. However, this is subject to provisions which control the way in which the case is considered and any decisions made, including the fact that no financial penalty may be imposed (as otherwise would be the case after the commencement of the Act).[40] In short, where a referral or appeal is pending or a right to appeal exists, that referral or appeal will be dealt with under the old regime up to the point at which a determination is made. Thereafter, the relevant procedures of the FSMA apply (including the "decision notice" regime—see paragraph 7.20 below) and continue to do so for the remainder of the disciplinary process.

The Listing Rules themselves continue in full force and effect pursuant to the Transitional Provisions Order and will be subject to further amendment pursuant

---

[35] FSA, *Consultation Paper 100: Proposed changes to the Listing Rules at N2* (June 2001) states that this exemption is likely to extend only to securities issued by a state or its regional or local authorities in accordance with Chap. 22 of the Listing Rules and securities issued by issuers as open-ended investment companies and authorised unit trust schemes listed in accordance with Chap. 21 of the Listing Rules.

[36] The Financial Services and Markets Act 2000 (Official Listing of Securities) (Transitional Provisions) Order 2001 (S.I. 2001 No. 2957. The "Transitional Provisions Order".).

[37] See FSMA, s. 74.

[38] See Art. 4 Transitional Provisions Order. Indeed, many of the transitional provisions reflect the fact that, whilst the 1986 Act (s. 142(a)) permitted securities to be admitted to the Official List either in accordance with Part IV of the 1986 Act or else outside the statutory provisions (*i.e.* non-Part IV securities), the FSMA brings all Official Listing within Part VI.

[39] See Arts 6–7 Transitional Provisions Order.

[40] See Arts 10–13 Transitional Provisions Order. See also *Consultation Paper 100*, Chapter 7 for a more detailed discussion of these transitional provisions and their application to disciplinary matters.

to FSA, *Consultation Paper* 100. The proposed amendments are largely conse-quential on the relevant provisions of the Act and, to the extent they are adopted, will result in substantial changes to Chapters 1 and 2 of the Listing Rules to take account of the significant alterations to decision-making and enforcement processes and to reflect the transfer of the sponsor regulation regime from a con-tractual to a statutory basis respectively (see paragraphs 7.19 and 7.20 below). In order for the timetable to be achieved and for the proposed amendments to be effective at N2, the rule making powers of the FSA, as Competent Authority, have already been brought into effect pursuant to various commencement orders.[41]

The UKLA has also used the introduction of the Act as an opportunity to pro-duce a draft guidance manual ("Guidance Manual")[42] which incorporates guid-ance in respect of the new powers and procedures contained in the Act, including the changes to the sponsor regime, the interrelationship of the Listing Rules with the market abuse regime and the power to fine directors and former directors for breaches of the Listing Rules. It formalises certain existing procedures and includes the UKLA's existing guidance notes, including the UKLA's newly revised guidance on the dissemination of price-sensitive information. The Guidance Manual also includes references to other regulatory process manuals to highlight certain pow-ers available to the FSA when it acts in a capacity other than as the Competent Authority, for example the "Enforcement Manual" the FSA proposes to use in rela-tion to the market abuse regime.[43]

The guidance given is not an exhaustive statement of an issuer's, sponsor's or director's obligations. However, to the extent that a person acts in accordance with guidance in the circumstances contemplated by that guidance, the UKLA will pro-ceed on the basis that the rule or requirement to which the guidance relates has been complied with.[44]

The LSE's Admission and Disclosure Standards

7.09 As a result of there being two separate regimes, one for the admission of securities to listing and one for their admission to trading, a company seeking to have its securities "officially listed on a stock exchange" now has to apply to the Competent Authority for its securities to be admitted to the Official List in accor-dance with the Listing Rules, as well as to the LSE for its securities to be admitted to trading in accordance with the Standards.

As an essential part of this regime, it is a condition of an application to be admitted to the Official List (and one of the principal changes in the Listing Rules flowing from the transfer of the Competent Authority function) that the securities for which the application is being made must be admitted to trading on an RIE.[45] It is also a continuing obligation that an issuer's securities must

---

[41] See the Financial Services and Markets Act 2000 (Commencement No.1) Order (S.I. 2001 No. 516) made on February 25, 2001 and the Financial Services and Markets Act 2000 (Commencement No. 3) Order (S.I. 2001 No. 1820) made on May 9, 2001.
[42] See FSA, *Consultation Paper 100a*. At the time of writing this the Guidance Manual was still the subject of consultation.
[43] See also Guidance Manual, Chapter 12.
[44] Other bodies have prosecuting powers under the Act and will not be bound by guidance in the Guidance Manual.
[45] Listing Rules, para. 3.14A. A copy of the application for admission to trading must also be submitted to the Competent Authority with all other "48-hour" documents (Listing Rules, para. 7.5(l)).

continue to be admitted to trading at all times[46] and, further, that an issuer must inform the Competent Authority of certain matters in relation to the trading of its securities, for example, if trading is about to be suspended.[47] Ultimately, the Competent Authority will cancel the listing of any security no longer admitted to trading on an RIE.[48]

The Standards do not require a sponsor or listing agent to be appointed for admission to trading but do require all applicants to identify a contact within their organisation, usually a director or senior employee, who will be responsible for communications with the LSE. The Standards also encourage issuers, so as to ease the burden on the issuer and their internal contact, to appoint a "nominated representative", which will be either the issuer's broker, financial adviser, lawyer or accountant.[49] The latest version of the Standards, published in May 2001, no longer state that when a sponsor is appointed under the UKLA's Listing Rules,[50] this party is the most logical choice for the role of the issuer's nominated representative although a sponsor would generally still be the most appropriate appointee for the role.

As a departure from its practice when it was Competent Authority, the LSE now expects to meet with any prospective applicant before admitting its securities to trading (although it retains a discretion not to do so in all cases, in particular in relation to companies transferring to the main market from AIM).[51] It requires that the timetable for admission of the securities to trading be discussed well in advance and in any event no later than the date on which draft documentation (including the listing particulars or prospectus) is submitted to the UKLA for approval.[52] Applications must be accompanied by copies of all relevant documentation, including prospectuses or listing particulars, and must cover all classes of security for which listing is sought.[53] Under the revised Standards, a new applicant must complete a further form "Form 2" which will be published on the LSE's "New Issues" list containing information such as the expected size of any offer, the retail portion and the anticipated market (*e.g.* the main market, techMARK, etc.) on which the securities are to be traded.[54] Applications can be refused on grounds that they may be detrimental to the orderly operation or reputation of the LSE's markets or that the applicant has not complied with the Standards or any special conditions.[55]

Admission to trading becomes effective when the decision of the LSE to admit the securities to trading has been announced through the Company

---

[46] Listing Rules, para. 9.44.
[47] Listing Rules, para. 9.44A.
[48] Listing Rules, para. 1.23A.
[49] Standards, r. 1.6.
[50] See Listing Rules, para. 2.3.
[51] Standards, r. 1.8. Whilst the Standards do not expressly state that any nominated adviser should attend any meeting, it is common practice for this to be the case. In relation to secondary issues of securities, timetables should be discussed in advance with the LSE at an early stage and submission of the application form contained at Form 1 (and relating to both primary and secondary issues of securities by an issuer) and other documentation (see r. 2.4) must arrive no later than 12.00 p.m., at least two business days before the application is considered.
[52] Standards, r. 1.7.
[53] Standards, rr. 1.1 and 2.4. The revised Standards state that AIM companies are able to transfer by way of a UKLA approved exempt listing document—see Standards, Pt 1, Chap. 2 and Listing Rules, paras 5.23A(c) and 5.24.
[54] Standards, r. 1.9.
[55] Standards, r. 1.4.

Announcements Office (the "CAO"). At present, listing and trading application procedures of the FSA, as Competent Authority, and the LSE are co-ordinated so that admission to listing and trading occur simultaneously; a single notice is posted on the Regulatory News Service ("RNS") of the CAO which confirms that admission to listing and to trading has taken place. It is open to question whether this dissemination medium would become centralised under the control of the FSA should other RIEs providing a primary market in listed securities enter the United Kingdom market or whether each new RIE would be required to create and operate its own information dissemination medium in conjunction with the FSA along the lines of the current model (this is considered in paragraph 7.10 below).

The revised Standards also formally introduce the concept of "Attribute Groups", which allow an issuer to seek admission to an indices or sub-set of the main market. Admission to an Attribute Group is determined in accordance with eligibility criteria (specific to each Attribute Group) published by the LSE from time to time.[56]

In terms of disciplinary powers, the LSE may suspend trading of securities should admission of the securities to listing be suspended or if it feels that a disorderly market has arisen. It also retains an absolute right to cancel trading in an issuer's securities. To complete the picture, the FSA, as Competent Authority, has stated that where circumstances arise which may justify it exercising its own powers of suspension, it intends to liaise closely with RIEs to ensure that suspensions can be arranged as quickly and efficiently as possible.[57] In practice, the UKLA and the LSE liaise to ensure that securities are suspended and/or cancelled simultaneously, with a joint notice being issued over the RNS. The LSE has retained its ability to censure an issuer privately and publicly.[58] Should a censure or trading cancellation (or, indeed, any matter concerning the LSE's interpretation of the Standards) be disputed, an issuer may lodge an appeal in accordance with the LSE's *Disciplinary and Appeals Handbook*.[59]

The main continuing obligation imposed on issuers by the Standards relates to the disclosure of information which would be likely to lead to substantial movement in the price of those securities.[60] These obligations are stated to be "similar" to the FSA's rules on disclosure but there are, unhelpfully, minor differences between the two in terms of the terminology used, which could ultimately lead to a divergence in interpretation.[61] The end result is that an issuer should consider whether additional disclosure is required pursuant to its obligations under either the Listing Rules or the Standards albeit that this is unlikely.

---

[56] Standards, r. 1.5. See, *e.g.*, the eligibility criteria published in relation to techMARK, extraMARK and landMARK.

[57] FSA, *Consultation Paper 37*, para. 4.6.

[58] Standards, r. 4.12(a).

[59] Standards, r. 4.13. At the time of writing, the revised *Disciplinary and Appeals Handbook* was not available. It is not thought that the appeals procedure, in terms of the committees to whom appeals can be brought, will alter significantly from that prescribed in the "old" Standards under which decisions could first be appealed to the Company Disciplinary Committee ("CDC") whose ruling could then be appealed to the Company Appeals Committee ("CAC"). Any appeal to the CAC had to be made within 20 days of the decision of the ruling of the CDC. The decision of the CAC was final.

[60] Standards, paras 3.1–3.10. The only other obligations relate to timetable for, *inter alia*, open offers and the obligation on listed issuers to pay fees (paras 3.11–3.12 and 3.13, respectively).

[61] The overlap between the Listing Rules and the Standards and the divergence in the use of terminology were criticised by respondents to the FSA's Consultation on the Transfer of the Competent Authority

A further consequence of the transfer of the Competent Authority function to the FSA appears in relation to the inspection and display of documentation. Whereas announcements made pursuant to the disclosure obligations in the Standards or the Listing Rules continue to be made via the CAO, the function of this office in relation to the inspection of documentation has now ceased. Where prospectuses/ listing particulars and other documentation are required by the Listing Rules to be published by making them available to the public for inspection, they must be displayed at the new Document Viewing Facility of the FSA.[62] In addition, the FSA's website[63] has a separate page relating to its function as the Competent Authority which, not later than one business day following the publication of the relevant document, notes that a document has been made available for inspection and states where the document can be inspected.

Dissemination of Price Sensitive Information

7.10   The Listing Rules and the Standards require issuers to disseminate certain prescribed information to the market, as well as price-sensitive information on an *ad hoc* basis.[64] This requirement developed while the LSE performed the role of Competent Authority and as a result of its obligation as an RIE under Part I of the 1986 Act to maintain an orderly market. The Listing Rules also require issuers to make further announcements where a disorderly market is apparent or the Competent Authority is concerned that one may develop, for example due to a leak of potentially price sensitive information.[65]

Despite the transfer of the Competent Authority function to the FSA, the actual method of dissemination remains the same, although this is seen by the FSA as being only a "transitional arrangement".[66] Issuers must submit announcements to the CAO and the announcement is then made to the market via RNS, which is, in this capacity, the sole distribution mechanism for regulatory information in the United Kingdom. There is no requirement of pre-notification to the LSE, as an RIE, nor to the Competent Authority. The United Kingdom market operates on the basis that regulatory information is used to support continuous trading and, consequently, there are no trading halts to allow the market to digest information as there are in certain other jurisdictions. RNS provides this information to subscribers who, in turn, distribute this to their own customers on a real time or delayed basis.[67]

Other methods of dissemination may be used by listed companies[68] but only on the basis that the announcement being made via alternative media (*e.g.* newspapers or newswire services) is not sent in advance of the announcement to be made via

---

function (FSA, *Consultation Paper 37*). Whilst the FSA agreed that the overlaps between the Listing Rules and an RIE's admission to trading rules should be kept to a minimum, it stated that as long as an RIE met its recognition requirements, which include requirements relating to information flow and proper market criteria, any additional rules are a commercial matter for the RIE itself.
[62] The Document Viewing Facility is located at: The Financial Services Authority, 25 The North Colonnade, Canary Wharf, London E14 5HS. See the amended Listing Rules, paras 5.33(c)(ii), 8.4, 8.13 (c)(ii) and 8.20(a). See *Consultation Paper 105* (August 2001) in relation to proposed changes to the Listing Rules in this area.
[63] *www.fsa.gov.uk*
[64] Listing Rules, Chaps 9 and 12. Standards, para. 3.1.
[65] Listing Rules, para. 9.4.
[66] Announced by the Treasury on December 7, 1999.
[67] For example, via Reuters and Bloomberg.
[68] This is enshrined in the Admissions Directive, Art. 17. See Listing Rules, para. 9.6.

the CAO. The provisions for dissemination after the CAO is closed for business also remain the same for the time being.[69]

Given that the two underlying tenets of this continuing obligation are the timely disclosure of all relevant information and the equality of treatment of all shareholders, the current system has been severely criticised. It is felt that the outdated input software[70] creates delays, not timely disclosure, and the whole system has limited access for some small institutional and nearly all private investors. In response to these criticisms,[71] the Information Dissemination Advisory Group ("IDAG") was constituted as an internal committee of the FSA and has now put forward proposals for review pursuant to its discussions with listed companies, RIEs, other information providers and private investors.[72] Indeed, one change that has already taken place is that the LSE has developed RNS so that it now permits announcements to be submitted via a secure internet based mechanism, available 24 hours a day, seven days a week.

IDAG's central proposal is to establish a regime where issuers are required to issue regulatory announcements via any one of an approved list of service providers, akin to RNS,[73] approved by the FSA pursuant to set criteria.[74] Issuers' obligations of disclosure would remain the same but the Listing Rules would name those service providers approved to disseminate the information. Ultimately, an issuer could pick one of a number of competing service providers to disseminate its price-sensitive information; the service provider would then, as before, pass the information onto its own subscribers for onward transmission. However, there will still be an emphasis on private investors continuing to rely on the internet to provide them with low cost access to information.[75]

THE IMPACT OF THE ACT ON LISTED SECURITIES

7.11   Part IV of the 1986 Act (as amended by the POS Regulations) has been largely implemented by Part VI of the Act, subject to the changes highlighted below. Offers to the public in the United Kingdom of unlisted securities are still regulated by the POS Regulations.

Applications by issuers for listing

7.12   There is no change to the principle that admission to the Official List may be granted only on an application made to the Competent Authority in such

---

[69] Listing Rules, para. 9.15.

[70] This is the "Direct Input Provider" system or "DIP" system. Companies can also submit announcements via 3.5" diskette, fax or by hand.

[71] See, in particular, FSA's Response to FSA Consultation Paper 37.

[72] See FSA Consultation Paper 92: Review of the Mechanism for Disseminating Regulatory Information by Listed Companies (May 2001).

[73] The FSA has already had preliminary discussions with, inter alia, the LSE, PR Newswire and Businesswire.

[74] See FSA, Consultation Paper 92, paras 3.8 and 5.8 for the high-level requirements any service provider may have to meet before they can become approved by the FSA.

[75] Alternative proposals, including a central FSA website, are also put forward in FSA, Consultation Paper 92 but are not favoured by the FSA at this stage. As it is likely that service providers will also send out non-regulatory announcements, it has been proposed that regulatory announcements should have specific proforma headlines so as to differentiate them.

manner as may be required by the Listing Rules[76] and that no application may be entertained unless it is made by or with the consent of the issuer of the securities concerned or from an issuer of a prescribed kind.[77] As before, an application for listing may also be refused if, for a reason relating to the issuer, the Competent Authority considers that granting admission would be detrimental to the interests of investors.[78] The Competent Authority may also refuse an application for listing under the Act if the issuer in question has failed to comply with any obligations to which it is subject pursuant to the listing of its securities in another EEA State.[79]

The Act also implements the relevant sections of the 1986 Act in prescribing that the Competent Authority must notify an applicant of its decision within six months of receiving the application or, if further information has been requested, within six months of receipt of that further information.[80] In practice, if an applicant falls within the suitability criteria laid down by the Listing Rules, the decision is likely to take considerably less than six months.[81] However, if an application may be refused, the Competent Authority must now provide the applicant with a statutory "warning notice" and, to the extent that the application is refused, the Competent Authority must also serve a statutory "decision notice"[82] on the applicant who has an automatic right of appeal to the Tribunal. The detail of these procedures, including specimen notices, are contained in Chapter 2 of the Guidance Manual (see also paragraph 7.20 below).

The Act also repeats the protections afforded to issuers and investors alike in the 1986 Act by providing that admission of securities to the Official List may not subsequently be called into question on the grounds that any requirement or condition for their admission has not been complied with.[83]

Cancellation and suspension of listing

7.13 The Act changes few of the provisions relating to the cancellation and suspension of listings on the Official List, although it does clarify the procedural aspects of such actions. The Competent Authority may, irrespective of when securities were admitted to the Official List and in accordance with the Listing Rules, cancel the listing of any securities where it is satisfied that there are special circumstances which preclude normal and regular dealings or suspend a listing where

---

[76] FSMA, s. 75(4) expands on this principle in that the Competent Authority may not grant an application for listing unless not only the Listing Rules have been satisfied (so far as they apply to the application) but also any other requirements imposed by the Authority in relation to the application have been complied with. Reg. 4 of the Financial Services and Markets Act 2000 (Official Listing of Securities) Regulations 2001 (S.I. 2001 No. 2956) defines who an "issuer" is for the purposes of Pt VI of the Act.

[77] These are set out in reg. 3 of the Financial Services and Markets Act 2000 (Official Listing of Securities) Regulations 2001 (S.I. 2001 No. 2956) and include private companies and "old" public companies. See FSMA, s. 75(3) and the 1986 Act, s. 143(3).

[78] FSMA, s. 75(5) reflecting s. 144(3)(a) of the 1986 Act.

[79] FSMA, s. 75(6) reflecting s. 144(3)(b) of the 1986 Act.

[80] FSMA, s. 76(1) reflecting s. 144(4) of the 1986 Act.

[81] To the extent that the Competent Authority does not notify the applicant of its decision, it is deemed to have refused the application; see FSMA, s. 76(2) reflecting s. 144(5) of the 1986 Act.

[82] See paragraph 7.20 below which deals with such "statutory notice decisions" and procedures in more detail.

[83] FSMA, s. 76(7) reflecting s. 144(6) of the 1986 Act.

it believes that the smooth operation of the market is, or may be, temporarily jeopardised or where the protection of investors so requires.[84]

The Competent Authority must now provide an issuer whose securities are to be or have been suspended or cancelled with a statutory written notice (called a "supervisory notice"[85]) of that fact stating, *inter alia*, the effective date of the cancellation or suspension (which may be immediate) and the reasons for the action. It must also inform the issuer of its right to make representations to the Competent Authority or to appeal to the Tribunal to the extent that any request for restoration to the Official List is refused. To the extent that the Competent Authority, having so warned the issuer, refuses to re-admit securities which have been suspended or cancelled, the issuer may again bring the matter before the Tribunal.[86] These procedures are detailed in FSA *Consultation Paper 100*, whilst detailed guidance on the UKLA's powers of suspension, cancellation and restoration (in each case at the request of the issuer concerned or otherwise) is contained in the Guidance Manual at Chapter 9.

Listing Particulars, Prospectuses and bringing securities to the Official List

General Principles

7.14 It has been argued that the 1986 Act appears to give the Competent Authority an unfettered right to set the parameters for admitting securities to the Official List.[87] However, the Act and the Listing Rules must be read alongside the minimum standards laid down by the Directives (including for these purposes the Public Offers Directive) and particularly those provisions relating to listing particulars and prospectuses. This position has not changed under the Act and nor indeed have most of the requirements in relation to the production and approval of such documentation.

As discussed in paragraph 7.07 above, historically, the Competent Authority has admitted to listing non-Part IV securities. As the definition of securities in the Act is more widely drawn (meaning that, potentially, all securities will be subject to Part VI), the UKLA has proposed that where a security is *not* subject to the Listing Particulars Directive, the Competent Authority will use its power under the Act to admit such securities by way of an equivalent offering document.[88] Accordingly, issuers of such securities will not be subject to the statutory provisions relating to compensation for false or misleading particulars, the general duty of disclosure set out in section 80 of the Act and the provisions relating to responsibility. However, in the case of securities that were non-Part IV securities but are subject to the Listing Particulars Directive, the UKLA has proposed that listing particulars (or prospectuses if appropriate) should be prepared.[89] As a consequence, an issuer of former

---

[84] FSMA, s. 77(1), (2) and (4), reflecting s. 145 of the 1986 Act. See also Listing Rules, paras 1.19 and 1.22. The definition of a cancellation (or "discontinuance") and a suspension is contained in FSMA, s. 78 (13)–(14).

[85] FSMA, s. 395(13).

[86] FSMA, s. 78(12).

[87] FSMA, ss. 74(4) and 79(4).

[88] 1986 Act, s. 144(1). See also FSMA, s. 79(1)(b).

[89] See FSA *Consultation Paper 100*. As a result issuers bringing securities to the official list pursuant to Chapter 24 of the Listing Rules will *not*, if the proposals are adopted, be able to do so by way of "equivalent offering document".

non-Part IV securities that are subject to the Listing Particulars Directive will be subject to the provisions of Part VI relating to listing particulars and/or prospectuses and, therefore, those relating to compensation for false or misleading particulars, the general duty of disclosure etc.

Subject to the above, the principle remains that in order to bring securities to Official Listing, listing particulars need to be published, unless the securities in question fall within the definition of "new securities", being securities which are to be offered to the public in the United Kingdom for the first time, in which case a prospectus must be published.[90] Any such document will need to be produced in accordance with the Listing Rules and vetted by the Competent Authority to the extent that the securities are to be admitted to the Official List (see also paragraph 7.18 below).[91] In general, the provisions of Part VI of the Act apply equally to prospectuses as they do to listing particulars.[92]

The provisions of the 1986 Act relating to the publication of advertisements have also been carried forward in the Act; such adverts need to be vetted and approved by the Competent Authority and failure to do so leaves the persons responsible open to possible criminal sanction.[93]

Persons responsible for particulars

7.15 The Financial Services and Markets Act 2000 (Official Listing of Securities) Regulations 2001[94] set out those persons who must take responsibility for listing particulars and supplementary listing particulars. These provisions were previously laid down in section 152 of the 1986 Act and only minor changes have been made in their migration to the Act; the categories of persons deemed responsible have not altered.[95] The effect of the 1986 Act is also replicated in that these provisions are extended to prospectuses, including non-listing prospectuses. (The consequences for persons responsible for producing such documents containing false or misleading information are dealt with in more detail in paragraphs 7.20–7.23, below).

The ability of the UKLA to certify a person as not having to take responsibility for a document has been removed. The reason for this is that the Act delegates to the Treasury the power to state who is responsible for such documentation and the Treasury did not feel that they could sub-delegate this power to the UKLA.

---

[90] FSMA, ss. 79, 84 and Sched. 11 see the 1986 Act, s. 144(2)–(2A) and Sched. 11A. Schedule 11 of the Act (amended by the Public Offers of Securities (Exemptions) Regulations 2001 (S.I. 2001 No. 2955) which extends the exemptions provided in Schedule 11 to units in a collective investment scheme) largely carries forward Sched. 11A of the 1986 Act and defines when an "offer" is made "to the public" and/or when it is deemed not to be an "offer to the public in the United Kingdom". It is unlawful for any securities to be offered to the public in the U.K. before a prospectus is published and to do so is a criminal offence (FSMA, s. 85).

[91] The Listing Rules themselves do not draw a distinction between a prospectus and listing particulars (para. 5.1(d)).

[92] FSMA, s. 86.

[93] FSMA, s. 98, reflecting s. 154 of the 1986 Act. The defences available under the 1986 Act have also been carried forward into the Act.

[94] The Financial Services and Markets Act 2000 (Official Listing of Securities) Regulations 2001 (S.I. 2001 No. 2956).

[95] The main change has been to replace the category of "international securities" under s. 152(5)–(6) (as modified by s. 142(3)(b)) of the 1986 Act with a new wider category of "specialist securities". This change has also been reflected in the proposed amendments to the Listing Rules in FSA, *Consultation Paper 100*. Reg.9(2) of the (Official Listing of Securities) Regulations appears to extend the category of persons *not* responsible for particulars relating to specialist securities to the issuer, whereas s. 152(5) of the 1986 Act states that the exemption only applies to current or prospective directors.

Paragraph 5.5 of the Listing Rules is expected to be amended and paragraphs 5.2 and 5.4 deleted accordingly.[96]

Disclosure and filing of particulars

7.16 The general duty of disclosure in listing particulars (and prospectuses) remains exactly the same as under the 1986 Act; such documents must contain all such information as investors and their professional advisers would reasonably require, and reasonably expect to find there, for the purpose of making an informed assessment of the assets and liabilities, financial position, profits and losses, and prospects of the issuer of the securities.[97] As before, this requirement is qualified in its application to information within the knowledge of any person responsible for the particulars or which it would be reasonable for him or her to obtain by making enquiries.[98] The general duty of disclosure is further qualified by the fact that regard must be had to the nature of the securities and their issuer, the nature of the persons likely to acquire them, the likely professional advice and knowledge any purchasers may already have and any further information which may be available to such advisers.[99]

The instances and grounds on which the Competent Authority may authorise certain exemptions from disclosure remain the same under the Act, limited as they are to a narrow set of circumstances based on public interest and serious detriment to the issuer. This means that they will only be rarely invoked.[1] Requests for variations and/or exemptions from disclosure (and, indeed, in relation to other applications of the Listing Rules) are dealt with in Chapter 6 of the Guidance Manual.[2] Where information is considered "essential" by the Competent Authority, no derogation can nor will be granted from the obligation to disclose it, even if it would be seriously detrimental to the issuer in question.[3] The Secretary of State or the Treasury may issue a certificate confirming that the disclosure of certain information would be contrary to the public interest.[4]

The provisions and penalties relating to the registration and publication of listing particulars and prospectuses are, in their effect, exactly the same as under the 1986 Act.[5]

Supplementary particulars

7.17 The provisions of the Act relating to the issue of supplementary listing particulars (and prospectuses) are carried forward from those in the 1986

---

[96] See FSA *Consultation Paper 100*, para. 6.14, 6.15, 8.14 and 8.15.

[97] FSMA, s. 80 reflecting s. 146 of the 1986 Act. This is without prejudice to any specific information required by the Listing Rules or by the Competent Authority (FSMA, s. 80(2)).

[98] FSMA, s. 80(3) reflecting s. 146(2) of the 1986 Act.

[99] FSMA, s. 80(4) reflecting s. 146(3) of the 1986 Act.

[1] FSMA s. 82, reflecting s. 148 of the 1986 Act. The issue of derogations under this section are rarely granted and must be formally approved by the Competent Authority in every instance. See the Listing Rules, para. 5.18.

[2] Annex I to Chap. 6 of the Guidance Manual sets out those Listing Rules in relation to which requests for variations must be made in writing.

[3] FSMA, s. 82(2). "Essential" information is that which a person acquiring securities of the kind in question would be likely to need in order not to be misled about any facts which it is essential for him to know in order to make an informed assessment (FSMA, s. 82(6)).

[4] FSMA, s. 82(3).

[5] FSMA, ss. 83 and 85 reflecting Pt IV, ss. 149 and 156B of the 1986 Act.

Act.[6] If there has been a significant change in any information included in particulars by virtue of an issuer's compliance with the general duty of disclosure under the Act, the Listing Rules or the specific requests of the Competent Authority or a significant new matter arises which would have had to be disclosed had it existed before the publication of the original particulars, then an issuer must submit supplementary particulars to the Competent Authority for approval.[7] Again, these obligations are not absolute and the obligation to publish supplementary particulars only relates to information of which the issuer is aware.[8]

Non-listing prospectuses

7.18   The POS Regulations incorporated provisions in Part IV of the 1986 Act allowing the Competent Authority to make listing rules which provided for a prospectus to be submitted to the Competent Authority for approval where, despite the fact the securities were being offered for sale for the first time in the United Kingdom, they were not the subject of an application for admission to the Official List.[9] This allows a prospectus to be recognised and used in other Member States where the relevant authorities are obliged to give it full effect on a mutual recognition basis. This regime is carried forward in section 87 and Schedule 11 of the Act and the Financial Services and Markets Act 2000 (Offers of Securities) Order 2001 which specifies, for this purpose, the provisions of the POS Regulations and reproduces the effect of certain provisions currently contained in the 1986 Act.[10] UKLA guidance on this area is set out in Chapter 6 of the Guidance Manual.

The Sponsorship Regime

7.19   For the first time the regime and basic framework from which the Competent Authority has developed the sponsorship regime is set out in statute thus clarifying the role, rights and duties of sponsors. Whilst none of these provisions extend the powers of the Competent Authority beyond their existing scope, certain procedural aspects of the sponsorship regime, as it stands at present, will require amendment.[11] In addition, the right of a sponsor to appeal any decisions regarding its accreditation (including its removal) and censure to the Tribunal is a change in existing practice.[12] The Act allows the Competent Authority, through the Listing Rules, to require an issuer to make arrangements with a sponsor for the performance by the sponsor of such services as are specified in eligibility criteria

---

[6] FSMA, s. 81 reflecting s. 147 of the 1986 Act.

[7] "Significant" means significant for the purpose of making an informed assessment of the kind mentioned in s. 80(1) of the FSMA; see also s. 146(2) of the 1986 Act.

[8] FSMA, s. 81(3)–(4); it is the duty of a person responsible for the listing particulars who is aware of a change to make the issuer aware of that change.

[9] 1986 Act, s. 156A. The detailed requirements for a "non-listing prospectus" are set out at the end of the Listing Rules, immediately prior to the Schedules.

[10] Financial Services and Markets Act 2000 (Offers of Securities) Order 2001 (S.I. 2001 No. 2958), Art. 3. The effect of this is to replicate the 1986 Act, s.156A(2)(6) inserted by the POS Regulations. Further provisions (including permitted advertisements under Schedule 11) are also contained in Part 4 of the Financial Services and Markets Act 2000 (Official Listing of Securities) Regulations 2001 (S.I. 2001 No. 2956).

[11] See FSA, *Consultation Paper 100.*

[12] See ss. 88(7) and 89(4). The proposed "root and branch" review of the Listing Rules, referred to in the FSA, *Response to FSA Consultation Paper 37*, will consider the role of sponsors more fully.

which are proposed to be contained in the Listing Rules and the Guidance Manual.[13]

The services required of sponsors under the Listing Rules will broadly replicate sponsors' responsibilities under the former contractual regime. The main changes relate to the procedural requirements imposed by the Act in relation to discipline (including censures), investigations, accreditation as a sponsor and cancellation of approval as a sponsor.[14] These procedures require the Competent Authority to issue statutory notices when it proposes to take any action. The Act also details the procedures whereby a sponsor may challenge the action the Competent Authority proposes to take (see paragraph 7.20 below). A sponsor cannot have a financial penalty imposed upon it.

The Competent Authority is currently consulting on proposals to remove the need for a public sector issuer or issuers of specialist and miscellaneous securities to appoint a listing agent.[15] The proposals mean that whereas, historically, an issuer was required to appoint a listing agent it will now be required to appoint an "authorised person" who will owe no responsibility to the Competent Authority. The reasoning behind this is that the Competent Authority feels that it has not exercised a significant regulatory function in respect of listing agents in the past.

Compensation, fines and censure

7.20   The material change introduced by the Act in this area is in relation to the ability of the Competent Authority to impose financial penalties for breaches of the Listing Rules. This is in addition to its existing ability to publicly and privately censure an issuer or applicant for listing and to publish information itself if an issuer has failed to do so.[16]

Before dealing with the detailed provisions of the legislation, it is worth noting that, in terms of structure at the FSA, the Quotations Committee, who were authorised to publicly censure, and the Quotations Appeals Committee, before whom appeals on censures were brought, are not going to be retained. They will be kept for a transitional period as there are various stages at which the new regime will take over. For example, if before N2 there has been an appeal against a decision of the Quotations Committee that has not been heard by the Quotations Appeal Committee or if an appeal may still be bought but has not been, the appeal can be heard by the Quotations Committee. Once a decision has been made (which cannot result in the imposition of a financial penalty) the UKLA will give effect to it by issuing a written notice under the Act (and the provisions of the Act apply to this notice) (see also paragraph 7.08 above).

In future, non "statutory notice decisions", for example appeals on an interpretation of the Listing Rules, will be made (after the UKLA's internal procedures have been exhausted) to the UKLA's Listing Authority Review Committee ("LARC"). It is proposed that this will be chaired by a managing director of the FSA and include the Director of Listing at the UKLA, the General Counsel to the FSA (or his

---

[13] See Guidance Manual, Chapter 4. This explains, in more detail than the Listing Rules, the eligibility criteria for sponsors. See also FSA *Consultation Paper 100*.
[14] FSMA, s. 89.
[15] See FSA, *Consultation Paper 100*.
[16] FSMA, s. 96 reflecting s. 153 of the 1986 Act.

delegate) and two ex-practitioners with market experience of listing matters. LARC decisions are final.[17] "Statutory notice decisions", being those where the Competent Authority intends, *inter alia*, to refuse an application for listing or approval as a sponsor, suspend or cancel a listing or impose a financial penalty or public censure, will be made by the Regulatory Decisions Committee ("RDC"). FSA *Consultation Paper 100* proposes that the chairman of the RDC will be an FSA employee with the rest of the committee made up of market practitioners and representatives of the public interest.[18] As has been noted throughout this Chapter, statutory notice decisions of the RDC may be taken on appeal to the Tribunal. Guidance in relation to Statutory Notice Decision-Making is laid down in detail in Chapter 10 of the Guidance Manual which also constitutes the UKLA's statement of procedure in this area pursuant to section 395 of the FSMA.

Compensation for false or misleading particulars

7.21 There is no change to the existing regime. A person responsible for the publication of listing particulars or prospectuses (supplementary or otherwise) which include any untrue or misleading statement or which omit any information required to be disclosed[19] and as a result of which an investor who has acquired or contracted to acquire securities in question suffers loss, is liable to pay that investor compensation.[20] No specific criminal liability can be incurred for untrue or misleading statements in documents bringing securities to the Official List; rather the general offence of misstatement made dishonestly or recklessly in the context of the issue or sale of the securities in question will apply.[21]

Schedule 10 to the Act carries forward the 1986 Act in terms of the exemptions it affords those responsible for the publication of particulars both in relation to general statements made within particulars and statements made in such documents by experts.[22] It also follows the 1986 Act in terms of its exemption provisions relating to correction notices, repetition of official statements, knowledge on the part of investor alleging loss and failure to publish supplementary particulars.[23]

These statutory liabilities are without prejudice to any other liability which may arise.[24]

---

[17] See Guidance Manual, Chapter 5, para. 5.8.

[18] The RDC will not be used in relation to a suspension of a listing of an issuer's securities where speed is often of the essence. Such decisions will be dealt with by UKLA executive procedures delegated by the RDC as will the cancellation of a listing at an issuer's request. The constitution and powers of the RDC are set out in the Decision making manual ("DEC") as approved by the Board of the FSA and operative for the purposes of the FSA's Handbook on September 3, 2001.

[19] Pursuant to FSMA, ss. 80 and 81, the Listing Rules, etc.

[20] FSMA, s. 90 reflecting s. 150 of the 1986 Act. This general principle is subject to the exemptions from the general duty of disclosure authorised under FSMA, s. 82 and to the underlying principle that if the particulars are required to include information about the absence of a particular matter, the omission from the particulars of that information is to be treated as a statement in the particulars that there is no such matter (FSMA, s. 90(3)).

[21] FSMA, s. 397 reflecting s. 47 of the 1986 Act.

[22] FSMA, Sched. 10, paras 1 and 2. A responsible person can avoid liability if he made such enquiries, if any, as were reasonable in the circumstances and reasonably believed that the statement was true and not misleading or, indeed, was properly omitted when the document was submitted for approval to the Competent Authority.

[23] FSMA, Sched. 10, paras 3–7, reflecting s. 151(3)–(6) of the 1986 Act.

[24] FSMA, s. 90(6).

Public censure and financial penalties

7.22 In addition to the statutory penalties in Part VI which can be imposed on an issuer for failing to file listing particulars or prospectuses with the Registrar of Companies prior to their publication[25] and offering securities to the public for the first time without publishing a prospectus,[26] the Competent Authority retains the right under the Act to censure an issuer for a breach of the Listing Rules[27] as well as the right to publish information itself concerning an issuer to the extent that it feels that an issuer has failed to do so.[28]

The major addition to the scope of the 1986 Act and the ability of the Competent Authority to deal with breaches of the Listing Rules is in the new power of the Competent Authority to impose financial penalties on issuers of securities and/or applicants for listing. Further, if it feels that a person, who was at the material time a director of the issuer or applicant, was knowingly concerned in the contravention by the issuer or applicant for listing, it may impose a penalty of such amount as it considers to be appropriate on that individual.[29] Alternatively, it may publicly censure any such individual, issuer or applicant for listing.[30] Part VI sets out the procedure which must be followed in taking any such action[31] and, in addition, it requires the Competent Authority to issue and consult on a policy statement on the imposition and level of financial penalties.[32] This the FSA did in the publication of *Consultation Paper 81* in January 2001 and the *Feedback Statement* on CP81 in July 2001.

The FSA has stated that it will not adopt a tariff of penalties for different kinds of contravention[33] but echoes the provisions of the Act by stating that in determining the amount of any penalty, the Competent Authority must have regard to the seriousness and context of the contravention set against the rule or requirement contravened, the extent to which the contravention was deliberate or reckless and whether the person on whom the penalty is to be imposed is an individual.[34] It must, as always, follow its disciplinary procedures (dealt with in more detail

---

[25] FSMA, s. 83(3)–(4).

[26] FSMA, s. 85(1)–(2).

[27] FSMA, s. 91(3).

[28] FSMA, s. 96(3), reflecting s. 153 of the 1986 Act.

[29] FSMA, s. 91(2). See FSMA, s. 91(7)(a). The Competent Authority is to be treated as knowing of a contravention if it has information from which the contravention can reasonably be inferred.

[30] FSMA, s. 91(3). Guidance Manual, Chapter 8 lays down detailed criteria which the Competent Authority must comply with when considering the making of a public or a private censure.

[31] FSMA, s. 92. The FSA must give the person concerned a statutory warning notice stating the reasons for the proposed action, the amount of the fine or content of the statement of censure, this must then be followed by a statutory decision notice. Matters may be referred to the Tribunal (FSMA, s. 92). Other persons who may be prejudiced must also be notified (FSMA, ss. 392 and 393).

[32] FSMA, ss. 93(1) and 94(2). The policy statement is expressed as being consistent with the statement of policy in respect of the imposition and amount of financial penalties in accordance with ss. 69 and 210 of the Act and as set out in Chapter 13 of the FSA's "final" *Enforcement Manual* ("ENF") published in May 2001 and now part of the FSA's Handbook.

[33] FSA, Consultation Paper 81: *Proposed Changes to the Listing Rules* (January 2001), para. 4.3 and FSA, *Feedback Statement on CP81* (July 2001), para. 3.33. This is mainly because it considers that there will be very few cases in which the circumstances are essentially the same to make the production of such a tariff worthwhile; it would ultimately inhibit the flexible and proportionate approach the Competent Authority intends to adopt in this area. FSA, *Feedback Statement on CP81*, para. 3.36 contains a hierarchy of breaches of the Listing Rules ranking such breaches in order of seriousness.

[34] FSMA, s. 93(2). In determining the policy on amounts of penalties to be levied the Competent Authority cannot have regard to the costs incurred in connection with the Competent Authority

in Chapter 13, below) as well as the detailed criteria and procedures set out in Chapter 8 of the Guidance Manual.

Over and above these statutory criteria, *Consultation Paper 81* and the Guidance Manual set out additional factors which may be relevant to the imposition and level of any financial penalty. These are:

- the amount of profits accrued or loss avoided as a result of the contravention;

- the conduct of the person before and following the contravention;

- the person's disciplinary record and compliance history;

- any action the FSA has taken in relation to previous similar behaviour;

- what action, if any, has been taken by other regulatory authorities; and

- any guidance previously given by the FSA.

In short, in determining whether to impose a financial penalty the Competent Authority will have regard to all the relevant circumstances of the contravention.[35]

The policy statement has been criticised for failing to take into account the relationship between penalties/censures under the Act and the market abuse regime as well as failing expressly to take into account whether another person/investor has a claim against an offender in respect of the same breach of the Listing Rules.[36] Further, the FSA has defended the amount of subjectivity the approach to financial penalties vests in the Competent Authority, arguing that there will often be subjective issues to consider when deciding whether to investigate potential breaches of the Listing Rules and, if so, whether to commence formal disciplinary proceedings.[37]

It should be noted that the Competent Authority may not take action against a person in relation to a breach of the Listing Rules after a period of two years beginning with the first day on which it knew of the contravention.[38]

Investigations

7.23   The Act provides for the appointment by the Competent Authority of persons to act as investigators to the extent that it believes there has been a breach of the Listing Rules by an issuer or applicant for listing, a director of an issuer or

---

function and, indeed, amounts paid to it by way of penalties can only be applied for the benefit of issuers of securities admitted to the Official List; albeit that this does provide a fair amount of scope; see FSMA, s. 100. Penalties are to be paid directly to the FSA.

[35] See FSA *Consultation Paper 81* which expands on each of the considerations that the Competent Authority will take into account. It is stressed in the FSA *Consultation Paper 81* and the *Feedback Statement on CP81* that the list of criteria is *not* exhaustive.

[36] See the response of The Law Society's Company Law Committee and The City of London Law Society's Company Law Sub-Committee to FSA *Consultation Paper 81*, Question 27. The Committees have also suggested that it would be very helpful if the UKLA were to publish, on a quarterly basis, the penalties imposed on a no-names basis, depending on the nature of the offence so as to allow scrutiny of consistency of approach and to act as a deterrent. It is not known whether the FSA will do so.

[37] FSA *Feedback Statement on CP81*, para. 3.34.

[38] FSMA, s. 91(6). This time limit does not mean that the action against the person needs to be concluded prior to the two year period expiring; rather the action by the Competent Authority only needs to be commenced prior to the end of this period.

an applicant for listing or by a sponsor.[39] An investigator may also be appointed in relation to alleged breaches of provisions of Part VI of the Act where criminal sanctions may be incurred. FSA *Consultation Paper 100* proposes to introduce this power of appointment into the Listing Rules in Chapter 1; any such appointment must be made and the conduct of the investigator after appointment must be in accordance with the detailed procedures laid down in the Guidance Manual. The Guidance Manual sets out the information the investigator can demand to see[40] (subject to certain qualifications in relation to banking confidentiality),[41] and gives detailed guidance on the admissibility of statements made to an investigator and the use of compulsory interviews.[42] It also contains guidance on publicity and announcements surrounding matters under investigation (during the course of and after the investigation has taken place).

To give the legislation teeth, section 177 of the Act creates three criminal offences in relation to non-co-operation with an investigator.

The Code of Market Conduct ("MAR 1"), the Listing Rules and the Market Abuse Regime

7.24 The FSMA provides that behaviour does not amount to market abuse if it conforms with a rule made by the FSA that expressly states that compliance with the rule does not amount to market abuse.[43] The Act does not, however, provide a blanket "safe harbour" for all FSA rules, including the Listing Rules nor does it do so in relation to rules promulgated by RIEs[44] (although the FSA has made it clear that RIE rulebooks do not permit or require behaviour which amounts to market abuse).[45] Understandably, concern has been expressed[46] that as compliance with certain Listing Rules would almost certainly bring an individual or body within the market abuse regime, actions taken in compliance with the Listing Rules should be exempt from enforcement action under MAR 1.

The FSA argues that the majority of the Listing Rules simply do not impact on the market abuse regime and it will only grant safe harbour status to those rules which expressly require or expressly permit behaviour which, without the safe harbour, would amount to market abuse or rules which require particular timings for an announcement, particular methods of dissemination, particular content for an announcement or a standard of care to be observed. Therefore, only specific

---

[39] FSMA, s. 97 and see Guidance Manual, Chapter 7. Criminal sanctions can be incurred for breaches of the provisions of Pt VI, *e.g.*, in relation to s. 85 which requires a prospectus to be issued when offering securities to the public in the U.K. for the first time and s. 83 which requires registration of a prospectus or listing particulars with the Registrar of Companies.

[40] FSMA, s. 413.

[41] FSMA, ss. 175(5) and 284(8).

[42] FSMA, s. 174.

[43] FSMA, s. 118(8).

[44] The FSA was not prepared to provide a safe harbour for all rules of RIEs, arguing that because some rules required a degree of subjective judgment in ascertaining whether compliance has been demonstrated, it would be unlawful for the FSA to delegate to an RIE interpretation of whether conduct amounts to market abuse. This is despite the fact that an RIE's rules are (especially as RIEs make the majority of their own rules) ultimately subject to arms length oversight by the FSA. See FSMA, s. 293.

[45] MAR 1.2.12G.

[46] The "concerns" themselves were in response to FSA *Consultation Paper 10: Market Abuse*.

Listing Rules have been rendered safe harbours[47] and it remains possible for behaviour which is permitted by the rules of an RIE or the Listing Rules to constitute market abuse.[48] Conversely, breach of the rules of an RIE or the Listing Rules do not in and of themselves give rise to a presumption that market abuse has occurred. Indeed, the FSA has acknowledged that compliance with the rules of an RIE or the Listing Rules (as well as other codes of conduct) will be relevant to any decision as to whether or not market abuse has taken place.[49]

The "final" text of the FSA's Code of Market Conduct[50] sets out those Listing Rules which will be granted safe harbour status; these fall generally into the following categories:

(i) rules which require public disclosure of accurate information and, therefore, a standard of care (*e.g.* Listing Rules, paras 9.3A and 17.24A);

(ii) rules which regulate timings of announcements, documentation and dealings (*e.g.* Listing Rules, paras 9.4, 9.10(j), 9.11, 9.12 and 9.14);

(iii) rules which allow the selective disclosure of relevant information before it becomes generally available (*e.g.* Listing Rules, paras 8.3, 9.4, 9.5 and 9.15);

(iv) rules which regulate the content of announcements (*e.g.* Listing Rules, paras 9.1, 9.2, 14(1)(a) and 14(1)(b)); and

(v) rules which regulate dealings in the listed securities of an issuer (*e.g.* Listing Rules, para. 9.15).

The Guidance Manual sets out the approach taken where conduct comes both within the scope of the Listing Rules and the market abuse regime.[51]

The introduction of the Act and the market abuse regime has also resulted in the FSA reconsidering its approach to breaches of a company's code of dealings by directors and relevant employees. On the basis that the UKLA has been moving towards a more disclosure-based regulatory regime it is now proposed that the Listing Rules be amended to allow the UKLA, where appropriate, to require a company to publish an announcement containing relevant details of any breach of a company's code of dealings by a director or relevant employee.[52]

THE IMPACT OF THE ACT ON UNLISTED SECURITIES

7.25 Unlisted securities do not need to meet the minimum standards laid down by the Directives in order to be traded on an RIE. A public offer of unlisted

---

[47] MAR 1.6.19P.

[48] MAR 1.2.8G.

[49] FSA *Consultation Paper 59*, para. 8.3. See also the response of The Law Society Company Law Committee and The City of London Law Society Regulatory Sub-Committee in relation to FSA, *Consultation Paper 76*.

[50] See *Market Conduct Sourcebook Instrument 2001* at MAR 1.7.3(3)–1.7.3(4) and MAR 1, Annex 1G. See also FSA *Consultation Paper 100*, Annex C ("Appendix to Chapter 1").

[51] See Guidance Manual, Chapter 12.

[52] See FSA *Consultation Paper 100* and proposed amendments to Chapter 16 of the Listing Rules. The factors the UKLA will take into account when deciding whether to require an announcement are set out in the Guidance Manual, Chapter 11.

securities in the United Kingdom is still regulated by the POS Regulations and this regime is largely unaffected by the introduction of the Act. For this reason, the POS Regulations, their application and the exceptions to them are not discussed here.

In terms of the hierarchy of regulation in this area, the FSA oversees the regime in relation to unlisted securities. However, no approval for any prospectus for unlisted securities needs to be sought from the FSA; rather it may authorise the omission of information from a POS Regulations prospectus or supplementary POS Regulations prospectus where its inclusion would otherwise be required by the POS Regulations.[53]

As it has in relation to its main market, the LSE has imposed certain further requirements for securities to be brought to its "junior" market, AIM. Indeed, issuers often come to this junior market because either their securities or the issuer itself do not meet the minimum standards laid down by the relevant EU legislation (and enshrined in the Listing Rules), as opposed to an actual desire to avoid those minimum standards. The LSE continues to regulate and oversee this market and yet, like the FSA in respect of unlisted securities,[54] does not pre-vet prospectuses in connection with an application for securities to be traded on AIM; rather it relies on an issuer's nominated adviser to confirm that the admission document complies with the relevant requirements of the POS Regulations and the AIM Rules.[55]

---

[53] See POS Regulations and Guidance Manual, Chapter 6, reg. 11(3). Such requests should always be made to the FSA in writing.

[54] Save in relation to FSMA, s. 87 applications.

[55] A derogation from the requirements to disclose certain information in an admission document relating to unlisted securities can be sought from the LSE, save in respect of a derogation where the document in question also constitutes a prospectus in which case the derogation must be sought from the UKLA.

CHAPTER 8

Market Abuse

DAVID TOUBE

INTRODUCTION

8.01 No other aspect of the FSMA has generated as many column inches in both the trade and national press or provoked as much heated discussion amongst practitioners and lawyers alike as Part VIII of the FSMA, which establishes the novel regime for policing and punishing market abuse. What renders the market abuse regime controversial is that:

- it extends the disciplinary powers of the FSA not only to authorised persons who have voluntarily submitted to the jurisdiction of the FSA, but also for the first time to unauthorised persons;

- it overlaps in certain important respects with the criminal offences of insider dealing under Part V of the Criminal Justice Act 1993 and the misleading statements and practices offence, formerly under section 47 of the 1986 Act, carried forward by section 397 of the FSMA;

- if a person against whom the FSA proposes to take enforcement action refers the matter to the Tribunal, he or she will not be afforded the full safeguards provided by the criminal justice process; and

- depending upon the manner in which the market abuse regime is operated, it is arguable that it may constitute, in substance, a criminal offence and that it may accordingly breach the process rights provisions provided by Article 6 and the substantive rights provided by Article 7 of the European Convention on Human Rights and Fundamental Freedoms ("ECHR"), given effect in the United Kingdom by the Human Rights Act 1998.

The market abuse regime has been criticised partly on the alleged ground that it is a device designed to achieve the punitive and deterrent goals of the criminal regime without maintaining certain of the protections provided by the criminal offences which the market abuse regime partially mirrors. Additionally, it has been suggested that it will be difficult at times to determine whether conduct constitutes market abuse, even with the assistance provided by the Code of Market Conduct ("COMC" or "MAR 1"), and that market participants may therefore conduct themselves in a manner which is unnecessarily defensive. By contrast, its supporters see it as an important bulwark against abuse in an area which has historically been underpoliced. Indeed, there have been only twelve successful prosecutions for insider dealing between 1990 and 2000.

It is worth mentioning, for the sake of completeness, that the market abuse regime is not the only method of curbing and punishing abusive behaviour. In particular, the FSA is empowered by the FSMA to institute proceedings for either the misleading statements and practices offence[1] or for insider dealing offences,[2] which in many circumstances will overlap with the market abuse regime. The FSA has indicated that it will apply the "realistic prospect of conviction" test drawn from the Code for Crown Prosecutors before launching criminal proceedings. Given that convictions under these sections have been notoriously difficult to achieve, it is not unreasonable to expect that proceedings for market abuse, which have been designed to be easier to pursue than the parallel criminal offences, will be more frequent than prosecutions.

DEFINITION OF MARKET ABUSE

8.02   Market abuse, in essence, is market manipulation or information abuse. Specifically, market abuse consists of behaviour which occurs in relation to "qualifying" investments "traded on" a prescribed market, which a regular user of that market[3] would regard as amounting to a failure to observe "the standard of behaviour reasonably expected of a person in his or their position in relation to the market". Although the FSMA does not specify precisely what is meant by "behaviour", MAR 1 makes it clear that behaviour includes not only dealing, but also arranging deals, causing or procuring or advising others to deal, disseminating relevant information, conducting corporate finance activities, and managing investments.[4] The behaviour in question must additionally fulfil one of the following three core tests[5]:

- the behaviour must be based on information which is not generally available to those using the market but which, if available to a regular user of the market, would or would be likely to be regarded by him as relevant when deciding the terms upon which transactions in investments of the kind in question should be effected. Information which may be obtained by "research and analysis" is to be regarded as "generally available" to market participants[6];

- the behaviour must be likely to give a regular user of the market a false or misleading impression as to the supply of, or demand for, or as to the price or value of, investments of the kind in question; or

- a regular user of the market would, or would be likely to, regard the behaviour as behaviour which would, or would be likely to, distort the market in investments of the kind in question.

---

[1] FSMA, s. 401.
[2] FSMA, s. 402.
[3] A "regular user" is defined as a reasonable person who regularly deals on that market in investments of the kind in question: FSMA, s. 118(10).
[4] MAR 1.3.1E.
[5] FSMA, s. 118(2).
[6] FSMA, s. 118(7).

"Behaviour" includes not only action but also inaction.[7] MAR 1 gives as an example of inaction which may breach the code, a person who fails to make a particular disclosure which they are under a legal or regulatory obligation to make.[8] It is not clear whether mere inaction, in the absence of any such duty, will be treated as capable of amounting to market abuse.

The FSA may take action, not only against a person who has engaged in abusive conduct, but also against a person who has required or encouraged another person to engage in market abuse.[9]

THE CODE OF MARKET CONDUCT ("MAR 1")

8.03   Additionally, the FSA has published MAR 1[10] which gives guidance to market participants as to behaviour which constitutes market abuse. The most important features of MAR 1, and, in particular, their application to each of the three classes of market abuse set out in the FSMA, are discussed below. The FSA intends to amend and update MAR 1 from time to time in order to reflect developments in market practice.

"TRADED ON A PRESCRIBED MARKET"

8.04   The Treasury has prescribed all those markets that are prescribed under the rules of the following bodies[11]:

- COREDEAL Limited;
- The International Petroleum Exchange of London Limited;
- Jiway Limited;
- LIFFE Administration and Management;
- The London Metal Exchange Limited;
- London Stock Exchange plc;
- OM London Exchange Limited; and
- Virt-x Exchange Ltd.

The FSA has taken the view that it would not be appropriate to provide a definitive list of investments which are traded on these prescribed markets, on the grounds that the speed of innovation in respect of new investments which may become tradable on investment exchanges would soon make such a task otiose.

---

[7] FSMA, s. 118(10).
[8] MAR 1.3.2.
[9] FSMA, s. 123.
[10] As required by FSMA, s. 119. See Market Conduct Sourcebook Instrument 2001 (MAR 1).
[11] The Financial Services and Markets Act 2000 (Prescribed Markets and Qualifying Investments) Order 2001 (S.I. 2001 No. 996), s. 118(3). All markets which are established under the rules of a U.K.-recognised investment exchange (Art. 4) and all investments of a kind specified for the purposes of s. 22 of the FSMA (Art. 5) are prescribed for the purposes of the market abuse regime.

However, MAR 1 itself provides objective guidance on whether an investment is traded on a prescribed market. Accordingly, MAR 1 provides that the following investments will be treated as traded on a prescribed market:

(i) investments which have not yet traded subject to the rules of a prescribed market, from the point they start trading subject to the rules of a prescribed market;

(ii) investments which are currently traded subject to the rules of a prescribed market; and

(iii) investments which have traded in the past and can still be traded subject to the rules of a prescribed market.[12]

The guidance supplied in MAR 1 makes it clear that none of the three core tests of market abuse will easily be satisfied if there is in fact no "ongoing market" on the prescribed market in the particular qualifying investment in question. MAR 1 suggests that the answer to the question of whether an ongoing market exists in fact will vary between exchanges, but ultimately will depend upon the frequency and volume of trading in the particular market.[13]

The FSMA makes it clear that the market abuse regime governs not only behaviour in relation to investments, but also "anything which is the subject matter, or whose price or value is expressed by reference to the price or value, of those qualifying investments" and investments whose subject matter is qualifying investments: for example, this will include a spread bet or a commodity by reference to which a qualifying investment which is derivative is priced.[14] MAR 1 also employs the concept of a "relevant product" to describe such a secondary product.

TERRITORIALITY

8.05 The behaviour in question must either occur on a prescribed market in the United Kingdom or must take place in relation to qualifying investments which are traded on a prescribed market that is either situated in the United Kingdom or which can be accessed electronically in the United Kingdom.[15] Similarly, a person may engage in behaviour on an overseas market which has an impact on a prescribed market in the United Kingdom, in which that person is also active. In those circumstances, the FSA will have regard to whether the person in question is in the United Kingdom, and to the rules and practices of the overseas market in deciding what action to take. However, it does not regard itself as bound by the rules, practices and conventions of that overseas market.[16]

The FSA will not necessarily take action against a person who is subject to the jurisdiction of an overseas agency, and who faces regulatory action under the rules of that agency. However, in certain circumstances, the FSA will work with the

---

[12] MAR 1.11.3G.
[13] MAR 1.11.4G.
[14] FSMA, s. 118(6); MAR 1.11.8E.
[15] FSMA, s. 118(5).
[16] MAR 1.2.9G.

overseas agency in order to take enforcement action in both jurisdictions.[17] Additionally, when considering whether to impose a penalty upon a person, the FSA will consider whether action is capable of being taken by an overseas agency and whether it is appropriate for it or the overseas agency to take such action.[18]

THE "REGULAR USER OF THE MARKET"

8.06 During the passage of the FSMA through Parliament, concerns arose relating to the breadth of application of the three core tests. The Government's answer was that the "regular user of the market" appropriately circumscribed the scope of behaviour which was caught by the market abuse regime. The "regular market user" was characterised by the then Economic Secretary to the Treasury, Melanie Johnson, as "the cousin of the courts' reasonable man".[19] The FSA describes the test as premised upon the notion of a "hypothetical, reasonable person" who is familiar with the markets and "whose judgement of behaviour is impartial and objective".[20] Further, this hypothetical person is taken to appreciate that standards between different markets may vary.

The analogy is apt: as with the "reasonable man" test, the "regular user of the market" test is designed to be an objective test. In deciding whether or not enforcement action is to be taken against a person, the FSA must take a view of those standards which such a regular user may properly expect. The required standard will not necessarily dictate that a single course of action is followed: a broad range of practices may meet the "regular user" test in any given situation.[21]

The FSA has repeatedly expressed the view that the "regular user" test is not an "actual user" test: rather, it is a test which looks to an objective, independent standard of what market conduct should be. In other words, more may be expected from market users than that they simply observe those standards and practices current in any particular market at any particular time. What that standard requires is a matter, at first instance, for the FSA, at second instance, for the Tribunal and ultimately, for the courts: it does not simply follow market practice, and in theory at least, it should not simply reproduce the FSA's own preferences. Nevertheless, the FSA has indicated that in most cases, generally accepted market standards are likely to be the same as the standards expected by the regular user.[22]

The FSA has indicated that where market standards differ from the standard which a "regular user" may properly expect, the FSA will be in a position to exercise its discretion to issue a "supervisory response"—the issuing of guidance or a statement to the markets— indicating that it regards that conduct as unacceptable, rather than taking enforcement action.[23]

The question which then arises is how market users are to determine whether the conduct in which they propose to engage is acceptable. Because the FSA is not the "regular user" it does not have the power to set the relevant standard, but merely

---

[17] ENF 14.11.3G.
[18] ENF 14.11.2G.
[19] Financial Services and Markets Bill, Standing Committee A, November 2, 1999, 10.30 a.m.
[20] *Policy Statement*, COMC, para. 5.3.
[21] *Policy Statement*, COMC, para. 5.7.
[22] MAR 1.2.11G.
[23] *ibid.*

to express a view—with which the Tribunal or the courts may disagree—as to what it may be. Therefore, the very difficulty in identifying, prospectively, what conduct the hypothetical regular market user will expect is likely to result in a substantial number of market users seeking advice from external counsel, if only because the FSA regards the taking of legal or other expert advice as a relevant consideration when considering whether a person has taken all reasonable precautions and exercised all due diligence to avoid engaging in market abuse.[24] Similarly, if action is subsequently taken against them, it is likely that suspected market abusers will endeavour to introduce expert evidence relating to both existing market practice and to the proper limits of the regular user test, although it is not particularly easy to foresee exactly what assistance such expert testimony will give the Tribunal and what weight will be given to such testimony if it is admitted.

In applying the regular user test, the FSA will evaluate the behaviour in question against the benchmarks set by:

- the characteristics of the market in question, the investments traded on that market, and the users of the market;

- compliance with the rules and regulations of the market in question and any applicable laws;

- any prevailing market mechanisms, practices and codes of conduct applicable to the market in question;

- the position of the person in question and the standards reasonably to be expected of that person at the time of the behaviour in the light of that person's experience, level of skill and standard of knowledge; and

- the need for market users to conduct their affairs in a manner that does not compromise the fair and efficient operation of the market as a whole or unfairly damage the interests of investors.[25]

At a second level, the FSA will consider, more generally, whether the behaviour in question conforms with generally accepted market standards. The FSA provides guidance upon the specific matters which it will regard as relevant in determining whether market abuse has taken place. Additionally, the FSA has set out a series of illustrative examples of conduct which meets the required standard in MAR 1 under each of the three statutory heads of market abuse. This guide does not seek to reproduce those examples, but will set out and consider the general matters which the FSA has indicated will guide its interpretive discretion.

SEEKING INDIVIDUAL GUIDANCE FROM THE FSA

8.07   It is open to market users to seek individual guidance from the FSA in relation to a proposed course of conduct. Contrary to the FSA's earlier policy on the giving of individual guidance, in which it made it clear that it will not operate

---

[24] ENF 14.5.1G.
[25] MAR 1.2.3E.

a formal "pre-clearance" mechanism for enquiries about market abuse,[26] the FSA has now confirmed that it will provide individual guidance on the applicability of MAR 1 and MAR 2 to corporate transactions. To this end, the FSA has established a specialist team within the Markets and Exchanges Division with a dedicated market conduct helpline.[27]

In seeking such clarification, it will be important both to make a "bona fide attempt to analyse the issue",[28] and to frame any request for guidance as precisely as possible—in particular, identifying the principal seeking the guidance: the FSA will be anxious not to provide firms with carte blanche to engage in conduct. Howard Davies put the point well before the Joint Committee on Financial Services and Markets:

"You have to be very, very clear about the terms of the transaction you are approving, because you do not want to approve something and then discover that, when it is actually effected, the transaction is rather different in crucial ways from the one that was put to you".[29]

Such guidance will not be analogous to a "no action letter" in the sense that the term is used in the United States of America. It will, however, be binding on the FSA, provided that it is in written form. Oral guidance will not be binding as such. However, a caller may request that the conversation be taped. As a result, it will be highly unlikely that the FSA will take action against the enquirer if the advice is followed.[30]

The FSA is concerned to ensure that its developing policy is understood by market participants; to this end, the FSA's Markets & Exchanges Division issues regular "Market Watch" newsletters. Further, interested institutions an trade associations, through the Market Abuse Co-ordination Project ("MACP") will have an opportunity to discuss issues arising from market developments, to consider the conclusions of projects carried out by various bodies and individual participants and generally, to be given a forum in which they are able to air their concerns about market conduct. The MACP was the brainchild of the Financial Law Panel—who will also be co-ordinating the MACP effort—together with a range of trade associations.

INTENT

8.08 One of the more controversial aspects of the definition of market abuse is that it does not require a person to *intend* to abuse the market. The absence of the element of intention from the definition of market abuse should assist the FSA in establishing that market abuse has taken place. Moreover, as the FSA pointed out in its evidence to the Joint Committee, intent in the criminal law is associated with criminal offences which carry the threat of imprisonment because they denote "serious moral culpability"[31]: as the market abuse regime is avowedly regulatory

---

[26] FSA, *Policy Statement, The FSA's approach to giving guidance and waivers to firms*, para. 23.
[27] The procedure on seeking guidance is set out in SUP 9.
[28] FSA, *Policy Statement, The FSA's approach to giving guidance and waivers to firms*, para. 17.
[29] Joint Committee on Financial Services and Markets, *First Report*, para. 274.
[30] FSA Market Watch Newsletter No. 1, September 2001.
[31] FSA, *Supplementary Memorandum, to the Joint Committee on Financial Services and Markets*, para. 7.

rather than criminal in nature, then—so the argument proceeds—intent should not be a necessary component of the regime.

Nevertheless, intent (or, at least, the state of mind of the accused) in various guises has a series of important roles to play within the market abuse regime. First, various definitions of market abuse in MAR 1 rely in part upon purpose for which a transaction is carried out.[32] At a second level the FSA will consider, *inter alia*, whether conduct was "deliberate or reckless" when deciding whether to take enforcement action.[33] At a third level, when the FSA considers whether, in response to a warning notice, the person under investigation has established either of the "defences" provided by section 123(2) of the FSMA, the question of the person's reasonable belief that his behaviour did not amount to market abuse is directly relevant. The FSA's guidance which governs its conduct following the issuing of a warning notice looks to a variety of factors, including that person's knowledge, skill and experience (which may affect the person's capacity to appreciate the consequences of their conduct) and whether that person can show that the conduct was engaged in for a legitimate purpose.[34] At a fourth level, market abuse which is carried out intentionally or recklessly may result in a higher penalty being imposed than might otherwise be the case.[35] In short, although a person's intention to abuse the market may not be directly relevant to the principal question of whether market abuse has been committed, it is nevertheless an important relevant consideration at subsequent stages of regulatory action.

REQUIRING OR ENCOURAGING

8.09   The FSMA empowers the FSA to take action, not only against a person who has engaged in market abuse, but also against any person who has required or encouraged another person to engage in conduct which would amount to market abuse if the "requirer" or "encourager" had itself engaged it the conduct in question.[36]

The FSMA itself does not elaborate further on the nature of conduct that will be held to amount to requiring or encouraging. However, MAR 1 provides guidance upon the various circumstances in which the FSA is likely to regard action as requiring or encouraging market abuse, and certain situations where the FSA will not take that view of the conduct in question.

The FSA has indicated that, when considering whether behaviour amounts to requiring or encouraging, it will consider the surrounding circumstances, including:

- acceptable market practices;

- the skill, experience and knowledge of the alleged encourager or requirer;

- the degree of control or influence which the encourager or requirer has over the encouraged or required.[37]

---

[32] *e.g.*, the description of an abusive squeeze: see, MAR 1.6.13E.
[33] ENF 14.4.2G(1)(b).
[34] ENF 14.5.1.
[35] FSMA, s.124(2); ENF. 14.7.4G(2).
[36] FSMA, s.123(1)(b).
[37] MAR 1.8.4G.

If early or selective disclosure of information by a person has taken place outside the scope of these circumstances, MAR 1 suggests that it will run the risk of being regarded as constituting requiring or encouraging, unless there is a legitimate purpose for the making of the disclosure.[38] The FSA has provided a series of examples of such legitimate purposes, which range from disclosures governed by the rules of the FSA, a prescribed market or the Takeover Code at one end of the spectrum to disclosures to a person's professional advisers at the other end.[39] The FSA recommends that in such circumstances, it will be prudent to provide the person to whom the information has been provided with a statement—which may be incorporated within a contract governing the relationship—warning that person from basing behaviour which might amount to market abuse on the information which they have received until it is generally available.

The position of intermediaries through whom a person carries out a transaction which amounts to market abuse is somewhat uncomfortable. At one end of the spectrum, if an intermediary knows that its customer is engaging in market abuse, the intermediary may well be regarded as having engaged in abusive conduct itself. At the other end of the spectrum, MAR 1 suggests that an intermediary which ought reasonably to have known that its customer was engaging in market abuse— for example, because the transaction appears to have no legitimate commercial rationale—may also be caught.[40] However, it may sometimes be difficult to determine whether an intermediary's conduct conforms with the code. For example, where a customer trades on information which is not generally available to those using the market, even if the intermediary ought to have known that this was the case, it cannot be said that the intermediary's conduct is based upon the information which the customer has, but which it has not imparted to the intermediary. Ultimately, the risk run by intermediaries may be determined by reference, at least in part, to the nature and extent of the interaction which takes place between the intermediary and its customer.[41]

MISUSE OF INFORMATION WHICH IS NOT GENERALLY AVAILABLE

8.10   The "misuse of information" head,[42] is in essence a species of market abuse that runs parallel to the insider dealing offences created by Part V of the Criminal Justice Act 1993. In short, in order to fall within this head of market abuse:

- the information must have a "material influence", *i.e.* it must be an influence, if not the only influence, on the conduct in question;

- the information must not be generally available;

- the information must be likely to be regarded by a regular user as relevant to the terms upon which a regular user would enter into transactions; and

---

[38] MAR 1.8.5G.

[39] MAR 1.8.6G.

[40] MAR 1.8.8G.

[41] FSA *Consultation Paper 76, Supplement to the Draft Code of Market Conduct*, para. 2.9.

[42] FSMA, s. 118(2)(a).

- the information must relate to matters which such a regular user would reasonably expect to be disclosed to users of the particular prescribed market.[43]

(a) "Information that is general available"

8.11 Information is treated as generally available when it has either been disclosed through research or analysis[44] and specifically:

- if it is disclosed under the rules of the market, or through an accepted channel for disseminating that information;
- if it is contained in records which the public may inspect;
- if the information has otherwise been made public; or
- if the information can otherwise be obtained by observation.[45]

(b) "Relevant information"

8.12 The question as to whether information is relevant is determined by reference to the regular user of the market test. Primarily, the FSA will be guided by the following considerations:

- whether the information is material;
- whether the information is current;
- whether the information is reliable; and
- whether there is other material information which is generally available to market users, and whether the information in question is different from the information which is generally available.[46]

Additionally, if the information relates to possible future developments which are not immediately subject to an expectation of disclosure, the FSA will look to both the degree of certainty that the developments will occur, and the significance of those developments were they to occur.[47]

(c) "Discloseable and announceable information"

8.13 The FSA is of the view that a regular user of the market will only reasonably expect information to be disclosed to other market users if it is either "discloseable information" or "announceable information".[48] Specifically, the FSA will treat information as discloseable if it is subject to a legal or regulatory disclosure requirement: for example, under the Takeover Code or the Rules of a Recognised

---

[43] MAR 1.4.4E.
[44] FSMA, s. 118(7).
[45] MAR 1.4.5E.
[46] MAR 1.4.9E.
[47] MAR 1.4.10E.
[48] MAR 1.4.12E.

Investment Exchange.[49] Announceable information differs from discloseable information in that, although it may not be subject to a specific disclosure requirement, it is nevertheless information which is routinely subject to a public announcement, such as information which is routinely announced by the Government.[50]

(d) Asymmetry between disclosure requirement in two linked markets

8.14   When considering its position—and framing its compliance procedures—in relation to the new regime, a firm may well need to reconcile the fact that it is subject to different disclosure requirements in relation to trading on different exchanges or markets even though there may be linkages between the investments or commodities traded. For example, a person might possess information which was disclosable to an equity market, but not to a commodity derivatives market. Alternatively, a commodity producer might wish to hedge its position in another market (for example, by dealing in a futures contract on a commodity derivatives market), before disclosing relevant information on, for example, an equity market. Under MAR 1, such conduct would not ordinarily amount to market abuse.[51]

In short, MAR 1 makes it clear that:

- where a disclosure obligation exists in relation to market A (*e.g.*, an equity market), dealing or arranging deals in relation either to investments traded on that market, or to related products—such as equity derivatives—on the basis of the disclosable information, will constitute market abuse; and

- however, if dealing or arranging deals takes place on market B (*e.g.*, a commodity derivatives market), in relation to which there is no disclosure obligation, market abuse will not take place.

Nevertheless, the FSA warns market participants that, although MAR 1 may not bite on such transactions, commodity producers whose equities are traded on an exchange may be subject to a wholly distinct disclosure requirement in relation to the equity market. The FSA gives the example of a commodity producer which discovers that its production of that commodity is lower than expected, and therefore decides to hedge its position in the commodity derivatives market. In these circumstances, although there may be no disclosure obligation ahead of trading in the commodity derivatives market, the producer may be obliged to disclose "significant news as soon as possible"[52] to the first market. In other words, although dealing in the second market in these circumstances may be permitted, the commodity producer may be in breach of its obligation under the listing rules in the first market.[53]

However, in these circumstances, a person who deals or arranges deals in the shares of, for example, a commodity producer on an equity market (or in derivatives related to the shares of the producer on a derivatives market) on the basis of relevant information which is not generally available and is discloseable or announceable in relation to that market will prima facie commit market abuse.

---

[49]   MAR 1.4.14E.
[50]   MAR 1.4.15E.
[51]   MAR 1.4.17E.
[52]   European Directive 79/279.
[53]   FSA *Policy Statement, COMC*, para. 6.11.

FALSE OR MISLEADING IMPRESSIONS

8.15   The second head of market abuse[54] broadly mirrors the misleading state-ments and practices offence carried forward in section 397 of the FSMA. Indeed, market abuse of this species has been treated as criminal as long ago as 1814 when in the well known case of *R v. De Berenger*,[55] a prosecution for "conspiracy by false rumours to raise the price of the public funds and securities" was successfully brought against the defendants who "by false reports, rumours, arts and con-trivances" spread the rumour that Napoleon Bonaparte had been killed, and that peace was to be declared, the intended result of which was to "raise the price of the Government funds".

Market abuse may be committed in a variety of circumstances. As in the *De Berenger* case, it may be carried out by a person who disseminates false or misleading information in order to "ramp" an investment: for example, by driving up its value by publishing false information and then selling a holding of shares in order to realise a profit created by the false or misleading information.[56] Equally, market abuse will occur when a person engages in "artificial" transactions (such as "wash trades") without any commercial rationale, which have the effect of creating the false or misleading impression that there is greater market activity in relation to that investment than is in fact the case.[57] Similarly, a person who is responsible for disseminating information through an accepted channel—such as a channel prescribed under the rules of a market—must not submit false or misleading information and is obliged to take reasonable care to ensure that information so submitted is not false or misleading.[58] The prohibition equally applies to engaging in a course of conduct which is likely to give a false or misleading impression.[59]

In order to be caught by this description of market abuse, the FSA is of the view that:

- the behaviour must be likely to give rise to, or to give an impression of, a price or value or volume of trading which is materially false or misleading; and

- "likely" means that there is a real and not fanciful likelihood of the effect which is feared, although the effect need not be "more likely than not".[60]

Additionally, the FSA will determine the likelihood of a false or misleading impression being created by reference to a variety of factors, including the experi-ence and knowledge of market users, the structure of the market, including its reporting, notification and transparency requirements, legal and regulatory requirements relevant to the markets, accepted market practices, the identity and position of the person whose behaviour is in question, and the extent to which the activity in question has been disclosed, and the nature of that disclosure.[61]

---

[54] FSMA, s. 118(2)(b).
[55] (1814) 3 M. & S. 66.
[56] MAR 1.5.15E.
[57] MAR 1.5.8E.
[58] MAR 1.5.18E.
[59] MAR 1.5.21E.
[60] MAR 1.5.4E. Also, see below under burden and standard of proof.
[61] MAR 1.5.5E.

Importantly, there is no requirement that a person have an interest in the investment in relation to which the false or misleading impression is created: an unhappy journalist who took revenge for being sacked by filling his final column with misleading information will still be caught by this head of market abuse.[62] However, the absence of an interest might go some way to showing that an actuating purpose of the behaviour was not to create a false or misleading impression.[63]

DISTORTING THE MARKET

8.16   The FSA regards the market distortion head of market abuse[64] as being aimed at behaviour which "interferes with the proper operation of market forces with the purpose of positioning prices at a distorted level". MAR 1 indicates that ordinarily, trading at times and in volumes beneficial to the market user has a positive effect on the liquidity of markets, and does not of itself amount to market distortion, as long as there is a legitimate commercial rationale behind the transaction: for example, entering into transactions close to the close of a market for the purpose of index tracking.[65] Neither does trading at high or low prices relative to the normal range of trading in an investment of itself establish that distortion is taking place. However, marking the close—for example, by buying or selling components of the FTSE-100 in high volume and at notably high or low prices, immediately prior to the close of trading in order to avoid paying out on a spread bet is likely to be treated as market distortion.[66] It is clear, therefore, that market distortion will be difficult in practice to separate from legitimate commercial activity. In order to meet this test, the behaviour must:

- be likely to distort the market in an investment; and

- "likely" meaning that there is a real and not fanciful likelihood of the effect which is feared. However the behaviour does not need to be "likely" on the balance of probabilities.[67]

Specifically, the FSA regards the following factors taken together as indicative of market distortion:

- entering into a transaction or transactions if one of the purposes of the transactions is to position the price of an investment at a distorted level, in particular if the timing of the transaction coincides with the time at which the price of an investment is relevant (*e.g.* the close of the FTSE-100). Indicators of price positioning behaviour includes the fact that a person has

---

[62] Indeed, that person may also commit the criminal offence created by FSMA, s. 397.
[63] MAR 1.5.16E.
[64] FSMA, s. 118(2)(c).
[65] MAR 1.6.10E.
[66] It may be difficult in practice, in circumstances such as these, to distinguish a legitimate motive for such a transaction (*e.g.* the unwinding of a hedge against a spread bet) from such an illegitimate commercial rationale. The FSA will need to consider the circumstances which surround the transaction in order to determine the true rationale for the transaction.
[67] MAR 1.6.4E.

an interest in the price or value of the investment, the relative volume or size of the transactions in question, whether the transaction resulted in an increase in the quoted price of the investment and whether the price paid for the investment has been successively or consistently increased by the person in question. However, MAR 1 makes it clear that the presence of these factors will not conclusively establish that market abuse has occurred[68]; and

- behaviour carried out for the purpose of engaging in an "abusive squeeze": that is, for the purpose of distorting the price at which other persons are forced to deliver or take delivery under a contract. For this purpose, the abusive squeezer must have both a "significant influence" over the supply of, demand for, or the delivery mechanisms relating to, an investment, and a position in that investment which provides for the delivery of the investment in question.[69] The FSA will take into account various factors in deciding whether the squeeze in question is legitimate or abusive, including whether the person is prepared to relax their influence in order to maintain an orderly market, the price at which that person is prepared to relax their influence, the extent to which the conduct gives rise to the risk of multi-lateral settlement default, the extent to which the price for delivery outside the settlement mechanisms of the market diverge from the price outside those mechanisms, and the relative divergence between spot and forward prices, or the relative expense of borrowing rates.

SAFE HARBOURS

8.17 The FSMA provides for a series of "safe harbours" from a charge that a market participant has engaged in market abuse. First, the Act provides that where behaviour conforms with a rule[70] which includes a provision to the effect that behaviour conforming with the rule does not amount to market abuse, that behaviour does not amount to market abuse.[71] Under this section, the FSA has made rules which provide for such safe harbours within the context of:

- the Conduct of Business rules relating to Chinese walls[72];

- certain aspects of the Listing Rules relating to share buy backs[73] and the timing, dissemination or availability, content and standard of care applicable to a disclosure, announcement, communication or release of information[74];

- the Price Stabilising Rules; and

---

[68] MAR 1.6.11E.
[69] MAR 1.6.14E.
[70] *e.g.*, rules made under FSMA, s. 143 endorsing the Takeover Code and the Rules Governing the Substantial Acquisitions of Shares, and Price Stabilising Rules made under FSMA, s. 144.
[71] FSMA, s. 118(8).
[72] COB 2.4.
[73] Listing Rules, r. 15.1(b).
[74] See MAR 1, Annex 1G.

- behaviour conforming with certain London Metal Exchange Rules.[75]

Secondly, a separate section provides that a person may rely upon a description in MAR 1 of behaviour which does not amount to market abuse as establishing conclusively that that behaviour is not market abuse.[76] The relevant safe harbours are set out in MAR 1 under each head of market abuse, and also include those of the Rules Governing the Substantial Acquisitions of Shares that have been endorsed.

Thirdly, the FSA is empowered to create, and has created, a special series of safe harbours in relation to the City Code on Takeovers and Mergers,[77] subject to Treasury approval (which has been received).

Finally, MAR 1 has evidential status in determining whether behaviour constitutes market abuse: a person accused of market abuse whose conduct conforms largely with MAR 1's description of behaviour which does not amount to market abuse, may nevertheless argue that substantial conformity with MAR 1 is evidence that his or her conduct does not constitute market abuse.[78]

It is outside the scope of this book to set out in full all of the safe harbours provided by MAR 1. Certain of the safe harbours specified by MAR 1 itself broadly mirror, and in some cases, go beyond, the defences to the criminal offences to which they run parallel. However, they have not been precisely reproduced in MAR 1.[79] For example, there is no specific safe harbour in the part of MAR 1 that concerns misuse of information equivalent to a key defence provided in insider dealing cases—that the defendant did not expect the dealing to result in a profit or the avoidance of a loss[80]—although it is arguable that this, broadly, is the effect of MAR 1. The essence of these safe harbours is set out below.

(a) Misuse of information

- **8.18** Dealing or arranging deals in circumstances that are required in order to comply with legal or regulatory obligations which pre-date the acquisition of the relevant information.[81]

- Dealing or arranging deals when in possession of relevant information, if that information did not influence the conduct in question.

The FSA will presume that the information did not influence the conduct under consideration if a firm's decision to engage in the conduct was taken before the information was in that person's possession and the terms upon which the transaction was to be entered into did not change after the information came into that person's possession. Furthermore, if the person in question is an organisation, the FSA will proceed on the basis that the information had no influence on the conduct if those individuals in possession of the information had no involvement in

---

[75] MAR 1.6.19P.
[76] FSMA, s. 122(1).
[77] FSMA, s. 120.
[78] FSMA, s. 122(2).
[79] FSA, *Policy Statement, COMC*, para. 6.21.
[80] Criminal Justice Act 1993, s. 53(1)(a).
[81] MAR 1.4.20P.

the decision to engage in the conduct, or did not behave in a manner which influenced the decision to engage in the conduct, or had no contact which could lead to the information being passed on with those persons who took the decision to engage in the conduct. Equally, information held by persons on one side of an effective Chinese wall or its equivalent will not be held to influence the decision of persons on the other side of that Chinese wall to deal.[82]

- Dealing or arranging deals based upon information as to any person's intention to deal or information relating to transactions which have already taken place is not market abuse, unless that information is in connection with a takeover bid or information relating to new offers, issues or placements.[83]

- Dealing or arranging deals which take place in connection with, and for the sole purpose of the acquisition or disposal of a stake in a company, and which take place for the sole benefit of the person making the acquisition or disposal, and the information consists of certain specified facts, including the kind, price and number of investments which are to be acquired or disposed of.[84] Therefore, a person's knowledge that it is to make a takeover bid in relation to a company does not place him in the absurd position of disqualifying that person from taking a stake in that company (which is also the general effect of the "market information" defence to the offence of insider dealing). However, transactions which do no more than provide an economic exposure to fluctuations in the share price of the company will be caught by MAR 1.

(b) False and misleading impressions

- 8.19 Transactions effecting either:

  — the taking or unwinding of a position for the purpose of arbitrage or differences in the taxation of income or capital returns generated by investments or commodities; or
  — lending or borrowing investments or commodities to meet a commercial demand

provided that a regular user of the market would regard the transaction as properly executed and the principal rationale for the transaction in question as a legitimate commercial rationale.[85]

- Making a report or disclosure that is expressly required or expressly permitted by FSA Rules, the Rules of a prescribed market, the rules of the Takeover Code or Rules Governing the Substantial Acquisitions of Shares or by any other applicable statute or regulation, as long as the report is made in the manner specified by the applicable legal or regulatory requirement.[86]

---

[82] MAR 1.4.21P–1.4.24P.
[83] MAR 1.4.26P.
[84] MAR 1.4.28P.
[85] MAR 1.5.24P.
[86] MAR 1.5.25P.

- An organisation does not commit market abuse if one of its employees disseminates information which he or she would know or could reasonably be expected to know was false or misleading, were that employee in possession of information held behind a Chinese wall, or its equivalent, and that employee did not in fact know and could not reasonably be expected to know that the information was false or misleading.[87]

(c) Distorting the market

8.20   The FSA has prescribed a single safe harbour in relation to activity which may be taken to distort the market. However, it is important to realise that market distortion may sometimes overlap with the creation of misleading impressions.[88] Accordingly, the relevant safe harbours may in principle also apply to conduct which amounts to market distortion.

The FSA has prescribed one safe harbour in relation to this head of market abuse: behaviour complying with the London Metal Exchange rules contained in "Market Aberrations: The Way Forward" governing the conduct of long position holders as a safe harbour.[89]

For the sake of completeness, the FSA has made it clear that the RIE rulebooks do not permit or require behaviour which amounts to market abuse.[90] Furthermore, certain specific RIE rules have been rendered safe harbours.[91] However, the FSA rejected the proposal that compliance with the rules of RIEs should themselves constitute a monolithic safe harbour, but that weight should be given to compliance with the rules of the exchange in determining whether market abuse has taken place. The rationale behind this approach is not simply that the FSA should not be fettered by the rules of an RIE from taking action (although the FSA has ultimate oversight of the rules of RIEs[92]), but specifically that abusive conduct may affect more than one market. However, it was suggested by Andrew Whittaker before the Joint Committee that:

> "Where an abuse arises only within a particular exchange, we would expect it to be that exchange that would take enforcement action: we ourselves would not get involved".[93]

Nevertheless, MAR 1 makes it clear that it is at least theoretically possible for behaviour which is permitted by the rules of an exchange to constitute market abuse.[94] Clearly, the interplay between the regulatory responsibilities of the RIEs and of the FSA will be of prime importance under the new regime.

---

[87] MAR 1.5.27P.
[88] MAR 1.6.7E.
[89] MAR 1.6.19P.
[90] MAR 1.2.12.
[91] *e.g.,* MAR 1.6.19P.
[92] FSMA, Pt XVIII.
[93] FSA, *Joint Committee on Financial Services and Markets, First Report,* para. 276.
[94] MAR 1.2.8G.

SAFE HARBOURS AND ENDORSEMENT: THE TAKEOVER CODE AND THE RULES GOVERNING THE SUBSTANTIAL ACQUISITIONS OF SHARES

8.21 In the absence of a safe harbour covering the key aspects of the Takeover Code, the foremost concern of the Takeover Panel was that participants in a takeover battle would make a "strategic" complaint to the FSA, which would be induced to consider taking enforcement action. The resulting regulatory action would, it was feared, introduce an element of uncertainty and delay into the takeover battle. On the final day of debate in the House of Lords, a compromise was reached.

The compromise took the form of a provision empowering the FSA to:

- endorse both the Takeover Code and the Rules Governing the Substantial Acquisitions of Shares.[95] As a result of the endorsement, the FSA may take enforcement action against firms and approved persons which breach the Takeover Code or the Rules Governing the Substantial Acquisitions of Shares, at the request of the Takeover Panel; and

- establish within MAR 1, with the approval of the Treasury, safe harbours covering behaviour required by the Takeover Code.[96] The FSA is empowered separately to create safe harbours governing the Rules Governing the Substantial Acquisitions of Shares.[97]

The rules which are so endorsed are set out in MAR 1.[98] The FSA is of the view that it has now endorsed all the relevant rules, and that those rules which remain unendorsed do not permit or require market abuse.[99]

One of the points of contention during the passage of the FSMA through Parliament was whether the FSA or the Takeover Panel should be entitled to determine whether the FSA or the Takeover Panel should police allegations of market abuse during takeover battles. Although it was made clear in the Lords that it would be improper for the final say to be given to the Takeover Panel, the position has been resolved by the requirement that the FSA must "keep itself informed of the way" in which the Takeover Panel interprets and administers the provisions of the Takeover Code which constitute safe harbours.[1] Moreover, the Enforcement Manual provides that the FSA will "attach considerable weight to the views" of the Takeover Panel as to whether conduct complies with the Takeover Code.[2]

The concerns of the Takeover Panel were also met by the FSA's policy that it will take into account the possibility that enforcement action will affect the timetable or the outcome of a bid. In particular, the FSA has indicated[3] that it will ordinarily

---

[95] FSMA, s. 143.
[96] FSMA, s. 120.
[97] FSMA, s. 122(1).
[98] MAR 1, Annex 2G.
[99] MAR 1 1.7.6E.
[1] FSMA, s. 120(3).
[2] ENF 14. 9.3G; MAR 1.2.8G.
[3] ENF 2.6.2G.

not take action—including applying for an injunction[4] or a restitution order[5]—against a person who is subject to the Takeover Code while a bid is current, unless:

- the person under investigation does not co-operate with the Takeover Panel;
- the person fails to comply with a Takeover Panel ruling;
- the Takeover Panel invites the FSA to consider using its powers;
- the behaviour involves securities which are outside the jurisdiction of the Takeover Panel; or
- the behaviour threatens the stability of the financial system.[6]

Furthermore, the FSA has suggested that it will only take action against a person when it considers that the Takeover Panel's powers will be insufficient.

The FSA has undertaken not to take regulatory action which is likely to have an adverse effect on the timing or outcome of a bid in all other circumstances without first consulting the Takeover Panel and giving due weight to its views. Likewise, if the Takeover Panel considers that conduct is in breach of the Takeover Code, the FSA has indicated that it would ordinarily not deploy its powers under the market abuse regime.[7] Similarly, the extent to which any behaviour complied with the Takeover Code, or whether guidance from the Takeover Panel has been sought and acted upon is a relevant factor in deciding whether the "defences" established by section 123(2) of the FSMA have been established.[8] Equally, co-operation with the Takeover Panel will be a factor which mitigates the level of any penalty that is imposed.[9]

JOURNALISTS' INTERESTS IN SECURITIES

8.22 MAR 1 will also bite on journalists (or for that matter, editors) who deal in investments in advance of the publication of a "buy" or "sell" recommendation in their publication or journal. The FSA's favoured response is to rely upon an "enhanced disclosure" obligation contained in the revised PCC Code of Practice.

The FSA's position was reached following discussions with the Press Complaints Commission ("PCC"), which led to the publication by the PCC of a note to editors containing "best practice" guidance on financial journalism.[10] The note builds upon the PCC's Code of Practice, which dictates that journalists must not use for their own profit financial information they receive in advance of its general publication, must disclose "significant financial interests" to the editor or financial editor, and must not buy or sell investments about which they have written recently or intend to write about.[11] The note to editors goes further than the Code of

---

[4] ENF 6.6.2G.
[5] ENF 9.6.12G.
[6] ENF 14.9.6G.
[7] ENF 14.4.2G(4).
[8] ENF 14.5.1G.
[9] ENF 14.7.4G(5)(b).
[10] Press Release, *PCC issues "best practice" guidance on financial journalism*, March 19, 2001.
[11] PCC, Code of Practice, clause 14.

Practice, in that it encourages editors to put in place safeguards against improper use of information by journalists, including voluntary external disclosure of investments that the journalist holds or has dealt in. Additionally, the note suggests that journalists apply the "Private Eye" test to any contemplated conduct: "if it would embarrass a journalist to read about his or her actions in 'Private Eye', and at the same time undermine the integrity of the newspaper, then don't do it".

It is worth noting briefly for the sake of completeness that the disclosure-based approach is mirrored in the exemption in the Financial Promotion regime which governs the publication of regulated communications by journalists.[12]

Process

8.23 The procedure which must be followed if enforcement action is taken under Part VIII of the FSMA is the child of compromise. As originally drafted, the FSA was in effect empowered to act as a court of first instance. The Tribunal was originally described as an "appeal" tribunal, and its primary function in market abuse cases was essentially conceived as being to check and to oversee exercises of power by the FSA. The FSA, by contrast, was empowered to exercise a primary, judicial power over those who it investigated.

To some extent, the power of the FSA is still judicial rather than administrative in nature, although the judicial flavour of its proceedings have been significantly diluted since the first draft of the FSMA. Nevertheless, the FSA's role is now akin in many ways to a prosecutor. It is for the FSA to frame the "charges"; however, unless an applicant chooses not to take his or her case to the Tribunal, ultimate discretion rests with the FSA itself. Moreover, the identities of the persons who investigate the circumstances giving rise to market abuse will be different from those which decide whether proceedings are to be brought.

Investigation of market abuse

8.24 Although the FSA is empowered to conduct a general investigation of a firm under section 167 of the FSMA, a specific power to investigate market abuse, misleading statements or practices and insider dealing is provided by section 168(2)(b) of the FSMA. The investigatory power under this subsection is extremely wide. Under section 173, an investigator is empowered to require any person who may be able to give information which may be relevant to the investigation to provide that information to the investigator. The power can be used to require such a person to provide documents to the investigator, or to answer questions posed by the investigator. Likewise, under section 175, the investigator has the power to require that documents be provided to the inquiry by a third party who possesses the document. Further, under section 175(2), the investigator is empowered to require that person, or various other persons including lawyers,[13] actuaries, accountants, controllers or employees of the person under investigation to provide an explanation of the document.

---

[12] The Financial Services and Markets Act 2000 (Financial Promotion) Order 2001, para. 20.
[13] FSMA, s. 413 preserves legal professional privilege: see ENF 2.10.

Although a person who is subject to investigation will ordinarily receive a written notice that it has appointed an investigator, the notification requirement does not apply to investigations into market abuse conducted within the scope of section 168(2).[14] However, as a matter of practice, the FSA has indicated that it will consider notifying the persons under investigation[15] as soon as their identities become clear, unless to do so would prejudice the ability of the FSA to conduct the investigation.[16] Although there is no statutory requirement to do so, the FSA will inform a person that an investigation has come to an end as soon as it considers it appropriate to do so.[17]

Following the *Saunders* case,[18] a statement made under compulsion to an investigator cannot be used against that person as evidence in any subsequent criminal proceedings, either by citing any answer as evidence or by asking questions relating to the answer previously given. Similarly, following the concern that the market abuse regime amounts in substance to criminal proceedings, the FSA has provided that such statements may not be used in proceedings in relation to market abuse proceedings action against that person.[19] Voluntarily-made statements may nevertheless be admitted in evidence. An explanation to this effect will be given by the FSA.[20] A person under investigation will also be informed of the right to be accompanied by a legal advisor.

ALTERNATIVES TO MARKET ABUSE PROCEEDINGS

8.25 A person who engages in conduct amounting to market abuse may find that it is in breach of the provisions of the several regimes which run parallel to the market abuse regime. For example, conduct may simultaneously breach:

- the criminal law;

- the Rules of a Recognised Investment Exchange;

- the Takeover Code and the Rules Governing the Substantial Acquisitions of Shares; and

- other statements of principles or rules made by the FSA, in particular, Principle 5 of the Principles for Businesses ("PRIN"), the relevant provisions of the Conduct of Business Sourcebook, and the Statements of Principle and Code of Practice for Approved Persons ("APER").

It should be mentioned that there will be circumstances where behaviour does not breach the market abuse regime but breaches one of these other provisions. Although certain aspects of the parallel regimes—such as elements of the defences to the criminal offences[21]—have intentionally been incorporated within MAR 1,

---

[14] FSMA, s. 170(2).
[15] ENF 2.12.4G.
[16] ENF 2.12.6G.
[17] ENF 2.12.7G.
[18] *Saunders v. U.K.*, No. 19187/91.
[19] ENF 2.10.4G.
[20] ENF 2.14.6G.
[21] FSA, *Policy Statement*, COMC, para. 6.21.

MAR 1 is not, and is not intended to be, a complete guide to prohibited market conduct.

In theory, a person may face double or even triple jeopardy in three separate judicial or quasi-judicial forums in respect of proceedings arising from the same course of conduct. In practice, the intention is that the overlap between the various regimes should be avoided. The interplay between the FSMA and the Takeover Code and the Rules Governing the Substantial Acquisitions of Shares is discussed above. Likewise, the FSA has stated that it will consider the extent to which the misconduct is capable of being addressed by, for example, disciplinary action by a Recognised Investment Exchange[22] before commencing action for market abuse. The FSA will attempt to co-ordinate any action which it proposes to take with the Recognised Investment Exchange or Recognised Clearing House[23] and is developing operating arrangements with each of the relevant United Kingdom authorities to that end.[24] Helpfully, the FSA is also empowered to require a Recognised Investment Exchange or Recognised Clearing House to limit or suspend or stop its disciplinary processes if it is necessary to do so.[25]

As noted above, in almost all cases which involve authorised persons, the FSA will also be presented with a choice between commencing market abuse proceedings and taking disciplinary action for breach of Principle 5 of the PRIN which requires a firm to "observe proper standards of market conduct". Furthermore, a approved person who commits market abuse will be likely to have breached Principle 3 of the APER which requires that an approved person observes "proper standards of market conduct in carrying out his controlled function". The Code of Practice indicates that compliance with the standards set out in MAR 1 and the IPC will "tend to show compliance" with Principle 3 of APER.

Disciplinary action by the person's SRO under the predecessor to Principle 5 was historically the method by which market abuse by the representatives of authorised persons was policed. However, the FSA considers that in circumstances where it is clear that market abuse has taken place it will take enforcement action against that person for market abuse. However, the FSA reserves the right to take action for breach of PRIN 5 or APER 3 in circumstances where it is satisfied that it would not be appropriate to deal with the case under the market abuse regime and where the "principal mischief" is regarded as the breach of the Principle, or where it is not clear what the principal mischief is.[26]

In certain circumstances, the FSA will therefore have a choice as to whether to commence criminal proceedings or to take civil action against the alleged offender under the market abuse regime. The interplay between these two parallel regimes is particularly instructive. The FSA does not intend to subject persons to the double jeopardy of both a prosecution and a sanction for market abuse.[27] First, guidelines[28] have been agreed between the various interested parties, including the

---

[22] ENF 2.6.2G(4)(a).
[23] ENF 14.9.1G.
[24] ENF 11.8.3G.
[25] FSMA, s. 128.
[26] ENF 14.8.
[27] ENF 15.7.4G.
[28] For guidelines on investigation of cases of interest or concern to the Financial Services Authority and other prosecuting and investigating agencies, see ENF, Annex 1G.

FSA, the Serious Fraud Office, the DTI, and the Crown Prosecution Service. In short, the FSA will be likely to have conduct of the case in circumstances where:

- market confidence or consumer protection issues arise;

- the FSA is best placed to prosecute take regulatory action including action for market abuse or other civil action against the person;

- the alleged offenders are authorised or approved by the FSA, or are issuers or sponsors of a security admitted or to be admitted to the official list;

- there is a need for FSA powers which may take immediate effect (such as the power to vary the permission of an authorised firm);

- assistance from an overseas regulatory authority is likely to be needed;

- the public interest favours achieving reparation for victims, which is likely to be undermined by a prosecution;

- criminal conduct is in a "grey area", but regulatory contraventions are clear; or

- parts of the case are best investigated with regulatory expertise.

In view of the last two factors in particular, it is likely that in many cases the FSA will be the preferred prosecutor. However, various other factors—including the lack of the power of the FSA to arrest suspected offenders and the possibility that the criminal conduct may in part lie outside the authority of the FSA as a prosecuting authority—may militate in favour of one of the other prosecutors having custody of the case in certain given circumstances.

Secondly, the FSA has stated that it will follow the "public interest" test set out in the Code for Crown Prosecutors in deciding whether it—or one of the other prosecuting authorities—should follow the criminal route.[29] The public interest test requires that the following two questions are answered in the affirmative:

- that there is sufficient evidence to provide a realistic prospect of conviction against each defendant on each charge; and

- that a criminal prosecution is in the public interest.

If the test is not met—which, given the difficulty of obtaining a conviction, may often be the case—then civil action will be considered. Further, the FSA has published a non exhaustive list of additional factors which it will consider when deciding whether to prosecute rather than take civil action:

- the seriousness of the misconduct;

- whether victims have suffered loss;

- the extent and nature of the loss;

---

[29] ENF 15.7.1, and see the Code for Crown Prosecutors in the Enforcement Manual, Annex 1G.

- the effect of the misconduct on the market;

- the extent of profits made or loss avoided;

- whether there are grounds for believing that the misconduct is likely to be continued or repeated;

- the relevant criminal, disciplinary and compliance history of the person under investigation;

- whether steps have promptly and voluntarily been taken to remedy the loss and resolve any systems failures which resulted in the conduct;

- the effects of a prosecution on achieving redress;

- whether the suspect has co-operated with the FSA in taking such measures;

- whether the case involves dishonesty or an abuse of a position of authority or trust;

- whether there is an individual who has taken a leading role in market abuse carried out by a group; and

- the personal circumstances of the suspect.[30]

The decision to investigate or to commence civil enforcement action under the market abuse regime will not be automatic in all cases where market abuse is suspected. Before an investigation into market abuse is commenced, the FSA will consider a variety of factors, including the seriousness of the abuse and its effect upon consumers or market confidence, the nature of the contravention, the context in which the contravention took place and any power of other regulatory authorities (such as a Recognised Investment Exchange or the Takeover Panel) to take regulatory action.[31]

At the second stage, once an investigation has taken place the FSA will consider taking enforcement action. In cases of market abuse, the FSA will consider a broad range of issues in deciding whether enforcement action should be taken, including:

- the nature and seriousness of the behaviour: how serious the breach of the Act was, whether the behaviour was deliberate or reckless, the duration and frequency of the behaviour, the impact of the behaviour on prescribed markets, the amount of any benefit gained or loss avoided and the loss or risk of loss caused to market users;

- the conduct of the person under investigation: how quickly, effectively and completely the behaviour was reported, whether the person co-operated in the investigation of the conduct, any remedial action taken by that person, whether the person complied with the rulings of any other regulatory body, and whether false or inaccurate information is provided to the FSA by the person;

---

[30] ENF 15.7.2G.
[31] ENF 2.6.2G.

- the degree of sophistication of the users of the market in question, the size and liquidity of the market, and the susceptibility of the market to market abuse;

- the adequacy of any action taken or to be taken by another regulatory authority;

- consistency with action taken by the FSA in previous similar cases;

- the impact—whether favourable or adverse—of any regulatory action upon the financial markets or the interests of consumers;

- the danger that the conduct will recur unless action is taken; and

- the disciplinary and compliance history of the person under investigation.[32]

THE WARNING NOTICE

8.26 If the decision is made to take enforcement action the suspected market abuser will receive a warning notice stating the amount of the penalty which the FSA proposes to levy upon that person or if the FSA has decided to issue a statement, the terms of that statement.[33] Upon receipt of a warning notice, further regulatory action may be prevented by establishing that the statutory "defences" apply. This will involve showing to the FSA's satisfaction that there are reasonable grounds to believe that the person:

- believed, on reasonable grounds, that his behaviour did not amount to market abuse; or

- took all reasonable precautions and exercised all due diligence to avoid engaging in market abuse.[34]

The person facing investigation may, in certain circumstances, be faced with a dilemma. Although statements made under compulsion to an investigator are subject to a privilege against self-incrimination, voluntary statements may be used against that person in subsequent criminal proceedings or in proceedings for market abuse.[35] A fine judgment may at times need to be taken as to whether the information which is provided to the FSA will prejudice the position of the person under investigation.

In deciding whether either of these two "defences" apply, the FSA's discretion is structured by the following considerations. First, if it is alleged that the person under investigation took all reasonable precautions and exercised all due diligence to avoid engaging in market abuse, the following non-exhaustive list of factors will be relevant:

---

[32] ENF 14.4.2G.
[33] FSMA, s. 126. The procedure which governs the issuing of a warning notice, and a specimen copy of such a notice, is set out at DEC 2.2 and Annex 5G to DEC.
[34] FSMA, s. 123(2).
[35] ENF 2.14.6G.

- whether the person under investigation took reasonable precautions to avoid committing market abuse;

- whether the behaviour was analogous to behaviour described in MAR 1;

- whether the FSA had issued any guidance and whether that guidance was followed;

- whether the behaviour complied with the rules of a prescribed market or any other regulatory requirement;

- the knowledge, skill and experience that can be expected from the person under investigation; and

- whether the person under investigation can show that the conduct was engaged in for a legitimate purpose and in a proper way.

Secondly, if it is argued that the person under investigation took all reasonable precautions and exercised all due diligence to avoid engaging in market abuse the following factors will be relevant:

- whether internal consultation procedures were followed;

- whether legal or other expert advice was sought and followed;

- whether advice from other market authorities was sought and followed;

- whether the FSA had issued any guidance and whether that guidance was followed; and

- whether the behaviour complied with the rules of a prescribed market or any other regulatory requirement.[36]

The decision notice

8.27 If the person under investigation fails to persuade the FSA that the statutory defences apply, and if the FSA decides to impose a penalty, it will serve a decision notice[37] on the suspected market abuser. The decision notice must either state the amount of any penalty which will be imposed[38] or, if the FSA decides to publish a statement that market abuse has occurred, instead of imposing a financial penalty the decision notice must set out the terms of the statement.[39]

Reference to the Tribunal

8.28 Once the FSA has issued a decision notice, the alleged market abuser has a choice: to accept the judgment of the FSA or to refer the matter to the Tribunal.[40]

---

[36] ENF 14.5.1G.
[37] FSMA, s. 127(1).
[38] FSMA, s. 127(2).
[39] *ibid*.
[40] FSMA, s. 127(4).

Any reference to the Tribunal must be received within 28 days of the date of the decision notice,[41] although the Tribunal has discretion to extend the time limit if it is satisfied that it would be in the interests of justice to do so.[42] Appeal from a decision of the Tribunal is to the Court of Appeal in England and Wales or the Court of Session in Scotland.[43] If the matter is referred to the Tribunal, and the FSA has decided to issue a statement, that statement will not be published until the matter is resolved by the Tribunal.

A legal assistance scheme established by the Lord Chancellor's Department[44] is available to persons once a decision notice has been issued: it is not available to assist with the legal costs which may be incurred, for example, during the course of making representations to the FSA after a warning notice has been issued. Importantly, the scheme is available only to persons who have been accused of market abuse, and is not available in the context of any other regulatory action which the FSA may take.[45] Although the legal assistance scheme is operated by the Lord Chancellor's Department, it is funded by the regulated community through the FSA. Legal assistance is available to cover preparation, advice, and representation in relation to:

- negotiations with the FSA;

- the preliminary, adjourned and main hearing of the Tribunal;

- arguments as to the aware of costs; and

- withdrawing a reference to the Tribunal.

Legal assistance will be means tested[46] and available to individuals and not to companies. Remuneration will be based broadly on rates of payment for work in the Crown Court under the Criminal Defence Service, and will in appropriate circumstances meet the costs of both a solicitor and one or more counsel.[47] Therefore, the rates may be sufficient to secure the assistance of a specialist sole practitioner with no significant overheads or high street criminal defence lawyer, but will not be sufficient to secure, for example, the services of a litigator at a city firm.

The FSA has indicated that, because the proceeds of market abuse penalties will be apportioned to the firms in the fee blocks to which the activity which gave rise to the penalty related, it is appropriate that the funding arrangements for the legal assistance scheme will also be levied in a parallel fashion.[48]

---

[41] The Financial Services and Markets Tribunal Rules 2001 (S.I. 2001 No. 2476), rule 4(2).

[42] *ibid.*, 10(2).

[43] *ibid.*, rule 23(1).

[44] FSMA, s. 134. The legal assistance scheme was introduced into the FSMA at a late stage in its progress through Parliament, after it had been argued that the market abuse regime would be treated as criminal in nature under the ECHR. Accordingly, Art. 6(3)(c) of the ECHR would require the provision of legal assistance in certain circumstances: see the Opinion by Lord Lester of Herne Hill Q.C. and Javan Herberg in the Joint Committee, *First Report*, Annex C.

[45] FSMA, s. 134(3).

[46] Lord Chancellors Department, *Consultation Paper, Legal Assistance Scheme* (June 2001). The Tribunal will grant assistance only where the person seeking assistance is financially eligible and if it is in the interests of justice to do so, and will take into account certain factors set out in the Order in exercising its discretion.

[47] Lord Chancellors Department, *Consultation Paper, Legal Assistance Scheme* (June 2001).

[48] FSA, *Consultation Paper 29: Second consultation paper on the FSA's post-N2 fee-raising arrangements*, para. 5.42.

THE BURDEN AND STANDARD OF PROOF

8.29   One of the most significant attractions to the Government and the regulator of the market abuse regime is that it is comparatively easy and less expensive to "prosecute". Although the offences overlap with criminal offences, the procedures for policing market abuse do not require the expense of a jury trial. Moreover, unlike a criminal offence, market abuse does not need to be proved "beyond reasonable doubt". Rather, market abuse is to be proved to a civil standard. The burden of proof in relation to market abuse is on the FSA; the FSA must be satisfied that a person has engaged in market abuse or has encouraged or required market abuse.[49] However, when considering whether either of the "defences" provided by section 123(2) applies, the burden of proof is reversed; it is for the person upon whom the warning notice has been served to satisfy the FSA that the defences apply.[50]

The FSMA itself provides some assistance as to the standard of proof which is required. The "reasonable market user" test is premised upon the likelihood of that hypothetical user regarding the conduct as a "failure on the part of the person or persons concerned to observe the standard of behaviour reasonably expected of a person in his or their position in relation to the market". MAR 1 itself suggests in various contexts that "likely" means that there is a "real and not fanciful likelihood" of the effect of the conduct, but that the effect "need not be more likely than not".[51] The FSA has suggested that the test also requires that the effect of the conduct be more than a "bare possibility".[52] However, the FSMA does not provide clear guidance upon the standard of proof required before it can be held that the person accused of market abuse engaged in the behaviour specified. The application of the standard of proof in cases of market abuse is likely to be fraught with difficulty in practice.

However, it has been suggested in various forums during the consultation upon, and passage of, the FSMA that the standard of proof which the Tribunal will expect in individual cases will be on something of a sliding scale: the more serious the allegation, the more will be required to discharge the burden of proof.[53] Although several attempts were made during the passage of the FSMA through Parliament to persuade the Government to include a provision raising the standard of proof in all cases, or in all serious cases, to the criminal standard, the Government would not be moved. In any event, the ECHR does not require that the standard of proof for criminal or quasi-criminal cases is "beyond reasonable doubt".

CONSEQUENCES OF A FINDING OF MARKET ABUSE

8.30   Various consequences may flow from a finding of market abuse. They are, in summary, as follows:

---

[49] FSMA, s. 123(2).
[50] FSMA, s. 123(1).
[51] MAR 1.5.4E(2).
[52] FSA, *Policy Statement, COMC*, para. 4.10.
[53] See, *e.g., Hornal v. Neuberger* [1957] 1 Q.B. 247.

- the imposition of an unlimited financial penalty by the FSA[54];

- publication by the FSA of a statement that a person has engaged in market abuse[55];

- an injunction restraining market abuse may be granted if the High Court is satisfied that there is a reasonable likelihood that a person will engage in, continue or repeat the market abuse[56];

- a "remedial" injunction, granted by the court on the application of the FSA, requiring a person to take steps remedying the market abuse[57];

- a freezing injunction if it is satisfied that a person may be engaging or may have been engaged in market abuse[58];

- a restitution order, made by the Court on the application of the FSA[59]; and

- the exercise by the FSA of the administrative power to require restitution.[60]

In any event, the FSA may also apply to the court for an injunction or a restitution order before any finding of market abuse has been made. Additionally, the court may grant an injunction restraining market abuse before abusive conduct has occurred if it is satisfied that there is a reasonable likelihood that any person will engage in market abuse.[61] The FSA will need to show a good arguable case for the granting of such injunctions.

THE LEVEL OF THE PENALTY

8.31 The power of the FSA to impose an unlimited financial penalty is constrained by section 124(2). That section requires that the FSA must have regard to the following matters:

- whether the behaviour in respect of which the penalty is to be imposed had an adverse effect on the market in question and, if it did, how serious that effect was. The FSA considers that the effect of the conduct on the market can be decided by reference to various factors including the risk of loss to other market users, the duration and frequency of the conduct, and the impact of the behaviour on the market. In addition, the FSA takes the view that the size of the penalty must be proportionate to the seriousness of the conduct;

- the extent to which that behaviour was deliberate or reckless. Intentional or reckless behaviour is likely to result in a higher penalty being imposed; and

---

[54] FSMA, s. 123(1).
[55] FSMA, s. 123(3).
[56] FSMA, s. 381(1).
[57] FSMA, s. 381(2).
[58] FSMA, s. 381(4).
[59] FSMA, s. 383.
[60] FSMA, s. 384.
[61] FSMA, s. 381(1)(a).

- whether the person on whom the penalty is to be imposed is an individual. The FSA will look to the financial resources of the person upon whom the penalty is to be imposed, and whether that person can show that serious financial difficulties will result from the imposition of a heavy penalty.[62]

In addition, the FSA will consider the extent to which the person made a profit or avoided a loss as a result of the conduct, whether the person co-operated with the FSA, the disciplinary and compliance history of the person under investigation, and whether any action is being taken by other regulatory authorities. Furthermore, the FSA will attempt to achieve consistency between similar cases in setting the level of any penalty.

PENALTY OR STATEMENT

8.32 When deciding whether to issue a penalty or to issue a statement, the FSA's discretion is structured by the following non-exhaustive list of factors:

- if a profit has been made or a loss avoided, it may militate in favour of the imposition of a penalty;

- the more serious the nature of the conduct, the more likely the FSA is to impose a penalty;

- co-operation with the FSA and voluntary compensation of victims may encourage the FSA to issue a statement rather than impose a penalty;

- the FSA will be guided by its conduct in other similar cases;

- the disciplinary and compliance history to the person under investigation; and

- the impact of a financial penalty on the person under investigation will be relevant considerations.[63]

Where a statement is to be issued, the FSA retains the discretion not to do so if publication would result either in unfairness to the person on whom a sanction is imposed, or prejudice to the consumers' interests.[64]

APPLYING FOR INJUNCTIONS

8.33 When the FSA is considering applying to the court for an injunction, it must consider whether an application for an injunction is the most effective way to deal with the matter. The FSA has indicated that it will be guided by the following factors:

- the potential impact of the conduct on the financial system;

---

[62] ENF 14.7.4G.
[63] ENF 14.6.2G.
[64] ENF 14.12.2G.

- the extent and nature of likely losses suffered by other users of the financial system;

- whether the conduct is likely to stop;

- whether steps will be taken by the person under investigation to ensure that the interests of consumers are adequately protected;

- where steps can be taken to remedy the market abuse;

- whether action has been required by another regulatory body, and whether that action has been taken;

- whether there is a danger that assets will be dissipated;

- the costs of applying for an injunction and the benefits which would result from such an injunction being granted;

- the disciplinary and compliance history of the person under investigation;

- whether other disciplinary powers will adequately address the conduct;

- whether another regulatory body can adequately address the conduct;

- whether there is information which indicates that the person under investigation is engaged in financial crime; and

- whether an injunction would affect the timetable or outcome of a takeover bid; in these circumstances, the Takeover Panel will be consulted.[65]

The FSA will also need to consider whether any other regulatory action which it may take against a regulated firm will be as effective as an injunction (which may be policed by subsequent action for contempt of court if it is not obeyed[66]).

RESTITUTION ORDERS AND THE ADMINISTRATIVE POWER TO REQUIRE RESTITUTION

8.34 The FSA has suggested that, in deciding whether to exercise its powers to obtain restitution or to apply for a restitution order, it will consider the alternatives open to the person who has suffered loss and the efficiency and cost effectiveness of those alternatives.[67] Accordingly, these powers are relatively unlikely to be used where the party seeking restitution is a market counterparty. In deciding whether to exercise its powers to obtain restitution, the FSA will take into consideration the following factors:

- whether quantifiable profits have been made which are owed to identifiable persons;

- the number of persons who have suffered losses and the extent of the losses, and if those losses are individually or collectively significant: the FSA may not take action if it takes the view that the claim may more efficiently pursued by the individual taking action against the firm;

[65] ENF 6.6.2G.
[66] ENF 6.7.2G.
[67] ENF 9.3.1G.

- the cost and benefit of the FSA obtaining redress;

- the availability of compensation or the assistance of the Financial Ombudsman Service;

- the availability of redress through the offices of another regulatory authority;

- the availability of civil proceedings;

- the solvency of the firm: if the solvency of the firm is at risk, the FSA may consider applying for an insolvency order;

- the availability of a compulsory insolvency order; administration order, bankruptcy order, or the appointment of receivers;

- the conduct of the persons who have suffered loss; and

- the context in which the conduct took place.[68]

It should be noted that when the FSA has applied to the court for an injunction or a restitution order in a case of market abuse, it may take that opportunity to request the court to impose a penalty for market abuse.[69]

THE EUROPEAN CONVENTION ON HUMAN RIGHTS AND FUNDAMENTAL FREEDOMS

8.35 During the course of the passage of the Act, the argument was raised in a number of quarters that the enforcement powers of the FSA were incompatible with the procedural rights provided by Article 6 and the substantive rights created by Article 7 of the ECHR which has been given force in the United Kingdom by the Human Rights Act 1998 ("HR Act").

A full discussion of Articles 6 and 7 of the ECHR is outside the scope of this book. However, at its broadest, the issue is this. It has been suggested that the market abuse regime is criminal rather than civil in nature. If the regime is criminal in nature, then the protections provided by Articles 6 and 7 all apply; if it does not, then only the protections provided by Article 6(1) are of relevance. That the market abuse regime is not described on its face as criminal does not prevent it from being criminal in nature. A court applying the ECHR must look "behind appearances [in order to] assess for itself whether a particular measure amounts in substance, to a penalty within the meaning of [Article 7]".[70] Moreover, even purely disciplinary offences have been held to amount in substance to criminal offences under Article 6.[71]

---

[68] ENF 9.6.2G–9.6.12G.
[69] FSMA, s. 129.
[70] *Welch v. U.K.*, (1995) 20 E.H.R.R. 247.
[71] *Engel v. Netherlands*, A 22 (1976); *Ozturk v. FRG* A 73 (1984). By way of contrast, in *The Securities and Futures Authority, ex p. Fleurose* unreported, April 26, 2001, which concerned the lawfulness of disciplinary action taken by the SFA against one of its members for market manipulation, Morison J. held that the SFA's disciplinary proceedings were civil in nature under the ECHR. However, as a member of the SFA, Fleurose had consensually submitted to its jurisdiction; it remains to be seen whether a court would take the same approach to an unauthorised person subject to proceedings under the market abuse regime.

Some commentators have advanced a more speculative argument which proceeds as follows. The European Court of Human Rights ("ECHR") has held that the specific safeguards listed in Article 6(3) are aspects of the overall requirement of fairness provided by Article 6(1).[72] Therefore, it has been argued that Article 6(1) may require, even in a case that is genuinely "civil", that certain of the "criminal" protections contained in Article 6(3) are provided to the applicant. This is not, however, an argument that has been explicitly considered in the context of purely civil proceedings by the ECHR.

To the extent that these arguments are well-founded, four consequences may therefore follow under the HR Act:

- both the Act and any subordinate legislation made under the Act (including MAR 1) would fall to be reinterpreted by the courts in order to achieve conformity with the ECHR[73];

- alternatively, to the extent that a court[74] could not reinterpret the Act in such a manner, it may make a "declaration of incompatibility"[75];

- any exercise of power by the FSA which had the effect of breaching Article 6 or 7 will be unlawful unless the FSA shows that as the result of one or more provisions of the Act, it could not have acted differently or in the case of one or more provisions of, or made under, the Act which cannot be read or given effect in a way which is compatible with Article 6 or 7, the FSA was acting so as to give effect to or enforce those provisions[76];

- finally, faced with an adverse finding by the United Kingdom courts, or if a declaration of incompatibility has been made, an individual may make an application to the European Court of Human Rights.

Following the publication of the *First Report* of the Joint Committee on Financial Services and Markets, the Government conceded that, although there were "reasonable arguments" that the imposition of penalties for market abuse were civil proceedings only under the ECHR, there was also a "real possibility" that the power to fine would be classed as criminal in nature.[77] Accordingly, concessions were made to "Strasbourg-proof" the FSMA in relation to the admissibility and use of statements made to an investigator in subsequent market abuse proceedings, the provision of safe harbours in MAR 1 and the availability of legal assistance before the Tribunal.

Applicants may invoke the HR Act if they are, or would be, victims of an act which is unlawful under the HR Act. A person is a "victim" only if he would be a

---

[72] *Edwards v. U.K.* (1992) 8 E.H.R.R. 96; *Rowe and Davis v. U.K.*, Application No. 28901/95, February 16, 2000.

[73] HR Act, s. 3.

[74] The courts which may make a declaration of incompatibility under the HR Act include the House of Lords, the Judicial Committee of the Privy Council in Scotland, the High Court of Justiciary sitting otherwise than as a trial court or the Court of Session; in England and Wales or Northern Ireland, the High Court or the Court of Appeal.

[75] HR Act, s. 4.

[76] HR Act, s. 6.

[77] *Memorandum* from H.M. Treasury to the Joint Committee on Financial Services and Markets (May 14, 1999).

victim for the purposes of Article 34 of the ECHR.[78] The question of who qualifies as a victim has been extensively discussed by the ECHR. It includes a body corporate.[79] It also includes those who are merely at risk of infringement of convention rights.[80] Nor does the applicant need to show that he has suffered detriment from the breach of convention rights.[81]

Article 6(1) of the ECHR explicitly applies to both the determination of an applicant's "civil rights and obligations" and to "any criminal charge" against the applicant. It provides an applicant with the following procedural rights:

- a fair and public hearing within a reasonable time by an independent and impartial tribunal established by law; and

- the public pronouncement of judgment.[82]

Article 6(2) provides that "everyone charged with a criminal offence shall be presumed innocent until proved guilty according to law".

Article 6(3) set out a series of minimum rights which apply to the determination of criminal charges:

- to be informed promptly, in a language which he understands and in detail, of the nature and cause of the accusation against him;

- to have adequate time and facilities for the preparation of his defence;

- to defend himself in person or through legal assistance of his own choosing or, if he has not sufficient means to pay for legal assistance, to be given it free when the interests of justice so require;

- to examine or have examined witnesses against him and to obtain the attendance and examination of witnesses on his behalf under the same conditions as witnesses against him; and

- to have the free assistance of an interpreter if he cannot understand or speak the language used in court.

Article 7 enshrines the principle against restrospectivity in criminal law; a person may not be held guilty of a criminal offence on account of any act or omission which did not constitute a criminal offence under national or international law at the time when it was committed. The principle against the creation of ex post facto criminal offences has also been held to include a requirement that the offence should be "clearly described by law", although the European Court of Human Rights has made it clear that this does not require that "the concrete facts giving rise to criminal liability should be set out in the statute concerned".[83] In any event, the FSA is of the view that "[MAR 1] does provide sufficient certainty to market

---

[78] HR Act, s. 7.
[79] *Autronic AG v. Switzerland* (1990) 12 E.H.R.R. 485.
[80] *Norris v. Ireland* (1988) 13 E.H.R.R. 186.
[81] *Johnston v. Ireland* (1987) 9 E.H.R.R. 203.
[82] *Handyside v. U.K.*, No. 5493/72 17 YB 228.
[83] FSA, *Policy Statement*, COMC, para. 4.6.

participants when they are deciding whether or not their behaviour amounts to market abuse".[84] Moreover, in a domestic context, Morison J. in the *Fleurose* case held that: "It is essential that general standards of conduct are set so that rogue traders are unable to evade their responsibilities through technical 'construction' arguments and such general rules as are a feature of many systems of professional regulation that are designed to ensure high standards of professional behaviour."[85]

The application of convention arguments such as these to the new market abuse regime, particularly as it applies to individuals who are not subject to the FSA's professional regulation by reason of authorisation or approval, will no doubt ultimately fall to be determined by the courts.

---

[84] *The Securities and Futures Authority, ex p.Fleurose*, unreported, April 26, 2001.

CHAPTER 9

Rules, Competition and Polarisation

DAVID TOUBE & JAI CHAVDA

INTRODUCTION

9.01   The FSA is invested with extensive powers to make rules, to prepare and issue codes, to give general guidance and to determine the general policy and principles which govern the performance of the various areas of activity for which the FSA is responsible. These delegated legislative powers lie at the very heart of the FSA's functions and form the nexus through which it exercises its authority. As noted above in Chapter 2, in exercising these "general functions",[1] the FSA is bound to:

- act in a manner which is both compatible with the regulatory objectives and which it takes the view is "most appropriate" for the purpose of meeting those objectives[2]; and

- considering the general functions "as a whole", to have regard to a set of "principles of good regulation".[3]

The sections which immediately follow this introduction divide the power to issue these various forms of delegated legislation up by category. However, it is important to realise that in the FSA *Handbook of Rules and Guidance* (the "Handbook")—the document which contains the best part of the delegated legislation and quasi-legislation issued by the FSA—rules and general guidance sit side by side, and codes and principles are integrated into the schema of the Handbook. Therefore, although it is important to bear in mind that there is an important distinction between the functions and legal effect of each of these species of regulation, their interaction in the context of the Handbook and elsewhere must also be properly understood.

The purpose of this Chapter is to provide an introduction to the nature and roles of, and of the distinction between the principles, rules, codes and guidance. The chapter then considers the manner in which the FSA rules and practices will be subject to competition scrutiny. A final section examines the reform of the rules on Polarisation. The schema to the Handbook itself—which contains the bulk of the

---

[1] FSMA, s. 2(4).
[2] FSMA. s. 2(1).
[3] FSMA, s. 2(3), as set out in Chapter 2 of this book.

principles, rules, codes and guidance made under the FSMA—is set out at Chapter 10 below. Although a detailed hermeneutical exercise of the Handbook itself is without the scope of this book, the most important aspects of the areas which are governed by the key parts of the Handbook are considered extensively elsewhere in this work, including the Chapters on authorisation, approved persons, enforcement, market abuse, and conduct of business.

RULES

9.02 The bulk of the FSA's rule making powers are located in Part X of the FSMA, which sanctions the issue of:

- general rules, which bind authorised persons in their carrying on of regulated and non-regulated activities which the FSA regards as "necessary or expedient" for the purpose of protecting the interests of actual or potential consumers;

- rules governing the communication or approval by authorised persons of communications falling within the financial promotion regime[4];

- client money rules[5];

- money laundering rules[6];

- price stablising rules[7];

- rules governing the disclosure and use of information held by authorised persons[8];

- rules endorsing the *City Code on Takeovers and Mergers and the Rules Governing Substantial Acquisitions of Shares*[9]; and

- rules prohibiting a manager of an authorised unit trust scheme[10] and persons who effect or carry out contracts of insurance[11] from carrying on a specified activity.

As the listing authority, the FSA is also empowered to make Listing Rules.[12] The FSA also retains the power to make unit trust scheme rules governing the operation of authorised unit trusts.[13] Finally, the FSMA invests the FSA with the power to make a wide variety of ancillary rules for diverse purposes, including rules applying to former underwriting members of the Society of Lloyds,[14] and rules applying

---

4 FSMA, s. 145.
5 FSMA, s. 139.
6 FSMA, s. 146.
7 FSMA, s. 144.
8 FSMA, s. 147.
9 FSMA, s. 143.
10 FSMA, s. 140.
11 FSMA, s. 141.
12 FSMA, Pt VI.
13 FSMA, s. 247.
14 FSMA, s. 322.

to members of designated professional bodies (such as solicitors or accountants) which may be exercised for the purpose of ensuring that clients are aware that the professional is not an authorised person.[15]

Before a rule is made, the FSA is obliged to publish it in draft and generally, to publish a cost benefit analysis of the impact of the rule and to conduct an extensive and thorough public consultation exercise before that rule is brought into force.[16]

WAIVERS

9.03   As under the 1986 Act regime, an authorised person may apply to the FSA for the modification or waiver of certain classes of its own rules.[17] The FSA may also revoke a previously granted waiver, after an opportunity has been given for representations to be made by the person who is affected by the revocation.[18] As under the previous regime, a waiver may be subject to conditions, and a rule may not be waived or modified unless it is satisfied that:

- compliance by the authorised person with the rules, or the unmodified rules, would be unduly burdensome or would not achieve the purpose for which the rules were made; and

- the modification or waiver would not give rise to in undue risk to persons whose interests the rules are intended to protect.

The FSA proposes to co-ordinate the granting of waivers, in order to ensure a consistency of approach between similar cases.[19]

FSA is ordinarily required to publish a waiver or modification of a rule—which it proposes to do on its website[20]—unless it is satisfied that to do so would be "inappropriate or unnecessary", taking into account the extent to which publication would prejudice the commercial interests of the applicant or its immediate group[21] to an unreasonable degree, and whether breach of the rule in question is actionable under section 150 of the FSMA or whether the publication of the rule would breach an international obligation of the FSA. A firm may object to the publication of a waiver, and if it fails to convince the FSA that details of a waiver should not be published, it may withdraw the application for the waiver.[22] The FSA may also simply delay publication of a waiver for as long as the grounds for delay subsist.[23] The full procedure which governs applications for waivers is set out at Chapter 8 of the FSA *Supervision Manual.*

---

[15] FSMA, s. 332.

[16] FSMA, s. 155(2)(a); see generally, Chapter 2 of this book.

[17] FSMA, s. 148: specifically, general rules (s. 138), insurance business rules (s. 141), price stabilising rules (s. 144), financial promotion rules (s. 145), money laundering rules (s. 146), control of information rules (s. 147), authorised unit rules (s. 247) and scheme particular rules (s. 248), and the rules governing auditors and actuaries (s. 340).

[18] SUP 8.8.

[19] SUP 8.9.

[20] SUP 8.6.9G.

[21] As defined in s. 148(11) of the FSMA.

[22] SUP 8.6.7G.

[23] SUP 8.6.8G.

GRANDFATHERING OF WAIVERS

9.04   Waivers are of course not a novel feature of the FSMA regime. Accordingly, at N2 the FSA has inherited from the previous regulators a certain number of firms which had been operating within the scope of waivers or similar concessions. The logistical difficulty presented by reconsidering each waiver in turn, in order to decide whether they should be grandfathered on the eve of N2 would have been significant. Accordingly, under transitional provisions[24] made by the FSA which may be found in the schedule of commencement and transitional provisions for the Supervision manual, waivers have temporarily and automatically been granted in respect of any provision which is substantially similar to a rule in the Handbook. Waivers have therefore not been grandfathered if the original rule to which they relate is not substantially similar, because, for example, the rule has either been modified in a manner which removes the need for the waiver, or has become general guidance which does not require a waiver, or has been altered in a manner which makes it impossible to apply the old waiver in the new context. The onus is on the firm to determine whether their waiver has been grandfathered, and/or whether there is a need to apply for new waivers or modifications.

The transitional provisions cover "written concessions". In other words, informal and oral concessions will not be grandfathered. Broadly speaking, the FSA considers the following to amount to such "written concessions" which are capable of being grandfathered:

- formal waivers and modifications of rules granted under the rulebooks of, for example, the SROs and other formal exercises of discretion under SRO Rules;

- written concessions from existing guidance, including 'concessions' from the standards in the FSA's *Guide to Banking Supervisory Policy*; and

- exemptions from rules, including exemptions under the SFA and IMRO Training and Competence Rules.

The majority of grandfathered waivers and written concessions have a life of only 12 months. However waivers granted in respect of matters now covered by the Interim Prudential sourcebooks and SUP 16.6 and 16.7 remain in place until these temporary rules are themselves replaced by the Integrated Prudential sourcebook.

PRINCIPLES

9.05   The foundation of the FSA's regulatory approach is the Principles for Business ("PRIN") which are located within Block 1—the "High Level Standards" block of the Handbook—and are themselves a species of rule. However, their position is fundamental to the regulation of firms; they are "a general statement of the fundamental obligations of firms under the regulatory system", and set the

---

[24] Made under s. 156(2) of the FSMA. Also see FSA, *Grandfathering of Waivers* (December 2000), and FSA, *Countdown to N2: Grandfathering* (July 2001).

boundaries of the concept of fitness and propriety. As such, they need to be read in conjunction with the "suitability" condition of the threshold conditions for authorisation. They apply fully to all firms, and are modified in their application to provide for the division between host and home state regulation for incoming EEA and Treaty firms.[25]

During the consultation process upon the PRIN, their number crept up from eight[26] to eleven—"one more than you-know-who", as the FSA humorously put it.[27] They are as follows:

1. *Integrity*: A firm must conduct its business with integrity.

2. *Skill care and diligence*: A firm must conduct its business with due skill care and diligence.

3. *Management and control*: A firm must take reasonable care to organise and control its affairs responsibly and effectively, with adequate risk management systems.

4. *Financial prudence*: A firm must maintain adequate financial resources.

5. *Market conduct*: A firm must observe proper standards of market conduct.

6. *Customers' interests*: A firm must pay due regard to the interests of its customers and treat them fairly.

7. *Communications with clients*[28]: A firm must pay due regard to the information needs of its clients and communicate information to them in a way which is clear, fair and not misleading.

8. *Conflicts of interest*: A firm must manage conflicts of interest fairly both between itself and its customers and between a customer and another client.

9. *Customers: relationships of trust*: A firm must take reasonable care to ensure the suitability of its advice and discretionary decisions for any customer who is entitled to rely upon its judgment.

10. *Clients' assets*: A firm must arrange adequate protection for clients' assets when it is responsible for them.

11. *Relations with regulators*[29]: A firm must deal with its regulators in an open and cooperative way, and must disclose to the FSA appropriately anything relating to the firm of which the FSA would reasonably expect notice.

---

[25] PRIN 3.1.
[26] FSA, *Consultation Paper 13* (October 1999).
[27] FSA, *Handbook Development No. 1* (December 1999).
[28] PRIN 3.4.1R. The FSA has made it clear that the application of Principle 7 to market counterparties requires only that that a firm communicates information in a way that is not misleading.
[29] "Regulators" means both the FSA and other domestic and overseas regulator with recognised jurisdiction: see PRIN 3.4.5R.

The use of high level principles as a means of circumscribing and defining the duties of authorised persons will be familiar at least to those firms which were authorised under the 1986 Act. Indeed, the primary source of the principles are the old Securities and Investments Board Statements of Principle.[30] Their value and purpose has been identified by the FSA as follows:

- *Coverage*: The use of wide ranging principles stated at a high level of generality ensures that the regulatory system will be able to respond to innovation, and that it will always be in a position to govern even those aspects of regulated activity not made the subject of a rule.

- *Consistency*: Because the FSA regards its regulatory response as premised upon and directed by the Principles they provide a degree of consistence and predictability as to the FSA's regulatory response.

- *Continuity*. The Principles incorporate certain aspects the approaches to regulation in the regimes which have been replaced, they provide a degree of continuity between the old and new regimes.

- *Cohesion*: The FSA takes the view that because the Principles themselves reflect the statutory objectives set out in the FSMA, "a Handbook built upon the foundations of the Principles will be more cohesive".[31]

In slightly greater detail, all the Principles apply to the conduct of regulated activities, activities which constitute dealing in investments as principal (but which are exempt under the Regulated Activities Order), ancillary activities in relation to designated investment business and the approval of communications falling within the financial promotion prohibition, with the exception of Principles 3, 4 and 11, which apply more generally to a firm's non-regulated business as well.[32] Principles 6–10 place requirements upon firms which govern their relationship with their clients or customers; the first five and the final of the Principles impose more general and wide ranging obligations upon firms. The distinction between clients and customers here is an important one: broadly speaking a customer is an actual or potential private or intermediate customer; a client also includes a market counterparty.

As noted below, breach of the PRIN may open a firm to disciplinary action by the FSA. It should be noted that fault is an element of each of the PRIN: the FSA must prove fault if action is to be taken against a firm.[33] However, breach of the PRIN in and of themselves cannot be used by a private person as the basis for an action for breach of statutory duty under section 150; they have been excluded from the scope of that section by PRIN 3.4.4R. However, breach of the Principles may well be accompanied by a concurrent breach of an actionable rule.

However, the PRIN are not the only high level standards to which firms are subject. Indeed, where appropriate, they should be read alongside the other components of the High Level Standards block of the Handbook, which are as follows:

[30] SIB Rules, Vol. 1, Statements of Principles
[31] FSA, *Policy Statement: The FSA Principles for Businesses, Response on Consultation Paper 13*, para. 6.
[32] PRIN 3.2.
[33] PRIN 1.1.7G: the role of fault will vary from principle to principle.

- Senior management arrangements, systems and control ("SYSC");

- The Statements of Principle and Code of Practice for Approved Persons ("APER")[34]; and

- Fitness and Propriety ("FIT").

FIT constitutes the FSA's criteria for assessing the fitness and propriety of approved persons and is discussed in Chapter 5, at paragraph 5.08. Likewise, APER sets out at a high level the personal responsibilities expected of approved persons when performing controlled functions; APER is further examined at paragraph 5.09. The SYSC are explored at paragraph 5.04.

BREACH OF RULES AND PRINCIPLES

9.06   Breach of a rule, or indeed the contravention of a principle made by the FSA, is not a criminal offence and does not render a transaction void or voidable.[35] Instead, the primary sanctions for breach of the rules are (depending upon the nature of the rule):

- the imposition of public censure[36] or a financial penalty[37] upon an authorised person;

- a requirement to pay restitution,[38] or an application to the court for an injunction[39] or, if appropriate a restitution order[40];

- the imposition of a penalty or the publication of a statement[41] or an application to the court to impose a penalty[42] in cases of market abuse; and

- ultimately the withdrawal of authorisation following the cancellation of an authorised firm's permission[43] and the issue of a prohibition order[44] to, or the withdrawal of approval[45] from an individual.

The exercise of the FSA's enforcement powers is dealt with fully in Chapter 13 of this book.

Additionally, the FSMA provides a private person who suffers loss as a result of the contravention of a rule[46] with a right of action for breach of statutory duty, unless the rule itself specifies that no such right of action may be brought.[47]

---

[34] Made under FSMA, s. 64.
[35] FSMA, s. 151.
[36] FSMA, s. 205.
[37] FSMA, s. 206.
[38] FSMA, s. 384.
[39] FSMA, s. 380.
[40] FSMA, s. 382.
[41] FSMA, s. 123.
[42] FSMA, s. 129.
[43] FSMA, ss. 33 and 45.
[44] FSMA, s. 56.
[45] FSMA, s. 63.
[46] With the exception of the listing rules and the financial resources rules: see FSMA, s. 150(4).
[47] FSMA, s. 150. *e.g.*, breach of the Principles in PRIN and the rules in SYSC are not actionable (PRIN 3.4.4R and SYSC 1.1.12R).

Guidance

9.07 Although guidance may be seen as a species of delegated legislation, it might more properly be termed quasi-legislation.[48] Although it may lack direct legal effect—in that compliance with or breach of guidance does not of itself impose or lift a legal burden from its subject—it nevertheless plays an important role in defining the discretion of the FSA, and moreover may give rise to a legitimate expectation. The FSA is empowered[49] to issue guidance upon the operation of both rules made under the FSMA and the FSMA itself or for the purpose of meeting the regulatory objectives.[50] Additionally, the FSA has a "catch all" ability to issue guidance in relation to any matter with respect to any other matters upon which the FSA wishes to provide information or advice. It is important to realise that, although FSA guidance will clearly be a persuasive factor, it amounts to no more the FSA's view as to the effect of the law, and that it is open to the courts to take a different view.[51]

Guidance falls broadly into two categories:

- *General guidance*, *i.e.* guidance which is intended to have continuing effect, in legible form, that is given either to persons generally, to regulated persons[52] generally or to a class of regulated person[53]; and

- *Individual guidance*, *i.e.* guidance which is given to one particular firm or other person in relation "its own particular circumstances or plans", in spoken or written form.[54] The FSA has indicated that it may convert to general guidance and publish individual guidance which is of general application.

Before general guidance is issued, the FSA is required to publish the guidance in draft, to conduct a cost benefit exercise, and to conduct a consultation exercise upon those rules[55] and to provide a copy of that guidance to the Treasury.[56]

Individual guidance may be issued following a "reasonable request"[57] from an authorised person,[58] or on the FSA's own initiative[59]; the FSA generally expects a firm to have conducted its own analysis of the situation in relation to which guidance is sought before the FSA is approached.[60] A particularly important issue

---

[48] G. Ganz, *Quasi-legislation: Recent developments in secondary legislation* (Sweet and Maxwell, 1987).

[49] FSMA, s. 157.

[50] FSMA, s. 2(2).

[51] SUP 9.4.4G.

[52] *i.e.* authorised persons or persons who are otherwise subject to rules made by the FSA: see FSMA, s. 157(2).

[53] FSMA, s. 158(5).

[54] SUP 9.1.2G.

[55] FSMA, s. 157(3).

[56] FSMA, s. 158(1).

[57] SUP 9.2.5G.

[58] Such requests should be addressed to the authorised person's to its usual supervisory contact at the FSA, or if the person is not authorised, to another appropriate department. A request for guidance relating to the Code of Market Conduct (MAR 1) should be addressed to the specialist team in the Markets and Exchange division: see SUP 9.2.2G.

[59] SUP 9.3.

[60] SUP 9.2.5G.

which arises in relation to individual guidance is the extent to which a person who receives such guidance may rely upon it in arguing that it has complied with a rule. The FSA is clearly alert to the possibility that a junior member of its staff may be wrong-footed by a request for oral advice, and that advice may later be cited against it in any action which the FSA may subsequently take. Accordingly, the FSA has made it clear that only compliance with current individual written guidance will ensure that the FSA will take the view that the rule to which the guidance relates has been complied with.[61] In addition, the extent to which guidance may be relied upon depends, *inter alia*, upon:

- the degree of formality of the original query and the guidance given;
- whether all relevant information was submitted with the request for guidance; and
- whether the backdrop of circumstances against which the guidance was given still exists.

In this regard, it should be noted that individual written guidance given in respect to market conduct will be binding on the FSA (see further paragraph 8.07).

The rule of thumb must therefore be to ensure that oral requests for guidance are followed up wherever appropriate to written requests for written guidance. Additionally, particular care will need to be taken framing a request for guidance in terms that are calculated to elicit a response which is likely to be appropriate, on a continuing basis, to the circumstances in mind. Finally, individual guidance which has been received should kept under review to ensure that the circumstances to which that guidance relates remain current.

Formal transitional provisions were not made in order to enable the grandfathering of guidance given to firms by their regulators under the old regimes. Instead, the FSA has expressed the view that, because:

- guidance is by its nature wholly dependent upon the backdrop of circumstances upon which it was based remaining unaltered; and
- is given in relation to a rule or to general guidance

to the extent that these two conditions continue to be satisfied, the individual guidance will continue to apply.[62]

Codes of Practice

9.08   The final species of quasi-legislation which the FSA is obliged to issue are the Codes of Practice. The two important Codes which have been issued under the FSMA are:

---

[61] SUP 9.4.1G.
[62] FSA, *Consultation Paper 89, Grandfathering Concessions and Individual Guidance*.

- The Code of Practice, which the FSA was obliged to issue as a consequence of having issued Statements of Principle regarding Approved Persons[63]; and

- The Code of Market Conduct ("MAR 1").

The impact of both these Codes are considered in context and in greater detail elsewhere in this work. Broadly speaking however, the APER Code of Practice specifies descriptions of conduct which, in the FSA's opinion, comply or do not comply with the Statements of Principle, and various factors which are to be taken into account in determining whether or not a person's conduct complies with the Statements of Principle.[64] Likewise, the COMC also describes conduct which the FSA believes amounts or does not amount to market abuse, and factors which are to be taken into account by the FSA in determining whether market abuse has occurred.[65] Compliance with express provisions of these Codes has evidential value in any subsequent proceedings brought by the FSA. However, there is an important distinction between the APER Code of Practice and the COMC; the former Code does not contain "safe harbour" provisions, whereas the COMC contains a series of safe harbours which, if complied with, protect a person from subsequent action from the FSA.

COMPETITION UNDER THE FSMA

9.09   This section deals with the extent to which competition issues in respect of regulation are addressed under Part X, Chapter III of the FSMA. There has been considerable debate on this, particularly in light of the coming into force of the Competition Act 1998[66] and the publication of the Cruickshank report on Competition in U.K. Banking ("Final Report")[67] along with its Interim Report into financial services.[68] It is against this background that the FSMA has sought to emphasise competition considerations through a system of internal and external scrutiny. In essence, the competition provisions seek to strike a balance between competition and adhering to the FSA's statutory objectives. The ideal level of regulation would avoid imposing such an onerous regulatory burden upon firms as to hinder their ability to compete internationally, while meeting the objective of fostering clean and orderly markets. This section examines the framework for competition analysis under the Act by looking at the two strands to competition scrutiny, together with the disapplication of the Competition Act 1998.

---

[63] FSMA, s. 64.
[64] FSMA, s. 64(3).
[65] FSMA, s. 119(2).
[66] In brief summary, it introduces prohibitions against anti-competitive agreements and dominant positions which are reflective of Articles 81 and 82 of the Treaty of Amsterdam 1997 (amending the Treaty of Rome 1957).
[67] Published on March 20, 2000.
[68] *Competition and Regulation in Financial Services: Striking the Right Balance ("Interim Report")*, published on July 22,1999.

THE FRAMEWORK FOR COMPETITION ANALYSIS UNDER THE FSMA

9.10   Under the new Act, regulating provisions[69] or practices[70] are stated to have a significantly adverse effect on competition if they have, intend or are likely to have, or if the actual effects, including likely or intended effects, encourage behaviour that has a significantly adverse effect on competition (section 159(2)). In addition, regulating provisions or practices that have, or are intended or likely to have the effect of encouraging exploitation of the strength of a market position, are taken to have an adverse effect on competition (section 159(3)).

"Internal" scrutiny is the first stage of competition analysis provided by the FSA. The "external" strand of scrutiny is firstly provided by the Office of Fair Trading ("OFT"), in particular by the Director General of Fair Trading ("DGFT")[71]—the head of the OFT—who under section 160 is required to keep under review, the Authority's regulating provisions and practices. The Competition Commission ("Commission")[72] is then required to investigate any report made by the DGFT which finds that certain regulating provisions and practices have a significantly adverse effect on competition or that they do not impede competition but the Commission is requested to consider the matter in any event (section 162). Under section 163, subject to certain circumstances, the Treasury must act if the Commission concludes that there is an unjustifiable adverse effect on competition. Each level of competition scrutiny is discussed in more detail below.

It should also be noted that as many of the provisions in the FSMA are dependent on a good deal of secondary legislation in the form of orders that the Treasury must make, therefore the Treasury too, will have to have due regard to competition considerations when drafting such orders. The Government relented to recommendation 14 of the Final Report of having to apply competition scrutiny *systematically to its policies and regulations in the financial services sector to ensure they are proportionate and minimise distortions to competition.*[73]

INTERNAL SCRUTINY

9.11   The FSA in discharging its general functions, *i.e.* making rules, preparing and issuing codes, giving general guidance and determining general policy and principles, must abide by its four statutory objectives as set out in section 2(2). However,

---

[69] Meaning rules, general guidance, statements of principle issued for Approved Persons and codes issued in respect of approved persons and market abuse, see s. 159(1)(a–d).
[70] Defined as practices adopted by the Authority in the exercise of functions under the Act, see s. 159(1).
[71] The DGFT is appointed by the Secretary of State for Trade and Industry and is assisted by the OFT which was set up under the Fair Trading Act 1973.
[72] The Commission is an independent public body, which replaced the Monopolies and Mergers Commission on April 1, 1999. The Commission has two types of roles: a reporting one and a judicial function. It is required to conduct inquiries into referrals made by the OFT or the Secretary of State for Trade and Industry into monopolies, mergers and in respect to the regulation of utility companies. Under the Competition Act 1998, an Appeals Tribunal is set up, which is required to hear appeals against decisions for infringements of the provisions of the act.
[73] See H.M. Treasury, *Competition in U.K. Banking, The Cruickshank Report—Government response,* (August 2000).

in discharging its general functions the FSA must also have due regard to the "principles of good regulation"[74] as set out in section 2(3) of the Act. Certain of these arguably relate indirectly to competition, but only (c) and (d) below, do so explicitly:

(a) the desirability of facilitating innovation in connection with regulated activities;

(b) the international character of financial services and markets and the desirability of maintaining the competitive position of the United Kingdom;

(c) the need to minimise the adverse effects on competition that may arise from anything done in the discharge of those functions[75];

(d) the desirability of facilitating competition between those whom are subject to any form of regulation by the Authority.

These principles of good regulation are a novel feature in the new regime and they serve to provide guidance to the FSA in adhering to the statutory objectives.[76] This is not to say that competition analysis was absent under the 1986 Act at the rule making stage, quite the contrary. Under the old regime, prior to a recognition or delegation order[77] being made or even in circumstances where changes were to take place, the Secretary of State had to send to the DGFT a copy of the rules (including statements of principle, regulations and codes of practice) and any guidance and other relevant particulars to the DGFT (section 122(1) of the 1986 Act).[78] The DGFT would then report to the Secretary of State expressing his opinion as to whether the above had, or intended or likely to have had, to any significant extent the effect of restricting, distorting, or preventing competition and if so, the likely effects. The Secretary of State would then have the final say before making any of the orders. Aside from the DGFT's role under the new Act, all of the competition analysis at the rule making stage (formerly undertaken by the DGFT) can now be seen to move from the DGFT to the FSA.

In this regard, it is noteworthy that the promotion of competition generally, is not a primary regulatory objective but merely part of several principles of good regulation. In parliamentary debate,[79] it was felt that a competition objective similar to the one in the Utilities Act 2000 should be inserted into the FSMA, where the primary objective necessitates the Secretary of State and the Authorities for gas and electricity to protect the interests of consumers wherever appropriate by the promotion of effective competition. Contrary to the opinion of certain members of the Joint Committee, that competition and the competitiveness of the United Kingdom financial services market should be incorporated into the statutory objectives, the Committee was satisfied with the way in which it was expressed

---

[74] FSA, *A new regulator for the new millennium* (January 2000), p. 5.
[75] This factor was only inserted after consultation.
[76] FSA, *A new regulator for the new millennium* (January 2000), p. 10.
[77] Under the Financial Services Act 1986, recognition orders in respect of SROs were made under s. 9, under s. 37 for investment exchanges and under s. 39 for clearing houses. S. 114 gave the Secretary of State the power to transfer any function (subject to s. 114(5) to a designated agency).
[78] As the first delegation order was made to the SIB under s. 114, the SIB was required to make the same notifications to the DGFT (s. 120 of the 1986 Act).
[79] *Hansard*, Vol. 610, Col. 47, February 21, 2000.

under the principles.[80] The Cruickshank Interim Report strongly advocated the insertion of a competition objective in the FSMA and thereby, internally balancing regulation and competition. It stated:

> "any complex public interest outcome that is not enshrined in the primary statutory duties is very unlikely to be adequately delivered."[81]

Whilst acknowledging this, the Government did not accede to having competition as a statutory objective which the FSA later explained as being due to the "very difficult trade off between the two objectives of regulation and competition".[82]

Although one could argue that competition alone would deliver consumer protection to a degree (*e.g.*, by enabling consumers to choose providers on the basis of price and quality), regulation for the sake of consumers may still be the domineering factor in the approach taken to regulation, in particular to address information asymmetries and market abuses.[83] The Government is very much aware of the importance of competition, and the Economic Secretary to the Treasury has said that:

> "It is vital that in fulfilling its statutory objectives the FSA continues to regulate in a way which does not unnecessarily distort competition. A healthy and competitive market is in the interests of consumers and practitioners, providing greater choice, innovation and opportunities for growth."[84]

In order for the FSA to strike the right balance between regulation and competition and ensuring competition concerns are considered at the outset when formulating policy and rules, the Economics of Financial Regulation ("EFR") (which is part of the Central Policy Division of the FSA) has published a guide for policy makers entitled, *Making Policy in the FSA; How to take account of competition*[85] to embed the competitive element into every policy which will eventually transpose itself into rules or practices. In summary, the guide stipulates that competition analysis must be carried out whenever the FSA exercises its general functions under section 2(4). From a variety of policy options the Authority must choose one that has minimal anti-competitive effect.

Having chosen the policy in question, the starting point of competition analysis will be by testing the chosen policy against two "diagnostic tools" which reflect the have regard factors that explicitly refer to competition in the Act. These being, the extent to which regulatory policy facilitates competition between regulated

---

[80] See the Joint Committee's *First Report*, May 14,1999, para. 46.
[81] *Interim Report*, Annex F, para. F.49.
[82] FSA, *Response to the Cruickshank Report on Competition and U.K. Banking*, para. 2.6. To illustrate this point the FSA gives the example of authorisation of new entrants where there is a difficulty in protecting consumer's interest and facilitating competition that more entrants would bring.
[83] In a speech to the Regulatory Policy Institute, Andrew Whittaker, General Counsel at the FSA, reiterated this point by stating that a competition objective would go against the grain of the other four objectives and, therefore, would present the FSA with an "unclear and confusing mandate" (April 27, 2001).
[84] Melanie Johnson commenting on the *Interim Report* on November 9, 1999.
[85] Central Policy Division (July 2000).

persons[86] (positive effects) and whether the policy gives rise to important adverse effects on competition (negative effects). Regard should also be had to special issues such as discriminatory effects of regulation against smaller or new entrant firms.

In all cases, the analysis should be checked by an adviser in EFR. However, if, according to the criteria[87] enlisted under each diagnostic tool shows that the effects are easy to understand and not substantial, a simple compatibility statement ought to be prepared showing how the policy accords with the statutory objectives and principles for good regulation. On the other hand, if the policy reveals adverse effects on competition or the consequences are complex, a detailed competition analysis must be carried out, necessitating the consultation of EFR. This will involve evaluating the existing level of competition in the specific area and analysing every aspect of it. There is also scope for policy makers to consult the OFT on a particular matter so as to reduce the chances of the DGFT making findings adverse to FSA's policy. This should all be set out in a consultation paper in addition to the compatibility statement. This analysis will be complementary to Cost Benefit Analysis ("CBA") which is considered below.

A CBA is a further way in which competition considerations are taken into account when making policies/rules. With the exception of making fee rules,[88] under section 155 of the Act, a CBA is required whenever the FSA makes any rules, (in addition to the competition analysis mentioned above) and competition is one of six "impacts"[89] taken into account when compiling a CBA.[90] This effectively, provides yet another platform for competition scrutiny. It should also be noted that the CBA's use extends beyond the consultation process, as the Commission in conducting its investigation, has to have due regard to the CBA relevant to the regulating provision or practice in question (paragraph 2(b) of Schedule 14). The FSA has the discretion not to carry out a CBA if it feels that the delay caused by doing so would prejudice the interests of consumers. There are a further two caveats in this respect: that in making an appropriate comparison (*i.e.* if the rules are made and the overall position if they are not made) it is felt that there will be no increase in costs or such an increase will be of minimal significance. However, in respect to these last two caveats, the FSA has endeavoured to carry out a preliminary CBA to avoid errors in policy making.[91] In instances where in the opinion of the Authority, rules made by the FSA differ significantly from the draft rules in consultation, the

---

[86] This type of analysis has already been attempted in relation to mortgages. See FSA, *A cost benefit analysis of statutory regulation of mortgage advice* (October 1999).

[87] For the first tool, policy makers are asked to assess how strong the existing market failures are for the following: information asymmetries; barriers to entry; barriers to exit; switching costs; excessive product differentiation; and market power and then whether the chosen policy reduces the failure in question. The second tool examines whether as a result of the policy in question, the following will lead to important adverse effects on competition: information asymmetries; barriers to entry; barriers to exit; excessive product differentiation; discrimination; market power; and the hindrance of innovation.

[88] FSMA, s. 155. Cost benefit analysis will not be required when making rules for the funding of the Legal Assistant Scheme, section 136(2)); Compensation Scheme, s. 213(1); funding of the Ombudsman Scheme s. 234; and Setting Fees, Sched. 1, para. 17.

[89] This forms part of step three (impact of the policy on the market) of a four-step process when conducting a CBA. See FSA, *Central Policy: "Practical Cost Benefit Analysis for Financial Regulators"* (June 2000).

[90] *ibid.*, p. 15.

[91] *ibid.*, p. 7.

Authority must publish the details of the difference and it should be accompanied by a CBA. To ensure that the most cost-effective regulatory policy is chosen, the FSA, as part of its general policy, will also apply a CBA to all of its policy options.[92]

EXTERNAL SCRUTINY

The DGFT

9.12   In spite of policies and rules of the FSA being subject to this internal competition analysis, the Act further goes on to make provision for external bodies to review regulating provisions or practices. Section 160 requires the DGFT, quite like under the 1986 Act, to keep regulating provisions and practices of the FSA under review.[93] This is in addition to section 2 of the Fair Trading Act 1973 ("FTA") under which the DGFT is under a duty to review and collect information on commercial activities that may adversely affect the interests, economic or otherwise, of consumers. These two provisions taken together may give the DGFT very wide powers to review regulating provisions and practices. If the DGFT considers that regulating provisions or practices taken alone, or together, or in combination with each other, has a significantly adverse effect on competition, he must make a report to that effect specifying the adverse effects on competition (section 160(2)).[94] If on the other hand, the DGFT decides that regulating provisions or practices do not have a significantly adverse effect on competition, then whether he chooses to make a report and publish it becomes discretionary (section 160(5)).

In making a report, the DGFT must send a copy of it to the Treasury, the Commission and the Authority, and publish it. In publishing a report, the DGFT must, as far as practicable exclude any matter relating to the private affairs of a particular individual or body, the publication of which in the opinion of the DGFT would or might seriously and prejudicially affect their interest (section 160(7) and 160(8). This does not apply when submitting a copy of the report to the Treasury, the Commission and the Authority (section 160(8)).

To aid the DGFT's supervisory role, under section 161(2), he is given the power to request information by way of notice from any person as is specified in the notice, although it must be in that person's custody or control. The scope of this power is extended in respect to persons carrying on a business under subsection 3 of the same section. Such persons are required to provide "information" as opposed to documents as specified in the notice which also specifies the time, manner and form in which such information should be presented. As expected, if the person from whom the information is requested fails to provide it, for whatever reason, the DGFT may urge the court to enquire into the case by certifying the non-compliance to the court (section 161(6)). If no reasonable excuse for refusing

---

[92] *ibid.* The FSA will also undertake a CBA when implementing an E.U. directive or other international agreement, or when the nature and category of persons to which the old rules apply, changes.
[93] The original provisions of the bill also contained a provision which required the FSA, when making regulating provisions or practices or removing them to notify the DGFT detailing any effects on competition, but with the additional scrutiny provided by the Commission, this has since been removed.
[94] FSMA, s. 160, subs. 2 and 4.

or failing to comply with the notice is tendered, the court may deal with the defaulter as if he were in contempt.

Past experience shows that the DGFT's monitoring role is quite proactive and pursuant to section 122 of the 1986 Act he has delivered some compelling reports. The most recent example is the report he published in relation to the rules on polarisation. This is discussed in greater detail at paragraph 9.16.

The Competition Commission

9.13 The Commission's role is a new feature in the Act. The potential role of the Commission first evolved in parliamentary debate but gathered pace during consultation and, again after the probing Cruickshank Interim Report. By analogy, it was believed that the position that is witnessed in the utility sectors should be used to build a similar review mechanism under the new regime.[95] This extra tier of external scrutiny was considered by the Interim Report and the Government to benefit the rule making process by not only acting as a further check on the decision made by the FSA but, also the DGFT's findings. It can also be seen to peg back this power which would otherwise have been wielded by the Treasury.

Under section 162(1), the Commission must investigate a report made by the DGFT in two instances. Firstly, if certain regulating provisions or practices are found to have a significant adverse effect on competition and secondly, that they do not have the same effect but the DGFT asks the Commission to consider the report in any case. The Commission must then make its own report unless it considers that as a result of a change of circumstances no useful purpose would be served by making a report, in which case it is obliged to make a statement setting out the change of circumstances (section 162(2)). It should be noted that the Commission has the power not to make a report under this section if it appears that the regulating provisions and practices subject of the referral have been abandoned by the FSA, although it must, at the request of the Treasury, provide any results it has come to until its decision to abandon.[96] Also under Schedule 14 of the Act, the Treasury may "assist" the Commission in making its report. It may give information in its possession to the Commission but only in so far as it relates to the investigation along with, "other" assistance relating to the report. The latter part of its support role may appear to be vague and, it could potentially allow the Treasury to dictate the course of the investigation. The Commission is obligated to have regard to any information passed onto it by the Treasury. Mirroring the provisions relating to the DGFT, the Commission is under a duty to pay due regard firstly, to representations made by persons it perceives to have a substantial interest in the matter, and secondly, to the CBA prepared by the FSA in conjunction with the regulating provisions and practices of the report (paragraph 2 of Schedule 14).

A report by the Commission must, as is expedient, give reasons for the conclusions it has reached. The report must stipulate the Commission's conclusion as to whether regulating provisions or practices taken alone or in conjunction with other

---

[95] *e.g.*, the Telecommunications Act 1984 required prior to implementation, the Commission to sanction that a rule is in the public interest.
[96] FSMA, Sched. 14, para. 3(3).

regulating provisions and practices, which are the subject of the report,[97] have a significantly adverse effect on competition (section 162(4)). If, however, the Commission concludes that there is a significantly adverse effect on competition then it should stipulate whether it feels that the effect is justified and if it considers it is not justified, then it should state what action if any the Authority should take. It should be noted that only when the Commission is considering whether the infringing regulating provisions or practices are justified or not, the Commission's conclusions must, as far as is reasonably possible, be set against the wider functions and obligations imposed on the FSA under the Act (section 162(6) and (7)), rather than competition concerns alone.

Again, like the DGFT, if the Commission makes a report, it must send a copy of the report to the Treasury, the Authority and the DGFT and should be published so as to bring it to the attention of the public.[98] It was originally proposed that the Treasury would have acted on the findings of the DGFT alone without referral to a body accustomed to reviewing competition matters in deciding what action to take over anti-competitive regulating provisions or practices. Pursuant to the Cruickshank recommendation of the involvement of a Competition Commission, the Commission can now recommend the course of action to be taken in instances where it finds that there is an anti-competitive effect. As a result, the Treasury's power is significantly confined by the Commission's findings and this is discussed in more detail below.

The Treasury

9.14 The Treasury's powers only come into play if the Commission concludes there is a significant adverse effect on competition (section 163(1)).

In its report to the Treasury, if the Commission comes to the conclusion that there is an adverse effect on competition and it is not justified, the Treasury is obliged to give a direction to the Authority in relation to the action which must be taken[99] and, in so doing, it must have regard to the course of action suggested by the Commission in its report (section 163(4)). There is, however, no need for the Treasury to give a direction if it considers the Authority has taken adequate action in response to the Commission's report, making it unnecessary for them to give a direction or that *exceptional circumstances* of the case make it inappropriate or unnecessary for them to do so (section 163(3)). An example of an "exceptional circumstance" is where there is a "grave risk to the financial system".[1] Although in such circumstance, the Treasury must make a statement giving reasons for their decision (section 163(10). The Authority may not be required to take any action that it does not have the power to take or which would be incompatible with any of the functions conferred, or obligations imposed on it by or under this Act. In circumstances where the Commission finds that the adverse effects on competition are justified but the Treasury, due to *exceptional circumstances*,

---

[97] This narrows their inquiry as they can only review their effect against other regulating provisions and practices that are referred to in the Report.
[98] The same caveats apply to the publication of Commission made reports that apply to reports published by the DGFT, in that matters relating to the private affairs of individuals or a body should be excluded where publication could seriously and prejudicially affect their interests (para. 4 of Sched. 14).
[99] FSMA 163(2).
[1] Explanatory Notes to the Act, para. 306.

requires them to act (section 163(5)), the Treasury may give a direction as they consider necessary.

In whatever circumstances the Treasury gives a direction, it must allow the Authority and any other person that is considered by the Treasury to be affected, to make representations and to have regard to any representation made (section 163(8)). In giving directions, the Treasury must make a statement giving details of the direction. In line with section 163(10), if a direction is given under section 163(5), again, it must provide their reasons for doing so. Any statements made by the Treasury must be published so as to bring it to the attention of the public and it must lay a copy before Parliament.

The Treasury can only overturn the decision of the Commission where exceptional circumstances prevail. In spite of the Interim Report recommendation of granting final responsibility for reviewing anti-competitive procedures to the Commission, this responsibility still (albeit in its weakened form) rests with the Treasury. However, this power is significantly weakened in comparison to the 1986 Act where the Secretary of State had to "consider" a report made by the DGFT.[2] This reflects the Government's realisation that competition is a specialised consideration which the Treasury is not adequately equipped to deal with. Conceivably, it would have been better to leave this to a body fully acquainted with anti-competitive practices, but the reason for not doing so can perhaps be explained due to maintaining a degree of Parliamentary accountability.

DISAPPLICATION OF THE COMPETITION ACT 1998

9.15 Due to the nature of regulatory requirements that regulated persons are expected to conform with, their resultant behaviour could possibly be construed as being anti-competitive and consequently falling foul of the Competition Act 1998. To obviate this possibility, section 164(1) states that the Chapter I prohibition[3] of the Competition Act 1998 does not apply to an agreement the parties to which may involve an authorised person or a person who is otherwise subject to the Authority's regulating provisions, but only to the extent that the agreement comprises provisions that are "encouraged" by any of the Authority's regulating provisions or practices.

Likewise, the Chapter II prohibition[4] does not apply to conduct of an authorised person or a person who is otherwise subject to the Authority's regulating provisions to the extent the conduct is encouraged by any of the Authority's regulating provisions (section 164(2)). It is interesting to note that such agreements or conduct could still fall foul of Articles 81 and 82 of the Treaty of Rome, as amended.

This immunity from competition law is carried over from the Financial Services Act 1986 (section 124) which exempted rules and practices of the SROs, RIEs and RCHs from the Fair Trading Act 1973, Restrictive Trade Practices Act 1976 and Competition Act 1980 as they were then.

---

[2] 1986 Act, s. 122(7).

[3] This prohibits agreements between undertakings, decisions by associations of undertakings or concerted practices which may affect trade within the U.K. and have as their object or effect the prevention, restriction or distortion of competition within the U.K. (s. 2).

[4] Any conduct on the part of one or more undertakings which amounts to the abuse of a dominant position in a market is prohibited if it may affect trade within the U.K. (s. 18).

In the first stages of the Bill the scope of the exemption was very much wider. In addition to covering those provisions "encouraged" by the FSA's regulating provisions or practices, it included those that were "contemplated". Further to the Interim Report this was deleted as it was feared that this would grant firms too much of a defence from a charge of falling foul of both the Chapter I and Chapter II prohibitions.

This three-tier competition scrutiny built on the principles of good regulation should provide a sound basis on which to ensure that regulatory provisions and practices do not unnecessarily hinder authorised firms' ability to compete in carrying on regulated activities. This protection is further supplemented by a necessary disapplication from the Competition Act 1998. However, this disapplication of the Competition Act 1998 is not an exemption from competition law in its entirety but only where agreements or conduct is required or encouraged by the FSA. Whilst it is true that as much as the potential impact of rules and practices are important, what is more significant is the actual impact these will have on competition. To address this concern, the Government will conduct a formal two-year review of the Act which will comment on the "actual" affects on competition of both the FSA and Government measures. This is reinforced by the FSA's Annual Report in which it will be prompted to show how its activities impact on competition.[5]

REVIEW OF THE POLARISATION RULES

9.16 The SIB introduced the polarisation rules in 1987 to rectify the perceived market distortions that were occurring due to the absence of a clear definition of "independent advice". At the time, the then DGFT concluded that polarisation, combined with financial regulation, the cost of compliance and the costs of the compensation and complaints procedures for IFAs[6] would significantly distort competition. The DGFT believed that these extra costs would reduce the number of IFAs. As the polarisation rules effectively removed an intermediate category of adviser, there would be an increase in the influence of tied advisers,[7] leading to a reduction in the information available to consumers on competing products.[8] In spite of the DGFT's findings, the Secretary of State permitted the rules to be promulgated because he concluded that otherwise the potential for market misconduct was rife. Ten years on, the DGFT's report revealed that the concerns expressed in

---

[5] H.M. Treasury *Competition in U.K. Banking, The Cruickshank Report—Government Response* (August 2000).
[6] IFAs are financial advisers who are not "tied" to any product providers and therefore, are seen to act on behalf of the investor. However, it is arguable that IFAs are not "independent" in the true sense of the word. IFAs operate product panels whereby they admit qualifying products onto their panels chosen according to a set criterion, which are then recommended by independent financial advisers. Commissions are negotiated after the products are chosen. There is a possibility that those IFAs that offer better rates of commission will actually qualify onto the panels and it is this arrangement which leads to the suggestion that IFAs could be construed as being tied. IFAs also operate "recommended product lists" on a similar basis.
[7] The tied sector comprises those advisers who are "company representatives"—employees of the product provider or "appointed representatives"—agents of the product providers and who can only offer advice on their company's products.
[8] OFT, *Securities and Investment Board: A report by the Director General of Fair Trading to the Secretary of State for Trade and Industry* (March 1987).

1987 were unfounded.[9] In particular, there had not been the dramatic reduction in independent advice predicted by the DGFT in 1987.

THE REVIEW PROCESS

9.17   In conducting the 1998 review, the DGFT used his powers under section 122(4) of the 1986 Act along with section 2 of the FTA 1973. Section 2 of the FTA imposes a duty on the DGFT to review the carrying on of commercial activities by suppliers of services to the extent that they may adversely affect the economic interests of consumers in the United Kingdom. The reason for this double barrel inquiry was to ensure that the consumer protection angle was covered. The DGFT reported to the Treasury[10] that the polarisation rules do adversely affect competition in the retail distribution sector (*i.e.* between IFAs and tied advisers) and, amongst product providers (providers of financial services products). The DGFT's findings are described in more detail below. As well as seeking the views of the DGFT, the Economic Secretary to the Treasury also sought the views of the FSA which, in turn, commissioned a report by London Economics (LE).[11] One of LE's main findings was that the rules on polarisation had an anti-competitive effect.

With the Treasury's approval of its proposals and the aid of the commissioned report from LE, the FSA set out its policy and consulted[12] on its proposals, which finally became effective from March 29, 2001.[13] The FSA has declared that the reformation of the rules will take place through a two-stage process.[14] The first stage will consist of relatively small changes where consumer detriment is believed to be minimal (see below) and, the second stage will be a far wider review on the rules of Polarisation but these will be developed in conjunction with consumer awareness measures.

IMPACT OF POLARISATION ON COMPETITION

9.18   At the retail distribution level, the DGFT felt that the polarisation rules may adversely affect competition between different types of advisers in two ways.[15] Firstly, the polarisation rules might prevent innovation in retail distribution. The DGFT commented that in well-functioning markets, the range of brands stocked by

---

[9] DGFT, *The Rules on the Polarisation of Investment Advice*, (August 1999), para. 7.6, p. 42 ("DGFT Report").

[10] Letter to Gordon Brown, dated August 3, 1999. See the DGFT Report, p. 1.

[11] LE, *Polarisation and Financial Services Intermediary Regulation* (July 2000) ("LE Report"). LE was asked to look at five options for change along with other ancillary matters. These options ranged from: introducing a new "intermediate" category of adviser—who could distribute products of more than one provider; to abolish polarisation for unit trusts and those products marked by CAT standards (CAT stands for fair Charges, easy Access and decent Terms); allowing tied advisers to "gap fill"—from other providers to supplement their own line of products; and retaining the rules on polarisation.

[12] FSA, *Consultation Paper 80—Reforming Polarisation: First steps* (January 2001) ("CP80") with feedback being published in March 2001.

[13] These took effect through designated rules amending the SRO's rules and will apply until N2 and thereafter the relevant rules that are to apply from December 1, 2001 can be found in COB 3 and 5.

[14] Howard Davies set this out in a letter to Gordon Brown dated November 1, 2000. See CP 80, Annex A, p. 10.

[15] DGFT Report, paras 7.8–7.10, p. 42.

retailers would be determined by consumer preferences and thus, there is scope for retail innovation. However, in the market for financial advice, retail innovation is hindered as a result of the rules on polarisation which impede various advisers competing between themselves. The permitted advice that could be given as a result of the rules also tempered the sale of products whose components were derived from different product providers. For example, cited in the Report are maxi ISAs[16]—a product whose life insurance component is provided by the life company but the unit trust from a range of companies. Under the current rules, advice on this by a tied adviser is not possible unless, for example, the provider of the life element of the product "buys in" and "packages" unit trusts from various other providers.

The DGFT was also of the opinion that if the polarisation rules were abolished, then additional rules would be required in order to make transparent to consumers any ties that the adviser may have with the product company and thereby, revealing any benefits derived from the product companies.[17]

The secondary competitive concern at the retail distribution level was that tied advisers were not able to offer advice on more competitive products, this again being to the customer's disadvantage.[18] However, the harm that this was perceived to cause could be mitigated by the tied adviser either referring the customer to an IFA or, product providers buying in the product of another company so as to widen their product range—so that products better match customer needs—or even, outsourcing aspects of their own product (an example of the latter being contracting out service elements such as marketing or even those relating to the make up of the product, *i.e.* fund management for unit trusts).

As noted above, competition between product providers was said to be affected in three ways.[19] First, there were said to be barriers to entry for first time market entrants, *i.e.* being debarred from adding their products to an adviser whom is already tied.[20] Nonetheless, the availability of alternative distribution channels (*e.g.* direct sales), the high number of product providers' products in the market, and the fact that tied advisers will sell the products of their associate providers (the product provider to whom they are tied) lessen these anti-competitive effects.

Secondly, polarisation might have competition-dampening effects. Although independent financial advice was readily available, a large proportion of business continued to go through tied channels. Much of the competitive pressure on providers came from competition between products sold through an independent adviser, and in the case of a tied adviser, this competition would take place only between the competing products of one provider or marketing group.

Thirdly, however, polarisation rules might have competition-enhancing effects. IFA product panels can be seen to stimulate competition between product providers who attempt to get admitted onto these panels. If the polarisation rules were removed, then this could result in fewer IFAs—as it would not be economically viable for IFAs to allocate resources into the research and other costs necessary to offer independent advice—and consequently, a reduction in competition between providers.

---

[16] *ibid.*
[17] DGFT Report, para. 7.12, p. 43.
[18] DGFT Report, para. 7.23, p. 43.
[19] DGFT Report, para. 7.17, p. 44–46.
[20] To illustrate the point, the Report cites the concern of unit trust providers of not being able to sell through banks. See para. 7.18.

The DGFT felt that these pro-competitive effects have more of a bearing in the market for life products than non life products such as unit trust sales, as consumers readily purchase these less complicated products directly without the need for advice.[21] Although it is conceivable that competition in this sense may be dampened, it may not be lost altogether since competition would still exist amongst product providers who seek to offer a range of products.

In sum, the DGFT concluded that competition between retailers was restricted or distorted to a significant extent by the polarisation rules. In retail markets, innovation was restricted by the rules. As regards competition between product providers, polarisation increased barriers to entry and dampened competition between providers, although the maintenance of a strong IFA sector might help to maintain competition. However, these effects on competition were found to differ according to the product in question, with the adverse effects of the rules on competition being significant in the case of units in collective investment schemes, but not in the case of life assurance and pensions.

EFFECTS OF POLARISATION ON CONSUMERS

9.19   On the surface, it appeared that the rules on polarisation had served its purpose. A survey conducted by the PIA found that 80 per cent of clients of IFAs correctly identified them as being tied advisers.[22] More worryingly, doubts remained over what customers understood by the distinction between these types of advisers and, the nature of "independent" advice. It was also found that around one third stated that a bank was the best place to seek independent financial advice, despite the fact that most banks sell tied products.[23] Nonetheless, the rules allowed the regulators to pin point who should be responsible for complying with the rules and who should shoulder the blame in the event consumers are given inappropriate advice.[24]

The DGFT found that on the whole IFAs appeared to offer consumers better quality advice on life products (the most complex investment products) than tied advisers, and as a consequence, a reduction in the amount of independent advice available would be detrimental to consumers. This is well documented by the persistency rates of products (*i.e.* the length of time customers persist with their chosen product).

For example, over 76 per cent of life policies purchased through IFAs were persisted for four years; compared to just over 60 per cent bought through company representatives (tied advisers) for the same period.[25] The DGFT Report recommended that advice on life insurance-linked products should continue to be polarised because, *inter alia*, the question of liability for improper advice would not be clear.[26]

In contrast, non-life products tended to be simpler and more transparent, and the removal of polarisation could have pro-competitive effects such as an increase

---

[21] This was contrary to LE's Report which found that over 40% of consumers sought advice when purchasing unit trusts. See Figure 23, p. 70.
[22] PIA, *Consumer Panel Report* (December 1998), Annex 5, p. 65.
[23] *ibid.*, Annex 1, p. 40.
[24] DGFT Report, para. 6.12, p. 36.
[25] PIA, *Fourth Survey of the Persistency of Life and Pensions Policies 1998*, Table 1, p. 5.
[26] DGFT Report, para. 6.21, p. 39.

in the number of products for selection from some advisers. Nevertheless, it was still important that consumers were aware, prior to making a purchase, of any bias their adviser might have and this liberalisation should be accompanied by status disclosure of the adviser.[27]

RECOMMENDATIONS AND EVENTUAL CHANGES

9.20   With these findings in mind, the DGFT made several recommendations,[28] and in so doing paid due regard to the double barrel nature of the inquiry. The recommendations of the DGFT, LE and the FSA are discussed in tandem below. It should be noted that these changes will directly impact upon tied advisers and the position of IFAs will be integral to the second stage review.

The DGFT's principal recommendation was that the polarisation rules should be retained only for advice on investment products linked to life insurance. Subject to financial promotion of packaged products (see below), this rather radical change has not been effected due to the market distortions that would result; for example, it would create anomalies between non life assurance and insurance based products that essentially have the same underlying investment vehicle.[29] LE vehemently opposed this on the grounds that it would distort competition between polarised and non-polarised investment products and, the potential danger of creating customer confusion as to adviser status. This no doubt constitutes a fundamental change and the FSA has said that this recommendation will form part of its second stage review on the rules of polarisation.[30]

The recommendations that applied to polarised advice included maintaining the rules regulating the independence of IFAs. For the moment, these have been retained, as IFAs are perceived to be an important source of impartial advice. Furthermore, the DGFT also recommended that commissions should not form part of the selection process for products to be included onto IFA product panels. The FSA in addressing this concern has deferred it to the second stage review of the rules on polarisation.[31]

The DGFT also recommended that specialist products should be recognised and sold in their own right as part of a tied adviser's product range, and the responsibility for advice provided in relation to this niche product should be taken by the lead adviser.[32]

One of the FSA's core proposals has done just this by allowing product companies to "adopt" Stakeholder Pension Schemes ("SHPs") manufactured by other product companies. SHPs were chosen in particular because of the stringent conditions under which they are sold. For example, charges of such pension schemes cannot exceed 1 per cent. The adoption of other product providers' products will

---

[27] *ibid.*
[28] See the DGFT Report p. 56.
[29] FSA CP 80, Annex A, p. 12.
[30] Howard Davies set this out in a letter to Gordan Brown, dated November 1, 2000. CP 80, Annex A, p. 10.
[31] *ibid.*, p. 15.
[32] LE's other main recommendation was that competition in the tied sector needed stimulating and accordingly, recommended the introduction of multi-tied advisers where tied advisers are able to offer products from a range of product providers. LE Report, para. 7.2.1, p. 58.

not be subject to FSA made criteria, as the FSA felt that to do so would fuse the distinction between IFAs and tied advisers.[33] It was believed better to leave this to the adviser's individual criteria. Arguably, this is undoubtedly the better option since a product company would be unlikely to select unfit products for fear of jeopardising its own reputation. However, as noted earlier, change was deferred for CAT standard ISA's until stage two of the consultation on the polarisation regime. This was done largely on the basis that immediate change resulted in little benefit and the fact that this change should take place once disclosure measures are finalised.[34] Concerns about product bias arising were eased by the overriding factor that in recommending an investment product, the investment adviser must ensure that it is suitable for customer needs.[35]

The DGFT also made recommendations in respect to non-polarised investment advice. This was done on the basis that if liberalisation were to take effect then someone should bear responsibility for non-polarised advice. Subsequently, he recommended that financial advisers with multiple ties should be directly authorised by the FSA. The FSA in response to this have said that they will monitor multi-tied advisers' compliance with the rules.[36] A related concern of the DGFT was that consumers should be aware of the type of products that they receive polarised advice on. This problem is resolved by the DGFT recommending that all investment advisers in giving non-polarised advice should disclose any ties/associations that they may have with product providers at the point of first contact with the customer. This is in order to achieve a greater standard of transparency.

Consumer awareness measures were unanimously recommended from all quarters. It was felt that any changes to polarisation should be accompanied by provisions which made clear to the consumer the nature of advice they receive. The FSA is currently in the midst of completing research on advisor status disclosure.[37] The FSA have committed themselves to publishing comparative tables on financial services products on the internet. Initially, this will cover investment products including personal pensions, endowments, investment bonds, unit trusts, ISAs and are likely to include mortgages.[38] The tables are purely for informational purposes and past performance of products will not feature in the tables as this could precipitate misselling.[39] Another internet initiative is the "interactive web quiz" that will help consumers with financial planning.[40]

The DGFT's more general recommendations included making recipients of tied advice aware that payment for advice is included in the commission paid to the

---

[33] FSA, *Policy Statement: Polarisation, feedback to CP 80* (March 2001), para. 3.18, pp. 9–10.
[34] As recommended by London Economics.
[35] FSA, *Policy Statement: Polarisation, feedback to CP 80* (March 2001), para. 3.20, p. 10.
[36] FSA, CP 80, Annex A, p. 15.
[37] This is scheduled to form part of the second stage consultation on polarisation.
[38] FSA, *Bulletin No. 2, Comparative Tables: Mortgages* (June 2001).
[39] Consultation on this was contained in FSA, *Consultation Paper 28: Comparative Information for Financial Services* (October 1999); and the FSA committed to this proposal in its response paper in June 2000. In raising consumer understanding about investment products, the FSA have published a discussion paper (Informing Consumers: a review of product information at the point of sale) along with a summary of research (Informed decisions? How consumers use key features. Consumer research 5) in November 2000. Also see FSA, Discussion paper: Treating customers fairly after the point of sale (June 2001).
[40] The website address is: *www.fsa.gov.uk/consumer/financial_planning*.

adviser by the product provider and that it is possible to negotiate rebates. The FSA considers the former to be another area in need of further review.

With respect to rebates,[41] this was believed to be a commercial issue that should be determined by advisers,[42] particularly as many receive low commission on regulated products. A case in point is the new SHP. The last of the DGFT's recommendations referred to equalising tax treatment for commission based advice with fee-based advice.

As a corollary to changing rules relating to the type of products that investment advisers may advise on, the FSA took a step further by extending the rules on financial promotion for packaged products (life products, units in regulated collective investment schemes or investment trust savings schemes). Currently, an inequality exists in that IFAs are able to advertise other firms' products by direct offer methods (*e.g.* newspaper supplements), but other firms, however, may only offer their own. This change was deemed necessary due to the potential impediment to fund supermarkets that offer investment funds (without advice), including those of other providers, over the internet.[43]

These changes mark a very cautious return to the pre-polarisation days. This small step is a welcomed one as many firms will be able to benefit from this loosening of the rules, although insurance companies and friendly societies will not be able to capitalise on these changes. Restrictions under section 16 of the Insurance Companies Act 1982 prohibit insurance companies from carrying on any activities other than in relation to insurance business. Similarly, friendly societies cannot undertake business that may compromise their traditional business.[44] Whilst these restrictions will cease for friendly societies at N2, the coming into force of the FSMA will be inconsequential for insurance companies as their restrictions stem from the E.U. First Life Directive (79/267). This first stage review of the polarisation rules could still be susceptible to further change if, under section 160 of the FSMA, the DGFT decides that they have a significantly adverse affect on competition, although this time the rules could be further reviewed by the Competition Commission.

---

[41] Rebates can be negotiated when advice is received from a commission-funded adviser, as payment for the advice is included in the commission paid to the adviser.

[42] FSA, CP 80, Annex A, p. 15. LE was of the opinion that this would mean merely formalising current market practice. It was also concerned about how this could be implemented for smaller IFAs (LE Report, p. 77).

[43] FSA, CP 80, p. 14.

[44] Incorporated societies and incorporated societies of unincorporated societies are able to offer SHPs (Friendly Societies Act 1992, Sched. 7).

CHAPTER **10**

FSA's Handbook:
Conduct of Business

JAMES PERRY

INTRODUCTION

10.01 Though the FSMA has been criticised because of its reliance on delegated legislation to put the regulatory flesh on the bare bones of the Act, it is unsurprising that the day-to-day conduct of regulated business will largely be governed by rules promulgated by the Authority. Indeed, though many of the "higher-level" issues discussed elsewhere in this volume are undeniably of critical importance, regulated firms might be forgiven for paying closer attention to the detailed FSA rules and guidance which, ultimately, will form the basis for their compliance regimes and monitoring programmes. The FSA's *Conduct of Business Sourcebook* ("COB") which was first published for consultation in late February 2000,[1] comprises the part of the FSA's *Handbook of Rules and Guidance* ("Handbook") which sets out the new conduct of business requirements for firms regulated by the statutory Authority, principally in relation to those firms' dealings with "private" and "intermediate" customers. The new Inter-Professionals Conduct ("IPC") chapter of the *Market Conduct Sourcebook* supplements COB by providing the rules and guidance which will apply when authorised firms deal or arrange deals with, or give specific advice to, a "market counterparty". COB is considered in some detail in paragraphs 10.03–10.25 below, while IPC is discussed at paragraph 10.26.

The statutory basis of the Authority's power to make rules and give guidance has already been discussed in Chapter 9, above. It is instructive to note that COB is in fact made pursuant to a number of separate rule-making powers under the FSMA, including:

- the "general rule-making power" (section 138);

- the power to make "non-regulated activity" rules (section 138(1)(b));

- the power to make rules relating to the holding of clients' money (section 139(1)); and

- the power to make "financial promotion rules" (section 145).

The breadth of these statutory powers gives some clue, at least, to the scope of the rules contained in COB (see below). In addition, COB contains a significant

---

[1] FSA, *Consultation Paper 45.*

amount of "general guidance" (defined in section 158(5) of the Act) which has been issued pursuant to the Authority's powers under section 157. As noted below, IPC is primarily guidance on the FSA Principles for Business and the FSA's understanding of "good market practice" in certain areas, though it does contain some rules. As noted in Chapter 9, it is particularly helpful that the FSA's stated policy is now to ensure that all such guidance will be incorporated in appropriate parts of the Handbook, where it will be most accessible to practitioners[2]; though the rulebooks of the SROs contained helpful guidance, it was often the case that guidance or regulatory policies were expressed outside the rulebook (generally in writing but sometimes not). It is to be hoped that the FSA's new policy will provide regulated firms with greater certainty than has been the case in the past.

THE FSA HANDBOOK

10.02 The FSA's Handbook represents the monumental product of more than 100 consultation papers, policy reports and other publications. Since the new regime was first mooted, the FSA has consistently stated that its new rulebook would significantly reduce the volume of the previous, different rulebooks and would strike a balance between "continuity and change". Consequently, both in COB and other parts of the Handbook, the process of integrating existing rules into a common framework has left much with which practitioners will be familiar; but, equally, a very large number of obvious and more subtle changes have been made. Also, the Handbook has to accommodate entirely new concepts such as the Code of Market Conduct, and new areas of regulation such as the Lloyd's regime.

Most of the Handbook comes into force on the day after N2—which, at the time of writing, is due to be December 1, 2001—though substantial parts will have come into force some three months earlier, on September 3, 2001. The materials which come into force on this earlier date are those which enable the FSA to deal with the broad range of regulatory applications now permitted under the FSMA including, most importantly, applications for permission (or new authorisation) under Part IV of the Act. COB, however, comes into force in its entirety on December 1, 2001 along with virtually all of the "Business Standards" block of the Handbook. As a technical matter, most of the Handbook (notably excluding the Redress block) was made by the FSA by instruments dated June 21, 2001, though the commencement date is September 3 or December 1, 2001 in almost all cases.

Various parts of the Handbook are considered elsewhere in this volume (including the chapters on authorisation, approved persons, enforcement and market abuse). A full review of the Handbook is certainly beyond the scope of this work! In brief, however, the scheme of the Handbook (together with the FSA's acronyms) is set out below:

Block 1—High Level Standards

- Principles for Businesses ("PRIN");
- Senior Management Arrangements, Systems and Controls ("SYSC");

---

[2] See FSA, *Policy Statement: The FSA's approach to giving guidance and waivers to firms* (September 1999), para. 6.

- Threshold Conditions ("COND");
- Approved Persons ("APER");
- Fitness and Propriety ("FIT"); and
- General Provisions ("GEN").

Block 2—Business Standards

- Interim Prudential Sourcebooks ("IPRU");
- Conduct of Business ("COB");
- Market Conduct ("MAR");
- Training and Competence ("TC"); and
- Money Laundering ("ML").

Block 3—Regulatory Process

- Authorisation ("AUTH");
- Supervision ("SUP");
- Enforcement ("ENF"); and
- Decision Making ("DEC").

Block 4—Redress

- Compensation ("COMP");
- Complaints against the FSA ("COAF"); and
- Dispute Resolution: complaints ("DISP").

Block 5—Specialist Sourcebooks

- Collective Investment Schemes ("CIS");
- Recognised Investment Exchanges/Clearing Houses ("REC");
- Lloyd's ("LLD");
- Professional Firms ("PROF");
- Credit Unions ("CRED");
- United Kingdom Listing Authority ("UKLA"); and
- Mortgages ("MORT").

In this Chapter, we concentrate on the section of Block 2 relating to Conduct of Business and the part of Market Conduct containing IPC.

THE SCOPE OF COB

10.03   COB will apply, to some extent at least, to all persons authorised under the FSMA (including "EEA firms" and "Treaty firms" qualifying for authorisation under, respectively, Schedules 3 and 4 of the Act). It replaces the diverse array of conduct of business and customer assets rules issued by the SROs, the RPBs and the FSA itself as well as the London Code of Conduct (though most of this Code, which was originally used by the Bank of England to regulate wholesale money market dealings between professionals, will now be reflected in IPC) and various statutory provisions formerly contained in banking, building societies and insurance legislation or orders. COB's potential general application to all regulated firms is confirmed by COB, 1.3.1R, which provides that the rules apply to firms in relation to all "regulated activities", except to the extent that a particular provision provides for a narrower application, and to "unregulated activities" to the extent specified. The scope of the "regulated activities" is defined by the RAO, which in turn means that a firm will generally not be subject to COB regulation in relation to an activity which is excluded under the RAO.[3] However, though the scope of COB extends to all kinds of "regulated activities" and to the firms which carry on such activities in the United Kingdom, the reality is that COB is principally concerned with the day-to-day regulation of those activities which used to be "investment business" under the 1986 Act. COB achieves this primary focus on "investment business" activities by using the separate, defined terms of "*designated investments*" and "*designated investment business*" which are designed, broadly, to incorporate the "investments" and activities which were regulated under the 1986 Act (including those long-term insurance contracts which were regulated under the 1986 Act and which fall within the RAO definition of "contractually based investments").[4] For example, therefore, the key rule on "suitability" of investment recommendations and decisions only applies to "designated investments" and not to deposits, general insurance policies and long-term protection policies, or regulated mortgages. In relation to the regulated Lloyd's activities of advising on membership of a syndicate and managing underwriting capacity, Chapter 12 of COB effectively "switches on" most of the COB Rules, subject to limited disapplications, as if the Lloyd's "investments" were designated investments. Conversely, regulated mortgages will be subject to their own special regime in the *Mortgage Sourcebook* (including financial promotion requirements which apply to a broad range of secured "qualifying credit" products and not just to regulated mortgages). Stakeholder pension schemes will be "designated investments" for the purpose of the new regime. Though the definitions of "designated investment business" and "designated investments" correspond closely to the 1986 Act and the new definitions in the RAO, the FSA has "sub-divided" some definitions where it has discerned policy reasons to do so. For example, "contracts for differences" have been sub-divided into (respectively) spread bets, rolling spot forex contracts and other contracts for differences for the purpose of the permission regime; and, for similar reasons, advising on pension transfers and pension opt-outs, and operating regulated or (separately) unregulated collective investment schemes, are included as separate investment activities.

Arguably one of the most important areas where COB represents an extension to the *status quo ante* is financial promotion. This is for two reasons. First, the general obligation on regulated firms relating to "fair, clear and not misleading" promotions[5] applies to non-real time financial promotions concerning deposits, general insurance contracts and long-term protection policies as it does to other regulated investments. However, the extremely detailed requirements of the rest of the financial promotion rules are disapplied in their entirety in the case of such "non-designated" investments,[6] and those persons wishing to promote such investments

---

[3] COB 1.3.2G(3). However, as was the case under the SFA Rules, dealing in investments as principal is treated as regulated notwithstanding any exclusion.

[4] "Designated investments" are those investments falling within Arts 75 (but only long-term insurance policies excluding "pure protection contracts"), 76 to 85 (inclusive) and 89 of the RAO. "Designated investment business" activities are, broadly, the activities which used to be investment business under the 1986 Act, but now including the "stakeholder pension scheme" activity.

[5] COB 3.8.4R.

[6] COB 3.2.3R. Reinsurance contracts are also excluded.

receive guidance from the FSA that they may (continue to) find it helpful to take account of the British Bankers' Association/Building Societies Association Code of Conduct for the Advertising of Interest Bearing Accounts (for deposits), the General Insurance Standards Council Code (for general insurance contracts) and the relevant ABI Code of Practice (for pure protection contracts).[7] The main practical change for persons marketing such products is that they may face disciplinary action by the FSA and/or a civil action at the suit of a "private person" (section 150 of the FSMA) if they fail in any case to live up to the general obligation to issue fair, clear and not misleading non-real time financial promotions.[8] However, these consequences may be avoided provided the conditions in Article 22 (in the case of deposits) or 24 (in the case of insurance) of the Financial Promotion Order are complied with; as long as certain basic information regarding the firm, compensation arrangements and (in the case of deposit-takers) capital is included, a promotion will be exempt and thus free from COB requirements (see further below and Chapter 6 relating to Financial Promotion, above).

The second reason is a product of the statutory definition of a "financial promotion". Under the 1986 Act, marketing activities were regulated if they constituted either "unsolicited calls" (section 56) or "investment advertising" (section 57). Section 21 of the FSMA has introduced a broader concept of regulated promotional activities, which includes (as well as unsolicited calls and advertising) solicited calls and other individual (or "one-to-one") communications, including "real-time promotions".[9] Consequently, the COB Rules on financial promotion are required to be broad enough to catch the new statutory concepts encompassed within section 21 and the Financial Promotion Order. The COB Rules on financial promotion are discussed further below.

Apart from "regulated activities", COB applies to "unregulated activities" to the extent specified in any COB provision. A number of COB rules[10] apply to a firm when it is conducting designated investment business or "activities in connection with designated investment business". This requirement for a connection with "real" investment activity provides some comfort that COB regulation will not stray too far into unregulated areas; the first draft of COB contained a more far-reaching attempt to catch "ancillary activities" held out as being for purposes similar to those of a regulated activity.

Though COB applies generally to regulated firms carrying on regulated activities (mainly being designated investment business), it has only limited relevance to business with or for "market counterparties". In relation to "inter-professional business" (see paragraph 10.26 below), only the rules relating to Chinese Walls, Client Classification and Personal Account Dealing will apply. In relation to other business with or for "market counterparties", the rules on Financial Promotions and Client Assets will apply and the rules regarding Inducements and Soft Commissions may also be relevant.[11]

---

[7] COB 3.8.6G.

[8] In this regard, see the FSA, *Policy Statement on COB*, paras 3.44–3.47 (inclusive) (February 2001) .

[9] See Chapter 6, above. Though "one-to-one" communications are caught by s. 21, they are the subject of an exemption in the Financial Promotion Order.

[10] *e.g.*, see certain of the rules in Chapter 2 of COB (rules which apply to all firms conducting designated investment business).

[11] COB 1.3.3G, 1.3.4R and 1.3.5G.

COB applies to all regulated firms, with some obvious but important exceptions (COB 1.2.1R). First, the rules on customer assets (covering money and other assets, including investments) do not apply to incoming EEA firms with respect to their passported activities in the United Kingdom since, in the case of such firms, the regulation of the holding of clients' money and assets is reserved to a firm's home state regulator in accordance with the ISD.[12] COB does not spell out the position in this respect of "Treaty firms" qualifying for authorisation under Schedule 4 of the FSMA. Secondly, the rules do not apply to the operators, trustees or depositaries of recognised EEA collective investment schemes in relation to their carrying on of regulated activities as such, except for the rules on financial promotion (though such "UCITS qualifiers" are reminded of the requirements elsewhere in the Handbook regarding maintaining scheme facilities in the United Kingdom). Thirdly, COB does not apply to authorised open-ended investment companies ("ICVCs"). Lastly, COB also does not apply to (FSA) authorised professional firms in relation to "non-mainstream regulated activities" except for specified provisions.

Importantly, however, the FSA's guidance in COB 1.3.2G(3) makes it clear that a firm will not be subject to COB Rules in relation to any aspect of its business activities which fall within an exclusion in the RAO, with the notable exception of exempt dealings as principal under Article 15 of the RAO. This guidance largely tracks the previous position under the rules of the SROs.[13] As a result, for example, conduct of business rules, including those relating to suitability and customer agreements, will not apply to advisory or dealing relationships between group companies.

Territorial scope

10.04   The territorial scope of COB is divided conceptually between:

- regulated and other activities governed by COB, except for financial promotions; and

- financial promotions.

In the case of regulated and other activities, the COB Rules will apply, broadly, subject to similar territorial limitations as those which existed in the SRO rulebooks. Activities carried on from an establishment maintained by a firm (or its appointed representative) in the United Kingdom will be subject to the full weight of the COB Rules, whether or not the firm's customer is in the United Kingdom (and apparently even if the establishment is not a permanent one). However, as was the case under SRO rules,[14] activities carried on by the firm from an office outside the United Kingdom, but with or for a client in the United Kingdom, will not be subject to the great majority of the COB rules *provided* that, if the office were a separate person, the activity *either* would fall within the "overseas person" exclu-

---

[12] Arts 8(3), 11(2), 17(4) and 18(2) of the ISD (93/22).
[13] *e.g.*, see r. 5–1 of Chapter 5 of the SFA Rules.
[14] *e.g.*, r. 5—1(2) of the SFA Rules.

sions in Article 72 of the RAO *or* would not be regarded as carried on in the United Kingdom. This is an important restriction on the territorial scope of the COB Rules for banks, securities firms and others with overseas branch offices, which otherwise would be required to comply with United Kingdom and local conduct of business requirements in respect of one and the same activity. For example, dealings in securities between the Singapore branch of a United Kingdom firm and a United Kingdom institutional client would not be subject to COB Rules; nor would dealings with private customers, as long as any financial promotions to the customers have been issued or approved where required by the United Kingdom firm in accordance with COB Rules. Also, private customers of the overseas branch must normally receive a written disclosure making it clear that, in some or all respects, the regulatory system overseas (including investors' compensation arrangements) will be different from that of the United Kingdom.[15] SRO Rules contained a similar requirement.

As one would expect, the COB Rules are also largely disapplied in the case of activities carried on by a United Kingdom firm from a branch in another EEA State under an "EEA [passporting] right"; this is consistent with the scheme of the ISD that the conduct of business rules of the host state may be applied to such activities carried on by a branch. This is subject, however, to the position in relation to custody and clients' money, where COB 9 on client assets will apply to the exclusion of host state rules.

There is a further territorial limitation, which relates to activities which are carried on otherwise than from a United Kingdom establishment or an EEA or other overseas branch. The COB will again not apply generally to such overseas activities.

The territorial scope of the COB regime for financial promotions is somewhat different, and relies on some of the concepts introduced in the Financial Promotion Order (discussed in detail in Chapter 6, above). Broadly, the position under COB 3.3 is that:

- a financial promotion *communicated* by a firm from a place within *or* outside the United Kingdom and *made to* or "*directed at*" persons within the United Kingdom will be subject to the financial promotion rules. For this purpose, COB uses the same tests as Article 10 of the Financial Promotion Order to determine whether or not a particular promotion is "directed at" the United Kingdom (though in COB the test is applied both to non-real time and real time promotions). Accordingly, as one would expect, promotions by overseas branch offices (including EEA passported branches) will generally be subject to COB Rules on financial promotions if "directed at" the United Kingdom (whether wholly or partly).

- a financial promotion *communicated* by others, *made to* or *directed at persons in the United Kingdom* and *approved* by a regulated firm will be subject to the financial promotion rules (see COB 3.3.2G). For example, therefore, a firm will be subject to the full COB Rules where it approves a promotion for an overseas group company or one of its clients with a view

---

[15] COB 5.5.7R.

to distribution in the United Kingdom. A firm is only permitted to approve *non-real time* promotions (COB 3.3.4G).

- a (non-real time) financial promotion *communicated* by others, not *made to* or *directed at persons in the United Kingdom* and *approved* by the firm will be subject to a few of the COB Rules,[16] including in particular the general obligation in COB 3.8.4R regarding the clarity and fairness of financial promotions. Though this appears logical, it represents a change because, under the rules of the SROs, overseas marketing was not subject to United Kingdom regulation. Therefore, for example, a United Kingdom corporate finance firm approving a private placement memorandum relating to a United Kingdom or French company for distribution entirely outside the United Kingdom (though approval is not strictly required under s.21 of the FSMA) will now have to ensure that the memorandum complies with the general obligation in COB 3.8.4R, unless one of the exemptions in COB 3.5R applies. If, however, a firm does *not* approve a document designed for distribution overseas, the position is different (see below). In the FSA's view, the fact that a firm approves a financial promotion means that recipients—wherever they may be—are entitled to expect that the communication will conform to basic standards.

- a financial promotion communicated by a firm from a place *inside* the United Kingdom and *made to* or *directed* at persons *outside* the United Kingdom will not be subject to COB regulation *unless* the promotion is an "unsolicited real time communication", in which case all those COB Rules particularly relating to real-time communications will apply.[17] A "real time communication" is defined in similar terms to the definition in Article 7 of the Financial Promotion Order, and means a financial promotion which is communicated in the course of a personal visit, telephone conversation or other interactive dialogue.[18] The effect of this treatment of unsolicited real-time communications is, however, to confirm that such communications to private customers outside the United Kingdom are effectively banned in the same way as unsolicited real-time communications to United Kingdom customers except in limited circumstances, including in particular where the promotion is exempt under the Financial Promotion Order.[19] Unsolicited real-time communications are also permitted in the context of an existing customer relationship where unsolicited promotions are envisaged by the customer, in the case of "packaged products" (except "higher volatility funds") and in the context of public takeover bids (as was the case under the 1986 Act). In relation to non-real time communications, the position under the Financial Promotion Order, and consequently under COB, was changed very late in the legislative process when the Treasury decided, subject to conditions, to exempt communications which are made to a person or persons outside the United Kingdom or which are directed solely at

---

[16] COB 3.8.4R, 3.11R (unregulated collective investment schemes) and 3.12.1–3.12.5 (communication and approval of financial promotions for overseas or unauthorised persons) will apply.
[17] COB 3.8.22R and COB 3.10 (as well as COB 3.11).
[18] COB 3.5.5 R(1).
[19] COB 3.10.3R(1).

persons outside the United Kingdom.[20] Consequently, the FSA revised its previous intention to subject overseas marketing to the general obligation of "clarity and fairness" under COB 3.8.4R, which preserves the *status quo ante* under the SROs' rules and will be welcomed by regulated firms.

- a financial promotion communicated by a firm from a place outside the United Kingdom (*e.g.* an overseas office) will not be subject to any financial promotion rules, if it is not made to or directed at persons in the United Kingdom.

- a little alarmingly, COB says that COB 3.11 (unregulated collective investment schemes) applies without any territorial limitation. However, scheme promotions which are made to overseas persons, or which are directed solely at overseas persons and United Kingdom "investment professionals" and high net worth persons", will be exempt under the Promotion of Collective Investment Schemes Order in any event. The purposes of this provision appear to be to limit the categories of overseas persons to whom a firm may promote unregulated CISs if the "overseas recipients" exemption does not apply (see Chapter 3 Annex 5); and to prevent a firm from communicating or approving a non-exempt direct offer promotion which is directed at overseas persons unless there is adequate evidence that it will be suitable for those persons (COB 3.9.5R(2)).

TRANSITIONAL PROVISIONS

10.05 The Act provides that rules made by the FSA may contain (*inter alia*) such transitional provisions as the Authority considers appropriate (section 156(2)). Given the potential implications which parts of COB have for regulated firms' systems and procedures, the FSA has chosen to exercise this power in respect of the introduction of COB. COB Rules and guidance come into force at "N2" (when most provisions of the new Act come into force and the Authority assumes its full regulatory powers), which at the time of writing had been announced as December 1, 2001. The FSA found that framing a set of transitional provisions which provided clarity and certainty while avoiding unnecessary burdens for firms was not at all straight-forward.[21] Originally, the FSA proposed a transitional period of 12 months from N2, during which firms could continue to comply with certain of the rules of their previous regulator (including rules regarding notices to and agreements with clients, and financial promotions).[22] In the event, the FSA responded after consultation with a far more wide-ranging and intricate set of transitional reliefs than had originally been envisaged.[23] Though the FSA's *Policy Statement* is extremely detailed, the basic approach adopted has been to produce a series of "Transitional Rules" (taking effect under section 156(2)) within three generic types:

[20] Financial Promotion Order, Art. 12 (see further Chapter 6, above).
[21] See the FSA's comments in the *Policy Statement on COB* at para. 3.4.1 (February 2001).
[22] See FSA, *Consultation Papers 45 and 57*.
[23] FSA, *Policy Statement: Conduct of Business Sourcebook—Transitional Arrangements* (July 2001).

- **Extra Time Provisions ("ETP")**: the effect of an ETP is to allow firms a "period of grace" after N2 to make the necessary systems and procedural changes to achieve full compliance with COB. In view of the time which had elapsed since its original proposals (with a 12-month grace period), the FSA fixed a transitional period of seven months, from N2 until July 1, 2001, for firms regulated by the FSA or one of the SROs and firms formerly on the "section 43 list", and a period of 12 months for firms formerly regulated by RPBs. The longer period for ex-RPB firms was intended to allow such firms to review details of the designated professional body ("DPB") rules to decide whether or not to opt into FSA authorisation (rather than Part XX exempt status under the FSMA). During the transitional period, a firm will be deemed not to breach a COB rule identified in the ETP if it can demonstrate compliance with the corresponding rule of its previous regulator (provided that that rule is "substantially similar" to the COB rule). The Transitional Rules contain ETPs in relation to (*inter alia*) financial promotions approved prior to N2; the client classification of "expert private customers"; and client money and assets.

- **Technical Timing Provisions ("TTP")**: TTPs apply to those COB Rules which require firms to fulfil obligations to customers at periodic intervals, such as those relating to periodic statements and periodic disclosures of soft commission. In these cases, a TTP will have the effect of providing a statutory defence for a firm that complies on or after N2 with the rules of its previous regulator in relation to an event occurring on or before N2. Therefore, assuming that N2 is December 1, 2001, a periodic statement issued by an investment manager to its clients covering the six-month period ending March 31, 2002 will not contravene COB 8.2 if it complies with the relevant SRO Rules (probably being those of IMRO).

- **Timeless Saving Provision ("TSP")**: a TSP allows a firm to rely upon documentation or compliance work undertaken in accordance with the rules of its previous regulator for an indefinite period. Significantly, many of the COB Rules relating to terms of business letters/ customer agreements, and suitability (including "know your customer" and understanding risk) will benefit from TSPs. Moreover, the TSPs may apply in some cases to work done, documents issued or transactions entered into before the end of the transitional period, as well as prior to N2.

There is some overlap between the different types of Transitional Rules, and in particular between ETPs and TSPs; moreover, the Transitional Rules are internally complex and need careful study before any conclusion can be reached that transitional relief will be available in a particular case. However, the importance of these rules cannot be doubted and goes beyond the attendant cost savings (significant though they may be). In legal terms, compliance with COB Transitional Rules will provide a statutory defence against disciplinary proceedings, or a civil action under section 150 of the Act, for a breach of a COB rule, provided a firm can discharge the burden of proving compliance with the corresponding rule of its previous regulator. This will not necessarily be easy, because the onus will lie with the firm to establish the "substantial similarity" between the respective rules and the validity of its work in accordance with previous regulatory rules, as well as establishing that any additional conditions specific to the Transitional Rule in question have been met (*e.g.*, in relation to "know your customer", that the circumstances of a private customer have not changed since the firm's last "fact-find").

If the Transitional Rules do not prescribe relief in relation to a particular COB rule (and the FSA's list is not exhaustive), firms will be obliged to apply for a waiver under section 148 of the Act if transitional relief is needed. However, it seems unlikely that such applications will be encouraged given their potential volume and the administrative complexity which they would entail for the regulator and firms alike.

THE DESIGN OF COB: RULES, EVIDENTIAL PROVISIONS AND GUIDANCE

10.06   The design of COB is slightly different from the SROs' rulebooks which practitioners will have been used to consulting. COB contains three kinds of provisions: rules, evidential provisions and guidance. Rules represent binding obligations placed on regulated firms, the breach of which may give rise to disciplinary action by the FSA and/or (in some cases) civil action for compensation.

Each evidential provision is linked, both logically and in the text of COB, to a particular rule, and may either tend to establish a firm's compliance with a linked rule (a positive provision) or, if breached, tend to establish a breach of the linked rule (a negative provision). If a firm breaches a negative provision, it will be presumed that it has also breached the linked rule, unless it can prove the contrary (so that the burden of proof, on balance of probabilities, lies with the firm). If a firm complies with a positive provision, it will be presumed that it has also complied with the linked rule, unless the FSA or another interested person (for example, a "private person" suing the firm under section 150 of the Act) can prove otherwise. Evidential provisions may also be two-way (*i.e.* positive and negative); COB confirms alongside each evidential provision whether it is positive, negative or both. For example, a "two-way" evidential provision is included in relation to terms of business (COB 4.2.10R and 4.2.11E), which states, broadly, that compliance with specific contents requirements will tend to establish compliance with the general Rule relating to "adequate" terms of business and customer agreements, while non-compliance will tend to establish the contrary. Though the concept is novel and significant, there are not many evidential provisions in COB.

Guidance is again linked to specific rules both physically and logically, but does not throw a burden of proof on a firm to establish compliance with a rule in the case of non-compliance with FSA guidance. Guidance is thus intended to be advisory in nature. The FSA has stated that, where a firm follows the FSA's guidance on a particular subject, in circumstances which are the same as those contemplated by the guidance, the firm will usually have the benefit of a "safe harbour" from disciplinary action. This stops short, however, of providing firms with an absolute safe harbour in such circumstances (see further Chapter 9, above). The FSA has tried to draft the guidance in COB so that it does not appear to place obligations on firms, as the Rules do.[24]

---

[24] See FSA's comments in the *Policy Statement on COB*, paras 3.22–3.27 (February 2001).

CLASSIFICATION OF CUSTOMERS

10.07   The need to distinguish between "retail" and "wholesale" business in the financial markets has been a constant theme of public debate on the new legislation. Indeed, the Chancellor mentioned the issue in the House of Commons when announcing his intention to introduce the FSMA.[25] Since primary legislation or a Treasury order would clearly be too inflexible a home for the definitions underlying the wholesale/retail distinction, they are to be found in COB; this mirrors the previous position under the 1986 Act and the SROs' Rules. The distinction is drawn under COB, as it was under the SROs' Rules, by classifying the objects of financial promotion and investment activity, namely market counterparties and customers.

The main purpose of a system of customer classification is to determine what protections under conduct of business rules should be provided to different kinds of persons. Under the SROs' Rules, this was achieved by classifying persons as market counterparties, non-private customers or private customers in relation to investment business carried on with or for such persons, and by applying limited customer protections to non-private customers, and little or no such protections to market counterparties. In addition, some dealings in investments and money market instruments between market counterparties and, in some cases, between market counterparties and non-private customers, fell outside the ambit of the SROs' Rules and were regulated instead under the London Code of Conduct policed by the Bank of England (and latterly by the FSA).

The new regime maintains and builds on the retail/wholesale distinction in two ways. First, provisions aimed principally at dealings between market counterparties in the wholesale securities and derivatives markets are to be found in the Market Conduct sourcebook (which incorporates the IPC and the Code of Market Conduct). Secondly, COB itself contains the important definitions of a "market counterparty", an "intermediate customer" and a "private customer", and is designed principally to provide different degrees of protection to, respectively, private customers and intermediate customers. In the main, COB does not concern itself with the protection of market counterparties. Most COB Rules are only expressed to benefit "customers", though a few (such as the COB rule on "inducements"[26]) are relevant to business with market counterparties. However, as mentioned above, the sections of COB on Client Assets apply to business between market counterparties, subject to permitted opt-outs or modifications of duties (as was the case under the SROs' Rules [27]).

The new definitions underlying the customer classification system were the product of lengthy consultation by the FSA. At a relatively early stage, it became clear that both the FSA and market practitioners were in favour of a clear, objective system of classification based on the characteristics of counterparties and customers (as was the case under the SROs' Rules), rather than the more complicated system under the "wholesale money market" regime, where classification depended

---

[25] *Hansard*, May 20, 1997 (Vol. 294, Col. 509).
[26] COB 2.2.3R.
[27] *cf.* Chapter 4 of the SFA Rules. See also *e.g.*, the opt-out in COB 9.3.9R relating to money held for market counterparties and intermediate customers.

(*inter alia*) on the relative size of different kinds of market deals between parties.[28] In the event, the FSA has settled on three definitions (market counterparty, intermediate customer and private customer) which in many respects closely resemble the three corresponding definitions under the SROs' Rules. The principal differences, however, are the following:

Market Counterparty

10.08 United Kingdom authorised persons and overseas financial services institutions are now in general treated as market counterparties. This represents a significant policy change from the position under the SROs' Rules, where such persons were only so treated in certain defined circumstances (including, under the SFA Rules, in the case of dealings in securities between members of an exchange and in the case of some "over-the-counter" deals; and, under the IMRO Rules, where the counterparty carried on similar investment business to the member firm and was either acting as principal or as agent for an unnamed principal). This change was the subject of considerable debate during the consultation period, which mainly centred on the protections which an authorised person acting as agent for its customers would be able or obliged to obtain for these customers if it was treated as a market counterparty by another authorised firm. In the event, the FSA retained the substance of the change while partly addressing the concerns raised (mainly from the fund management industry[29]). In the case of "inter-professional business" covered by IPC between authorised firms (or between an authorised firm and an overseas professional), Firm 1 will be a market counterparty of Firm 2 even if Firm 1 has underlying customers *unless* both firms have agreed that Firm 1 should be classified as an intermediate customer.[30]

As indicated below, "inter-professional business" includes dealing and arranging deals and giving transaction-specific advice in relation to securities and derivatives. Consequently, in relation to a very broad range of business, fund managers, investment advisers and other professional agents will be classified as market counterparties unless the authorised person expressly agrees otherwise (which, of course, he is not bound to do). In the case of non-inter-professional business, however, Firm 1 must be treated as an intermediate customer if it has an underlying customer (or even if it does not, if it has not indicated that it is acting on its own behalf) or if it is a life office, and the protections for customers under COB will therefore apply.[31] This means, for example, that a fund manager delegating discretion over all or part of a portfolio to a second manager must be treated as an intermediate customer (since discretionary investment management services are not covered by IPC); and the same would be true in the case of a United Kingdom or overseas firm acting for clients in the context of corporate finance business.

In addition, a new provision has been included for "large intermediate customers" to opt-up from intermediate customer status to that of market

---

[28] See FSA's response to comments on *Discussion Paper: The Future Regulation of Inter-Professional Business* (June 1999).

[29] FSA, *Policy Statement on COB*, paras 5.16–5.19 (inclusive) (February 2001).

[30] COB 4.1.7R(2).

[31] COB 4.1.7R(3). Regulated collective investment schemes must be treated as private customers.

counterparty.[32] This right of opt-up, which had found considerable support in the consultation process, will apply in the case of companies having (broadly) either called up share capital of at least £10 million (or its equivalent in another currency), or which have a balance sheet total of 12.5 million euros, a net turnover of 25 million euros and an average number of employees during the year of 250 (the euro-based tests being derived from FESCO[33] published standards). This opt-up for bodies corporate will not require the client's consent, provided it is given a written warning that it will lose protections under the regulatory system, and the authorised person has taken reasonable steps to ensure that the notice/warning is delivered to a person authorised to take such a decision for the client (which may, in practice, be easier said than done). It remains to be seen how often firms will be able to use this opt-up provision in practice. In addition, there are similar opt-up provisions for partnerships, trusts (including OPS, SSAS or stakeholder pension schemes), and local/public authorities, but in the case of such clients written consent to the opt-up will be required.

Intermediate Customer

10.09 Though the term "intermediate customer" is new, the components of the category are actually very similar to those of the "non-private customer" class under the SROs' Rules. There are, however, various changes, including the addition of listed companies, "special purpose vehicles" (*e.g.* in relation to securitisation or repackaging transactions) and unregulated collective investment schemes as new categories of intermediate customers, irrespective of the size of the company, vehicle or scheme. In addition, the threshold figure for share capital or net assets of an (unlisted) company has been set at £5 million, irrespective of the number of shareholders. The definition also clarifies that a regulated collective investment scheme (or its trustees) may not be treated as an intermediate customer (though, of course, the manager of such a scheme may be treated as a market counterparty or an intermediate customer).

Private customers

10.10 COB also retains the concept of "expert" private customers being treated as intermediate customers[34] with their consent though, interestingly, it appears that this consent does not have to be in writing as long as it is "informed" and the firm can demonstrate that consent has actually been given. As always, however, reasonable care needs to be taken to determine the customer's experience and understanding for this purpose. In this case, and in the case of "large intermediate customers" who have been opted up to market counterparty status by notice or agreement, a firm must review all classifications at least annually to ensure that they remain appropriate to the designated investment business carried on with or for each such client (unless no such business has been carried on with or for any such client during that 12-month period).[35]

---

[32] COB 4.1.12R.
[33] See Chapter 17, below, in relation to FESCO.
[34] COB 4.1.9R.
[35] COB 4.1.15R.

APPLICATION OF COB RULES

10.11 The treatment of, respectively, market counterparties, intermediate customers and private customers under the COB Rules is similar to the previous position under the conduct of business rules of the SROs. As noted above, COB has very limited application to market counterparties. As was the case for "non-private customers", many of the COB Rules will either not apply, or will be limited or modified in their application, to business undertaken with or for intermediate customers. For example, the COB Rules on financial promotion, including those relating to direct offer promotions and real-time and non-real time promotions are disapplied in the case of promotions to intermediate customers.[36] This general disapplication was introduced into COB very late in the drafting process (in June 2001, after the "final" version of COB which was published the previous February); it is, however, welcome, because it avoids the need for firms to categorise intermediate customers as "exempt" under one or other of the categories in the Financial Promotion Order for this purpose (which could be difficult and time-consuming). The COB Rules on "suitability" and "know your customer" are also disapplied in the case of advice and recommendations to intermediate customers (including discretionary as well as advisory intermediate customers). In addition, rules on customer agreements, the provision of risk warnings, and the marketing of "packaged products" (*e.g.* life policies and regulated collective investment schemes) will still be disapplied or modified for business with intermediate customers.[37] Intermediate customers will also be permitted to opt-out of various customer protections, including those relating to best execution, the holding of clients' money and the provision of periodic portfolio statements and contract notes or trade confirmations.[38]

The application of COB to corporate finance business was the subject of much debate during the FSA's consultation process. Initially, the FSA proposed to apply most of COB to corporate finance business (to the extent it was capable of applying), which would have been a considerable change from the more relaxed regime applying under the rules of the SFA. In the event, the final version of COB made in June 2001 largely replicates the SFA's regime[39]; many provisions of COB, including those relating to customer agreements and most of those relating to dealing, are expressly disapplied. Interestingly, the whole of COB 3 (in relation to financial promotion) will apply to corporate finance business, which was not the case under SFA Rules; however, as noted above and in paragraph 10.15, below, there are various exemptions from the rules on financial promotion which are likely to apply to communications made by corporate finance firms (including those relating to takeover promotions).

---

[36] COB 3.2.5R(1).
[37] See COB 4.2.5R (customer agreements); COB 5.4 (customers' understanding of risk); and COB 6.1 (packaged products).
[38] See COB 7.5.4R (best execution); COB 8.2.6R (periodic statements); and, COB 9.3.9R (clients' money).
[39] COB 1.6.4R.

E-COMMERCE

10.12 The need to ensure that COB Rules accommodated the extraordinary growth in online financial services was another important theme of the FSA's consultation on the draft COB. In the event, the COB Rules do not say a great deal about e-commerce (whether by way of rules, evidential provisions or guidance), though this is largely because the key issues of the provision of material "in writing", and the obtaining of customers' signatures, are dealt with in the General Provisions in the FSA Handbook,[40] which provide that (unless a contrary intention appears) any communication, notice, agreement or other document is deemed to be "in writing" if it is in legible form and capable of being reproduced on paper, irrespective of the medium used. Consequently, any requirement that a document be signed may also, apparently, be satisfied by an electronic signature. Firms should note, however, the FSA's reminder in its guidance in COB 1.8.3G that the rule does not (and indeed cannot) affect any other legal requirement which may apply in relation to the form or manner of executing a document or agreement. For example, therefore, particular local legal requirements may apply where a customer agreement is entered into under a foreign law; and, at the time of writing, any document entered into as a deed under English law requires "wet" signatures by the parties and their witnesses. The FSA has given additional guidance in relation to electronic communications with customers that a firm must be able to demonstrate that the customer wishes to communicate using this media (which may be achieved, it is suggested, by a suitable provision in a terms of business letter or customer agreement); and, when entering into an agreement on-line, that a firm must make it clear to a customer that a contract with legal consequences will result.[41]

In addition, the FSA has given useful guidance on the use of the internet and other electronic media in the context of financial promotions (COB 3.14). *Inter alia*, the guidance clarifies the FSA's intention to distinguish between "real time communications" delivered through electronic media (*e.g.* interactive company presentations or "chat rooms") and non real time communications, including e-mails and promotions contained in a firm's website. Therefore, for example, the ban on unsolicited real time communications to private customers will have to be considered in the context of any on-line marketing campaign involving "real time interaction" with customers, in the same way as it would in the case of telephone calls. Conversely, promotional material accessed by a customer through a firm's website will generally be treated as non-real time, with the result that such material may (subject to exceptions, including in particular unregulated collective investment schemes) be read by the general public but must comply with the detailed COB Rules on financial promotion. The FSA's guidance also includes specific guidance on issues including the electronic provision of "key features" documents relating to packaged products; restrictions relating to unregulated collective investment schemes; and confirmatory guidance relating to hypertext links, which may be financial promotions but *not* solely because any website to which a link leads constitutes a financial promotion.[42]

---

[40] GEN 2.2.14R and 2.2.15G.
[41] COB 1.8.2G.
[42] COB 3.14.5G (specific guidance); and see guidance in AUTH relating to hyperlinks.

Some important changes

10.13 COB is very lengthy and detailed, and a full critique of its provisions is well beyond the scope of a work which aims to introduce the reader to the FSMA itself. It should, however, be of some comfort to regulated firms leafing through the (many) pages of COB that there is much with which they will be familiar. Important changes have, however, been made; some of these are noted below.

Polarisation

10.14 The segregation of "tied agents" (on the one hand) and independent financial advisers (on the other) was one of the cornerstones of the 1986 Act. Under this regime, known as "polarisation", advisers have either to be independent and advise on "packaged [investment] products" drawn from the entire market, or alternatively to represent one product company (and its "marketing group") and to sell only its products. The "packaged products" to which the polarisation regime applies comprise life insurance (other than "pure protection policies"), pensions (including stakeholder schemes), regulated collective investment schemes, investment trust savings schemes and ISAs/PEPs where life policies and regulated collective investment schemes are components. The polarisation regime, which was originally intended to eliminate confusion about the status of advisers in the retail market and to make product companies and advisers directly accountable to customers, has subsequently attracted considerable criticism from various quarters. Ultimately, the Director General of Fair Trading ("DGFT") reported to the Chancellor under section 122 of the 1986 Act on the polarisation rules' effect on competition in the retail marketplace. The DGFT reported in 1999,[43] *inter alia*, that the polarisation rules restricted or distorted competition to a significant extent by preventing some innovation in retail markets; and, in particular, that the polarisation rules should be retained for life and pension products but eliminated in the case of regulated collective investment schemes. The DGFT's Report is considered further in Chapter 9. Subsequently, the FSA proposed a two-stage reform of the polarisation regime, beginning—prior to N2—with the relaxation of the SRO's polarisation rules in relation to stakeholder pension schemes ("SHPs") (introduced in April 2001) and direct offer financial promotions for packaged products.[44] A proposal also to relax the rules in relation to "CAT standard" ISAs was deferred pending the second stage of the FSA's review, which will be considerably more wide-ranging. Consequently, COB allows product providers and marketing associates to "adopt" the SHPs of more than one firm, and to make direct offers of different packaged products (including through on-line "fund supermarkets" in the case of regulated collective investment schemes).

Financial Promotions

10.15 The section of COB on financial promotions is, at first glance, the most intimidating, partly because of its length and partly because it uses defined terms and concepts which are new. In reality, however, many of the rules themselves have

---

[43] Office of Fair Trading, *The Rules on the Polarisation of Investment Advice* (August 1999) (OFT 264).
[44] See the FSA *Policy Statement on Polarisation: Feedback to CP80* (March 2001). The changes to the polarisation rules are now reflected in COB 3 and 5.

been carried over from the conduct of business rules of the SROs, though there is a substantial amount of new guidance. The main change is that various rules, including the general obligation relating to "fair, clear and not misleading promotions" are applied to non-real time promotions relating to deposits, general insurance contracts and "pure protection contracts" (COB 3.8.4R), though the rules relating to "direct offer" financial promotions do not apply to such "investments". In reality, the main consequence of this for firms communicating or approving promotions relating to such banking or insurance products is that they may face disciplinary or (in the case of promotions to "private persons" and fiduciaries or representatives for such persons[45]) civil action if the general requirements of the rules in COB 3.8 are not complied with.

The new rules cover, for the first time, solicited "real time promotions", being solicited telephone calls, personal visits or other interactive dialogue. Such promotions were not regulated under the 1986 Act unless in any case the view was taken that they constituted "investment advertisements" (which was not generally the case). As a result of this change, the former SFA rule on "unsolicited calls" made on private customers has been translated into a new COB rule on real time financial promotions to private customers (solicited and unsolicited), though the practical requirements of the rule are largely the same as the old SFA rule.[46] As noted above, unsolicited real time promotions are only permitted in very limited circumstances, including where they constitute "exempt financial promotions" (so that, in any event, the COB Rules on financial promotions do not apply). Unsolicited real time promotions to private customers are only possible if the promotion is exempt; or is made in the context of an established existing customer relationship where such promotions are envisaged by the customer; or relates to the sale of a "packaged product" (other than a "higher volatility fund"); or is made in connection with a United Kingdom or EEA takeover.[47]

The COB Rules on financial promotion do not apply to promotions which are exempt under the Financial Promotion Order (including promotions to or directed at overseas recipients, and "one-off communications" which are non-real time or solicited real time promotions). In addition, the FSA has specified[48] some other types of communication which are exempted from the financial promotion rules, including:

- most importantly, promotions to market counterparties and intermediate customers (see above). It should be noted, though, that a promotion to an "expert" intermediate customer will only be exempt if the promotion relates to an investment in which the customer is expert;

- brief corporate image advertisements or quotations of prices or yields;

- a personal quotation or illustration form; and

- "takeover promotions", being promotions governed by the City Code on Takeovers and Mergers or which have been exempted from the requirements

---

[45] See s. 150 of the Act, and Art. 6 of the Financial Services and Markets Act 2000 (Rights of Action) Regulations 2001 (S.I. 2001 No. 2256).
[46] COB 3.8.22R.
[47] COB 3.2.5R and COB 3.10.3R.
[48] COB 3.2.5R.

of the City Code by the rules of the Code or by a ruling of the Takeover Panel, and promotions subject to takeover regulation in other EEA States.

The "final" version of COB produced in February 2001 also contained a special exemption for "one-off" promotions, but this has become less relevant because the Financial Promotion Order itself now contains an exemption for such communications (which in turn means that COB Rules on financial promotion will not apply to any such communication).

Another helpful late change to COB 3 was the confirmation that a firm may "re-communicate" a financial promotion of another firm without re-confirming compliance with the rules under COB 3.6, unless the first firm is aware, or ought reasonably to be aware, that the promotion has ceased to be clear, fair and not misleading or that the second firm has withdrawn the promotion.[49] This new rule should help IFAs and other brokers who distribute promotions prepared by product providers, though it is a little unclear how the first firm "ought reasonably to be aware" of any factual change unless it has taken at least some of the steps which it would have taken under COB 3.6 to check a promotion's compliance (which may partly defeat the evident purpose of this Rule).

One helpful new feature in the financial promotion rules is the introduction of FSA guidance on various different kinds of specific and "direct offer" financial promotions[50] This guidance covers promotions of AVC schemes, PEP or ISA transfers, bond funds, "guaranteed" products, Phased Retirement Pensions, "High Income" products, Stock Market bonds, so-called "hybrid bonds", and personal pensions and stakeholder pension schemes.

Record Keeping

10.16 The FSA has proposed a number of changes to the time limits for the retention of records relating to regulated business (see above). Briefly, for pension transfers and opt-outs the minimum retention period remains "indefinite"; for other life and pensions business (including stakeholder pensions) the minimum retention period is six years, which represents a doubling of the minimum period in respect of all relevant documents for SFA regulated firms and in respect of most documents for IMRO regulated firms. For all other business, the minimum retention period is set at three years; this represents a halving of the period for PIA regulated firms and a reduction of two years for IMRO regulated firms in respect of dealing and allocation records. These time limits are different from the five-year record keeping requirements under the Money Laundering Regulations,[51] but the FSA is evidently persuaded that, for the time being at least, these inconsistencies are not prejudicial given the different focus of the respective sets of rules. However, the FSA has said that it will look at a possible rationalisation of these time limits in the future.[52] As a practical matter, firms reviewing COB for the first time should note that the requirements for different kinds of records (e.g. financial promotions, dealing, client assets, etc.) are contained in the different sections of COB relating to each respective subject.

---

[49] COB 3.6.5R(3).
[50] COB 3, Annex 4G.
[51] S.I. 1993 No. 1933.
[52] FSA, *Policy Statement on COB*, para. 3.34 (February 2001).

Terms of Business and Customer Agreements (COB 4.2)

10.17 Apart from an exclusion for overseas customers (subject to conditions), the COB Rules require "two-way" customer agreements to be entered into between an authorised firm and a private customer for discretionary investment management, contingent liability transactions, stock lending or underwriting. The last two items represent an extension as far as SFA regulated firms are concerned. Further, in all other circumstances, the COB Rules require that all customers should receive terms of business in connection with designated investment business (though, except as stated above, these terms do not need to be signed by the customer). This requirement is also a new one for former SFA regulated firms; however, in practice, such firms almost invariably issue terms of business, engagement letters or other contractual documentation in any event. However, former SFA regulated firms will no longer be required to issue two-way agreements for discretionary management business with intermediate customers. Helpful guidance has also been given in relation to the time at which terms of business must be provided[53]; a firm is not required to provide information that, by its very nature, is unavailable when terms of business are initially issued. For example, some information such as investment objectives and restrictions may only become apparent once a "know your customer" fact-find has been completed.

Suitability (COB 5.3)

10.18 The former PIA requirements for "suitability letters" (or "reason why" letters) in the case of recommendations to private customers concerning packaged products have been extended to former SFA and IMRO member firms, but a special exclusion has been inserted for investment managers which make a personal recommendation to buy or sell units or shares in a regulated collective investment scheme.[54] However, firms (including private client stockbrokers formerly regulated by SFA) will nonetheless need to issue such letters for unit trust and OEIC recommendations which are not made in the course of an investment management relationship. An exemption has also been included for overseas customers who are not present in the United Kingdom at the time of acknowledging consent to the recommendation. An initial proposal to extend the suitability requirement to intermediate, as well as private, customers was not carried forward.[55]

Cancellation and Withdrawal (COB 6.7)

10.19 A few changes have been made to the regime for cancellation or withdrawal from "cancellable investment agreements", including making the provision of cancellation rights for cash deposit ISAs mandatory (it having been voluntary under the previous legislation because of the narrower definition of "investments" under the 1986 Act); and the introduction of cancellation or withdrawal rights for occupational pension scheme contracts and pension transfers (as well as stakeholder pension schemes generally). As was the case under the 1986 Act, some

---

[53] COB 4.2.5G.
[54] COB 5.3.19R.
[55] FSA, *Policy Statement on COB*, paras 5.43 and 5.44.

agreements will only be cancellable if a firm provides advice, such as purchases of authorised unit trusts and shares in OEICs.

Allocation

10.20 The automatic seven day period for allocating transactions in overseas securities, formerly located in the IMRO Rules, has been discontinued. The new COB rule and evidential provision[56] requires that allocation of an aggregated transaction, or a series of transactions, in "designated investments" should take place within one business day following the execution of the transaction, unless in the case of an intermediate customer the firm has agreed with the customer that the period for allocation may be extended to five business days. This extends to transactions in United Kingdom securities a relaxation generally afforded by IMRO to transactions in overseas securities (although the customer's express agreement is now required). The new strict requirement for prompt allocations to private customers may give rise to some difficulties in practice in overseas markets (which may be less liquid and/or have slower or less reliable price information). The old practice of "stock warehousing" will now, apparently, become less common.

Confirmation of Transactions/Periodic Statements (COB 8.1 and 8.2)

10.21 Broadly, the new rules carry forward the provisions found in the SROs' rulebooks. Helpfully, the IMRO practice of allowing an investment manager not to provide customers with contract notes/trade confirmations, where the manager has taken reasonable steps to establish that the customer does not want to receive them, has been carried forward. However, there is a new requirement for former SFA member firms to send periodic statements to non-discretionary intermediate customers, to whom such firms were not previously required to send periodic statements (though such customers can opt not to receive such statements if they wish).

Client Money and Assets (COB 9)

10.22 The requirement for firms holding client money to calculate their Client Money Requirement on a daily basis, which was a requirement of the SFA's Client Money Rules, has been adopted in COB. This will represent an increase in the frequency of calculation required of firms formerly regulated by IMRO and PIA, which are likely to have performed such calculations on a weekly or even monthly basis. This is likely to result in such firms incurring one-off costs to enable their systems to cope with the change; many firms seem likely also to require additional back-office support to handle the daily calculations required. Changes have also been made to the frequency and methods required for reconciliations of "safe custody investments"; in particular, it is now generally required that firms should perform a reconciliation of safe custody investments every 25 business days where those investments are not held by the firm (subject to a possible extension up to every six months if the firm is unable to obtain statements on a monthly basis from third party managers of unit trusts, OEICs or other mutual funds).[57] The FSA will

---

[56] COB 7.7.5R and 7.7.6E.
[57] COB 9.1.85R and 9.1.87R.

be undertaking a more fundamental "risk-based" review of the holding of client assets following N2.[58]

Packaged products: marketing

10.23 Firms will now not be required to send "follow-up" key features in hard copy form when customers choose to buy packaged products using electronic media. However, for the time being at least, "with profits guides" for private customers, and stand-alone "key features" documents for life products, have been retained.[59]

Fair and Clear Communications

10.24 Interestingly, the FSA has included Principle 7 as a COB rule specifically to give customers who are "private persons" the right to sue for breach pursuant to section 150 of the Act.[60] The rule requires that when, in the scope of, or in connection with, its designated investment business, a firm communicates information to a customer, it must take reasonable steps to do so in a way which is clear, fair and not misleading. It is possible that the FSA might ultimately use its power under section 150(3) of the Act to make a breach of this rule actionable at the suit of a person other than a "private person".[61]

Best Execution (COB 7.5)

10.25 At the time of writing, it appears likely that the FSA will consult practitioners in the latter part of 2001 regarding possible changes to the "best execution" regime. The relevant issues were flagged in a Discussion Paper issued by the FSA in April 2001, which raised (*inter alia*) whether the use of a price benchmark (*e.g.* SETS in the United Kingdom equity market) is the best way of encouraging firms to achieve "the best price"; whether regulators should require firms to have access to a minimum number of "execution venues"; whether there should be greater disclosure to customers of execution policies adopted by firms; and to what extent there should be a trade-off between price and other elements of a customer's order (*e.g.* timing). In addition, "soft commissions" are due to be reviewed by the FSA following N2.

INTER-PROFESSIONAL CONDUCT

10.26 In essence, inter-professional conduct ("IPC") represents the "light touch" regulation for dealings between market counterparties which has frequently been presaged by the Government and the FSA. The starting point for IPC is that market professionals require less regulatory protection than the consumer, and that a radically different approach to regulation in the area is therefore essential. Thus, to a significant extent, the Rules and Guidance in

---

[58] FSA, *Policy Statement on COB* para. 5.75 (February 2001).
[59] FSA, *Policy Statement on COB* paras 5.53–5.60 (inclusive).
[60] COB 2.1.2G and 2.1.3R.
[61] See in this regard Art. 6 of the Financial Services and Markets Act 2000 (Rights of Action) Regulations 2001 (S.I. 2001 No. 2256) for the circumstances where a non-private person may now bring an action under s. 150.

IPC[62] have been made with the FSA's "market confidence objective" (of maintaining confidence in the financial system) in mind, though the objective to protect consumers is also relevant in as much as many of the dealings between market counterparties which are regulated by the IPC will be undertaken by one or both of the parties for the benefit of a third-party consumer.

There are, in the main, three sources for the Rules and Guidance appearing in IPC:

- the London Code of Conduct, which was the code policed by the Bank of England and subsequently the FSA, which regulated wholesale market dealings between the "listed institutions" which were exempt persons under section 43 of the 1986 Act;

- the FSA Statements of Principle which were published under the 1986 Act, and which have been replaced by the new "Principles for Businesses"; and

- various items of guidance and rulings given by the SFA in respect of certain market practices and behaviour.

In addition, some requirements formerly applying to section 43 "listed institutions" under the so-called "Grey Paper"—including, for example, requirements on record-keeping and client money segregation—now appear mainly in COB and other parts of the FSA's Handbook.

It will be apparent from the sources of IPC that it is principally intended to apply to firms dealing in the wholesale financial markets, which used to be section 43 listed institutions or members of the SFA (or, in some cases, both). However, the scope of IPC has a potentially broader application. IPC applies to all authorised firms, except for service companies,[63] "UCITS qualifiers" and insurance companies and friendly societies which are not covered by the single market directives (MAR 3.1.1R). It covers the following regulated activities (and related ancillary activities) where they are undertaken with or for a "market counterparty":

- *dealing* in an "inter-professional investment";

- acting as an *arranger* (or name-passing broker) in respect of an inter-professional investment or agreeing to do so; and

- giving *"transaction-specific advice"* in relation to an inter-professional investment or agreeing to do so (MAR 3.1.2R).

For this purpose, "inter-professional investments" include all of the investments previously regulated under 1986 Act except for long-term insurance contracts (which are "contractually based investments") and units or shares in collective investment schemes,[64] and rights in respect of either of them. However, the list

---

[62] The Rules and Guidance are, as in the case of COB, made under the FSA's rule-making power in s. 138 and its power to issue guidance in s. 157, respectively.

[63] Service companies' sole investment business is the making of arrangements enabling or facilitating deals for market counterparties and intermediate customers.

[64] Except that interests in overseas unincorporated vehicles are included in the RAO definition of "shares"—and this definition is also adopted for the purpose of IPC.

excludes deposits, general insurance contracts, long-term protection policies, Lloyd's underwriting capacity and syndicate membership, stakeholder pension schemes, regulated mortgages and funeral plan contracts. "Transaction-specific advice" is, in essence, limited to advice given for the purpose of or in connection with dealing or arranging services that the firm is already providing or which it wishes to provide to the counterparty in question. Despite these limitations, it will be apparent that IPC applies to a broader range of authorised firms than simply those which hold themselves out as dealers or brokers in the wholesale markets; for example, authorised insurance companies and investment managers will fall within the scope of IPC in respect of their dealings with or for market counterparties, even though IPC will not catch their respective regulated insurance and asset management activities. By way of illustration, an investment manager which, for instance, deals in a security or a derivative for a client classified as a market counterparty (*e.g.* a company classified as a large intermediate customer) will be subject to IPC, and not COB, in relation to both the market and the client side of the dealing transaction, but it will be subject to COB in relation to its discretionary management responsibilities (though most COB Rules will not apply if the client is a market counterparty). Further, it is important that persons who are classified as market counterparties will retain that classification for IPC and non-IPC business, except for authorised firms and overseas professionals, which may be intermediate customers in relation to non-IPC business (see above).

The territorial application of IPC is different from that of COB, in that it only applies to inter-professional business carried on from an establishment maintained by a firm in the United Kingdom (MAR 3.1.4R). Consequently, the activities of an overseas branch of a United Kingdom authorised firm are not covered, since the FSA envisages that local professional market rules will apply instead. Conversely, of course, United Kingdom regulated branches of overseas firms (including EEA passported firms) will be subject to IPC in relation to inter-professional business. However, strangely, IPC's territorial scope is apparently extended by the FSA's guidance in IPC that IPC transactions carried out by unauthorised persons or overseas offices of United Kingdom firms but subsequently "booked" to a United Kingdom regulated firm will sometimes be treated as a transaction executed by the United Kingdom firm. This may result in a conflict between United Kingdom requirements and overseas conduct of business rules.

IPC's relationship with COB is relatively straightforward, in that COB does not apply where IPC applies (though, as noted above, it is possible for both COB and IPC to apply to different aspects of a single transaction). IPC expressly clarifies its relationship with COB in respect of particular activities by providing that IPC does not apply to them.[65] In particular, corporate finance business has been excluded from the ambit of IPC, in view of the special treatment already afforded to such business under COB. However, the FSA has given guidance in an annex to IPC that some activities, such as dealing, carried out in connection with corporate finance business, may be subject to IPC. The inter-relationship between IPC and the Code of Market Conduct ("COMC") is more complex, in that there are various points of convergence and dissimilarity. IPC is concerned with dealings between regulated firms, whereas COMC applies also to unregulated persons where their actions have

---

[65] MAR 3.1.3R.

an impact on a "designated market". IPC covers a wide range of investments, since it is not limited to investments having some connection with on-exchange transactions; however, it should be borne in mind that COMC also covers non-exchange traded investments where they are related to exchange-traded investments or indices (*e.g.*, an OTC option referenced to the FTSE-100 Index). IPC and COMC are similar in that they are both concerned with FSA's "market confidence objective", but IPC is mostly silent on the question of "abusive behaviour" in deference to COMC. Though aspects of IPC apply to on-exchange business, the rule on non-market price transactions ("NMPTs") is "switched off" where the rules of an exchange govern the transaction in question,[66] though COMC will obviously apply if the NMPT constitutes abusive behaviour in relation to a designated market.

The FSA has given guidance in IPC that nothing therein should be read as qualifying or modifying COMC, or the Principles and Code of Practice for Approved Persons (MAR 3 Ann 1G). In addition, though IPC provides guidance on the application of the FSA's Principles for Businesses, it does not limit or qualify those Principles in any respect. In this regard, IPC states[67] that it has three main purposes:

- to increase certainty by explaining how the FSA's Principles for Businesses apply to IPC business;

- to set out rules for inter-professional business in cases where it is not appropriate to rely on the Principles alone; and

- to set out the FSA's understanding of some "good market practices" and conventions.

In fact, most of IPC represents guidance on how the FSA proposes to interpret the Principles (including, in particular, Principle 5 relating to proper standards of market conduct). However, as noted above in relation to COB, failure to follow such guidance in the circumstances to which the guidance relates will not, of itself, mean that an authorised person will be presumed to have breached an FSA Principle or that the burden of proof to establish compliance with the Principle will lie with the authorised person. Conversely, compliance with guidance in the circumstances envisaged will usually (but not inevitably) provide a "safe harbour" from disciplinary action in respect of a breach of a Principle. The FSA has stated in relation to the role of guidance that a regulated firm has "latitude to make commercial and operational judgements about how [it is] going to meet regulatory requirements".[68]

The FSA has also decided to publish in an Annex to IPC some general guidance on "good market practice" in relation to all kinds of inter-professional business (MAR 3 Ann 3G). This Annex includes some statements which practitioners may regard as obvious (such as that a firm should agree expressly all economic terms of a transaction before committing itself), but also helpful general guidance on matters including limit orders, out-of-hours dealing, settlement errors and the use of master agreements (which are encouraged by the FSA). Specific market or industry codes are not endorsed in IPC (since the FSA has no power to do so except in the case of

---

[66] MAR 3.5.6R
[67] MAR 3.2.1G.
[68] FSA, *Consultation Paper 47: The Inter-Professionals Code* (May 2000), para. 1.18.

the City Code on Takeovers and Mergers), though guidance is given that the FSA will take into account different standards and practices operating in markets when interpreting the Principles as they apply to inter-professional business.[69] In relation to activities falling outside the scope of the FSMA which used to be regulated under the Grey Paper regime and the London Code of Conduct (*e.g.* currency and money market dealings), the FSA and the Bank of England are evidently collaborating to ensure that standards required by the new Non-Investment Products Code produced by the Bank of England will be compatible with IPC (see further below).

Though the scope of IPC is wider than the London Code of Conduct as regards the firms affected, it is narrower in relation to the range of financial instruments covered, since the London Code regulated wholesale market dealings in spot and forward foreign exchange, bullion and wholesale deposits, which were not regulated "investments" under the 1986 Act. To ensure that inter-professional dealings in these instruments remain under some regulatory scrutiny, the Bank of England has co-ordinated and produced a Non-Investment Products Code ("NIP Code") which is intended to dove-tail with IPC and provide the same flexible, sensible regulation which was a feature of the London Code. There will, however, be no direct replacement for the informal mediation procedure run for firms subject to the London Code. The FSA has concluded that this service would be inappropriate in cost/benefit terms given the wider constituency of authorised firms subject to IPC, but nonetheless recommends market counterparties to use mediation or alternative dispute resolution ("ADR") procedures to resolve market disputes. It is nonetheless a pity, but perhaps inevitable, that the advent of the statutory regulator has ended the central mediation procedure.

A breach of any rule in IPC will not give rise to a civil right of action for the aggrieved market counterparty. This is consistent with the genesis and objectives of IPC and with the fact that, in reality, IPC mainly constitutes guidance for market counterparties.

---

[69] MAR 3.8.1G.

CHAPTER 11

Controllers and Control of Business Transfers

JAMES PERRY

INTRODUCTION

11.01   This Chapter deals with two separate parts of the FSMA which will be of particular interest to those in the financial services industry who are customarily involved in major business transactions, including mergers and acquisitions and business transfers. Paragraphs 11.02–11.10 deal with the regulation of "changes in control" of United Kingdom authorised firms (Part XII of the FSMA); paragraphs 11.11–11.13 analyse the new law relating to insurance business transfers and banking business transfers (Part VII of the FSMA).

PAST REGULATION OF CONTROLLERS

11.02   The FSMA represented a good opportunity to rationalise the various different regimes governing changes of "control" in United Kingdom financial services businesses. Convergences in business areas such as bancassurance and investment banking have created global behemoths involved in all kinds of financial services, but these giants found (in the United Kingdom at least) that when they wished to merge, acquire or co-venture, they were faced with differing consent requirements operated by a variety of United Kingdom regulators. It is true to say that some important differences were eradicated by the enactment in the United Kingdom of the single market directives,[1] which introduced (at different times) new conditions to acquiring or increasing control over a regulated firm, but some differences nonetheless remained. The structure of investment business regulation in the United Kingdom meant that, even after the introduction of new "change of controller" requirements in the Investment Services Regulations 1995, the SROs under the 1986 Act continued to operate their own restrictions on the control of their members. Even though these restrictions were amended to take account of the new requirements for controllers of ISD "investment firms", there were still anomalies. Strictly speaking, a change of control in an ISD investment firm was required to be notified to the relevant United Kingdom regulator both by acquirer (under the 1995 Regulations) and by the member firm (under SRO Rules);

---

[1] The requirements were contained in the Second Banking Co-ordination Directive (89/646); the Third Non-Life Insurance Directive (92/49); The Third Life Insurance Directive (92/96); and the Investment Services Directive (93/22). See, in this regard, para. 1 of Sched. 3 to the Act.

a change of control in a non-ISD regulated firm would normally be approved within 28 days after notification, while the same process for an ISD firm was in theory subject to a three month waiting period under the 1995 Regulations (as prescribed by the ISD). Perhaps most importantly, the SRO Rules caught changes of control in overseas firms with a regulated United Kingdom branch (other than incoming passported EEA firms), with the result that large international corporations with a small United Kingdom presence frequently required a United Kingdom regulatory approval for a transaction with little or no relevance to the United Kingdom branch. The respective statutory requirements for changes of shareholding control in a bank or insurance company were similar, but some requirements pre-dating the single market directives remained, and the definitions of a "controller" included senior executive officers as well as shareholder controllers. Thankfully, these distinctions have now been consigned to the history books.

CONTROLLERS UNDER THE FSMA

11.03 The primary requirement is that a person who proposes to take a step which would result in him acquiring:

- control over a United Kingdom authorised person;

- an additional kind of control over a United Kingdom authorised person; or

- an increase in a kind of control which he already has,

must notify the FSA of his proposal (section 178(1)). Unfortunately, it is not entirely clear what is meant by "taking a step which would result" in a person acquiring control. It must include entering into an unconditional contract to acquire control. It might conceivably include more preliminary steps, such as the Board of directors of the acquirer approving the transaction, or even the arrangement of acquisition finance, if that is the last pre-condition to a transaction. What if an acquisition contract is conditional on E.C. or United Kingdom merger clearance, or on FSA approval itself (as has been customary)? It seems that, strictly speaking, the acquirer might only be required to notify the FSA under section 178(2) (and not section 178(1)) within 14 days after he has become aware that the condition has been satisfied and that he has thereby acquired control "without himself taking any step". If this is correct, it is certainly unwelcome, because the potential consequences of the FSA objecting to control which has already been acquired include disenfranchisement and/or sales of shares (section 189), which would be avoided if prior notification and approval were required. Despite this, it seems likely that the existing practice of buyers entering into acquisition agreements conditional on FSA approval will continue, though the statutory basis for such prior notification is at best unclear.

The procedure for post-notification of acquisitions of control (section 178(2)) will be important in other cases too. For example, it might be necessary if a shareholder in a company exceeds one of the control thresholds following a buy-back of shares by the company, or if a parent undertaking learns *ex post facto* that a subsidiary has acquired shares in a United Kingdom authorised person. As prescribed by the single market directives, the FSA has three months from the date when it receives notice in which to approve the application or to serve a warning notice objecting to the new control (section 183(3)) or imposing conditions upon it (section 185(3)). An objection or imposition of conditions may subsequently lead to an FSA decision notice and a reference to the Financial Services and Markets Tribunal (section 186(5)). The FSA is also given power to specify a period during which its approval of the acquisition will remain effective (so that the acquisition must be completed in that period) (section 184(3)). If no period is specified in the FSA's notice of approval, the approval will be effective for one year.

Before approving an acquisition or increase of control over a United Kingdom authorised person, the FSA is required to comply with such requirements as to consultation with authorities outside the United Kingdom as may be prescribed by the Treasury (section 183(2)). The Treasury has prescribed requirements for the FSA to consult with relevant EEA competent authorities where it receives a notice of control from an EEA firm that is an ISD investment firm or a BCD credit institution (or from a parent undertaking of such a firm or institution) and that notice relates to a United Kingdom authorised investment firm or credit institution and which indicates that the acquirer is or proposes to become a parent undertaking of the United Kingdom firm.[2] These requirements originated in the single market directives and were also reflected in the Investment Services Regulations 1995.[3]

11.04 For this purpose, a "United Kingdom authorised person" means a United Kingdom incorporated company or an unincorporated association formed in the United Kingdom (other than a United Kingdom operator, trustee or depository of a recognised collective investment scheme, or a United Kingdom authorised OEIC) (section 178(4)). This is broader than the corresponding requirements under previous legislation, which only applied to United Kingdom firms entitled to a passport under the single market directives (including the ISD), though non-ISD members of SROs were still subject to contractual requirements obliging them to obtain the regulator's consent to some changes of ownership. Early drafts of the Bill extended the requirements to authorised persons incorporated or formed outside the United Kingdom (and the EEA), but this was not carried forward. The new statutory requirements do mean, however, that an acquirer of control in a non-ISD United Kingdom firm will commit an offence if he does not comply with the notification requirements (section 191(1)), whereas a breach of the SRO Rules merely had disciplinary consequences for the member itself (if it was aware of the acquisition).

It is a criminal offence punishable by a fine to fail to comply with the notification requirements in relation to an acquisition or reduction in control, or to acquire control while the three month period following the FSA's receipt of the notice of control is running or before the FSA has reached its decision following the issue of a warning notice (section 191). A person who acquires control in the face of a notice of objection may be punished on conviction on indictment by imprisonment or an unlimited fine, or both. In addition, as indicated above, the FSA has an array of powers to "freeze" the rights attaching to shares acquired in

---

[2] The Financial Services and Markets Act 2000 (Consultation with Competent Authorities) Regulations 2001 (S.I. 2001 No. 2509).
[3] S.I. 1995 No. 3275, reg. 42(2)).

contravention of a notice of objection or a condition on its approval imposed by the Authority, and to apply to the court for an order that particular shares should be sold (though an order may not be made if a reference to the Financial Services and Markets Tribunal in respect of a notice of objection has been or may still be made).

As under the single market directives, the threshold level of "control" which triggers the requirement for notification and FSA approval is 10 per cent of the shares or voting power in the authorised person or its parent undertaking (section 179(2)). Any acquisition of shares or voting power which takes a new or existing controller over 10 per cent, 20 per cent, 33 per cent or 50 per cent thresholds, or which results in the controller becoming a parent undertaking of the United Kingdom firm, will trigger a requirement for FSA approval (section 180). Any reduction in control through these percentage thresholds must also be notified to the FSA (either before the reduction, or within 14 days afterwards if the reduction occurs without the controller taking any step), though there is no requirement for FSA approval (sections 181 and 190). In addition, control is acquired where a person (the acquirer) is able to exercise significant influence over the management of the authorised person or its parent undertaking by virtue of his shareholding or voting power in either. The definition of an acquirer includes, separately or together, the acquirer itself and any of "its associates" (which, in the case of a body corporate, includes directors and subsidiary undertakings (section 422(4)). In this respect, the drafting of this part of the FSMA has usefully clarified that a person may become a "controller" even if the relevant shares or voting power are held entirely by his associate, which was unclear under previous legislation.[4] The definition of an "associate" is nonetheless a broad one.

11.05 Importantly, the definition of "control" has been significantly narrowed following earlier drafts of the Bill, which caught persons exercising management "influence" over authorised persons (a nebulous concept). Further, chief executive officers, managing directors or other senior officers, whether of authorised firms or parent undertakings, are not included as "controllers" (though they may certainly be "associates" of a controller). This represents a change for United Kingdom credit institutions and insurers.

The Act now specifies "approval requirements" with which the Authority must be satisfied in relation to an acquisition or increase in control (section 186). These are that:

- the acquirer is a fit and proper person to have the control over the authorised person that he has or would have if he acquired the control in question; and

- the interests of consumers would not be threatened by the acquirer's control or by his acquiring that control.

The second limb of these approval requirements is interesting, in that it is not expressly limited to consideration of the authorised firm's own customers or business. Therefore, the FSA appears to be empowered—if it is so minded—to consider the effect of a particular acquisition on the broader United Kingdom financial

---

[4] *cf.* the Investment Services Regulations 1995, para. 46(2).

services market, which would certainly extend the Authority's jurisdiction well beyond the historic role of the financial services regulator, and close to the province of the competition regulators. It seems doubtful, though, that the FSA will interpret its powers this widely. More helpfully for acquirers, it appears that the FSA may only issue a decision notice objecting to the acquisition or imposing conditions if the approval requirements are not met. It appears, though, that a decision notice may also be given *after* approval has been given if the FSA becomes aware of matters which satisfy it that the approval requirements are not met or that a condition imposed under section 185 has been breached (section 187(3)).

At the very end of this Part of the Act, section 192 contains an extremely wide power for the Treasury to amend the cases where a person is treated as acquiring, increasing or reducing control, whether by varying, removing or adding a case, and similarly to amend the cases where a person is treated as being a "controller". Apparently, therefore, the law as it stands may in time be re-written by statutory instrument. Perhaps more helpfully, the Treasury is also given power (following an amendment made during the passage of the Bill through the House of Lords) to provide for exemptions from the obligations to notify imposed by sections 178 and 190 of the Act. It is not yet known whether any exemptions will be prescribed by the Treasury; it should be borne in mind in this regard that the Treasury's freedom is limited by the relative requirements of the single market directives. No exemption has been timetabled to come into force on N2, except in relation to friendly societies and building societies.[4a]

The Treasury has prescribed certain transitional provisions in relation to notices of control served before N2. In essence, the new regime under Part XII of the Act will be deemed to apply to any such outstanding application (see The Financial Services and Markets Act 2000 (Transitional Provisions) (Controllers) Order 2001, (S.I. 2001, No. 2637)).

REGULATION OF CONTROLLERS BY THE FSA

11.06 Chapter 11 of the FSA's *Supervision Manual* ("SUP") significantly extends the statutory requirements referred to above, as well as providing guidance on the statutory obligations and specimen copies of the forms of notification which will have to be completed by intending and existing controllers.

The FSA has extended the statutory requirements in the following key ways:

Overseas firms

11.07 Though the statutory requirements only apply to the acquisition or reduction in control over a United Kingdom company or unincorporated association, the FSA must also be notified if a person acquires or ceases to have control over an "overseas firm", or if an existing controller of an overseas firm becomes or ceases to be a parent undertaking of the firm.[5] An "overseas firm" is an authorised person whose registered office is not in the United Kingdom, including passported

---

[4a] See The Financial Services and Markets Act 2000 (Controllers) (Exemption) Order 2001 (S.I. 2001 No. 2638) and the Financial Services and Markets Act 2000 (Controllers) (Exemption) (No. 2) Order 2001 (S.I. 2001 No. 3338).

[5] SUP 11.4.4R.

EEA firms and Treaty firms. An obligation to notify the FSA is placed upon the United Kingdom regulated overseas firm itself, rather than the controller, presumably since there is no corresponding statutory requirement or enabling provision. The FSA has stated that this notification requirement has been imposed to enable the Authority to monitor overseas firms' continuing satisfaction of Threshold Conditions.[6] However, the FSA's approval of a new controller of an overseas firm is not required, since such a requirement could only be imposed by legislation, and thus the notification requirements themselves are less prescriptive than in the case of changes in control of United Kingdom incorporated firms. In particular, once a person has become a controller of a United Kingdom regulated overseas firm and has notified the FSA, no further notification is required for any subsequent increase of control (e.g. if the controller meets any of the 20 per cent, 33 per cent or 50 per cent thresholds), unless and until the controller becomes a parent undertaking of the firm. The timetable for the notification of acquisition of control in an overseas firm is, however, the same as in the case of United Kingdom incorporated firms under the FSMA (including the 14-day "window" in cases where control is acquired "without taking a step"). Though these requirements extend the position under the FSMA, they are actually less onerous than the previous requirements imposed on some non-United Kingdom incorporated members of SROs, who were required to obtain the regulator's approval to certain changes of control, except in the case of members which were passported EEA firms.

Notifications by regulated firms

11.08   The FSMA places obligations on controllers to make notifications to the FSA. The FSA has imposed parallel requirements on United Kingdom incorporated firms themselves,[7] so that the FSA will be notified of a change in control from two separate sources. The FSA also makes it clear in guidance that this obligation applies whether or not the controller himself has given or intends to give a notification in accordance with his obligations under the Act.[8] Further, these requirements are supplemented by an obligation on regulated firms (United Kingdom and non-United Kingdom incorporated) to take reasonable steps to keep themselves informed about the identity of their controllers (which, the FSA says, will include monitoring the company's shareholder register, public announcements and the exercise of voting rights at general meetings[9]). In practice, however, the "parallel" requirements for notifications by regulated firms and controllers will develop in most cases towards a "joint" notification by the parties; the FSA has given guidance that this is permitted[10] and has stated that, in such cases, a single "Controllers Form A"[11] may be completed by and on behalf of the buyer and the target. Even if separate notifications are needed for any reason, the form of notification required from regulated firms is briefer than the "Controllers Form A" to be completed by controllers themselves.[12]

---

[6] SUP 11.2.3G.

[7] SUP 11.4.2R.

[8] SUP 11.4.9G.

[9] SUP 11.4.10R and 11.4.11G.

[10] SUP 11.5.8G.

[11] Controllers Form A can be found, along with Controllers Form B in relation to individuals, respectively in Annex 4D and 5D to SUP 11.

[12] SUP 11.5.1R (note, however, the requirement for a regulated firm to include "any other information of which the FSA would reasonably expect notice").

Individuals

11.09 A person acquiring or increasing control over a United Kingdom incorporated firm is required to complete the FSA's "Controllers Form A" in relation to itself, and also "Controllers Form B" in relation to certain of its key managers. In the case of companies, the individuals will be the chief executive and one other director; in the case of partnerships, the managing partner (or equivalent) and one other individual partner.[13] Though completion of this Form B, which must be signed by the individuals concerned, does not mean that the individuals will themselves be "controllers" of the regulated firm, it does entail potential consequences (*e.g.* in the case of a false declaration).

Changes in circumstances of existing controllers

11.10 Regulated firms (United Kingdom and non-United Kingdom incorporated) are subject to a potentially onerous new requirement to notify the FSA immediately upon becoming aware of certain "material matters" in relation to a controller, including any legal action or investigation which might put into question the integrity of the controller; any significant deterioration in the financial position of a controller; substantial changes or series of changes in the controller's governing body; and any controller which is authorised in another EEA state under single market directives ceasing to be so authorised.[14] Though these requirements are intended to enable the FSA to monitor the regulated firm's continuing compliance with the Threshold Conditions, they do require firms to make judgments about the relative significance of events which they may not be best placed to make. As a result, firms may be tempted to make notifications on a "failsafe" basis, which would obviously be unsatisfactory in view of the purpose of the rule. The FSA has tried to give some comfort to firms through guidance that it does not expect them to put in place systems and procedures to monitor the occurrence of material events, though it does expect a firm to make enquiries of controllers if it becomes aware that a material specified event may occur or has occurred.[15]

BUSINESS TRANSFERS: GENERAL

11.11 Some important parts of the FSMA have attracted considerable public debate, while others have attracted less attention outside the regular respondents to consultation papers. Park VII of the Act, relating to the "control" of insurance business transfer schemes and banking business transfer schemes, is certainly an example of the latter. However, the new law in this part of the Act has fundamentally reshaped the way in which many sales, transfers and re-organisations of United Kingdom (and indeed non-United Kingdom) banking and insurance businesses will be regulated. The basic requirement is that no qualifying "insurance business transfer scheme" or "banking business transfer scheme" is to have effect unless it is sanctioned by an order of the court (section 104 of the FSMA). In two

---

[13] SUP 11.3.8D.
[14] SUP 11.8.1R.
[15] SUP 11.8.5G.

important respects, this is new. First, while transfers of long-term insurance business by United Kingdom authorised insurers have for many years required court approval,[16] transfers of general insurance businesses have proceeded subject to the approval of the competent United Kingdom regulator (originally the Department of Trade and Industry; then the Treasury's insurance division; and latterly the FSA itself). This distinction has been consigned to the history books, with little public debate. Secondly, the transfer of banking businesses, including deposits accepted by a bank, has not been directly governed by any United Kingdom statute or E.C. directive (unlike insurance transfers), though various celebrated banking mergers have been complex enough to require a private Act of Parliament to allow them to proceed.[17] Now, virtually all transfers of businesses by United Kingdom authorised deposit–takers will, prima facie, be subject to court approval, irrespective of the scale of the business to be transferred and the numbers of customers involved. As noted below, however, the Treasury is empowered by regulations to provide exemptions from the statutory restrictions; it seems that this power is not to be used before N2, but may be used thereafter.

Significantly, the Treasury apparently has no immediate plans to bring section 104 into force for banking business transfers, although it will be brought into force at N2 for insurance business transfers. However, much of the remainder for Part VII comes into force on N2 in relation to both types of schemes; in relation to banking transfers, the Treasury's intention appears to be to enable companies to use the Part VII procedure but not to make it mandatory (which is welcome).

BANKING BUSINESS TRANSFER SCHEMES

11.12   The new regime applies to any transfer of a business wholly or partly including the accepting of deposits if:

- the transferor is a United Kingdom company or unincorporated association with a permission to accept deposits in the United Kingdom; or

- the transferor is an overseas company or association with a permission to accept deposits in the United Kingdom and the transferee will carry on the business in the United Kingdom,

unless the deposit-taker is a building society or credit union, or the proposed scheme is a merger or division of a public company governed by section 427A(1) of the Companies Act 1985 (in which case it is an "excluded scheme"). The types of business transfers caught are therefore very broad; the sale of a non-United Kingdom branch by a United Kingdom authorised bank will be caught, even though (within the EEA) there is no E.C. directive compelling such "home state" approval, and there may be parallel requirements for approval or notification in the state where the branch is located. There is no exclusion or relaxation for small business transfers or intra-group transactions, even though, in such cases, it might be possible to obtain the consent of all of the depositors to the proposed

---

[16] Insurance Companies Act 1982, ss. 49–52(B) (inclusive) and Sched. 2C.

[17] *e.g.,* the merger between Lloyds Bank Plc and TSB Group plc in November 1995.

transfer. While section 104 is not in force, this does not matter much, but it would be problematic when it is. Any section 104 requirement for court sanction would also apply to the transfer of a portfolio of deposits which forms part of a far larger transaction which would not otherwise require court approval (*e.g.* the sale of a securities trading business). In this regard, some hope of future change is provided by section 117, which allows the Treasury to modify or amend Part VII by regulations, which seems appropriate at least in the case of smaller transactions where all or a prescribed majority of depositors so agree. It is to be hoped that Treasury regulations will address these concerns, though this has not been timetabled to occur before N2 (presumably because section 104 is apparently to be left in abeyance).

The requirements and conditions for applications in relation to banking schemes (and indeed insurance schemes) are set out in the Act and in Treasury regulations to be made under section 108.[18] An application for approval may be made by the authorised firm or the transferee or by both (section 107(2)). A notice stating that the application has been made must be published in the *London, Belfast* and *Edinburgh Gazettes* and (unless the court waives the requirement) in two national newspapers as well. The FSA must approve the notice before publication.[19] While these requirements are clearly borrowed from Schedule 2C of the Insurance Companies Act 1982, it is helpful that the Schedule 2C requirements for the production of an expert report and the compulsory distribution of a scheme document (including terms of the scheme and a summary of the report) to customers and shareholders have *not* been applied to banking schemes; the only "trade-off" for this is that a statement setting out the terms of the scheme has to be sent free of charge to any person who requests it (whether or not he or she is a customer or shareholder of the bank). The court may only sanction the scheme if[20]:

(a) a certificate has been obtained from the transferee's home state regulator confirming the adequacy of the transferee's financial resources;

(b) if the transferee is an EEA credit institution, the FSA has also certified that the home state regulator has been notified of the proposed scheme and either that it has responded or that a period of three months since the notification was made has elapsed;

(c) the court is satisfied that the transferee is duly authorised in the place to which the business is to be transferred (which may not be the United Kingdom, if the transferor is a United Kingdom incorporated bank) or will be authorised before the scheme takes effect; and

(d) the court considers that, in all the circumstances, it is appropriate to sanction the scheme.

---

[18] At the time of writing, these regulations were still in draft; see The Financial Services and Markets Act 2000 (Control of Business Transfers) (Requirements on Applicants) Regulations 2001, contained in the Treasury's Consultation Document (March 2001). This Chapter refers to these draft regulations, which are subject to change.

[19] *ibid.*, reg. 5(2) and (3).

[20] FSMA, s. 111.

The court is also given broad powers (again derived from Schedule 2C) to make provision for the transfer of property and other matters[21]; and, as one would expect, any provision for the transfer of property or liabilities will be effective to vest the same in the transferee.[22] The court's (and the Act's) powers do not, however, extend to overseas contracts and property, and the court may therefore direct the transferor (if the transferee so requires) to take "all necessary steps" to secure that the transfer becomes fully effective under the law of the overseas territory (though, in the absence of a similar court procedure, this may be easier said than done).[23]

In relation to transfers of non-United Kingdom branches by United Kingdom banks, it seems strange that a court procedure should be prescribed (without the compulsion of an E.C. directive) when—as the Act itself admits—the concomitant benefit of statutory vesting cannot be achieved.

INSURANCE BUSINESS TRANSFER SCHEMES

11.13   As noted above, the sanction of the English or Scottish courts has long been required in the case of transfers of long-term insurance business. Consequently, the FSMA's requirements for insurance business transfer schemes draw heavily from a body of law with which practitioners will already be very familiar. However, the extension of these requirements to transfers of general business—which were subject to separate procedures for regulatory approval under Schedule 2C— is entirely new and has not been fully explained. Some general insurers may regret that, for example, group reorganisations will now be subject to a public (and expensive) court procedure rather than the FSA approval process with which they are familiar.

A scheme may only be an insurance business transfer scheme if, among other things, it results in the relevant business being carried on from the transferee's establishment in an EEA State; in this respect, the requirements are narrower than those applying to banking transfers by United Kingdom companies.[24] Most transfers of general or long-term business by United Kingdom authorised insurance companies will require court approval, except most obviously where the business consists of direct insurance policies written by the United Kingdom passported branch of an EEA insurance company, in which case approval will be reserved to the EEA firm's home state regulator or courts (under the E.C. insurance directives). Conversely, the transfer of a book of reinsurance business by the United Kingdom branch of an EEA passported firm will be subject to court approval.[25] There are four prescribed kinds of "excluded scheme", including any transfer by a friendly society, and the transfer by a United Kingdom incorporated insurer of reinsurance business written elsewhere in the EEA, provided that the scheme has been approved by a court in an EEA state or by the host state regulator.[26] However, even in the case

---

[21] FSMA, s. 112.
[22] FSMA, s. 112(3).
[23] FSMA, s. 112(4).
[24] FSMA, s. 105(1).
[25] FSMA, s. 105(2)(b).
[26] FSMA, s. 105(3).

of an excluded scheme (other than a transfer by a friendly society), the parties may (but are not obliged to) apply to the court for an order sanctioning the scheme (section 105(4)).

The basic effect of Part VII and the Treasury regulations, taken together, is to replicate much of what was contained in Schedule 2C in relation to long-term business transfers, and to apply it to transfers of general business as well. Therefore, the Schedule 2C requirement that the scheme should be reported on by an independent actuary is translated into a requirement for a "scheme report", prepared by a skilled person nominated or approved by the FSA, in relation to any insurance business transfer scheme (section 109). Any person, including any employee of the transferor or the transferee, who alleges that he would be adversely affected by the carrying out of the scheme, and the FSA itself, are entitled to be heard at the court hearing of the application (section 110).

This right of audience is complemented by requirements in the draft Treasury regulations to publish notices in the *London, Belfast* and *Edinburgh Gazettes* and two United Kingdom national newspapers and (if the business includes EEA policies) two national newspapers in the relevant EEA State(s) as well,[27] and to send free of charge a statement setting out the terms of the scheme, and a summary of the expert's scheme report, to all policyholders and members of each party and to anyone else who requests it (*e.g.* employees or even competitors).[28] As under Schedule 2C, however, the court is given discretion to waive these requirements except for the publication of *Gazette notices*, which may be particularly helpful in the case of group reorganisations and some smaller transactions.[29] Copies of the transfer application itself and the scheme report must be available for public inspection at the United Kingdom offices of the parties, and elsewhere in the EEA if the business includes EEA policies, for at least 21 days beginning with the date of publication of the *Gazettes* and newspaper notices.[30]

Apart from these information requirements, the court may only sanction an insurance business transfer scheme if various authorisation, certification and consent requirements are satisfied, most of which are ultimately derived from the E.C. insurance directives.[31] In relation to the transferee, a certificate is required from the FSA or the transferee's home state authority regarding the adequacy of its solvency margin. Also, importantly as regards the timetable for these transactions, schemes which include direct insurance policies where another EEA State is the state of the commitment (in relation to long-term business) or the state where the risk is situated (in relation to general business) will have to be notified to the regulator in the other EEA State; and the FSA must certify that the regulator has been notified and that it has either consented to the scheme or that a period of three months has elapsed without consent being refused. Consequently, many schemes will take some months to implement, and schemes involving general business seem likely to take longer than previously.

The court has broad powers when it sanctions a scheme to make further provisions (section 112). It seems likely (though not entirely free from doubt) that this

---

[27] Treasury Regulations, reg. 3(2).
[28] *ibid.*, reg. 3(4).
[29] Treasury Regulations, reg. 4(2).
[30] *ibid.*, reg. 3(5).
[31] FSMA, s. 111 and Sched. 12.

may include provision for the transfer of the benefit of outwards reinsurance contracts. The FSA evidently agrees with this view, though it also has suggested that reinsurers should be informed of any proposed scheme (which is, of course, normal practice).

Once a court order has been made sanctioning a scheme, policyholders in other EEA States may still have rights under local law to cancel a policy which is part of the transferred business. For this purpose, notice of the court order or the execution of any transfer document is required to be published in the EEA state concerned, to enable affected policyholders to consider whether or not exercise such rights as they may have.[33]

Finally, one welcome aspect of Part VII is that it has preserved the ability for public companies to effect reorganisations or arrangements with members or creditors under sections 425 to 427A of the Companies Act 1985, in conjunction with a scheme under this Part of the FSMA. If these two statutory procedures are used in parallel, the FSA must be sent copies of the statutory reports prepared by the transferor and the transferee under Schedule 15B of the Companies Act 1985.[34]

---

[32] FSA, *Consultation Paper 110: Insurance Business and Friendly Society Transfers* (September 2001), para. 3.17.
[33] FSMA, s. 114.
[34] Treasury Regulations, reg. 3(7).

CHAPTER 12

Collective Investment Schemes

ROGER WALSOM

INTRODUCTION

12.01 The concept of a collective investment scheme was introduced into English law by the 1986 Act. This followed the Directive on Undertakings for Collective Investment in Transferable Securities[1] (the "UCITS Directive") which was promulgated in 1985 with a view to harmonising the rules relating to such undertakings across the European Union (discussed further below).

Other than a few specific changes of detail, referred to below, the FSMA leaves the substance of the 1986 Act intact in relation to collective investment schemes although the order and layout of the relevant statutory provisions has been changed somewhat in an attempt to make it more logical and more consistent with the drafting approach adopted elsewhere in the FSMA. Thus, the basic definitions of a collective investment scheme and related concepts are set out in sections 235 to 237 of the FSMA, the basic restrictions on promotion of collective investment schemes are set out in sections 238 to 241 and the detailed exceptions and operational restrictions are dealt with in certain statutory instruments and ancillary regulations as described below.

Because few substantive changes have been made by the FSMA in this area, much of the following summary would apply equally to the law under the 1986 Act as to that under the FSMA, except where specifically indicated.

The main consequence if an arrangement constitutes a collective investment scheme is that, unless it falls within one of certain fairly rigid categories of permitted schemes (*i.e.* an authorised unit trust, an authorised open-ended investment company or a recognised overseas scheme), it cannot be marketed except to certain specific categories of person even if the general pre-condition (in section 21 of the FSMA) for marketing most other investments is satisfied, namely approval by an authorised person.

The policy rationale behind this relatively draconian position is presumably that (as will be seen) the nature of a collective investment scheme means that the participants will be agreeing to allow some third party to have day-to-day control where the participants might not themselves be expert in the subject matter of the scheme. Whether that is any more true in the case of collective investment schemes than, say, certain types of individual discretionary investment management is perhaps questionable.

The restrictions on promotion of what are now known as unregulated collective investment schemes have a long history, having first appeared in the Prevention

---

[1] Directive 85/611, as amended by Council Directive 88/220.

of Fraud (Investments) Act 1944, and reflect the distinction in tax treatment between such schemes and authorised schemes, with the latter benefiting from an exemption from taxation on capital gains (currently in section 100(1) of the Taxation of Chargeable Gains Act 1992). If a collective investment scheme is unauthorised and constitutes a "unit trust scheme" (*i.e.* a scheme "under which the property is held on trust for the participants": section 237(1) of the FSMA), the scheme will, unless it is a qualifying limited partnership,[2] be liable to capital gains tax (section 99(1) of the Taxation of Chargeable Gains Act 1992) and so is likely to be tax inefficient.

The definition of a collective investment scheme can also be relevant in determining: whether participation in an arrangement constitutes an investment (and is therefore regulated by the FSMA); whether the person operating the arrangement requires authorisation; and whether and to what extent the rules in the *Conduct of Business Sourcebook* ("COB") and in the specialist *Collective Investment Schemes Sourcebook* (the "CIS Sourcebook") will apply.

In broad terms, COB sets standards for the marketing and selling of collective investment schemes and for the management and custody or holding of scheme assets whereas the CIS Sourcebook sets out the product regulation requirements for the regulated schemes themselves. COB therefore replaces the rules of IMRO (generally the appropriate regulator in respect of collective investment schemes) and the CIS Sourcebook replaces the Financial Services (Regulated Schemes) Regulations 1991 (as amended) and the Financial Services (Open-ended Investment Companies) Regulations 1997 (discussed below). However, guidance currently in the IMRO Rules on valuation and pricing, and on the correction of pricing and box management errors, is now in the CIS Sourcebook. In the case both of COB and the CIS Sourcebook, the existing rules have largely been carried forward with few major changes in policy.

DEFINITION

12.02 It is, therefore, worth examining the definition of a collective investment scheme in some detail. Section 235(1) of the FSMA defines it as:

> "(1) ". . . any arrangements with respect to property of any description, including money, the purpose or effect of which is to enable persons taking part in the arrangements (whether by becoming owners of the property or any part of it or otherwise) to participate in or receive profits or income arising from the acquisition, holding, management or disposal of the property or the sums paid out of such profits or income.
>
> (2) The arrangements must be such that the persons who are to participate ("participants") do not have day-to-day control over the management of the property, whether or not they have the right to be consulted or to give directions.

---

[2] A qualifying limited partnership is exempted from the normal tax consequences of being unauthorised by the Income Tax (Definition of Unit Trust Scheme) Regulations 1988 (S.I. 1988 No. 267), the Capital Gains Tax (Definition of Unit Trust Scheme) Regulations 1988 (S.I. 1988 No. 266) and the Stamp Duty and Stamp Duty Reserve Tax (Definition of Unit Trust Scheme) Regulations 1988 (S.I. 1988 No. 268). These are expected to be replaced by corresponding regulations under the FSMA.

(3) The arrangements must also have either or both of the following characteristics:

  (a) the contributions of the participants and the profits or income out of which payments are to be made to them are pooled;
  (b) the property is managed as a whole by or on behalf of the operator of the scheme."

Subsection (4) provides that, where separate parts of the property are pooled, this will not of itself give rise to a single collective investment scheme unless rights in one part of the property can be exchanged for rights in another.

A collective investment scheme might therefore be summarised, broadly, as an arrangement whereby two or more persons or companies participate financially in any type of property (including cash) over the management of which they do not have day-to-day control and either (a) the contributions of those persons *and* the money from which amounts are paid to those persons are pooled *or* (b) the property is managed as a whole by someone else.

There are a few points to note. First of all, the property need be nothing to do with investments: it could, for example, equally be land, a car or a racehorse. Secondly, there is no definition of "pooled" but the word would generally be understood to imply some sort of co-mingling or collective ownership. However, it should be noted that a collective investment scheme can still exist even if there is no pooling of anything. Thirdly, the "operator", who must manage the property as a whole, is not defined (except in the case of a unit trust scheme with a separate trustee or in the case of an open-ended investment company), and therefore presumably simply means the person who in fact operates or manages the scheme. Again, this is not an essential requirement (provided in that case that there is some pooling) but it will still be a requirement that the participants do not have day-to-day control over the property; and this is most likely to be the case where someone else (the operator) does have such control, by managing it as a whole.

Therefore, one can distil the definition further to: management in common of cash or other property by one person on behalf of others who have a financial interest in it but do not have day-to-day control.

It can therefore be seen that the scope of the definition is potentially extremely wide and covers arrangements relating to assets which would not otherwise be regulated. It is the element of separate management and/or pooling, rather than the nature of the underlying asset, which determines whether or not an arrangement constitutes a collective investment scheme. A profit motive is not, of itself, required as part of the definition although, as the word "investment" suggests, the legislation is primarily directed at situations where some element of investment motive is likely to be involved, and this is reflected in a number of the exceptions, which will be considered below.

EXCEPTIONS

12.03 By virtue of the Financial Services and Markets Act 2000 (Collective Investment Schemes) Order 2001 (the "CIS Exemption Order"),[3] the following are not collective investment schemes:

---

[3] S.I. 2001 No. 1062.

Individual investment management schemes

12.04   These will not be collective investment schemes if:

(a)   the property of the scheme generally comprises shares or other securities or certain types of insurance;

(b)   each participant is entitled to a part of the underlying property of the scheme and able to withdraw that part at any time;

(c)   contributions to the scheme or profits or income from the scheme are not pooled; and

(d)   the underlying property of the scheme is managed as a whole by the operator only in the sense that the parts of the underlying property to which different participants are entitled are not bought and sold separately except on a person becoming or ceasing to be a participant.

Therefore, in essence, the exception covers situations where the underlying property of the scheme relates to certain types of investments which are held for each participant separately but where the relevant property may be bought or sold for more than one participant simultaneously as part of a single transaction. The most obvious example is a PEP or ISA but note that, curiously, a pure cash ISA would not be covered (and the PIA have previously indicated that it would not be covered by the common account exception referred to below). It is arguable that a PEP or ISA (or at least one falling within this exception) would not have fallen within the definition of collective investment scheme even without this exception in view of the requirements for (effectively) separate beneficial ownership of the underlying property, no pooling and no management as a whole apart from on joining or leaving the scheme. Whilst one can understand the desire to avoid any doubt on the matter, the fact that the exception is thought necessary suggests that a PEP, ISA or similar arrangement which does not precisely satisfy the requirements of the exception would constitute a collective investment scheme. It is generally assumed that the not uncommon contractual requirement to pay a transfer charge to leave a PEP or ISA, or to wait a reasonable period while the administrative formalities are dealt with, would not mean that the PEP or ISA would be outside the exception for failing to permit a participant's part of the underlying property to be withdrawn "at any time" but the position might be less clear if, as a condition of withdrawal or transfer, an exorbitant fee is charged or, even if in practice but not in theory, a minimum period of notice is applied.

Enterprise initiative schemes

12.05   Where shares (or cash awaiting investment) are held pursuant to a scheme under Chapter III of Part VII of ICTA 1988, the scheme will not be a collective investment scheme provided that each participant is entitled to a part of the underlying property and:

(a)   qualifying shares under the scheme (*i.e.* in respect of which, broadly, relief under section 306 of ICTA 1988 has not been disallowed or withdrawn) can be withdrawn from the scheme at any time after five years from the date of issue of the shares (if listed in an EEA state or dealt in on a recognised investment exchange) and after seven years from the date of issue in other cases;

(b) non-qualifying shares can be withdrawn from the scheme at any time after six months from the date on which they cease to be qualifying shares;

(c) any cash in the scheme which has been conditionally or unconditionally committed to the acquisition of shares can be withdrawn at any time;

(d) the minimum contribution to the arrangement is £2,000; and

(e) the same requirements as in (c) and (d) above for individual management arrangements are satisfied or, in the case of (d), would be satisfied except that the operator of the scheme is entitled to exercise all or any of the rights conferred by shares within the scheme.

This exception is directed at Enterprise Investment Schemes. It will be noted that requirement (e) offers slightly greater flexibility than (d) above for individual management arrangements as to the rights which the operator may have to manage the scheme, although PEPs or ISAs are likely to entitle the operator of the scheme to exercise at least some of the rights attaching to the shares in the scheme and it seems inevitable that it will exercise such rights in practice.

Pure deposit-based schemes

12.06 This exception applies where the whole of each participant's contribution is a cash sum held by an authorised or exempted person on deposit where the deposit is lent to others or used to finance any other activity of such authorised or exempted person.

Scheme not operated by way of business

12.07 Arrangements which are not operated by way of business are excluded. This would cover, for example, a syndicate of private individuals who operate an investment club or who each have shares in a racehorse. Questions sometimes arise in relation to trustees, but the answer is likely to turn on whether or not they are acting in the capacity of professional trustees.

Debt issues

12.08 Arrangements will not be a collective investment scheme if the rights or interests of the participants comprise *only one* of the following:

(a) debentures issued by a single body corporate;

(b) debentures convertible into shares of any single issuer;

(c) debentures issued by any government;

(d) debentures issued by a single issuer (other than a body corporate) guaranteed by any government; or

(e) warrants which confer rights in respect of the shares or debentures referred to in (a) to (d) above of the same issuer as issued the warrants.

An open-ended company is in certain circumstances not regarded as a body corporate for the above purposes. Inclusion in the arrangements of a professional counterparty to a currency or interest rate swap will not generally prevent the exception from applying. This exception therefore covers securitisation or bond issues under which an entity (frequently a newly formed company based off-shore) issues debentures in respect of which the interest and capital will normally be paid from an underlying portfolio of assets. The words in italics are new and make clear that the arrangement must relate to only one of the specified types of investment.

Common accounts

12.09   Arrangements will not be a collective investment scheme if they relate to money held in a common account on the understanding that the contribution of each participant will be applied:

(a) in making payments to him; or

(b) in satisfaction of sums owed by him; or

(c) in the acquisition of property for him or the provision of services to him.

"Common account" is not defined but the exception would cover the client account operated by solicitors or other professional advisers.

Certain funds relating to leasehold property

12.10   A trust fund within the meaning of section 42(1) of the Landlord and Tenant Act 1987 will not be a collective investment scheme. This covers sinking funds for service charges payable by residential tenants.

Certain employee share schemes

12.11   This covers a scheme relating to securities in a company or group of companies where the participants in the scheme are group employees or former employees (or their respective spouses or children) and the scheme is to enable or facilitate the holding of such securities by or for the benefit of such persons or transactions in such securities between them or for their benefit. The scheme may be operated by a group company or a person who under the scheme holds shares or debentures in the group as trustee. This would therefore cover most ESOPs and other share incentive schemes.

This exemption is no wider than the corresponding exception in paragraph 36 of Schedule 1 of the 1986 Act, but it is obviously considered wide enough as the additional similar exemption in section 75(6) of the 1986 Act has not been repeated in the FSMA. Section 75(6) applied where the participants were all current or previous employees of a company in the same group as the operator of the scheme (or members of their families), and the property of the scheme comprised shares or debentures in that group. This was largely duplicative as, although section 75(6) (unlike paragraph 36 and the new exception) did not impose a condition as to the purpose of the scheme, there are probably few likely circumstances covered by this omitted exemption which would not also be covered by the retained one.

Schemes entered into for commercial purposes related to existing business

12.12 This exception will apply where each participant carries on a business other than investment business and he enters into the arrangements for commercial purposes related to that other business. However, it must not just be a participant's participation in the arrangements which means that he will carry on that other business; and it will still be investment business for these purposes even if one of the exclusions from what normally constitutes a regulated activity applies. These last two points are both changes to the exception in the 1986 Act made by the CIS Exemption Order.

The general thrust of this exception is fairly clear but some points are worth noting. Each participant must have another recognisable business which is not investment business. Participation by a newly formed company set up specifically for the purpose of participating in the arrangement (or indeed an existing company), which does not carry on a non-investment business (even though it is part of a group of companies which does so), would cause the arrangement to fall outside the exception for *all* participants. The wording of an earlier draft of the CIS Exemption Order would have meant that a contemplated future business, rather than just an existing business, could suffice, but this wording has not found its way into the final version. It would seem that the type of non-investment business need not be the same for each of the participants.

This is an important exception and would cover, for example, arrangements between one or more property companies, or developers participating in the development and resale of properties or sites; but, if a financier is also party to the arrangement as part of its investment business, the exclusion will not apply to any of the participants.

Group schemes

12.13 This covers an arrangement where each of the participants is a body corporate in the same group as the operator. An example might be where one company in a group is used as a channel to invest surplus funds of the group on a pooled basis and allocates the profits to members of the group. Appointment of a professional operator outside the group would therefore cause the arrangement to be outside the exception. The reference to "body corporate" would include overseas companies.

Franchise arrangements

12.14 These are defined to mean arrangements under which a person earns profits or income by exploiting a right conferred by those arrangements to use a trade mark or design or other intellectual property or the goodwill attached to it. So, if A allows B to carry on a business using A's logo etc. in return for a share of the profits or revenues, this will not be a collective investment scheme.

Trading schemes

12.15   It will not be a collective investment scheme simply because participants are to receive payments or other benefits (which are wholly or mainly funded out of the contributions of other participants) as reward for introducing other participants but in the meantime those contributions are managed as a whole by or on behalf of the operator.

Timeshare schemes

12.16   This exception covers schemes under which the rights or interests of the participants are timeshare rights as defined in the Timeshare Act 1992. This is a new exception introduced under the FSMA. Previously, it would have been necessary to rely on the next exception, but that might have been problematic if the predominant purpose behind the timeshare was to make a profit by holding the property as an investment.

Other schemes relating to use or enjoyment of property

12.17   This exception applies where the predominant purpose is to enable the participants to share in the use or enjoyment of property *(other than shares or other regulated investments)*, or to make its use or enjoyment available gratuitously to others.

Under the 1986 Act, this exception was limited to arrangements relating to the use or enjoyment of a particular property, but the new exception is less restrictive in that it will still apply where the scheme relates to more than one property or to property generally. However, the words in italics have been introduced under the FSMA to make clear that investment-related arrangements are not covered by the exception.

Schemes involving the issue of certificates representing investments

12.18   It is not a collective investment scheme if the rights or interests of the participants are certificates conferring rights to shares, debentures or rights to acquire, dispose of or convert any investment. This would cover depositary receipts.

Clearing services

12.19   This covers clearing services operated by an authorised person, a recognised investment exchange or a recognised clearing house. It would therefore include, for example, the activities of CREST.

Contracts of insurance

12.20   Unit-linked life policies will normally be investments but they will not be collective investment schemes.

Funeral plan contracts

12.21   A scheme for paying funeral expenses will not be a collective investment scheme.

Individual pension accounts

12.22 Accounts in which pension assets are held will not be collective investment schemes.

Occupational and personal pension schemes

12.23 Except for personal pension unit trusts which are set up as feeder funds, these will not be collective investment schemes.

Bodies corporate

12.24 A building society, friendly society or provident society will not be a collective investment scheme.

Similarly, any other body corporate, other than an open-ended investment company or a limited liability partnership under the Limited Liability Partnership Act 2000,[4] will also not be a collective investment scheme. Bodies corporate include overseas companies. An open-ended investment company is one:

(a) where the property of the scheme is beneficially owned and managed by or on behalf of the company and the purpose of the company is the investment of its funds with the aim of spreading investment risk and giving its members the benefit of the results of such management; and

(b) in respect of which a reasonable investor would expect that he would be able to realise, within a period appearing to him to be reasonable, the value of his securities in the scheme and be satisfied that this would be on a basis calculated wholly or mainly by reference to the value of the property in the scheme.[5]

For the purposes of (b), any actual or potential redemption or purchase of shares under Chapter VII of Part V of the Companies Act 1985 by a United Kingdom company or under corresponding provisions in another EEA State *or in another territory designated by the Treasury*[6] is disregarded.

The wording of (a) above is the same as in the 1986 Act but (b) is new as are the words in italics. These changes were introduced to the FSMA by amendment in the House of Lords. The changes follow criticisms of the previous wording in the 1986 Act which required only that the participants be entitled to have their securities redeemed or purchased or (other than under Chapter VII of Part V of the Companies Act 1985 or corresponding provisions under the law of any other EEA State) that their securities were, in fact, redeemed or purchased.[7] There were doubts as to whether, for example, the right of a shareholder to have his shares in a United Kingdom company redeemed or purchased even as a one-off or on a future date or subject to a condition precedent would cause that company to be regarded as open-ended and therefore a collective investment scheme and, if so, from what

---

[4] A limited liability partnership created under the Limited Liability Partnership Act 2000 will be a body corporate: Limited Liability Act 2000, s. 1(2).

[5] FSMA, s. 236.

[6] This power to designate other territories was added by the FSMA, s. 236.

[7] 1986 Act, s. 75(8)(b)(i).

date. A United Kingdom investment trust (which, despite its name, is not a trust but a closed-ended body corporate) would not normally be regarded as a collective investment scheme under the previous or the new wording (but see below).

The previous wording did not require the redemption or purchase to be linked to asset value although an alternative ground upon which a scheme could previously be regarded as a collective investment scheme was where the company ensured that its securities could be sold on an investment exchange at a price related to the value of the property to which such securities related.[8] This has not been repeated in the FSMA.

Clearly, the new wording in (b) is closer to the substance of what most people would regard as open-ended. However, doubts still remain: for example, no guidance is given as to the length of period before realisation which a reasonable investor would regard as reasonable. Since the period would surely depend on the type of scheme and, as no particular type of scheme is assumed in the wording of (b), a relatively long period might be reasonable for certain types of scheme. To this extent, the definition is somewhat circular and arguably, therefore, any scheme which provides for realisation on a basis calculated wholly or mainly by reference to the value of the underlying property of the scheme is potentially a collective investment scheme. Query whether it could ever extend to a United Kingdom investment trust with a fixed life or fixed redemption date, at least as the relevant date approaches? In debates on the Bill in the House of Lords the Government spokesman (Lord McIntosh) said that the test was intended to be "based on the overall impression that the reasonable investor would get when he is considering investing . . . It does not concern a particular point in time at the end of a company's life".[9] In subsequent debates, he said that such a company would *probably* fall to be considered as a closed-ended company through its life".[10] The FSA have expressed a similar view in their consultative guidance on the definition of open-ended investment companies,[11] apparently on the grounds that the fixed life or fixed redemption date was always part of the company's constitution, that the wording in (b) has to be applied in relation to the company as a whole at the pre-investment stage for a hypothetical reasonable investor and nothing about the company fundamentally changes as the relevant date approaches. However, as the guidance also indicates that it is possible for a closed-ended company to become open-ended and vice-versa (although not to be both at the same time), it is not clear that this is a wholly convincing answer. Also, clarity is not greatly increased by the FSA's view in the guidance that the period before realisation which a reasonable investor regards as reasonable could depend, for example, on differences in the investment objectives that a reasonable investor might be seeking to achieve.

Drawing a distinction between the words "would expect" and "be satisfied" in the wording in (b) above, the FSA guidance says that the reasonable investor could expect to be able to realise his investment within what he believes to be a reasonable period even though he does not have a contractual entitlement or option to do so if, for example, the company in practice regularly redeems or repurchases its shares or

---

[8] 1986 Act, s. 75(8)(b)(ii).
[9] Vol. 611 H.L. March 30, 2000.
[10] Vol. 612 H.L. May 9, 2000.
[11] FSA, *Consultation Paper 104: The Authorisation Manual, Supplementary Consultation on Certifications, Financial Promotion and related activities, and Open-ended Investment Companies* (August 2001).

has a publicly declared policy or intention of doing so (but that the latter might not suffice if what happens in practice differs from the declared policy or intention).

The FSA guidance seems to be on firmer ground in suggesting that the ability to trade a company's shares on a stock exchange or other secondary market would not, of itself, be sufficient to satisfy a reasonable investor that his investment would be realised wholly or mainly by reference to the value of the underlying assets—after all, such a market would not necessarily continue to exist or might not produce a price equal to his proportionate share of the value of the underlying assets. The position could, of course, be different if the company has given an undertaking to intervene in the market to ensure that the market price reflects such value. The reference in the wording in (b) to the value of the property in the scheme could be construed as suggesting gross rather than net asset value but no doubt this is not intended and this is assumed in the FSA guidance.[12]

The FSA guidance also recognises that difficult questions can arise if a company has redeemable and non-redeemable shares; and the FSA guidance concludes that, if a company has mainly the former (even if they are redeemable only after a stated period), a company is likely to be an open-ended company.

The existing wording in (a) has also given rise to questions as to the degree of investment risk spreading that is necessary; but it would seem that a holding of only a relatively small number of investments might be sufficient so long as a diversification objective could genuinely be discerned. On this point, the FSA guidance says only that the level of risk involved in each of the investments is not relevant so long as the range of different investments demonstrates that the aim was to spread investment risk.

Ultimately, no doubt the FSA guidance is correct in concluding that the definition of an open-ended company is intended to cover a company which, looked at as a whole, is of an open-ended nature with variable funding.[13] However, it seems unfortunate that a definition intended to clarify ambiguities in the 1986 Act, and the application of which can have significant regulatory and tax consequences, should be so inherently uncertain.

One continuing anomaly is that a Delaware or Scottish limited partnership, because it is a body corporate, would probably not be a collective investment scheme whereas an English limited partnership, which would not be a body corporate but would normally be regarded as closed-ended, would be a collective investment scheme. However, a limited liability partnership created under the Limited Liability Partnership Act 2000 will be a body corporate,[13a] but is capable of being a collective investment scheme.[14] A professional partnership without limited partners would not normally be a collective investment scheme as the partners would have day-to-day control over management of the partnership property and such property would not be managed as a whole by an operator.

The Treasury now has the power (in section 236(5)) to change the definition further by order, thus preserving flexibility for the future.

---

[12] FSA, *Consultation Paper 104*, para 2.9.3.
[13] FSA, *Consultation Paper 104*, para. 2.4.5.
[13a] See n.4 above.
[14] The Financial Services Act 1986 (Extension of Scope of Act and Meaning of Collective Investment Scheme) Order 2001 (S.I. 2001 No. 1421). A similar order is expected to be introduced under the FSMA.

Restrictions on promotion

12.25 As mentioned earlier, section 21 of the FSMA generally prohibits the communication, in the course of a business, of an invitation or inducement "to engage in investment activity" other than by an authorised person; and participation in a collective investment scheme would be regarded as engaging in investment activity for these purposes.

In addition, section 238 states that, subject to specific exemptions discussed below, an authorised person "must not communicate an invitation or inducement to participate in a collective investment scheme" unless (a) it is an authorised unit trust scheme, an authorised open-ended investment company or a recognised overseas scheme (collectively referred to as "regulated schemes", all other schemes being unregulated); or (b) the communication originated outside the United Kingdom and is not "capable of having an effect" in the United Kingdom. "Communicate" includes causing a communication to be made and "participate" means becoming a participant (and such definitions are used in this Chapter). In broad terms, therefore, the marketing of unregulated collective investment schemes in or from the United Kingdom is generally not permissible even by an authorised person. As under the 1986 Act, breach of this restriction is not a criminal offence but (as a result of section 241) investors are entitled to claim for any loss; and the other sanctions for breach of the conduct of business rules will apply. Also, as noted below, a breach of section 238 will generally also give rise to a breach of section 21, which is a criminal offence.

In certain respects, the language of section 238 (and its differences to the corresponding wording in the 1986 Act) mirrors that in section 21 dealing with financial promotion generally. As with section 21, the word "promotion", while a useful shorthand, is not used in section 238 other than in the heading and a reference to the FSA's power to issue exemption orders. The words "communicate", "invitation" and "inducement" and the territorial scope have already been discussed in the context of section 21 in Chapter 6 above and that discussion will not be repeated here.

Whereas the prohibition in section 21 applies only to invitations or inducements communicated in the course of business, and does not apply if made or approved by an authorised person, the prohibition in section 238 applies only if the communication has been made by an authorised person (which, by virtue of Schedules 3 and 4 to the FSMA, includes EEA firms covered by the single market directives or "Treaty firms" established and authorised in another EEA State). However, this does not mean that anyone other than an authorised person may promote a collective investment scheme with impunity, as section 21 will normally still apply (assuming that the invitation or inducement is communicated in the course of a business). Therefore, the communication (if not made by an authorised person) must be approved by one, but section 240 prohibits such approval of a communication relating to a collective scheme where the communication would have been prohibited (by section 238) if made by the authorised person.

The corresponding restriction in the 1986 Act (section 76) also applied only to authorised persons (and, by virtue of paragraph 23 of Schedule 7 to the Investment Services Regulations 1995 and paragraph 25 of Schedule 9 to the Banking Coordination (Second Council Directive) Regulations 1992, to investment firms or financial institutions established and authorised in another EEA State) and the

1986 Act contained no equivalent of section 240. However, this potential loophole was closed by the SIB prohibiting (by rule 7.04(3) of the Financial Services (Conduct of Business) Rules 1990) firms authorised by it (and investment firms or financial institutions established and authorised in another EEA State) from approving under section 57 of the 1986 Act (the equivalent of section 21 of the FSMA) investment advertisements relating to collective investment schemes other than in certain limited circumstances. The SFA, IMRO and the PIA adopted similar rules.

Unlike section 21, it is doubtful if the language of section 238 extends the scope of the restrictions on promotion of collective investment schemes much in practice beyond what it was as a result of the corresponding provisions of the 1986 Act. This is because the 1986 Act generally prohibited not only the issue or causing to be issued in the United Kingdom of any advertisement inviting persons to become or offer to become participants in a collective investment scheme, or containing information likely to lead directly or indirectly to their doing so, but also advising or procuring a person in the United Kingdom to do so.

Nevertheless, section 76 of the 1986 Act has generally been interpreted so that an intermediary who merely passed on to its client an advertisement issued by another authorised person would not have issued the advertisement or caused it to be issued. Therefore, if the intermediary did not advise or procure his client to become a participant, he would not be acting contrary to section 76 (and so would not have to ensure that an exemption applied). Similarly, if the intermediary was an authorised person, or a person who in the ordinary course of business acquired or disposed of the same kind of property as in the scheme, the authorised person who had issued the advertisement would not have been in breach as section 76(2) provided an exemption for advertisements issued to such persons.

Now, however, the intermediary would be regarded as having communicated an invitation or inducement and so would be caught by section 238 unless falling within one of the exemptions, described below. Section 240 states that, for purposes of determining whether there has been a breach of section 21, an approval in breach of section 238 is deemed not to have been given. Therefore, a breach of section 238 will generally also give rise to a breach of section 21; and a breach of section 21 (unlike section 238) is a criminal offence.

Section 238 authorises the FSA and/or the Treasury to issue exemptions from the restrictions on promotion although, in the case of the FSA, the exemptions must relate to the promotion of specific types of scheme other than to the general public. This, in turn, is defined to include "promotion" (as noted above, the only use of the word in this Chapter of the Act apart from in the headings) in a way designed to reduce, so far as possible, the risk of participation by persons for whom participation would be unsuitable.

EXEMPTIONS FROM RESTRICTIONS ON PROMOTION

12.26   The exemptions from the promotion of unregulated collective investment schemes are now set out in the Financial Services and Markets Act 2000 (Financial Promotion) Order 2001[15] (the "Financial Promotion Order"), the Financial Services

---

[15]   S.I. 2001 No. 1335 as amended by Article 2 of S.I. 2001 No. 2633.

and Markets Act 2000 (Promotion of Collective Investment Schemes) (Exemptions) Order 2001[16] (the "CIS Promotion Order") and rule 3.11 and Annex 5R of COB.

The Financial Promotion Order (which deals with exemptions to section 21 rather than section 238) has already been discussed in Chapter 6 above, and, as the general exemptions to section 21 apply equally to collective investment schemes, they will not be discussed further here. However, the following additional exemptions to section 21 apply specifically to collective investment schemes:

(a) non-real time and solicited real time communications (the meanings of which are discussed in Chapter 6 above) by the operator of a Designated Territory Scheme or Individually Recognised Scheme (discussed below) to persons in the United Kingdom who are participants in that or any other such scheme of that operator where the communication relates to any such scheme (Article 40); and

(b) invitations or inducements communicated by an open-ended investment company to any person reasonably believed to be, or to be entitled to become, a member or creditor or holder of shares, debentures or warrants of that company (Article 44).

Operators of authorised unit trusts and open-ended investment companies (and of Member State Schemes, discussed below) will always be authorised, and so they do not need these specific exemptions.

The exemptions to section 238 in the CIS Promotion Order are in most respects substantially similar to the corresponding exemptions to section 21 in the Financial Promotion Order discussed in Chapter 6 above, and so the discussion will not be repeated here. However, the exemptions to section 21 in the Financial Promotion Order relating to exempt persons, mere conduits and certain communications by journalists and unauthorised members of a profession are not repeated for purposes of section 238 in the CIS Promotion Order (because they are less relevant in the context of the CIS Promotion Order which is intended to benefit authorised persons). Also, the exemptions relating to communications from outside the United Kingdom in the CIS Promotion Order are slightly different and cover:

(a) "solicited real time communications" made from outside the United Kingdom relating to an unregulated scheme operated and managed outside the United Kingdom (Article 9); and

(b) "non-real time and unsolicited real time communications" made from outside the United Kingdom by an authorised person to a "previously overseas customer" relating to such a scheme (Article 10).

The wording in quotation marks are defined in a similar way to those in the Financial Promotion Order (as to which see Chapter 6 above). The exemption in relation to communications to persons outside the United Kingdom is the same in the CIS Promotion Order as in the Financial Promotion Order. Also, as noted

---

[16] S.I. 2001 No. 1060 as amended by Article 3 of S.I. 2001 No. 2633.

above, communications originating outside the United Kingdom and not capable of having an effect in the United Kingdom are exempted by section 238 itself.

This approach, of repeating many of the exemptions to the general prohibition on marketing investments by unauthorised persons specifically in relation to the marketing by unauthorised persons of collective investment schemes, is new. The approach is, however, logical insofar as it seeks to put authorised persons marketing unregulated collective investment schemes in no worse position than unauthorised persons promoting other types of investments.

In addition, the CIS Promotion Order contains an exemption which applies to a "non-real time communication" or a "solicited real time communication" communicated by the operator of an unregulated collective investment scheme to persons believed on reasonable grounds to be entitled to units or shares in that scheme (Article 18).

Rule 3.11 and Annex 5R of COB 3 contain further specific exemptions to section 238 for the promotion of unregulated collective investment schemes by authorised persons. These exemptions are based on those contained in the Financial Services (Promotion of Unregulated Schemes) Regulations 1991[17] (the "Unregulated Schemes Promotion Regulations"), and Annex 5R adopts a similar tabular format as the Unregulated Schemes Promotion Regulations, although there are certain differences.

Thus, as before, the main exemptions are that an unregulated collective investment scheme may be promoted to:

(a) a person who is (or was within the previous 30 months) a participant in such a scheme if the promotion is of that scheme, or of another scheme with a "substantially similar" underlying property and risk profile in terms both of liquidity and volatility, or of a scheme which is intended to absorb or take over the other scheme's assets or which is offered as an alternative for cash in the liquidation of that other scheme;

(b) a person in relation to whom reasonable steps have been taken to ensure that investment in the scheme is suitable and who is an established or newly accepted customer (*i.e.* one obtained without breach of COB) of the person doing the promoting—previously the exemption specifically required information to be sought about the person's circumstances and investment objectives but this is still implied by the requirement for suitability;

(c) current or former officers or employees (or certain relatives thereof) of the company doing the promoting, or a group company, provided that the scheme is either limited to cash or shares or debentures in the employing company or a connected company and the said categories of persons are the only participants in the scheme or is a limited partnership scheme where the employer or a connected company will be the unlimited partner and such persons will be some or all of the limited partners (under the previous law, the limited partnership exemption would also appear to have required the said categories of persons to be the only participants);

---

17 1991 (Rel. 101).

(d) certain categories of non-private investors (now called intermediate customers), such as companies or partnerships with net assets of at least £5 million and trusts with gross assets of at least £10 million, though the scope of the exemption has been widened slightly.

In addition, certain new exemptions have been added. For example, category (c) above has been extended to include such officers, employees or relatives where their participation in any type of scheme is to facilitate their co-investment with their employer or companies in the same group, or clients of such a company, whether such co-investment is direct or through a family trust or another intermediate vehicle. This exemption, unlike (c) above, will therefore cover employee participation in the normal English limited partnership structure where, to avoid a breach of the 20-partner limit (although the DTI is currently considering removing this limit[18]), the employees might participate indirectly in the partnership interest of a special purpose corporate limited partner rather than themselves be limited partners.

Certain exemptions contained in the Unregulated Schemes Promotion Regulations are, however, not repeated in Annex 5R: for example, the exemption previously in the Unregulated Schemes Promotion Regulations allowing promotion of a scheme to those whose names appear on a list (lawfully compiled by an unconnected company) of persons willing to receive details of that type of scheme.

Section 239 of the FSMA repeats section 76 of the 1986 Act in providing that regulations may exempt single property schemes from the restrictions on promotion of collective investment schemes and, as the definition of a single property scheme is the same in each Act, presumably the existing regulations under the 1986 Act will be adopted or adapted for the purpose. These are the Financial Services Act 1986 (Single Property Schemes) (Exemption) Regulations 1989.[19] Such a scheme is one where the underlying property consists of a single building, or group or adjacent buildings, managed by one operator and the units or shares in which are, or are to be, dealt in on a recognised investment exchange. Since 1997, the London Stock Exchange has permitted single property vehicles to obtain a Stock Exchange listing. These regulations, which set out a number of detailed requirements for a scheme to qualify, recognise two basic types of scheme: a corporate-based scheme where the investors will acquire shares in a special purpose company, coupled with property income certificates (known as "PINCs"); and single property ownership trusts (known as "SPOTs") where the investors become beneficiaries in the SPOT. In either case, the property must be situated, and the operator and (if applicable) trustee established, in the United Kingdom or another Member State.

These exemptions relate to the categories of person to whom the scheme is promoted but, as noted in the introduction above, the restrictions on promotion also do not apply to certain types of scheme, namely authorised unit trusts, authorised open-ended investment companies and recognised overseas schemes. Each of these will be considered briefly in turn following a brief discussion of the UCITS Directive.

---

[18] DTI, *Consultation Document: Removing the 20 Partner Limit* (April 4, 2001).
[19] S.I. 1989 No. 28.

UCITS DIRECTIVE

12.27 A UCITS (an undertaking for collective investment in transferable securities) is an open-ended scheme for spreading investment risk by collective investment in transferable securities. The objective behind the UCITS Directive was to enable a UCITS formed in one Member State, and complying with the rules of that state within the parameters laid down by the UCITS Directive, to be sold freely in any other Member State.[20] However, the UCITS Directive has largely failed in this objective because, for example:

(a) the UCITS Directive leaves Member States free as to how to tax locally incorporated schemes and amounts paid by offshore schemes to local investors—the tax treatment is often the most important aspect of a scheme;

(b) schemes must still comply with local laws and rules as to marketing (for example sections 21 and 238 of the FSMA and COB in the United Kingdom)—although understandable, this inevitably increases the expense and difficulty of launching a pan-European scheme;

(c) the UCITS Directive requires a management company wishing to market its products in another Member State to have a permanent establishment in that state or to appoint a paying and redemption agent in that state—this is a further hurdle to launching a pan-European scheme;

(d) the UCITS Directive was deliberately limited in scope so as to cover only those types of schemes which were allowed to be marketed to the public in every Member State—thus only schemes which invest principally in publicly traded securities are covered.

There have been several attempts to widen the scope of the UCITS Directive. In 1988, the European Commission proposed to widen its scope to include investments in bank deposits, cash funds, money market funds, traded options and futures and units of other UCITS. It was also proposed to allow management companies to have a single licence entitling them throughout the European Union to manage the assets of investors on a pooled basis. The Investment Services Directive[21] (which aims to achieve this in the case of discrete asset management) does not apply to fund management on a pooled basis although, in the United Kingdom, an operator or trustee of a UCITS constituted in another member state is automatically authorised in respect of that UCITS scheme (paragraph 1 of Schedule 5 to the FSMA which re-enacts a similar provision from the 1986 Act). In May 2000, the European Commission renewed these proposals and restated its commitment, first made in 1973, to completing the single market in financial services by 2005.

The UCITS Directive applies to all UCITS "situated" within a Member State and provides that this will be wherever its management company's registered office

---

[20] Member States include for this purpose members of the European Economic Area (currently E.U. Member States and Iceland, Liechtenstein and Norway).

[21] Directive 93/22.

is situated. A UCITS may be a trust, an investment company or a common fund constituted by contract but must not be closed-ended. A unit trust or unlisted investment company is generally required to have a depositary which is independent of the management company but based or operating in the same Member State as that in which the management company is incorporated and the UCITS Directive lays down a number of requirements for depositaries. The only restriction specific to the management company is that it cannot engage in any business other than the management of unit trusts and investment companies. This latter provision was reflected in section 83 of the 1986 Act, in relation to authorised unit trust schemes but is omitted from the FSMA (as indeed it was in relation to the Authorised Corporate Director of an authorised open-ended investment company when this new vehicle was introduced in 1996). Whilst there have been proposals to remove the requirement from the UCITS Directive it remains there for the time being and, in the meantime, any management company taking advantage of the relaxation in the FSMA will, therefore, not be able to rely on the UCITS Directive when seeking to sell products elsewhere in the European Union even though they would otherwise have been covered by the Directive.

A UCITS cannot invest:

(a) more than 10 per cent of its assets in non-publicly traded securities (unless the securities are to be listed within 12 months)[22];

(b) more than 5 per cent of its assets in any one entity (or 10 per cent so long as the holdings of more than 5 per cent do not in aggregate exceed 40 per cent of its assets)[23];

(c) more than 80 per cent of its assets in government securities and no more than 35 per cent of its assets in the securities of any single government;

(d) more than 5 per cent of its assets in other UCITS and nothing at all in non-UCITS schemes;

(e) in more than 10 per cent of the securities of any entity;

(f) in precious metals; and

(g) in derivatives except for purposes of "efficient portfolio management" (*i.e.* hedging of risk rather than speculation).

A UCITS is also prohibited from borrowing, except up to 10 per cent of its assets on a temporary basis,[24] and it may not grant loans or act as guarantor.

Because it is of the essence of a UCITS that it is open-ended, the units of a UCITS must generally be re-purchased or redeemed on demand out of the assets

---

[22] A relaxation allegedly exploited by the fund manager of certain Deutsche Morgan Grenfell unit trusts to invest in a much higher percentage of securities which were not ultimately listed. As a result, AUTIF members have voluntarily agreed to limit their investments in non-publicly traded securities to 10% including securities expected to be listed within 12 months.

[23] This is a problem for funds tracking an index, such as the FTSE-100, which represents as to more than 10% the securities of any one entity. To avoid a breach, they have to track a modified index in which no one entity represents more than 10%.

[24] An investment company may also borrow up to 15% of its assets (including any temporary borrowings) to acquire premises required to carry on its business.

of the UCITS unless the UCITS ensures that its units have a value on the Stock Exchange which is close to their net asset value.

The UCITS Directive requires the UCITS to publish a prospectus which must contain specified information, be kept up to date, be filed with the local regulatory authorities and be supplied free of charge to any potential investor together with the latest audited annual financial statement and half yearly report. The contents of annual and half-yearly reports are also prescribed and they must be produced within a certain time after expiry of the period to which they relate.

AUTHORISED UNIT TRUSTS

12.28 To be authorised, a United Kingdom unit trust scheme must be one of the types prescribed by the CIS Sourcebook, which replaces the Financial Services (Regulated Schemes) Regulations 1991 (as amended).[25] The permitted types are: securities funds (including schemes dedicated to Government and other similar securities), money market funds, futures and options funds, geared futures and options funds, property funds, warrant funds, umbrella funds, funds of funds and feeder funds (the latter being for personal pensions only and in any event subject to review by the FSA). Detailed rules are prescribed for each type of fund. Of those types of fund, only securities funds and warrant funds, and umbrella funds investing in securities and/or warrants, fall within the UCITS Directive.

Like its predecessor, the CIS Sourcebook sets out detailed regulations relating to investment and borrowing powers and other operational matters for authorised United Kingdom unit trust schemes and it makes few real changes of substance in relation to such schemes. However, one significant change (which will bring the rules for authorised unit trust schemes closer to those for authorised open-ended investment companies) is that the CIS Sourcebook permits expenses to be allocated to capital rather than income in wider circumstances than previously. A number of the amendments made by the CIS Sourcebook in relation to authorised unit trusts, and authorised open-ended investment companies, are summarised in Part Two of the FSA's *Consultation Paper on the CIS Sourcebook* issued in August 2000.[26]

Contrary to continental European practice, and to the position in relation to authorised open-ended investment companies as described below, dual pricing continues to be permitted (and, until 1999, was required) for such schemes so that units are issued at an offer price and redeemed at a bid price, the difference representing the bid/offer spread. The FSA is reviewing making single pricing mandatory[27] but, in the meantime, the CIS Sourcebook sets out separately the requirements for single pricing and dual pricing and has conformed the procedures for each method of pricing in certain respects.

Certain fundamental structural requirements for authorised United Kingdom unit trust schemes are dealt with in sections 242 to 261 of the FSMA which largely reproduce, albeit with some changes, the substance of sections 77 to 85 of the 1986 Act. This is not surprising as certain provisions of those sections and the

---

[25] 1991 (Rel. 148).

[26] FSA, *Consultation Paper 62.*

[27] This has been under review since September 1998: see FSA, *Consultation Paper 14.*

underlying regulations set out, in relation to United Kingdom authorised unit trusts, the requirements laid down by the UCITS Directive. Thus, an application for authorisation must still be made by the manager and trustee; the manager and trustee must be independent of each other; they must each be incorporated in the United Kingdom or another European Union or EEA State and have a place of business in the United Kingdom and be an authorised person[25] with permission to act as manager or (as the case may be) trustee; any provision in the trust deed exempting the manager or trustee from liability for failure to exercise due care is void; and the participants in the scheme must be entitled to have their units redeemed at a price related to the net asset value or the manager must be required to ensure that participants can sell their units on a stock exchange at a similar price.

Whereas, under section 78(7) of the 1986 Act, applicants for authorisation had to be informed of a decision within 6 months after the application is received, section 244 says that an application must be determined within 6 months of receipt of a completed application and an incomplete application must be determined within 12 months of receipt of the application. As before, the FSA can issue a certificate that a scheme complies with the UCITS Directive although it is now made clear, reflecting previous practice, that this will be done only on request (section 246 of the FSMA).

As noted above, the requirement in section 83 of the 1986 Act that the manager cannot carry out any activity other than managing collective investment schemes has not been repeated in the FSMA, although it remains a requirement of the UCITS Directive. Similarly, the provision in section 81(4) of the 1986 Act, that rules issued in relation to authorised unit trust schemes shall not impose limits on the remuneration of the trustee or the manager, has been omitted.

Other new provisions are that application may be made to the FSA to modify or waive the rules in relation to a particular scheme (section 250) and that an auditor who has breached the rules applicable to authorised unit trust schemes may be disqualified by the FSA from being the auditor of any other authorised unit trust or open-ended investment company (section 249).

As before, any proposed alterations to the scheme, or any proposal to replace the manager or the trustee, must be notified to the FSA in advance and the FSA has one month in which to object, pending which the proposal cannot become effective; and any proposed change to the trust deed requires a certificate from a solicitor that the trust deed still complies with the regulations.

Similarly, the FSA still has similar powers to revoke a scheme's authorisation (section 256), or to require the manager to stop issuing and/or redeeming units under the scheme or to require the scheme to be wound up (section 257) or to apply to the court for the manager and/or the trustee to be replaced (section 258) if, amongst other things, there has been a breach of the regulatory requirements in relation to the scheme. The provisions relating to the procedures for giving of directions, refusal and withdrawal of authorisations, etc. have, however, been expanded and (no doubt with a view to avoiding a breach of the Human Rights

---

[28] Qualification under the European "passport" provisions of the Investment Services Directive or the Banking Consolidation Directive as an investment firm or financial institution established and authorised in another EEA State is not sufficient for this purpose.

Act 1998) there is now generally a right to challenge adverse decisions of the FSA relating to such matters by referring them to the Financial Services and Markets Tribunal (which is discussed further in Chapter 14 below).

OPEN-ENDED INVESTMENT COMPANIES

12.29 Until the Companies Act 1980, a United Kingdom company could generally not acquire its own shares. In 1980 this was permitted subject to certain conditions (now contained in Chapter VII of the Companies Act 1985). However, it was not until the Open-Ended Investment Companies (Investment Companies with Variable Capital) Regulations 1996[29] (the "1996 Regulations"), which set out the basic corporate framework, and the Financial Services (Open-Ended Investment Companies) Regulations 1997[30] (the "1997 Regulations"), dealing with detailed operational matters, that a truly open-ended investment company (christened an "OEIC" by the Treasury), which can issue new shares when required and redeem existing shares on request at any time by any shareholder, became permissible. It was introduced following claims by the United Kingdom fund management industry that marketing collective investment schemes to investors in continental Europe was made more difficult by the greater familiarity of such investors with the open-ended investment company than the unit trust (and with single pricing for issue and redemption rather than the dual pricing prescribed for United Kingdom authorised unit trusts). However, the success of the new vehicle in overcoming this difficulty will have been constrained by the fact that the requirement for United Kingdom funds to apply withholding tax on distributions still remains.

In order to avoid the need for primary legislation, the 1996 Regulations (and, in turn, the 1997 Regulations) were introduced under section 2(2) of the European Communities Act 1972, which allows the Government to introduce secondary legislation on any matter where the purpose is to implement in the United Kingdom the requirements of an E.U. Directive. These regulations were therefore introduced by way of implementation of the UCITS Directive and, as a result, the only types of open-ended investment company permitted were those covered by the UCITS Directive, namely, securities funds, warrant funds and umbrella funds investing in securities and/or warrants. Proposals were put forward by the Treasury in 1996 to permit open-ended investment companies also to invest in the same range of funds as non-UCITS authorised unit trusts, but these proposals did not proceed following the change of Government in 1997. It has therefore always been envisaged that the rules relating to unit trusts and open-ended investment companies would ultimately converge so far as consistent with their respective structures and this is intended to be advanced under the FSMA.

Accordingly, the 1996 Regulations and the 1997 Regulations are now to be replaced by the Open-Ended Investment Companies (Investment Companies with Variable Capital) Regulations 2001[31] (the "ICVC Regulations") and the CIS Sourcebook respectively. As with their predecessors, the former set out the basic corporate framework (*i.e.* a blend of normal company law and the rules relating to

---

[29] S.I. 1996 No. 2827.
[30] 1997 (Rel. 168).
[31] S.I. 2001 No. 1228.

authorised unit trusts) for ICVCs (being the new terminology for United Kingdom authorised open-ended investment companies) and the latter deals with more detailed operational matters.

Thus, the ICVC Regulations stipulate that the head office must be in the United Kingdom, there must be at least one director, who must be a body corporate and an authorised person (though there can be other directors so long as they are "fit and proper" and have appropriate experience and expertise), there must be an independent depositary, who is incorporated in an E.U. or EEA Member State and has a place of business in the United Kingdom and to whom the property of the company must be entrusted for safekeeping, and the shareholders must be entitled to have their shares redeemed or repurchased upon request at a price related to net asset value or be entitled to sell their shares on an investment exchange at a similar price. The ICVC Regulations also set out, in terms which are similar to those for authorised unit trusts, the procedures for authorisation and revocation of authorisation of open-ended investment company status including (unlike the 1996 Regulations) a right of referral to the Tribunal. Unlike under the 1996 Regulations, registration of ICVCs will now be the responsibility of the FSA rather than the Companies Registry.

On the other hand, the CIS Sourcebook contains similar provisions to those in the corresponding regulations relating to authorised unit trusts dealing with more detailed operational matters such as the mechanics of issue and redemption of shares, investment and borrowing powers and procedures for meetings, etc. One significant difference, introduced in the 1997 Regulations and repeated in the CIS Sourcebook, is that (in response to the demands of the United Kingdom fund management industry, referred to above, which also prompted introduction of the ICVC) single pricing is prescribed for the issue and redemption of shares by ICVCs, without the dual pricing alternative currently permitted for authorised unit trusts, although levying of a redemption charge on a redemption or cancellation of shares, and/or a so-called dilution levy (intended principally for large deals) on the issue, redemption or cancellation of shares, is permitted. As with authorised unit trusts, the CIS Sourcebook allows ICVCs greater flexibility than previously in relation to charging expenses to capital although the provisions differ in detail. This and a number of other amendments made by the CIS Sourcebook are summarised in Part Two of the FSA's *Consultation Paper on the CIS Sourcebook* issued in August 2000 referred to earlier.

Unlike previously, however, the ICVC Regulations and the CIS Sourcebook have been issued by virtue of powers under the FSMA and so are not limited by the constraints of the UCITS Directive. Therefore, the types of permissible fund for an ICVC are now the same as described above for an authorised United Kingdom unit trust scheme (except for feeder funds which, as noted above, are in any event subject to review). Indeed, the CIS Sourcebook now deals with ICVCs as well as authorised United Kingdom unit trust schemes and the rules for each have generally been conformed so far as practicable.

RECOGNISED OVERSEAS SCHEMES

12.30 There are three basic categories of these:

(a) schemes constituted (by contract, trust or as an open-ended company) and authorised in another Member State of the European Union or the EEA ("Member State Schemes")[32];

(b) schemes authorised in other designated countries or territories ("Designated Territory Schemes")[33];

(c) individually recognised overseas schemes ("Individually Recognised Schemes").[34]

Member State Schemes

12.31 Such a scheme will be deemed to be recognised in the United Kingdom, subject to the FSA receiving at least two months' notice from the operator of the scheme of its intention to promote the scheme in the United Kingdom, and the FSA not objecting within that period. If the FSA does object, the operator has 28 days in which to make representations (as compared with 21 days previously under section 86(5) of the 1986 Act) and, if the FSA does not then withdraw its objection, the matter may be referred to the Tribunal.

If a Member State Scheme is recognised, then (except for rules relating to marketing[35]) the FSA's COB Rules do not apply to the operator, trustee or any depositary in relation to such a scheme (and who will be deemed to be authorised under the FSMA in connection with the scheme[36]), as the scheme will be similarly regulated by the home state, but the operator must maintain an address for service of notices and certain other facilities in the United Kingdom. Also, COB Rules on the promotion of regulated collective investment schemes will apply. Thus, while such a scheme may be promoted in the same manner as a United Kingdom authorised unit trust or ICVC, if there is a breach of the restrictions on promotion of such a scheme (*i.e.* a breach of the exemptions from the full restrictions) the FSA may impose the full restrictions on promotion of the scheme as apply to unauthorised United Kingdom schemes. This is subject to the right of the operator to make representations and ultimately to challenge the decision with the Tribunal. The procedure for allowing the operator to make representations has been expanded and the right to apply to the Tribunal is new.

Designated Territory Schemes

12.32 The power of designation is vested in the Treasury and the Treasury must be satisfied that the law and practice in the relevant territory affords to

---

[32] FSMA, s. 264.
[33] FSMA, s. 270.
[34] FSMA, s. 272.
[35] FSMA, s. 266.
[36] FSMA, Sched. 5.

United Kingdom investors at least "equivalent" protection to a comparable authorised United Kingdom scheme and (a new requirement in section 270(2)(b) of the FSMA) that there is, or will be, adequate co-operation with the regulatory authorities in the relevant territory.[37] So far only Jersey, Guernsey, the Isle of Man and Bermuda have, in relation to specific categories of scheme, been so designated.

Application for approval of the scheme is made to the FSA and the FSA has two months in which to object (previously it was four months). If the FSA objects, the operator may apply to the Tribunal. As with Member State Schemes, detailed regulation of the scheme is left to the home state but the operator must maintain an address for service of notices and certain other facilities in the United Kingdom. Unlike Member State Schemes, the operator will require separate authorisation if conducting investment business in the United Kingdom, for example selling shares or units in the scheme where an exemption does not apply.

Individually Recognised Schemes

12.33 These are other schemes managed outside the United Kingdom where the FSA is satisfied that the protection for participants in the scheme, the scheme's constitution and management and the powers and duties of the operator and (if applicable) trustee or depositary, are all "adequate" having regard to comparable United Kingdom authorised schemes.

The scheme must be an open-ended investment company or, failing that, the operator must be a body corporate. In any event, the scheme must be open-ended in the same sense as a United Kingdom authorised scheme but with the difference (newly introduced by section 272(15) of the FSMA) that the requirement for participants to be able to redeem their units at a price related to net asset value or to be able to sell their units on an investment exchange at a similar price is expressly stated not to imply that such redemption or sale must be immediately on demand.

The operator and (if applicable) trustee or depositary must each be an authorised person or must at least be a fit and proper person to act as such and must be willing and able to co-operate with the FSA in relation to the sharing of information, etc. The operator must also maintain an address for service of notices etc. and certain other facilities in the United Kingdom. However, the requirement in section 88(5) of the 1986 Act that the operator has a representative in the United Kingdom who is an authorised person and authorised to act generally on behalf of the operator has been omitted (perhaps because such a general authority could have adverse tax consequences).

The period in which the FSA must determine a complete application and an incomplete one is the same as for an authorised United Kingdom unit trust, namely 6 months and 12 months respectively after submission of the relevant application. This is a new provision as, under the 1986 Act, there was no time limit for Individually Recognised Schemes. Unlike with a Member State Scheme or a Designated Territory Scheme, where regulation is largely left to the home state or territory, the procedures in the event of a refusal or withdrawal of recognition, or for the giving of directions, by the FSA or on a proposed change of operator or (if applicable)

---

[37] However, this provision has now been proscribed by the World Trade Organisation: Standing Committee A (December 2, 1992, c. 1122).

trustee or depositary, and the right for the operator to apply to the Tribunal, are similar for purposes of an Individually Recognised Scheme to those applicable to authorised United Kingdom unit trust schemes discussed earlier.

The above requirements for recognition are generally considered to be difficult to satisfy and, so far, very few Individually Recognised Schemes have been recognised.

FUTURE DEVELOPMENTS

12.34 In February 2001, the CIS Sourcebook was published[38] in what was supposed to be its "final" draft form. A small number of amendments, principally in relation to warning notices and decision notices, were published in March 2001[39] and these were incorporated in a revised version published in June 2001.[40] However, certain issues relating to collective investment schemes are still being considered by the FSA which could give rise in due course to further changes.

For example, as noted above, mandatory single pricing for authorised unit trusts is contemplated and the existing rules relating to single pricing for ICVCs are being reviewed. Also, following an earlier consultation paper in June 1998,[41] the FSA intends to produce formal proposals for consultation permitting limited issue and limited redemption funds.

The FSA has stated that it intends to keep the rules relating to collective investment schemes under review and would be willing to amend them if necessary in the light of developments in the market and consumer needs. It has also said that it will consider whether the product regulation regime might be simplified by, for example, relying more on principles than detailed rules.

On the international front, the European Commission has published certain proposals for the amendment of the UCITS Directive (*e.g.*, to cover a wider range of funds and to relax certain of the investment limitations) which, if implemented, would require consequential amendments to the rules.

Therefore, as a result of both domestic and international developments, the rules relating to collective investment schemes are unlikely to remain static.

---

[38] FSA, *Policy Statement: The Collective Investment Scheme Sourcebook* (February 2001).
[39] FSA, *Consultation Paper 85: Collective Investment Scheme Sourcebook— Consultation on warning and decision notices in relation to applications* (March 2001).
[40] *The Collective Investment Scheme Sourcebook Instrument 2001.*
[41] FSA, *Consultation Paper 11: Limited issue and limited redemption funds.*

CHAPTER 13

Enforcement

WILSON THORBURN

INTRODUCTION

13.01   The Act imposes on the FSA statutory obligations to monitor compliance with the requirements imposed by the Act[1] and enforce the provisions of and made under the Act.[2] This Chapter outlines the powers which the FSA has to enforce the provisions of the Act. The FSA views the proportionate and effective use of its enforcement powers as playing an important role in helping it to achieve its statutory obligations and in particular maintaining public confidence in the regulatory regime.

The FSA has also professed a concern to ensure that its powers are exercised in a manner that is transparent, proportionate and consistent and to this end has published the *Enforcement Manual* ("ENF")[3] which sets out its policy and criteria governing the exercise of its powers.

INVESTIGATIONS

Referral to Enforcement

13.02   In some circumstances, matters will be referred directly to the enforcement division of the FSA. Often, however, matters which might give rise to disciplinary proceedings will first be uncovered by the FSA in exercising its supervision functions. During the consultation process, concerns were expressed as to the factors and processes that would be applied in deciding to refer a matter from supervision to enforcement. The FSA has given some guidance on this[4] and has stated that it recognises the need to ensure that its internal interface processes are consistent and fair. The FSA has indicated that firms will normally be informed by their usual supervisory contact that a matter has been referred to the enforcement division. It appears therefore that this will be an after the fact notification so that there will be no notification to a firm that the FSA is considering the referral of a matter, nor therefore any formal ability to make submissions to the FSA so as to influence its decision. The pre-conditions for the appointment of investigators are dealt with below and the FSA has indicated that where the statutory preconditions are satisfied investigators will generally be appointed shortly after a case has been referred to the enforcement division.

---

[1] FSMA, Sched. 1, para. 6(1).
[2] FSMA, Sched. 1, para. 6(3).
[3] See Enforcement Manual Instrument 2001.
[4] FSA *Policy Statement: Regulatory processes manuals*, (May 2001), para. 3.5.

General power to require information

13.03 The FSA has a general power[5] to require information and documents from firms. The power can be exercised by the FSA by a notice in writing or by an officer authorised by the FSA. In either case the power applies to information or documents that the FSA reasonably requires in connection with the exercise of its functions under the Act. In addition the FSA may require that the information be verified and documents be authenticated. It may also require an explanation of documents. The power is exercisable in respect of an authorised or formerly authorised firm, persons connected with the firm,[6] certain persons (*e.g.*, operators) in respect of CISs and RIEs and RCHs. This power is the FSA's basic power to require information and will be used by the FSA principally in the supervision context and in the enforcement context prior to the appointment of investigators. Where investigators have been appointed those investigators will have the more extensive powers discussed below.

Investigation powers

13.04 The FSA has two statutory powers to appoint investigators. For ease of understanding these are referred to as the section 167 and section 168 powers. Under section 167, the FSA can appoint persons to carry out general investigations and under section 168, it can appoint persons to carry out investigations in particular cases. The statutory pre-conditions for appointment of persons under these two sections are different as are the powers which the investigators may exercise. The FSA has set out a non-exhaustive list of examples of the types of concern which might prompt it to carry out investigations and thus exercise one of these powers.[7] They are that there are circumstances which suggest that:

- a firm, or an approved person within a firm may have acted in such a way as to prejudice the interests of consumers;

- a firm, or an approved person within a firm may have acted in breach of the requirements of the legislation or rules;

- a firm may no longer meet the threshold conditions or an approved person within a firm may not be a fit and proper person to perform controlled functions;

- a firm may have been used or may be being used for the purposes of financial crime or laundering the proceeds of crime;

- the FSA should be concerned about the ownership or control of a firm including whether a person who has acquired influence over the firm meets the requirements for FSA approval; and

- the conduct of certain types of regulated activities in which a firm is involved are a cause of serious public concern over the way in which these activities are being conducted.

---

[5] FSMA, s. 165.
[6] FSMA, s. 165(11) (connected persons include: a member of the firm's group, a controller of the firm, other members of a partnership of which the firm is a member and officers, managers, employees and agents of corporate firms).
[7] ENF 2.5.5G.

General investigations

13.05 Where the FSA has general concerns about a firm or appointed representative, but the circumstances do not suggest a specific breach or contravention it may appoint investigators under the section 167 power. Investigators will usually be members of the FSA's staff.

The FSA may, where it appears to it that there is good reason for doing so, appoint investigators to conduct an investigation into:

- the nature, conduct or state of the business of an authorised person or of an appointed representative;
- a particular aspect of that business; or
- the ownership or control of an authorised person.

If the investigator thinks it necessary for his investigation he may also investigate the business of a person who is or has at any relevant time been a member of the group, of which the subject of the investigation is a part, or a partnership, of which the subject of the investigation is a member (section 167(2)). In addition, investigators may also be appointed under this power in relation to formerly authorised firms or appointed representatives in relation to business carried on when it or he was an authorised person, or the ownership and control of a formerly authorised person when it was authorised. The section 167 power does not relate to approved persons. It should also be noted that the definition of "business" for the purposes of section 167 is wide and includes all of a firm's business even that part which does not consist of regulated activities.

Specific investigations

13.06 Where circumstances suggest that certain specified contraventions or offences (for instance, a breach of the general prohibition, insider dealing, market abuse, breach of an FSA rule, misconduct by an approved person) have occurred it is likely that the FSA will appoint investigators under the section 168 power, as the investigators' powers are wider than those of investigators appointed under the section 167 power. An investigation which is commenced under the section 167 power may become a section 168 power investigation if it subsequently appears that the requirements of the section 168 power are satisfied. The FSA has indicated that in circumstances where the scope of the investigation changes in this way it will "normally" notify the person under investigation.[8]

Powers of investigators

13.07 Investigators appointed under the section 167 power have the following powers:

- to require the person under investigation or any person connected (section 171(4)) with it or him to attend before the investigator to answer questions

---

[8] ENF 2.5.11G.

or otherwise to provide such information as the investigator may require; and

- to require any person to produce specified documents or documents of a specified description.

These powers may only be exercised to the extent that the investigator considers the question, or provision of information or documents to be relevant to the purposes of the investigation (section 171(3)).

Investigators appointed under the section 168 power have additional powers, but the extent of these depends upon the subsection of section 168 under which they have been appointed. The majority of investigations are likely to be under section 168(4). Such investigators have the powers of section 167 investigators, but in addition, where satisfied that it is necessary or expedient for the purposes of the investigation, have the power to require any person to attend to answer questions or otherwise provide such information as he may require for the purposes of the investigation.

Investigators appointed under section 168(2) (which are broadly investigations into insider dealing, market abuse and breaches of the restrictions on financial promotion or the general prohibition) may in addition if they consider that any person is or may be able to give information which is or may be relevant to the investigation require that person to answer questions, provide information, produce specified documents and give the investigator all assistance in connection with the investigation which he is reasonably able to give (section 173).

In addition, section 175 provides that where the investigator has the power to require production of a document and it appears that the document is in the possession of a third person, the investigator may use that power in relation to the third person.

Restrictions on the FSA's powers

13.08 There are a small number of restrictions on the powers outlined above. Section 413 provides that a person may not be required to produce, disclose or allow inspection of "protected items" which are essentially items benefitting from legal professional privilege.

Banking confidentiality is also preserved save where the person to whom the duty of confidentiality is owed is the subject of the investigation or where the requirement for disclosure is specifically authorised by the FSA.

The Act also deals with the admissibility of statements made to investigators (section 174). It provides that statements made to investigators in compliance with an information requirement cannot generally be used in criminal proceedings in which the person who made the statement is charged with an offence or in market abuse proceedings brought against that person. This restriction does not however apply to proceedings for offences such as making false statements or providing false or misleading evidence. Statements made voluntarily are not subject to this restriction.

The FSA has stated[9] that its investigators may not always use their statutory powers, but that where they do so they will at all times make this clear to those

---

[9] ENF 2.11.2G.

persons to whom their enquiries are addressed. Given the different uses which may be made of voluntary and compelled statements it is important that the FSA does so and that the person under investigation is aware whether any interview is voluntary, compulsory or under caution and the effects of this.

Reports on firms by skilled persons

13.09   The FSA also has a power to require a firm, any other member of its group or a partnership of which it is a member (or a person who at any relevant time has been one of the above) to provide it with a report by a skilled person on any matter in relation to which the FSA has or could require the provision of documents or information under its general information gathering power (section 165). The skilled person must be nominated or approved by the FSA and (although this would appear to follow from the first condition) appear to the FSA to have the skills necessary to report on the matter concerned. The FSA has consulted separately[10] and at some length on the circumstances in which it will exercise this power. The FSA has indicated that it is likely to use this power as opposed to its own investigation powers where its objectives include obtaining expert analysis and/or recommendations for remedial action rather than gathering historic information or evidence. In cases where the investigation is likely to require the use by the FSA of its statutory powers, the FSA is unlikely to require only a report by a skilled person although this may be required in conjunction with the appointment of investigators.

Notification and publicity

13.10   Save in the case of specified circumstances (section 170(3)), the FSA must give persons who are the subject of an investigation written notice of the appointment of an investigator.[11] Such notice must specify the provision under which the investigator is appointed and state the reasons for the investigator's appointment. Notification need not be given of the appointment of an investigator under the section 168 power to investigate insider dealing, market abuse or breaches of the restriction on financial promotion or the general prohibition. Other appointments under the section 168 power need not be notified if doing so would be likely to result in the investigation being frustrated.

Given the general requirement of notification in respect of an investigation it is strange that where there is a change in the scope or conduct of an investigation notice of that change need only be given where in the FSA's opinion the person under investigation is likely to be significantly prejudiced if not aware of the change (section 170(9)). This provision prompted a number of responses during the consultation process, however the FSA has stated[12] that it will not apply an additional or alternative test but will simply apply the statutory test thus only giving notice where it considers it likely that significant prejudice might result from a failure to notify. Those the subject of the investigation should therefore be aware that the initial notification of investigation will only set out the scope of

---

[10] FSA, *Consultation Paper 91: Reports by skilled persons* (May 2001).
[11] FSMA, s. 170(2).
[12] FSA, *Policy Statement, op. cit.* (May 2001), para. 6.5.

investigation at that time and that the scope may well increase or change without notice to them.

Conversely, although the Act does (rather oddly) not require the FSA to provide notification of the termination of an investigation, the FSA has confirmed[13] (as must be right) that it will, where it has notified a person of the commencement of an investigation and subsequently decided to discontinue its investigation, confirm this to the person concerned.

In relation to publicity of investigations the FSA's basic position is that it will not normally make public the fact that it is or is not investigating any particular matter or any of the findings or conclusions of an investigation.[14] In exceptional circumstances, the FSA may, however, publicise the existence of an investigation and examples of such circumstances are set out in the Enforcement Manual.[15]

Preliminary findings letter

13.11   Before considering whether to recommend the initiation of enforcement action the FSA will generally send a preliminary findings letter to the person under investigation. The FSA has indicated that it will normally do this unless it is not practicable to do so, such as in urgent cases. The letter will set out the facts which the FSA considers relevant and will invite the person named to confirm that they are complete and accurate. The FSA will take any response received in time (usually 28 days) into account. Where the FSA decides not to take any further action it will communicate this decision promptly to the person named.

INJUNCTIONS AND OTHER INTERIM RELIEF

13.12   The FSA has two powers to take immediate action in urgent cases. It can apply to the Court for an injunction (interdict in Scotland) either under the statutory provisions in the Act,[16] or under the Court's inherent jurisdiction. It can also use its own initiative power to vary a firm's Part IV permission on an urgent basis.

Injunction applications

13.13   The Act contains two provisions permitting the FSA to apply to the court for injunctions in cases of breaches or likely breaches of the provisions of the Act or rules[17] and in cases of actual or likely market abuse.[18]

Under section 380, the FSA can apply to the court for an injunction against any person (whether authorised or not). Where the court is satisfied that there is a reasonable likelihood that that person will contravene a relevant requirement, or has contravened a relevant requirement and there is a reasonable likelihood that the contravention will continue or be repeated, it may make an order restraining the contravention. Ultimately, of course, an injunction is a discretionary remedy

---

[13] ENF 2.12.7G.
[14] ENF 2.13.1G.
[15] ENF 2.13.3G–2.13.6G.
[16] FSMA, ss. 380 and 381.
[17] FSMA, s. 380.
[18] FSMA, s. 381.

and its grant will therefore always be a question for the Court's discretion. The Court may also make an order requiring the person concerned and any other person who appears to have been knowingly concerned in the contravention to take steps to remedy it. Where the Court is satisfied that any person may have contravened a relevant requirement or have been knowingly concerned in such a contravention it may in addition make a freezing order restraining such persons from dealing with or disposing of their assets.

In this context, a relevant requirement is defined[19] as a requirement imposed by or under the Act or imposed by or under any other Act and whose contravention constitutes an offence which the FSA has power to prosecute under the Act, for instance, insider dealing. The FSA has similar powers in section 381 to apply to the Court for injunctions relating to market abuse.

In addition to the statutory powers[20] to seek asset freezing injunctions, the FSA may ask the Court to exercise its inherent jurisdiction to grant such an order. In such cases the FSA will need to show a good arguable case, but unlike under the statutory provision will not need to show that a contravention has already occurred or may have already occurred.

On the grant of an injunction the party requesting the injunction is usually required by the Court to give a cross undertaking such that if it is subsequently decided that the injunction should not have been granted and its grant has caused loss the applicant will make good that loss. It is worth noting that the FSA (and other law enforcement bodies) are not usually required to give such undertakings.[21]

The FSA has set out at some length[22] the factors which it will take into account when deciding whether to seek an injunction either under its statutory powers or the Court's inherent jurisdiction.

The FSA's own initiative powers to vary a Part IV permission

13.14   In the normal course, the FSA must give notice of its intention to vary a firm's permission. The firm has the right to refer such a decision to the Tribunal and the variation will not take effect until it is no longer open to review. In certain circumstances, the FSA can give notice that its decision to vary a firm's permission will take effect immediately or on a specified date. The FSA may only do so if it reasonably considers it necessary for the variation to take effect immediately (or on the specified date) having regard to the ground on which it is exercising its own initiative power (section 53(3)).

The FSA has indicated[23] that it will consider exercising its own initiative powers as a matter of urgency where it has serious concerns about a firm which need to be addressed immediately and it is appropriate to use its statutory powers immediately to ensure those concerns are addressed. The FSA has given examples of the circumstances likely to give rise to such serious concerns[24] which include:

---

[19] FSMA, s. 380(6).

[20] FSMA, ss. 380(3) and 381(3).

[21] *SIB v. Lloyd Wright* [1993] 4 All E.R. 210.

[22] ENF 6.6.2G.

[23] ENF 3.5.11G.

[24] ENF 3.5.12G.

- information indicating significant loss, risk of loss or other adverse effects for consumers;

- information indicating that a firm's conduct has put it at risk of being used for the purposes of financial crime;

- evidence that the firm has submitted to the FSA inaccurate or misleading information so that the FSA becomes seriously concerned about the firm's ability to meet its regulatory obligations; and

- circumstances suggesting a serious problem within a firm or within a firm's controllers that calls into question the firm's ability to continue to meet the threshold conditions.

The FSA has also set out[25] a list of the factors which it will take into account in considering the urgent exercise of its own initiative power.

DISCIPLINE OF AUTHORISED FIRMS AND APPROVED PERSONS

Introduction

13.15 By far the majority of enforcement proceedings brought by the FSA will be against authorised firms and approved persons. Actions can and will be brought against others in relation to, for example, market abuse and breaches of the general prohibition and such actions are dealt with later in this Chapter. The FSA's general approach to disciplinary proceedings is succinctly set out in the *Enforcement Manual*.

> "Disciplinary measures are one of the regulatory tools available to the FSA. They are not the only tool, and it may be appropriate to address many instances of non-compliance without recourse to disciplinary action. However, the effective and proportionate use of the FSA's powers to enforce the requirements of the Act, the rules and the Statements of Principle will play an important role in buttressing the FSA's pursuit of its regulatory objectives."[26]

This theme that disciplinary measures are but one of the regulatory tools available to the FSA has been a recurring theme in the development of the new regime. Equally however, there can be no doubt that the FSA views disciplinary measures as an important tool in demonstrating that regulatory standards are being upheld.

The remedies available to the FSA as a result of disciplinary action are public statements and censures and financial penalties. In addition where the FSA considers that a firm's continuing ability to meet the threshold conditions or an approved person's fitness and propriety is called into question other measures are available to the FSA including[27]:

---

[25] ENF 3.5.13G.
[26] ENF 11.2.1G.
[27] ENF 11.2.3G.

- variation or cancellation of permission and the withdrawal of a firm's authorisation;

- the withdrawal of an individual's status as an approved person; and

- the prohibition of an individual from performing specified functions in relation to regulated activities.

Private warnings

13.16 In circumstances where the FSA determines that formal disciplinary action is not appropriate, but that nevertheless it has concerns regarding the behaviour of a firm or approved person the FSA may issue a private warning.[28] The FSA considers that this will be helpful in that it will make the firm or approved person aware that they came close to being subject to formal disciplinary action. The FSA may also issue private warnings to persons who are not authorised, for instance, in relation to potential cases of market abuse, or breach of the general prohibition.

Private warnings will invite the person to whom they are addressed to submit comments on it. Private warnings together with any comments received in response to them will form part of the firm's or approved person's compliance history. The FSA will be able to take them into account in considering whether to commence disciplinary action in relation to future breaches. However, if disciplinary action is commenced, prior private warnings may not be taken into account in determining whether a breach has taken place, or in determining the level of sanction, if any, to be imposed.

In addition to private warnings the FSA may also indicate to a firm in ordinary correspondence that it has concerns about a particular aspect of the way it conducts its regulated activities. This will also form a part of a firm's compliance history.

Criteria for disciplinary action

13.17 The FSA has set out[29] a non-exhaustive list of the factors which it will take into account in determining whether to take disciplinary action. These include:

- the nature and seriousness of the suspected breach;

- the conduct of the firm or the approved person after the breach;

- the previous regulatory record of the firm or approved person;

- guidance given by the FSA;

- action taken by the FSA in previous similar cases; and

- action taken by other regulatory authorities.

In considering each case these are the factors which the FSA expects to take into account most often. It has, however, emphasised that it will assess all the

---

[28] ENF 11.3.1G.
[29] ENF 11.4.1G.

circumstances of each case. Whilst the FSA has stated that it will not take disciplinary action for all breaches of requirements and that other regulatory tools may be appropriate in certain cases, the FSA views the enforcement of regulatory requirements through formal disciplinary action as essential to the fulfilment of its statutory objectives.[30]

Action against approved persons

13.18 The FSA has stated[31] that the primary responsibility for ensuring compliance with a firm's regulatory obligations rests with the firm itself and that therefore, normally, the FSA's main focus in considering disciplinary action will be the firm rather than approved persons. Whilst this may be of some comfort nevertheless it will remain the case that approved persons will personally be the subject of FSA disciplinary action. In particular, onerous obligations are placed on those individuals approved for significant influence functions and it is clear that the FSA views them as having a major part to play in ensuring that firms are properly organised so as to comply with their obligations.[32]

The FSA will, however, only take disciplinary action against approved persons where there is evidence of "personal culpability".[33] This will arise where the approved person's behaviour was deliberate or where their standard of behaviour was below that which would be reasonable in all the circumstances; essentially a negligence test. An individual will not be in breach where he has exercised due and reasonable care when assessing information and has reached a reasonable conclusion which he has acted on. The test for personal culpability was the subject of significant comment during the consultation process and as originally drafted referred to behaviour falling below the standard which the FSA would expect. Commentators were concerned that this test would allow the FSA to apply a subjective and not necessarily consistent approach. As a result, the FSA has adopted the more objective standard set out above, although whether in practice there is much difference between the two is a moot point.

The FSA may only bring disciplinary action against an approved person where the statutory test[34] is met; that is, he is guilty of misconduct and the FSA is satisfied that it is appropriate, in all the circumstances, to take action. An approved person will be guilty of misconduct where he has failed to comply with a Statement of Principle, or been knowingly concerned in a breach of a requirement by the firm (section 66(2)). However, the FSA has stated[35] that it will not discipline approved persons simply on the basis of what it calls vicarious liability. In particular, individuals approved for significant influence functions will not be disciplined simply because a regulatory failure has occurred in the part of the business for which they are responsible.

---

[30] FSA, *Policy Statement, op. cit.* (May 2001), para. 6.44.
[31] ENF 11.5.1G.
[32] SYSC.
[33] ENF 11.5.3G.
[34] FSMA, s. 66(1).
[35] ENF 11.5.6G(2).

Statements of Principle and Code of Practice

13.19 The Act permits the FSA to issue Statements of Principle relevant to the conduct expected of approved persons.[36] The FSA has chosen to do so and has issued seven such Statements of Principle. Statements of Principle 1–4 are relevant to all approved persons. Statements of Principle 5–7 are only relevant to those approved persons approved for significant influence functions. The Statements of Principle only apply to the approved person in relation to the performance of his controlled function.

Where it issues Statements of Principle, the FSA is obliged (section 64(2)) to issue a Code of Practice[37] the purpose of which is to help determine whether or not an approved person's conduct complies with the Statements of Principle. The Code of Practice contains examples of conduct which, in the opinion of the FSA would be a breach of a Statement of Principle and sets out some of the factors which the FSA will take into account in assessing an approved person's conduct. The Code does not include any "safe harbours", in other words descriptions of conduct which, if complied with, would insulate an approved person from disciplinary action.

The Code does, however, have what is referred to as "evidential status". This means that conduct at odds with the Code will tend to establish non-compliance with the relevant Statement of Principle, but such a finding is not determinative. It should be noted that the guidance interspersed throughout the Code is not binding and does not form part of the Code. As such it does not have evidential status.

DECISION MAKING

Introduction

13.20 Following consultation on the *Enforcement Manual* and other manuals, the FSA has removed from these all of the material relating to its decision making processes and has placed this in a separate decision-making manual ("DEC").[38] The manual explains and gives guidance on the FSA's decision making and other procedures for giving statutory notices such as warning notices. In addition, the manual covers the FSA's procedures where it decides to apply to the Courts for insolvency orders, injunctions and restitution orders or to prosecute criminal offences. The manual also fulfils the FSA's obligation (section 395) to publish a statement of its procedure for the giving of statutory notices.

The Regulatory Decisions Committee ("RDC")

13.21 The FSA has two types of internal decision making procedures. First, decisions taken by the RDC and secondly, decisions taken by committees of senior FSA staff under executive procedures. In the enforcement context, nearly all relevant decisions will be taken by the RDC. The FSA has set out an explanation of

---

[36] FSMA, s. 64(1).
[37] See Statements of Principle and Code of Practice for Approved Persons Instrument 2001.
[38] See Decision Making Manual Instrument 2001.

the split between decisions to be taken by the RDC and decisions taken under executive procedures.[39]

The RDC is to be a body outside the FSA's management structure and apart from its chairman none of its members will be FSA employees. The members, who will be appointed by the FSA Board, will be composed of current and recently retired practitioners with financial services industry skills and knowledge and other suitable individuals representing the public interest. The RDC is accountable to the FSA Board for its decisions. The decision making manual sets out procedures for meetings of the RDC.[40]

Discipline procedure

13.22   In the majority of cases where the FSA proposes to exercise its powers in the enforcement context, it is obliged to use the warning notice and decision notice procedure.[41] A warning notice gives the recipient details about the action which the FSA proposes to take and about the right to make representations. A decision notice gives the recipient details about the action which the FSA has decided to take.

Warning notice procedure

13.23   Where FSA staff consider that action is appropriate they will recommend to the relevant decision maker (either the RDC or FSA staff under executive procedures) that a warning notice be given. The decision maker can accept the recommendation and give the notice, or decide not to take further action, although a private warning may be given.

A warning notice must[42]:

- be in writing;
- state the action which the FSA proposes to take;
- give the FSA's reasons for the proposed action;
- state whether the recipient is entitled to access to FSA material and if so the nature and extent of the right; and
- notify the recipient of a reasonable period (which may not be less than 28 days) in which he is entitled to make representations to the FSA.

In addition, where appropriate, the warning notice will contain a statement that the mediation scheme is available. This is considered below.

Representations to the FSA

13.24   The FSA has indicated[43] that the period for making representations will normally be 28 days, although the recipient of the notice may request an extension of time by writing to the FSA within 14 days of receiving the notice.

---

[39] DEC 4.1.1G.
[40] DEC 4.2.8G *et seq.*
[41] DEC 2 Annex 1G.
[42] FSMA, s. 387.
[43] DEC 4.4.3G.

Representations may be written and/or oral.[44] If the recipient wishes to make oral representations, he must notify the FSA of this at least five business days prior to the end of the period for making representations. The recipient of the notice may appoint a representative (who need not be legally qualified) to make representations on his behalf.

Decision Notice

13.25 If no representations are received, the matters in the warning notice will be considered to be undisputed and a decision notice will be given accordingly. Where representations are made the decision maker will consider them and will issue a decision notice or a notice of discontinuance as appropriate.

A decision notice must[45]:

- be in writing;

- give the FSA's reasons for taking the action to which it relates;

- state whether the recipient is entitled to access to FSA material and if so the nature and extent of the right; and

- identify any right to refer the matter to the Tribunal and the procedure for doing so.

The action set out in the decision notice may be different from that set out in the warning notice, but must be under the same part of the Act (section 388(2)). If it is decided not to take the action proposed in a warning notice, the FSA is required to give a Notice of Discontinuance (section 389).

Final notice

13.26 The FSA must[46] give a final notice if the matter is not referred to the Financial Services and Markets Tribunal ("Tribunal") within the relevant period or following the outcome of any Tribunal proceedings and appeal. A final notice sets out the terms of the statement, order, penalty or other action to be taken and gives details of when the action takes effect.

Access to FSA material

13.27 In certain cases[47] (including most enforcement actions), the recipients of warning and decision notices will have a right of access to FSA material (section 394). The material concerned is:

- the material on which the FSA relied in taking its decision; and

- any secondary material which in the opinion of the FSA might undermine that decision.

---

[44] DEC 4.4.6G and 4.4.7G.
[45] FSMA, s. 388(1).
[46] FSMA, s. 390.
[47] FSMA, s. 392.

This obligation, which is akin to the disclosure process in civil proceedings, is an entirely new one to the FSA and its predecessor bodies. The ability to view this material will be of assistance in assessing whether to refer the FSA's decision to the Tribunal. However, in the absence of Tribunal proceedings, there are no effective checks on the FSA's compliance with its obligations and the FSA will need to be thorough in identifying the relevant information particularly in relation to the second category.

The right of access is qualified in a number of respects:

- access is not permitted to excluded material (section 394(2));

- access is not permitted to material relating to a case involving another person, if it was only taken into account for comparison purposes (section 394(2)(b)); and

- the FSA may refuse access to particular material if in its opinion allowing access would not be in the public interest or would not be fair having regard to the likely significance of the material to the person concerned and the potential prejudice to the commercial interests of another person which would be caused by the material's disclosure (section 394(3)). In this case, the FSA must give written notice of its refusal and the reasons for it.[48]

Excluded material is defined (section 394(7)) as material which:

- has been intercepted in obedience to a warrant issued under any enactment relating to the interception of communications;

- indicates that such a warrant has been issued or that material has been intercepted in obedience to such a warrant; or

- is a protected item[49] (essentially privileged material).

Where access is refused on the basis that the material concerned is a protected item the FSA must give written notice of this decision and the existence of the protected item.

Third Party Rights

13.28 In those cases where there is a right of access to FSA material there will also be what are referred to as third party rights (section 392). These provide[50] that where a warning notice identifies a person other than the recipient and in the FSA's opinion the notice is prejudicial to that person then that person must be given a copy of the warning notice unless this would be impracticable or the third party has been given or is being given a separate warning notice about the same matter. Other notices issued by the FSA relating to the same matter must also be provided and the third party also has rights to refer the matter to the Tribunal and to obtain access to FSA material.

---

[48] FSMA, s. 394(5).
[49] FSMA, s. 413.
[50] FSMA, s. 393.

Supervisory Notice Procedure

13.29 In certain circumstances,[51] for instance variation of a firm's Part IV permission, the FSA can take action by way of the supervisory notice procedure. Initially a first supervisory notice is issued. The notice must[52]:

- give details of the action;

- the date when the action is to take effect;

- the reasons for the action;

- set out the right to refer the matter to the Tribunal; and

- set out the right to make representations to the FSA.

The FSA will consider any representations received. If the FSA decides to take the proposed action, to take action in a different way or decides not to rescind action that is already effective then a second supervisory notice must be given.

If the FSA has decided to take the action set out in the first supervisory notice or has decided not to rescind action already taken the notice must inform the person named of his right to refer the matter to the Tribunal. If the FSA decides to take action, different from that proposed in the first supervisory notice the second supervisory notice must be in the same form as a first supervisory notice. If the FSA decides not to take action or to rescind action which is already effective, then it must inform the person concerned in writing.

Settlement and mediation

13.30 In the past, the rules of the SROs have provided the opportunity for settlement discussions to take place in order to resolve disciplinary proceedings. This opportunity will remain and the FSA has indicated[53] that settlement discussions may take place on an informal basis following the giving of a warning notice by the FSA. In addition where the warning notice indicates an intention to bring disciplinary action against a person, the mediation scheme will be available where settlement discussions have broken down.

Settlement

13.31 The FSA has indicated that whilst there is no bar to settlement discussions prior to the issue of a warning notice, it believes that such discussions are likely to be less productive until a warning notice is issued.[54] The counter argument to this is of course that the later in the process settlement discussions take place, the more entrenched the parties' respective positions have become and the less likely it is that settlement discussions may succeed.

Should a proposed settlement be reached, its terms will be recorded in writing. This document will set out a statement of facts, any breaches admitted and the

---

[51] DEC 3, Annex 1G.
[52] DEC 3.1.5G.
[53] DEC, App. l, 1.1.1G.
[54] DEC, App. 1, 1.2.1G.

proposed action to be taken. It will then be considered by the RDC who may accept or decline the proposed settlement. If it declines the proposed settlement it may invite the FSA and the person concerned to enter into further discussions to try to achieve a settlement.

A controversial aspect of this procedure is that during its consideration of the proposed settlement the RDC may ask to meet with the FSA staff involved or the person concerned, and may meet with either party without the other being present. During consultation a number of people raised concerns about the possibility of FSA staff meeting with the RDC in the absence of the person concerned. The FSA's response was that the RDC's role is not to adjudicate disputes and its proceedings are not adversarial. The FSA does not therefore consider that this breaches the requirement for separation between its staff and the FSA. Whilst this may be the case some may think this a curious decision by the FSA as it is important that the RDC must not only be independent of the FSA staff, but seen to be so independent.

Mediation

13.32 Where it is not possible to reach an agreed settlement by informal discussions the person concerned may elect to submit the case to mediation. This is a new departure in financial services regulation which mirrors the trend towards alternative dispute resolution encouraged in the new Civil Procedure Rules. The mediation proposals received strong support during the consultation process. They are to be operated for one year as a pilot scheme during which time there will be an ongoing review and evaluation of the scheme.[55]

The mediation scheme will be available only in enforcement cases involving disciplinary matters and market abuse.[56] Some respondents to consultation suggested that the scope should be extended to areas such as fitness and propriety, the exercise of the FSA's own initiative powers (*e.g.*, variation of permission) and criminal cases. The FSA has indicated that it is not at this stage minded to extend the scope of the scheme, but has said this will be kept under review as part of its review of the pilot scheme.[57]

The scheme will be administered by the Centre for Dispute Resolution ("CEDR") which will provide a panel of experienced mediators with suitable expertise and experience. Where a case is referred to mediation the parties will send a joint notice in agreed form to the mediation provider and the secretary to the RDC. The mediation notice will commit each party to use their best endeavours to progress the mediation in a timely manner. There is provision, where a mediation is taking place, to ask the RDC to extend the time for making representations to the RDC in respect of the warning notice in order to permit the mediation to take place. In the first instance, such extension may be a maximum of 14 days although a further extension of 14 days may be granted thereafter. The total extension may not exceed 28 days save in exceptional circumstances.[58]

There is therefore a maximum period of 56 days from issue of the warning notice for informal settlement discussions to take place and fail, to commence a mediation;

---

[55] FSA, *Policy Statement, op. cit.* (May 2001), para. 7.21.
[56] DEC, App. 1 1.4.1G.
[57] FSA, *Policy Statement, op. cit.* (May 2001), para. 7.22.
[58] DEC, App. 1 1.6.3G-1.6.4G.

appoint a mediator, prepare submissions, for the mediation to take place and then, if it is unsuccessful, for representations on the warning notice to be prepared and submitted. This appears to be a rather over ambitious timetable certainly in a case of any significance or complexity and it will be of interest to see how often it is necessary to resort to exceptional circumstances to justify the grant of a longer extension.

Procedure

13.33 The mediation provider will in each case recommend a mediator to the parties. If either party does not agree the proposed mediator, the mediation provider will seek to obtain agreement of the parties to another mediator from the panel. If no agreement is obtained within seven days of the mediation notice, a mediator will be appointed by the mediation provider.[59]

The mediation provider will then liaise with the parties and mediator to agree a date for the mediation and a timetable for the submission of case summaries and exchange of documents. These must be provided to the mediator at least a week before the mediation.

Authority to settle

13.34 The area which provoked most comment during the consultation process was the fact that any proposed settlement arising from a mediation will have to be approved by the RDC. It is normally a key feature of commercial mediations that they are attended by representatives of each party who have full authority to agree settlement terms. However, in FSA mediations, the FSA will be represented by the FSA staff who initially recommended that disciplinary action be taken and they will need to refer any proposed settlement to the RDC. The FSA has indicated that it will endeavour to ensure that relevant members of the RDC are available for consultation by telephone, but even this will only enable an indication of the RDC's view to be given.[60] The FSA has raised the possibility that members or a sub-committee of the RDC may attend the mediation, but at this stage the FSA is not able to confirm whether this will be a practical or possible solution. Again, this is an area which will need to be watched carefully to see whether the mediation process is compromised.

Costs

13.35 Each party will be responsible for half of the mediation costs.[61] The anticipated costs will be invoiced in advance of the mediation. Legal or other costs incurred by either party will be that party's sole responsibility.

The Tribunal

13.36 The Tribunal will bring about a major change in the way in which disputes between the regulator and the regulated are determined. Whereas currently matters such as the discipline of regulated persons and firms are determined by

---

[59] DEC, App. 1 1.7.2G(1).
[60] DEC, App. 1 1.7.9G(2).
[61] DEC, App. 1 1.7.11G(2).

tribunals established under the rules of and administered by the SROs, the Tribunal is to be established under Part IX of the Act[62] and will be administered by and operate under rules prepared by the Lord Chancellor's Department.

The Tribunal will therefore be staffed and operated independently of the FSA. The individual members of the Tribunal will be selected from panels of legally qualified and lay persons appointed by the Lord Chancellor. The Tribunal's permanent staff will also operate as part of and be funded by the Lord Chancellor's Department. This structure is intended to ensure that disputes are resolved by a truly independent body and was no doubt, at least in part, driven by the need to comply with the European Convention on Human Rights ("ECHR"). Indeed, the Guidance Notes to the rules state that they "... aim to be fair and even-handed to all parties, and to be compatible with the European Convention on Human Rights".

A person who receives a decision notice (or a supervisory notice) has the right to refer the FSA's decision to the Tribunal. Under the Act,[63] any such reference must be made within 28 days of the date on which the decision notice was given although the Tribunal may provide an extension to this period on application.

THE TRIBUNAL RULES

Reference notice

13.37   Where a person ("the applicant") refers a matter to the Tribunal he must do so by way of a written notice ("the reference notice"[64]). The reference notice must be filed (and copied to the FSA) so as to be received by the Tribunal not later than 28 days after the date of the FSA notice being referred. On receipt of the reference notice, the secretary of the Tribunal will acknowledge it and usually[65] enter details in the public register.

The applicant may apply to the Tribunal for an extension to the time limit for making a reference. The Tribunal will extend the time limit where it would be in the interests of justice to do so. The FSA has the opportunity to make representations on any such application.

Statement of case

13.38   Within 28 days of receipt of the secretary's acknowledgment of the reference notice the FSA must file and serve (on the applicant) a statement of case which sets out all the matters and facts relied upon by the FSA in support of the action referred, together with the reasons for the referred action and the statutory provisions under which it is taken.[66]

The FSA may seek an extension of the time limit for filing and serving its statement of case. If the FSA fails to file a statement of case within the relevant time period the Tribunal may of its own initiative direct that the FSA file a statement of case by a specified date.

---

[62] FSMA, s. 132 and Sched. 13.
[63] FSMA, s. 133(1).
[64] Financial Services and Markets Tribunal Rules 2001 (S.I. 2001 No. 2476, r.4) ("Tribunal Rules").
[65] Unless a direction to the contrary has been made, see below.
[66] Tribunal Rules 2001, *op. cit.*, r.5.

Applicant's reply

13.39 Within 28 days of receiving the statement of case the applicant must file and serve a reply.[67] The reply must contain the grounds on which the applicant relies, the matters in the statement of case which are disputed and the reasons for disputing them. The applicant may apply for an extension to the period for filing and serving the reply.

Disclosure

13.40 The FSA's statement of case must (rule 5(3)) be accompanied by a list of:

- the documents on which it relies in support of the proposed action; and

- the further material which in the opinion of the FSA might undermine its decision.

The applicant's reply must be accompanied by a list of all the documents on which it relies in support of its case.

Following the filing and service of the applicant's reply the FSA must give disclosure of any further material which might be reasonably expected to assist the applicant's case as disclosed by the applicant's reply and which was not included in the FSA's original list (rule 7). This disclosure must be provided within 14 days of receipt of the applicant's reply.

Lists of documents served need not include (rule 8):

- in the case of the FSA, documents relating to a case involving another person which has been used for comparative purposes only; and

- in the case of either party, documents excluded from legal proceedings by section 17 of the Regulation of Investigatory Powers Act 2000.

In addition, either party may make an application to the Tribunal to permit it not to disclose a document on the ground that its disclosure:

- would not be in the public interest; or

- would not be fair having regard to the likely significance of the document to the applicant in relation to the referred matter and the potential prejudice to the commercial interests of a person other than the applicant which would be caused by disclosure of the document.

Directions

13.41 The Tribunal may give directions to the parties at any time in order to assist it in determining the issues and generally to ensure the just, expeditious and economical determination of the reference (rule 9). The Tribunal may make such directions on its own initiative or the application of either party. Where a party

---

[67] Tribunal Rules 2001, *op. cit.*, r.6.

applies to the Tribunal for directions and the other party objects, the Tribunal need only give the parties an opportunity to make representations if it considers it necessary. The Tribunal will need to ensure that it exercises this power carefully in order to ensure that its procedures are seen as fair. Where the Chairman decides it is appropriate he may hold a pre-hearing review.

The hearing

13.42 The Tribunal may determine the matter without an oral hearing in unopposed cases and where the parties agree (rule 16). Otherwise, there will be an oral hearing.

The hearing will normally be in public, but there is provision for all or part of the hearing to be held in private in certain circumstances. The procedure at the hearing will be determined by the Tribunal but the parties will be entitled to (rule 19):

- give evidence;
- call witnesses;
- question any witnesses; and
- address the Tribunal.

Evidence may be admitted by the Tribunal whether or not it would be admissible in a court of law.

Decisions of Tribunal

13.43 The Tribunal's decisions are public although where all or part of the hearing is in private all or part of the decision may be kept private (rule 20).

Costs

13.44 Unlike tribunal proceedings before the SROs, the Tribunal will have the ability to make a costs order against either party (rule 21). The making of a costs order is in the discretion of the Tribunal, but it shall not make an order without giving the paying party an opportunity to make representations. The Tribunal may either fix a sum for costs itself or order that the costs be assessed by an appropriate court official. It will be interesting to see whether the ability for a successful applicant to receive his costs from the FSA encourages more Tribunal cases to be brought than has been the case in the past.

Appeals

13.45 The Tribunal's decision may be appealed to the Court of Appeal[68] (or Court of Session in Scotland), but permission is required. An application for permission may be made at the hearing or within 28 days of the decision. If the Tribunal refuses permission the applicant may seek permission from the Court of Appeal or Court of Session.

---

[68] FSMA, s. 137.

ACTIONS WHICH CAN BE TAKEN BY THE FSA

Disciplinary measures

13.46   The two potential disciplinary measures available to the FSA in disciplinary proceedings against firms or appointed persons are[69]:

- public statements and censures; and

- financial penalties.

Other measures are available to the FSA where it is necessary to take protective or remedial action (other than disciplinary action) or where a firm's continuing ability to meet the threshold conditions or an approved person's fitness and propriety is called into question. These include[70]:

- variation or cancellation of permission and the withdrawal of a firm's authorisation;

- the withdrawal of an individual's status as an approved person; and

- the prohibition of an individual from performing regulated activities.

The subject of action by the FSA is however unlikely to make technical distinctions between disciplinary action and other action. In any event, the two are not mutually exclusive and the FSA may well take disciplinary action in conjunction with other enforcement action.

Public statements and censures

13.47   The FSA may issue a public statement or censure in four circumstances[71]:

- the FSA may issue a public censure on a firm where it considers that the firm has contravened a requirement imposed on it by or under the Act (section 205);

- the FSA may issue a public statement of misconduct on an approved person[72] where it considers that he is guilty of misconduct;

- the FSA may issue a public statement[73] where a person has engaged in market abuse; and

- the FSA may issue a public statement[74] where there has been a contravention of the listing rules.

Where the FSA proposes to issue a public statement or censure it must follow the warning notice and decision notice procedure.

---

[69] ENF 11.2.2G.
[70] ENF 11.2.3G.
[71] ENF 12.1.1G.
[72] FSMA, s. 66.
[73] FSMA, s. 123.
[74] FSMA, s. 91.

Despite the potential reputational damage, public statements are regarded by the FSA and generally as a less serious penalty than a fine. The FSA has set out[75] a list of factors which it will consider in determining whether it is appropriate to issue a public statement or censure.

Financial Penalties

13.48 The FSA may impose a financial penalty in the same circumstances in which it can issue a public statement or censure.

With the exception of certain penalties for late returns the FSA does not propose to adopt a tariff of penalties for different types of contravention as it considers that there will be very few cases in which all the circumstances are essentially the same. Instead the FSA will consider all the relevant circumstances of a case when determining the level of financial penalty. The FSA has set out a list of factors which it will take into account in determining the level of any financial penalty.[76]

Where the FSA proposes to impose a financial penalty it must follow the warning notice and decision notice procedure.

Variation of permission

13.49 The FSA may on its own initiative vary a firm's Part IV permission in three circumstances[77]:

- where it appears to the FSA that[78]:

  — the authorised person is failing or likely to fail to satisfy the threshold conditions;

  — the authorised person has failed during a period of at least 12 months to carry out a regulated activity for which he has a Part IV permission; or

  — it is desirable to exercise the power in order to protect the interests of customers or potential customers.

- where a person has acquired control over a United Kingdom authorised person who has a Part IV permission and that it appears to the FSA that the likely effect of the acquisition of control on the authorised person or on any of its activities is uncertain;[79]

- in support of an overseas regulator.[80]

Where the FSA proposes to vary a firm's Part IV permission it must follow the supervisory notice procedure. The FSA's own initiative power (and its use of this power in support of an overseas regulator) includes a power to cancel a firm's permission. Where the FSA proposes to cancel a firm's permission it must follow the

---

[75] ENF 12.3.
[76] ENF 13.3.3G.
[77] For a further disussion on this see Chapter 4, para.4.06.
[78] FSMA, s. 45.
[79] FSMA, s. 46.
[80] FSMA, s. 47.

warning notice and decision notice procedure. The FSA has set out its policy as to the variation of a firm's permission.[81]

Cancellation of permission

13.50   The FSA will consider cancelling a firm's permission in two main circumstances[82]:

- where the FSA has very serious concerns about a firm or the way its business is or has been conducted; and

- where the firm's regulated activities have come to an end and it has not itself applied for cancellation of its permission.

The FSA's power to vary a permission can be used in urgent cases. Its power to cancel a firm's permission can only be used following the warning notice and decision notice procedure, any subsequent referral to the Tribunal, and any appeal. In some circumstances the FSA may use its power to vary a permission on an urgent basis and subsequently go on to cancel it.

Withdrawal of approval

13.51   Where the FSA considers that an approved person is no longer a fit and proper person to perform the function to which his approval relates it may withdraw his approval (see paragraph 5.08 above).[83] Where the FSA proposes to withdraw an approval it must follow the warning notice and decision notice procedure. In addition, the FSA must give interested parties (essentially the approved person's employer) a copy of its decision notice where it proposes to withdraw an approval. Interested parties have an independent right to refer the FSA's decision to the Tribunal. The FSA has set out[84] a list of factors which it will take into account in considering whether to withdraw an approved person's approval.

Where the information available to the FSA casts doubt on a person's fitness and propriety to be involved in regulated activity conducted by firms generally, the FSA may consider making a prohibition order against him as well as withdrawing his approval.

Prohibition of individuals

13.52   All individuals whether or not they are approved may be subject to a prohibition order. A prohibition order may prohibit the individual concerned from carrying out specified functions in relation to regulated activities, or all regulated activities and may apply to specified classes of firms or all firms. The FSA has indicated[85] that it will use this power where it considers that an individual presents

---

[81] ENF 3.5.
[82] ENF 5.5.1G.
[83] FSMA, s. 63(1).
[84] ENF 7.5.2G.
[85] ENF 8.1.2G.

such a risk to consumers or to confidence in the market generally that it is necessary either to prevent him from carrying out any function in relation to regulated
activities or from being employed by any firm, or to restrict the functions which he
may carry out or the type of firm by which he may be employed.

The FSA has identified three general circumstances in which it will consider
using this power in respect of approved persons:

- where the person has shown a lack of honesty, integrity or financial soundness which represents a serious danger to consumers, firms or the market in
  general which cannot be adequately dealt with in another way;

- where the person has displayed such a serious lack of competency or training that consumers, firms or the markets in general are at risk; and

- where a person has been repeatedly disciplined for conduct which would
  not on its own warrant a prohibition but has not altered his conduct in light
  of those proceedings or has continued to carry out controlled functions for
  which he no longer has approval.

In respect of individuals who are not approved persons, a prohibition order may
be appropriate where persons have shown themselves to be unfit to carry out
functions in relation to regulated activities. It is a criminal offence to carry out a
function in breach of a prohibition order.

Where the FSA proposes to issue a prohibition order it must follow the warning
notice and decision notice procedure. The FSA has set out factors which it will take
into account in considering whether to make a prohibition order.[86]

Variation or revocation of prohibition orders

13.53   At any time after a prohibition order has been made the individual may
apply to the FSA to have the order varied or revoked.[87] In considering such an
application, the FSA will consider all relevant circumstances. The FSA will not
generally grant an application to vary or revoke a prohibition order unless it is satisfied that the proposed variation will not result in a reoccurrence of the risk to
consumers or confidence in the financial system that resulted in the order being
made. The FSA will not revoke a prohibition order unless satisfied that the individual is fit to carry out functions in relation to regulated activities.

Where the FSA proposes to refuse an application for variation or revocation of a
prohibition order it must follow the warning notice and decision notice procedure.

Restitution and redress

13.54   The FSA has powers to:

- apply to the court for a restitution order where a person (whether authorised or not) has breached a requirement of the Act or been knowingly

---

[86] ENF 8.5.2G.
[87] ENF 8.9.1G.

concerned in such a breach[88] or has engaged in, required or encouraged others to engage in, market abuse[89];

- require restitution by a firm which has contravened a requirement of the Act or been knowingly concerned in such a contravention[90]; and

- require restitution where a person (whether authorised or not) has engaged in or encouraged others to engage in market abuse.[91]

These powers will be used principally to obtain redress for consumers. The FSA has indicated[92] that the circumstances in which it is likely to use its powers to obtain restitution for market counterparties will be limited. Therefore, for instance, where a firm has mis-sold ISAs to consumers the FSA is likely to seek restitution for those consumers, but where an approved person has, in breach of Statement of Principle 3[93] (high standards of market conduct) artificially inflated the price of a share, the FSA is unlikely to seek compensation for market counterparties who have bought at the artificially inflated price.

The FSA has set out[94] the factors which it will consider in determining whether to exercise these powers. In addition, it will also consider other ways in which those who have lost might obtain redress. During the consultation process, some suggested that where investors were in a position to bring their own legal proceedings to recover losses the FSA should not consider exercising its restitution powers. The FSA's view is that this would not be appropriate and that in certain circumstances it will be appropriate for it to exercise its powers rather than requiring individuals to take their own proceedings. For example, where a particular practice which is widespread in the industry has resulted in restitution claims it will be more cost effective for the FSA to take action on behalf of all investors involved.

Insolvency proceedings

13.55 The FSA's insolvency powers relate to currently or previously authorised persons (firms), current or previous appointed representatives and those who are carrying on or have carried on a regulated activity in contravention of the general prohibition. Under the Act, the FSA has powers to:

- seek Administration Orders[95];

- present a petition for a winding-up[96];

- be heard in the voluntary winding-up of an authorised person (other than an insurance company carrying on long term insurance business)[97]; and

---

[88] FSMA, s. 382.
[89] FSMA, s. 383.
[90] FSMA, s. 384(1).
[91] FSMA, s. 384(2).
[92] ENF 9.3.2G.
[93] See para. 9.05 for further discussion.
[94] ENF 9.6.
[95] FSMA, s. 359.
[96] FSMA, s. 367.
[97] FSMA, s. 365.

- present a petition for the bankruptcy of an individual (who is or has been an authorised person or who is in breach of the general prohibition) (sequestration of the estate of an individual in Scotland)[98] where an individual appears to be unable to pay or have no reasonable prospect of being able to pay a regulated activity debt.

The FSA has indicated[99] that it will take full account of the principle that recourse to the insolvency regime is a step to be taken for the benefit of creditors as a whole and will take full account of the fact that the court will have regard to the public interest when considering whether to windup a body on the just and equitable ground. When considering whether to exercise its insolvency powers the FSA will consider all the facts of each particular case including the other powers available to it and consumers under the Act and other legislation. The FSA's policy in relation to exercising these powers has been set out by the FSA.[1]

The FSA also has powers:

- to challenge company and individual voluntary arrangements[2];

- to apply to the court for orders against debt avoidance[3];

- to be informed of and heard on third party petitions[4]; and

- to be involved in insolvency regimes (*e.g.* administrations, winding-ups and receiverships.[5]

Intervention against incoming firms

13.56 In certain circumstances, the FSA has the power[6] to intervene against incoming firms, that is EEA or Treaty firms. In such cases the FSA may be entitled to impose any requirement which it would be entitled to impose when varying an authorised person's Part IV permission.

Where the FSA proposes to intervene against an incoming firm it must use the supervisory notice procedure. In addition, in certain cases, the FSA must adopt an additional procedure for requiring the firm to remedy the situation.[7]

Disqualification of auditors and actuaries

13.57 The FSA has certain powers[8] to disqualify auditors and actuaries appointed by firms. The FSA has set out its policy on the disqualification of auditors and actuaries.[9] Where it proposes to do so it must follow the warning notice and decision notice procedure.

---

[98] FSMA, s. 372.
[99] ENF 10.4.
[1] ENF 10.6.
[2] FSMA, ss. 356, 357 and 358.
[3] FSMA, s. 375.
[4] FSMA, s. 361.
[5] FSMA, s. 362.
[6] FSMA, ss. 194 and 195.
[7] FSMA, s. 195.
[8] FSMA, ss. 249 and 345.
[9] ENF 17.4.

Collective investment schemes

13.58   The FSA has enforcement powers in relation to:

- Authorised Unit Trusts ("AUTs");

- ICVC's; and

- recognised schemes.

In relation to AUTs, the FSA has powers to:

- revoke the authorisation of an AUT[10];

- give directions[11]; and

- apply to court for the removal of a manager or trustee or the winding-up of an AUT.[12]

The FSA has similar powers in relation to ICVCs.[13]
In relation to recognised schemes, the FSA has powers to:

- suspend promotion of a scheme constituted in another EEA state[14];

- revoke recognition of a scheme[15]; and

- give directions.[16]

Where the FSA proposes to exercise any of these powers it must follow the supervisory notice or warning and decision notice procedures as appropriate.[17]

Disapplication Orders against members of the professions

13.59   Members of designated professional bodies (for instance, The Law Society) are permitted to carry on certain regulated activities under supervision and regulation by their professional body and as such may be entitled to an exemption from the general prohibition.[18]

The FSA has the power under section 329 to disapply this exemption if it appears to the FSA that the person concerned is not a fit and proper person to carry on regulated activities under the exemption. Where the FSA proposes to exercise this power it must use the warning notice and decision notice procedure.

---

[10] FSMA, s. 254.
[11] FSMA, s. 257.
[12] FSMA, s. 258.
[13] Open-ended Investment Companies Regulations 2001 (S.I. 2001 No. 1228).
[14] FSMA, s. 267.
[15] FSMA, s. 279.
[16] FSMA, s. 281.
[17] ENF 16, Annex 1G.
[18] FSMA, s. 327.

Market abuse

13.60 The provisions relating to market abuse and the ability for the FSA to take enforcement action in respect of it are dealt with in Chapter 8, above.

Criminal offences

13.61 The FSA has the power to prosecute criminal offences arising under the Act (section 401). In addition, the FSA has the power to prosecute insider dealing under Part V of the Criminal Justice Act 1993 and breaches of the money laundering regulations (section 402). The FSA's prosecution powers are limited to England, Wales and Northern Ireland. The Crown Office is the prosecuting authority in Scotland.

The FSA's general policy is to pursue criminal prosecution in all appropriate cases. In considering whether a case is appropriate for criminal prosecution the FSA will apply the Code for Crown Prosecutors. In relation to breaches of the money laundering regulations, the FSA will also have regard to whether the person concerned has complied with the Guidance Notes for the Financial Sector produced by the Joint Money Laundering Steering Group.[19] The FSA may take civil proceedings in conjunction with criminal proceedings.

The Code of Crown Prosecutors contains two principal tests. In each case the FSA must consider whether:

- there is sufficient evidence to provide a realistic prospect of conviction ("the evidential test"); and

- having regard to the seriousness of the offence and all the circumstances, criminal prosecution is in the public interest ("the public interest test").

In some cases, the FSA may decide to issue a formal caution rather than to prosecute an offender.[20] In such cases, the FSA will follow the Home Office Guidance on the cautioning of offenders.[21] The FSA will not issue a caution unless satisfied that:

- there is sufficient evidence of the offender's guilt to give a realistic prospect of conviction;

- the offender admits the offence; and

- the offender understands the significance of a caution and gives informed consent to being cautioned.

European Convention on Human Rights and Fundamental Freedoms

13.62 One of the issues which attracted the most attention during the progress of the Act through Parliament was the compatibility of the FSA's enforcement powers and proceedings with the rights provided by Article 6 and 7 of the ECHR which has now been adopted in the United Kingdom by the Human Rights Act 1998.

---

[19] ENF 15.4.1G.
[20] ENF 15.6.1G.
[21] Home Office Circular No. 18 (1994).

Article 6(1) applies to both civil and criminal proceedings and provides for a fair and public hearing within a reasonable time by an independent and impartial tribunal established by law and the public pronouncement of judgment.

Articles 6(2) and (3) only apply to criminal charges and provide for the presumption of innocence and the minimum rights which apply to criminal charges:

- to be informed promptly, in a language which he understands and in detail, of the nature and cause of the accusation against him;

- to have adequate time and facilities for the preparation of his defence;

- to defend himself in person or through legal assistance of his own choosing or, if he does not have sufficient means to pay for legal assistance, to be given it free when the instances of justice so require;

- to examine or have examined witnesses against him and to obtain the attendance and examination of witnesses on his behalf under the same conditions as witnesses against him; and

- to have the free assistance of an interpreter if he cannot understand or speak the language used in court.

Article 7 provides that a person may not be held guilty of a criminal offence on account of any act or omission which did not constitute a criminal offence under national or international law at the time when it was committed.

Clearly, all of these rights will be relevant in respect of criminal offences prosecuted by the FSA. After much debate as to whether the market abuse regime is criminal or civil in nature the Government, although not conceding that the market abuse regime was criminal, granted concessions relating to the admissibility of statements, the provision of safe harbours in the Code and the availability of legal assistance before the Tribunal in order to ensure that the market abuse regime would comply with the Convention.

Despite some suggestions to the contrary, the Government has always considered the FSA's other enforcement powers to be civil in nature and following the decision of Morison J. in R. v. The Securities and Futures Authority, ex p. Fleurose,[22] it appears clear that the Courts would, if asked, reach the same conclusion and therefore only the protections of Article 6(1) will apply to such proceedings.

---

[22] Unreported, April 26, 2001.

CHAPTER 14

Regulation of the Market Infrastructure: Investment Exchanges and Clearing Houses

WILLIAM CHALK

INTRODUCTION

14.01   The Act has superseded Chapter IV of Part I of the 1986 Act in relation to the regulation and accreditation of Recognised Investment Exchanges ("RIEs") and Recognised Clearing Houses ("RCHs") through which the majority of all securities are issued and traded in the United Kingdom.

The FSA retains its responsibility to ensure that all RIEs,[1] continue to meet the recognition requirements and obligations laid down in the 1986 Act, and now Part XVIII of the Act. The transfer of the Competent Authority function from the London Stock Exchange (the "LSE") to the FSA has not affected this responsibility and, in fact, the role of the FSA has expanded. Whereas previously, recognised body status could only be granted by the FSA to those exchanges with a physical presence in the United Kingdom, the FSA has now assumed jurisdiction from the Treasury in relation to overseas investment exchange applicants as well.

It is important to appreciate the distinction between the "recognised body" regime and the "authorised persons" regime (dealt with in Chapter 4, above). Under the 1986 Act and the FSMA, recognised bodies are exempt bodies[2] operating under their own separate regime. This permits them to perform certain activities which would otherwise require them to become authorised persons.[3] Recognised bodies are regulators in their own right, making rules governing the conduct of their constituent members and monitoring and ensuring compliance with those rules. Although they are overseen by the FSA, the FSA has no power to make rules applying to recognised bodies other than in relation to notification rules. The FSA may only give guidance on the interpretation it proposes to follow in respect of each recognition requirement and the factors it is likely to consider in assessing a recognised body's compliance with a recognition requirement.[4] In

---

[1] A full list of current RIEs and RCHs is set out Appendix 3.
[2] FSMA, s. 285(2).
[3] See the 1986 Act, ss. 36(1) and 38(1); and FSMA, ss. 285(2) and (3). In the Treasury's *Consultation Paper "The Financial Services and Market Bill: A Consultation Document"* (July 1998), it was announced that these special arrangements would continue and RIEs/RCHs would retain their exempt status.

contrast, authorised persons are subject to the rules made by the FSA, regulating the conduct of their regulated activities. Further advantages in recognised body status lie in the immunity granted to each body and their employees for acts or omissions in the conduct of their regulatory functions[5] and in the fact that senior staff do not have to become "approved individuals".[6]

THE IMPACT OF THE ACT ON THE RIE/RCH REGULATORY REGIME

Overview of legislative changes

14.02   The legislation, including provisions concerning recognition and revocation of recognised body status, in relation to United Kingdom investment exchanges and clearing houses was largely contained in sections 36 to 39 of the 1986 Act, with the main body of the recognition requirements contained in Schedule 4 of the 1986 Act (as amended by The Traded Securities (Disclosure) Regulations 1994).[7] The provisions relating to overseas exchanges and clearing houses were laid down in section 40 of the 1986 Act. Default rules,[8] being those rules applicable in the event that a member of an investment exchange or clearing house becomes unable to meet its obligations in respect of "market contracts", were contained in Parts I and II of Schedule 21 to the Companies Act 1989 for United Kingdom exchanges and clearing houses and in Part III of Schedule 21 for their overseas equivalents. The overall regime of competition scrutiny relating to recognised body status was contained in Part XIV of the 1986 Act.[9]

Part XVIII of the Act largely carries forward the body of the old regime. In addition, the Act empowers the Treasury to make regulations setting out the requirements which must be satisfied in order for an investment exchange or clearing house to become and retain recognised body status[10] and, as a result, the "RIE Regulations"[11] were laid before Parliament on April 10, 2001. The RIE Regulations contain the recognition requirements and default rules for both United Kingdom investment exchanges and clearing houses and, again, largely reproduce Schedule 4 of 1986 Act, as amended. The RIE Regulations do, however, contain certain new requirements which are discussed later in this Chapter. The Act also deals with the procedural aspects of the grant and revocation of recognition and competition scrutiny, previously contained in the 1986 Act, as well as the entirety of the recognition requirements for overseas investment exchanges and clearing houses.

---

[4] FSA, *Consultation Paper 39*, para. 5.14.
[5] FSMA, s. 291(1). This was initially not the case in the early stages of the legislation.
[6] Market infrastructure providers may elect to function as recognised bodies or as authorised persons; there is no requirement in law to act in one or other capacity.
[7] The actual procedures relating to applications for grants, refusals and revocations of recognition were contained in ss. 9–11 of the 1986 Act. The full reference for the statutory instrument is the Traded Securities (Disclosure) Regulations 1994 (S.I. 1994 No. 188).
[8] These prevent liquidators from attempting to unwind contracts made through RIEs or RCHs.
[9] 1986 Act, ss. 119–120 and 122–123.
[10] FSMA, s. 286.
[11] The Financial Services and Markets Act 2000 (Recognition Requirements for Investment Exchanges and Clearing Houses) Regulations (S.I. 2001 No. 995).

The RIE and RCH Sourcebook

14.03   One way in which the regime arguably has been enhanced is by the publication of the RIE and RCH Sourcebook (the "Sourcebook"),[12] which now forms part of the FSA's Handbook.[13] It is based on the FSA's interpretation of the statutory provisions governing recognised bodies as well as the RIE Regulations, the proposed Code of Market Conduct in respect of market abuse and other materials including the Regulated Activities Order.[13a] In addition, it consolidates all of the FSA's guidance and, in particular, guidance in relation to the FSA's new powers to give directions, its new role approving and overseeing overseas bodies and the new notification rules.[14]

The Sourcebook is divided into chapters which deal in turn with recognition requirements (REC 2), notification rules (REC 3), supervisory practice and procedure by the FSA (REC 4), applications for recognition by both United Kingdom (REC 5), overseas exchanges and clearing houses (REC 6) and fees (REC 7). In each case, the Sourcebook sets out on a clause by clause, regulation by regulation, basis the legislative framework of each of the provisions[16] and, in relation to each clause or regulation, provides the FSA's guidance. It is stressed throughout that the FSA does not regard standard approaches as the only way in which any requirement or obligation can be met and actively encourages applicants or recognised bodies to discuss alternative approaches with it. The FSA's guidance is not binding on recognised bodies.[17]

Despite the fact that the FSA is required to issue this guidance, concern has been expressed that the Sourcebook will lead to recognised bodies being treated more like authorised persons, with less recognition of their relative autonomy as exempt persons under the Act; that this is symptomatic of a failure by the FSA to acknowledge the regulatory role performed by recognised bodies; and that the FSA has over-concentrated on commercial matters which are not its concern. It remains to be seen whether these criticisms have any basis; indeed, the FSA has expressly stated that it does not expect a significant increase in the regulatory burdens on recognised bodies as a result of the introduction of the Sourcebook.[18]

---

[12] The abbreviation and/or "module" for the Sourcebook within the FSA Handbook is "REC" and is used to signify references within the Sourcebook both by the FSA as well as for the purposes of this Chapter. For example, "REC 1" refers to Chapter 1 of the RIE and RCH Sourcebook.
[13] This "specialist sourcebook" was made by the Recognised Investment Exchange and Recognised Clearing House Sourcebook Instrument 2001 on June 21, 2001 (albeit that REC 7, in relation to fees, was made on July 19, 2001). The only changes made between this version and the "final" text published in April 2001 were of a "minor and technical" nature and included the addition of provisions on methods of notification to ensure consistency with the approach taken elsewhere in the FSA's Handbook (see REC 3.2). The commencement date for REC was September 3, 2001 in relation to applications for recognition, waivers/modifications of notification rules and fees. The commencement date for the rest of REC is December 1, 2001.
[13a] The Financial Services and Markets Act 2000 (Regulated Activities) Order 2000 (S.I. 2001 No. 544).
[14] These new notification rules replace the Financial Services (Notification by Recognised Bodies) Regulations 1995 made by the FSA.
[16] Either from the Act, the RIE Regulations or the Companies Act 1989.
[17] FSA, *Consultation Paper 39*, para. 5.9.
[18] See REC 4.

The RIE Regulations

14.04 The Treasury has set out in the RIE Regulations the requirements which United Kingdom investment exchanges and clearing houses must meet to be, and continue to be, recognised under the Act.[19] The requirements themselves are set out in the Schedule to the RIE Regulations, although the FSA may take into account all relevant circumstances when considering whether recognised body status should be granted.[20] The Regulations also provide that the recognition requirements will be satisfied notwithstanding the delegation of functions to a third party.[21]

Parts I and III of the Schedule to the RIE Regulations set out the recognition requirements relating to investment exchanges and clearing houses respectively.[22] The respective requirements are broadly similar and focus on the sufficiency of financial resources, the fitness of the entity, person or body to perform the designated functions, the existence of safeguards for investors (including satisfactory arrangements for the timely settlement and recording of transactions) and disciplinary and complaints procedures. Investment exchanges must also ensure that appropriate media exist for the dissemination of relevant information to market users (*e.g.* price sensitive information) and that rules are in place to allow it to oblige an issuer to make a disclosure and/or suspend trading of an offending issuer's securities.[23]

The underlying tenet of the requirements is that the body in question must be able and willing to promote and maintain high standards of integrity and orderly and fair dealing by persons using the facilities of the exchange or clearing house. An investment exchange must also limit dealings to investments in which there is a proper market.[24] In addition, a body must be able and willing to co-operate with and share information with the FSA[25] and have sufficient financial resources for the proper performance of its functions.[26] Parts II and IV[27] to the Schedule lay down the default rules required of investment exchanges and clearing houses.[28]

As discussed, the RIE Regulations carry forward the body of the former requirements; however, they are more explicit, allow clearing houses to become recognised bodies without being tied to an investment exchange and allow for more delegation of a recognised body's functions.

---

[19] FSMA. s. 290.

[20] Recognition requirements in relation to investment exchanges and clearing houses are contained in Parts I and II and Parts III and IV respectively of the Schedule to the RIE Regulations.

[21] RIE Regulations, paras 6(2) and 6(3).

[22] Some requirements in Part I to the Schedule to the RIE Regulations refer to "investments", which are defined in reg. 3(1) by reference to s. 22 of the Act. The investments specified for the purposes of that section were contained in Part III of the Financial Services and Markets Act 2000 (Regulated Activities) Order 2001 (S.I. 2001 No. 544).

[23] RIE Regulations, Sched., Pt I, paras 4(2)(c) and 5(2). These provisions largely carry forward the provisions of the Traded Securities (Disclosure) Regulation 1994 (S.I. 1994 No. 188).

[24] *ibid.*, para. 4(2)(b).

[25] *ibid.*, para. 6 and Pt III, para. 20.

[26] *ibid.*, para. 1(1) and Pt III, para. 16(1).

[27] These requirements were previously contained in Pts I and II of Sched. 21 of the Companies Act 1989.

[28] See reg. 8 to the RIE Regulations which means that default rules are only required in relation to types of market contract which are actually relevant to an investment exchange or clearing house. FSMA, s. 286(4) provides that a "market contract" is a contract to which Pt VII of the Companies Act 1989 applies as a result of s. 155 of that Act or a contract to which Pt V of the Companies (No.2) (Northern Ireland) Order 1990 applies as a result of Art. 80 of that Order or any other category of contract prescribed by the Treasury as such (although there has been no such prescription to date).

The principal changes under the Act

U.K. recognised bodies

14.05 **Recognition requirements and default rules.** The default rules for both RIEs and RCHs have been carried across largely unchanged from the Companies Act 1989. There are, however, several new recognition requirements and, while some of these only applied to RIEs in the draft RIE Regulations,[29] they have now been extended to RCHs as well. Whilst the substance of the requirements is set out in the RIE Regulations, guidance in relation to these requirements is set out in REC 2. The guidance emphasises the fact that recognition requirements must be satisfied at all times while a body is recognised and by applicants for recognised body status before recognition is granted. The same standards apply both on initial recognition and throughout the period that recognised body status is held.[30]

New recognition requirements have been introduced in relation to the suitability of the person concerned to perform the recognised functions, the internal systems and controls of the recognised body, access to facilities (*i.e.* membership security), financial crime and market abuse, the provision of custody services by recognised bodies, disciplinary and appeal procedures and provisions relating to the investigation of complaints. A further requirement for RIEs is that the rules of a particular exchange must allow for certain prescribed action to be taken against an issuer of securities to the extent that it has not complied with an obligation of disclosure,[31] including the ability to publish price-sensitive information to the extent that it feels that an issuer has failed to do so. The guidance in the Sourcebook reflects all of these new provisions and also covers those that have been carried forward from the former regime.

The Treasury has been given the ability to permit referrals to the Tribunal from some RIE and RCH disciplinary proceedings in order that disciplinary decisions of recognised bodies are consistent with decisions of the Tribunal (pursuant to Part VIII of the Act).[32]

14.06 **Notification requirements.** The Act empowers the FSA, as opposed to the Secretary of State, to lay down rules requiring recognised bodies to supply it with information.[33] This is in addition to information relating to changes to its core particulars, submitted on its application for recognition. The Act now allows the FSA to waive or modify any of its notification rules on the application of, or with the consent of, the recognised body to the extent that compliance is considered to be unduly burdensome and there is no undue risk to those whom the rules are meant to protect.[34]

The new notification rules and guidance in relation to them are set out in REC 3.

---

[29] Published in February 1999.
[30] REC 2.1.2.
[31] RIE Regulations, Sched., Pt 1, para. 5, reflecting the amendment to Sched. 4 of the 1986 Act by the Traded Securities (Disclosure) Regulations 1994.
[32] See FSMA, s. 300(1) and (2).
[33] FSMA, s. 293(1), see also ss. 293(5)–(7) in relation to changes to particulars which must also be supplied to the FSA (these do not apply to overseas recognised bodies; see FSMA, s. 293(8)).
[34] FSMA, s. 294.

A large number of changes and additional notification obligations have been added to the existing requirements.[35] Indeed, one of the main concerns expressed in response to the draft Sourcebook was that the notification rules required recognised bodies to supply information which was not of proper regulatory interest, was of questionable value to the FSA and, further, was particularly burdensome for recognised bodies to provide. As a result, the FSA has eased some of the burden and refocused its attention at a higher level of a recognised body's operation, for example, now only requiring the provision of information on disciplinary matters relating to certain key individuals as opposed to all officers and employees.[36] Whether these concessions have gone far enough remains to be seen.

14.07 Supervision, revoking recognition and complaints about recognised bodies. The Act extends the power of the FSA by giving it the ability to give directions to, and order specific actions to be taken by, a recognised body to the extent that it thinks that the body has failed or is likely to fail to satisfy any one of its recognition requirements (or, indeed, any other obligation).[37] Whilst the FSA must hear any representations made in response to such directions, there is no formal right of appeal.[38] This ability coincides with the introduction of "risk-based supervision" for United Kingdom recognised bodies; being an approach to supervision which focuses on key risk factors for each supervised entity and, therefore, on their continuing ability to satisfy the recognition requirements or to comply with the Act. In turn, this approach allows the FSA to prioritise risks across the entirety of its regulatory responsibilities and allocate resources accordingly. To this end, the FSA intends to draw up, in consultation with the recognised body, and implement a supervision programme for each body.[39]

The grounds upon which the FSA may revoke a recognition order, being the failure of the recognised body to satisfy the recognition requirements or any other obligation imposed by the Act, have been carried forward from the 1986 Act, as have the procedures for doing so. The substance of the procedures themselves has been extended to the FSA's new power to give directions.[40] If recognition is to be revoked (or, indeed, an application for recognition (see below) is to be refused), the FSA must give written notice of its intention to the body concerned[41] and take such other reasonably practicable steps to bring the notice to the attention of members and publish the notice in a manner which it considers appropriate. [42] The notice, which must state the reasons for the action being taken, must draw the attention

---

[35] Although they largely re-enact the Financial Services (Notification by Recognised Bodies) Regulations 1995.
[36] REC 3.5.
[37] FSMA. s. 296.
[38] Directions are enforceable by injunction (England and Wales) or an order for specific performance (Scotland), see FSMA, s. 296(3).
[39] REC 4.
[40] FSMA, ss. 296 and 298. The time limit for making representations in the face of such an order for revocation (and now in relation to any directions given by the FSA) has been reduced from three to two months—see FSMA, s. 298(4) compared with s. 11(5) of the 1986 Act. A revocation order is not effective for three months after it has been made (unless the RIE or RCH has consented to a shorter time period) and may contain such transitional provisions as the FSA thinks necessary or expedient—see FSMA, s. 297.
[41] FSMA, ss. 290(5) and 298(1)(a).
[42] FSMA, ss. 290(5) and 298(1)(b) and (c).

of those likely to be affected by it to their right to make representations in relation to the order. [43]

REC 4 provides the FSA's guidance on its power to revoke recognition orders, its approach to handling complaints[44] and its new power to issue directions under the Act, as well as under Part VII of the Companies Act 1989 in relation to default proceedings. The guidance given seeks to ensure that the FSA receives sufficient comfort that recognised bodies are continuing to satisfy their recognition requirements and that the FSA's supervisory resources are allocated, and supervisory effort is applied, in ways which reflect the actual risks to the regulatory objectives laid down by the Act.[45]

14.08 Applications for recognition. A body corporate or an unincorporated association may apply for recognition as a United Kingdom recognised body under the Act.[46] The only change to this area is that an application should be made to the FSA as opposed to the Secretary of State. Authorised persons under Part III of the Act may apply for recognition but the principle that it is not possible to be both an authorised person and a recognised body is retained (because under the FSMA one cannot be both an authorised person and an exempt person).

The Act provides that the FSA must pass an applicant's rules, guidance and clearing arrangements (the "regulatory provisions"), together with all such (other) information in its possession[47] as will assist the DGFT in order that he may produce a report on whether any of the applicant's regulatory provisions or practices have a significantly adverse effect on competition or whether they require or encourage exploitation of the strength of a market position.[48] In turn, the DGFT must send a copy of this report to the Treasury, the Commission and the FSA.[49] Once a body has been recognised, the DGFT has the capacity to review its regulatory provisions and practices on the same basis as under section 160 of the Act.

Both the scope of the DGFT's and the Commission's powers are the same as they are in respect to the FSA (as discussed in Chapter 10 above), when reviewing the regulatory provisions and practices of recognised bodies.[50] However, in addition to the two circumstances in which the Commission is required to investigate a report made by the DGFT under section 162, the Commission will also investigate a finding by the DGFT that an applicant body's regulatory provisions are anti-competitive or that they are not but the DGFT requests the Commission to consider the report in any event.[51] Again, the Treasury's powers are essentially the same as under section

---

[43] FSMA, ss. 290(5) and 298(2) and (3).
[44] The approach included in the Sourcebook follows the existing approach taken in this area: the FSA expects complainants to make full use of the internal complaints handling arrangements at the relevant RIE and, where appropriate, of any independent complaints commissioner. The FSA is not a court of appeal but is required to have procedures in place to investigate complaints from a procedural point of view—see FSMA, s. 299.
[45] REC 4.1.3.
[46] FSMA, ss. 287 and 288, reflecting the 1986 Act, Pt I, Chap. III, ss. 37 and 39.
[47] FSMA, s. 303(2).
[48] FSMA, s. 303(3). The interpretation of "significantly adverse effect" in FSMA s. 302 mirrors FSMA, s. 159.
[49] FSMA, s. 303(5).
[50] FSMA, ss. 304 and 306.
[51] FSMA, s. 306.

163 with the only significant difference being that directions under Part XVIII are of a "remedial" nature.[52] This means that the Treasury may only direct the FSA to revoke a recognition order or give such directions to the body in question as specified by the Treasury.[53]

Furthermore, representations under section 310,[54] in contrast to the nature of representations under section 163(8), can be made specifically on the DGFT's report and the Commission's report by the body in question and any other affected person. Indeed, representations can be made on whether and, if so, how the Treasury should make a recognition order or issue a remedial direction.[55]

Most importantly, the Treasury's approval is required before the FSA can make a recognition order and it may override the findings of the DGFT and the Commission albeit only in "exceptional circumstances".[56] To the extent that the Treasury does decide to refuse an application it must take appropriate steps to allow the applicant (and any other affected parties) to make representations.[57] REC 5 sets out guidance for applicants, including the regime of competition scrutiny to which any application will be subject. In addition, for reasons previously noted, sections 311 and 312 disapply Chapters I and II Competition Act prohibitions[58] respectively on a similar basis to section 164.

It should be remembered that even if all of the recognition requirements are met, the FSA is not obliged to grant recognised status but, if it does not, it must follow the same procedure as it would in order to revoke recognised status.[59] It should also be noted that the DGFT has the ability to investigate recognised bodies on an ongoing basis in relation to competition issues.[60]

Overseas recognised bodies

14.09 Recognition facilitates the participation of overseas investment exchanges and clearing houses in the United Kingdom markets. The level of involvement which United Kingdom authorities need to have in relation to the daily affairs of an overseas recognised body is greatly reduced as compared with the authorised persons regime. This is due to the fact that the FSA relies upon the supervisory and regulatory arrangements in the country where the body's head office is situated, although the FSA's new power to issue directions does extend to such bodies.

It is now the FSA, and not the Treasury, that has jurisdiction to grant recognised

---

[52] However, the Treasury will issue a normal direction where it decides to act even though the Commission has found that the adverse effect on competition is justified (s. 308(6)).

[53] FSMA, s. 308(8).

[54] There are three circumstances when representations can be made: when the Treasury is considering whether to (i) turn down an application to be recognised (FSMA, s. 307), (ii) issue a remedial direction where the Commission has found that there is an unjustifiable effect on competition (FSMA, s. 308(2)), and (iii) issue a direction even though the adverse effects on competition are justified but the Treasury, in light of exceptional circumstances, decides to act (FSMA, s. 308(6)).

[55] FSMA, s. 310(2).

[56] FSMA, ss. 290(2) and 307.

[57] FSMA, s. 310.

[58] These exclusions fall away after six months from the day on which the recognition order is revoked (FSMA, s. 311(8)).

[59] FSMA, s. 290(5).

[60] FSMA, s. 305.

status to overseas investment exchanges and clearing houses. REC 6 sets out the recognition requirements (as laid down by the Act) as well as the procedures and competition scrutiny to which an application will be subject. It also details the on–going supervision requirements a body will need to observe.

The recognition requirements themselves carry forward the provisions of the 1986 Act and are the only recognition requirements applicable to overseas recognised bodies.[61] In short, the FSA must be satisfied that investors are afforded protection equivalent to that offered by an equivalent United Kingdom recognised body (effectively meaning that the requirements in the RIE Regulations are brought into play); that the applicant must be willing and able to co-operate with the FSA; that it must be adequately supervised in the country of its head office; and that the applicant and/or its home supervisory authority must be willing and able to share information with the FSA.[62] In addition, a new requirement has been introduced requiring the existence of adequate default rules and procedures in relation to market contracts.[63]

The regulatory regime and guidance issued in this area broadly mirrors the Treasury's former approach and the FSA has stated that it intends to continue to rely heavily on home territory supervision of overseas recognised bodies.[64] However, the Act does require the submission of an annual report to the FSA, the Treasury and the DGFT covering a range of matters related to the special overseas recognition requirements and any competition issues. As a result, the Sourcebook includes a number of notification rules specifying matters and incidents on which the FSA requires information from overseas recognised bodies.[65]

REGULATION OF THE MARKET INFRASTRUCTURE IN THE FUTURE

14.10   In response to the rapid transition to electronic trading and the resultant changes to and fragmentation of the structure of capital markets (including the emergence of alternative trading systems ("ATSs")) the FSA has embarked on a fundamental review of its regulation of market infrastructure as a whole and not just in relation to recognised bodies.[66] The main tenet of this review is to ensure that the benefits brought by electronic trading and ATSs are not undermined by regulation that fails to respond quickly and efficiently enough to accompanying changes in market structure and participant roles but still, above all else, supports market confidence.

The FSA sought views on the regulation of various mechanisms emerging for the trading of "exchange-traded" investments and on how best to deal with potential market fragmentation, leading as it has to the blurring of roles between investment exchanges and authorised persons/firms. It also canvassed opinion on

---

[61] See REC 6.3.1.

[62] FSMA, ss. 292(3)(a),(c) and (d), reflecting the 1986 Act, s. 40(2).

[63] FSMA, s. 292(3)(b).

[64] FSA, *Consultation Paper 39*, Chapter 5, para. 5.52.

[65] FSMA, s. 295. The notification rules in the RIE and RCH Sourcebook are made by the FSA pursuant to FSMA, s. 295(3).

[66] See FSA, *Discussion Paper: "The FSA's approach to regulation of the market infrastructure"* (January 2000) and the FSA, *Feedback Statement on the Discussion Paper* (June 2001).

the increasing concentration and organisation of trading within some "over the counter" markets (ATSs), which have raised issues previously only relevant to exchange-based markets. This, in turn, has lead to its focusing on the reliability and efficiency of central trading mechanisms.

Ultimately, the FSA believes that in order to support market confidence it may be necessary to take greater account of broader trading activity in an investment when considering the regulation of the underlying trading mechanisms. This may lead to the introduction of comparable regulatory requirements for all significant trading mechanisms in a particular market sector, irrespective of whether investment exchange trading systems are involved.

The FSA intends to work closely with other European regulators to develop a "consistent, proportionate and graduated" regulatory approach to regulating all market infrastructure providers ("MIPs", *e.g.* RIEs, RCHs, ATSs, authorised firms, etc.) at the European level. In addition, the FSA is considering implementing its new risk-based approach to supervision as a basis for supervising all MIPs within the existing regulatory structure to ensure that their activities do not jeopardise the "fair, efficient and safe operation of United Kingdom markets".[67] The FSA has also stated that following the completion of FESCO's work[68] on developing common European standards for ATS regulation, the FSA will consider whether it needs to propose new rules and/or guidance for the implementation of these standards in the United Kingdom. The review is on-going.

---

[67] *Feedback Statement*, para. 2.6.
[68] The Forum of European Securities Commissions. At the time of writing, responses to the consultation are currently being reviewed.

CHAPTER 15

Regulation of Lloyd's

JEREMY HILL

INTRODUCTION

15.01 For those who were involved, whether as campaigners for the external regulation of Lloyd's or seeking to preserve the regulatory independence of Lloyd's through self-regulation, there may have been a sense of déjà vu about some of the debate and consultation processes preceding the FSMA as certain of the issues debated at the time of the Lloyd's Act 1982, and again preceding the Financial Services Act 1986, resurfaced.

Regulation of Lloyd's has not proved an easy subject, in part because of the need to avoid prejudicing through too intrusive a regulatory regime the role of Lloyd's as a major world insurance market, employer and contributor to the United Kingdom's invisible earnings. The governance of Lloyd's was scrutinised to some degree at the time of the private Bill which became the Lloyd's Act 1982, but at least the discussions at that time were held against a backcloth in which Lloyd's was relatively free of scandal. By the time of the Financial Services Bill, however, the Lloyd's scandals of the 1980s were well underway with the Howden Affair and PCW and the creation of one of the first action groups of wronged members of Lloyd's (or "Names")—why, angry Names wanted to know, can the activities of Lloyd's underwriting agents escape from the regime of SIB and the SROs under the 1986 Act when other agents in the financial world who handled and invested client money (and, unlike Lloyd's agents, did not have absolute power to take underwriting decisions on behalf of, and pledge the entire wealth of, Names with unlimited personal liability), were subject to regulation and independent regulatory supervision under the 1986 Act?

Although the Names failed to win the argument on that occasion, the massive losses of the late 1980s and early 1990s that nearly brought Lloyd's to destruction (the underwriting years 1988 to 1992 produced losses for Names of £9,502 million equating to an average of 66.2 per cent loss on capital) and the years of action groups, litigation and claims culminating in the Lloyd's Settlement in 1995, seemed likely to ensure that even if it survived, Lloyd's would not escape from external supervision and regulation under the FSMA. The FSA has now stepped into the seat vacated some years ago by the Bank of England as the ultimate regulator of Lloyd's, but with a direct duty to regulate and powers to intervene in Lloyd's which have never before been granted to an external body. Even after the implementation of Part XIX of the FMSA in connection with Lloyd's, Lloyd's own regulatory powers live on, to a significant extent, at least on a day-to-day basis, and the internal committee, regulatory and market system at Lloyd's as run by the Council of Lloyd's remain largely untouched—at least until the FSA may decide to exercise its powers of intervention or Lloyd's fails to implement any of the detailed requirements set out in the new *Lloyd's Sourcebook*[1] ("LLD") proposed by the FSA.

LLOYD'S POSITION IN THE WORLD INSURANCE MARKET

15.02 Before moving on to consider exactly what Lloyd's is, and then considering how Lloyd's fits into the framework of the FSMA, it may be worthwhile to ask the question whether Lloyd's is still of any real significance in the modern global insurance market.

Although direct comparisons between Lloyd's and insurance and reinsurance companies are complicated by Lloyd's three year accounting rules and the fact that Lloyd's results exclude returns on the capital base deposited at Lloyd's whereas insurance companies earn and account for substantial investment income from their underwriting capital, let alone the fact that since part of Lloyd's Chain of security includes the unlimited (and unquantified) assets of its unlimited liability members, the following figures give some indication of the relative significance of Lloyd's:

- for the 2001 underwriting year, Lloyd's had a total underwriting capacity of £11,063 million of which over 80 per cent is provided by corporate Members;

- there were only 2,852 individual Members still underwriting for the 2001 year of account; in 1988 there were 32,433 individual Members;

- in 2000, the United States accounted for 35 per cent of Lloyd's gross premium income (equivalent to U.S.$5.9 billion), exceeding the United Kingdom marketplace for the first time ever;

- Lloyd's free assets exceed £18 billion;

- 68 per cent of FTSE 100 companies and 83 per cent of Dow Jones Industrial Average corporations purchased insurance at Lloyd's in 2000;

- 63 per cent of the capital backing at Lloyd's is provided by major international insurers; and

- Lloyd's was the world's second largest commercial insurer in 1999 with net premiums written of U.S.$9,940 billion; Lloyd's was also the eighth largest reinsurer in the world.

There are certain other fundamentals which place Lloyd's in a stronger position, not least as to influence and reputation, than bare statistics may indicate:

- Lloyd's record for paying valid claims is exemplary; the old adage about each Lloyd's Name being liable in respect of claims on business underwritten by him to the full extent of his wealth, even down to his cufflinks, may no longer be true in the majority of cases (limited liability corporate Names now far outnumber and in terms of underwriting capacity far

---

[1] See Lloyd's Sourcebook Instrument 2001.

outweigh the remaining traditional individual unlimited liability Names)
but even in its darkest days during 1988 to 1992 when Lloyd's losses
exceeded £9.5 billion, all valid insurance claims were still paid;

- London remains the leading (some would say the only true) insurance market in the world and even though the amount of underwriting capital at the
  disposal of the insurance companies in the London market may dwarf the
  premium income capacity of Lloyd's, many large and specialist insurance
  risks are led by Lloyd's underwriters and only then subscribed by the
  following insurance companies market; Lloyd's remains the primary market
  for many specialist insurance risks and no single insurance entity insures all
  the types of risk which are insured at Lloyd's;

- Lloyd's has a licence to transact insurance business in over 100 countries;
  this fact has not been lost on the U.S. and non-United Kingdom insurers
  who have set up operations as corporate members of Lloyd's, underwriting
  on syndicates managed by managing agents in which they have a stake, if
  not control; these entities are in concept identical to insurance companies,
  yet by establishing in Lloyd's have an almost global franchise—in stark contrast to the local licensing and regulatory requirements of each of the States
  of the United States; and

- Lloyd's has, since 1997, allowed itself to be scrutinised by rating agencies to
  obtain an overall security rating for Lloyd's globally; Lloyd's rating of "A"
  (excellent) from AM Best and "A+" (strong) from Standard & Poor's,
  assists to demonstrate the ability of Lloyd's to pay claims.

THE PRINCIPAL COMPONENTS OF LLOYD'S

The Society

15.03   Lloyd's is a society incorporated by statute; to use its statutory name—
"The Society of Lloyd's incorporated by Lloyd's Act 1871"—and the provisions of
the 1871 Act are in many cases still in force today, having operated successfully to
turn the collection of merchants and insurers who then operated from premises in
the Royal Exchange into a formal self-regulating society with a rulebook and a
Council.

The Corporation

15.04   Often confused with the Council, the Corporation of Lloyd's has no
statutory or legal persona, but is the part of the Lloyd's machinery which operates
the market, employs staff, handles member's deposits and is the general func-
tionary of the Society.

The Council of Lloyd's

15.05   The Council has overall responsibility to regulate and direct the membership of Lloyd's and the insurance and reinsurance business transacted at
Lloyd's. The Council alone has the power to make byelaws governing the operation

of the Society and has substantial rulemaking and disciplinary powers. Its members and Lloyd's are immune from legal actions by Members, Lloyd's brokers and Managing and Members' Agents in respect of the exercise of its functions under *Lloyd's Acts, Byelaws or Regulations*. Since 1993, the Council has delegated many of its functions to the Market Board and the Regulatory Board, although it retains the exclusive power to make byelaws.

The Market Board

15.06 The Market Board is primarily charged with advancing the interest of Members, handling relations with governments and media, and providing cost-effective services in areas common to all Members (*e.g.*, premium processing, claims handling, policy issuance and central accounting). It also sets standards in areas affecting Lloyd's reputation, efficiency and standards of conduct for those trading at Lloyd's.

Members of Lloyd's

15.07 Until 1994, all Members of Lloyd's were individuals who had to be proposed for membership of the Lloyd's "club" and pass interview procedures at which their suitability and financial means to underwrite would be assessed, and the rewards and risks of membership (particularly unlimited personal liability) would be explained by Lloyd's representatives. The membership of Lloyd's has been recorded since 1771, in which year Lloyd's had 79 Members; by 1814, that figure had risen to 2,150 (a level that was not attained again until 1947). Membership of Lloyd's grew rapidly and more than doubled during the 1980s, peaking at over 34,000 in 1989. This growth in membership was helped by a long run of profitable years at Lloyd's (until the huge losses of 1988 to 1992) but was also driven by favourable tax status and a relatively low deposit ratio to the amount of premium income that could be accepted, coupled with the attraction that assets used for Lloyd's membership purposes could "earn money twice over" (*e.g.*, the family farm could be pledged to secure a bank guarantee to provide a Lloyd's deposit to permit underwriting at Lloyd's whilst still continuing to produce a separate agricultural income); during the years 1950–1987, high rate tax-paying Members of Lloyd's would on average have made a positive post-tax return every year. When Lloyd's was hit by huge catastrophic losses in the late 1980s, however, the real asset base of the membership was shown to be insufficient in many cases when Names were faced with their share of the aggregate £9.5 billion losses.

In order to provide new underwriting capital to secure the future of the Society in the face of an exodus by individual Names, Lloyd's instituted a Reconstruction and Renewal plan ("R&R") which included the introduction of new corporate members with limited liability, and in 1994 corporate entities were for the first time admitted to underwriting membership of Lloyd's and provided some £1,595 million of new underwriting capacity.

Corporate membership was only made commercially practicable, however, by a separation of the liability for the old loss-making years (which had been hit by catastrophe and asbestosis losses) from the new underwriting years in which corporate members would participate—there would be little or no commercial incentive to new corporate Members to join Lloyd's if the RITC process (see below) operated as normal and passed the old year liabilities forward to later underwriting years of account on which the corporate members participated.

Lloyd's solution, of which there could be no guarantee of success at the time that corporate members first joined Lloyd's, was to create a firebreak between the 1992 and prior underwriting years of account and the 1993 and post years by prohibiting Managing Agents from reinsuring the 1992 and prior years' risks forward into subsequent years of account and instead requiring them to be reinsured into a new DTI authorised company which came to be Equitas. The assumption by Equitas of the long tail liabilities of Lloyd's Members in respect of 1992 and prior years means that Lloyd's has less exposure to long tail risks (assuming that the reinsurance holds up) than many of its competitors.

Members' Agents

15.08   Although the Managing Agents manage Names' underwriting activities on the relevant syndicates, the primary role in looking after a Names' Lloyd's affairs is entrusted to his Members' Agent. The number of Members' Agents still active in the Lloyd's market has declined from 110 in 1984 to only five ongoing Members' Agency groups for the 2001 year of account, but the underwriting capacity managed by the remaining Members' Agents is significant, being £3,441,641,279 for the 2001 year of account. The role and responsibility of the Members' Agents was the subject of considerable litigation in the cases that were consolidated as "The Lloyd's Litigation", and the duties of Members' Agents were summarised by the Court of Appeal in *Brown v. KMR Services Limited*[2] as being:

- to advise the Name which syndicates to join and what amounts of premium income capacity to allocate to each syndicate;

- to keep the Name informed at all times of material factors which may affect the Name's underwriting;

- to provide the Name with a balanced portfolio and appropriate spread of risk; a balanced spread of business on syndicates throughout the main markets at Lloyd's (*i.e.* marine, non-marine, aviation, motor);

- to monitor the syndicates on which it places the Name, and to make recommendations as to whether the Name should increase his share on a syndicate, join a new syndicate, reduce his share or withdraw;

- to keep regularly in touch with the syndicates to which the Name belongs; and

- to advise and discuss with the Name the prospects and past results of syndicates on which he could be placed.

These are onerous duties, and ones in which many Members' Agents were found wanting; not only were they liable for negligent or inappropriate syndicate selection decisions but in "The Lloyd's Litigation" they were held liable for the negligence and breaches of agency agreement by Managing Agents on whose syndicates they

---

[2] [1995] *Lloyd's Law Reports*, Vol.2, p.513.

had placed Names—although a consequence of the contractual agency relationships under which the Members' Agent had the primary duty for the Names' Lloyd's affairs and then delegated in turn to the Managing Agent the performance of the Names' underwriting business, this was a cruel blow for Members' Agents since the contractual arrangements under which they were found liable in law for the acts and omissions of Managing Agents were in a format prescribed by Lloyd's and imposed on Members' Agents and Managing Agents alike.

The Regulatory Board

15.09 The Regulatory Board is responsible for establishing rules to protect the interest of Members while upholding their contractual obligations to policyholders and ensuring regulatory compliance world-wide. The Regulatory Board is also responsible for solvency matters and oversees the disciplinary functions exercisable by the Council.

The Syndicates

15.10 Members of Lloyd's, either individuals (with unlimited liability) or corporations or Scottish Limited Partnerships (with limited liability) conduct insurance business in Syndicates, each of which is run by a Managing Agent. A Syndicate is not a legal entity and no legal relationship exists among the constituent Members on a Syndicate. The rights and obligations of each Member participating in a Syndicate are several and not joint or joint and several. A Syndicate is a group of Members on behalf of whom insurance business is accepted by an Active Underwriter who is employed by the Managing Agent. Reference to "Syndicate stamp" or a "Syndicate list" is the list of Members participating through a Syndicate and their respective percentage share of the Syndicate's underwriting capacity for a calendar year. Each year of account of a syndicate accepts business for 12 months during each calendar year and then remains open until the Syndicate purchases a reinsurance policy to transfer all risks it has written (known as reinsurance to close or RITC), usually at the end of 36 months. Each year, the Syndicate is reconstituted with changes made necessary by deaths, resignations, sales of syndicate membership, increases or decreases of underwriting capacity by existing Members and/or by the addition of new Members. Some Syndicate stamps consist of many dozen Members, while some consist of one Member only. Corporate Members may, if owned by or under common ownership with a Managing Agent, elect to participate only on one or more Syndicates managed by that Managing Agent; individual Members will tend to underwrite on a selection of syndicates so as to spread risks/rewards. The only limitation on the total amount of premium income a Member is eligible to receive is his overall premium limit ("OPL") which must not exceed the multiple prescribed by the Council by reference to the amount of the Members' Funds at Lloyd's.

Each Syndicate is managed by a Managing Agent which oversees the accounts, the investments and the administration of the Syndicate. The Managing Agent employs the underwriters that negotiate and accept risks for Members on the Syndicate. The lead underwriter is known as the "Active Underwriter" to distinguish him or her from "deputy underwriters" or the other underwriting Members of the Syndicate. In most cases, officers or directors of the Managing Agent also serve as the Active Underwriter. The relationship between the Managing Agent and each Member is one of agent and principal.

A Member may not withdraw from a Syndicate during the year, nor until the year of account is closed. Usually, this occurs at the end of 36 months after the year of account commenced. Thus, no one else on the Syndicate is or can become liable for the risks attributable to the premiums the Member has received. If a Member resigns from a Syndicate (or from Lloyd's altogether, for that matter), he continues to participate in all open years of account on all Syndicates through which he accepted risks until each year of account has been closed by RITC and any profits or losses have been declared, *i.e.* for a period of at least three years from the first day of the most recent open year of account.

The role and duties of a Managing Agent

15.11   The principal role of a Managing Agent is to determine the underwriting policy of the Syndicates it manages and to make arrangements for the underwriting of risks. Managing Agents must appoint and supervise one or more individuals to be the Active Underwriters for each of their Syndicates, pricing and accepting risks on behalf of the Syndicate Members.

The role of a Managing Agent includes the approval and supervision of arrangements for:

- the acceptance and pricing by the Active Underwriter of the risks to be underwritten and the receipt of the premiums agreed with brokers;

- the agreement and settlement of claims made against the Syndicate;

- the negotiation and management of the Syndicate's reinsurances;

- the management of the investments held in the Premiums Trust Fund of each Syndicate Member;

- the management and control of the Syndicate's expenses;

- monitoring and controlling the premium income earned by the Syndicate;

- the maintenance of accounting records and statistical data for the Syndicate and the preparation and audit of the Syndicate's accounts;

- making, where necessary, cash calls on Members to provide for underwriting losses;

- compliance with relevant domestic and overseas taxation and legislative requirements; and

- the approval of the premium for and effecting the reinsurance required to close each year of account.

The standard form Managing Agent's agreement in the format as prescribed by Lloyd's Byelaws gives the Managing Agent (and hence the Active Underwriter) absolute discretion as to the risks (including reinsurance to close) which may be underwritten on behalf of a Member; a Member has no right to interfere or even participate in, underwriting decisions made on his behalf by the Managing Agent, notwithstanding that the Member's assets are being used to back the underwriting of insurance and reinsurance business by the Managing Agent.

The Premiums Trust Funds

15.12   Under provisions of the Insurance Companies Act 1982 ("ICA"), each Member is required to establish one or more Premiums Trust Funds ("PTFs") into which all premiums received must be paid. The primary purpose of the trust funds is to ensure that premiums are available to meet claims from insureds without being open to claims from non-insurance creditors of the Member. Pursuant to the PTF, the Member assigns to his PTFs the premiums, and all income arising from investment of the premiums, whilst those premiums are held in trust for the payment of claims and related expenses under insurance and reinsurance policies signed in his name.

The beneficiaries of a Member's PTFs are the policyholders and those claiming in their stead; the Member is the equivalent of the settlor of the trust and he (or his estate) is also the residuary beneficiary. Monies may be withdrawn from the PTFs only to pay claims, return premiums, pay reinsurance premiums and pay expenses. When the relevant year of account is closed, any profit achieved can be released from the PTFs to the Member in accordance with Lloyd's system of accounts.

The PTFs are beyond the reach and the control of a Member until the relevant year of account has closed. Since all premiums are required to be paid into the PTFs, a Member has no discretion whatsoever to limit or reduce the size of these funds. No broker has any authority to remove any monies from the PTFs. The PTFs exist for the benefit of the policyholders.

Chain of Security

15.13   When an insured loss is incurred and payment has been approved, the first source of funds to pay the claims are the funds in the Member's PTFs. If these funds are exhausted the Member is called upon to meet the shortfall from his or its reserves or deposits or by the introduction of cash from his or its assets. If these sources are also exhausted and any part of a claim remains to be paid, the Central Fund could, at the discretion of the Council, be used to satisfy the claim. The ultimate link in the chain of Lloyd's security is thus the Central Fund which is held and administered by the Council primarily as a fund of last resort available (at the discretion of the Council) for the protection of Lloyd's policyholders. Members contribute to the Central Fund each year based on a percentage of their allocated overall premium limit (the rate for 2000 was 1 per cent for all Members).

Lloyd's System of Accounts

15.14   Under the Lloyd's accounting system, Members' underwriting results are stated by "year of account". As a general rule, each year of account is a one-year venture that is fully accounted for and settled at the 36-month period. To close a year of account, RITC must be purchased with respect to that year's liabilities, known and unknown. Only after such reinsurance is purchased is the year of account officially closed and the profit, if any, distributed. No distribution may occur until after the year of account has closed. The three-year accounting system was designed to ensure that when a year of account is closed, written premium has been fully earned, returned premiums have been accounted for, a proportion of the losses have been settled and an amount for outstanding and incurred but not reported losses has been established on the basis of mature data in order to set the appropriate premium to purchase RITC.

Reinsurance to Close

15.15 When the year of account is usually set to close at the end of 36 months, the RITC is determined. A Syndicate's entire portfolio is usually reinsured to cover claims that may subsequently be made against Members on the reinsured Syndicate's year of account, including any earlier accounts reinsured to close therein. Usually, this is accomplished by transferring the entire portfolio to the next subsequent open year of account of the Syndicate or another Syndicate by means of indemnity reinsurance. The ceding Syndicate's year of account is then closed and underwriting profit or loss is ascertained for the closed year. Members on the assuming reinsuring Syndicate receive reinsurance premium income, salvages, reinsurance recoveries and late-arriving direct insurance premiums according to the percentage that each Member's underwriting capacity allocated to the Syndicate bears to the Syndicate's total underwriting capacity; they also assume the risk of losses and pay all subsequent claims and expenses. The Member subscribing to the original policy remains liable in law, but benefits from the reinsurance effected through RITC, such reinsurance may be subscribed to by the same Member if the Member participates on the reconstituted Syndicate, as will be the case with the New Syndicate.

The calculation of the premium for the RITC involves the exercise of significant judgment and draws on the experience of the Active Underwriter in assessing the outstanding known claims, claims incurred but not reported to the Syndicate and any further claims which are considered likely to arise.

While exercising absolute discretion in determining the RITC, the Managing Agent and the Active Underwriter must consider both the interests of the Members paying the premium and the interests of the Members accepting the premium; however, no Member or group of Members has the right to approve or veto the RITC. The premium must be equitable between the two groups of Members. The Syndicate's independent auditor is required to pay particular attention to the determination of the RITC in issuing his opinion on the Annual Report and profit for a closed year of account.

Solvency Test

15.16 Each Member is subject to a solvency test administered by Lloyd's to demonstrate that the Member has sufficient acceptable assets at Lloyd's to meet such Member's underwriting liabilities. The solvency test is carried out even after a Member has ceased underwriting and will continue until all accounts in which it participates are closed by RITC.

The exercise is carried out in respect of the Member's underwriting through all of such Member's Syndicates. Open year of account and run-off year of account surpluses, together with the profits of a year of account in the process of closing on all Syndicates in which the Member participates, are set off against open year of account and run-off year of account deficiencies and losses of a year of account in the process of closing. Any deficiency will be set against the Member's Funds at Lloyd's. Any shortfall must be made good by the Member transferring cash or investments from its own resources into its PTFs. If a Member does not transfer cash or other acceptable investments to make up this shortfall, the amount of such deficiency will be provided for against the Member's Funds at Lloyd's, with the effect that the Member's OPL would be correspondingly reduced for the succeeding year of account.

New Members will receive no profits from Syndicates through which they participate until, at the earliest, the middle of the fourth year after they commence underwriting. Meanwhile, their solvency position will be calculated at the 12- and 24-month periods based, in part, on market-wide reserving percentages. Furthermore, the Members will incur expenses before such, if any, premium income is received for their account. The Managing Agent expenses and Lloyd's charges will be paid from the PTFs.

Annual Audit

15.17   Under the ICA, every Member must submit his underwriting accounts each year to an audit, which must be conducted by an independent auditor approved by the Council and in accordance with the guidelines issued annually by the Council and approved by the Treasury (and in future the FSA). Reserves must at least equal the minimum percentages prescribed by the Council of the premium income for the various classes of business underwritten by a Member. If, during the course of an annual audit, it is found that a Member's assets are insufficient to meet his estimated underwriting liabilities, he will be required to lodge additional assets to cover the shortfall or otherwise be obliged to cease underwriting, and the full amount of his Lloyd's deposit and, if necessary, the Central Fund can be earmarked to cover such liabilities.

REGULATION OF LLOYD'S PRE-FSMA

15.18   Before the FSMA came into effect with regard to Lloyd's, there had been very iittle external statutory or regulatory control over Lloyd's. The Lloyd's Acts 1871–1982 provided the framework within which Lloyd's could govern itself and granted wide powers of internal regulation of its Members and those using the Lloyd's marketplace—indeed, given the public debate surrounding the powers to be vested in the FSA and the extent to which the Authority should or should not be subject to immunity from suit, it may come as a surprise to learn that Lloyd's already enjoys statutory immunity. Under section 14 of Lloyd's Act 1982, the immunity applies not only to protect Lloyd's from liability in damages at the suit of current members of the Lloyd's "community" (a term that includes Names, brokers and underwriting agents and the directors and managers thereof) but even extends to those who have at any time been members or even applied to become members of that community (irrespective of whether the application was successful) and grants Lloyd's immunity from suit save where the act or omission complained of was done or omitted to be done in bad faith or was of a purely routine or clerical nature (*i.e.* it involved no exercise of discretion by the Society's employee in question).

External regulation of Lloyd's has hitherto been concerned largely with the solvency of Lloyd's Members and of the Society of Lloyd's as a whole. Lloyd's has been outside the regulatory ambit of the 1986 Act, notwithstanding that the activities conducted by Managing Agents include substantial handling of client monies and investment activities, and that the syndicate selection advice given by Members' Agents, let alone their initial advice to would-be Names as to the benefits and pitfalls (unlimited personal liability included) of Lloyd's membership and advice on participation in Lloyd's capacity auctions or otherwise on the disposal of syndicate membership rights, may appear similar to the giving of investment advice and hence a regulated activity under the Act.

The powers of self regulation given to the Council of Lloyd's under the Lloyd's Acts created a regulatory system which to an outside observer might make Lloyd's akin to one of the SROs under the 1986 Act indeed, in *R. v. Lloyd's of London, ex p. Briggs and others*,[3] Counsel for the applicant Names who had obtained leave to move for judicial review against Lloyd's sought to draw this very comparison and gave examples of SROs being adjudged or conceded to be within the scope of judicial review citing, *inter alia, Bank of Scotland v. Investment Management Regulatory Organisation Ltd.*[4] The Court, however, did not accept the analogy and held, *per* Leggatt L.J., that:

" . . . Lloyd's is not a public law body which regulates the insurance market . . . the Department of Trade and Industry does that. Lloyd's operates within one section of the market. Its powers are derived from a private Act which does not extend to any persons in the insurance business other than those who wish to operate in the section of the market governed by Lloyd's and who, in order to do so, have to commit themselves by entering into the uniform contract prescribed by Lloyd's. In our judgement neither the evidence nor the submissions in this case suggest that there is such a public law element about the relationship between Lloyd's and the Names as places it within the public domain and so renders it susceptible to judicial review."

The Financial Services Act 1986

15.19 The Act did not include general insurance business within its scope and thus much of Lloyd's activities automatically fell outside the ambit of the Act. Membership of Lloyd's, and syndicate membership rights, are not included in the definition of "investment" in Part 1 of Schedule 1 of the Act, and hence Part 2 of Schedule 1 which defines "investment activity" does not catch most of the activities of Managing Agents and Members' Agents. The investment activities necessary to enable custodian and investment management of Members' deposits at Lloyd's and PTF monies are recognised in section 42 of the 1986 Act which treats Lloyd's and Managing and Members' Agents as "exempted persons" in respect of

---

[3] [1993] *Lloyd's Law Reports*, Vol. 1, p.176.
[4] [1989] S.L.T. 432.

investment business carried on by them for the purposes of or in connection with the carrying on of insurance business at Lloyd's.

At the time of the Financial Services Bill, as well as the unrest in certain quarters as to whether Lloyd's should be brought within the regulatory framework proposed by the Bill (particularly given the very significant investment management role conducted by underwriting agents at Lloyd's) there was also disquiet amongst external Names (*i.e.* those who did not actually work within the Lloyd's market place) at the fact that, notwithstanding the scandals involving Lloyd's in the early 1980s the "working Names" (*i.e.* those Names who as well as being underwriting Members worked in the Lloyd's market as brokers or underwriting agents) still held 16 seats on the Council of Lloyd's whilst the external Names held eight seats, with four seats in addition being for nominated members of the Council. This, it was argued, allowed the participants in the Lloyd's market who were to be regulated to actually dictate the degree of self-regulation which Lloyd's should impose on them. The scandals involving Lloyd's in the early 1980s prompted the Governor of the Bank of England to procure the appointment of a Chief Executive at Lloyd's and Lloyd's sought to introduce other controls through regulatory byelaws passed between 1982 and 1986. The Fisher Report had been prepared at the behest of Lloyd's itself and laid the groundwork for what became the Lloyd's Act 1982; Fisher had taken account of the need to protect sections of the Lloyd's community including external Names as passive investors in Lloyd's. In January 1986, Leon Brittan, Secretary of State for Trade and Industry, announced the appointment of a Committee of Inquiry chaired by Sir Patrick Neill, Q.C. to report on Regulatory Arrangements at Lloyd's. Neill's terms of reference were:

> "To consider whether the regulatory arrangements which are being established at Lloyd's under the 1982 Lloyd's Act provide protection for the interests of Members of Lloyd's comparable to those proposed for investors under the Financial Services Bill (now Act)."

When Neill reported in December of that year, his Committee put forward some 70 recommendations for further action in the regulatory field at Lloyd's seeking to put Names who transacted business at Lloyd's on a par with the protections which would be available to City investors under the 1986 Act. Excluding members of the Council of Lloyd's, a total of 274 individuals or organisations gave evidence to the Neill Committee which may indicate the strength of feeling amongst external Names.

Although Neill was complimentary as to the pace and scale within which the Council of Lloyd's had used their powers under the Lloyd's Act 1982 to institute reforms at Lloyd's and having rejected the argument that new external supervision of Lloyd's should be instituted (whether along the lines of the SIB or otherwise), Neill recognised that all conflicts of interest whether between external or working Names, or between Lloyd's and Names generally, whether at the level of principle or practice, were resolved by the Council of Lloyd's and that it was a "major weakness" for the composition of the Council to be such that the balance of initiative on regulatory as well as on market matters rested with the working Names; to redress this weakness, Neill recommended that the balance of the Council should be modified so that the working Names would cease to have a majority; Neill recognised that no new primary legislation would be required to institute this change and that the Council of Lloyd's could rely on its powers under section 3(3) of the Lloyd's Act 1982 which enabled it by byelaw to increase or decrease the number of members of the Council. Having escaped from external regulation under the 1986 Act, Lloyd's moved swiftly to address Neill's concern by adopting his recommendation; one important factor which Neill recognised in declining to recommend new external supervision of Lloyd's was that no case had been presented alleging that the self-regulatory regime then in place at Lloyd's had damaged the interests of Lloyd's policyholders—the primacy of Lloyd's policyholders' interests being a theme which was followed through into the FSA's view of Lloyd's.

Whatever the rights or wrongs of excluding Lloyd's and its Members and Managing Agents from the requirement to be authorised under the 1986 Act, the landscape at Lloyd's changed radically after the 1986 Act became law, including by:

- the introduction of pre-emption rights on syndicate membership—Names now had a right to remain on their chosen syndicates from year to year and a pre-emptive right to take up any new capacity made available on those syndicates;

- the introduction of capacity auctions enabling syndicate participations to be traded in auctions organised and held by Lloyd's—hence attaching realisable value to Names' syndicate participations;

- the grant to Managing Agents of the right to buy syndicate participations from Names on syndicates managed by those Managing Agents through the mechanism of a capacity offer (similar in concept, and documentation, to a takeover offer for securities) coupled with a compulsory purchase right once a 90 per cent capacity level had been secured to squeeze out Names who did not accept the offer (akin to compulsory acquisition under sections 428 *et seq.* of the Companies Act 1985 following a successful takeover offer); and

- the admission of limited liability corporate Names to Lloyd's and permitting Managing Agents to own, or be under common ownership with corporate Names

These developments led to a very different role for the reduced number of Members' and Managing Agents in the market—syndicate analysis and selection became more scientific, investors in the new corporate vehicles in Lloyd's wanted forecasts of investment returns, PTF monies needed to be wisely invested to maximise returns for corporate shareholders, advice was needed as to if, or when, syndicate capacity should be bought or sold in the Lloyd's capacity auctions and syndicate participation rights needed valuing in the face of capacity offers made by the syndicate's Managing Agent—all of which presented a picture far more akin to that of conducting investment business under the 1986 Act.

Insurance Companies Act 1982

15.20 By the end of the 1990s there had developed at Lloyd's a new vehicle ("Integrated Lloyd's Vehicle") which had many of the features of a small or medium-sized insurance company (but not one writing life insurance). Often owned by a public listed company or a non-United Kingdom insurer (Bermudan in particular) these vehicles combined ownership of a Lloyd's limited liability Corporate Member underwriting as often the only Name on a Lloyd's syndicate managed by a Managing Agent owning, or under common ownership with, the Corporate Member; underwriting capacity and insurance risk underwriting decisions were thus in the hands of the same corporate grouping.

Notwithstanding the similarities with an insurance company and in spite of the scale of business transacted at Lloyd's, Integrated Lloyd's Vehicles, Lloyd's and its membership have not been subject to the authorisation requirements that apply to insurance companies under the ICA; nor, unlike insurance companies, has the ownership or control of Lloyd's Members or underwriting agents been subject to regulation by the Treasury. The general prohibition contained in section 2(1) of the ICA whereby "no person shall carry on any insurance business in the United Kingdom unless authorised to do so [by the Secretary of State]" is expressly stated not to apply to insurance business underwritten by a Member of Lloyd's.

When it comes to solvency of Lloyd's and its Members, however, the Treasury (in succession to the DTI) has had, and after the FSMA, the FSA will have, oversight under Part IV of the ICA as supplemented by the Insurance (Lloyd's) Regulations 1983.[4a] The solvency and security arrangements imposed on Lloyd's and its Members include: the requirement for insurance premiums to be held in PTFs on terms approved by the Treasury; an annual auditor's certificate to be provided to the Treasury confirming that each Member has sufficient assets available to meet his liabilities; a margin of solvency to be maintained under risk-based capital requirements which set the requisite underwriting capital requirements; and an annual global statement for Lloyd's collectively to show the character of the insurance business carried on there; Lloyd's also produces and publishes audited accounts for the Society, including the Corporation.

E.U. Directives

15.21   Lloyd's is also provided for in the various E.U. Directives applicable to insurance, in particular the Third Non-Life Directive which provides a "single passport" to Lloyd's Names, as it does to other insurers established and regulated in the EEA enabling them to operate throughout the EEA subject to having complied with the requirements of their home state regulations.

PRINCIPLES ENSHRINED IN THE FSMA

15.22   The FSA could have taken the view that a single tier of regulation was appropriate for Lloyd's and that the FSA should be the only regulator, thus ending once and for all self-regulation at Lloyd's and the multitude of Byelaws, Regulations, Codes of Conduct and Bulletins that constitute Lloyd's internal rulebook.

The FSA appears to have treated Lloyd's with some caution in instituting a detailed consultation process by launching its *Consultation Paper 16* in November 1998— "The future regulation of Lloyd's"—and then engaging in further consultation on

---

[4a] S.I. 1983 No. 224.

the responses received to that paper.[5] The Paper makes it clear that the FSA recognises "Lloyd's unique characteristics, its recent history and the current rapid change in this market, especially its capital structure". The FSA also recognises "that innovation has been a key feature of the Lloyd's market over the years and that regulation which sought to remove risk entirely would also stifle innovation and involve an unjustifiable level of costs for those in the market".[6] As to the recent history of Lloyd's and the question of whether allowing self-regulation to continue had been the right approach, the FSA comments that:

> "It is clear with hindsight that through the 1970s and 1980s Lloyd's self-regulation did not match the standards of the time in other financial markets, let alone those now expected . . . Lloyd's did improve its own regulation over [the 1990s] and in the last few years this has been substantially transformed, as attested by various independent reviewers, including rating agencies. We are determined that this standard should be maintained and, where possible, enhanced, and we shall use our powers to ensure that this is the case."[7]

The beneficiary of this approach is to be the Lloyd's policyholder; notwithstanding that the stated failings of Lloyd's caused more extensive damage to the interests of the Society and its Members than to policyholders (whose valid claims were paid at all times), the FSA is clear that the interests of policyholders are paramount, as is clearly the position which the DTI, Treasury and FSA have taken to protect the consumer who purchases insurance products from insurance companies:

> "Our primary concern will be the protection of Lloyd's policyholders against the risk that valid claims may not be paid. In carrying out this responsibility we shall take particular account of the risks which can arise from poor underwriting risk, and concentrations of risk.
>
> We shall also have regard to the position of Lloyd's Members, the providers of the market's capital, as consumers of certain advisory and custodial services."[8]

FSMA PROVISIONS REGARDING LLOYD'S

15.23 On first reading, it would appear that the FSMA has ended Lloyd's own powers of regulation by:

- giving the Authority powers in respect of Lloyd's equivalent to the powers which the FSA has over all regulated firms;

- bringing the Society within the ambit of the FSMA and making it subject, as an authorised person, to the FSA;

---

[5] See FSA, *Response Paper on Consultation Paper 16: The Future Regulation of Lloyds* (November 1998) and FSA. *The Lloyds return* (December 1999).
[6] FSA, *Consultation Paper 16*, para. 54.
[7] FSA, *Consultation Paper 16*, para. 55.
[8] FSA, *Consultation Paper 16*, para. 8.

- requiring Managing agents, Members' agents and anyone outside Lloyd's who offers advice in relation to Lloyd's syndicates to be authorised;

- giving the FSA express duties to keep itself informed as to the way the Lloyd's market (and regulated activities therein) operate and are supervised and regulated.

However, having now brought Lloyd's within the FSMA and made it subject to the authority of the FSA, the Act then allows the Council of Lloyd's, so long as it does so to the satisfaction of the FSA, to continue its day to day regulation of the Society and the insurance operations conducted at Lloyd's, as well as permitting it to keep its primary regulations in place and continue as the proponent of primary regulation at Lloyd's. In the event that the FSA wishes to intervene, it can exercise its powers directly or via the Society and/or Council of Lloyd's.

Lloyd's is also permitted to retain its disciplinary powers although, again, this is entirely without prejudice to the FSA's powers of investigation, and disciplinary proceedings—whether Lloyd's or the FSA, or both, subject any Lloyd's participant to investigation or disciplinary proceedings—will depend on the facts of the case and on which body has the most appropriate powers.

Part XIX of the FSMA contains the new regulatory regime to which Lloyd's, its members and its authorised participants such as underwriting agents are to be subject.

General duty of the FSA regarding Lloyd's

15.24 The FSMA imposes express statutory duties on the FSA with regard to Lloyd's. The FSA must keep itself informed about the way in which the Council of Lloyd's exercises its supervisory and regulatory powers over the Lloyd's market and the way in which regulated activities (hence not just the conduct of insurance and reinsurance business, but also the activities of Managing and Members' Agents) are carried on (section 314(1)). The FSA is also mandated to keep under review the desirability of exercising its powers in respect of Lloyd's, either directly or through the Council or Society of Lloyd's (section 314(2)).

Extent of Lloyd's authorisation under the FSMA

15.25 The FSMA treats Lloyd's as though it had made an application for (and been granted) permission to carry on regulated activities under the FSMA as an authorised person, hence effectively grandfathering Lloyd's. The FSMA only authorises Lloyd's for the following specific purposes (section 315(2)):

- arranging deals in contracts of insurance written at Lloyd's;

- arranging deals in participation in Lloyd's syndicates; and

- activities carried on in connection with or for the purposes of either of the foregoing.

The width of the description "arranging deals in participation in Lloyd's syndicates" would appear broad enough to catch all the activities at Lloyd's (such as capacity auctions, capacity offers and conversion schemes) which have arisen since the enactment of the 1986 Act—indeed, given that the FSA recognises the difficulty in predicting how Lloyd's will develop in the future, the width of these definitions may be deliberate in that it gives scope for new business methods and practices which will nevertheless be caught by the FSMA without the need for additional regulation.

Managing and Members' Agents will have to be authorised persons under the FSMA because the activities they carry out are now to be regulated activities under the FSMA. The FSA also has stated that it intends to make rules under section 59 of the FSMA which will specify controlled functions in the case of certain regulated activities—these controlled functions will apply not only to Managing and Members' Agents, but also certain key positions within the Society itself.

Managing and Members' Agents who are already approved by Lloyd's under its relevant Byelaws will effectively be grandfathered, as will persons carrying out regulated functions within these organisations, subject in all cases to the FSA's right to cancel, restrict or impose additional conditions. Going forward, new applicants for authorisation as Managing or Members' Agents will have to go through an application process for authorisation on a basis similar to that in place for authorised persons in other sectors, including by meeting fitness and propriety criteria.

Members of Lloyd's, whether individual unlimited liability Names or limited liability corporate Names, will not require to become authorised specifically under the provisions of the FSMA—the actual business of underwriting insurance risks at Lloyd's is not a regulated activity—and will continue to be subject to direct regulation by the Council of Lloyd's under its powers derived from Lloyd's Acts 1871–1982.

Mention was made above of the fact that (notwithstanding claims to the contrary brought by action groups of dissident Names who argued both in England and the United States that membership of Lloyd's was a "security" and hence should be subject to securities laws—which had therefore been flouted by Lloyd's and its underwriting agents) neither syndicate membership nor underwriting capacity constituted as "investment" for the purposes of the 1986 Act—hence the various activities specified in that Act as constituting "investment business" did not apply in these instances to Lloyd's (*per contra* any attempt to market or conduct such activities in the shares of Corporate Members or in "conversion schemes" through which unlimited liability individual Names can convert to be shareholders in one or more limited liability corporate Names or the holding company thereof).

The FSMA fills that gap by making it clear in Schedule 2[9] and subject to the FSMA that both syndicate underwriting capacity and syndicate membership are "investments" and subject to the FSMA—hence "investment business" which requires authorisation now includes everyday activities in Lloyd's.

Powers of intervention vested in the FSA

15.26 Sections 316 and 318 of the FSMA set out the routes that the FSA can take if it wishes to intervene in Lloyd's. Although the consultation processes to be followed before any intervention are the same, the methods of intervention differ:

---

[9] FSMA, Sched. 2, Pt II, para. 21.

- under section 316, the FSA can make an "insurance market direction" in writing in respect of either a Member of Lloyd's or the entire Membership of Lloyd's in order to enforce the "general prohibition" or to apply a "core provision"; and

- under section 318, the FSA can (instead of giving an insurance market direction under section 316 or at the same time as, or following, the giving of an insurance market direction) give a direction to the Council of Lloyd's or to the Society of Lloyd's (acting through the Council) or to both the Council and the Society in respect of any particular Member of Lloyd's, or the entire Membership of Lloyd's; unlike a "market direction" which is made by the FSA directly, a direction under section 318 is made via the governing body of Lloyd's and can be made in respect of Managing and Members' Agents at Lloyd's as well as in respect of Names.

The other main difference between section 316 and section 318 is the scope of intervention available under either section.

If the FSA wished to give a direction to Lloyd's to make the Council exercise its powers generally towards a specified object or to exercise a specific power towards a specified objection (perhaps opening up Lloyd's marketplace to a wider franchise? steering Lloyd's towards closer integration with the London market so as to reduce costs and strengthen common practices in a single London Market?) it would be likely to use its powers under section 318.

Under section 316, the FSA can enforce the "general prohibition" or a "core provision" in relation to the carrying on of an activity regulated by the FSMA relating to contracts of insurance written at Lloyd's. The "general prohibition" as set out in section 19 is that no person may carry on or purport to carry on any regulated activity in the United Kingdom unless that person is an authorised person, or an exempt person. Thus, the FSA may be more likely to take direct action under section 316 in cases of (say) insolvency in the event of the Lloyd's equivalent of Independent (the exercise of the FSA's powers in the event of insolvency of authorised persons being one of the "core provisions") whilst in the event that any action needed to be taken against a Managing Agent and Lloyd's appeared not to be adopting a sufficiently firm stance, the FSA can take action under section 318 by issuing a direction to the Council of Lloyd's.

It remains to be seen how these powers of intervention will be exercised and in view of the fact that the FSA has allowed Lloyd's to continue to exercise the powers it has under its current Byelaws the FSA presumably has a high level of confidence in both the internal Lloyd's rulebook and the manner in which it polices itself. It should be borne in mind, however, that the FSA has a statutory obligation under section 314 of the FSMA to keep itself informed about Lloyd's, and for the discharge of the general functions for which the FSA was established, which require (section 2 of the FSMA) the need for the FSA to have regard to:

"the desirability of facilitating innovation in connection with regulated activities[10] . . . the international character of financial services and markets

---

[10] FSMA, s. 2(3)(d).

and the desirability of maintaining the competitive position of the United Kingdom . . . "[11]

which could be significant in the context of Lloyd's as it adapts to a rapidly changing global insurance market.

Prior to giving any direction under section 316 or 318 of the FSMA, the FSA is obliged to enter into a consultation process. As the first step in that process, the FSA must publish a draft of the proposed direction, accompanied by a cost benefit analysis and a notice advising that representations about the proposed direction may be made to the FSA within a specified time. Prior to making the proposed direction, the FSA must then have regard to any representation it receives and, if at the end of the process the FSA makes the proposed direction, it is obliged to publish an account detailing (in general terms only) the representations (if any) made to it and its response to them and if the final direction issued by the FSA is different from the draft which it originally published in any manner which is in the opinion of the FSA significant, then the FSA is obliged (in addition) to publish details of the difference(s) and a cost benefit analysis.

Former underwriting members

15.27   In view of the severe decline in the total number of Members of Lloyd's, there is now a significant body of former underwriting Members of Lloyd's (the FSA puts the figure at 25,000) who continue to have personal liability in respect of insurance business written on their behalf whilst they were active underwriting Members of Lloyd's. The risks of default by such former underwriting Members are recognised in section 320 of the FSMA which as well as permitting such former underwriting Members to perform contacts of insurance underwritten by them (irrespective of whether they have become authorised persons) also gives the FSA power to impose on former underwriting Members such requirements as appear to the FSA to be appropriate in order to protect policyholders against the risk of default by former underwriting Members. Any former underwriting Member on whom the FSA does impose a requirement, however, is entitled to refer the matter to the Tribunal.

Transfer of insurance business underwritten at Lloyd's

15.28   Under the ICA, a mechanism was provided under Schedule 2 of that act whereby portfolio transfers of life or non-life insurance business could be undertaken, with section 85 of the ICA providing that a portfolio transfer could similarly be effected by or to a Lloyd's syndicate provided that only the transferor or transferee (and not both) were Members of Lloyd's and provided that the Committee of Lloyd's had impliedly sanctioned the transfer by appointing one person to act on behalf of the Syndicate Members concerned. To preserve these mechanics in the case of Lloyd's, section 323 of the FSMA provides that the Treasury may by order provide for the application of any of Part VII of the FSMA (which contains the portfolio transfer provisions applicable to insurance companies) to schemes for the transfer of the whole or any part of the business carried on by current or former Members of Lloyd's.

---

[11] FSMA, s. 2(3)(e).

Prudential Supervision

15.29 Prior to the implementation of the FSMA, solvency at Lloyd's was effectively measured on three levels: first, the solvency of each syndicate was calculated; secondly, each Member's individual solvency was calculated so as to ensure that, taking into account any current or historic surplus or deficit, the Member had a (variable) margin of solvency in addition to sufficient assets to meet underwriting liabilities; thirdly, as a global solvency measure, Lloyd's was required to file a Statutory Statement of Business with the Treasury in a prescribed form to show that the Society had total assets in excess of liabilities available to meet the minimum margin of solvency. The FSA stated that its policy would be to seek to apply to Lloyd's insurance business the same standards and approach to prudential regulation as were applied to United Kingdom authorised insurance companies; they also concluded that the risk based capital system under which Lloyd's reviewed the asset backing requirements for Members so as to seek to match regulatory capital with underwriting business exposure should be maintained, but in addition there would be changes to the detail of existing prudential regulation, including a new Lloyd's Return to be submitted to the FSA in respect of each year, new asset valuation rules applicable to each class of Member, asset diversification requirements[12] and further detailed changes which have subsequently been set out in the Lloyd's *Sourcebook* published by the FSA in June 2001.

Compensation

15.30 There always have been important differences in the security underlying policies of insurance underwritten at Lloyd's when compared to policies underwritten by insurance companies (at least those authorised in the United Kingdom). The insurers under Lloyd's policies are the various Syndicate Members who have subscribed for a percentage of the risk under the policy and have thereby accepted personal liability (unlimited liability in the case of individual Members of Lloyd's) in respect of the insurance risks underwritten. Notwithstanding that those risks may be passed elsewhere through contracts of reinsurance or passed to a succeeding Syndicate year of account by way of RITC (see above) the original subscribing Syndicate Members are always liable as a matter of contract to the original insured. In the event that valid claims by the policyholder were not met, the policyholder would have to follow through the chain of security at Lloyd's, which would start with the monies in PTF, move on to the Lloyd's deposit held on behalf of the defaulting Name(s) and then the Names' non-Lloyd's assets, and if still unsatisfied would have available as a fund of last resort the resources of the Lloyd's Central Fund—the Central Fund, however, is available at the discretion of the Council of Lloyd's and is not available directly as a right to aggrieved Lloyd's policyholders. When comparing the Lloyd's chain of security with the assets available to a policyholder with a United Kingdom insurance company, it would be apparent that not only are the assets of the insurer easier to identify (and the insurers annual Treasury returns will be available for public inspection) but in the event of the insolvency of the insurer the insured may as a statutory right be entitled to protection from the Policyholders Protection Board.

---

[12] FSA, *Consultation Paper 66: Prudential requirements for Lloyds insurance business* (August 2000).

During the crisis at Lloyd's the position was reached in 1994 and 1995 (when the Central Fund became a key part of the Lloyd's Settlement) that the Central Fund had insufficient assets to cover the solvency shortfalls of Lloyd's Members and in order to cover these shortfalls the net assets of the Society and a credit for part of a double count in respect of insurance losses which were already protected by errors and omissions insurance reserves had to be taken into account. The burden of the huge losses at Lloyd's in past years has now been substantially removed from the Central Fund following the Lloyd's Settlement and the reinsurance of liabilities relating to the 1992 and prior underwriting years in to Equitas. The FSA clearly recognises the significance of the Central Fund in the protection of Lloyd's policyholders because in the *Lloyd's Sourcebook* the FSA provides both guidance (to the effect that Lloyd's should seek to ensure that the Central Fund provides protection for policyholders at least equivalent to that available to other policyholders under the Financial Services Compensation Scheme[13]) but also provides rules requiring Lloyd's to report to the FSA quarterly on the net market value of the Central Fund, payments that have been made from it, claims made or circumstances notified against it.[14]

THE *LLOYD'S SOURCEBOOK*

15.31 The FSA published *Consultation Paper 48*, the *Lloyd's Sourcebook* in May 2000, and having received responses (although only eight in total) in March 2001 published the *Lloyd's Sourcebook*.[15] The *Sourcebook* in the form published will form part of the FSA's *Handbook of Rules and Guidance* and the text of the rules is now in final form and has been approved by the FSA's Board.[16] The final text of the *Lloyd's Sourcebook* is therefore now available to add a high degree of detail to the proposals on which the FSA has consulted in its various consultation papers.

The *Lloyd's Sourcebook* contains a mixture of guidance, regulations and (in limited circumstances only) formal directions given by the FSA under section 318 of the FSMA. The *Sourcebook* now gives a clearer and more detailed picture of the route that the FSA wishes Lloyd's to follow in the following areas:

Provision of information

15.32 In order to enable the FSA to perform the regulatory functions vested in it under FSMA, Chapter 2 of the *Sourcebook* sets out directions and guidance to Lloyd's on the provision of information, including that Lloyd's must immediately inform the FSA if it becomes aware that any matter likely to be of material concern to the FSA may have arisen in relation to (i) the regulated activities for which Lloyd's has been granted permission; or (ii) underwriting agents; or (iii) approved persons acting for and on behalf of underwriting agents.[17] This Directive is designed to enable the FSA to fulfil its monitoring and enforcement obligations. The FSA has also issued directives that Lloyd's must inform the FSA if it commences

---

[13] LLD 3.2.1G.
[14] LLD 3.3.2R.
[15] FSA, *Policy Statement, the Lloyd's Sourcebook: Feedback on CP48 and CP66.*
[16] This was approved with other parts of the FSA, *Handbook of Rules and Guidance* on June 21, 2001; see Lloyd's Sourcebook Instrument 2001.
[17] LLD 2.3.1D.

investigations or disciplinary proceedings relating to apparent breaches of the
FSMA or requirements made under the FSMA (including any general principles or
other rules) by an underwriting agent or any person who carries out controlled
functions for or on behalf of an underwriting agent.[18] Chapter 2 also sets out
guidelines for co-operation between the FSA and Lloyd's in investigations or action
taken by the FSA in respect of underwriting agents or approved persons carrying
out controlled functions for and on behalf of underwriting agents,[19] and furthermore sets out a reciprocal guideline as to how Lloyd's should give the FSA
adequate notice of changes it proposes to make to its byelaws and requires Lloyd's
to consult interested parties on any proposed changes to byelaws and advise the
FSA about the consultation undertaken and responses received.[20]

Capacity transfer market

15.33 Mention is made above of the Lloyd's capacity auctions which enable, at
limited times of the year, syndicate capacity to be transferred. Chapter 4 of the
Lloyd's Sourcebook imposes a requirement on the Society to make appropriate
byelaws governing conduct in the capacity transfer market and sets out standards
which the byelaws must ensure are met[21]; in view of the fact that the Lloyd's capacity
transfer market has been in operation for a number of years and Lloyd's already
has rules covering some of the matters which the FSA has sought to cover by
requirements and guidelines (the prohibition of unfair and abusive practices and
dissemination of price sensitive information, for example) it remains to be seen
what new features Lloyd's will feel obliged to include in its byelaws; the FSA has,
however, required Lloyd's to provide a report at the end of each quarter in which
the capacity transfer market operates.[22]

Complaints from policyholders and members

15.34 Chapter 6 of the *Lloyd's Sourcebook* includes an insurance market direction given in the interests of policyholders which makes Members of Lloyd's subject to the compulsory jurisdiction of the Financial Ombudsman Service with
respect to the carrying on of insurance business and enables the complaints of policyholders (insofar as eligible for consideration by the Financial Ombudsman Service) to be dealt with under the rules of that Service.[23] With regard to complaints
from Members, the FSA has taken the view that the Financial Ombudsman Service
is not in a position to deal with complaints from Members about the conduct of
activities within the Lloyd's Market, by the Society itself, or by underwriting agents
and that separate rules and guidelines are therefore required[24]; to this end, the
FSA has issued a requirement that Lloyd's must establish and maintain effective
complaint handling arrangements for Members including a procedure as to how
complaints are made, processed and the implementation of independent dispute

---

[18] LLD 2.4.1D.
[19] LLD 2.5.1G.
[20] LLD 2.6.2G and 2.6.3G.
[21] LLD 4.2.1R and 4.2.2G.
[22] LLD 4.3.1R.
[23] LLD 6.1.2G and 6.2.1.D.
[24] LLD 7.1.4G.

resolution schemes.[25] As to compensation arrangements for individual Members of Lloyd's, the Financial Services Compensation Scheme will not be available to compensate current or former Members if claims against underwriting agents (other than claims for losses arising only from underwriting or investment risk) are not satisfied and therefore separate rules and guidance are required[26]; Chapter 8 of the *Lloyd's Sourcebook* requires the Society to maintain byelaws to establish appropriate and effective arrangements to compensate current and former Members if underwriting agents are unable or are likely to be unable to satisfy claims relating to regulated activities[27]; the arrangements to be put in place are to have a governance structure that is operationally independent from the Society[28] and in setting the limit for compensation payable for a single loss the Society is to have regard to the compensation payable by the Financial Services Compensation Scheme for claims relating to similar regulated activities.[29]

---

[25] LLD 7.2.1R.
[26] LLD 8.1.4G.
[27] LLD 8.2.1R.
[28] LLD 8.2.4G.
[29] LLD 8.2.6G.

CHAPTER 16

Mutual Societies

VIVIENNE DE CHERMONT

INTRODUCTION

16.01   The term "mutual" is often loosely applied to an entity, some or all of whose customers are also in legal terms its owners. As used in the FSMA, however, the expression "mutual societies" refers to friendly societies, building societies, industrial and provident societies and credit unions. Given that the purpose of the FSMA was to provide both a single statutory framework and a single regulator for financial services businesses in the United Kingdom, it was to be expected that some rationalisation of the regulation of mutual societies would be included in the Act.

Mutual societies originated on a largely informal (and initially unincorporated) basis principally in the nineteenth century under the umbrella of friendly societies, often limiting their participants to a small geographical area. Although later assuming different names according to the purpose for which they were established, these societies were usually set up with the common aim of pooling subscriptions or other funds for the benefit of some or all of the participants. By the twentieth century, their role as providers of actually quite distinct types of financial services, often akin to deposit-taking or insurance and the consequent need for some form of defined status and regulation, had been recognised in the form of a collection of different statutes. These were principally:

- the Building Societies Act 1986;
- the Friendly Societies Acts 1974 and 1992;
- the Industrial and Provident Societies Act 1965; and
- the Credit Unions Act 1979.

GOVERNMENT PROPOSALS

16.02   In its March 1999 Progress Report,[1] the Treasury noted that the existing legislation relating to mutual societies performed a mixture of functions. On the one hand, it provided a means of establishing a legal status for the society itself (as distinct from its members), which was entirely independent of the Companies Acts, setting out a framework for registration and, in some cases, incorporation. On the other, the legislation also sought to regulate to some degree the conduct of

---

[1] H.M. Treasury, *Financial Services and Markets Bill Progress Report* (March 1999).

business by this mixed bag of financial services providers. The legislation also established the Registry of Friendly Societies (with a Chief Registrar), the Building Societies Commission and the Friendly Societies Commission which between them carried out a mixture of both prudential regulation and what the Treasury termed "corporate code" functions akin to the regulation of ordinary companies in relation to building societies and friendly societies.

So far as the FSMA was concerned, the Government's intention was that any of the existing legislative provisions relating to the financial services businesses of mutual societies should be brought within the scope of the Act in much the same way as has occurred for the first time in relation to deposit-taking and insurance business. This requires the transfer of regulatory functions in respect of such matters to the FSA and the repeal of much existing of the legislation dealing with the prudential or conduct of business control of mutuals, so that this can be encompassed within the FSA's own rules. Since much[2] of the business conducted by mutual societies is practically indistinguishable from the type of deposit-taking and insurance activities carried on by banks and insurers, there must be considerable logic in seeking parity of regulation as between the same types of business, notwithstanding that they are conducted by different forms of provider.

Corporate code provisions more closely aligned to the Companies Acts framework for ordinary companies, on the other hand, serve a very different purpose. These provisions effectively define the mutual entity to which they relate—without them, the mutual would have no recognisable independent existence in law. Thus, the legislation embodying these is, by and large, to be retained. Responsibility for overseeing this aspect of the regulation of mutuals is not, however, to be left with the existing Commissions and Registry. Instead, those functions are being split between the Treasury (which will take on most of the powers previously vested in the Commissions and the Registry to make orders or regulations) and the FSA (which will pick up the remainder and, in practice the majority, of these functions under its rule-making powers).

FSMA PROVISIONS

16.03　As in other areas of the new financial services regime, the FSMA itself has done little more than establish the framework under which these proposals will be implemented, leaving it to secondary legislation to bear most of the burden of actually achieving this. The FSMA therefore has little but the basics to impart in Part XXI.

Transfer of functions

16.04　Each of sections 334(1), 335(1) and 336(1) are in substantially identical terms and empower the Treasury by order to transfer any of the functions of the Friendly Societies Commission, the Registry of Friendly Societies and the Building Societies Commission respectively to the FSA and any functions which are not so transferred to the Treasury. In relation to friendly societies, section 335(2) and (3)

---

[2] Not all friendly societies engage in the types of activity covered by the FSMA, however, and those that do not are not intended to be subject to the FSMA authorisation regime or the FSA's rules.

include similar provisions in respect of the central office of the registry of friendly societies and the assistant registrar of friendly societies for Scotland.

To enable the Treasury to tidy up "loose ends", each of sections 334, 335 and 336 empowers it to make orders providing that the existing regulatory bodies will cease to exist. In practice, this will happen only after the Treasury has exercised its supplemental powers under section 339 to ensure that the relevant transferee of functions also takes on the relevant property, rights and liabilities of the transferor and has the necessary powers to continue investigations, disciplinary or legal proceedings.

Section 337 also gives the Treasury power by order to dismantle the Building Societies Investor Protection Board, so as to achieve the desired unification under the FSMA umbrella of investor protection and compensation schemes.

Repeal of existing legislation

16.05 Schedule 18 to FSMA contains some changes to the existing legislation for mutual societies (as does Schedule 22, which covers repeals of existing legislation generally). For the most part, these changes are fairly limited. Some consist in the removal of existing statutory restrictions on what certain types of mutuals may do to bring them more in line with each other (*e.g.*, the amendments in Part II of Schedule 18, which are designed to remove the restrictions on incorporated friendly societies forming or acquiring control of subsidiaries and put them on a more even footing with building societies in this respect).

Others are intended to set the scene for the FSA in future to perform the supervisory or registration role currently held by one or other of the Commissions or the Registry. Thus, Schedule 18 repeals sections 44–50 of the Friendly Societies Act 1992 (which regulate registered and incorporated friendly societies in the conduct of insurance business), so that these functions may pass to the FSA through application of the general FSMA prohibition on conducting insurance business without authorisation. It also repeals section 9 of and Schedule 3 to the Building Societies Act 1986, which deal with the authorisation of building societies, since this will also now be encompassed within the general prohibition and FSA authorisation under the FSMA.

These legislative amendments were deliberately included in FSMA itself, rather than allowing the Treasury to deal with them in its secondary legislation, so as to ensure that the Treasury's powers under delegated legislation were restricted and did not extend (as the Treasury itself confirmed)[3] to introducing deregulatory measures.

MUTUAL SOCIETIES ORDER

16.06 The first draft of this was issued, along with the Treasury's first *Consultation Document* on the subject, in March 2001. A very short period of consultation was allowed for comment on the draft Order, since the Government's intention was to ensure that proposed changes to the regulation of mutual societies

---

[3] H.M. Treasury, *Mutual Societies Order—A Consultation Document* (March 2001).

were generally effective at N2. To this end, the Order[4] was made with no further consultation on July 18, 2001.

Credit unions represent an exception to this. Although the Government's main proposals for mutuals were set out in March 1999, it was not until October of that year that the decision was taken to include credit unions within the FSMA framework. To allow sufficient time for consideration of the legislative changes this will bring about, it is currently intended that the FSA's powers under FSMA will not be extended to credit unions until July 1, 2002. The Order therefore contains only interim arrangements for such bodies, which are discussed in more detail below.

Although no further draft Order was issued or consultation invited following the draft Order issued in March 2001, that draft was produced with input from the Building Societies and Friendly Societies Commissions as well as the Registry of Friendly Societies and trade associations and there was little by way of substantive change to the Government's proposals for mutuals before the Order was made.

Transfer of functions in the Order

16.07 Schedule 1 sets out, in a convenient table form, those functions of each of the existing mutual regulators, which are to be transferred to Treasury. Article 4 of the Order makes it clear that all other functions of the registrars, central office and the Commissions pass to the FSA.

In keeping with the Government's stated intention, all the Treasury powers appear to be powers to make orders or regulations in respect of corporate governance or existence matters (*e.g.*, making regulations for the conversion of friendly societies into companies or regulations about the form and content of annual accounts). The longest list of Treasury powers relates to the functions of the Building Societies Commission, which is to be expected, given that the legislation relating to building societies has been the most developed in recent years.

Article 9 *et seq.* of the Order provide that, as soon as practicable after commencement (N2), each of the existing regulators must produce reports for Parliament and/or the Treasury (as the case may be) and, in the case of the Commissions, produce within seven months of commencement, a statement of accounts. Article 8 then includes automatic provisions for each of the regulators to cease to exist once these requirements have been complied with. Article 11 completes the picture, with similar provisions for the provision of reports and accounts by and the cessation of the Building Societies Investor Protection Board.

Amendments to legislation

16.08 Schedules 3 and 4 (dealing with amendments to and repeal of existing legislation respectively) of the Order are extensive. The amount of cross-referencing they require to existing legislation inevitably makes for a fairly tedious read and it is helpful that the Treasury has set out fairly clearly the guiding purpose behind these amendments.

Since no new registrations have been effected under the Friendly Societies Act 1974 since the 1992 Act was passed, amendments to the former are relatively limited. The same is true in relation to the Industrial and Provident Societies Act

---

4 The Financial Services and Markets Act 2000 (Mutual Societies) Order 2001 (S.I. 2001 No. 2617).

1965, which does little more than establish the incorporation and registration framework for these societies. Since it does not contain any real financial services regulatory provisions, most of the Act is intended to remain in place, with the functions of the registrars transferred to either the FSA or the Treasury.

In respect of the other statutes, the following points are worth mentioning specifically:

- bodies corporate established pursuant to specific Acts of Parliament, such as friendly and building societies, derive their entire existence and powers from that statute. Thus, the provisions under the Friendly Societies Act 1992 and the Building Societies Act 1986, which set out (and include restrictions on) what the society may do, such as the "principal purpose" requirement for building societies, have been retained;

- the prohibition contained in the Friendly Societies Act 1992 on carrying on insurance without an authorisation from the Commission will effectively be superseded by the FSMA general prohibition on effecting and carrying out insurance as a regulated activity without an authorisation or exemption. The same applies to building societies in relation to acceptance of deposits. The draft Order contained detailed proposals for transitional "grandfathering" in respect of existing authorisations, so that these were expressly converted into FSMA authorisations with a Part IV permission. These provisions were dropped from the final version of the Order;

- rights of appeal to the Friendly Societies Appeal Tribunal under sections 58 to 61 of the Friendly Societies Act 1992 and to the Building Societies Appeal Tribunal under the Building Societies Act 1986 are to be replaced by rights to refer an FSA proposal to exercise its powers, to the Financial Services and Markets Tribunal established under Part IX of FSMA;

- section 68 of the Friendly Societies Act 1992 imposes obligations on societies, which are more onerous that those applicable to ordinary companies, by requiring the maintenance of systems of control in respect of the society's business and records and of inspection and report. A similar point arises under section 71 of the Building Societies Act 1986. Schedule 3 to the Order contains provisions amending these, the Government's intention being to allow the FSA instead to make whatever rules it considers appropriate. The idea is evidently to align prudential requirements as between friendly societies and insurance companies and as between building societies and banks in this respect;

- the dispute resolution arrangements in sections 80 to 84 of the Friendly Societies Act 1992 and in sections 83, 83A and 84 of the Building Societies Act 1986 currently remain in place, rather than being subsumed within the FSMA single Ombudsman Scheme, on the basis that the types of disputes covered by these provisions differ from those intended to be dealt with under the Ombudsman Scheme;

- provisions dealing with the way in which friendly and building societies merge, transfer their businesses or convert into companies (which provisions are required because they are creatures of statute, rather than ordinary companies) by and large remain, since they are an integral part of the statutory basis for the establishment of these types of bodies corporate;

- the principal powers of the Building Societies Commission to regulate the business of societies for the protection of shareholders and depositors contained in sections 41 *et seq.* of the Building Societies Act 1986 will disappear, as this is an area which is intended to be dealt with under FSA rules. Certain powers currently in that Act are, however, to be retained and transferred to the FSA. These are:

  — power to direct restructuring of business (section 36);
  — power to make prohibition orders (section 36A);
  — power to petition for winding up (section 37); and
  — power to direct transfers of engagement or business (section 42B).

Credit Unions

16.09   In keeping with the Government's wish to allow credit unions more time to consider and adjust to the imposition of the new FSMA regime in relation to their deposit-taking activities, the Order contains only interim arrangements intended to take effect at N2 up until July 1, 2002. The Order effects the transfer of the existing prudential functions of the registrars under the Credit Unions Act 1979 to the FSA and the Treasury at N2 but without making the amendments and repeals to that Act which would be required, if regulation of deposit-taking were to be conducted under the FSMA provisions from that date.

There is, accordingly, a transitional exemption from the general prohibition in respect of deposit-taking for all credit unions contained in Article 6 of the Financial Services and Markets Act 2000 (Exemption) Order 2001, which will expire on July 1, 2002. The repeals in respect of the Credit Unions Act 1979 contained in Part V of Schedule 18 of FSMA will also take effect only from July 1, 2002.

The *Consultation Document* issued by the Treasury in March 2001 confirms, however, that in keeping with its overall approach to the future regulation of mutuals, the current prudential requirements of the Credit Unions Act 1979 (such as the limit on the maximum number of members, restrictions under section 11 on the loans which can be made and restrictions on investments) will disappear, either through the operation of Schedule 18 to the FSMA or by Treasury order, to be replaced by FSA Rules where appropriate.

CHAPTER 17

What Next for Financial Services? Looking to the Future

JAI CHAVDA

INTRODUCTION

17.01 The more we steer towards an integrated global financial services market place, the more important it is to keep a watchful eye on those regulatory developments at the European level which are likely in time to impact direct upon United Kingdom law. The most marked changes at the European level have largely been driven by the race to complete the internal market for financial services before the year 2003 and an integrated financial market by 2005.[1] To facilitate the meeting of this target, the E.U.'s Economic and Finance Ministers ("ECOFIN") commissioned a report on the regulation of European securities markets, from a committee chaired by Alexandre Lamfalussy which became known as "The Committee of Wise Men" ("Committee"). This report seeks to, within the powers prescribed under the Treaty of Rome 1958 ("Treaty") as amended by the Treaty of Amsterdam 1997, accelerate the current E.U.[2] legislative process and thereby to keep pace with changes taking place in the financial services market. This Chapter will briefly set out framework for reform which has been established, and will briefly discuss the current state of recent European legislative proposals.

LAMFALUSSY PROPOSALS

17.02 The Committee of Wise Men's *Report on the Regulation of European Securities Markets* ("Lamfalussy Report") was commissioned by ECOFIN on July 17, 2000. The Committee made an "Initial Report" on November 7, 2000 in response to which the Council requested the Wise Men to clarify certain matters and make a "Final Report" in February 2001. This it did, and the Final Report was published on February 15, 2001. The Final Report was formally endorsed by the

---

[1] Presidency conclusions at the Lisbon European Council (March 23–24, 2000) (DOC/00/8).
[2] The E.U. comprises 15 Member States: Austria, Belgium, Denmark; Finland, France, Germany, Greece; Ireland, Italy, Luxembourg, the Netherlands, Portugal, Spain, Sweden and the United Kingdom.

European Commission ("Commission"), the European Council ("Council") and the European Parliament ("Parliament").[3]

Broadly, the Committee's mandate comprises of three main elements, the focus of which was to be the securities markets. They are as follows:

- to assess the conditions under which regulation was implemented in the securities markets in the E.U.;

- to determine how the mechanism for regulating the securities markets in the E.U. can best respond to developments in the securities markets; and

- to eliminate barriers and obstacles to an integrated financial market by proposing scenarios for adapting current practices in order to ensure greater convergence and co-operation in day-to-day implementation, taking into account new developments in the market.

Drivers for change

17.03   The rationale behind reform is the desirability of promoting an integrated financial market and securities market in the E.U., accordingly, the Committee made its findings against the backdrop of the Financial Services Action Plan ("FSAP").[4] The FSAP was formulated by the Commission in which it set out 43 (legislative and non-legislative) measures that the Commission deemed necessary to effect a fully integrated financial market. The sense that there is a pressing need for reform at the European level is driven by the belief that it is imperative that the European securities markets—which are believed to be half the size of those in the U.S.[5]—must be developed in a manner which enables the E.U. to pose a series challenge to other global markets. Reform, it is reasoned, will itself bring economic benefits to Member States within the E.U. The Committee's core proposals accordingly have focused on oiling the wheels of the European legislative processes, and removing the more significant obstacles to the furtherance of a fully integrated European securities market. These obstacles have included[6]:

- the slow speed of E.U. legislative mechanisms has resulted in legislation failing to meet the pace of change in the financial markets. Under the current legislative process, Parliament and the Council have to agree a proposal made by the Commission through a co-decision procedure of these two institutions. The average time taken for the co-decision process to be exhausted and agreement to be reached is two years and, the process is particularly tortuous in the financial services area. A case in point is the

---

[3] The Lamfalussy proposals were adopted by a Council Resolution at the Stockholm summit March 23–24, 2001 (DOC/01/6) with Parliament passing a resolution on March 15, 2001 (B5-01773/2001).
[4] *Financial Services—Implementing the framework for financial markets: Action Plan* (COM(1999)232), (May 11, 1999).
[5] Final Report, p. 10.
[6] Other obstacles were also raised but these were deemed to be outside the scope of the Lamfalussy Report and should be dealt with in the next trade round.

proposed Take-over Directive which was first considered over 12 years ago and has recently been rejected[7];

- the slow speed of regulatory processes themselves;

- the absence of E.U.-wide regulation in key areas such as prospectuses and market abuse (see below);

- inconsistent implementation of existing legislation by the Member States. There is perceived to be an underlying need for more co-operation between Member States;

- there is a mismatch between the core principles which underpin Directives with the rules purporting to implement those principles;

- there has been a failure to prioritise, against the backdrop of the FSAP, those measures that are likely to have the most significant impact in the shortest time; and

- there has been inadequate convergence of regulatory and supervisory structures within Member States.

The starting point of the Lamfalussy Report is the proposal that there should be a series of "overarching principles" on which all European financial services and securities legislation should be based.[8] These overarching principles in many ways resemble the statutory objectives under the FSMA and include core principles such as maintaining confidence in the European securities markets; to ensure an adequate level of consumer protection; and to promote competition.[9] More specifically, the Wise Men, using these overarching principles as a basis for change, have recommended a four level approach on which the current European legislative process should be overhauled.

Four level approach

17.04

- *Level one*: Framework principles for legislation to be decided on existing E.U. legislative procedures;

- *Level two*: Establishment of two committees—these being the European Securities Committee ("ESC") and the Committee of European Securities Regulators ("CESR");

- *Level three*: Increased co-operation among E.U. securities regulators to achieve standard implementation of Level one and two legislation;

- *Level four*: Commission to vigorously enforce E.U. Law.

---

[7] This Directive came close to agreement when a conciliation committee of the Council and Parliament agreed on the proposal on June 6, 2001 but was subsequently rejected by Parliament's plenary session on July 4, 2001.
[8] The Lamfalussy Report suggests that these could be accommodated by enacting them as a framework regulation by the Council and Parliament or even by amending the Treaty.
[9] Final Report, p. 22.

Level one

17.05   The Level one approach seeks to alter the nature and content of directives and regulations. Essentially, the proposal would create a dichotomy between framework principles (that is, those provisions setting out the core principles of a directive) and implementing measures (those details of the directive that are to be delegated to Level two: see below). Whilst the Commission would still retain its right to promulgate proposals, it would also be empowered to suggest the species of implementing details to be delegated to Level two. In doing so, it is required to undertake background work such as canvassing market participants in an open and transparent manner, while seeking the views of Member States and, in the case of Parliament, entering into non-binding agreements on the scope of implementing powers that could be delegated to Level two. The former would set out the political choices of the Parliament and the Council. These would be set at a general level but would specify the nature and extent of technical implementing measures to be taken at Level two, together with setting the boundaries within which certain delegated measures may be adapted without recourse to the Parliament and Council. The purpose of this mechanism is to ensure that Parliament and Council are not only fully informed of the delegations they are making but that they are also actively involved in deciding on the content and extent of the delegation.

A good illustration of this process in action is provided by the Commission proposal on the single prospectus directive,[10] which has been drafted in accordance with the Lamfalussy Report. Article 3(1) of that proposal provides that any offer of securities to the public in a Member State should be accompanied by the publication of a prospectus (framework principle). Article 3(2) and 3(3) provides for derogations to the obligation set out in Article 3(1). Further, Article 3(4) provides that the terminology and exemptions to Article 3(2) and (3) may be clarified and adapted by the Commission who shall be assisted by the ESC. The Commission proposal for a directive on insider dealing and market manipulation (market abuse)[11] is premised on the same structure. Article 5 of this directive prohibits any natural or legal person from engaging in market manipulation—examples of such behaviour are laid down in section B to the Annex of this directive. Again, in following the structure outlined in the Lamfalussy Report, examples of such behaviour can be amended by the Commission in conjunction with the ESC.

The new legislative procedure is in many ways preferable to the existing practice. Under the current legislative procedure, species of abusive behaviour would have been detailed in the directive, and once made there would be no scope for amending the examples to cover new types of abusive behaviour, not specifically covered by the directive. However, under the new procedure, the Commission with the ESC can, within a much shorter period, amend the examples in order to catch innovative types of abusive behaviour. An analogy can be drawn with the broad framework created by section 118 of the FSMA which establishes the market abuse "offence", on the one hand, and the flexible COMC on the other. In short, the new procedure would allow E.U. legislation to respond appropriately and expeditiously to developments in securities markets and removes a major source of delay: the

---

[10] COM (2001) 280 final.
[11] COM (2000) 281 final.

need for Parliament and the Council to agree upon specific technical implementing measures.

The distinction between Level one framework principles and Level two implementing measures is not easy to make. However, the European Court of Justice has in previous case law indicated that "all essential elements"[12] should be included in the basic legislation that is those provisions that should appear in the Commission's proposal. It is not yet clear as to what can be delegated to the comitology process at Level two. According to Article 202 of the Treaty, only "powers for the implementation of the rules" can be delegated from the normal Level one co-decision procedure. As to what is or is not essential, the Interinstitutional Agreement on Comitology[13] (as to which see below) agreed by the Parliament, Council and the Commission states that the use of comitology process refers to "applying the essential provisions of basic instruments as well as measures designed to adapt or update certain non-essential provisions of a basic instrument".[14] In summary, core provisions of a directive or regulation must be set out in the Commission's proposal and agreed by co-decision of Parliament and the Council, whereas implementing measures at Level two will be provisions which are intended to give effect to the core provisions in the legislation agreed at Level one.

Level two

17.06 The change recommended under Level two may not be as profound as first thought. Level two essentially builds on the comitology process which is currently in place. Comitology is the process whereby the Commission implements E.U. legislation according to its implementing powers that have been delegated to it by the Council. Through "comitology committees" representatives of Member States assist the Commission in carrying out the implementing powers conferred on it. In accordance with the same principle, the purpose underpinning the creation of the ESC and CESR is to complete the implementing measures as agreed in Level one of this structure. The interface between the two committees is that the ESC will perform primarily regulatory functions in order to fortify the framework legislation while the CESR will be a "consultative body" also performing advisory functions—gauging the opinions of industry and consumers. The CESR will be modelled on the structure of the Forum of European Securities Commissions ("FESCO")[15] and will subsume its functions.[16]

17.07 **ESC.** The ESC will take on the functions of the "High Level Securities Supervisor's Committee" established by the Commission on an informal basis in 1985. It is envisaged that the ESC will carry out three key roles. First, it will perform the function of a regulatory committee. Secondly, it will act in an advisory capacity to the Commission to assist, amongst other things, with Level one legislation.

---

[12] See ECJ, December 17, 1970, Koster, 25/70, ECR 1161, para. 6.

[13] Council Decision of June 28, 1999 laying down the procedures for the exercise of implementing powers conferred on the Commission (1999/468/EEC).

[14] *ibid.*

[15] FESCO was pioneered in 1997 by the Statutory Securities Commissions of the EEA to meet the challenges of creating a pan-European market in financial services. It aims to provide an expert opinion to the European Commission on regulatory/supervisory issues pertinent to financial services.

[16] Art. 9.3 of the Charter of the European Securities Regulators (Ref: FESCO/01–070e).

Finally, it will advise the Commission on the construction of Level two mandates for the CESR. The ESC's constitution will comprise "high level" Member States' nominees who are expected to serve for sufficiently long periods in order to facilitate good working understandings between Committee members. The ESC is expected to operate in a transparent and open manner and report to the Parliament when required. The ESC will come into being once it receives its first implementing powers.[17]

17.08   CESR. FESCO have agreed a charter for the CESR.[18] Its role is threefold: to enhance co-ordination among Member States securities regulators; to act as an advisory group to assist the Commission; and to aid the Commission in preparing the drafting of implementing measures.

As mentioned above, FESCO will be renamed CESR and the Committee will be composed of a senior representative from each Member States' competent authorities for the regulation and supervision of securities.[19] Unlike the ESC, the CESR will also allow competent bodies from countries of the EEA who are not members of the E.U. to attend its meetings. Although, it would appear these representatives can contribute to debates and discussions, they may not be involved in the "decision making" process (Article 1.2 of the Charter). Membership of the CESR is further extended to "observers" where it is in the "common interest to work together" (Article 1.2). The Commission can also send a representative to CESR meetings and is able to "actively participate in all debates", subject to confidential matters being discussed (Article 3.31). Again, voting will be held by a qualified majority to mirror the voting process of the ESC. The CESR's first meeting took place on September 11, 2001 at which they ratified the Charter.

Consultation and transparency is impressed upon every aspect of the CESR's work. The methods of consultation employed by the Commission and more recently FESCO have come under criticism for being inadequate or even, in the case of the latter body, absent. The Lamfalussy Report appears to have paid heed to these comments and has, as a result, recommended that consultation should be carried out according to a specified procedure to be set out in the CESR's statutes and rules of procedure.[20] A novel aspect of consultation is the issue of a "concept release". This is an instrument to gauge public opinion at first instance. The release would highlight the problem and suggest options and ask for input on what type of regulatory approach would be appropriate.[21] The CESR may also establish consultation groups with the objective of encouraging dialogue with market participants and consumers.

So what are the differences between the two committees? While both committees will act in an advisory capacity to the Commission, the respective levels at which they will function will differ. The Commission may consult the ESC when

---

[17] The Lamfalussy Report recommended that in the interim it should be set up as an advisory committee. The ESC's first meeting was held on September 21, 2001.

[18] Charter of the European Securities Regulators (Ref: FESCO/01-070e).

[19] These representatives can be accompanied by "appropriate experts" (Art. 1.1 of the Charter).

[20] The Commission appears to have promptly responded to these comments as in its proposal for reforming the ISD, the Commission has launched an "open" consultation procedure in which an open hearing will be held.

[21] Once a regulatory approach has been decided, a draft proposal would be released by the ESC for consultation for a further three months.

drafting legislative proposals before they are put before both Parliament and the Council. Having consulted the ESC, the Commission could then ask the CESR to prepare technical details for the implementing measures. These measures will then be submitted to the ESC in accordance with the comitology provisions, which will then vote on the draft measures according to a fixed timetable. In an attempt to ensure a cohesive link between the two committees, the chair of the CESR will participate at the meetings of the ESC as an observer and the Commission will be represented at all meetings of the CESR.

Due process requires that these proposals are subject to certain checks and balances; specifically that they are transparent; that the institutional balance between the Parliament, Council and the Commission is respected; and that they are in conformity with the structure of the Treaties. The Lamfalussy Report attempts to achieve this end by:

- ensuring that Parliament will be fully informed of the contents of the CESR's emerging advice and resulting Commission proposals. The CESR is also obliged to submit a copy of its annual report to Parliament and more importantly, the chair is required to report periodically to Parliament when requested;

- the two committees and the Commission will keep in "close contact" with Parliament, sending all documents as required;

- the Commission will attempt to publish in an indicative form, drafts of more important implementing measures; and

- before the Commission makes a proposal to the ESC and after the ESC has voted on it, Parliament will have sufficient time to check the proposal against implementing powers defined by co-decision in Level one; Article 8 of the Interinstitutional Agreement on Comitology provides Parliament with a *droit de regard* which enables Parliament to vote a resolution stating that the Commission has exceeded the implementing powers conferred on it, meaning that a redraft would be necessary taking "utmost account" of Parliament's opinion.

Although these measures have been designed to protect the position of the Parliament, since the publication of the Lamfalussy Report, Level two implementing measures have met with some resistance from Parliament. In particular, some members have voiced concerns that the balance of power between the *status quo*—that is, the three European institutions—is compromised. Equally, concerns have been voiced in relation to the nature of the powers vested in the ESC. Parliament's principal concern is that once a proposal has been decided by the co-decision procedure, it would have no scope for reviewing the "implementing provisions" that the ESC together with the Commission concoct.[22] Accordingly, the fear is that the procedure effectively gives the ESC a free hand to determine crucial parts of legislation. As a result, Parliament wishes to have something akin to a "call back" procedure where it has the right to scrutinise these implementing provisions with the

---

[22] Robert Goebbels at the Economic and Monetary Affairs Committee on June 19, 2001.

Commission. At the time of writing, these arguments were still ongoing and it is likely that some type of *ex-ante* agreement, which allows Parliament to review these implementing measures, will be brokered.

Level three

17.09   The objective at this level is for Member States to implement E.U. law "within a framework of enhanced and strengthened co-operation and networking between regulators with a view to ensuring consistent and equivalent transposition of the Level one and two legislation".[23] Put singly, it requires the implementation of E.U. law to be standardised across the E.U. by encouraging Member States to work together. The ESC's role is central to this and in order to facilitate common transposition of Level one and two, it is required to:

- formulate guidelines for the administrative regulations to be adopted at the national level;

- issue joint interpretative recommendations and set common standards on matters not covered by E.U. legislation which could eventually become E.U. law by virtue of the Level two procedure;

- to review regulatory practices aimed at ensuring effective enforcement throughout the Union and define best practice; and

- periodically to conduct peer reviews of regulatory practices in Member States, reporting their result to the Commission and ESC.

Decisions at this level would have to be taken by consensus, and they would not be binding. It may well be that a political resolution would be needed in order to mandate regulators to carry out this essential work. The Committee further recommended more fundamental changes such as encouraging governments to establish indepent regulators or to increase the involvement of market participants in the regulatory process.

Level four

17.10   Level four is a subset of Level three and would require enforcement at two levels—first, enforcing E.U. law, and secondly, the regulatory system itself. Under the first head, the Commission should be charged with a high level responsibility for ensuring that E.U. law is complied with. Under the second, national regulators of the Member States would assume their role to enforce E.U. law in their respective Member States. The Committee encourages a two-way dialogue between the regulator and the private sector with the national regulators reporting to the Commission any potential infringements. The Committee was also keen to see established a process which monitors and reports the effectiveness of the four level regulatory structure.

To this end, an inter-institution Monitoring Group comprising two external independent nominees was proposed with the aim of keeping the progress towards

---

[23] Final Report, p. 37.

a single financial market under review; the three European institutions would pay particular consideration to its findings. The Monitoring Group is required to produce half-yearly reports.

The Stockholm Council meeting concluded that the new regulatory structure should be operational from the beginning of 2002 and that there would be a full and open review of the four level process in 2004. However, if it becomes clear from the efforts of the Monitoring Group that progress is not being made then there is scope for the review to be brought forward. If the review reveals that the approach does "not have any prospect of success" then the only other option left, according to the Lamfalussy Report, would be to amend the Treaty in order to set up a single E.U. regulatory authority to oversee financial services.

Significant proposals made under the FSAP

17.11 A detailed assessment of the current legislative developments under the FSAP umbrella would indeed be beyond the scope of this work. Hence, the discussion below will briefly focus on the more significant changes with a fleeting reference to other measures under the FSAP.

E-commerce

17.12 In this area there are broadly, two main initiatives: the E-commerce Directive[24] and the proposal for the Distance Marketing of Consumer Financial Services.[25] The objective is to facilitate e-commerce in the E.U. though the ideal appears to be to "level the playing fields" in which on-line and off-line economic businesses are carried on.

The E-commerce Directive seeks to establish a coherent legal framework within which the free movement of *"information society services"* across all Member States can be achieved. Information society services are those provided by a *"service provider"* and cover *"any service normally provided for remuneration, at a distance, by means of electronic equipment for the processing and storage of data, and at the individual request of a recipient of a service"*.[26] This definition covers an array of economic activities, provided over the internet. In principle, therefore it could encompass financial services firms executing contracts on-line, and those providers offering recipients on-line information relating to financial services. However, certain types of financial services, such as those related to the taking up and carrying out of insurance business and advertising of UCITS[27] are specifically excluded from the scope of the Directive. The Directive also regulates *"commercial communications"*, these being advertising or sales promotion, and *"unsolicited real-time communications"* (respectively, Articles 6 and 7). The Directive does not affect the right of the parties to a contract to choose an applicable law. Furthermore, the Directive exempts service providers from liability where they are no more than mere conduits: that is, where they have no knowledge or control over the information which is transmitted or stored (section 4 of the Directive).

---

[24] Directive 2000/31. Member States are required to implement this directive before January 17, 2002.
[25] Made in October 1998.
[26] See Directive 1998/34, as amended by Directive 1998/48.
[27] E-commerce Directive, Annex.

The E-commerce Directive builds upon Article 49 of the Treaty to enable cross-border provision of services. It is premised upon the application of the principle of "home country control" under which service providers are to be subject to the laws and rules of the country in which it is authorised. The place where a service provider is "established" is deemed to be where the service provider's core economic activity is carried on (Article 2 (c)). Once the home state is ascertained, the service provider will have to comply with the "co-ordinated field",[28] requiring it to become authorised to carry on the information service activity as well as conforming to conduct of business type rules relating to the service provided. The co-ordinated field will as a matter of principle be the responsibility of the home Member State and, subject to certain derogations;[29] this principle cannot be occluded by other Member States (known as the "internal markets" clause). Thereafter, the service provider can effectively exercise its "EEA passport". This approach is a notable digression from the normal principles of home state and host state supervision under Articles 10 and 11 of the ISD, whereby prudential supervision is the domain of the home state and the supervision of conduct of business is the responsibility of the host state where an activity is carried on. The "home state approach" taken by the E-commerce Directive has, however, been eagerly endorsed by information service providers who have also lobbied extensively for reform of the ISD along the lines of the E-commerce Directive. To put the issue in its proper context, a significant fear of ISPs—which appears well-founded—has been that the jurisdiction afforded to host states under the ISD will limit the natural growth of on-line financial services and information busnesses through the application of differing and incompatible national conduct of business regimes. The "home state" approach in the E-commerce Directive has thus been seized upon (with the support of many regulators, including the FSA) as the basis for reform of the ISD (see below).

Whereas the E-commerce Directive establishes a legal framework for the passing of commercial information over the internet, the Distance Marketing of Consumer Financial Services[30] proposal on the other hand, attempts to regulate the marketing of contracts for retail financial services (including all insurance products as covered by the existing E.U. insurance directives) that are negotiated at a distance, *i.e.* those that do not require the physical presence of the parties to the contract. In this regard, it should be noted that the proposed Directive is concerned with the manner in which these services are marketed and not with product regulation. The reasoning behind this proposal was that it was important to promulgate a legal framework which ensures that consumers have optimum choice when selecting

---

[28] Defined in Article 2 of the Directive as "requirements laid down in Member States' legal systems applicable to information society service providers or information society services, regardless of whether they are of a general nature or specifically designed for them".

[29] *ibid.* Art. 3(4)(a). This is subject to Member States taking measures for public policy or even for the protection of investors. This "roll back" derogating provision is heavily criticised in the Huhne Report as arguably it denies businesses and consumers the benefits from a full home country control dichotomy. In addition to these general based derogations, there are also specific exceptions. Although on the face this appears to be a disadvantage, in effect this could be seen to liberalise internet related activity in these fields as Member States can potentially apply less stringent conditions on firms established in their country than prescribed by the Directive. The downside to this is that a firm wishing to circulate investment advertisements across the E.U. may need to comply with more than one set of rules.

[30] This Directive is the parallel of Directive 97/7 on distance contracts for goods and services. Directive 97/7 expressly excludes financial services from its remit.

financial services on a cross-border basis, whilst at the same time ensuring consumers are granted an adequate level of protection. Similar to the E-commerce Directive, this proposal sets out information requirements that consumers should be given prior to entering into a contract. Uniquely, the Directive also would give customers the right to withdraw without penalty from a financial service contract for a period of 14 days. This "cooling-off" period can be extended by Member States to 30 days.[31]

Article 9 of the E-commerce Directive imposes an obligation on Member States to ensure that the execution of contracts on-line should neither be hindered nor deprived of legal validity.[32] In this regard, the Commission further expressed its concern about the difficulty of harmonising different rules relating to financial services contracts. The endeavour[33] to review contract law in this field was subsequently fulfilled in the Commission Communication of July 2001 which proposes four different options for converging rules of contract.[34]

Another issue that the Commission felt needed to be addressed in order to foster consumer confidence, was in the area of providing consumers adequate redress when entering cross border financial services contracts. The answer to this was provided by the introduction of a "FINancial Services Complaints Network" ("FIN-NET") which pools alternative dispute resolution ("ADR") bodies across Member States so as to create a network. In the instance that a consumer in a Member State has a dispute with a financial services firm located in another Member State, that consumer can have the dispute resolved in his country of residence.[35]

Other measures

17.13 The reform of the ISD is at the heart of the FSAP and the Commission has launched consultation—in accordance with the Lamfalussy recommendation—on amending the ISD.[36] The basis for change is to build upon the existing ISD but in a way that captures changes in the securities markets. For example, the Commission proposes to tighten the definition of a "regulated market", together with addressing the regulation of new species of trading platforms such as Alternative Trading Systems ("ATSs") and, broadening the range of investment services to which the ISD is to apply. Pursuant to the Commission's earlier concerns about investment firms being hindered in the exercise of their single passport rights,[37] conduct of business rules as applied to the cross-border provision of services, are proposed to be vested in the home state regulator. This reform would effectively shift

---

[31] The right to withdraw does not apply to certain types of financial services contracts such as insurance policies.
[32] Contracts such as those of surety and collateral securities furnished by persons acting outside their trade, business or profession fall outside of Article 9.
[32] Communication from the Commission to the Council and the European Parliament on E-commerce and Financial Services COM (2001) 66 final.
[34] COM (2001) 398 final.
[35] Compare with the European Extra Judicial Network ("EEJ-NET") which sets up contact points in each Member State which, in the event of a consumer cross-border dispute will assist the consumer in lodging a complaint to the body in the Member State where the service provider is located.
[36] Overview of proposed adjustments to the Investment Services Directive: Working document of DG Internal Market, (July 2001).
[37] Communication from the Commission to the European Parliament: Upgrading the Investment Services Directive (93/22).

regulatory and supervisory responsibilities wholesale to an investment firm's home country regulator. However, in the case of branch operations, a firm will still have to comply with the conduct of business rules of the state in which the branch is established. As noted above, this change in policy would also be consistent with the E-commerce Directive. It is also envisaged that the "full weight" of conduct of business rules should not apply to "professional" investors in the same way that it does to "retail" investors. Other proposed changes include clarifying the conditions under which market participants and regulated markets may access clearing and settlement facilities.

It should be noted that a significant number of regulatory initiatives have emanated from international bodies such as the International Organization of Securities Commissions (IOSCO)[38] which has been an important source for certain initiatives.[39] Valuable proposals relating to the capital adequacy of banks have also originated from the Basel Committee on Banking Supervision[40] ("Basel Committee") with a proposal for a new Basel capital accord being published in January 2001. The Commission's proposal[41] for a change in capital charges very closely follows the Basel Committee's except that, importantly, the Commission's proposals will also apply to investment firms. The Basel Committee and the Commission will carry out a further round of consultation in the early part of 2002.

It goes without saying that the deadline set by the Lisbon Council is somewhat challenging. The Lamfalussy proposals certainly go some way towards smoothing the rule-making process but by the same token it relies on the three European institutions working very closely together and more importantly, co-operating each step of the way. It is the latter point on which much of the proposals set out under the FSAP will hinge. This is a period of massive change for European financial services and the proposals that have been issued under the Lamfalussy structure— and the reaction which they engender—will without doubt provide a serious indication as to whether the recommendations will come to fruition.

---

[38] IOSCO is an international forum which enables national securities market regulators to co-operate and achieve certain standards of regulation in order to maintain efficient and sound domestic and international securities markets.

[39] *Report on Securities Activity on the Internet* (June 2001) and *Investigating and Prosecuting Market Manipulation Report* (May 2000) both by IOSCO's Technical Committee.

[40] Established by the Central Bank Governors of the Group Ten of Countries in 1974.

[41] These were published in February 2001.

APPENDIX 1

List of Abbreviations

1986 Act	Financial Services Act 1986
2BCD	Second Co-ordination Banking Directive (89/646)
Act	Financial Services & Markets Act 2000
ADR	American Depository Receipt
A & O	Apportionment and Oversight Function
AIM	Alternative Investment Market
APER	The Statements of Principle and Code of Practice for Approved Persons Instrument 2001
ATS	Automated Trading Systems
AUTH	Authorisation Manual Instrument 2001
AUTIF	Association of Unit Trusts and Investment Funds
Authority	Financial Services Authority
BCD	Banking Consolidation Directive (2000/12/E.C.)
BSC	Building Societies Commission
CAC	Company Appeals Committee
CAO	Company Announcements Office
CAT	fair Charges, easy Access and decent Terms
CBA	Cost Benefit Analysis
CCA	Consumer Credit Act 1974
CDC	Company Disciplinary Committee
CEDR	Centre for Dispute Resolution
CESR	Committee of European Securities Regulators
CIS Promotion Order	Financial Services and Markets Act 2000 (Promotion of Collective Investment Schemes (Exemptions) Order 2001 (S.I. 2001 No. 1060)
CIS Exemption Order	Financial Services and Markets Act 2000 (Collective Investment Schemes) Order 2001 (S.I. 2001 No. 1062)
CIS Sourcebook	Collective Investment Schemes Sourcebook Instrument 2001
CIS	Collective Investment Scheme
COAF	Complaints Against the FSA Scheme Instrument 2001
COB	Conduct of Business Sourcebook Instrument 2001
COB Rules	FSA-made Conduct of Business Rules
COMC	Code of Market Conduct
Commission	The Competition Commission
COMP	Compensation Sourcebook
Compensation Scheme	Financial Services Compensation Scheme
Competent Authority	U.K. Listing Authority
COND	Threshold Conditions Instrument 2001

CRED	Credit Unions Sourcebook
CUCR	Common Unsolicited Calls Regulations 1991
DEC	Decision Making Manual Instrument 2001
DGFT	Director General of Fair Trading
DISP	Complaints Sourcebook Instrument
DPB	Designated Professional Body
DTI	Department of Trade and Industry
ECHR	European Convention on Human Rights and Fundamental Freedoms
EEA	E.U. states and Iceland, Liechenstein and Norway
EFR	Economics of Financial Regulation, FSA Central Policy Division
ENF	Enforcement Manual Instrument 2001
ESC	European Securities Committee
ESOP	Employee Stock Ownership Plans
ETP	Extra Time Provisions
E.U.	European Union: Austria, Belgium, Denmark, Finland, France, Germany, Greece, Holland, Ireland, Italy, Luxembourg, Portugal, Spain, Sweden and the U. K.
FESCO	Forum of European Securities Commissions
Financial Promotion Order	Financial Services and Markets Act 2000 (Financial Promotion) Order 2001 (S.I. 2001 No. 1335)
FIT	The Fit and Proper test for Approved Persons Instrument 2001
FSA	Financial Services Authority
FSAP	Financial Services Action Plan
FSMA	Financial Services and Markets Act 2000
FTA	Fair Trading Act 1973
GEN	General Provisions and Glossary Instrument 2001
GISC	General Insurance Standards Council
Guidance Manual	UKLA Guidance Manual
HR Act	Human Rights Act 1998
IBRC	Insurance Brokers Registration Council
ICA	Insurance Companies Act 1982
ICTA 1988	Income Corporation and Taxes Act 1988
ICVC Regulations	Open-Ended Investment Companies (Investment Companies with Variable Capital) Regulations 2001 (S.I. 2001 No. 1228)
IDAG	Information Dissemination Advisery Group
IFA	Independent Financial Adviser
IMRO	Investment Management Regulatory Organisation
IOSCO	International Organisation of Securities Commissions
IPC	Inter-Professional Conduct
IPRU	Interim Prudential Sourcebook
IPRU (INS)	The Integrated Prudential Sourcebook for Insurers Instrument 2001
IPRU (INV)	Integrated Prudential Sourcebook for Investment Businesses Instrument 2001

ISD	Investment Services Directive (93/22/EEC)
ISPs	Internet Service Providers
Lamfalussy Report	The Committee of Wise Men's Report on the Regulation of European Service Markets
LARC	Listing Authority Review Committee
Listing Regulations	The Stock Exchange (Listing) Regulations 1984
LLD	Lloyd's Sourcebook Instrument 2001
LSE	London Stock Exchange
MAR	Market Conduct Sourcebook Instrument 2001
MAR 1	Code of Market Conduct
MAR 2	Price stabilising rules
MAR 3	Inter-professional Conduct
MACP	Market Abuse Co-ordination Project
Member States	the countries that comprise the E.U.
ML	Money Laundering Sourcebook Instrument 2001
MLRO	Money Laundering Reporting Officer
MORT	Mortgages Sourcebook
N2	December 1, 2001
N3	9 months after N2; the date when mortgage regulation comes into force
NIP	Non-Investment Products Code
OEIC	Open-Ended Investment Companies
OFT	Office of Fair Trading
Ombudsman	Financial Services Ombudsman Scheme
OPL	Overall Premium Limit
OPS	Occupational Pension Scheme
PCC	Press Complaints Commission
PIA	Personal Investment Authority
PINCs	Property Income Certificates
POS Regulations	The Public Offers of Securities Regulations 1995 (S.I. 1995 No. 1537)
PR	Personal Representative
PRIN	Principles for Business Instrument 2001
PROF	Professional Firms Sourcebook Instrument 2001
PTF	Premiums Trust Funds
RAO	Regulated Activities Order (S.I. 2001 No. 544)
RCH	Recognised Clearing House
RDC	Regulatory Decisions Committee
REC	Recognised Investment Exchange and Recognised Clearing House Sourcebook Instrument 2001
RIE	Recognised Investment Exchange
RITC	Reinsurance to close
RNS	Regulatory News Service
RPB	Recognised Professional Bodies
R&R	Reconstruction and Renewal Plan
SEC	Securities Exchange Commission
SFA	Securities and Futures Authority

SHP	Stakeholder Pension Scheme
SIB	Securities and Investment Board
Sourcebook	Relevant parts of the FSA Handbook
SPOTs	Single Property Ownership Trusts
SPV	Special Purpose Vehicle
SROs	Self-regulatory organisations
Standards	LSE Admission and Disclosure Standards (May 2001)
SUP	Supervision Manual Instrument 2001
SYSC	Senior Management Arrangements, Systems and Controls Instrument 2001
TC	Training and Competence Sourcebook Instrument 2001
Tribunal	Financial Services and Markets Tribunal
TSP	Timeless Saving Provision
TTP	Technical Timing Provisions
UCITS Directive	Undertakings for Collective Investment in Transferable Securities Directive (85/611)
UKLA	U.K. Listing Authority

APPENDIX 2

List of Useful Website Addresses

Association of Unit Trusts and Investment Funds (AUTIF)
http://www.investmentfunds.org.uk

British Bankers Association (BBA)
http://www.bba.org.uk

Bank for International Settlements (BIS)
http://www.bis.org/

DG Internal Market/Financial Services
http://europa.eu.int/comm/internal_market/en/finances/index.htm

European Central Bank (ECB)
http://www.ecb.int/index.html

Financial Services and Markets Act 2000
http://www.legislation.hmso.gov.uk/acts/acts2000/20000008.htm

Forum of European Securities Commissions (FESCO)
http://www.europefesco.org

Financial Law Panel (FLP)
http://www.flpanel.demon.co.uk

Financial Services Authority (FSA)
http://www.fsa.gov.uk/

Financial Services Consumer Panel
http://www.fs-cp.org.uk/

H.M. Stationery Office
http://www.hmso.gov.uk/

H.M. Treasury
http://www.hm-treasury.gov.uk/

International Financial Services London (IFSL)
http://www.britishinvisibles.co.uk

International Organization of Securities Commissions (IOSCO)
http://www.iosco.org/iosco.html

Law Society
http://www.lawsociety.co.uk

London Investment Banking Association (LIBA)
http://www.liba.org.uk

London Stock Exchange (LSE)
http://www.londonstockexchange.com

The Takeover Panel
http://www.thetakeoverpanel.org.uk

U.S. Securities Exchange Commission (SEC)
http://www.sec.gov

List of Recognised Investment Exchanges and Recognised Clearing Houses

To date, the FSA has recognised the following:

(i) **Domestic RIEs—**

London Stock Exchange
Virt-x Exchange Limited
London Metal Exchange
International Petroleum Exchange
London International Financial Futures and Options Exchange
OM London Exchange (formerly OMLX)
COREDEAL
Jiway

(ii) **Domestic RCHs—**

European Central Counterparty Limited (EuroCPP)
London Clearing House
CRESTCo

(iii) **Overseas RIEs—**

NASDAQ LIFFE, LLC Futures Exchange
NASDAQ
The Swiss Stock Exchange (SWX)
New York Mercantile Exchange (NYMEX)
Cantor Financial Futures Exchange (CFFE)
Sydney Futures Exchange (SFE)
Chicago Mercantile Exchange (CMF)
Chicago Board of Trade (CBOT)
EUREX (Zurich)
Warenterminbörse Hannover
New Zealand Futures and Options Exchange (NZFOE)

To date, there are no recognised overseas clearing houses.

Index